PEARSON CUSTOM PUBLISHING

MANAGING PEOPLE

Compiled from:

*Organising and Managing Work:
Organisational, managerial and strategic behaviour in theory and practice*
Second Edition
by Tony Watson

Human Resource Management: A Contemporary Approach
Sixth Edition
Edited by Julie Beardwell and Tim Claydon

Essentials of Organisational Behaviour
Third Edition
by Laurie J. Mullins

Contemporary Human Resource Management: Text and Cases
Third Edition
by Tom Redman and Adrian Wilkinson

Human Resource Management
Eighth Edition
by Derek Torrington, Laura Hall, Stephen Taylor and Carol Atkinson

Human Resource Management
Seventh Edition
by Derek Torrington, Laura Hall and Stephen Taylor

Introducing Human Resource Management
Sixth Edition
by Margaret Foot and Caroline Hook

ALWAYS LEARNING PEARSON

Harlow, England • London • New York • Boston • San Francisco • Toronto • Sydney • Auckland • Singapore • Hong Kong
Tokyo • Seoul • Taipei • New Delhi • Cape Town • Sao Paulo • Mexico City • Madrid • Amsterdam • Munich • Paris • Milan

Pearson Education Limited
Edinburgh Gate
Harlow
Essex CM20 2JE

And associated companies throughout the world

Visit us on the World Wide Web at:
www.pearsoned.co.uk

This Custom Book Edition © Pearson Education Limited 2012

Compiled from:

Organising and Managing Work:
Organisational, managerial and strategic behaviour in theory and practice
Second Edition
by Tony Watson
ISBN 978 0 273 70480 5
Copyright © Pearson Education Limited 2002, 2006

Human Resource Management: A Contemporary Approach
Sixth Edition
Edited by Julie Beardwell and Tim Claydon
ISBN 978 0 273 72285 4
Copyright © Longman Group Limited 1994
Copyright © Financial Times Professional Limited 1997
Copyright © Pearson Education Limited 2001, 2010

Essentials of Organisational Behaviour
Third Edition
by Laurie J. Mullins
ISBN 978 0 273 75734 4
Copyright © Laurie J. Mullins, 2006, 2011; Chapters 2 and 4 © Laurie J. Mullins and Linda Carter 2008;
Chapter 3 © Linda Carter 2008

Contemporary Human Resource Management: Text and Cases
Third Edition
by Tom Redman and Adrian Wilkinson
ISBN 978 0 273 71633 4
Copyright © Tom Redman and Adrian Wilkinson 2001, 2006, 2009

Human Resource Management
Eighth Edition
by Derek Torrington, Laura Hall, Stephen Taylor and Carol Atkinson
ISBN 978 0 273 73232 7
Copyright © Pearson Education 2011

Human Resource Management
Seventh Edition
by Derek Torrington, Laura Hall and Stephen Taylor
ISBN 978 0 273 71075 2
Copyright © Prentice Hall Europe 1987, 1991, 1995, 1997
Copyright © Pearson Education Limited 2002, 2005, 2008

Introducing Human Resource Management
Sixth Edition
by Margaret Foot and Caroline Hook
ISBN 978 0 273 74098 8
Copyright © Pearson Education Limited 1996, 2011

All rights reserved. No part of this publication may be reproduced, stored in a retrieval system, or transmitted in any form or by any means, electronic, mechanical, photocopying, recording or otherwise, without either the prior written permission of the publisher or a licence permitting restricted copying in the United Kingdom issued by the Licensing Agency Ltd, Saffron House, 6–10 Kirby Street, London EC1N 8TS.

ISBN 978 1 78086 176 0

Printed and bound by Antony Rowe.

MANAGING
PEOPLE

PEARSON

We work with leading authors to develop the strongest educational materials bringing cutting-edge thinking and best learning practice to a global market.

Under a range of well-known imprints, including Financial Times/Prentice Hall, Addison Wesley and Longman, we craft high quality print and electronic publications which help readers to understand and apply their content, whether studying or at work.

Pearson Custom Publishing enables our customers to access a wide and expanding range of market-leading content from world-renowned authors and develop their own tailor-made book. You choose the content that meets your needs and Pearson Custom Publishing produces a high-quality printed book.

To find out more about custom publishing, visit www.pearsoncustom.co.uk

Contents

Semester 1	**CONCEPTS AND CONTEXTS**	**1**

Managing work and managing people in the workplace 3
Chapter 1 'Organising and managing work: study, critique and practice'
in *Organising and Managing Work:*
Organisational, managerial and strategic behaviour in theory and practice
Second Edition
by Tony Watson

The wider context of managing people 39
Chapter 4 'Human resource management and the labour market'
by Tim Claydon and Amanda Thompson
in *Human Resource Management: A Contemporary Approach*
Sixth Edition
Edited by Julie Beardwell and Tim Claydon

Organising people – responses to control 81
Chapter 4 'Organisations and people: orientations, emotions and mischief'
in *Organising and Managing Work:*
Organisational, managerial and strategic behaviour in theory and practice
Second Edition
by Tony Watson

Managing and motivating 137
Chapter 8 'Managing, motivating, leading and tasking'
in *Organising and Managing Work:*
Organisational, managerial and strategic behaviour in theory and practice
Second Edition
by Tony Watson

Working together – team working 181
Chapter 6 'Work Groups and Teams'
in *Essentials of Organisational Behaviour*
Third Edition
by Laurie J. Mullins

HRM as a concept 225
Chapter 10 'Organising and managing human resources'
in *Organising and Managing Work:*
Organisational, managerial and strategic behaviour in theory and practice
Second Edition
by Tony Watson

Semester 2   **PROCESSES AND PRACTICES**   **273**

Entering the workplace: selection and assessment   275
Chapter 4 'Selection'
in *Contemporary Human Resource Management: Text and Cases*
Third Edition
by Tom Redman and Adrian Wilkinson

Getting on: the development of the human resource   305
Chapter 18 'Learning and development'
in *Human Resource Management*
Eighth Edition
by Derek Torrington, Laura Hall, Stephen Taylor and Carol Atkinson

Just desserts – rewarding and performing   337
Chapter 13 'Employee reward'
by Amanda Thompson and Alan J. Ryan
in *Human Resource Management: A Contemporary Approach*
Sixth Edition
Edited by Julie Beardwell and Tim Claydon

Employment relations – control, conflict and commitment   379
Chapter 8 'Industrial relations'
in *Contemporary Human Resource Management: Text and Cases*
Third Edition
by Tom Redman and Adrian Wilkinson

Employee wellbeing   401
Chapter 11 'Health, safety and wellbeing'
in *Introducing Human Resource Management*
Sixth Edition
by Margaret Foot and Caroline Hook

Where next? The future of work   449
Chapter 34 'The future of work'
in *Human Resource Management*
Seventh Edition
by Derek Torrington, Laura Hall and Stephen Taylor

INDEX   467

Semester 1
CONCEPTS AND CONTEXTS

MANAGING WORK AND MANAGING PEOPLE IN THE WORKPLACE

CHAPTER 1

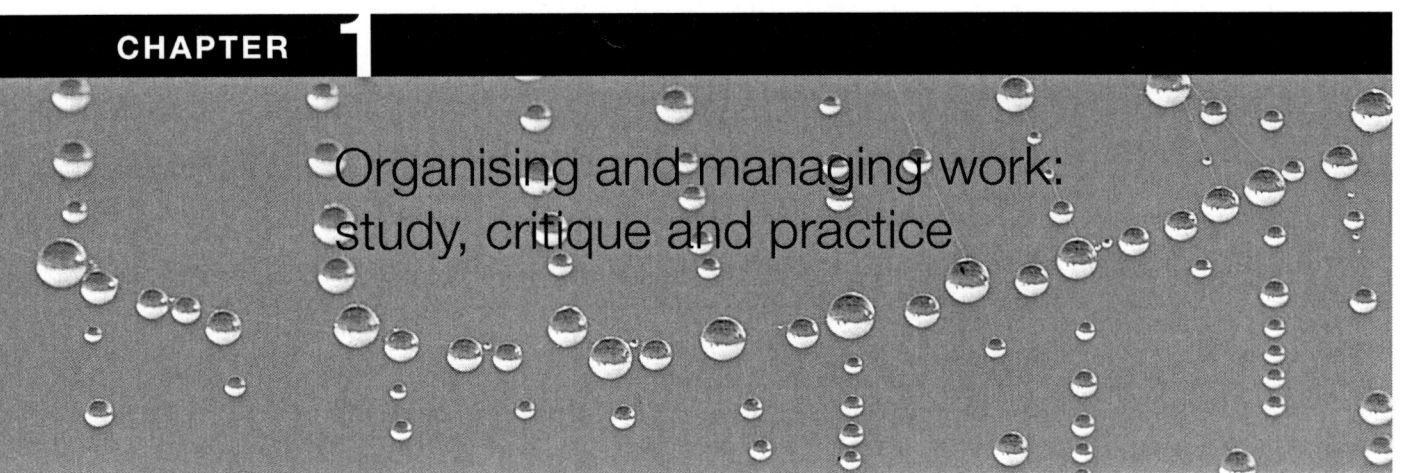

Organising and managing work: study, critique and practice

Objectives

Having read this chapter and completed its associated activities, readers should be able to:

- Appreciate the value of a 'management of work', rather than a 'management of people' or a 'management of systems' approach as a starting point for thinking about work organisations and their management.
- Understand the contribution which various social science disciplines make to the academic study of the organising and managing of work.
- See how the study of work organisation and management relates to associated studies like those of strategy, human resource management, organisation theory, management learning and critical management studies.
- Recognise continuity between social science thinking and a critical form of common sense.
- Understand the value of studying the organising and managing of work in a critical way.
- Discriminate between frameworks, perspectives, theories and research findings in terms of how useful (or 'true') they are when it comes to relating theory and practice.
- Use concepts in a social scientific way in the analysis of organisational and managerial practices.
- Distinguish between two broad ways of 'framing' human behaviours and organisational patterns: the systems-control and the process-relational.

The management of work

To create the goods, services and quality of life that people look for in the modern world, rather complex patterns of cooperative human behaviour have to be orchestrated or 'managed'. The academic study of the organising and managing of work involves taking a step back from our day-to-day involvement in these patterns of behaviour and trying systematically to understand how they come about. Such a study can also help us achieve a better quality of productive cooperation than we typically manage in contemporary work organisations.

We study work organisation and its management because we are interested in the various individual human motivations, interests, values and meanings which play a part in bringing about the patterns of behaviour we see in workplaces ranging from shops, offices and factories to schools, hospitals and universities. But the study also has to concern itself with the ways in which these human activities and meanings themselves come to be an influence on the people that are involved in them. Once human beings create institutions and structures, like work organisations and managerial practices, their lives become significantly shaped by them. One of the things which makes the study of the organising and managing of work so challenging is that it has to understand how individual choices and initiatives, on the one hand, and already existing and *emerging* organisational and societal structures and patterns, on the other, both play their parts in social life. And these two influences – of human action and structural context – do not work separately. They are inextricably intertwined. This means that we must be careful not to overemphasise either the 'people' side of work organising and managing or the 'organisational systems' aspect of work patterning. The intention of *Organising and Managing Work* is to go beyond the tendency, seen in both academic programmes and the everyday thinking of organisational practitioners, to oversimplify these issues by treating organising in a one-sided manner as primarily a matter of, to put it very simply, either 'managing people' or 'managing systems'.

The notion of 'managing people' is widely and popularly used in the organisational world. There are, however, three major problems of thinking about organising and managing work in such terms. First, there is the problem of whether it is realistic even to contemplate the possibility of managing people. Is it at all reasonable, especially in a modern democratic society, to assume that there are people about who are willing to be 'managed' – to subjugate themselves to the wills of 'bosses' at work? Surely not. In fact, it can be argued that one of the main ways that members of the human species differ from other animals is that they are active agents in the shaping of their lives. However meek or submissive particular individuals might be, each human being is nevertheless always the owner and shaper of their own identity, to some degree. As far as the historical record can tell us, no human group in the history of the human species has yet found another group over which it could exert complete control. And this applies even in the extreme conditions of slave societies or extermination camps, where human beings have still demonstrated what looks like an

FIGURE 1.1 Managing people is like trying to herd cats

inherent tendency of the species: to be recalcitrant; to resist being managed. There is a very popular cliché that one hears day after day in work organisations to the effect that 'managing people is like trying to herd cats'.

One hears engineering managers say that 'managing engineers is like trying to herd cats'; health service managers saying 'managing medical workers is like trying to herd cats'; retail managers saying 'managing shop workers is like trying to herd cats' and university faculty deans saying 'managing academics is like trying to herd cats'. There is probably no sphere of work where this cliché has not been applied (it is nearly as common as 'You need to be mad to work here'!). But there is an important insight behind the cat herding cliché: human beings are indeed inherently 'unmanageable' in the same way that cats are inherently 'un-herdable'.

A second problem with the idea of managing people is a rather important ethical one. It can be argued that a manager does not have the moral right to direct, manage or 'boss' any individual in their area of responsibility *as a whole person* or in *the totality of their workplace behaviour*. Instead, they have a limited authority to give instructions to employees in tightly prescribed and limited areas of activity. The moral basis of that authority lies in its purpose – to fulfil those work tasks in which the employees have contractually agreed to participate. Employees in modern democratic societies do not sign a contract of employment on the assumption that managers appointed by their employer will have the right to manage them as a person. The manager is appointed to manage the work tasks – and as part of this has limited rights to instruct people.

But these rights only exist as means to specific organisational ends and not because of any 'right to command' over the person as a whole. It is thus morally improper to encourage a view of managerial and organisational work based on a principle of 'managing people'.

The third problem with the people management idea is that a focus on people or indeed on 'organisational *behaviour*' tends to leave blurred the part played by structures, systems, cultures, processes and the rest. It is, in effect, to focus on human behaviours at the expense of paying attention to the performance of the systems within which those behaviours occur.

It has perhaps been in recognition of the problems inherent in shaping work activities by directly focusing on people, rather than structures and processes, that we see an alternative emphasis in managerial thinking and organisation theory existing alongside the people management emphasis. This is what is often called 'systems thinking'; a way of looking at patterns of activity which has some significant virtues, but which has some considerable weaknesses too. Identifying those weaknesses, and going beyond them, is to be a key theme of Chapter 2. But what we can say, for the moment, is that replacing the idea of 'managing people' with the idea of 'managing systems' is rather problematic. Just as with the 'management of people' approach, the 'management of systems' approach founders on a fundamental problem with one of its key assumptions. This is the assumption that once a sensible and coherent system of operating has been devised by systems designers, the people who are to be employed to operate those systems will unquestioningly fulfil the roles in the systems allocated to them. Once again the issues of human self-expression and the universal tendency of people to resist the power of others arises. Of course, people will go along *up to a point* with the instructions of 'people managers' and, of course, people will go along *up to a point* with the requirements of the working systems within which they undertake employment. But their willingness to 'go along' with the requirements of others or fit into the demands of systems is tightly bounded. Recognition of the extent of that boundedness is vital to any realistic understanding of how work organisation and management can realistically be achieved – especially in societies whose cultures emphasise concepts of political freedom, personal expression and social and economic choice.

How do we get away from these two rather limited ways of thinking about the organising and managing of work? The suggestion is that we turn away from a focus on both the management of people and the management of systems and adopt a focus on the management of work itself. The most helpful starting point for any consideration of organisational and managerial behaviour is neither the 'people' nor the 'systems'. It is, instead, the work tasks that are to be carried out and the working relationships associated with those tasks that are managed. It is tasks and relationships which are organised and 'managed', not the people who carry out the tasks. It is the tasks and relationships which have to be shaped, in a relatively predictable and therefore relatively systematic way, not systems as such. And an important insight which follows from the adoption of this management of work focus is the recognition that work tasks are always *to an extent managed by everyone involved in those tasks*. Work management is not simply what people formally designated as 'managers' do. To say this is not, however, to play down the significance of the work done by people holding managerial posts. This immensely important type of work is closely examined in Chapter 3. And careful examination of what managers actually do makes it clear that effective managers recognise that much of the shaping or managing of work tasks is done by those nominally under the control of designated managers – albeit to different degrees in different circumstances.

Studying the organisation and management of work

The field of study covered in *Organising and Managing Work* is broader than that which is typically covered by traditional 'Organisational Behaviour' programmes taught in schools of business and management and, as was explained earlier, it is very different in its emphasis from courses in 'people management'. It can usefully be labelled 'work organisation and management studies' – an activity which is treated here as a social scientific form of activity.

Work organisation and management studies — Concept

The analysis of the human aspects of work organisation and its management which draws on the social sciences to develop insights, theories and research findings with a view to informing the choices, decisions and actions of people who have a practical involvement with organisations.

We need to note several things about this way of characterising our field of study.

- What is studied is the 'human aspects of work organisation and its management'. This language is not meant to imply that attention is only paid to 'human aspects' at the level of the human individual. The focus is on work *organisation* and management, which means that patterns of human activity and thinking going beyond the level of the individual are as important as thinking about the human individual. The concern is with the interplay of factors at the level of human initiative and choice and factors at the level of social, political and economic context, or structure.

- The subject *informs* the choices, decisions and actions of people involved in practices in organisations. There is no question of developing an academic study which can tell people what they should do in the complex area of work management. The area is far too complex for there to be any basic rules or even sets of guidelines about 'how to do management'. Not only this but, given the moral factors which must come into every human situation where power and authority are involved, it would be quite wrong for a textbook to attempt to provide guidance in this way. What it can do, however, is to provide insights into the range of factors and issues which are relevant to any particular choice (of, say, job design or planning an organisational change programme). The actual choice or decision that is made is a matter for those

- involved in the particular organisational situation – with all the political, moral and specific local considerations coming into play alongside the insights which can be derived from academic study of the managing and organisation of work.

- Reference is made to 'organisational practitioners' rather than 'managers' as the potential 'users' of the subject. This is done in recognition of the fact that people other than those formally designated as managers are closely involved in the way work tasks are managed. If there are social scientific ideas which would be helpful to a manager in an organisational situation wishing to have their understanding enhanced by academic thinking then surely those ideas are going to be equally relevant to anyone else concerned with that situation. This would be the case regardless of the person's formal authority in the organisation or, for that matter, their degree of commitment to official organisational policies.

- The social sciences are 'drawn on' in the study. 'Organising and managing work' is not seen as a social science in its own right. A variety of social science disciplines can be turned to to provide research findings, theoretical resources or insights that might be helpful in understanding organisational issues. This does not mean, however, that we simply turn in a random or *promiscuous* manner to the vast bank of social science materials every time we wish to analyse a particular situation. Each individual is likely to build up their set of preferred social science concepts as their learning proceeds. They then turn to the books and journals for further insight, as the need arises, and incorporate the new learning into their ever-developing personal framework of understanding.

The social scientific study of the organising and managing of work has tended to draw primarily on the social science disciplines of sociology, psychology and social psychology. And it supports the contributions of the main disciplines with insights from economics, political science and anthropology. The key concerns of each of these are outlined in Table 1.1.

All of these disciplines can be seen as providing resources which can be drawn upon when wishing to understand the organising and managing of work in general or any particular organisational situation or problem in particular. Many of the human issues that can arise in the organisational context do not fall into any one obvious disciplinary territory and many of them might use ideas from more than one discipline. Bearing this in mind, see how you get on with Activity 1.1.

Activity 1.1

Read the story about Rose Markey taking over as the manager of The Canalazzo restaurant (Case 1.1), thinking about the issues which Rose is going to have to deal with to satisfy her employers. Following the characterisations of the six social sciences set out in Table 1.1, note the factors or issues that you think might be identified as, respectively, psychological, social–psychological, sociological, economic, political and anthropological.

Table 1.1 Focal and supporting social science disciplines for studying the organising and managing of work

Focal social science disciplines	Supporting social science disciplines
Psychology focuses on individual characteristics and behaviour and on such matters as learning, motivation and individual ('personality') differences	**Economics** supports the sociological concern with the economic context and, also, the psychological concern with decision making (through its attention to 'rational' decisions made by economic actors)
Social psychology focuses on group characteristics and behaviour, on roles, attitudes, values, communication, decision making and so on	**Political science** supports the sociological concern with power and conflict and the social–psychological concern with decision making (through its concern with the state and other institutions handling matters of power and difference of interest)
Sociology focuses on structures, arrangements or patterns and how these both influence and are influenced by individual and group behaviour. It is concerned with the structure of the social and economic system as well as with the organisational structure and issues of technology, conflict, power and culture	**Anthropology** supports the social–psychological concern with norms, values and attitudes and the sociological concern with cultures (both organisational and societal) with insights taken from the study of non-industrial or 'less advanced' societies about such things as rites, rituals, customs and symbols

Rose takes over The Canalazzo restaurant

Case 1.1

Rose Markey had been working for a national chain of restaurants for only a couple of years when they asked her to take over a restaurant which they had recently acquired. They had bought The Canalazzo restaurant from the Italian family which had established the business some 20 or so years previously. The family had decided to return to Italy and to warmer summers. The company had originally put in one of their older managers to run the newly acquired restaurant. However, they were very disappointed with what was being achieved. Their Director of Finance argued that the turnover of the business simply did not justify the investment that had been made in the purchase of the business and in the redecoration of the premises. When they challenged the first manager they had put in, he talked of his resentment at being asked to move to a new part of the country at the age of 55. He persuaded the company to give him an early retirement settlement so that he could return to the part of the country he had lived in for most of his life. They were pleased to do this because it was clear, the human resources manager told Rose, that this man's poor motivation and attitude to customers was increasingly being reflected in the way the staff of the restaurant went about their work.

When Rose arrived at the restaurant she soon learned that her predecessor had clashed on several occasions with local police officers about serving late drinks. This was likely to get back to the magistrates and the restaurant would be in danger of failing to have its drinks licence renewed when it was next due for review. The manager's defence was that he was simply following local customs in the town whereby customers would have a night out that would bring them into the restaurant only after spending most of the evening in a public house. It was not his fault, he said, that the police officers and the magistrates all lived outside of the town and did not know about this.

When it came to the problems with the staff, Rose found that her predecessor had set up a strongly hierarchical set of relationships among them. This seemed to be accepted, albeit grudgingly, by the people who worked in the kitchen. But it was resented by the waiting staff who were largely part-time workers studying at the local university. Not only this, but the group of waiters – who all knew each other from the university – and the kitchen workers, all of whom had left school at 16, tended only to speak to members of their own group.

The chef, who was a middle-aged Italian, regularly fell out with the headwaiter – a woman a dozen years younger than him. Their respective ideas about how young female staff should be treated were poles apart and these differences led to frequent arguments. Overall there was very little coordination between the kitchen and the restaurant. All of this, Rose decided, seriously affected the quality of service the customers received.

Perhaps psychological factors will be the first to suggest themselves here, ranging from issues of differences of personality and temperament among different employees of the restaurant to ones of motivation and personal commitment. The varying sets of attitude in the restaurant are clearly a matter of social–psychological interest, as are the problematic patterns of communication and the way the two groups of kitchen and restaurant staff have developed to create a division among the junior staff as a whole. All of this feeds into the sociological factors and issues. There is a power structure within the restaurant and this has elements which relate to sociological variables such as age, gender and ethnicity – all of which relate to the way society as a whole is organised. But there are also sociological factors about the way the restaurant fits into the local economy and community, both as a provider of services and a source of employment. Here there is a clear overlap with economic issues of market organisation and this, in turn, relates to the most obvious economic issues of financial performance, turnover (and, by implication, profitability) and investment. Issues of a formal political nature (i.e. relating to issues of the role of the state) are present with regard to the police and magistrates, and there are obvious informal 'political' issues running right through the whole set of relationships in the restaurant. This is in addition to whatever the 'informal' politics of the relationship between local police officers and restaurant managers might be. Anthropological issues of informal customs might also be involved but, more obviously, the anthropological notions of custom and ritual are highly relevant to the patterns of restaurant use which influence the pattern of work that has to be managed by Rose Markey and the rest of the staff of The Canalazzo.

Work organisation and management studies and associated fields of study

We have now distinguished between, on the one hand, social science disciplines like sociology, social psychology, economics and anthropology and, on the other hand, the field of study that we are calling the organising and managing of work. But there are other fields of study which draw on the social science disciplines to study aspects of work organisation and its management. In fact, the field of study with which *Organising and Managing Work* is concerned brings together material and ideas from several of these. In the traditional curricula of business and management schools we will come across the subjects of Strategy (or 'strategic management'), HRM (Human Resource Management),

Organisational Behaviour (OB), Organisation Theory (OT, or Organisation Studies, OS), Critical Management Studies (CMS) and Management Learning. There are courses or modules in all of these, there are academic journals focusing on each of them and there are textbooks dealing with each one of them.

The field of study covered by the present text incorporates elements of all of these. But this is not done in a spirit of scholarly imperialism. It is done in order to provide a broader base for subsequent study than OB courses have tended to do. OB programmes often form part of the foundational level of business and management studies programmes. And they should thus provide ideas that can be built upon later than in broad strategic management or HRM modules or in more focused modules in such areas as management learning or critical management studies. But they typically do little bridging over into these areas. *Organising and Managing Work* tries to provide precisely this kind of bridging. It does this by actually incorporating into itself as a field of study some of the ideas and materials of strategy, HRM, OT, CMS and management learning.

Figure 1.2 shows the relationship between the 'organising and managing of work' field of study and the fairly standard business school subjects of OB, Strategic Management and HRM and the other fields of Organisation Theory/ Organisation Studies, Management Learning, and Critical Management Studies. OB tends to focus on the human behaviours associated with the internal functioning of organisations, with an eye on what will be helpful to managerial practitioners in this area. Organisation Studies (or 'Organisation Theory') looks at some of the same issues but with greater attention to how organisations relate to their societal contexts. It also has a primarily academic focus – concerning itself first and foremost with scholarly understanding rather than with the

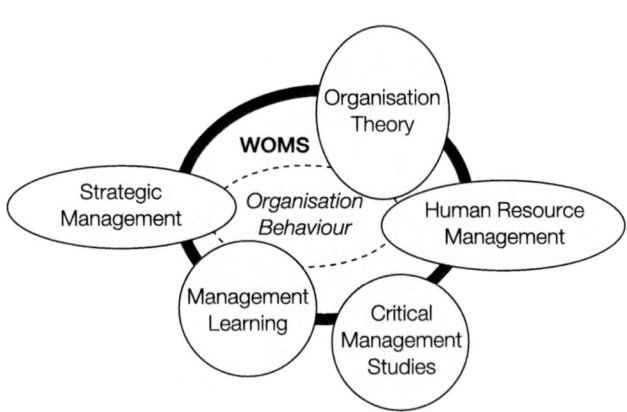

FIGURE 1.2 Work Organisation and Management Studies (WOMS) and associated fields of study

implications of such understandings for practice. The OS and OT materials are to be found in journals such as *Organisation Studies* and books like Tsoukas and Knudsen (2003), Vibert (2004) and Hatch (2006). Organisation Studies/Theory has also been more concerned with taking a critical stance than OB, something which has also informed the emergence of Critical Management Studies – in effect an application of the more critical ideas of Organisation Theory directly to issues of managerial activity (see the Further Reading on critical approaches in organisation and management studies p. 32).

Management Learning is another emergent field of specialist study with its own academic journal, *Management Learning*, and a concern to bring together theoretical developments in the understanding of human learning processes with issues of both educating and 'developing' managerial practitioners. *Organising and Managing Work* is informed by this development in its recognition of the central importance of issues of learning to all aspects of the organisation and management of work. And this is learning which, it is argued, needs to go beyond simple or 'everyday' common sense.

Common sense and social science in the study of work organisation

One of the first thoughts occurring to anyone trying to make sense of the problems we saw earlier arising with regard to The Canalazzo restaurant might be that 'common sense' is likely to be just as helpful as ideas from psychology, sociology or anthropology. It has, nevertheless, been a tradition of social science teachers to contrast social science thinking with common-sense thinking and to argue that social science analysis is to be preferred to common sense. But an alternative response might be to say, 'It all depends on what you mean by common sense.' This is necessary, in fact, because there are two quite different usages of the term 'common sense' that often get muddled up. It is useful to distinguish between *everyday common sense* and *critical common sense*.

Everyday common sense *Concept*

Analysis based on unthought-out, taken-for-granted, immediately 'obvious', everyday assumptions about the world and human activity within it.

Everyday common sense is necessary for 'getting by' in our daily lives. We all make quick assumptions about what is going on around us, drawing on all kinds of stereotypes, half-remembered experiences and simplistic cause–effect connections. This is necessary to cope with our daily lives. We would not cope with life if we stopped, sat back and deeply pondered on every eventuality that faced us between getting up in the morning and going to bed at night. But perhaps we can see why social scientists claim that their more analytical style of thinking has advantages over this. In the work context, for example, individuals frequently offer woefully simplistic generalisations such as 'People only go to work for the money' – typically adding, 'It stands to reason' or, 'It's obvious' or, 'It's common sense isn't it?' This is a good example of everyday common sense, based as it is on easy, unthought-out, taken-for-granted assumptions. Assumptions like these make life simpler – at first sight, anyway. But such assumptions are often dangerous guides to action on matters of any importance or complexity such as designing a pay system or 'reward structure', for example.

We therefore turn to critical common sense as a style of thinking which involves being deliberately logical or rational about things in the way that is common to all human beings when they are alertly and critically putting their mind to whatever matter is in hand.

Critical common sense *Concept*

Analysis based on the basic logic, rationality, hard-headedness to be found in human beings whenever they step back from the immediate situation and critically put their minds to an issue or problem.

This is the kind of common sense that we can more reliably use as a guide to action when more complex matters of work organisation and management arise. It is an activity of the same order as that in which the scientist engages. Science, in this view, is essentially a formalised version of critical common sense. Scientific thinking – in principle if not always in practice – is the more formal, systematic and painstakingly analytical application of critical common sense.

Critical common sense analysis tends to start from a consideration of the most obvious or likely explanation of what is going on; the everyday common sense explanation in fact. But it then goes on to ask whether things are really as they seem at first. Alternative explanations are considered and attention is paid to available evidence in judging the various rival explanations. We can see the two types of common sense compared in Table 1.2 and the managerial implications of applying each of them, in this case in deciding for or against a performance-related pay system.

Table 1.2 Two types of common sense in practice

Everyday common sense and pay	Critical common sense and pay
If you pay employees in proportion to their output they will produce more than if they get the same wage whatever they turn out	Pay for output might work. But employees might prefer the comfort of a steady work rate and the security of a steady wage. They might resent the pressures of a bonus system on group relations
They will clearly work better under a performance-related pay system	It would be wise to find out what particular employees' requirements are before deciding for or against a performance-related pay system

The considerations about performance-related pay connected in Table 1.2 to a critical common sense way of thinking about work behaviour are indeed similar to ones which have emerged from social science research and theorising about the relationship between pay and behaviour. See, in particular, the 'expectancy' theory of work motivation explained in Chapter 8. Similar arguments to these critical common sense ones were developed in the light of one of the famous Hawthorne experiments – the Bank Wiring Observation Room experiment – by Roethlisberger and Dickson (1939).

The critical study of organising and managing

A critical common sense frame of mind is obviously relevant to any kind of practical human endeavour. But it has particular relevance to academic work – and especially to studies that claim to be scientific. Scientific analysis, as has already been suggested, can be understood as an especially rigorous or systematic application of critical common sense. And this would suggest that we could not do social science at all without being critical in the sense of constantly questioning taken-for-granted ideas and practices. However, there has been a growing trend of questioning the extent to which social science study of work behaviour and managerial practice has been sufficiently critical.

The crux of the problem that all writers and researchers interested in managerial issues have to face up to is the fact that managerial activities are always and inevitably implicated in issues of power and relative advantage and disadvantage between human groups and human individuals. Everyone engaged in management research and management education is therefore faced with a dilemma. How do they reconcile providing knowledge that might help improve the effectiveness of work activities with the fact that in doing so they might help some people ('managers' and the employers of managers, say) more than others ('the managed', for example)? Helping make work organisations more efficient or more effective is not a politically neutral matter.

In a world where valued resources tend to be scarce and there is continuous competition for the goods, services and rewards provided by work organisations, any intervention can involve one in taking sides between the relatively advantaged and the relatively disadvantaged. The social scientist is in danger of becoming a 'servant of power', as an early polemic on such matters put it (Baritz, 1960, p. 39). A desire to avoid this problem is something shared by all of those associated with the emergent 'critical management studies' movement (see the Further Reading on critical approaches in organisation and management studies p. 32). A radical strategy adopted by some critical management thinkers amounts, in effect, to 'going on the attack' against managerial ideologies and activities that are felt by the critical scholar to be 'wrong' or 'harmful'. Critical research and writing would, for example, offer its students 'an appreciation of the pressures that lead managerial work to become so deeply implicated in the unremitting exploitation of nature and human beings, national and international extremes of wealth and poverty, the creation of global pollution, the promotion of "needs" for consumer products etc.' (Alvesson and Willmott, 1996, p. 39). Such a critical management study is committed to exposing the political implications of managerial work with an ambition of helping achieve 'emancipatory transformation' – the transformation of both people and society. And, in the workplace itself, a 'critical' version of the concept of empowerment is called for, 'empowering employees to make more choices and to act more effectively to transform workplace relations' (Thompson and McHugh, 2002, p. 18).

These advocates of critical management studies, critical management education and critical organisation studies want their work to help change the balance of power in the worlds of work and employment. But they are not just critical of the existing patterns of power prevailing in organisations and society at large. They also aim their critical fire at the type of writing and teaching which constitutes the orthodoxy in contemporary business and management schools. And the main thrust of this critique is against the assumption behind much of this orthodoxy that success in managerial and organisational work comes from acquiring, developing and applying *skills* and *techniques* – skills and techniques which are neutral and 'innocent' in a political sense. Issues of power, inequality, conflict (at interpersonal, group and class levels), gender and ethnicity are either ignored or treated as peripheral matters which, from time to time, get in the way of smooth organisational functioning. Sympathy with this latter criticism has been an important inspiration for the writing of the present text and it informs the critique of what is called the *systems-control* orthodoxy and its displacement by a more realistic and politically sensitive *process-relational* frame of reference. But the whole text is underpinned by a particular notion of a critical organisation and management study, which is summarised in Figure 1.3. It is a notion that shares much ground with the work being produced under the flag of 'critical management studies' but its overlap is only partial, as the earlier Figure 1.1 suggested.

The conception of a critical organisation and management study adopted in *Organising and Managing Work* differs from that taken by some of the critical thinkers whose ideas were looked at above. This is primarily with regard to the issue of arguing for 'transformation', at both the personal and the social levels. It is felt that the choices that these transformations would entail are a matter for political and moral debate in society generally and for contestation within organisations themselves. They are not transformations which social science can or should push people towards. What the social sciences can do is to illuminate or inform those debates with information and insights derived from both research investigations and theoretical reflections. And if these insights, research contributions and theories are going to have any real potential to *make a difference* to practices in the world outside the classroom and library, there has to be openness about the fact that all social science analysis is itself value-laden. To contribute to either societal or organisational debates about how work tasks are to be organised and managed as if this were simply a matter of deciding which power-neutral technique or procedure to adopt would be dishonest at the moral level and misleading at the level of informing practice.

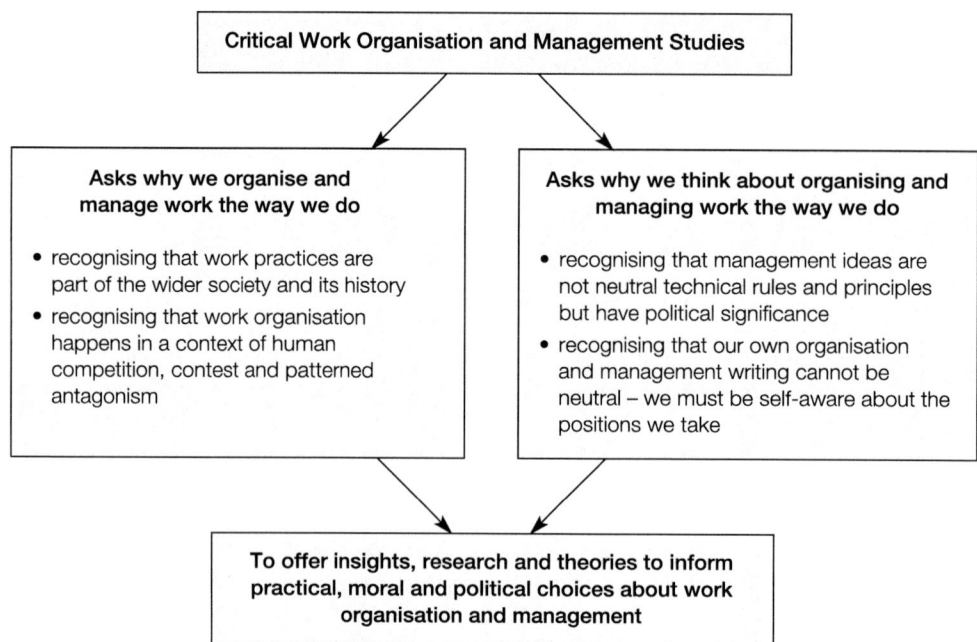

FIGURE 1.3 A critical study of work organisation and management

This means that no study of organisations and management can claim to be objective or in some sense 'value-free'. A critical study of organisation and management must keep asking questions of itself – as the words on the right-hand side of Figure 1.3 suggest. This entails recognising that the management and organisational ideas that are dealt with are not matters of technique or neutral principles, devoid of political significance. It also requires a degree of self-awareness in writing and teaching and a commitment to judiciously revealing our own biases and moral inclinations where this is necessary to help the reader or student take one's inevitable partiality into account. This principle was followed early in the present chapter where the notion of 'people management' was *engaged with* as a matter of morality as well as pragmatic realism.

The writing of the early part of this chapter was also relevant to the words on the left-hand side of Figure 1.3. The essence of critique is *questioning* and a critical study has to ask questions about the organisational activities that it is studying as well as constantly questioning what it is producing itself in its 'literature'. Accordingly we raised questions earlier in the chapter about the practice of speaking of organising work in terms of 'the management of people' or 'the managing of systems' as opposed to 'the management of work'. This argument will be built upon as *Organising and Managing Work* develops. And, as we ask questions about how and why work organisation practices are as they are, we will constantly bear in mind that work organisations are only in an extremely limited way a separate phenomenon from the economy and society of which they are part. They did not historically 'evolve' in the working out of some divine or abstract principle of increasing organisational efficiency. The hierarchy of jobs in today's organisations, for example, is both an outcome of and a contributor to the hierarchy of class and status which has developed in society as individuals and groups have competed with each other for advantage over the years. By the same token, markets do not exist 'out there' as part of the 'economic context' of business organisations. They are *made* by organisational initiatives as much as they are served by organisations. A critical perspective also requires us constantly to observe that differences of interest – and the frequent alignment and realignment of interests – are inherent in organisations. They permeate the managerial strata of organisations as well as underlying the basic tensions between employees and employers.

Activity 1.2

Quickly reread Case 1.1 and how Rose Markey 'took over' at The Canalazzo restaurant. Then read the sequel to that story (Case 1.2), 'Rose and The Canalazzo under threat'. Make a note of all the ways in which an understanding of both parts of The Canalazzo story would require attention to factors to which, it is argued above, a critical study of organisation and management draws attention. The wording on the left-hand side of Figure 1.3 is a starting point for your analysis.

Rose and The Canalazzo under threat   Case 1.2

After six months of managing The Canalazzo restaurant, Rose Markey prepared for her annual performance appraisal at the headquarters of the company which owned the restaurant. She was still finding her job quite a struggle. She had begun to adjust to living in the north of the country, having only ever lived in the south previously. She had established good relationships with the local police and the worry about losing the drinks licence had disappeared. However, she was having difficulties with the chef, who resented a woman being in charge of the restaurant. The problems with the chef were exacerbated by the fact that the kitchen staff seemed pleased to see her discomforted whenever she got into an argument with him. And the kitchen staff's uncooperative attitude towards the waiters had got worse. They knew that Rose was a university graduate and frequently mocked her southern middle-class accent in the same way they regularly mimicked what they called the 'posh' accents of the largely student waiting staff. They saw Rose and the waiters as people who were only in their present jobs as a means towards something better later on.

In spite of these difficulties, Rose felt sure she could succeed in improving the restaurant's popularity. She believed she could win over the chef in the long run, by encouraging him to develop some more adventurous menus and attracting a new clientele. This, she thought, would encourage him to discipline his kitchen staff more effectively – especially with regard to their relationships with the waiters.

Rose was excited about explaining all of this to the manager who was to do her appraisal. However, before she could even begin to talk about what she was doing, he told her that the company was considering closing the restaurant. A rival had ousted the chief executive of the company. The new managing director wanted, she said, to take the whole business 'up-market'. A restaurant in a northern town with a declining local economy did not 'fit into the new scheme of things'. Rose was to be offered redundancy – the terms of which she was invited to go and discuss with the human resources manager.

When Rose found the HR manager, he immediately invited her to go to a nearby wine bar for a drink. He explained that as an old friend of the former managing director he had felt it wise to seek a job with another business. He had been successful in this and therefore felt able, he said, to let Rose know that he believed she had been badly treated. He said that the possibility of closing the restaurant had arisen before Rose had been moved there. Rose had been chosen to take the Canalazzo job because one or two of the headquarter's managers felt that her 'face did not fit'. She was not only the one graduate trainee manager they employed. She was the only one with a black face.

The story of Rose and The Canalazzo involves many of the normal problems that someone is likely to face when trying to manage work – in a struggling restaurant or anywhere else. Alongside the obvious problems about the nature of the market for the particular services offered, and the need to achieve better coordination of the restaurant's division of labour, are a whole series of interpersonal and intergroup relationship problems. But most of these relate in some way to the patterns of conflict, inequality and discrimination existing in the wider culture and society. A critical organisation and management study would take all of this into account in an analysis of what was occurring. This would take it well beyond attention to orthodox issues of motivation, leadership and group relations. But it would also recognise the wider pattern of economic ownership which was relevant to issues in The Canalazzo and observe the way in which boardroom politics can affect what happens at a local workplace level in an organisation. There are politics at every level – workplace, organisation and society. A critical work organisation and management study would see these as centrally important matters, not merely as ones providing the 'context' in which the basic day-to-day application of managerial techniques and motivational skills have to be applied.

By now, after twice visiting The Canalazzo restaurant, two things should be apparent about analysing all the complexities of organisational and managerial behaviour as it occurs in 'real life' (as opposed to how it appears in the idealised world of standard management texts). First, as we saw in Activity 1.2, we have to look critically at facets of social, cultural, political and economic life that go way beyond a simple search for efficient management techniques. A whole series of moral issues arise in the Canalazzo story. Second, as we saw in Activity 1.1, we have to turn to a range of social science sources for help in analysing these matters. But each of these social sciences itself has a range of perspectives, models, concepts, theories and research studies on which we might draw when analysing whatever organisational or managerial issues interest or concern us. How do we choose between these?

Good, better and bad theories of organising and managing

One of the distinctive features of the present book (See Introduction, p. xix) is a concern with doing more than simply leaving readers more or less to decide for themselves which models, theories or ways of looking at organisations they prefer. However fair and reasonable this may seem at first, it avoids the issue of advising students of work organisation and management about what broad criteria they might apply to any piece of research or theorising they come across when trying to understand organisational or managerial practices. And this militates against taking a critical stance with regard to the study of work organisation and management itself. How do we make judgements about the relative value of one piece of analysis or knowledge compared with another?

To deal with this question we have to get involved with issues of *epistemology*. This is the branch of philosophy that deals with the relationship between the way the world is and the knowledge we have of that world. And it has a specific concern with the sort of truth claims that can be made for particular propositions or pieces of knowledge. This might seem a rather complex issue for us to get involved in here, something we can leave to philosophers while we get on with looking directly at organisations and their management. However, we really cannot duck the matter. It is vital to any understanding of how we relate 'theory and practice'.

Whether we like it or not, we all make epistemological judgements every day of our lives. We may have to decide, for example, 'how much truth there is' in the story we just read in our newspaper about an imminent business takeover. We might be concerned with 'how much truth there is' in the picture of society painted by the politician whose speech we have just listened to. Or we might be anxious about 'how much truth there is' in stories we have heard about a local school 'failing' and being closed down. Broadly speaking there are three approaches or 'theories' we can apply to such matters – approaches we can also take to the sort of accounts and analyses we come across when studying organisations and management. These are shown in Table 1.3.

In everyday life we apply all three ways of deciding the validity of a piece of knowledge. We do this in organisational contexts as much as we do in the other areas of life used in the examples in Table 1.3. But the approach to making judgements is obviously the most relevant to deciding what practices we are going to follow in any situation, in the light of the knowledge about that situation which is available to us. In the case of deciding which of the two tourist guides to trust, we would clearly be wise to apply the pragmatist 'theory of truth'. We would similarly be wise to apply this principle if we were considering taking a job with a particular organisation and had available to us, say, both the organisation's recruitment brochure and an article written by a researcher who had carried out participant observation research in that organisation. Which of these two 'pieces of knowledge' is the 'truer' one, we would tend to ask. And we would ask ourselves this question because we would be concerned to decide the most appropriate way to behave when entering the organisation. We would, in

Table 1.3 Three ways of deciding the 'truth' of knowledge

Three ways of deciding the 'truth' of an item of knowledge	For example . . .
Correspondence theories of truth judge an item of knowledge in terms of how accurately it paints a picture or gives a report of what actually happened or 'is the case'	A jury is asked to apply this principle (qualified by the notion of 'beyond reasonable doubt') when deciding between the accounts given by the prosecution and the defence. A judgement has to be made as to whether 'x' actually did or did not kill 'y'
Coherence/plausibility theories of truth judge an item of knowledge in terms of how well it 'fits in with' everything else we have learned about this matter previously	We might apply this principle when deciding whether a piece of gossip about somebody we know is true or false. We ask whether or not it fits with everything else we have seen of them and heard about them
Pragmatist theories of truth judge knowledge in terms of how effectively one would fulfil whatever projects one was pursuing in the area of activity covered by the knowledge, if we based our actions on the understanding of those activities which it offers	We might apply this principle when comparing what a promotional tourist brochure says about a foreign city we are going to visit and what is said in a book by an independent author drawing on their first-hand experiences. We have to decide which account of that city we are going to heed when deciding what to wear, how to address local people, how to find food that we like, or avoid being robbed

this respect, be applying a pragmatist theory of truth claims in the same way that we do when we compare the account of a product given in the manufacturer's advertisement and a report on the product published by an independent consumer association.

In the light of these examples, it is clear that a philosophical pragmatist approach to judging the sorts of material one comes across in studying organisations and management is invaluable. The wisdom of such an approach derives from two main things:

- It is impossible when looking at organisational issues to have enough information – free of interpretation, free of biased reporting, free of the tricks of human memory and free of ambiguity – to apply the correspondence theory of truth. This applies to social life in general as well as to organisations specifically. Because everything we are told about the world is mediated by language and interpretation, we can never receive an account which accurately reports or 'mirrors' that world.

- There are no absolute truths or 'final laws' which social scientific analysis can offer with regard to organisations or any other aspect of social life. One proposition, theory or research study can be judged to be truer than another, however. But this is only to the extent that it will tend to be a *more trustworthy, broad guide to practice* in the aspect of life it covers than the other. It cannot be wholly correct, totally true, or completely objective. One piece of knowledge is simply more useful than the other as an account of 'how things work' which we can use to inform our practices.

This pragmatist approach to judging the validity of the sorts of material we are going to study derives from a particular school of philosophy, the pragmatist philosophy of Charles Pierce, William James and James Dewey as well as, in part, the neo-pragmatist thinking of Richard Rorty (see Further Reading on epistemology and philosophical pragmatism, p. 32). It is important here to recognise that we are using the term 'pragmatist' in a more specific way than it tends to be used in everyday conversation, where it tends to mean 'expedient'. We are not using the word in the same way as the manager who says, 'Let's be pragmatic about this and get the job done, never mind what we ought to be doing in theory or according to the company's principles'. That manager was talking about doing something that was expedient or convenient, in the specific circumstances of the moment. This is not what we mean when we talk of philosophical pragmatism. What we talking about is something not dissimilar to the relatively straightforward notion of *critical common sense* looked at earlier. Pragmatist thinking leads us to the eminently sensible critical common sense practice of reading management and social science books (or considering any other kind of knowledge for that matter) and asking ourselves, 'To what extent should I take into account this knowledge when deciding what to do in practice?' If one theory, one research study, or even one piece of fictional writing, is thought to be more helpful in informing our practical projects than another, then it is a *better* theory, article or book. It is 'truer' in the philosophical pragmatist sense of 'true'. And note that this truth comes from the capacity to *inform practices*. It is in this that the truth lies. It is not a matter of a piece of knowledge or information being true because it is simply 'useful'. A lie can clearly be useful. To tell lies can be expedient. But where lies tend to fall apart is when one tries to base human practices on them. This is the sense in which lies are 'untrue' in philosophical pragmatist terms.

We also need to recognise that philosophical pragmatism avoids an absolute notion of truth. Instead, to put it simply, it regards some things as truer than others. One cannot produce a piece of academic research which presents the complete truth about an aspect of the world. The logic of science has to be understood as one of constantly looking for theories or explanations which are truer than those which preceded them (cf. Popper, 1963). But no absolute truth is achievable. In pragmatist terms, we will never have a body of knowledge upon which we can base our practices or projects in the world and which will give us complete success every time. However, there are some pieces of knowledge that will enable us to 'do better' if we take them as guides to action than if we utilise others. Truthfulness to the pragmatist is a relative matter.

To emphasise the relevance of pragmatist criteria for evaluating pieces of organisational and management knowledge is not to argue for completely turning our backs on the other criteria for judging truth. The concept of justice applied in many societies requires us to work with the correspondence theory of truth, for example, in courts of law or other types of judicial or bureaucratic enquiry. Yet even here, as we noted earlier, the ultimate impossibility of this is recognised in the acceptance that a judgement can only achieve a reliability which is 'beyond *reasonable* doubt'. We are therefore much safer, for most purposes, applying the more modest pragmatist criterion for judging truth claims. And we are certainly much safer applying this approach than making too much use of coherence or plausibility theories of truth. We apply these all the time – when, for example, we ask how one statement on some issue 'stacks up against' everything else we have heard on that matter. At the level of ordinary or everyday common sense we have to do this. But it is not good enough when we are engaged in the more rigorous and critical common sense type of thinking which we frequently have to do in the complex area of organising and managing work. Too many poor theories in the organisational and management sphere have an immediate plausibility, one that soon disappears when rigorous and critical common sense is applied to them.

The pragmatist style of thinking is also relevant, in a very basic way, to the arguments set out earlier for the *critical analysis* of work and organisational behaviours. Doing this, it was argued, involved appreciating that work organisation happens in a context of contest, inequality and conflict and that management ideas are more than neutral rules, principles or guides to action; they always have political significance. Knowledge of organisations and management which gives full recognition to these matters, according to the pragmatist principles, would be better – as a set of resources for informing practice – than knowledge which ignored them. This is because an organisational practitioner, managerial or non-managerial, would be better placed to succeed in whatever their purposes might be if they were informed in this way. We might go as far as to say that an individual who tried to undertake any kind of organisational task without a strong awareness of the political dimension of organisational life would be a fool! It follows from this that critical thinking is equally relevant to a manager, a non-managerial worker or someone wishing to challenge and undermine the whole enterprise. To put this another way, there cannot be 'managerially biased' knowledge – other than inadequate or misleading knowledge. If there is work organisation knowledge which helpfully informs the practices, projects and purposes of managers, then it is likely to be equally helpful to anyone else operating in that context – including someone wishing to oppose 'managerial' initiatives. The same principle applies to other spheres of human activity. Knowledge which helps a government rule can also help an opposition to bring it down, for example. Knowledge which helps a police force fight crime can equally help criminals carry out crimes more successfully, for example.

As far as *Organising and Managing Work* is concerned, everything in the book is intended to inform people involved in the management of work – whatever the nature of that involvement might be. The book should be helpful to those designated as 'managers'. But it should be equally relevant to someone whose 'project' is to have a quiet life at work, make an investment or customer decision about a work organisation or set out in some way to oppose the managers of an organisation. And, to put this style of 'active reading' into practice from the start, it can be useful to apply it to one of the most popular items ever taught to students of organisation and management: Maslow's hierarchy of needs theory.

Assessing a popular 'motivation theory' critically and pragmatically

A central place has been given for half a century or so in management education and organisational studies to certain thoughts of one particular mid-twentieth century American writer, Abraham Maslow (1943, 1954, 1968). Indeed, Maslow's 'hierarchy of needs' theory of motivation has come to play an iconic part in the study of organisational behaviour and courses on management. This is in spite of it having emerged from a body of work which is very much at odds with more recent thinking and values in psychological and social science research (Cullen, 1997). Countless teachers and students of areas of human endeavour ranging from organisation behaviour and supervisory management to nursing education and consumer behaviour have drawn and redrawn the triangle shown in Figure 1.4 – this being used to illustrate Maslow's at first sight plausible notion that human beings in their lives and activities generally work *upwards* through a particular sequence of 'needs'. People are said generally to seek to satisfy 'lower order' *physiological* and *safety* needs before moving upwards to satisfy 'higher order' *social* and *esteem* needs. At the top of the hierarchy is an idealised notion of perfect human fulfilment called '*self-actualisation*'. This is something that people allegedly seek to satisfy once they are well fed, safe, socially integrated and 'well thought of' by others.

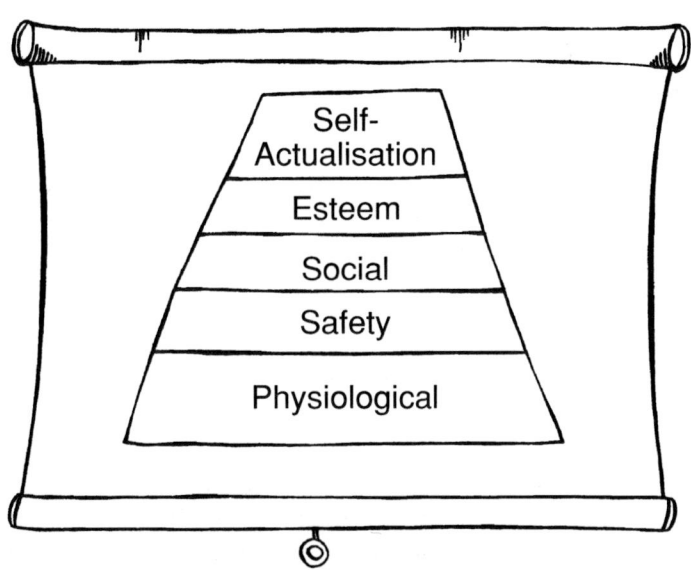

FIGURE 1.4 The ubiquitous hierarchy of needs model

At the level of everyday common sense (p. 10) there is some logic in this. If we wish to 'motivate' a starving worker running away from a hungry lion it is not unreasonable to consider chasing away the lion and giving them a loaf of bread in return for them performing as we require. Once the worker is getting plenty to eat and has had their 'safety needs' met, it seems equally reasonable to expect to have to offer some further incentives to gain worker cooperation: giving them the satisfactions of sociability with other human beings and making them feel esteemed or 'highly thought of'. Perhaps, beyond this, the only incentive that the worker can be offered is an opportunity to self-actualise or somehow to 'become everything that they would most want to be'.

The so-called 'hierarchy of needs' theory has some appeal at the everyday common sense level then. But before we turn to philosophical pragmatist criteria to help us reach a more critically commonsensical evaluation, let us first look at this theory in its social and political context in the way that fits with that requirement shown in Figure 1.2 whereby critical organisational and management studies 'asks why we think about organising and managing the way we do'. To understand why we think about 'motivation' in the hierarchy of needs way we have to note its origins in the particular setting in which Maslow was working. This was one, within the increasingly comfortable middle classes of the USA, where it was plausible to expect people who were 'doing well' to seek to 'get even more out of life'. The message from Maslow's popularisers to employers in the increasingly affluent sections of certain mid-twentieth-century societies was, in effect, 'if you want to get more out of your increasingly comfortable employees you had better think of some extra things to give them'. The ultimate 'extra' that successful industrial capitalism could offer people was the opportunity to achieve the total opposite of the 'alienation' that so many social commentators had worried about as a consequence of industrialism and capitalism. Maslow's message was corporate capitalism's answer to the Marxist fear of work under capitalism leading to dehumanising and the *alienation* of people (p. 448). Instead of people being separated from their essential humanity, as Marxists and other radical critics of capitalism feared, they could be rewarded not just with the material and social rewards of economic success but also with the chance to become everything that a human being could possibly become – the chance to realise their essential humanity, whatever that might be. This was self-actualisation.

Any critical study of organisational and managerial behaviour must pay attention to these ideological implications of what is probably the most frequently taught and most commonly remembered single 'theory' in the business and management studies curriculum.

Having identified the ideological roots of Maslow's thinking, we can move on to apply the normal social scientific critical rigour to the theory itself. Each of the three types of 'truth claim' that can be made for knowledge, set out above (p. 18) can be applied to the hierarchy of needs theory's claim that people only seek to satisfy 'higher order' needs once they have satisfied the lower level ones.

The *correspondence* criterion for judging the 'truth' of a theory might be applied by testing whether the sequence of 'need fulfilment' posited in the theory accords with what we see to 'be the case' if people are systematically studied meeting their needs in a research laboratory. Research psychologists have attempted to do this and found that people simply do not follow the sequence suggested by Maslow (Rauschenberger, Schmitt and Hunter, 1980). On these grounds, then, the theory fails.

On the *plausibility* criterion, which would judge the theory to be true if it fitted with everything else we know, we have already seen that there are some grounds for acceptance. But the plausibility of the theory soon drops away once we move beyond the everyday common sense mode of thinking (p. 10) in which truisms play an important part ('it's obvious isn't it?' we often say when thinking at the unreflective *everyday common sense* level). The *critical common sense* advocated earlier requires us to step back and critically put our minds to what at first seems credible.

So what about the *philosophical pragmatist* principle of judging truth claims? This requires us to ask how helpful the theory would be in informing our practices were we to find ourselves in the situation of trying to 'motivate' people at work. And here we can turn to the case of Campbell Toon, a manager and a management student whom we see in Case 1.3 applying, in effect, both critical common sense thinking and the philosophical pragmatist principle. He does not use these terms himself but the principles they represent are implicit in what he says to the researcher.

Activity 1.3

Read Campbell Toon's conversation with the researcher in Case 1.3 and his experience-based rejection of the Maslow theory of motivation and reflect on:

- why you think so many people seem to remember the 'hierarchy of needs' theory (or the triangular representation of it at least) and not the more complex theories that deal with 'motivation';

- the extent to which the hierarchical sequence of need satisfaction is followed in your own life (following the approach that Campbell takes to analysing the place of different aspects of need satisfaction in his personal life).

Campbell Toon confronts the Maslow triangle   Case 1.3

During a management class the researcher had reported the outcomes of some 'ethnographic experiments' he had done with other management students. During one of these events, a year or more previously, a student had uttered what the researcher took to be the very significant words, 'Motivation, that's Maslow isn't it?' (Watson, 1996a). Most of the current class reacted positively to the researcher's argument that these words perfectly captured the sort of 'surface learning' that can occur in management education when the topic of study becomes 'what this or that American professor wrote years ago' rather than how academic theorising relates to the actual practices of people involved in organising and managing work. Campbell Toon, however, was especially vocal in his attack on what he called 'Maslow's bloody magic triangle', arguing that he had been 'foolish enough to think that what he studied on management courses should be relevant to his practice as a manager'. When he visited the researcher's office after the class to collect a copy of the journal article reporting the study, he agreed to a tape recording of a conversation with the researcher. The researcher speaks first.

I hope, Cam, that I wasn't going too far in the class by asking the course members to be critical of both themselves and the material they have to study.

No, I don't think so. I think that you are right that too many lecturers and too many students simply go through the motions of drawing that dreaded triangle as an alternative to engaging with serious attempts to understand what it really means to have to motivate people at work. I'm not sure, though, whether you are right that people keep reproducing the triangle in their lectures and in their assignments as a magic ritual or a magic charm because they are actually frightened by – what was it you said?

'The frightening realities of managerial work', or some such thing, probably. No, I was just speculating that perhaps the endless drawing of the triangle by teachers and students is equivalent to people crossing themselves when they see a funeral pass by. You know, it's a sort of whistling in the dark when you are frightened because you don't really know what you are doing. But, leaving all that aside, I'm interested in your point that you did try to apply this thinking in your work.

Yes, I was facing some big problems in the packaging business where I work. It was made clear to me that the productivity levels in my part of the factory were not good enough. I knew I had to get more out of people. I had no sticks to beat people with – they were all doing a reasonable job, even if they rarely showed any kind of initiative and hardly ever helped each other out with problems. Generally, people seemed to me to be complacent. The firm was ostensibly doing well and people were reasonably paid and were secure in their jobs. When I tried exhorting people to speed up a bit, to work together a bit more when problems arose and to look for smarter ways of doing things, they just smiled at me and carried on in the same way. So you can see that when it came to the classes on motivation I was dead keen to see what these 'theories of motivation' would have to offer. The Maslow thing clicked with me when we covered it. The lower level needs of my people were all satisfied, I concluded, and therefore to motivate them to do more I had to offer them something at the 'higher order' level. I saw that Herzberg's job enrichment principle ('Herzberg spelled without a "t"', I remember the lecturer saying) was a way of applying the Maslow theory. I therefore set about rearranging the jobs of my people so that there was more variety in their tasks and, by taking away a level of supervision, they were given more freedom to choose how to do the work. In introducing this I really played up the 'social needs' bit by pointing out that they would need to work more closely together and would find this socially rewarding. I gave even more emphasis to the 'esteem' need by making the point very strongly that I had a high opinion of my staff and that the firm had perhaps been insulting their abilities by supervising them so closely and prescribing every little detail of how to do things.

And did this work?

Did it hell. After only a week and a half I had to get some tight supervision back. The simple truth of the matter is that my people *did not want to have their jobs enriched*. Well, this is not entirely true. Two or three of them were persuaded by my arguments. I had a sort of post mortem talk with two of these. They told me that they agreed that people ought to find some of the fulfilment in their work that they tended to get with their families or in their hobbies. However, I inferred from what they told me that most of their work mates were happier getting their social, esteem and fulfilment needs satisfied outside of work and that they were happy 'cruising along' at work. But when I put it to them that 'money was not a motivator' they just laughed at me and said that had the new system lasted a little longer they were all going to put in a wage claim. When I expressed some shock they said, 'Sod money as a motivator. First, there's no way any factory worker is ever going to feel that they are paid enough. And, second, it would simply be unfair to leave people on the ordinary factory rate when they were now doing some of the old supervisor's job'.

One might argue that you had just been naïve here as a manager and that you can't really blame old Maslow for your naïvety.

I accept that. But your class last week made me think a lot about why, as management students, we often fail to test the material we are offered against our own work experiences, let alone common sense. Somehow, with me though, the confrontation with Maslow's magic triangle had encouraged me to *switch off* my common sense. When you think hard about the so-called hierarchy of needs, it doesn't stack up, does it? I am Jewish and I get a good deal of my self-esteem and an awful lot of the social rewards in my life from belonging to my culture. The meeting of these social and esteem needs, I have to say, comes before I meet my need to eat or my need to make love to whoever I fancy. The rules of my religion and my community define what and when I eat and who I can have sex with. If I was in the Israeli army, like my cousin recently was, I would put the need to belong to my community and my personal prestige needs, as a defender of my community, way before even my need for safety. Yet Maslow's simplistic scheme has us all working up through the satisfaction of the more basic physiological and safety needs towards the higher social or esteem ones. It is nonsense – there is simply no straightforward sequence to how people pursue their needs. And Maslow's whole notion of human beings seems to be one in which people live outside of culture. What I said about being Jewish would apply, in various ways, to members of any other culture of course.

Well, I'm sure he wasn't unaware of all of these things but the 'theory of motivation' that has been extracted from his writings and presented to generations of management students does seem to do just this. It reduces people, with all their choices, preferences, values and cultural influences to need-led little machines.

So this doesn't say a lot for business school education does it?

Well perhaps not. But, to be fair, I am sure that you covered other motivational theories that would be closer to your own commonsensical thinking and would helpfully, in my favourite phrase, 'inform your practice'. Do you not remember coming across something called 'expectancy theory' – an approach which stresses the importance of finding out just what your own particular employees actually want, rather than wasting time reflecting on human 'needs' in general? And did you not look at 'equity theories' and their emphasis on how ideas about fairness influence people's motivation (as happened with your people)? All of that would have been very useful to you as a manager, I suggest. And, of course, I would argue that the ideas about work orientations and implicit contracts that some of us use in this area are even more useful.

I confess that I just didn't take in these other theories – 'process theories' I think they called them. They just seemed to be more complicated – and more difficult to remember.

Well, you're not alone there. In the research paper you will see evidence that the vast majority of the three hundred or so students who took part in the events covered in the project, one year on, could remember practically nothing of the 'process theories' they studied.

For them motivation was Maslow?

Something like that.

On pragmatist grounds, then, it would seem that only very weak truth claims can be made for Maslow's theory. What Campbell Toon has to say, however, has a significance way beyond the hierarchy of needs theory specifically or to motivational theories generally. The conversation raises serious questions about the role that traditional management education plays in the management learning processes of those who take the courses and use the standard textbooks. This connects back to the earlier arguments for applying critical common sense to the questions that surface whenever we really want to understand the complex issues that arise with organising and managing work. Both parties to the conversation reflect on why the particular motivational theory of which they are so critical should be given such massive attention within management education. Cam recognises the relevance of information (and images) being easy to remember. The researcher speculates, at an anthropological level, about a possible symbolic role for the 'magic triangle' as some kind of talisman that helps management tutors and management students alike cope with the ambiguities and anxieties involved in studying something as complex and daunting as managerial practice (see Watson, 1996a). This issue of 'managerial angst' and the 'controlling the uncontrollable' expectations that are put on managers will be returned to in Chapter 6 (pp. 229–34).

Campbell's thoughts about how he does not move through a sequence of need satisfaction that remotely resembles the hierarchical models in his own life are especially significant. As he points out, every one of us lives within a culture. This means that satisfying 'needs' that can be characterised in social, esteem or 'self-actualisation' terms could be seen as having precedence over the satisfaction of so-called lower order ones – contrary to the hierarchical model. Is there anyone who could say that they regularly satisfy their physiological needs for food, drink, sex or to urinate without first considering the norms of the social groups to which they belong or prior to reflecting on what sort of esteem they will be held in if they prioritise their hunger, thirst, lust or full bladder over a need to 'belong' or a need to be admired? Of course not. One's 'motivations', in work or elsewhere, are matters of one's cultural location, personal identity, work orientation, values and life priorities and how these lead to exchanges in particular circumstances – like the exchange that people make through an implicit contract with a particular employer at a particular time.

Furthermore, it is unlikely that any of us would be able to point to any kind of sequential pattern at all in the way we go about managing our lives and handling our 'needs'. Maslow's desire to impose a particular order on people's need satisfaction behaviour is an example of the type of *linearity* in theorising about human behaviour that we will critically examine in Chapter 3. And, as we will also see in Chapter 3, matters of work motivation and orientation simply cannot be reduced to something as simple as 'needs'. While it is reasonable to talk of people 'needing' food and water, it becomes much more difficult to use the language of needs when considering matters like pursuing promotion to a high status position or trying to obtain a company car. 'Wants' would be a more realistic notion here, as would be the concepts of *expectancy* and *equity* that are used in some of the more process-oriented motivational theories that we shall meet in Chapter 8. But what are 'concepts' and how might we most effectively use them in our study of the organising and managing of work.

Concepts, perspectives and two ways of framing reality

Concepts
Concept

Concepts are the working definitions that are chosen or devised to make possible a particular piece of scientific analysis. They are the way scientists define their terms for the purpose of a specific investigation. They therefore differ from dictionary definitions which tend to have a much more general applicability.

In our everyday lives, we often look for *correct definitions* of phenomena, ones that will be generally helpful to us when communicating within a broad public language. If we wish to analyse phenomena with the greater degree of rigour and focus that distinguishes scientific analysis, however, we find ourselves having more carefully to *conceptualise* phenomena. This means devising working definitions which are helpful to us in trying to analyse and understand some aspect of the world. Thus an economist will conceptualise money more rigorously than the person in the street will 'define' it. Psychologists will do similarly with regard to 'intelligence' – working with different concepts of intelligence at different times. What this means is that in engaging in an enterprise like writing *Organising and Managing Work*, one develops concepts that are useful to one's purposes. One does not turn to a dictionary for the universally 'correct' definition. Thus, every time there is a 'defining of terms' in this book (usually using the device of a 'concept box'), it is done to be *helpful* to the purposes of the book – and *useful* to the readers who are interested in improving their understanding of how work is organised and managed. The whole enterprise of the book is based on the notion that some ways of conceptualising, 'management' or 'organisation', say, are more useful than others. The intent is not to find a 'correct' definition of what 'management' or 'organisation' is but to use concepts that help us critically engage with the world.

Although in the subsequent chapters we will be offering conceptualisations of management and of organisations that are helpful in analysing and thinking about work activities and their shaping, it is important to stress that concepts should not be seen as free-standing entities that can be used without being made consistent with other concepts being used in that same analysis. To analyse any area of human life we need 'bundles' or sets of concepts that are all compatible with each other, logically and in terms of the deeper assumptions underlying the concepts (Watson, 1997a). Thus, for any given analysis, one develops a conceptual framework or theoretical perspective that is appropriate to the purpose in hand. Thus a psychologist studying certain types of problem will want a set of linked concepts of, say, intelligence, personality, learning, motivation and so on.

Whilst it is the case that the individual social scientist will choose concepts appropriate to the particular piece of research that they are engaged in at any particular time, it is nevertheless true that each of us – both in our formal analytical endeavours and in our general thinking about life – tend to build up bundles of concepts that we find most helpful, these adding up to the personal analytical frames of reference that we take through life. These are, in the broadest sense of the word, 'theories' (systematic ideas about how the world works, we might say). These schemes are often and very usefully referred to as ways of 'framing reality'.

> ### Framings of reality *Concept*
>
> These are broad ways of looking at the world that people adopt to make sense of various aspects of human life – work organisation and management being one of these. The framework that we use with regard to any particular aspect of life will incorporate:
>
> - basic general assumptions about human beings ('people's characters are decided before birth', for example);
> - conceptualisations of various dimensions of the specific area being considered (concepts of organisational culture or work identity, for example);
> - broad ideas about how these various dimensions relate to each other (how organisational cultures relate to organisational structures, for example).

The notion of 'discursive framing' in human life will be examined in Chapter 3 (p. 102). For the moment we need simply to emphasise that the way we 'frame' reality influences how we both think and act in the world. We might, for instance, 'frame' *management* as essentially an activity in which intelligent and trained individuals decide how work should be done and then instruct less able and knowledgeable individuals to act accordingly. If we do this, we are likely to act differently when we get into management situations (as either the 'boss' or the 'worker') than we would if we 'framed' management as a process involving the bringing together of different types of knowledge, understanding and priorities to get work tasks done.

To help organise the present book, all the time applying the philosophical pragmatist principle of developing frameworks which better inform human practices, a basic distinction between *systems-control* and *process-relational* ways of framing the realities of human life generally and organisational activities specifically is used. These two framings will be unfolded in the next two chapters. For the moment, however, it is useful to see these two broad ways of thinking about human beings and about work organisations set out alongside each other. The first two columns of Table 1.4 (p. 30) derive from the thinking to be set out in Chapter 2 and the third and fourth columns relate to Chapter 3. The broad shape of the thinking behind these two chapters is presented here in part to offer a road map of the terrain over which we are about to travel. But it is also offered to show the parallels that exist between the issues to be covered at the organisational level and the issues to be covered at the level of the human being. This is not to say that organisations can be treated as if they were people. It is, instead, to recognise that there are clear parallels in the way we think about human beings on the one hand and work organisations on the other.

The most important point to stress before we move on is that, whilst it is *not* being argued that the systems-control way of framing is wrong or untrue and the process-relational framework is right or true, it will be argued, in pragmatist terms, that there are real and practical advantages in moving beyond systems-control ways of framing reality towards process-relational ones. This is fully in line with the intention behind *Organising and Managing Work* not to duck the issue of whether some ideas, theories or frames of reference relating to the organising and managing of work might be *better* than others. It is to be argued that all of us will be better placed to cope in the world of work management if we adopt thinking that can be broadly conceived of as part of a process-relational way of framing reality than if we follow the more traditional or orthodox systems-control style of thinking.

Table 1.4 is something that can helpfully be referred back to after Chapter 2 and 3 have been read. In the next chapter we will see how the systems-control way of framing organisational and managerial activities derives from modernist and universalistic aspirations to maximise control over human circumstances and does this through encouraging a notion of organisations as large goal-based controllable mechanical systems and individuals as small need-oriented systems. It will be argued that a more useful way of framing organisational realities – and indeed the broader human realities that we will consider in Chapter 3 – is to focus instead on the processes of emergence in the patterning of relations between people, organisations and the wider social world.

Summary

In this chapter, the following key points have been made:

- The most helpful way to think about issues of work organisation and management is not to focus on either the management of people or the management of systems but to focus on the management of work tasks and the relationships involved in fulfilling those tasks. This involves looking at all those activities which contribute to the management of work tasks, only then considering how such activities are divided up between people who have the title of 'manager' and those who do not.

- The field covered in the present text is the study of the human aspects of work organisation and its management which draws on the social sciences to develop insights, theories and research findings with a view to informing the choices, decisions and actions of organisational practitioners.

- This field of study is linked to, and incorporates elements of, several other established and developing academic subjects, including management learning, critical management studies, strategic management and human resource management.

Table 1.4 Systems-control and process-relational ways of framing organisations and people

Systems-control framing of organisations	Process-relational framing of organisations	Systems-control framing of people	Process-relational framing of people
The organisation is an *entity*: a system of managerially designed rules and roles existing on its own terms	Organisations are *relational phenomena*: sets of relationships and associated understandings	The individual person is an *entity* which exists on its own terms with an essential or 'true' self	People are *relational* beings: their individuality only becomes possible as a result of relating to others
The organisation is based on an *organisation design* with a set of structural and cultural characteristics	Organisations are *emergent patterns* resulting from processes of exchange, negotiation, conflict and compromise	The individual possesses a more or less fixed set of *personality* traits	People are always in a process of 'becoming': they have *emergent identities*
The organisation operates to ensure the completion of the *organisational goals* it was designed to fulfil	Organisations are *strategically oriented* in the sense that those in charge of them strive to ensure that they survive in the long term	People have sets of needs which create *motives* propelling them towards particular behaviours	People are *sense making* and *project oriented* rather than need led: in the light of how they interpret their situation they make *exchanges* with others to deal with their material and emotional circumstances
The organisation is a rational *system of rules and procedures* which ensures the completion of tasks that ensure corporate goal fulfilment	Organisations operate with *both reason and emotion*: the feelings of managers, workers and customers are as relevant to their behaviours as is their rational pursuit of material interests within formal corporate procedures	People at work are capable of suppressing emotions so that their engagement in *rational analysis* and decision making is unaffected by feelings and values	People are *simultaneously rational and emotional*: their feelings about the world and their reasoning capacities mutually influence each other
The organisation is an expression of universally applicable organisational and managerial principles	Organisations all follow modernist bureaucratic principles, but their functioning also reflects the economic, cultural and political circumstances of their societal setting	People, regardless of the society in which they live, play the role of worker, manager or whatever according to the logic of modern systems of employment and work organisation	People are cultural animals: they make sense of the world and their work activities in the light of the culture and values of the society and communities of which they are a part

- The social science disciplines drawn upon by *Organising and Managing Work*, and their analytical styles, are not essentially different from 'common sense' thinking. In fact, they have a close continuity with what can be called 'critical common sense'.

- In the spirit of 'critical common sense', the style of work organisation and management studies adopted here can be identified with certain aspects of the emergent tradition of 'critical management studies'. This entails continually asking, first, why

- work is organised and managed in the way it is and, second, why we think about and study work and its management in the ways we do. It also involves continuous recognition of the extent to which work organisation happens in a context of human competition, context and patterned antagonism as well as recognising that management ideas are not neutral technical rules and principles but always have political significance.

- To be able to relate what we study to issues of practice in the organisational and managerial world we need some criteria for judging the relative merits of the theories, research studies and other materials that are available to us. The most useful criterion we can apply to judging theories, and the rest, is one derived from pragmatist philosophy. There is no way of judging absolute truth or validity. But some accounts can be seen as 'truer' than others. It is suggested that one piece of material may be judged to be 'truer' than another to the extent to which it better informs human practices or 'projects' in the aspect of human activity with which it deals.

- In spite of a growing interest in processual thinking, an almost fetishistic level of attention is given to 'motivation theories' in business and management education and, especially to Maslow's 'hierarchy of needs' theory. This latter theory has enormous weaknesses and has little value as a guide to human practice. But it nevertheless has an important ideological significance in how employment relationships have been thought about in more affluent societies over the past half century. It may also have a symbolic role in the handling of managerial angst.

- Concepts are vital tools for social scientific analysis and are different from dictionary definitions in that they are devised for the specific purpose of a given analysis. Concepts are drawn together into conceptual or theoretical frameworks. Such frameworks are, again, devised for specific studies. But all of us develop personal ways of looking at the world which are broadly of a similar nature: they help us make sense of the world around us and influence how we act in the world. These perspectives can be understood as ways of 'framing realities'. There are two basic ways of framing the realities of the organising and managing work: a systems-control framing and a process-relational framing. The latter has greater promise as a frame of reference that will inform the practices of anyone involved in organisational situations.

Recommended reading

A stimulating and accessible overview of a critical style of thinking about organising and managing is provided by Chris Grey in his *A Very Short, Fairly Interesting and Reasonably Cheap Book about Studying Organization* (London: Sage, 2005). This book is nicely complemented by the collection of pieces edited by Mats Alvesson and Hugh Willmott, *Studying Management Critically* (London: Sage, 2003). For a coverage of the variety of different theoretical positions on organisations that gives useful background to the systems-control/process-relational scheme used in *Organising and Managing Work* see the book written by Mary Jo Hatch with Ann Cunliffe, *Organization Theory: Modern, symbolic and postmodern perspectives*, 2nd edition (Oxford: Oxford University Press, 2006). And for a fuller explanation of how one can apply pragmatist thinking to research on managing and organising see the Tony Watson article 'Theorising managerial work: a pragmatic pluralist approach to interdisciplinary research' (*British Journal of Management*, 8: 3–8, 1997).

Further reading

Further reading Critical approaches in organisation and management studies

Alvesson, M. and Deetz, S. (1999) *Doing Critical Management Research*, London: Sage

Alvesson, M. and Willmott, H. (1996) *Making Sense of Management: A critical introduction*, London: Sage

Alvesson, M. and Willmott, H. (eds) (2003) *Studying Management Critically*, London: Sage

Fournier, V. and Grey, C. (2000) 'At the critical moment: conditions and prospects of critical management studies', *Human Relations*, 53(1): 7–32

Grey, C., Knights, D. and Willmott, H. (1996) 'Is a critical pedagogy of management possible?' in R. French and C. Grey (eds) *Rethinking Management Education*, London: Sage

O'Connor, E.S. (1999) 'The politics of management thought: a case study of Harvard Business School and the human relations school', *Academy of Management Review*, 24(1): 117–131

Perriton, L. (2000) 'Verandah discourses: critical management education in organizations', *British Journal of Management*, 11(3): 227–237

Prasad, P. and Capruni, P.J. (1997) 'Critical theory in the management classroom: engaging power, ideology, and praxis', *Journal of Management Education*, 21(3): 284–291

Reynolds, M. (1997) 'Towards a critical management pedagogy' in J. Burgoyne and M. Reynolds (eds) *Management Learning: Integrating perspectives in theory and practice*, London: Sage

Reynolds, M. (1998) 'Reflection and critical reflection in management learning', *Management Learning*, 29(2): 183–200

Reynolds, M. (1999) 'Grasping the nettle: possibilities and pitfalls of a critical management pedagogy', *British Journal of Management*, 10(2): 95–184

Sotorin, P. and Tyrell, S. (1998) 'Wondering about critical management studies', *Management Communication Quarterly*, 12(2): 303–336

Steffy, B.D. and Grimes, A.J. (1986) 'A critical theory of organisational science', *Academy of Management Review*, 11(2): 322–336

Watson, T.J. (1994) 'Towards a managerially relevant but non-managerialist organisation theory' in J. Hassard and M. Parker (eds) *Towards a New Theory of Organizations*, London: Routledge

Willmott, H. (1997) 'Critical management learning' in J. Burgoyne and M. Reynolds (eds) *Management Learning: Integrating perspectives in theory and practice*, London: Sage

Wilson, F. (2004) *Organizational Behaviour and Work: A critical introduction, 2nd edition*, Oxford: Oxford University Press

Further reading Epistemology and philosophical pragmatism

Davidson, D. (1986) 'A coherence theory of truth and knowledge' in E. Lepore (ed.) *Truth and Interpretation*, Oxford: Blackwell

Gallie, W.B. (1952) *Pierce and Pragmatism*, Harmondsworth: Penguin

Haack, S. (1996) 'Pragmatism' in N. Bunnin, and E.P. Tsui-James (eds) *The Blackwell Companion to Philosophy*, Oxford: Blackwell

James, W. (ed. D. Olin) (1992) *Pragmatism in Focus*, London: Routledge

Mounce, H.O. (1997) *The Two Pragmatisms*, London: Routledge

Putnam, H. (1995) *Pragmatism*, Oxford: Blackwell

Rorty, R. (1980) *Philosophy and the Mirror of Nature*, Oxford: Blackwell

Rorty, R. (1982) *Consequences of Pragmatism*, Brighton: Harvester

Rorty, R. (1989) *Contingency, Irony, and Solidarity*, Cambridge: Cambridge University Press

Tsoukas, H. (1989) 'The validity of idiographic research explanations', *Academy of Management Review*, 14: 551–561

Tsoukas, H. (1998a) 'Forms of knowledge and forms of life in organized contexts' in R. Chia (ed.) *In the Realm of Organization*, London: Routledge

Tsoukas, H. (1998b) 'The word and the world: a critique of representationalism in management research', *International Journal of Public Administration*, 21(5): 781–817

Urmson, J.O. (1989) 'Truth' in J.O. Urmson and J. Rée (eds) *The Concise Encyclopedia of Western Philosophy and Philosophers*, London: Routledge

Watson, T.J. (1997) 'Theorising managerial work: a pragmatic pluralist approach to interdisciplinary research', *British Journal of Management*, 8 (special issue): 3–8

THE WIDER CONTEXT OF MANAGING PEOPLE

Chapter 4

Human resource management and the labour market

Tim Claydon and Amanda Thompson

Objectives

- To explain the nature and composition of the UK labour market.
- To identify the major social forces responsible for shaping the nature and extent of people's engagement with paid employment.
- To highlight developments in the nature of work and employment in the late twentieth and early twenty-first centuries and to show how these trends have influenced organisational requirements for labour.
- To present a critical assessment of workers' experiences of employment in contemporary Britain.

Introduction

This chapter is concerned principally with the size, composition and condition of the UK labour market and more specifically with how the labour market shapes employers' choices concerning people management and utilisation. An appreciation of labour markets and how they operate is especially relevant for students of HRM, as it claims to offer a strategic approach to managing people. A strategic stance is considered attractive because it offers organisations scope to select an appropriate employment system and a set of complementary HR practices to 'fit' the external operating environment, placing the firm in a better position to exploit competitive advantage. From a practical perspective therefore, knowing and understanding labour market issues is likely to be of prime value to the organisation in its bid to formulate a strategic approach to HRM and support the wider aim of achieving superior business outcomes.

We divide the chapter into four main sections to draw upon a range of contemporary labour market issues and consider the significance of each for the practice of HRM. In the first we discuss the nature of labour markets and the considerations that influence the employment strategies of firms. In the second we explore recent political and social developments and the implications of these for the supply of labour. The third section explores the changing nature of work and employment and is designed to focus on emergent themes in employers' demand for labour. The final section of the chapter considers key dimensions of job quality and discusses these in relation to workers' experiences of employment in contemporary Britain.

The nature of labour markets

The most general definition of the labour market is that it consists of workers who are looking for paid employment and employers who are seeking to fill vacancies. The amount of labour that is available to firms – *labour supply* – is determined by the number of people of working age who are in employment or seeking employment and the number of hours that they are willing to work. This number will be determined by the size and age structure of the population and by the decisions made by individuals and households about the relative costs and benefits of taking paid employment. These decisions are influenced by various factors, one of which is the level of wages on offer. Generally speaking, a higher wage will attract more people into the labour market while a lower wage will attract fewer, as long as other factors, such as the level of welfare benefits and people's attitudes towards work, remain constant.

The number of jobs on offer to workers – *labour demand* – is the sum of people in employment plus the number of vacancies waiting to be filled. The demand for labour is determined by the level of demand for the goods and services produced by firms in the market. When sales and production are rising, firms' demand for labour rises. When sales fall and production is cut back, firms' demand for labour falls. This is illustrated by widespread job losses in the car industry during 2008–09, following a collapse of sales due to the recession. For example, BMW announced 850 job losses at its Mini production plant in Oxfordshire in February 2009 following a 35 per cent drop in sales.

The simplest view of the labour market is that it is an arena of competition. Workers enter the arena in search of jobs and employers enter it in search of workers. Competition between employers for workers and between workers for jobs results in a 'market wage' that adjusts to relative changes in labour demand and supply. Thus, when labour demand rises relative to labour supply, the market wage rises as firms try to outbid each other for scarce labour. When labour demand falls relative to labour supply, the market wage falls as workers compete with each other for the smaller number of available jobs.

Competition means that no individual firm can set a wage that is out of line with the competitive market wage. Neither can workers demand such a wage. Should a firm try to offer a wage that is below the market rate, it will be unable to hire workers. Should a firm set a wage above the market rate, it will go out of business because its costs of production will be above those of its competitors. For the same reason, workers who demand a wage higher than the market rate will price themselves out of jobs. No firm will hire them because to do so would increase their costs of production relative to those of their competitors.

While it is undeniable that competitive forces operate in the labour market to a degree, few would seriously pretend that this is a wholly accurate description of the real world. There are limits to competition between firms and among workers. Wages do not respond instantly to changes in labour demand. Nor is there a uniform wage in the labour market. Empirical research has shown that rates of pay vary between firms, even in the same industry and operating in the same local labour market (Nolan and Brown, 1983). Other employment policies also vary among firms. For example, some firms employ labour on a hire and fire basis and make heavy use of casualised forms of employment such as temporary work while others offer long-term employment security and career development. The policies that employers adopt are influenced to a great extent by the characteristics they seek in their workforce:

- **The need for a stable workforce.** A stable workforce is advantageous to employers because it reduces the costs of labour turnover, i.e. disruption of production due to the unplanned reductions in the workforce that result from workers leaving, costs of recruitment and selection, such as the financial costs of advertising for recruits and the cost in terms of management time spent in recruiting and selecting replacements, and the cost of training new recruits. These costs may be particularly high where skilled labour is scarce and replacements hard to find, or where employers have invested considerable amounts in training workers. In these situations employers have a strong interest in limiting the extent of labour turnover.

- **The need for worker cooperation in production**. A central issue in managing people at work is how to manage their performance. One way of trying to ensure that workers supply the required level of effort is by subjecting them to direct controls (Friedman, 1977). Traditionally, this took the form of direct personal supervision by a superior and externally imposed discipline. Today, direct supervision is supplemented with electronic surveillance, 'mystery customers' and customer questionnaire surveys in a managerial effort to make workers' effort levels increasingly visible. However, there are limits to the extent that employers can rely on direct controls. This is because the nature of the product or the production process often makes it difficult to define what the appropriate effort levels are for each worker and to measure how hard they are actually working. Therefore employers have to rely on sufficiently motivated workers using their initiative to ensure efficiency and quality in the production of goods and the delivery of services. This makes it difficult for managers to impose effort levels without the workers' agreement. Heavy reliance on supervision and surveillance may also be counterproductive because of the resistance that it can generate among workers. The alternative is to encourage workers to exercise *responsible autonomy* at work (Friedman, 1977). In other words, it may be more cost-effective for managers to offer positive incentives to ensure that workers cooperate voluntarily with management and use their job knowledge and their initiative to maintain and improve efficiency and quality.

> **STOP and think**
>
> *What types of workforce will have low turnover costs and why? What types of workforce will have high turnover costs?*

The greater the employer's need for a stable, highly cooperative workforce, the more likely they are to introduce policies to retain workers and create a basis for mutual trust and cooperation. These policies, which are associated with the 'best practice HRM' principle of treating employees as valued assets rather than disposable commodities (see Chapter 1), *internalise* employment by fostering long-term employment relationships and giving workers a degree of protection from external labour market pressures. They include guarantees of long-term employment security, opportunities for training and internal promotion, fringe benefits and pay that is higher than the market rate. However, these policies are themselves costly. Therefore the extent to which employers seek to internalise employment depends on the cost of labour turnover and the extent of the limits to direct control. Where these are low, employers are more likely to treat labour as a disposable commodity, in other words *externalising* the employment relationship.

> **Activity**
>
> Recently two academics undertook a study of how construction companies use contingent labour, i.e. subcontractors and workers supplied by agencies. They found widespread use of contingent labour, but many firms would have made less use of contingent labour had it not been for the difficulties they had in recruiting directly employed workers. The researchers also found that the vast majority of employers valued long-term relationships with workers even when using contingent contracts and tried to develop long-term relationships with suppliers, especially in the case of subcontract labour and to a lesser extent with temporary agencies.
>
> Source: Forde and Mackenzie (2007).
>
> **Question**
>
> What advantages are there for construction industry employers in using contingent labour?

> Why, in view of these advantages do the great majority of construction employers value long-term employment relationships and seek to foster long-term links with suppliers of contingent labour?

It is clear that employers make strategic choices concerning the extent to which they internalise or externalise employment but these choices are influenced by the specific labour market contexts in which individual firms operate. Two key elements of this context are the overall state of the labour market and the way in which the labour market is segmented, giving rise to advantaged and disadvantaged labour market groups. To be able to understand how these influences operate, we first need to examine the two sides of the labour market; labour supply and demand.

The supply of labour

'In being bought and sold in the labour market, labour becomes a commodity' (SCER (Scottish Centre for Employment Research), 2001: 5). It follows that firms in competition with one another for labour will be interested in the current and future availability of this commodity. Conventionally, the process of human resource planning involves forecasting the supply and demand for labour so that suitable plans can be put in place to address situations of labour shortage or surplus. Despite the apparent logic of this approach Taylor (2008) reports that the use of formalised human resource planning is in decline as employers find it impossible to predict labour supply and demand with any degree of accuracy in a climate of uncertainty. Even so, some understanding of where the future supply of labour can be sourced from and how plentiful that source is expected to be is important in informing employers' actions in the labour market.

The number of people seeking work in the labour market is influenced by factors relating to the size and composition of the population. Within this section of the chapter we consider the main demographic factors affecting total labour supply, namely population and population change, the age structure of the population, gender and ethnicity.

Population

National population trends

The supply side of the labour market derives from the country's population, specifically men aged between 16 and 64 years and women between the ages of 16 and 59 (working age), so information on the total size of the current population and predictions of future patterns of population growth and decline are important for estimating the current and future supply of labour.

Population is affected by birth and death rates. When live births exceed the number of deaths a net natural population increase arises and when mortality rates exceed birth rates a net natural decline in population occurs. Population change is also influenced by net migration; that is the effect caused by people moving into and out of the country. In the 1950s and 1960s population growth was largely attributable to net natural change. Within this period, a relatively stable death rate coupled with the baby boom that followed the Second World War triggered net natural growth. In the 1980s the net inflow of migrants began to increase, in other words the number of people coming to live in the United Kingdom began to surpass the number leaving, thus switching the key trigger for population growth from net natural change to the effects of migration. In 2004, for example, nearly 222,600 more people migrated to the United Kingdom than left it. This net inflow represents the highest since the present methods of estimation began in 1991. The net effects of migration are forecast to continue to play a significant role in population growth alongside net natural change (ONS, 2006). The ONS (Office for National Statistics) (2008a) projects that migration patterns coupled with an increased birth rate and lower deaths will result in a situation where natural change and net migration become roughly equally responsible for population growth during the period 2006 to 2011. However, in the following decade (2011 to 2021) natural change will once again be the main contributory factor to population change.

Latest data from the ONS (2008a) shows that the population of the United Kingdom has been climbing steadily since 1971 and had reached 60.6 million people by 2006. UK Snapshot (ONS, 2007) predicts that the population of the United Kingdom will grow by around 10.5 million in the period 2006–31, edging above the 71 million mark by 2031 (see Table 4.1 below).

As Table 4.1 shows, growth is expected to be greater in England compared with the rest of the United Kingdom and slowest in Scotland. In a slight move away from trends that began in the 1980s, where net migration has consistently been the key source of population growth in recent decades, from 2006 to 2031 net natural change in the population rather than net migration will be the main driver of population expansion (53 per cent of growth attributable to net natural change and 47 per cent to net migration). A main source of natural population growth in the United Kingdom over the period is predicted to be an increase in births to migrants. The overarching prediction is thus that as much as 69 per cent of the population growth experienced in the period 2006–2031 will be either directly or indirectly linked to migration.

The way in which the country's population expands, whether as a result of natural change or migration patterns, affects the gender composition, age profile and ethnic diversity of the labour market. Changes to the composition of the labour supply may call into question the appropriateness of established human resource management practices aimed at attracting and retaining suitable labour. At a local level, patterns of regional population density resulting from a combination of natural causes, international migration *and* internal migration (the movement of people between regions within the United Kingdom) lead to variations in the *amount* of labour available in different parts of the country. While labour tends to move to parts of the country where work is more plentiful (ONS, 2001), those organisations relying on local labour in areas of the country with low population density and/or net population loss are confronted with a different set of labour market circumstances from those operating in areas of higher population density. The age profile, ethnicity and skills mix of workers in local labour markets can also vary considerably, affecting the *type* of labour available. These factors combine to pose different employment challenges and opportunities for firms operating in different regions of the country.

Regional population trends

Regional populations form an interesting focal point for study with important implications for the supply of labour. ONS (2008a) shows that at Local Authority level in England the greatest net accumulation in population occurred in Milton Keynes, Buckinghamshire, where the population increased by over 78 per cent in the period 1981–2006. Next were Tower

Table 4.1 Projected populations of the constituent countries of the United Kingdom

	2006	2011	2016	2021	2026	2031
United Kingdom	60587	62761	64975	67191	69260	71100
England	50763	52706	54727	56757	58682	60432
Wales	2966	3038	3113	3186	3248	3296
Scotland	5117	5206	5270	5326	5363	5374
Northern Ireland	1742	1812	1868	1922	1966	1999

Source: 2006-based national population projections, Office for National Statistics.

Hamlets (in London) and East Cambridgeshire; in both of these areas population rose by 47 per cent in 1981–2006. Regional populations reflect births and deaths and the effects of international and internal (within the UK) migration. Some interesting patterns are evident in terms of internal migration; the capital has seen the greatest net loss through internal migration for at least the last three decades, losing an average of 60,000 people annually to other parts of the UK, while the Devonshire Local Authority of Torridge was home to the highest net population gain from internal migration in 2006 (ONS, 2008a: 9). The effects of international migration can, of course, counter the net losses of within-UK (internal) migration, so whilst the number of people moving out of London to other parts of the UK exceed those moving to London from within the UK, London's population continues to rise as a consequence of the inflow of international migrants. In fact, London remains the most popular destination for international migrants with 170,000 of the 191,000 people coming in to the United Kingdom in 2006 settling in London (ONS, 2008a).

Age structure of the population

The age structure of the population is a key determinant of labour supply as firms draw employees from the portion of the total population that is of working age. The age structure is closely associated with past trends in migration; such trends, referred to in the section above, can also be used to explain regional differences in the population's age profile as migrants establish communities in certain areas of the country. ONS (2008a) shows that white ethnic groups, particularly the white Irish population, have an older age structure than other ethnic groups as a consequence of past fertility and immigration patterns. Among non-white ethnic groups, younger age profiles are exhibited within groups migrating to the United Kingdom relatively recently whilst, as might be expected, those groups with an earlier history of large-scale migration to the United Kingdom have now begun to contain larger proportions of people within older age brackets. For example in 2005, 32 per cent of the Pakistani community and 34 per cent of the Bangladeshi population in the United Kingdom was under the age of 16 and just 5 per cent and 4 per cent respectively of these groups were aged over 65. In the same year just 3 per cent of the country's Black African population were aged 65 and over. In contrast, 13 per cent of Black Caribbeans were aged 65 plus (ONS, 2008a), large-scale migration from countries such as Jamaica and Trinidad having taken place several decades prior to the large-scale arrival of migrants from Pakistan, Bangladesh and African countries.

Activity

Examine the information provided in the table below summarising the age structure of the populations of Eastbourne and Leicester at the time of the last census in April 2001. These Local Authorities are in very different parts of the country, Eastbourne is a seaside resort on the South coast of England and Leicester, a major city in the East Midlands. The ethnic profile of the two towns is also considerably different; according to Census data 2001 the population of Eastbourne is 92.47 per cent white British compared with 60.54 per cent in Leicester. Leicester has a large Indian population (25.7 per cent) and is home to other white and non-white ethnic groups.

Age structure of the population	Eastbourne	Leicester
% of the resident population aged 0–4	5.31	6.83
% of the resident population aged 5–15	12.69	15.46
% of the resident population aged 16–19	4.32	5.92
% of the resident population aged 20–44	30.49	38.75
% of the resident population aged 45–64	22.47	19.52
% of the resident population aged 65 or over	24.72	13.52
Average age of the population (years)	43.2	35.5

Source: Census 2001 (ONS, 2001).

> **Questions**
>
> 1 Suggest why the proportion of residents over the age of retirement in Eastbourne is almost double the proportion of those aged 65 and over in Leicester.
> 2 Explain why Leicester has a greater proportion of residents in all age brackets below 65.
> 3 Consider the possible implications of the above data for the current and future supply of labour in Leicester and Eastbourne.

As well as past trends in migration, the age structure of the total population and of regional populations is affected by trends in births and deaths. Records show a fairly erratic pattern in the number of live births occurring in the United Kingdom at different phases throughout the twentieth century (ONS, 2006). Notable decreases in the number of births occurred during the two world wars (1914–18 and 1939–45) and after a sharp increase immediately after the First World War, births fell again and remained relatively low for most of the inter-war period. A further baby boom occurred after the Second World War causing another, more modest, upsurge in the late 1980s and early 1990s as the baby boomer generation produced their own children. The smaller cohorts of women born in the 1970s (reaching their reproductive peak in the 1990s), coupled with lower fertility rates (fewer children born per woman), led to a decline in births by 2000 (ONS, 2008a). ONS data (2008a) shows that births reached their lowest point since 1977 in 2001 (at around 670,000) but have risen again every year since. Birth projections are set to follow an upward trajectory until 2020 before relapsing; the increased trend is attributed to an increase in births to mothers born outside of the UK whose child-bearing patterns perhaps bear more relation to norms in their country of origin than to the prevailing trend for lower fertility rates displayed among non-migrant women in the United Kingdom.

Together with birth rates, the age structure of the population is influenced by the death rate (number of deaths as a percentage of the population). The ONS (2008a) reports that every year since 1901, with the exception of 1976, there have been fewer deaths than births in the United Kingdom. In 2006 (ONS, 2008a) there were 572,000 deaths in the United Kingdom and deaths are expected to remain below 600,000 per annum until the late 2020s. After this time deaths are predicted to increase because those born in the postwar population boom in the 1950s and the 1960s baby boom years will be approaching old age. Effectively, death rates in the United Kingdom have fallen due to the combined factors of stable absolute death figures and a growing population. General improvements in living standards, changing occupational structure from hard physical labour to office/white collar work and advancements in health and medicine have contributed to increased life expectancy for both men and women. Recently figures also show that male life expectancy is increasing at a faster rate than women's, thus closing the gap between the sexes. Taking into account the continued improvements in mortality rates assumed in the 2006-based principal population projections, it is calculated that women born in the United Kingdom in 2006 can expect to live to the age of 91.5 and men to the age of 88.1 (ONS, 2008b); this contrasts sharply with the life expectancy of men and women born at the start of the last century, a time when boys could expect to live to just 45, and girls to 49. Projections of life expectancy based on 2006 data predict a continuation of past trends, adding some substance to the claim 'by this time tomorrow you can expect to live for five hours longer!' (Jah, 2006: 6).

We have seen in this section that the age structure of the population is affected by migration, births and deaths. While some non-white ethnic groups display relatively young age profiles, the overall picture in the United Kingdom is of an ageing population. In short, 'over the last 35 years the population aged under 16 has decreased from around 14.3 million to 11.5 million while the population aged 65 and over has increased by 2.3 million' (ONS, 2008a: 3). As we have seen, these recent trends in the age structure of the population can be attributed to lower fertility rates combined with declining mortality rates amongst the eld-

Table 4.2 UK life expectancy 2005–07

	Years			
	At birth		At age 65	
	Males	Females	Males	Females
United Kingdom	77.2	81.5	17.2	19.9
England	77.5	81.7	17.3	20.0
Wales	76.7	81.1	16.9	19.6
Scotland	74.8	79.7	16.0	18.7
Northern Ireland	76.2	81.2	16.8	19.7

Source: Office for National Statistics: Interim Life Tables 2005–07.

erly. Such trends show little sign of abating; on the contrary it is projected that the number of people over the age of 65 will exceed the number aged under 16 by 2021 (ONS, 2008a).

In terms of human resource management, the implications of changes in the age structure of the population are numerous, particularly where labour market conditions are tight. The following points indicate some of the challenges presented by an ageing population:

- The prospect of a shrinking pool of people of working age as the 'baby boomers' born in the 1950s and 1960s move into retirement.
- Intensified competition for school leavers/young workers.
- Identifying employment strategies to attract and retain older workers.
- Meeting the needs and aspirations of older workers in work.
- Career management and development.
- Managing sickness absence.
- Growing elder care responsibilities for those in employment.
- Concerns over the adequacy of pension arrangements.

In addition, employers are obliged to comply with the Employment Equality (Age) Regulations implemented on 1 October 2006. The regulations make it unlawful for employers to discriminate on the grounds of age by denying someone employment, dismissing someone, refusing to provide training, denying someone a promotion, retiring an employee before the employer's usual retirement age (if there is one) or retiring an employee before the default retirement age of 65 without an objective justification.

> **STOP and think**
>
> *How might employees' care responsibilities for elderly relations impact upon their presence and attention to paid work?*
>
> *Do you think elder care will soon begin to pose a greater challenge to employers and employees than childcare? Why?*
>
> *What measures, if any, do you think employers should introduce to assist employees with elder care responsibilities?*

The gender composition of the population

ONS (2008a) reports that more boys than girls have been born every year in the United Kingdom since 1922, however there are more females than males in the population. In 2006, there were 30.9 million females compared with 29.7 million males (ONS, 2008a: 2). Analysis of the country's population by gender and age in 2006 shows that although there are more male than female children, the number of women in the population overtakes the numbers of men by the 25–34 age group; this pattern is attributable to a higher mortality rate among young adult males in the 16–24 age group. In the older age groups (post-retirement age) the gap between the number of men and women in the population broadens; in 2006 there were three times as many women as men in the United Kingdom aged over 90 (ONS, 2008a). However, as we noted earlier, male life expectancy is improving at a faster rate than women's and so contributing to an expansion of the male population at older ages.

As 'the inflow of females has always been higher than the outflow' (ONS, 2006: 17) net in-migration further explains expansion in the country's female population. In every year since 1994 the outflow of males *and* females from the United Kingdom has been lower than the inflow of both sexes into the country, causing a net in-migration effect to both the male and female population with most of the increase being among the female population. In 2003 for example, the net gain for the United Kingdom's female population was more than 15,000 higher than the net gain to the male population (ONS, 2006: 17). It is highly probable that, at least in numerical terms, the labour market will benefit from net in-migration as migrants (both in and out) are least likely to be over the age of retirement, or children under the age of 15 (ONS, 2006: 18).

Later in the chapter we consider the ways in which gender shapes people's experiences of work. In particular, we explore the interplay of gender and age and look at gendered roles within the family to understand differences in the patterns of male and female participation in the labour market.

Ethnicity and the population

In previous sections we have referred to migration and demonstrated that in the postwar period the United Kingdom has granted residency to people from a variety of different countries including Pakistan, India, Bangladesh, China, parts of Africa and the Caribbean and more recently from countries within Eastern Europe. As a consequence, a number of distinct minority ethnic groups have joined the nation's historically white British heritage to form a more multicultural, ethnically and religiously diverse Britain. The census collects ethnicity data by asking people which group they see themselves belonging to. When the census was last conducted in April 2001 it showed England's population to be 87 per cent white British, 3.9 per cent white other, 1.3 per cent mixed, 4.6 per cent Asian, 2.3 per cent Black and 0.9 per cent Chinese and other (ONS, 2001). In terms of religious denomination, almost 70 per cent of respondents considered themselves to be of Christian religion and white British ethnicity. Other main faiths include Pakistani Muslims, Indian Hindus, black Caribbean Christians, Indian Sikhs and black African Christians. The next census, due to take place on 27 March 2011, will reveal changes to the ethnic composition of the United Kingdom over the decade.

While in general terms the total population is becoming more ethnically diverse, certain local authority districts contain high concentrations of (non-white) ethnic minority groups, in excess of the national average of 9 per cent non-white (ONS, 2001). The census conducted in 2001 shows that 16 of the 20 authorities with the highest concentrations of non-white ethnic minority groups are London boroughs (ONS, 2001); of these Newham and Brent both have a majority non-white population (61 per cent and 55 per cent respectively). Outside London, Leicester, Slough, Birmingham and Luton record the highest concentrations of non-white ethnic minority groups. In some other regions of the country (for example, the south-west and the north-east), non-white ethnic minority groups form a very small percentage of the population, significantly below the national average.

The limited geographical spread of non-white ethnic minority groups means that some local labour markets remain practically monocultural whilst others are considerably diverse. In 2003, a report by the Strategy Unit for the Cabinet Office on the position of ethnic minorities in the labour market showed that men and women from non-white ethnic minority groups tend to be disadvantaged in the labour market compared with whites. They were less likely to be active in the labour market than whites, more likely to suffer high levels of unemployment and when they were in work, people from ethnic minority groups as a whole had lower levels of occupational attainment and progression than white people. These results held even when factors such as age, gender and qualifications were controlled for and the report concluded that this was partially explained by racism and discrimination in the labour market (Strategy Unit, 2003).

Similarly, Heath and Cheung (2006), in a report commissioned by the Department for Work and Pensions, found ongoing evidence of 'ethnic penalties' in the labour market. In particular they found that a number of ethnic minority groups, notably Pakistani, Bangladeshi, Black Caribbean and Black African men, continue to experience higher unemployment rates, greater concentration in routine and semi-routine work and lower hourly earnings than members of the comparison group of British and other whites. Women from these ethnic minority groups also experience higher rates of unemployment than the comparison group but for those in work, average hourly earnings tend to match or exceed those of white women. Heath and Cheung drew particular attention to the levels of disadvantage experienced by Pakistani and Bangladeshi groups, where male unemployment and levels of male economic inactivity are high. In addition, where individuals from these groups are in employment they are disproportionately represented in semi-routine and routine work. The differentials Heath and Cheung found are not confined to those born and educated outside the United Kingdom; indeed the ethnic penalties they refer to also appear to be experienced by second generation ethnic minority groups who were born and schooled in the United Kingdom.

We return to the issues of disadvantage and discrimination in employment in Chapter 6, where the key subject of debate and discussion is the role of HRM in addressing workplace discrimination and embracing diversity.

The workforce

The workforce is conventionally drawn from the segment of the population between the ages of 16 and state retirement age, although some men and women will continue to work beyond the state pension age. However, not everyone of working age will be in employment at any one time. Figure 4.1 is a useful framework for analysing the activities of people of working age.

A proportion of those over the age of 16 will not be in work or seeking work; this portion of the workforce is classified as *economically inactive*. There are a number of reasons why people might be economically inactive. This group typically includes those with caring

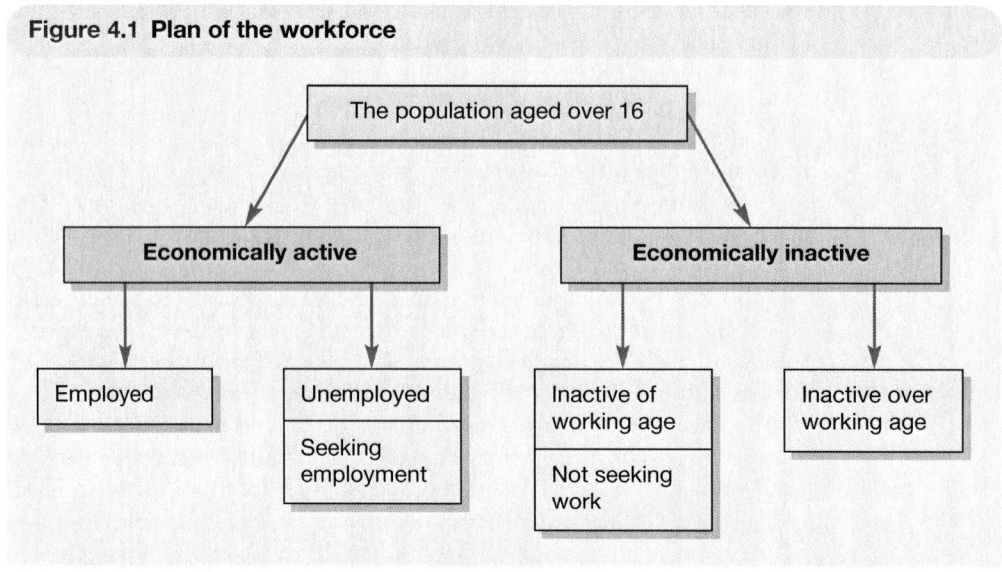

Figure 4.1 Plan of the workforce

Source: Adapted from *SCER Report* 1 (2001: 10).

responsibilities for children or other dependents, those who have retired from work, students, people who are incapacitated through ill-health or disability and those choosing not to work or seek work. People within this group may voluntarily decide to enter (or re-enter) the labour market once their circumstances alter. Others may need to be enticed back to work through incentives and/or government-orchestrated benefit reforms. The government is, at the time of writing, in the midst of reforming the welfare framework designed to help people into work, whilst supporting those who are genuinely incapacitated. An independent review commissioned by the Department for Work and Pensions (Gregg, 2008) sets out a vision for a more differentiated regime geared around the needs of three broad groups; a 'work-ready' group, a 'progression to work' group and a 'no conditionality' group. Those who fall into the last group include lone parents and partners with a youngest child under the age of one, and certain carers who would be eligible for Employment and Support Allowance (ESA) with no conditions attached. The proposals set out in the independent review are reflected in a White Paper currently making its way through Parliament. The revised benefits regime, expected to become law sometime in 2010, is part of the government's drive to get 1 million of the 2.6 incapacity benefit claimants back into work (Phillips, 2008).

The amount of labour available to firms at any one time is determined by the number of people of working age who are in employment or seeking employment, in other words those classified as *economically active*. ONS (2008a), using data drawn from the Labour Force Survey (LFS), shows that over the period 1971–2007 the number of both economically active and economically inactive people has increased. Much of the increase in the number of those in work or actively seeking work is attributable to the increased participation of women in the workforce since the 1970s. However, despite an increase in the number of those economically active, the economic activity rate (that is the percentage of the population in a given age group who are economically active) has not moved accordingly. This can be explained by an overall expansion in the working-age population in the corresponding period. By the second quarter of 2007 (ONS, 2008a) 29.5 million people of working age (16–64 for men and 16–59 for women) in the United Kingdom were economically active and 7.9 million people of working age were economically inactive.

The employed segment of the workforce contains those in paid work; this incorporates those working full time or part time, temporarily or permanently as employees (under a contract *of service*), workers (under a contract *for services*) or on a self-employed basis. A number of factors affect individuals' propensity to take work, including the availability and proximity of suitable employment opportunities, travel links, the levels of pay and benefits offered, the type of contract offered and so forth. These factors also influence people's decisions to move between jobs within the labour market.

The employment rate (the proportion of the working-age population of the United Kingdom in employment) is subject to fluctuations associated with the economic cycle and shows variations both within and between different regions of the country. There are also different trends for men and women, some differences according to educational attainment and differences at different age brackets. In the second quarter of 2007, the employment rate in the United Kingdom stood at 74 per cent, a full percentage point down on the previous quarter (ONS, 2008a) and the latest first release labour market statistics (ONS, 2009) show that the employment rate for the period November 2008 to January 2009 was 74.1 per cent. The employment rates of men and women of working age have converged considerably since 1971, the result of the male employment rate falling and women's employment rate rising. In the second quarter of 2007, the employment rate for working age women was 70 per cent whilst for men of working age it was just 9 percentage points higher at 79 per cent, this compares to a gulf between the sexes of 33 percentage points in 1971 (ONS, 2008a). In geographical terms there are also notable differences in employment rates, for example three London Boroughs, Hackney, Newham and Tower Hamlets had employment rates below 60 per cent in quarter two of 2007 whereas South Northamptonshire enjoyed an employment rate of 90 per cent; differences between Local Authorities are often more marked than differences between the regions of England (South West, East Anglia, North East etc.) or between England, Scotland and Wales (ONS, 2008a).

Those seeking work are typically registered as unemployed, but also include those who have recently left work but are not eligible to claim unemployment benefit, for example, those who have been made redundant. Job seekers might also include recent school leavers and those completing programmes of study in further and higher education. The term *unemployed* is used to describe those people who are currently not in work but would like to be. Unemployed workers must be able to show that they are actively seeking work as a condition for receiving unemployment benefits. The unemployed group consists of people affected by different types of unemployment:

- *Long-term unemployment or structural unemployment* – those unemployed as a result of the demise of whole industries or distinct occupations, for example mineworkers, shipbuilders, textile workers.
- *Frictional unemployment* – those temporarily out of work because they are between jobs.
- *Seasonal unemployment* – those made jobless as a result of seasonal fluctuations in the availability of work. Seasonal unemployment is characteristic of land workers and those whose work is connected with holiday seasons.

It is also likely that some of those registered unemployed will never work again as they lack the skills and competencies sought by employers. This group of unemployed workers is sometimes referred to as the *residual* unemployed.

Unemployment rates are also subject to variation across regions of the United Kingdom. Headline estimates for November 2008 to January 2009 (ONS, 2009) place the North East as the region suffering from the highest unemployment rate (8.8 per cent), whilst the rate is lowest in the South East at 4.4 per cent. Nationally the unemployment rate in the United Kingdom stood at 6.5 per cent (2.03 million people) in the period November 2008 to January 2009, an increase of 0.5 of a percentage point on the previous quarter (equivalent to 165,000 people). Although unemployment is rising and the economy officially slumped into recession in January 2009, following two successive quarters of negative economic growth, unemployment has yet to reach levels commensurate with those experienced in 1984 when 3.3 million were unemployed.

Patterns of labour market participation

This section of the chapter explores patterns of participation in paid employment by gender, parental/family status, age and ethnicity.

The operation of the labour market is influenced by broader societal developments, government ideology and policy, and the behaviour of employees and employers. In social terms, attitudes to marriage and partnership and men and women's respective responsibilities for childcare and domestic duties shape the labour market decisions made by individuals, couples and families. In so far as government policies are concerned, those concerning issues such as the school curriculum and funding for post-compulsory education affect the skills set and level of educational attainment with which young people join the labour market and also influence the age at which young people enter employment. As we saw earlier, the government also acts to stimulate labour supply by implementing policies designed to get the unemployed into work and schemes to encourage the economically inactive to enter into employment.

Some people's ability to find employment is constrained by their inability to understand the labour market and acquire and exploit 'social capital' (SCER, 2001: 17). In other words, some people will lack the necessary information and contacts to search for and take advantage of employment opportunities. The SCER notes that this is particularly likely to be the case for the unemployed and for new entrants to the labour market. However, the SCER also states that 'even with the right information, skills and qualifications, there still exist barriers to full or appropriate labour market participation for some people . . . one such barrier is discrimination, typically race and sex discrimination' (2001: 18). Whilst anti-discrimination legislation exists to help eradicate unfair discrimination in employment, employers' policies and practices may still harbour prejudice and unfairness, resulting in patterns of disadvantage in the labour market for certain groups and individuals.

Patterns of male and female participation in employment

Over the last 30 years or so the employment rates of men and women have converged considerably. A major doorway to the world of work has clearly opened up for women but, as we shall see, the career paths and fortunes of men and women in the labour market are often distinctly gendered.

One of the deeper influences attributable to gender that serves to structure women's participation in paid employment is domestic work. Women continue to perform the bulk of housework and to shoulder the primary responsibility for childcare in the majority of households and this shapes the amount of paid work they do. A glimmer of change is offered by Hardill *et al.* (1997) who present evidence of a small move towards more egalitarian relationships in professional/managerial, dual-career households, but this is dashed by Laurie and Gershuny (2000) who find that women continue to do more than 60 per cent of the domestic work even in couples where both partners work full time.

A major element of domestic work is childcare. Table 4.3 below (Labour Force Survey, 2008) clearly shows the differences in employment and unemployment rates, economic activity and economic inactivity rates of men and women of working age with and without responsibilities for the care of dependent children. It also shows differences between mothers and fathers in couples and lone mothers and lone fathers. This indicates that parenthood affects the employment rates of mothers and fathers in different ways; while mothers of working-age were marginally *less* likely to be in employment than working age women without any dependent children, fathers were much *more* likely to be in employment than men of working age without dependent children. Lone mothers experienced the lowest activity rate and employment rate of all groups and the highest economic inactivity rate.

> **STOP and think**
>
> *Why might 'couple' mothers (but not lone mothers) display economic activity rates not dissimilar to women of working age without any dependent children?*

While parenthood continues to affect women's employment rates disproportionately to men's, the proportion of working-age mothers with dependent children who are in employment has risen from 47 per cent in 1973 to 67 per cent in 2004 (EOC, 2006). In 2004, in all but the youngest age category (mothers aged 16–24 with dependent children) the majority of married *and* lone mothers of working age were engaged in paid employment. The employment rate of married and cohabiting mothers in the United Kingdom is particularly strong; in the second quarter of 2007 it was 72 per cent, 2 percentage points ahead of the employment rate for all women of working age (ONS, 2008a). The speed with which women return to work following maternity leave has also hastened significantly in the period since 1979; according to EOC figures (2006) 70 per cent of mothers are back at work eight months after giving birth, compared with just 15 per cent in 1979. The average amount of time women spend away from waged work for general family care is falling rapidly too (Bradley, 1999). Women have undoubtedly come a long way in terms of labour market participation but, as we shall see, there are still gender-based inequalities that segment the experiences of and opportunities for different sorts of women.

Table 4.3 Labour market summary for working-age people with and without dependent children, by sex[1,2] (United Kingdom, January–December 2008, not seasonally adjusted)

Thousands and per cent

	Couple parents with dependent children[3]			Lone parents with dependent children				People without dependent children[4]			All working-age people		
	Couple mothers	Couple fathers	Total	Lone mothers	Lone fathers	Total		Women	Men	Total	Women	Men	Total
Levels ('000s)													
Economically active	4,084	5,160	9,244	1,034	108	1,142		8,228	10,917	19,145	13,345	16,186	29,531
In employment	3,951	5,030	8,981	933	98	1,031		7,816	10,187	18,003	12,700	15,315	28,015
Unemployed	133	130	263	101	10	111		411	730	1,141	645	871	1,516
Economically inactive	1,447	345	1,792	651	41	692		2,582	2,976	5,558	4,680	3,362	8,042
Total	5,531	5,506	11,036	1,685	149	1,834		10,810	13,893	24,703	18,025	19,548	37,573
Rates (%)													
Economic activity rate	74	94	84	61	73	62		76	79	77	74	83	79
Employment rate	71	91	81	55	66	56		72	73	73	70	78	75
Unemployment rate	3	3	3	10	10	10		5	7	6	5	5	5
Economic inactivity rate	26	6	16	39	27	38		24	21	23	26	17	21

1 Men aged 16–64 and women aged 16–59.
2 Dependent children are children under 16 and those aged 16–18 who are never-married and in full-time education.
3 Includes people in married and cohabiting mixed-sex couples, same-sex couples and civil partnerships.
4 Figures for people without dependent children may include parents whose children live in a separate household from them. The Labour Force Survey does not ask people whether they have any children who live in a different household.

As with any sample survey, estimates from the Annual Population Survey are subject to a margin of uncertainty.

Source: Annual Population Survey Household Dataset, Labour Force Survey (2008)

Ethnicity and patterns of labour market participation

Employment participation rates for ethnic minorities are significantly lower than those for the population as a whole. In the first quarter of 2008, 68.1 per cent of ethnic minority people of working age were either in work or seeking work compared with 78.8 per cent among the population as a whole. The employment rate among ethnic minorities was 60.5 per cent as against 74.6 per cent for the population as a whole, while unemployment was higher among ethnic minorities at 11 per cent compared with 5.2 per cent of the entire workforce (ONS, 2008c). It has been argued that low participation rates among ethnic minorities are related to low levels of educational attainment and low skills, aspects of family structure, poor access to childcare, poor housing and a lack of public transport facilities (Strategy Unit, 2003). However, research by Wadsworth (2003) found that age, region and educational attainment explained hardly any of the difference in employment rates as between ethnic minorities and British-born whites.

There are noticeable variations in activity and employment rates as between different ethnic minority groups. For example, the employment rate among people of Indian origin is 69.4 per cent compared with just 42.9 per cent among Bangladeshis (ONS, 2008c). Activity and employment rates also vary within each ethnic group, generally being higher among British-born members of ethnic minorities than among immigrants (Wadsworth, 2003). Also, ethnic minority women are less likely to participate in employment than men, with the differential tending to be greater among immigrants relative to British-born ethnic minorities. Nonetheless, British-born Indian women had the same employment rate – 73 per cent – as British-born white women in 2002 (Wadsworth, 2003).

Labour demand

Aggregate demand for labour

The aggregate demand for labour consists of total employment plus unfilled vacancies. As the demand for labour is derived from the demand for goods and services it follows the economic cycle, rising in upswings and falling in recessions. Changes in labour demand are reflected in changes in the unemployment rate.

Low levels of unemployment are usually taken as a sign that the economy is growing and is in good shape. For employers however, the combination of record employment, low unemployment and high numbers of economically inactive people creates a labour market that is referred to as a 'tight labour market'. Tight labour markets mean that employers have to compete more actively for workers and workers have a wider choice of employment opportunities. This will lead to higher rates of labour turnover as workers leave organisations for better jobs elsewhere. In response, firms may be forced to increase pay. They may also adopt other policies aimed at retaining employees, since vacancies arising from labour turnover will be hard to fill. Therefore there will be more internal promotion and redeployment and this may necessitate increased investment in training. While these responses might be seen as moves towards internalising employment, they are not driven by the technical and skill requirements of production or a long-term employment strategy, but by immediate pressures from the labour market. These pressures may be reinforced by stronger trade union bargaining power as a result of low unemployment and unfilled vacancies. Once established, these employment practices may become embedded, although employers may seek to reverse them should labour demand slacken and unemployment rise.

Tight labour markets characterised the period from 2001 until 2008. There was low unemployment, a record number of people in employment and a large number of economically inactive people. All this meant that many employers experienced recruitment difficulties and skill shortages, although these problems were eased by an inflow of immigrant workers, including those from countries such as Latvia, Poland and Slovenia, which joined the EU on 1 May 2004 (CIPD, 2005). However, during 2008 the economy moved into recession as a result of the 'credit crunch', the ensuing financial crisis and global recession. As economic activity has slumped, unemployment has risen sharply, to 7.1 per cent in January–March 2009 compared with 5.4 per cent the year before. 286,000 workers were made redundant in January–March 2009 and the number of job vacancies was 232,000 fewer than in the same period in 2008 (ONS 2009a). The fall in labour demand has meant that tight labour market conditions have given way to a 'slack' labour market in which there are more people seeking work than there are jobs available. Employers do not replace workers who leave because they need a smaller workforce as demand for their product falls. Where they do need to fill vacancies, many prefer to hire on a temporary basis in view of uncertainties about future demand.

Whereas tight labour markets improve the bargaining position of workers relative to employers, the reverse is true when labour demand falls. Workers' and unions' anxiety about job losses may lead them to accept lower wage increases or even lower absolute wages in order to save jobs. They are also more likely to support changes to production methods in order to improve the chances of company survival, even if this leads to some job losses.

As well as examining changes in aggregate demand for labour we need to look at how the employment experience of different labour market groups varies as the result of structured patterns of inequality of employment opportunity. As we shall see, slack labour markets are likely to have disproportionate effects on those who are already disadvantaged in the labour market, such as those with little education and low skill levels and those who are subject to various forms of discrimination. We also need to examine the changing pattern of demand for labour in the long run and how it affects different labour market groups.

Labour market inequality

The quality of jobs on offer in the labour market varies. Some workers are in 'good jobs' with high earnings, good working conditions, employment security and opportunities for training and career development. Others are in 'bad jobs' with low status and pay, poor working conditions, little access to training and few if any opportunities for promotion. How good and bad jobs get created has been a matter of ongoing debate surrounding the theory of labour market segmentation. One line of explanation, advanced by two economists, Doeringer and Piore (1971), is based on the analysis of employers' labour requirements outlined earlier. Some firms face strong pressures to internalise the employment relationship in order to train, develop and retain suitably skilled workers and gain their voluntary cooperation in production. Others do not and are able to meet their labour requirements by following the commodity labour approach and externalising the employment relationship.

Another explanation (Gordon et al., 1982) is that some firms enjoy monopoly power in their product markets and are able to use this power to increase the selling price of the product, thereby increasing profits. Some of these companies are faced by workers who have developed strong trade unions that can use their bargaining power to gain a share of these profits in the form of high wages and other benefits, including job security provisions. At the same time, management seeks to limit union solidarity and bargaining power by dividing the workforce into horizontal segments and offering the prospect of promotion to those who are cooperative and trustworthy. Firms that are unable to use monopoly power to raise their prices do not have surplus profits to share with trade unions, so terms and conditions of employment are less favourable. Since it is more likely that large, rather than small firms are able to exercise monopoly power, primary sector employment is concentrated in large, rather than small firms.

One of the central predictions of the labour segmentation thesis is that there will be little movement of workers between the primary and secondary sectors of the labour market. Workers in the primary sector are unwilling to move to the secondary sector and the high level of employment security that they enjoy means that they are unlikely to be forced to through job loss. Workers who make up the disadvantaged segments of the labour market are unable to move up into the primary sector because employers see them as undesirable candidates for jobs. Primary sector employers want disciplined, cooperative workers with good work habits, so when selecting from among applicants for jobs, primary sector employers will tend to reject those with unstable employment histories that involve frequent unemployment and job changes, because they will assume that this indicates a poor quality worker. This will automatically rule out secondary sector workers, regardless of their personal qualities, since by definition secondary workers are in unstable, insecure jobs. It is also the case however, that because of their experience of poor work, some secondary sector workers will tend to develop negative attitudes and poor patterns of work behaviour that reinforce employers' prejudices against secondary sector workers as a whole.

These explanations for labour market segmentation emphasise the way in which firms' employment decisions influence the wider labour market by dividing it into advantaged and disadvantaged groups. However, the question of whether the labour market *is* divided into primary and secondary sectors as a result of employers' labour policies has generated considerable debate. Numerous empirical studies to test the theory have been carried out in Britain and the United States, with mixed results (see Joll et al., 1983; King, 1990 for a discussion of these).

What is not in doubt is that the quality of the jobs that people do is not determined simply by their abilities, educational attainment and skills acquired through training. The chances of someone being in a good or a bad job are also influenced by their membership of particular socio-economic groups. There is clear evidence that the labour market is segmented along lines that reflect 'broader social forces leading to discrimination within the labour market' (Rubery, 1994: 53).

Discrimination in the labour market means that workers' chances of gaining access to 'good' or 'bad' jobs are unfairly influenced by non-work characteristics such as gender, race, class, work-unrelated disability and age. Thus two equally skilled workers will find themselves in different sectors of the labour market because one is a white male from a middle-class social background and the other is a working-class black woman. This reflects deep-seated patterns of discrimination within society in general as well as in the labour market. Here we focus on how gender and ethnicity influence people's experiences in the labour market.

Women and ethnic minority groups occupy a disadvantaged place in the labour market. Women's employment disadvantage reflects deep-seated societal norms concerning the family and the respective roles of women and men in domestic roles and paid work. The domestic roles played by many women mean that their employment opportunities are restricted geographically and contractually. This is particularly true of women with children. In the absence of highly developed systems of state support for childcare, childcare responsibilities mean that many women cannot travel long distances to work and also that they cannot work 'standard' hours. Therefore they are invariably restricted to part-time work in the immediate locality. This means that they have limited choice of employment and therefore little bargaining power and may have to accept secondary sector terms and conditions of employment. Ethnic minority workers, as well as facing racial prejudice and discrimination, may be faced with additional limits to their choice of employment because they live in areas where business activity is low and public transport facilities are poor (Strategy Unit, 2003). For these reasons it is also likely that women and ethnic minority workers will be disproportionately affected by unemployment generated by recession. This is because they are less able to compete for such jobs as are available should they lose their current employment and it is easier for employers to discriminate against women and ethnic minorities when there are many people competing for a limited number of jobs. It is true that unemployment has risen faster for men than for women in the current recession with unemployment among men standing at 7.8 per cent and that for women at 6.1 per cent, but this reflects the different distribution of male and female employment across sectors, with men more commonly employed in manufacturing, construction and transport – the sectors hardest hit by recession – than women, who are disproportionately employed in the relatively more secure public sector areas of education, health and public administration (ONS, 2009b: 4.1).

Gender-based inequalities in employment opportunity

The social forces identified above mean that there are major differences in the types of work that men and women tend to do and the way in which male and female employment is segregated by time. Patterns of occupational segregation are strongly in evidence in the labour market, creating a division between male and female work. Bradley (1999) suggests that 66 per cent of men and 54 per cent of women work only or mainly with their own sex, with women typically crowded into administrative and secretarial work, catering, cleaning and caring occupations and men in skilled trades, construction and information technology (EOC, 2005). As shown in Table 4.4, patterns of vertical segregation also loom large with men continuing to dominate highly rewarded, senior roles in politics, business, media and culture and the public and voluntary sectors (Equality and Human Rights Commission, 2008: 5–7).

Men's and women's jobs are also segregated by hours of work. In 2007 there were 5.1 million female and 1.3 million male part-time workers clearly demonstrating that women are disproportionately represented in part-time work (ONS, 2008a). Generally women are more likely than men to work part-time, but particularly so if they have dependent children. Thirty eight per cent of women with dependent children worked part-time compared with only 4 per cent of men with dependent children (ONS, 2008d). Whilst part-time working is most closely associated with mothers, students and semi-retired older people are also attracted to working in this way (Hakim, 1998). Part-time working is invariably low-paid and this is reflected in the stubbornly persistent gender pay gap that exists between women working part-time and men working full-time (Longhi and Platt, 2009).

Table 4.4 Women's share of a selection of senior ranked roles in five consecutive years 2003–2008

Role	2003 % women	2004 % women	2005 % women	2006 % women	2007–08 % women
Members of parliament	18.1	18.1	19.7	19.5	19.3
Local Authority Council leaders	n/a	16.6	16.2	13.8	14.3
Directors in FTSE 100 companies (executive and non-executive directors)	8.6	9.7	10.5	10.4	11.0
Small businesses with women the majority of directors	12.3	14.4	12.0	14.0	n/a
Editors of national newspapers	9.1	9.1	13.0	17.4	13.6
Directors of major museums and art galleries	21.1	21.1	21.7	17.4	17.4
Chief executives of national sports bodies	14.3	6.3	6.7	6.7	13.3
Local authority chief executives	13.1	12.4	17.5	20.6	19.5
Senior ranks in the armed forces	0.6	0.8	0.8	0.4	0.4
Senior police officers	7.5	8.3	9.8	12.2	11.9
University vice chancellors	12.4	15.0	11.1	13.2	14.4
Health service chief executives	28.6	27.7	28.1	37.9	36.9

Source: Commission for Equality and Human Rights (2008: 9–7)

Female heterogeneity

The population, and hence the labour market, comprises different sorts of women, fractured by age, class, ethnicity, qualification level, background and experience. So, while generalisations about the relative positions of men and women in employment serve some purpose, an understanding of the different employment experiences of groups *within* these two broad categories is more useful.

While we have seen that women are typically casualties of segregation in employment, some women will be in a more advantageous labour market position than other women (and some men). For example, in quarter two of 2007, 86 per cent of women who had a degree were in employment compared with 39 per cent of women who did not have any qualifications (ONS, 2008a). Some of these female graduates will be mothers who have been able to return to well paid jobs following maternity leave, something women without qualifications are less likely to be able to do. Some women are making significant strides in training and occupations traditionally dominated by men, for example, women now comprise the majority of medical students, there was a 24 per cent rise in the number of female law students between 1971 and 1990, and a 61 per cent rise in women entering managerial work (Crompton, 1997).

Management is one of the areas in which women have made most progress. In 2004, 34 per cent of all managers or senior officials were female (ONS, 2005). However, a closer look at the gender composition at different levels of management and at management in different sectors reveals patterns of horizontal and vertical segregation *within* management careers. The dominance of men in the most senior management positions is aptly illustrated by the following findings from the Cranfield Female FTSE Index 2008 (Sealy, 2008):

- Alliance Trust tops the female FTSE index with three women on its board of seven members (43 per cent) including a female chairman and a female chief executive officer (CEO). AMEC and Marks and Spencer are joint second in the ranking with 33 per cent female boards. In joint fourth place each with three female directors (representing 30 per cent of the board) are RSA Insurance and Sainsbury's.
- Although there was an increase in the number of female CEOs in FTSE 100 companies between the 2007 index and the 2008 report, there are still only five female CEOs and three regional or divisional CEO posts held by women.
- 16 companies in the FTSE 100 have female executive directors – this is, however, only four more than in 1999 – the list includes Marks and Spencer, Pearson, Tesco, Lloyds TSB, HBOS, Royal and Sun Alliance, Legal and General.
- The total number of female executive directors across all FTSE 100 companies is 17 (4.8 per cent of the total).
- There are 114 female non-executive directors (NEDs) (14.9 per cent of the total).
- The total number of female directorships is 131 (11.7 per cent of the total).
- 22 FTSE 100 companies have exclusively all male boards.
- Of the 149 new appointees to the boards of FTSE 100 companies, only 16 (10.7 per cent) were female (the 2007 index showed 20 per cent of new FTSE 100 directorships going to women).
- Pearson (10th position with a 23 per cent female board) is the only FTSE 100 company with two female executive directors.
- There are only two female chairmen in the FTSE 100 (Baroness Hogg at 3i and Lesley Knox at Alliance Trust).

A similar picture emerges in the professions. Women make up some 40 per cent of those working in the autonomous liberal (traditional) professions, for example law, medicine, veterinary science, accountancy and teaching (EOC, 2001), but there are still some very entrenched areas such as engineering and sciences that are heavily male-dominated. Again, even where women formed a sizeable proportion of the profession as a whole, their share of higher-level jobs is low and they tend to be channelled into different branches of the profession to men as the following example illustrates:

- Women made up 34 per cent of hospital medical staff in 1999 (compared with 26 per cent in 1989).
- The number of female general practitioners increased by a similar amount in the same period.

But...

- Men made up 79 per cent of consultants (the highest grade) and 95 per cent of consultant surgeons.
- Women made up 38 per cent of paediatric consultants, 32 per cent of the psychiatry group and over 20 per cent of gynaecologists.

Source: EOC (2001)

A report by a working party of the Federation of Royal Colleges of Physicians (Federation of the Royal Colleges of Physicians of the United Kingdom, 2001) drew similar conclusions. It found that despite over 50 per cent of graduates being women, there were fewer women than might be expected in the acute medical specialties, academia and positions of seniority. Gender segregation is also evident in the teaching sector, where women remain over-represented in primary and nursery teaching and less well represented in secondary schools, further and higher education and in positions of leadership across the sector. Their pay and promotion prospects also lag behind men's (Shepherd, 2008).

Higher-level qualifications therefore, afford women greater opportunities within the labour market, but do not entirely safeguard against disadvantage. Even relatively advantaged women, such as those in the esteemed professions, find that their roles and opportunities for advancement are limited because of their gender; 'Women can stretch the ties that bind but cannot sever them' (Marlow and Carter, 2004: 16). Moreover, if highly educated women remain at a disadvantage in employment terms, this is even truer of less educated women from lower income and lower social class backgrounds (Taylor, 2002b).

Ethnically based labour market inequality

People from ethnic minorities experience disadvantage compared to whites in terms of their access to employment, their level of occupational attainment, and pay. Average unemployment among ethnic minority workers in autumn 2007 was 11.8 per cent compared with 5.9 per cent across the workforce as a whole (National Audit Office 2008: 14). Heath and Cheung have found that men and women in most ethnic minority groups face what they call 'ethnic penalties' in the labour market, i.e. disadvantages that cannot be explained by factors such as educational achievement and appear to be related to ethnicity alone. Ethnic minority men are paid less than white men. Ethnic minority women earn as much or more than white women, but this is mainly because they are more likely than white women to take full-time jobs, which are better paid than part-time jobs. Ethnic minorities in general are less likely than whites to be employed in professional and managerial occupations and more likely to be in semi-routine and routine occupations (Heath and Cheung, 2006).

These disadvantages could theoretically reflect differences in education and skills. We know that unemployment is higher and wages are lower among lower educated, unskilled workers. However, these disadvantages remain even when educational qualifications are taken into account. Most ethnic minority workers are paid less than white workers having the same educational qualifications. This means that the return to investments in education, that is the amount that each extra year of education beyond minimum school leaving age adds to lifetime earnings, is lower for most ethnic minority groups than for comparable white workers. Thus the National Audit Office report to Parliament in 2008 observed that:

> Employer discrimination puts ethnic minorities at a disadvantage. Research by the Department for Work and Pensions shows that ethnic penalties exist not only in accessing the labour market but also in occupational achievement and pay. There is considerable evidence that unequal treatment by employers on grounds of race or colour is likely to be a major factor underlying the pattern of ethnic penalties.
> (National Audit Office 2008: 18)

Ethnic heterogeneity

Although people from ethnic minorities as a whole are disadvantaged in the labour market, there is noticeable variation in the experience of different ethnic groups and between men and women within ethnic groups. Differences have also been found between members of ethnic minorities born in Britain and more recent immigrants (Wadsworth, 2003).

Unemployment varies considerably between groups; for example in Spring 2007 the unemployment rate among Bangladeshis at 18 per cent was more than twice as high as that for Indians at 8 per cent (National Audit Office 2008: 14). Levels of occupational attainment also vary between different ethnic minority groups, as shown in Table 4.5 below. Chinese and Indians of both sexes are more likely to be in professional and managerial occupations than whites, as are black African and black Caribbean women. With the exception of Indians and Chinese, ethnic minority workers are more likely to be in semi-routine or routine occupations than whites.

There are also variations in average earnings across ethnic minorities. Thus Indian and Chinese men's average hourly earnings in the period 2001–04 were 5 per cent higher and 11 per cent higher respectively than British and other white men's earnings. All other ethnic minority men earned less than British and other whites. Black Caribbean workers' average hourly earnings were 90 per cent of whites'; Pakistanis' earnings were 80 per cent and Bangladeshis received just 59 per cent. Ethnic minority women's earnings were as high or higher than those of British and other white women. Chinese earned 16 per cent more than whites while the lowest paid, the black Africans, earned 98 per cent (Heath and Cheung, 2006). At first glance this is surprising, but it is explained by the fact that ethnic minority women are less likely to take part-time jobs than white women. Full-time jobs are noticeably better paid than part-time jobs, and it is this that accounts largely for the apparent lack of pay disadvantage among ethnic minority women.

Table 4.5 Occupational attainment among ethnic groups in the UK 2001–2004

	Proportion (per cent) of ethnic group in			
	High and low professional and managerial occupations		Semi-routine and routine occupations	
	Men	Women	Men	Women
British/other white	41.8	37	24.5	31.1
Black African	38.8	43	35.6	33.2
Black Caribbean	30.8	39.4	36.5	31.9
Indian	45.3	37	23.7	31.2
Pakistani	27.9	30	29.7	39
Bangladeshi	17.8	20.7	50.2	52.9
Chinese	46	41.6	18.2	26.7

Source: Heath and Cheung (2006: 15).

All ethnic minorities apart from the Chinese experience ethnic penalties relating to access to employment. Once in employment, most groups – apart from Indians and Chinese – face ethnic penalties in terms of access to professional and managerial jobs and in terms of pay. Black Africans pay the highest penalty in this respect. From Table 4.5 this group appears quite successful, particularly women, who are more likely to be in professional and managerial roles than whites. However, they remain significantly under-represented when qualifications are taken into account. Black Africans are more highly qualified than whites in the UK. Some 27 per cent have degrees compared with 18 per cent of whites and only 11 per cent have low or no qualifications compared with 13 per cent of whites. On the basis of their qualifications a higher proportion of black Africans should be in professional and managerial occupations and black Africans should also have higher average earnings than whites, rather than lower.

The presence of disadvantaged groups in the labour market increases the range of options open to some employers by allowing them to fulfil their requirements for a stable, cooperative workforce without having to offer the positive incentives associated with internalised employment relationships (Rubery, 1994). This is because, as indicated above, disadvantaged groups have few employment alternatives so they have to take what they can get. The absence of better alternatives makes these jobs more attractive than they would otherwise be and therefore more highly valued by workers. This is reflected in the willingness of many disadvantaged workers to remain with their employer and cooperate with management in order to keep their jobs. This is illustrated in Box 4.1.

> **STOP and think**
>
> *Is it rational for an employer to refuse to hire workers on the basis of their ethnicity or nationality? Do employers who hire ethnic minority workers nevertheless benefit from the presence of racism in society as a whole?*

Changing patterns of demand

The period since the 1980s has seen significant changes in the pattern of demand for labour and therefore in the types of jobs available to workers. These shifts reflect inter-linked changes in the structure of the economy, government policy for the labour market, and employers' labour requirements.

A shift of employment from manufacturing to services

The proportion of workers employed in manufacturing has declined in the UK, USA and all the major European Union economies since the 1960s. This reflects the effects of economic

---

Box 4.1 **Advantages to employers of using immigrant labour from Eastern Europe**

Recent research carried out for the Joseph Rowntree Foundation into the position of Central and Eastern European immigrant workers in the UK found that immigrant workers from Central and Eastern Europe often had skills and qualifications that were significantly higher than those needed in their jobs. Many of these workers were willing to take low-paid work in the UK because there were even fewer employment opportunities in their home countries. The research also found that employers regarded them as 'high quality workers for low-skilled work' and that employers 'were often trying to balance the requirement for workers who were easy to hire and fire on the one hand but were also reliable and easy to retain'.

Source: Anderson *et al.* (2006: 115).

growth and rising incomes on people's consumption patterns. As people get richer, the proportion of their income that they spend on manufactured goods declines (although people may still spend more money on them in absolute terms) and the proportion spent on services increases. This means that output and hence employment grow faster in the service sector than the manufacturing sector. This trend is reinforced by the fact that the long-run rate of growth of labour productivity is higher in manufacturing than in services. Higher productivity growth plus slower growing demand mean slower growth or even decline of employment in manufacturing.

The decline of manufacturing has been particularly rapid in the UK since 1980. This has reflected additional forces such as the effects of government monetary and exchange rate policy during the 1980s, which raised the price of British exports in foreign markets and cheapened foreign imports; the long-term inability of UK manufacturing to respond adequately to foreign competition; and organisational restructuring whereby manufacturing firms have tried to cut costs by hiving off certain 'non-core' and specialist activities, such as security, cleaning and catering to outside suppliers of these services. This has meant that the workers who used to deliver these services are now counted as being in the service sector rather than manufacturing. The trend of employment away from manufacturing towards services is predicted to continue, as shown in Table 4.6.

The growth of service sector employment has been a major factor in the increase in part-time employment in the UK and has therefore expanded employment opportunities for women with dependent children and also, more recently, young people in full-time education.

> **STOP and think**
>
> How specifically has the growth of the service sector boosted part-time and female employment?

Changes in the occupational structure of employment

The occupational structure refers to how employment is apportioned among different jobs in the economy. Changes in the occupational structure of employment reflect changes in the types of skill demanded by employers. The declining relative importance of manufacturing means that, over time, the share of occupations associated with manufacturing has also declined while the share of occupations associated with the delivery of business services, retail services, etc. has increased. Changes in the occupational structure also reflect changes in the demand for skills *within* industries. These changes are generated by new technologies and by organisational changes that alter the way in which goods are produced and services delivered; for example, the introduction of new robotic equipment has reduced the requirement for semi-skilled workers in vehicle manufacture. Over the last 25 years the effect of technical

Table 4.6 Changes in the distribution of employment by broad sector 1982–2012 (percentage share of total employment)

	1982	1992	2002	2007*	2012*
Primary goods and utilities	5.2	3.5	2.2	2.0	1.8
Manufacturing	22.7	16.6	13.2	11.7	10.5
Construction	6.7	7.0	6.3	6.1	5.9
Distribution, transport, etc.	28.3	29.5	29.6	29.5	29.6
Business and other services	16.5	21.1	25.6	26.9	28.6
Non-marketed services	20.6	22.7	23.1	23.8	23.6

*Projected figures

Source: Wilson et al. (2006: 26)

change has been to increase demand for skilled workers relative to unskilled workers. A national survey of skills trends for the period 1986–2001 found evidence of an overall increase in the skill requirements of jobs, with the proportion of jobs requiring degree qualifications increasing from 9.7 per cent to 17.3 per cent over the period and the proportion requiring no qualifications falling from 38.4 per cent to 26.5 per cent. (Felstead *et al.*, 2002).

We can see further evidence of this in the way in which the occupational structure has changed since the early 1980s. From Table 4.7 we can see that the most highly skilled groups – managers and senior officials, professionals, and associate professional and technical occupations – increased their overall share of employment from 28.3 per cent in 1982 to 40.2 per cent in 2002. Meanwhile the share accounted for by the remaining categories fell from 71.8 per cent to 59.8 per cent. The projections suggest that by 2012 the three most highly skilled categories will have increased their share to 45.1 per cent while that of the rest will fall to 55 per cent.

We need to be careful in interpreting what these trends mean for actual employment opportunities. They do not mean that there will be no job vacancies in declining occupations. The figures in Table 4.7 refer to the total number of jobs in each occupation that results from its net expansion or decline – the 'expansion demand' (Wilson *et al.*, 2006). However, we also need to take account of the fact that in addition to net growth or decline, there will be a demand for workers to replace those leaving occupations, mainly for reasons of retirement. Replacement demand means that, although total employment in an occupation may be declining, there will still be a large number of jobs on offer within it at any one time. For example, employment in elementary clerical and service occupations (e.g. filing clerks, check-out operators) is predicted to fall by 408,000 over the period 2002–12 but replacement demand is estimated at 1,108,000. This means that there will be a net labour requirement of an extra 647,000 workers over that period, higher than for most of the professional and associated professional groups, which are predicted to grow (Wilson *et al.*, 2006: 73). It may be for this reason that employers report skill shortages in skilled trades and personal services. These reported shortages do not relate to a dearth of applicants to vacancies, but to what employers see as a lack of necessary skills among applicants. For example, the 2007 National Employers' Skills Survey reported that 48 per cent of applicants to skill shortage vacancies in skilled trades lacked technical and practical skills (Learning and Skills Council, 2008: 37).

Higgs (2004) observes that in response to a shortage of skills in certain areas, some employers have elected to focus on potential ability rather than current ability when hiring staff,

Table 4.7 Changes in the occupational structure (percentage share of total employment)

	1982	1992	2002	2007*	2012*
Managers and senior officials	10.7	12.6	14.9	15.4	16.2
Professional occupations	8.0	9.4	11.3	12.2	12.9
Associate professional and technical occupations	9.6	11.3	14.0	15.1	16.0
Administrative, clerical and secretarial occupations	15.5	15.8	13.2	12.2	11.4
Skilled trades	17.0	14.6	11.4	10.2	9.1
Personal service	3.7	4.9	7.3	8.2	9.4
Sales and customer service	6.1	6.7	7.9	8.5	9.0
Transport and machine operatives	11.8	9.7	8.4	7.7	7.2
Elementary occupations	17.7	15.0	11.6	10.4	8.9

*Projected figures

Source: Wilson *et al.* (2006: 58).

this approach, he suggests 'opens up a larger talent pool and at the same time offers potential employees skill development as part of the "deal" to attract and retain them' (Higgs, 2004: 20). However, in the light of the evidence of continuing discrimination against women and ethnic minorities in the labour market, employers could also put more effort into making fuller use of the skills and abilities of workers from disadvantaged labour market groups.

While employers claim to experience skill shortages in specific areas, there is evidence of a growing mismatch between the qualifications held by workers and those required in their jobs. The supply of workers with intermediate qualifications, i.e. Levels 2 and 3, is outstripping the demand for them and a growing proportion of workers as a whole are in jobs where they are over-qualified. This proportion increased from 30.6 per cent in 1986 to 37 per cent in 2001 (Felstead et al., 2002). Bevan and Cowling (2007) cite studies that find that between 33 per cent and 55 per cent of workers in the UK are in jobs that under-utilise their skills. This suggests that, in general, the demand for skilled labour has not kept pace with the increased supply of qualified workers, so more people are experiencing job dissatisfaction as a result of the mismatch between their qualifications and the demands of their jobs. This is confirmed in the latest report of the UK Commission for Employment and Skills, which finds that there are 'too few high performance workplaces, too few employers producing high quality goods and services, too few businesses in high value-added sectors' (UKCES, 2009: 10).

This growing mismatch may be in part a reflection of a growing polarisation of employment in the UK (Bevan and Cowling, 2007). While there has been an overall shift in favour of more highly skilled jobs, some of the most rapid growth has been in low-skilled jobs such as sales assistants and check-out operators, telephone sales workers and security guards. One study found that employment growth was concentrated among the best paying and the worst paying jobs. Those in the top 20 per cent of the pay distribution and those in the bottom 10 per cent increased their share of total employment while the share of the rest declined (Goos and Manning, 2003). This suggests that the labour market is polarising into good jobs and bad jobs as intermediate jobs decline.

> **Activity**
>
> Review the sections of this chapter that discuss differences in employment opportunity between socio-economic groups and then consider the likely consequences of polarisation of employment for these different groups.

Changing forms of employment

During the 1980s and 1990s, senior managers initiated programmes of organisational change aimed at reducing costs and increasing the speed with which their organisations could respond to changes in market conditions. A central feature of organisational change programmes was workforce 'restructuring' that involved large-scale reductions in headcount, achieved partly through redundancies, early retirement and non-replacement of departing workers and partly by contracting out non-core and specialist services. This was accompanied by the reorganisation of work and in many cases, wider use of part-time, fixed-term contract and temporary labour and in a minority of cases, highly casualised forms of employment such as zero hours contracts (Cully et al., 1999; Millward et al., 2000). These changes were aimed at increasing managers' ability to achieve greater *numerical labour flexibility*, in other words to be able to adjust the size of the workforce more easily in response to changes in demand.

The result was that, although the total number of jobs grew, there was a net reduction in the number of *full-time* jobs in Britain during the 1990s. All of the growth in employment was accounted for by a growth of part-time jobs, which increased from 22.9 per cent of total employment in 1992 to 24.6 per cent in 1999. The early and mid-1990s also saw an increase in the share of fixed-term and temporary employment from 5.9 per cent in 1992 to 7.6 per cent in 1997. These developments led some to argue that the full-time, permanent job was likely to become the exception rather than the rule (Bayliss, 1998). However, while part-time employment continued to increase its share of total employment after 1997, reaching 25.8 per cent in 2004 before levelling off and dropping slightly to 25.5 per cent at the end of 2008, the trend of temporary and fixed-term employment has been downward, the share falling to 5.5 per cent in 2008 (ONS 2005, 2009c). Full-time, permanent jobs continue to be the most common form of employment.

> **STOP and think**
>
> *What factors might explain why the share of employment accounted for by temporary and fixed-term jobs has fallen back in recent years while that of part-time jobs has continued to rise?*

Labour market outcomes: the quality of employment

In this section of the chapter we examine how changes in the labour market have affected the quality of employment experience. How should we assess the quality of jobs? What indices should we use? Traditionally, economists have used pay as the measure of job quality. Other social scientists have stressed the level of skill as a key measure on the grounds that skilled work not only provides workers with better pay but also more variety, personal autonomy and involvement and ultimately more control over their effort. We have seen that there has been an overall trend towards increased skill requirements in jobs, so on the face of things at least it seems plausible that the quality of jobs available in the labour market has, on balance, improved. However, recent research has uncovered unexpected disjunctures between skill and other measures of job quality such as employment security, the ability to control one's level of effort and exercise control over how the job is done. In this section we review evidence relating to these dimensions of job quality to assess whether recent changes in the demand for labour have improved the quality of employment experience in the UK.

Job security

Job security is generally regarded as an important factor determining job quality. Employment security has also been linked positively to skill level, with skilled workers enjoying greater job security than unskilled workers. Management-led organisational change during the 1980s and 1990s led to a growth of concern at what appeared to be an increase in employment insecurity. It was argued widely in the press and by some academics that organisational restructuring and associated changes in patterns of labour demand were creating a new era of insecurity for workers, who were faced with higher risks of job loss and increased costs of job loss, leading to a subjective sense of employment insecurity (see Heery and Salmon (2000) for a review of these arguments).

The risk of job loss is affected by movements in the labour market, particularly changes in the rate of unemployment. The risk of job loss is greater when unemployment is rising than when it is constant or falling. However, during the 1990s some observers argued that the risk of job loss was increasing independently of the level of unemployment; in other words for any given level of unemployment the risk of job loss was higher than it used to be. Proponents of this argument pointed to redundancy dismissals and the replacement of permanent, full-time jobs with part-time and temporary jobs among previously secure groups such as managerial and professional workers and public sector workers, and some argued these developments marked the end of internalised employment relationships that offered 'jobs for life' and clear career paths linked to length of service. Supporters of the insecurity thesis also argued that the costs of job loss had risen because the level of social security payments had fallen relative to average wages and workers who had lost permanent full-time jobs were less able than previously to find equivalent replacements because of the trend away from full-time, permanent jobs to part-time and temporary jobs. They also argued that these developments generated heightened feelings of insecurity among workers. However, the idea that workers were entering a new age of employment insecurity was challenged by other observers, who argued that it was largely a media creation that had been fuelled by some well-publicised but unrepresentative instances where permanent, full-time employees had been replaced by freelance workers on fixed-term contracts, mostly in the media themselves (Doogan, 2001).

The empirical evidence showed that there had not been a step increase in employment insecurity during the 1990s. While there was a slight increase in the proportion of workers in jobs lasting less than one year between 1991 and 1998, there was also an increase in the proportion of people employed in long-term jobs, i.e. those lasting ten years or more (Sparrow and Cooper, 2003: 77). Neither was there a long-term increase in people's feelings of employment insecurity. In fact, fewer workers felt they were likely to lose their job in 2001 compared with 1987 or 1996 and more felt there was virtually no chance of losing their job (Green, 2004). The 'employment insecurity debate' subsided as quickly as it had arisen, figuring less and less in public discussion as we moved into the new millennium. However, while it is true that the structural basis for long-term employment has not been undermined, if the rise in unemployment that began in 2007–08 continues for another year or so, as seems likely at the time of writing, workers will feel more insecure as the chance of losing their job increases and the likelihood of finding another lessens. There is also evidence that the recession is forcing more male workers who really want permanent or full-time jobs to take part-time or temporary jobs (ONS, 2009c). For these workers, the quality of employment has declined.

Activity Discuss with fellow students your perceptions of your own job security or insecurity. What factors influence your assessment?

Worker discretion and autonomy

Worker discretion and autonomy are usually associated with skill. In fact, the skill content of a job is partly defined in terms of the extent to which workers are required to exercise their own judgement in deciding how the job should be done, the other elements being task complexity and variety. The fewer the prescribed instructions to workers and the greater the number of decisions that workers have to make in the course of the job, the more skilled it is (Noon and Blyton, 1997). We have already seen that changes in the demand for labour have led to an increase in the average skill requirements of jobs. But does this mean that workers are enjoying increasing influence and control over how they work? The trend towards work intensification noted above suggests that workers have been losing control over effort levels and the pace of work. What has happened to their ability to influence other aspects of their work?

Various studies have cast doubt on how far recent upskilling of jobs has been accompanied by increased discretion and control for workers. Ramsay *et al.* (1991) found that white-collar workers in local government reported increased supervision following the introduction of information technology. Dent (1991) found that doctors and academics were being subject to increased bureaucratic control and a large survey carried out by Gallie *et al.* (1998) found that skilled workers were subject to increased supervision, particularly when they worked with new technology.

National survey data also show that the overall increase in skill levels has not been accompanied by increased worker discretion; if anything the reverse has occurred. The proportion of all workers reporting that they had a great deal of choice over the way they did their job fell from 51.8 per cent in 1986 to 38.6 per cent in 2001, a decline of 13.2 percentage points.

While all broad occupational categories reported a decline in discretion, it was most marked among professional workers, where the proportion reporting that they had a lot of choice over how they did their work fell from 71.5 per cent to 38.3 per cent, a drop of 33.4 percentage points (Green, 2006: 105).

Rather than the shift in favour of more skilled jobs providing workers with greater control over their work, there has been a marked overall decline in discretion, particularly among professionals, who are among the most highly skilled workers. The reasons for this probably include the effects of new technology, financial pressures in the public sector, the spread of subcontracting and the increased public accountability to which professions have been subjected in the interests of improving public services such as health and education. New technologies allow the implementation of routine processes and the closer monitoring of individual workers. Professional workers are also concentrated in the public sector, where government-imposed financial constraints have encouraged closer managerial control of professional workers. At the same time, political pressure to reform and improve public services has involved criticisms of established standards and practices among professional groups that have led to managerial interventions to limit professional autonomy.

> **STOP and think**
>
> *Identify as many examples as you can of politically inspired managerial interventions that have affected public service sector professional workers. Here is one to start you off – the National Curriculum in schools.*

Effort and work pressure

Since the 1980s, many have argued that work pressure has been increasing on two fronts in the UK. First, managers have been putting workers (and each other) under increasing pressure to work long hours. The prevalence of the 'long hours culture' in the UK is indicated by the fact that average working hours are higher than elsewhere in the European Union (EU). The British government has been accused of supporting a long hours culture by seeking to limit the effect of the EU Working Hours Directive in the UK. Second, since the mid-1980s analysts have argued that work is being intensified; in other words, workers are being made to work harder during their working hours.

Green (2006) notes that there is a widespread perception that work is encroaching on other aspects of life, restricting the time available for non-work activities and subjecting people to increased time pressures. This has fuelled recent discussion of 'work–life balance' (see below). Statistical evidence, however, shows that there has not been a long-term increase in average hours worked in the UK. Average hours worked per employed person fell from the 1950s to the 1980s. The decline was halted during the 1980s but has resumed since. In 2003, average annual hours worked per employed person were 1673 compared with 1767 in 1990, 1713 in 1983 and 1833 in 1979 (Green, 2006: 46). At the end of 2008, average weekly working hours for full-time workers stood at 37. What have increased are working hours per household as the proportion of households where all the adults are working has grown. The growing proportion of women with dependent children who are in work has been a major influence here. According to Green, it is the increase in the total hours worked per household rather than an increase in hours worked per worker that has made it more difficult to balance work and non-work activities and put people under pressure of time. Even so, there was widespread dissatisfaction over working hours among the UK workforce as a whole at the beginning of the millennium. Boheim and Taylor (2004) found that over 40 per cent of male and female full-time workers were dissatisfied with their hours of work, with the majority wanting to work fewer hours.

If the average amount of time that workers spend in work has not increased since the 1980s, people are nevertheless working harder during working time. Workers' self-reports during the 1990s showed that the amount of effort required of them increased, that they had to work faster to cope with their workload and that were increasingly working under a great deal of tension. Thus the proportion of workers reporting that they worked at very high speed all the time or almost all the time rose from 17.3 per cent in 1992 to 25.6 per cent in 2001 and the proportion agreeing or strongly agreeing that they worked under a great deal of tension rose from 48.4 per cent to 58.4 per cent over the same period (Green, 2006: 54). A growing proportion of workers also reported that they found it difficult to unwind after work, that they kept worrying about work problems after work and that they felt 'used up at the end of a workday' (Green, 2006: 156). Moreover, work pressure remains an important issue. The 2008 CIPD Absence Survey found that a third of responding organizations reported an increase in work-related stress over the previous year while only 11 per cent reported a decrease. The most common cause of work-related stress, cited by 56 per cent of respondents, was workload (CIPD, 2008: 26).

Work intensification has been driven mainly by the 'effort-biased' nature of technical change (Green, 2006), which enables management to exercise closer control over workers' effort. A clear example of this is the automated call distribution technology that is used in call centres. This ensures that call centre operators receive a continuous stream of incoming and outgoing calls, setting the pace of work in a similar way to the assembly line of an automated manufacturing plant. Another factor contributing to work intensification may be change in the labour market environment, particularly the decline of collective bargaining. This has given employers greater freedom to introduce new pay systems that are designed to extract higher effort from workers (Green, 2006).

> **STOP and think**
>
> *Think about your own workplace. What systems and technologies are in place to regulate your effort? Have you noticed an increase or decrease in the intensity of your work over time?*

Responses to work pressure – the quest for 'work–life balance'

Declining job satisfaction over hours and workload during the 1990s led to a growing demand for an improved balance between work and non-work aspects of life among workers generally. Therefore work–life balance is not just about finding ways of combining work with the need to care for children or older relatives. We need to take a wider view of work–life balance and not just see it in terms of the 'family friendly' agenda. Work–life balance is in fact a broader issue of how to deal with the conflicting demands of corporate profitability on the one hand and the concerns of workers who are under work pressure and strain on the other (Taylor, 2002a).

What do we mean by work–life balance?

Work–life balance is not an easily defined term. The word 'balance' suggests the search for equilibrium between work and life; a settled point perhaps at which work and the rest of life's activities can comfortably reside side by side. Noon and Blyton (2007) suggest work–life balance is about individuals being able to run their working lives and non-work lives without pressure from one detracting from the other. Part of the problem associated with the notion of striking a balance or equilibrium, however, is that work and non-work aspects of life are entwined rather than being separate, compartmentalised spheres. For example, we might read a report for work on the train on the way home, we may look up the cinema screening times on the internet at work or chat to colleagues about non-work related issues during working hours; in essence what we are doing is seeking to find ways to *integrate* work and other aspects of our lives in ways that are workable and beneficial. However, Noon and Blyton also point out that while individual and household adjustments to help bring about a better work–life balance are important, we also need to consider how they are shaped by action at community, organisational and societal levels. Consequently, they argue that it is necessary to consider four different levels of inter-related response to the problem of work–life imbalance to identify the conditions for achieving satisfactory work–life balance. These are shown in Figure 4.2 below.

The following sections briefly examine statutory intervention in the work–life balance arena and ways in which employers have responded to the work–life balance needs of employees.

Work–life balance and government policy

Legal imperatives for employers to address issues of work–life balance began to emerge at the end of the 1990s. In 1998 we saw the introduction of the Working Time Regulations, aimed at limiting the working week to a maximum of 48 hours and requiring employers to formally secure an 'opt-out' agreement with those employees willing to contract in excess of the 48-hour cap. On the heels of the Working Time Directive, the Employment Rights Act 1999 contained provisions to bolster the position of working parents and carers within the workplace whilst the Employment Act 2002 introduced a right to request flexible working for parents of children under the age of six, later to be extended to those with care responsibilities for adults (see Chapter 11 for further details of the legislation).

The UK government's concern for work–life balance was formally highlighted in Spring 2000 at the launch of the Work–Life Balance Campaign (Hogarth *et al.*, 2000). The campaign sought to alert employers to the business case in favour of introducing practices to help employees strike a better balance between work and other aspects of their lives. Importantly, the campaign sought to promote the merits of work–life balance *for all*, rather than just those with caring responsibilities. The Department for Education and Employment conducted a baseline study (Hogarth *et al.*, 2000) to assess how far employers operated work–life balance practices and to provide a comparator for future survey results. There have subsequently been two further surveys, one in 2003 conducted by MORI (Stevens *et al.*, 2004) and the

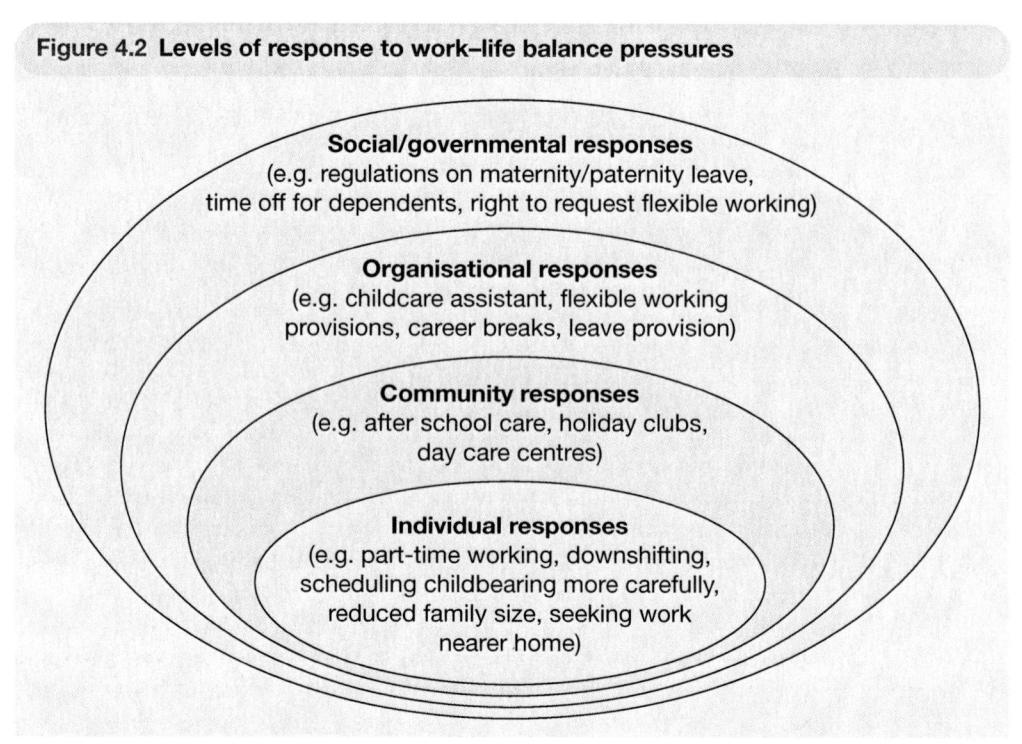

Figure 4.2 Levels of response to work–life balance pressures

Social/governmental responses
(e.g. regulations on maternity/paternity leave, time off for dependents, right to request flexible working)

Organisational responses
(e.g. childcare assistant, flexible working provisions, career breaks, leave provision)

Community responses
(e.g. after school care, holiday clubs, day care centres)

Individual responses
(e.g. part-time working, downshifting, scheduling childbearing more carefully, reduced family size, seeking work nearer home)

Source: Noon and Blyton (2007: 368).

latest in 2006 by researchers at the Institute for Employment Studies (Hooker *et al.*, 2007). The most recent survey is encouraging and appears to provide evidence that employers are engaging with the work–life balance agenda to the satisfaction of their employees. The availability of data from both the baseline survey and the second work–life balance survey has proved a useful source of comparison and has given analysts involved in the third survey the opportunity to begin to examine possible trends in the availability of, and demand for, flexible working arrangements, employees' perceived views of the feasibility of flexible working arrangements, take up patterns and so forth. Some of the key findings from the third survey are included within the following sub-section alongside other empirical evidence.

Organisational responses to work–life balance

There are potentially strong business reasons why employers should offer arrangements to employees to help achieve a better integration of work and non-work aspects of their lives. Clutterbuck (2004) suggests that creating an enabling culture in which employees can amend and re-apportion the time and attention they pay to work to meet their particular needs and circumstances can be a source of sustainable competitive advantage. More specifically, Edwards and Wajcman (2005) refer to international survey evidence to show that graduates care more about work–life balance than pay when they are selecting an employer, the implication being that employers who attend to the work–life balance needs of their employees are more likely to be employers of choice in the competitive graduate market. However, finding the right blend of organisational interventions to help individuals is complex; work–life balance is a movable target in the sense that different people have different ideas of what constitutes a satisfactory work–life balance. Sparrow and Cooper (2003) suggest that organisations can help employees to address work–life balance through practices that offer employees the opportunity to negotiate a wider range of options in relation to their patterns of work. They suggest two categories of practices. First, the provision of specific organisational arrangements to enable employees to split work and non-work aspects of their lives; for example, options to work part-time or full-time, to work in school term-time only or to job share. Second, practices that enable individuals to draw their own lines between and around work and non-work; for example, unpaid leave, career breaks, parental leave, sabbaticals, paid holidays. Work–life balance strategies are thus often associated with the provision of greater flexibility in terms of working arrangements.

In practice, employers' responses to work–life balance have been mixed. According to the WERS 2004 survey (Kersley *et al.* 2006), most managers (65 per cent) felt that it was up to individual employees to balance their work and family responsibilities. Managers in private sector organisations were more likely than those in the public sector to take this view and in line with this, fewer private sector than public sector employees reported finding their managers sympathetic to their work–life balance dilemmas. Managers in smaller workplaces, single independent establishments and non-union workplaces were more likely to say that it was up to individuals to manage their own work–life balance than were managers in larger workplaces, establishments that were part of a larger organisation, and workplaces where unions were recognised. Managers in organisations where more than half the workforce was female were less likely to believe individuals should take responsibility for their own work–life balance than workplaces that were male-dominated, so that more females than males found their managers to be understanding of their responsibilities outside of work. Nevertheless, comparison of WERS 2004 and WERS 1998 data show that some flexible working arrangements had become more widely available in 2004 (Kersley *et al.* 2006).

In work undertaken for the National Centre for Economic Research, Wood (1999) provides a framework for identifying and explaining why some firms seem to be willingly and proactively adopting work–life balance initiatives while others are more reluctant and reactive. Table 4.8 below presents Wood's four-fold theoretical classification of employers' motives for introducing work–life balance initiatives.

Table 4.8 Wood's theoretical classification of employers' responses to work–life balance

Institutional theory	Organisations whose behaviour shows them to be eager to reflect broader societal values in their practices conform to *institutional theory*. Typically these firms operate in the public sector and need to be seen to be proactive, or they are large private sector firms in the public gaze for whom there is visible kudos to be earned from setting the lead in developing and implementing work–life balance solutions. Additionally firms with trade union presence are more likely to conform.
Organisational adaption theory	Organisations in which societal norms are interpreted in ways that are seen to be consistent with the views and interests of senior management. Firms conforming to *organisational adaption theory* are likely to be drawn towards work–life balance initiatives because of specific organisational circumstances. Such firms may be especially reliant on a predominantly female workforce or require skill sets that are difficult to secure and retain so employee retention issues are critical. *Organisational adaption theory* also captures the propensity of firms to implement work–life balance initiatives when existing working patterns and systems are conducive to or compatible with them.
High-commitment theory	Organisations with developed HRM systems and practices, where it is understood that mechanisms to help employees achieve a better work–life balance may in turn engender greater levels of employee commitment.
Practical response theory	Organisations who display a rather more *ad hoc* approach to the development and introduction of work–life balance initiatives; resorting to implementing work–life balance practices if they are perceived to be beneficial in helping to address particular organisational difficulties.

Source: Wood (1999).

The WERS 2004 findings give some support to Wood's analysis. In line with the prediction of *institutional theory*, flexible working arrangements in support of work–life balance were generally found to be more prevalent in larger workplaces that were part of a wider organisation, large organisations, unionised organisations and the public sector. In addition, consistent with *organisational adaption theory*, most of the practices (with the exception of flexi-time and home-working) were more common where more than half of the workforce were female (Kersley *et al.*, 2006: 251).

> **STOP and think**
>
> *Think of an organisation you have worked for where some work–life balance practices were available. Why do you think this organisation elected to develop and introduce WLB initiatives?*

Trends in the provision and take-up of work–life balance initiatives

We have seen that the WERS 2004 survey showed that the majority of employers did not think they should take any responsibility for employees' work–life balance. However, the *Third Work–life Balance Survey* (Hooker *et al.*, 2007) reported a significant increase in the availability of most flexible working arrangements since 2003 (the time of the *Second Work–Life Balance Survey*, Stevens *et al.*, 2004). The most commonly available working arrangements cited by employees in the 2006 survey were part-time working (69 per cent said this would be available), the ability to reduce hours for limited periods (54 per cent) and flexi-time (53 per cent). Just over a third of employees thought their employers would be amenable to term-time working and a similar proportion said compressed hours would be an option (working normal weekly hours in a shorter time frame e.g. 37.5 hours over four days rather than five). If we compare these responses with the WERS 2004 data on the availability of different forms of flexible working, presented in Table 4.9 below, it appears that there are some significant mismatches between employees' perceptions of the likelihood of being able to taking advantage of certain forms of flexible working and what managers are willing to offer, particularly in relation to flexi-time, term-time working and compressed hours.

Take-up of these flexible working options, in other words the proportion of people making use of flexible working arrangements, has actually changed little since the *Second Work–Life Balance Survey* in 2003. Almost half (49 per cent) of those who had the option to use flexi-time had done so in the preceding 12 months, 44 per cent of those who could work from home made regular use of the arrangement, and 38 per cent took advantage of part-time working where it was available. Other flexible working practices were less commonly used; 24 per cent took advantage of compressed working hours where they were offered while under a fifth of employees who could reduce their hours for a limited period had done so in the preceding 12 months and just 12 per cent took their employers up on the option to job share. When employees were asked why they had not worked flexibly when they had the chance to do so, 41 per cent said that they were happy with their current working arrangements. Few mentioned organisational barriers to take-up and the survey also found that there were lower levels of unmet demand than reported in the 2003 survey, suggesting that more employees now have access to the working patterns they prefer.

These findings suggest that most employees do not think that their ability to take advantage of flexible working is being obstructed by their employer. In contrast however, another study into attitudes to flexible working and family life by Houston and Waumsley (2003) found that many employees feared that using flexible working practices would be career

Table 4.9 Availability of flexible working arrangements

Flexible working arrangements	Per cent of workplaces offering the arrangement to some employees
Reduced hours	70
Increased hours	57
Change working pattern	45
Flexi-time	35
Job sharing	31
Homeworking	26
Term-time only	20
Compressed hours	16

Source: Kersley et al. (2006: 206).

Table 4.10 Reasons given for not working flexibly by employees who had not worked any of the flexible arrangements

Concerned about career progression	1%	Other	3%
Concerned about job security	1%	Don't know	4%
No children/no childcare needs	1%	Employer would not allow it	6%
Hadn't thought of it	1%	Financial reasons	10%
On contract/fixed hours	1%	Doesn't suit domestic arrangements	11%
Just don't want to	1%	Job doesn't allow it	17%
Concerned about colleagues' workload	1%	Happy with current arrangements	41%
Want to work full-time	2%	No need/not necessary/not applicable	8%
Too much work to do	3%		

Source: Hooker et al. (2007: 69).

damaging. This was particularly true of managers, who were significantly more likely to feel that they had to put work before their family and personal life in order to progress than were skilled or semi-skilled workers, and more men were of this opinion than women. The reason for the discrepancy between the two studies is unclear but may be attributable to sampling and methodological differences.

Despite the optimistic findings of the *Third Work–Life Balance Survey*, progress in addressing work–life balance issues will continue to be uneven, given the trend to smaller workplaces combined with limited trade union presence. Moreover, even in those organisations where opportunities for flexible working are offered, barriers to their take-up by employees remain; 'organisations need not only to have policies for work–life balance in place, but also an underlying culture that supports employees who use flexible working options' (Noon and Blyton, 2007: 373). Obstacles to take-up include the irreducible nature of work tasks in many cases, possible damage to career prospects resulting from taking flexible work options and for low earners, loss of earnings resulting from some options. Workers may also be unwilling to take advantage of work–life balance initiatives because they are worried that it will generate hostile responses from colleagues who are unable or do not wish to do so (Sparrow and Cooper, 2003).

Job quality – an assessment

What can we conclude about the quality of working life at the end of the first decade of the new millennium? The evidence that we have reviewed in this section suggests that in important respects workers' experience of employment deteriorated during the 1980s and 1990s. Although there was no general, long-term increase in job insecurity, work became more intense and pressured and workers had less control over how they did their jobs. At the same time, the increase in the number of households where all adults are working led to difficulties of balancing work and non-work areas of life. These changes were responsible for a significant decline in job satisfaction among British workers, with just over 40 per cent of workers reporting high levels of job satisfaction in 2001 compared with just over 50 per cent in 1992 (Green, 2006: 154). More optimistically, since the end of the 1990s the incidence of long hours working has declined and the process of work intensification has halted. The proportion of workers working long hours peaked at 36 per cent in 1995 and fell to 30 per cent by the end of 2002 (Green, 2003: 140). While work was more intense in 2001 than in 1992, the trend to intensification halted in 1997 (Green, 2003: 144). Therefore we are working harder in 2009, though not on average longer, than in 1980 or 1990 and opportunities for flexible working are more readily available; we are subject to more extensive, if sometimes less obvious, controls at work and more of us are likely to be in jobs for which we are over-qualified. This is not a particularly encouraging picture, especially when looked at alongside the increasing inequalities in income and wealth that have characterised the last 25 years.

Conclusion: labour market developments, job quality and the implications for the employment relationship

The evidence discussed in this chapter suggests that, despite the widespread rhetoric of high-commitment and high-involvement and the tendency among advocates and practitioners of HRM to present the employment relationship in terms of mutual consent, it continues to be characterised by conflicts of interest. Currently these centre on hours of work, work intensity, lack of discretion and control over how work is performed, and structured inequalities in the labour market.

The main labour market developments from 1997 to 2007 were sustained growth of employment accompanied by increasing inequality in the distribution of pay as a result of the polarised nature of employment growth. While employment and pay have risen for all groups of workers since 1993, the *relative* position of less-skilled workers in terms of unemployment, access to jobs, and pay is worse than it was at the start of the 1980s. This is despite recent government interventions such as the national minimum wage and measures aimed at improving the employability of young school leavers (Goos and Manning, 2003). Moreover, the 'credit crunch' and recession in 2008 have led to a rapid rise in unemployment that will have disproportionate effects on the most disadvantaged sections of the population.

In addition, long-standing patterns of inequality and disadvantage remain. The difference in employment rates between women and men has not really changed over the last ten years, the employment rate among women remaining 11 percentage points below that of men. Neither has there been much change in the quality of jobs occupied by women. They are still concentrated in occupations and industries where rates of pay are low and working conditions are poor. While the overall pay gap between women and men has narrowed, it is the minority of women who are working full-time in higher-paid occupations who have benefited. This group have also benefited from statutory maternity leave provisions, which have given them the right to return to their jobs after childbirth. The pay gap for the majority of working women, who are in part-time jobs, has not narrowed and may even have increased slightly (Robinson, 2003). Moreover the position of these women, employed mainly in low-skill occupations, has deteriorated to an even greater extent than that of low-skilled men in relation to unemployment, access to employment, and pay (Gregg and Wadsworth, 2003).

Established patterns of labour market inequality between ethnic minorities and whites have also persisted. There has been an increase in the employment rate and a consequent reduction in the employment gap relative to whites among some, but not all, British-born ethnic minority groups and a slight reduction in the degree of occupational segregation. However, there is less evidence for a reduction in the pay gap. The position of ethnic minority immigrants has shown no sign of improving relative to whites (Wadsworth, 2003).

These features of the contemporary labour market suggest that there are serious long-term issues to face. First, it is clear that there has been a mismatch between the way managers are organising work and designing jobs on the one hand and how workers' job aspirations are developing on the other. Widespread job dissatisfaction has weakened employees' commitment to their employers and eroded the goodwill that is necessary for cooperative behaviour in the workplace. Recent attention to work–life balance issues may go some way to addressing these issues but as long as, in the words of the UK Commission for Employment and Skills (2009: 10), there are 'too few high performance workplaces, too few employers producing high quality goods and services, too few businesses in high value-added sectors' there will continue to be too many people in jobs for which they are over-qualified and in which they find insufficient fulfilment.

Second, discrimination against ethnic minorities, women and older workers represents a waste of human resources since it leads to under-utilisation of skills possessed by these groups. However, employers individually may benefit from the presence of disadvantaged groups who can be exploited because they lack alternative job opportunities. Therefore there is a case for stronger state intervention to combat unfair discrimination in the labour market. There is also a case for strengthening workers' rights to trade union membership and representation.

Finally, the evidence reviewed in this chapter should lead you to think about the nature of HRM and the extent of its adoption in the UK. What do we consider to be HRM? Is it a set of practices aimed at generating high levels of employee commitment or high performance through employee involvement? If so, there would appear to be little evidence that it has spread widely in the UK since the 1980s.

Summary

- Labour markets are often seen as arenas of competition in which forces of supply and demand determine wage and employment levels. In reality however, there are limits to competition in labour markets.
- Employers have some freedom to make a strategic choice between internalising or externalising the employment relationship. Their choices are influenced although not completely determined by the nature of their labour requirements and by features of the labour market context in which they operate.
- The aggregate supply of labour – the size of the workforce – is determined by demographic factors such as the size and age structure of the population and by social and political factors that influence the participation rate of different socio-economic groups within the population. In the UK differential participation rates can be observed between men and women of different age groups and different ethnic groups.
- Aggregate labour demand consists of total employment plus unfilled vacancies. The demand for labour is derived from the demand for goods and services. In conditions of low unemployment – tight labour markets – employers have to compete more actively to attract and retain workers.
- The demand for labour is segmented into jobs offers of varying quality. Unfair discrimination along lines of gender and ethnicity mean that women and ethnic minorities are disadvantaged in terms of access to good jobs.
- There has been a long-term change in labour demand away from manufacturing to services. This has been an important force driving the long-term growth of part-time employment and women's employment.
- Since the 1980s there has been a shift in the occupational structure of labour demand mainly towards highly skilled occupations but also leading to the growth of some low-skilled occupations. There has been a relative decline in intermediate occupations.
- Since the 1980s managers have restructured their organisations and their workforces. This has involved a retreat from internalised employment relationships.
- Contrary to what might have been predicted from the overall trend towards more highly skilled work, the quality of jobs has deteriorated in terms of work pressure and worker autonomy, although not in terms of job stability leading to falling levels of job satisfaction compared with the early 1990s. The demand for better work–life balance is a recent response to growing work pressure.
- Declining job satisfaction and the presence of disadvantaged groups in the labour market indicate the continued presence of conflict in the employment relationship.

Questions

1. Explain the factors that influence the differential labour market participation rates of women and men and ethnic minorities and whites.
2. How has the structure of demand for labour changed since the 1980s?
3. Why have levels of job satisfaction declined since the early 1990s?
4. Who have been the main beneficiaries of changes in the labour market since the 1980s and who have been the main losers?

Case study

Stuck on the 'mummy track' – why having a baby means lower pay and prospects

From the moment they give birth, women get stuck on a 'mummy track' of low pay and low prospects as their wages fall and never fully recover – even when their children have left home, a new study has found.

Far from being a liberating release, the point when their children start school marks another sudden slump in the average growth of women's pay compared with male wages, according to the report by the Institute for Fiscal Studies.

Before they have children, the average hourly wage for female workers is 91 per cent of the male average but declines to 67 per cent for working mothers juggling jobs and childcare.

Their wages relative to men then stagnate for 10 years before showing a modest recovery, reports the study, *Newborns and New Schools*. But even when children have left home, the average hourly wage for their mothers remained at 72 per cent of the male average.

Rather than facilitate a large-scale return to the workforce for women, the moment their children enter full-time school accelerates relative wage decline. The average wage growth over two years for women before having children was 11 per cent, but fell to 8 per cent for women with newborn children. While it recovered to 9 per cent for those with pre-school children, it fell again to less than 5 per cent when their children entered school. The aggregate proportion of mothers in work before their children began school compared with afterwards only rose slightly from 53 per cent in June to 57 per cent when term began in September.

'There is a huge assumption that suddenly because the child is at school the mother can return to work,' said Gillian Paull, a co-author of the study for the Department for Work and Pensions. 'But school hours are far too short to cover most jobs and school brings with it a new set of responsibilities in terms of children needing input from parents and parents being involved in school life. Finding childcare that fits around school hours and the holidays is difficult unless you pay for expensive full-time care.'

Only a small part of this gender wage gap is because mothers choose to work part time. For full-time workers, the gender wage ratio suffered a similar slump between childless women and working mothers, with a decline from women commanding 94 per cent of male wages before children to just 74 per cent for those with children and 79 per cent for the group after children.

When researchers took account of other factors which might determine the gender wage gap such as gender differences in demographic background, educational attainment and work characteristics and conditions they still found 'a substantial "unexplained" gender wage gap' of 11 per cent for those before children, 30 per cent for those living with children and 23 per cent for those whose children have grown up or left home.

'The million-dollar question is: "Are the wage levels different because working mothers are treated differently or is it that they choose a different way to behave in the labour market?"' Dr Paull said.

Working mothers could be suffering a wide pay gap because of pure discrimination. Or, controversially, some employers claim they do not pay as much because working mothers are not as productive as men. Third, Dr Paull said, it could be that women were choosing jobs that fit in with the demands of motherhood, finding work that was less physically demanding, for instance, so they could devote more energy to their families.

'Too many women get stuck on a "mummy track" of low pay and low prospects. The pay gap for women working part-time, at nearly 40 per cent, has barely improved since the Sex Discrimination Act was introduced 30 years ago,' said Caroline Slocock, the chief executive of the Equal Opportunities Commission.

'Many women choose to work part-time, but they don't choose low pay. Four in five part-time workers – 5.6 million people, most of whom are women – are working in jobs which do not use their potential, because flexible and part-time work is too often low-status and underpaid. This is a colossal waste of talent for employers and the economy as well as individuals.'

The IFS study is published days before the Women and Work Commission reports to Tony Blair after spending 18 months looking at the problem of the gender pay gap. The Prime Minister is expected to help launch the report next month, which is expected to outline radical proposals to help women return to well-paid work.

Children represent a 'major part' of the gender pay gap, according to Margaret Prosser, who chairs the Women and Work Commission. 'Once women have

Case study continued

children, their job choices are hugely constrained, either because they have to choose local work which provides fewer options or choose part-time employment, where there are few jobs at a professional or senior level.'

Lady Prosser said she was not surprised that figures showed women's pay stagnating even years after they have raised young children.

'The majority of women who have children want to spend some time with those children. What they would like is work that is sufficiently flexible but what they do not want is work that is always at the bottom of the ladder.

'There is no silver bullet answer to this. There has to be a whole range of policy proposals around educational choices, encouragement for girls and more widely available childcare facilities.'

Source: from Stuck on the 'mummy track' – why having a baby means lower pay and prospects, *The Guardian*, 20 January 2006 (Barkham, P.), Copyright Guardian News & Media Ltd 2006.

Questions

1 To what extent do you believe that women get stuck on the 'mummy track' because they *choose* to prioritise responsibilities to their children over and above paid work?

2 Are New Labour's promises to improve access to affordable childcare and plans to introduce school 'wrap around time' (the provision of breakfast clubs and after school activities to extend the school day) the 'green light' needed for working mothers to be able to compete on equal terms with men in the workplace?

3 Whilst organisations might not deliberately set out to discriminate against working mothers, consider ways in which norms and expectations in the contemporary workplace may make it difficult for working mothers to gain promotion and hence access to better paid positions. What steps could organisations take to help more women off the 'mummy track'?

Activity

You have been invited to a campus debate to discuss the proposition outlined below:

> Given employers' demand for low skill workers to fill low-paid jobs in the service sector, the existence of receptive pockets of labour (for example, working mothers, students, migrant workers) prepared to accept these jobs is beneficial for organisations and the economy at large.

Using the article 'Stuck on the Mummy track' as a starting point, consider positions both *in support of and against* the above statement. You should be able to draw upon several segments of this chapter to inform your arguments.

References and further reading

Adkins, L. (1995) *Gendered Work, Sexuality, Family and the Labour Market*. Buckingham: Oxford University Press.

Anderson, B., Ruhs, M., Rogaly, B. and Spencer, C. (2006) *Fair Enough? Central and Eastern European Migrants in Low-Wage Employment*. York: Joseph Rowntree Foundation.

Bayliss, V. (1998) *Redefining Work: An RSA Initiative*. London: Royal Society for the Encouragement of Arts, Manufactures and Commerce.

Bevan, S. and Cowling, M. (2007) *Job Matching in the UK and the European Union*. Research Report RR25 Sector Skills Development Agency. www.employment-studies.co.uk.

Boheim, R. and Taylor, M.P. (2004) 'Actual and preferred working hours', *British Journal of Industrial Relations*, 42, 1: 149–66.

Bradley, H. (1999), *Gender and Power in the Workplace: Analysing the Impact of Economic Change*. Basingstoke: Macmillan.

Browning, G. (2005) 'The search for meaning', *People Management*, 13 December: 38–39.

CIPD (2005) *A Barometer of HR Trends and Prospects, Overview of CIPD Surveys*. Wimbledon: CIPD.

CIPD (2006) 'Jobs blow to women as economic slowdown hits consumer services', Press Release, Wimbledon, CIPD, 15 March.

CIPD (2008) *Absence Management: Annual Survey Report 2008*. Wimbledon: CIPD.

CIPD and KPMG (2006) Labour Market Outlook, *Quarterly Survey Report*, Wimbledon, CIPD Spring.

Clutterbuck, D. (2004) *Managing Work–Life Balance in the 21st Century*. London: CIPD.

Connor, H., Tyers, C., Davis, S. and Tackey, N. (2003) *Minority Ethnic Students in Higher Education*. London: DfES.

Cooper, C. (2005) 'Another year down?' *People Management*, 13 December: 36–37.

Crompton, R. (1997) *Women and Work in Modern Britain*, Oxford: Oxford University Press.

Cully, M., Woodland, S., O'Reilly, A. and Dix, G. (1999) *Britain at Work. As Depicted by the 1998 Workplace Employee Relations Survey*. London: Routledge.

Dent, M. (1991) 'Autonomy and the medical profession: medical audit and management control' in C. Smith, D. Knights and H. Willmott (eds) *White-Collar Work: The Non-Manual Labour Process*. Basingstoke: Macmillan, pp. 65–88.

Doeringer, P.B. and Piore, M.J. (1971) *Internal Labor Markets and Manpower Analysis*. Lexington, MA: Heath.

Doogan, K. (2001) 'Insecurity and long term employment', *Work, Employment and Society*, 15, 3: 419–41.

Drucker, P. (2001) 'Beyond the information revolution' in A. Giddens (ed.) *Sociology: Introductory Readings*. Cambridge: Polity Press.

DWP (2005) Speech given by the Rt Hon Alan Johnson MP, Secretary of State for Work and Pensions, 7 February, www.dwp.gov.uk.

Edwards, P. and Wajcman, J. (2005) *The Politics of Working Life*. Oxford: Oxford University Press.

EOC (2001) *Women and Men in Britain: Professional Occupations*.

EOC (2005) *Facts about Men and Women in Britain 2005, an EOC Fact Sheet*.

EOC (2006) *Then and Now; 30 years of the Sex Discrimination Act, an EOC Fact Sheet*.

Equality and Human Rights Commission (2008) *Sex and Power 2008*. London: EHRC.

Federation of the Royal Colleges of Physicians of the United Kingdom (2001) *Women in Hospital Medicine: Career Choices and Opportunities*, Report of a Working Party of the Federation of Royal Colleges of Physicians. June.

Felstead, A., Gallie, D. and Green, F. (2002) *Work Skills in Britain 1986–2001*. Nottingham: DfES publications.

Forde, C. and Mackenzie, R. (2007) 'Getting the mix right? The use of labour contract alternatives in UK construction' *Personnel Review*, 36, 4: 549–63.

Friedman, A. (1977) *Industry and Labour*. London: Macmillan.

Gallie, D., White, M. and Cheng, Y. (1998) *Restructuring the Employment Relationship*. Oxford: Clarendon Press.

Goos, M. and Manning, A. (2003) 'McJobs and MacJobs: The growing polarisation of jobs in the UK' in R. Dickens, P. Gregg and J. Wadsworth (eds) *The Labour Market under New Labour: The State of Working Britain*. Basingstoke: Palgrave, pp. 70–85.

Gordon, D.M., Edwards, R. and Reich, M. (1982) *Segmented Work, Divided Workers: The Historical Transformation of Labor in the United States*. Cambridge: Cambridge University Press.

Green, F. (2003) 'The demands of work', in R. Dickens, P. Gregg and J. Wadsworth (eds) *The Labour Market under New Labour: The State of Working Britain*. Basingstoke: Palgrave, pp. 137–49.

Green, F. (2004) 'The rise and decline of job insecurity', *Department of Economics Discussion Paper*. Canterbury: Kent University.

Green, F. (2006) *Demanding Work: The Paradox of Job Quality in the Affluent Economy*. Oxford: Princeton University Press.

Gregg, P. (2008) *Realising Potential: A Vision for Personalized Conditionality and Support*. An Independent Report to the Department for Work and Pensions.

Gregg, P. and Wadsworth, J. (2003) 'Labour market prospects of less skilled workers over the recovery' in R. Dickens, P. Gregg and J. Wadsworth (eds) *The Labour Market Under New Labour: The State of Working Britain*. Basingstoke: Palgrave, pp. 87–97.

Hakim, C. (1998) *Social Change and Innovation in the Labour Market*. Oxford: Oxford University Press.

Hardill, I., Duddlestone, A. and Owen, D.W. (1997) 'Who decides what? Decision making in dual career households', *Work, Employment & Society*, 11, 2: 313–26.

Heath, A. and Cheung, S.Y. (2006) *Ethnic Penalties in the Labour Market: Employers and Discrimination*. DWP Research Report 341.

Heery, E. and Salmon, J. (2000) 'The insecurity thesis' in E. Heery and J. Salmon, (eds) *The Insecure Workforce*. London: Routledge, pp. 1–24.

Higgs, M. (2004) 'Future trends in HR' in D. Rees and R. McBain (eds) *People Management Challenges and Opportunities*. Basingstoke: Palgrave, pp. 15–31.

Hogarth, T., Hasluck, C., Pierre, G., Winterbotham, M. and Vivian, D. (2000) *Work–life Balance, 2000: Baseline Study of Work–Life Balance Practices in Great Britain*. Warwick: Institute for Employment Research, Warwick University.

Hooker, H., Neathley, F., Casebourne, J. and Munro, M. (2007) *The Third Work–Life Balance Employee Survey: Main Findings*, Institute for Employment Studies, Department of Trade and Industry, Employment Relations Research Series No. 58.

Houston, D., and Waumsley, J.A. (2003) *Attitudes to Flexible Working and Family Life*. Bristol: Policy Press.

Hudson, M. (1999) 'Disappearing pathways and the struggle for a fair day's pay', in B. Burchell, D. Day, M. Hudson, D. Ladipo, R. Mankelow, J. Nolan, H. Reed, I. Wichert and F. Wilkinson, *Job Insecurity and Work Intensification: Flexibility and the Changing Boundaries of Work*. York: Joseph Rowntree Foundation, pp. 77–93.

Jah, A. (2006) 'The future of old age', *The Guardian*, 8 March 2006, p. 6.

Joll, C., Mckenna, C., McNab, R. and Shorey, J. (1983) *Developments in Labour Market Analysis*. London: George Allen & Unwin.

Kersley, B., Alpin, C., Forth, J., Bryson, A., Bewley, H., Dix, G. and Oxenbridge, S. (2006) *Inside the Workplace: First Findings from the 2004 Workplace Employment Relations Survey*. London: DTI.

King, J.E. (1990) *Labour Economics*, 2nd edn. London: Macmillan.

Laurie, H. and Gershuny, J. (2000) 'Couples, work and money' in R. Berthoud and J. Gershuny (eds) *Seven Years in the Lives of British Families*. Bristol: Polity Press, pp. 45–72.

Learning and Skills Council (2008) *National Employer Skills Survey 2007: Main Report*. Coventry: Learning and Skills Council.

Leonard, D. and Speakman, M.A. (1986) 'Women in the family: companions or caretaker?' in V. Beechey and E. Whitelegg (eds) *Women in Britain Today*. Milton Keynes: Open University Press, pp. 8–76.

LFS (2008) Annual Population Survey, Office for National Statistics, www.statistics.gov.uk.

LFS (2006) 'Ethnic minorities in the labour market: Autumn 2005', *LFS Update*, www.emetaskforce.gov.uk.

Longhi, S. and Platt, L. (2009) *Pay Gaps and Pay Penalties by Gender and Ethnicity, Religion, Disability, Sexual Orientation and Age*. London: Equality and Human Rights Commission.

Marlow, S. and Carter, S. (2004) 'Accounting for change: professional status, gender disadvantage and self-employment', *Women in Management Review*, 19, 1: 5–17.

Miller, H. (1991) 'Academics and the labour process' in C. Smith, D. Knights and H. Willmott (eds) *White-Collar Work: The Non-Manual Labour Process*. Basingstoke: Macmillan, pp. 109–38.

Millward, N., Bryson, A. and Forth, J. (2000) *All Change at Work? British Employment Relations as Portrayed by the Workplace Industrial Relations Survey Series*. London: Routledge.

National Audit Office (2008) *Department for Work and Pensions. Increasing Employment Rates for Ethnic Minorities. Report by the Comptroller and Auditor General*. London: The Stationery Office.

Nolan, P. and Brown, W. (1983) 'Competition and workplace wage determination', *Oxford Bulletin of Economics and Statistics*, 45, 269–87.

Noon, M. and Blyton, P. (2007) *The Realities of Work: Experiencing Work and Employment in Contemporary Society*, 3rd edn. Basingstoke: Macmillan.

ONS (2001) Census 2001.

ONS (2005) *Labour Market Trends*, 113, 12.

ONS (2006) *Social Trends*, No. 36, 2006 edn, Office for National Statistics. Basingstoke: Palgrave MacMillan.

ONS (2007) *National Projections*, UK Snapshot, Population, www.statistics.gov.uk.

ONS (2008a) *Social Trends*, No. 38, 2008 edn. Office for National Statistics. Basingstoke: Palgrave MacMillan.

ONS (2008b) *Life Expectancy Continues to Rise*, UK Snapshot, Health, www.statistics.gov.uk.

ONS (2008c) *Labour Force Survey*, Spring 2008.

ONS (2008d) *More Women in Work But Half in Part-time Jobs*. Office for National Statistics News Release, 26 September 2008.

ONS (2009) *First Release Labour Market Statistics March 2009*. www.statistics.gov.uk 18 March 2009.

ONS (2009a) *National Statistics Online* 22 May www.statistics.gov.uk/cci.nugget.asp?ID=12.

ONS (2009b) *The Impact of the Recession on the Labour Market*. www.statistics.gov.uk/downloads/theme_labour/Impact-of-recession-on-LM.pdf.

ONS (2009c) *Economic and Labour Market Review*, April, Table 2.03. www.statistics.gov.uk/elmr/04_09/2.asp.

Phillips, L. (2008) 'Benefits claimants forced to look for work', *Personnel Management*, 29 December: 13.

Ramsay, H., Baldry, C., Connolly, A. and Lockyer, C. (1991) 'Multiple microchips: the computerised labour process in the public service sector', in C. Smith, D. Knights and H. Willmott (eds) *White-Collar Work: The Non-Manual Labour Process*. Basingstoke: Macmillan, pp. 35–64.

Robinson, H. (2003) 'Gender and labour market performance in the recovery', in R. Dickens, P. Gregg and J. Wadsworth (eds) *The Labour Market Under New Labour*. Basingstoke: Palgrave, pp. 232–47.

Rubery, J. (1994) 'Internal and external labour markets: towards an integrated analysis', in J. Rubery and F. Wilkinson (eds) *Employer Strategy and the Labour Market*. Oxford: Oxford University Press, pp. 37–68.

Scottish Centre for Employment Research (2001) *SCER Report 1 – Understanding the Labour Market*, Department of Human Resource Management, University of Strathclyde.

Sealy, R. (2008) *The Female FTSE Report 2008: A Decade of Delay*. Cranfield: Cranfield University.

Shepherd, J. (2008) 'Women teachers still losing out to men, says report', *Education Guardian*, 27 March.

Sparrow, P.R. and Cooper, C.L. (2003) *The Employment Relationship: Key Challenges for HR*. London: Butterworth Heinemann.

Stanworth, C. (2000) 'Flexible working patterns' in D. Winstanley and J. Woodall (eds) *Ethical Issues in Contemporary Human Resource Management*. Basingstoke: Palgrave, pp. 137–55.

Stevens, J. Brown, J. and Lee, C (2004) *The Second Work–Life Balance Study: Results from the Employees' Survey*. Department of Trade and Industry, Employment Relations Research Series No. 27.

Strategy Unit (2003) *Ethnic Minorities and the Labour Market: Final Report*. London: Cabinet Office.

Taylor, R. (2002a) *The Future of Work–Life Balance*. Swindon: Economic and Social Research Council.

Taylor, R. (2002b) *Britain's Diverse Labour Market*. Swindon: Economic and Social Research Council.

Taylor, S. (2008), *People Resourcing*, 4th edn. London: CIPD.

TUC (2005) *Challenging Times*, London: TUC.

UK Commission for Employment and Skills (2009) *Ambition 2020: World Class Skills and Jobs for the UK*. London: UKCES and www.ukces.org.uk.

Wadsworth, J. (2003) 'The labour market performance of ethnic minorities in the recovery' in R. Dickens, P. Gregg and J. Wadsworth *The Labour Market under New Labour: The State of Working Britain*. Basingstoke: Palgrave, pp. 116–33.

Wilson, R., Homenikou, K. and Dickerson, A. (2006) *Working Futures: New Projections of Occupational Attainment by Sector and Region 2002–2012*. Volume 1: *National Report*. Coventry: Institute for Employment Research, University of Warwick.

Wood, S. (1999) 'Family-friendly management; testing the various perspectives', *National Institute Economic Review*, 168 (1): 99–116.

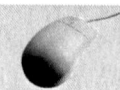

For multiple-choice questions, exercises and annotated weblinks related to this topic, visit **www.pearsoned.co.uk/mymanagementlab**.

ORGANISING PEOPLE – RESPONSES TO CONTROL

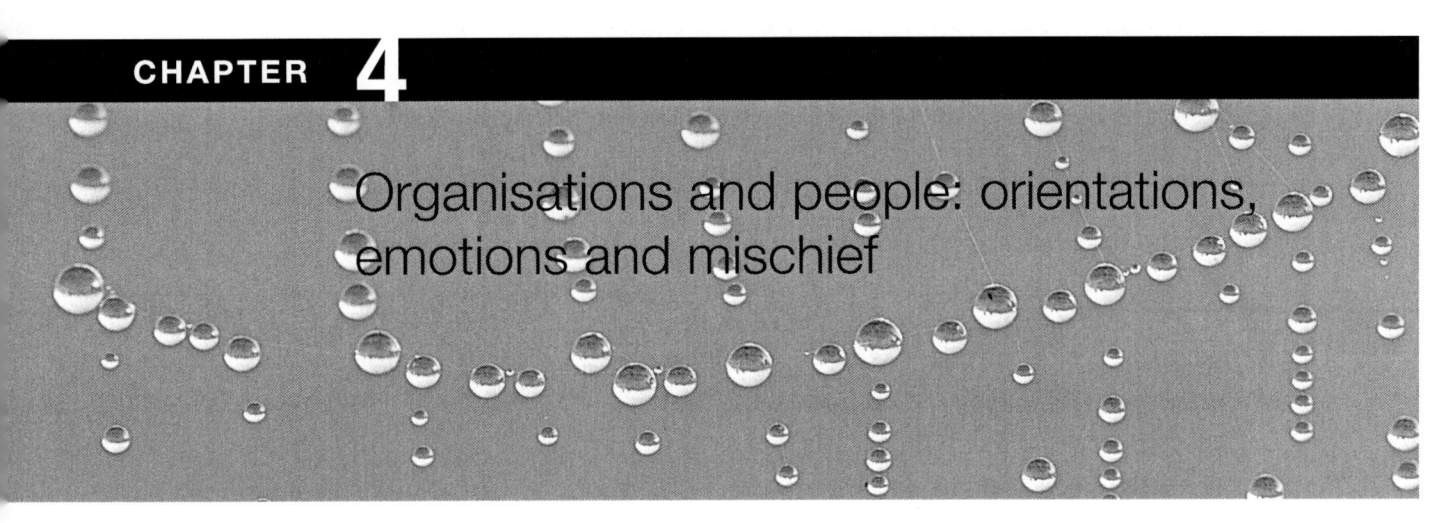

CHAPTER 4

Organisations and people: orientations, emotions and mischief

Objectives

Having read this chapter and completed its associated activities, readers should be able to:

- See how a *strategic exchange* perspective can be developed within a process-relational frame of reference to help us understand particular aspects of the relationship between people and organisations.
- Recognise the importance of the *implicit contract*, which is made between the employee and the employing organisation, to an understanding of work behaviour and organisational relationships.
- Apply the concept of *work orientation* to people's involvement in work organisations, appreciating that organisational employees are better understood not as 'motivated' to work in particular ways but as 'oriented' to their work circumstances by the meanings they both bring to the organisation in the first place and by the way these meanings change as they move on through their life and work careers.
- Understand the importance of matters of *emotion* and *feelings* in the work context and come to terms with the fact that these permeate every aspect of organisational activity.
- Recognise that an emotional dimension is sometimes deliberately built into the design of certain kinds of work and that people in various kinds of work, including management, find themselves engaging in *emotional labour*.
- Appreciate how emotional matters are involved in situations of individual stress and how the experience of stress, or work-related distress, can best be understood in terms of an interplay of factors in the organisational circumstances and factors in the individual's own life – especially their 'personal resources'.
- See how practices that can be characterised as *organisational mischief* – from fiddles and sabotage to sexual, joking and 'play' activities – all relate to matters of power, identity and negotiated order in the workplace.
- Recognise the particular significance of sexuality and humour in both challenges and adjustments to organisational controls.

Shaping lives and shaping organisations: a strategic exchange perspective

Within the process-relational way of framing human and organisational activities that has been unfolded over the previous chapters we can now develop a more tightly focused perspective to help us deal with specific aspects of the relationships between organisations and people who work in them. This is the *strategic exchange* perspective. It is intended to draw our attention to two things. First, attention is drawn to the *parallel* that exists between human beings and organisations: the fact that both people and organisations, albeit in different ways, have to make exchanges of various kinds with the world in order to survive in that world into the future. And, second, attention is drawn to a key *link* that exists between people and organisations: the exchanges that occur between organisations and people as part of their survival processes. The idea of organisations existing without some kind of giving to and taking from 'people' is clearly ridiculous. It is possible, however, to envisage people surviving without trading with organisations. But that would only be possible in a very simple society where there were no bureaucratised state bodies or commercial enterprises with which people have to deal in order to participate in society. In modern societies it is out of the question for anyone to contemplate living without some kind of give-and-take relationship with enterprises, institutions, firms and corporations.

The importance of exchange in human existence generally was stressed in Chapter 3 where it was pointed out that people's physical and psychological survival depends upon give-and-take exchanges with others. People exchange meaning-giving and emotional resources as well as material goods or necessities (p. 95). And a proportion of these exchanges is inevitably with organisations – in activities ranging from the buying goods and services from an organisation to the entering of an employment relationship with one of them. It was also recognised that human beings are 'strategic' in the sense of actively shaping their lives, identities and their biographies. People are 'strategic and situationally sensitive' (pp. 94–5): people always act with regard to their specific context, given their broader projects in life and what they currently regard their identity to be.

Although the lives of all of us are influenced and constrained by the social-structural, cultural and other circumstances in which we find ourselves, none of us can simply lie back and adopt a totally passive stance towards the world. It is true, of course, that people vary considerably in how purposefully active ('proactive') they are in shaping their lives. But human survival, in both the physical and psychological senses of the term, requires of everyone a degree of strategic initiative-taking, a degree of life shaping and the pursuit of survival projects. In Table 1.4 (p. 30), where process-relational thinking is contrasted with systems-control ideas about human beings, it was pointed out that people are not best understood as 'need-led'. Rather, they are sense-making and project-oriented creatures who, in the light of how they interpret their situation, make exchanges with others to deal with their material, psychological and emotional circumstances.

People can be seen, then, always to be striving to come to terms with the circumstances in which they find themselves and to shape their existence. Their 'biography' does not just write itself. People, in part, have to be the authors of their identities and biographies. They therefore pursue their projects in life and manage their continuously emerging identities through exchanging meanings and resources with others and, as we argued in Chapter 3, through a 'dialogue' with their cultures. And, here, there is a parallel with organisations.

Organisations are most certainly not people. But their future existence, just like the future existence of the human individual, depends on their making exchanges with others – in this case with customers, suppliers, employees and so on. Both organisations (as sets of understandings and arrangements), and the people involved in them (as individuals with identities and biographies) are shaped and shape themselves to continue their existence into the future. This shaping may be relatively deliberate ('planned') or it might be very reactive, haphazard even.

Strategic exchange *Concept*

> As both individuals and organisations shape themselves and are shaped to continue their existence into the future, the exchange of material and symbolic resources occurs (a) between individuals and others in their social worlds (including employing organisations) and (b) between organisations and their internal and external constituencies upon which they are resource dependent (including employees).

The concept of strategic exchange draws attention to the interplay that occurs between how people involved with work organisations shape and make sense of their lives and the way organisations themselves are strategically shaped. People make many exchanges, materially and symbolically, with the whole range of people whom they encounter in their lives. The exchange they make with the work organisations in which they become involved, typically in an employment relationship, is an important one for many people. And organisations themselves would be nothing without exchanges made with all of those who become attached to the organisation as owners, workers, managers and so on. The exchange between such individuals and the organisation is represented in Figure 4.1. This exchange is a contractual one – a point we will develop shortly.

This 'interplay' between individual and organisational exchange processes, at the heart of which is a specific contractual exchange, will be seen in many of the cases that we shall encounter in coming chapters. The interplay can be seen in an especially clear way in the story of Peter Brodie in Chapter 5 (Case 5.2, p. 177). We will see there how this chief executive of a charity was simultaneously working to shape his own life and that of the Youth Links organisation which employs him. We will see how the organisation was being shaped, and

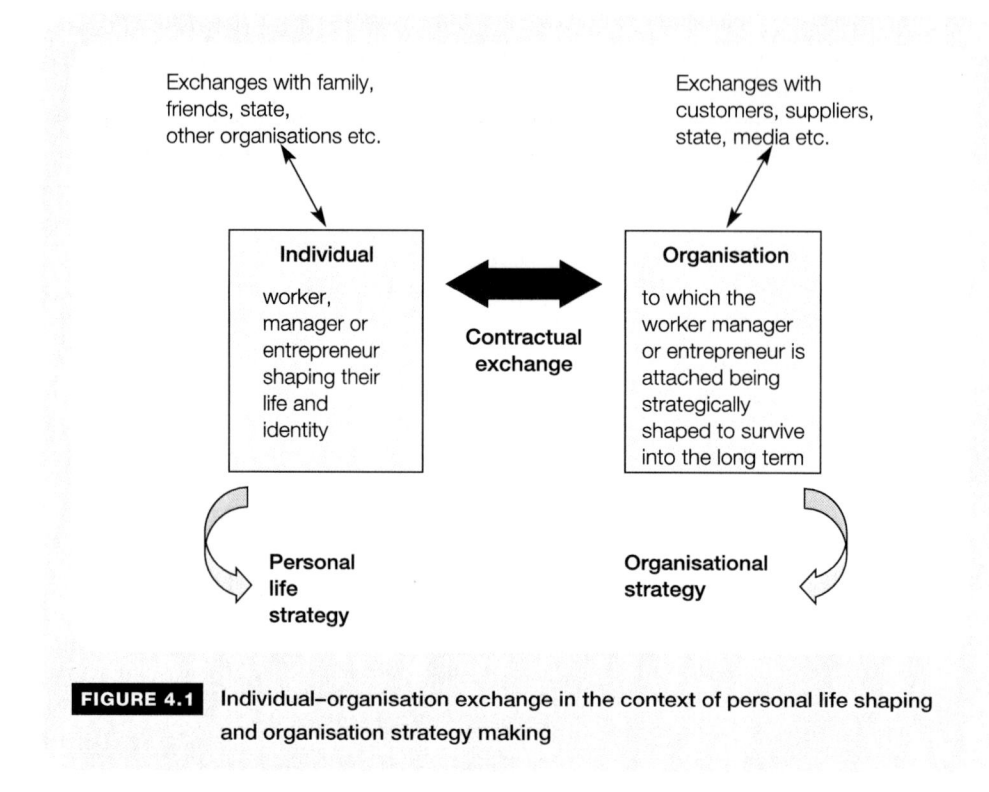

FIGURE 4.1 Individual–organisation exchange in the context of personal life shaping and organisation strategy making

taken forward into the future, through processes of economic, political and social exchange. These exchanges were managed by Peter to ensure that the resources of effort, support, accommodation and so on, needed by the organisation to survive and continue into the long term, were obtained from employees, politicians, police officers, landlords and the rest. He did all this in a way that shaped and expressed his own life and identity at the same time as it shaped the enterprise he was running. And we will see similarly striking evidence of this type of interaction between individual's life-shaping efforts and the strategic managing of a guitar-making firm in Case 9.4 (p. 388) where the entrepreneurial individuals who created a business confront, at the same time, questions about where they are going with their personal lives and questions about the future of the Strath Guitars. In this case the two are very tightly interrelated indeed.

The focus of the present chapter is not so much on the organisational shaping side of the picture presented in Figure 4.1 but on the exchange that occurs between workers and organisations generally. Although we are focusing on one side of the picture, it is vital to recognise that this exchange would not come into being were it not playing a part in the other side of the picture. Organisations, in principle at least, do not pay and otherwise reward people for involvement that has no significance for the strategic shaping of the enterprise as a whole.

Implicit contracts and orientations to work

Our main concern for the present is with the exchange that occurs between organisations and the people working in organisations. This exchange is identified in Figure 4.1 as one of contractual exchange. There is a trade, a 'deal' at the heart of the exchange relationship. And much of this contract is implicit. The normal way for people in a modern society to join a work organisation is to enter into an exchange with that organisation whereby they trade their application of skills and capabilities for a bundle of 'rewards' including cash, security, status, work satisfaction, opportunity for advancement and so on. Certain elements of this exchange are formally agreed and a very limited proportion of it is written in a formal contract of employment or perhaps a more short-term formal contract of engagement. However, the bulk of the 'understanding' that comes about between the employer and the worker is unwritten and is, in large part, unstated. The concept of implicit contract first started to be used (Levinson *et al.*, 1966) at about the same time as the work orientation concept, to which we shall shortly connect it, and is related to the concepts of *effort bargain* (Behrend, 1957, Baldamus, 1961) and *psychological contract* (Schein, 1978). (See also Further Reading on work orientations, implicit and psychological contracts, p. 160.)

Implicit contract *Concept*

The tacit agreement between an employing organisation and the employed individual about what the employee will 'put in' to the job and the rewards and benefits for which this will be exchanged.

The implicit contract is clearly a relational matter. It is an exchange between an individual who is seeking employment as part of the way they are strategically shaping their lives to take them into the future and an employer who requires their services to shape its activities to take it into the future. It takes the form of a set of understandings negotiated between the employee and the employer, much of which is unlikely to have been explicitly stated, let alone written into a formal contract. There will be unstated understandings about such matters as how long the job is likely to last, what sort of career advancement might be available or how much overtime can be earned. Inferences will be made about how willing the employee will be to take orders from managers and how adaptable the employee will be if organisational circumstances change. What all of this means is that the employment relationship is a highly ambiguous one. It is also a potentially fragile one, given the very different power positions of the employee, on the one hand, and the employer on the other (an observation central to Marx's classic critique of class relations in capitalist societies).

As the individual approaches the organisation to seek work, they take into the potential relationship more than just the skills and working capacities that they possess. As the strategic exchange perspective highlights, the individual also takes with them an identity and a biography as well as various values and feelings or emotions about the world. The human being approaching engagement with the organisation is a whole human being, not just a human resource. But, as they approach an organisation, many of these aspects of their lives and identities will, in the light of their particular life circumstances at the time, inform a particular meaning which they attach to the work and the job they are going into: a *work orientation* (or 'orientation to work').

Work orientation *Concept*

The meaning individuals attach to their work which predisposes them both to think and act in particular ways with regard to that work. There is an *initial orientation* at the point of entry to work and this is liable to change as circumstances and interests change within the continuing employment relationship.

At the stage of approaching engagement with the organisation we can refer to an initial orientation to work, in recognition of the fact that it is liable to develop and change once they have joined the organisation. The concept of orientation to work has its origins in sociological studies that were carried out in the 1960s in Britain. Goldthorpe, Lockwood and their colleagues (1968) developed the concept as they recognised the inadequacy of need-based motivational analyses for understanding the groups of employees that they studied. The concept of work orientation was seen as a more realistic tool for analysing what employees were seeking when they took certain jobs. The researchers argued that to understand the way different groups of workers behaved one should examine what those workers' jobs meant to them and what calculated choices they were making when entering that particular employment. Some people had an orientation to work that caused them to seek jobs which offered promotional opportunities or the opportunities to apply manual skills, for example, while others sought simply to maximise the money they could earn and *discounted* opportunities, say, for job interest or career advancement. Clearly these choices were made in the light of the abilities and aptitudes which people possessed as well as their value preferences. Most famously the study showed that many of the people working in the car assembly factory had chosen this work to maximise the income they could then spend on their families. And this meant forgoing the potentially more satisfying, but lower paid, work that they could have taken, should they have so chosen.

A way of linking the concepts of work orientation and implicit contract, as well as identifying some of the elements of the employment bargain is suggested in Figure 4.2. This recognises that the individual's 'understood deal' or *perceived implicit contract* is at the centre of their work orientation. It does not exist 'in the head' of the worker in isolation from their relationship with the employer but it does play a key part in how they *enact* their work roles and their

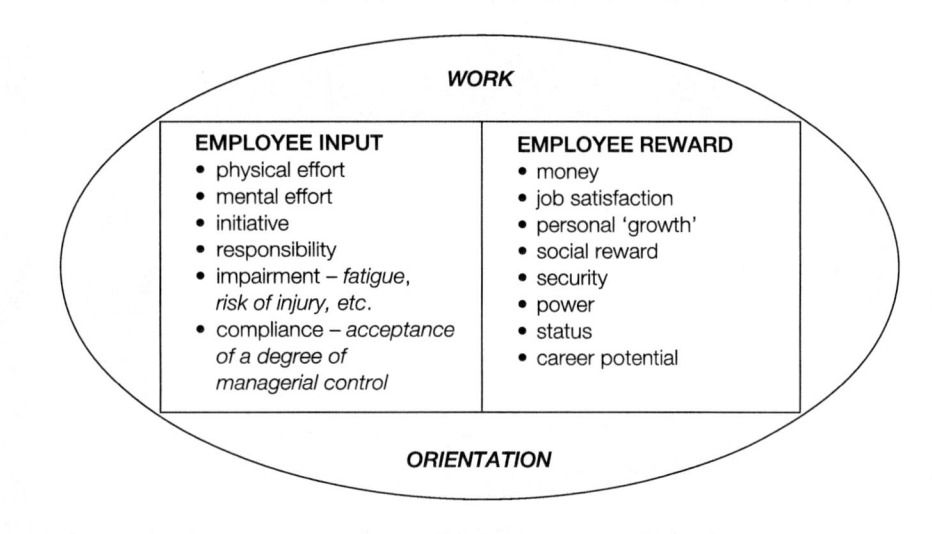

```
                              WORK
   ┌─────────────────────────┬─────────────────────────┐
   │ EMPLOYEE INPUT          │ EMPLOYEE REWARD         │
   │ • physical effort       │ • money                 │
   │ • mental effort         │ • job satisfaction      │
   │ • initiative            │ • personal 'growth'     │
   │ • responsibility        │ • social reward         │
   │ • impairment – fatigue, │ • security              │
   │   risk of injury, etc.  │ • power                 │
   │ • compliance – acceptance│ • status                │
   │   of a degree of        │ • career potential      │
   │   managerial control    │                         │
   └─────────────────────────┴─────────────────────────┘
                           ORIENTATION
```

FIGURE 4.2 The individual worker's perception of their implicit contract with the organisation

relationships with the managers in the employing organisation. Every employed individual, in the light of their current circumstances, their self-identities, life projects and the rest, has a notion of what they are exchanging with the employer: what mix of *inputs* of physical and mental efforts, the taking of responsibility, willingness to take risks of accident, stress and acceptance of managerial control is being traded with the employer for a particular mix of money, job satisfaction, social reward (satisfaction of serving the community, say), employment security, status, and opportunity to wield power, develop skills and advance a career.

This way of looking at people's work meanings and behaviours takes us a long way from the old-fashioned debates about whether people generally 'go to work mainly for the money' or seek employment for some other reason. Such 'either–or' thinking is simple-minded and of little value in understanding either work behaviour generally or the behaviour of particular groups of worker. In practice, every one of us has our own bundle of expectations and wants that we take into the strategic exchange we make with an employing organisation. There may be times in the life of each of us when we prioritise, say, money over job interest or security over high pay. But such a situation is recognised in this process-relational focus on orientations and implicit contracts as something which is particular to a particular person at a particular time and in particular circumstances. This is not to say that the concept cannot, to a certain extent, also be applied to groups, however.

A pattern of similar orientations may be seen across groups of employees who are similarly placed in the organisation or have come to the organisation from similar situations. It would tend to be the case that highly qualified senior staff would have different orientations, as a group, from unskilled and temporary manual workers, say. And it is possible that a different pattern of orientation might be found amongst people coming from one ethnic grouping, age or gender group rather than another, within the same organisational area of activity. Clearly, the cultural or age-group expectations of different groups of employees will vary, as will the bargaining strength which different types of prospective employee will take into their negotiation of an implicit contract – these varying with the skills, competencies or experiences they have to 'trade'. And, in circumstances where there is a formal trade union or other group representation, the bargaining over some aspects of the contract of employment will actually take place collectively. Nevertheless, even where there are clear patterns of orientation across groups of organisational members, it is necessary to recognise the variations that occur between individuals, albeit within these group patterns.

To understand any individual's or group's work behaviour we have to look at how they are predisposed to act in certain ways in the light of their orientation at that time and their perception of the deal they are making with the employer. We have to consider how they *enact* their role within the organisation, in other words. This, however, has to be set in the context of the employees' lives before they enter the organisation. We can see the importance of this in the case of Ravi Barr and how he came to be in the management job that he now does, by looking at the *initial orientation* which he brought to his present employing organisation. To look at processes of work entry and 'occupational choice', as it has traditionally been called, in the process-relational way, which a focus on work orientation involves, means once again turning away from the kind of *serial thinking* which was criticised in the previous chapter. Orthodox thinking tends to see the process of work entry as one in which we develop our interests, values and aptitudes as we grow up and go through education and then make a *choice* of occupation or career to fit this. Thus 'choice' precedes entry into a job or occupation. But, in practice, it does not work as simply as this, as Ravi Barr's story illustrates. What is the outcome of choice and what is adventitious, or a matter of circumstance and chance, is far from straightforward when we look at how people come into the sort of work we find them in at any point in their lives, in practice.

Activity 4.1

Read the conversation with Ravi Barr in Case 4.1 and consider the following questions:

- To what extent did Ravi 'choose' his career? Did he 'make a choice' of career and then enter it. Or did he 'find himself' in a job and then give this the rationale of a choice? Or was it a combination of these two?

- How has Ravi's work orientation changed over time, from the work he did in the family business, to the part-time jobs he took as a student, to the jobs he has done in the organisation he joined when he left school?

- How has Ravi 'managed' his identity? Because he has lived 'between two cultures', as he puts it, he is especially conscious of how identity is not a 'given' or fixed thing.

Ravi Barr gets oriented   Case 4.1

Tell me how you came to be a human resources manager, Ravi?

It was pure accident really. I was working as a supervisor in one of our shops, a job which I took when I got chucked out of university in my second year. I had always liked playing with computers, would you believe, and when a job came up in the home electrics department, as it was then called, I jumped at the chance. They said they wanted someone to build up that side of the department's business and I thought this would suit me. In fact it built up quite fast and I was soon spending a lot of my time recruiting new staff and training people on the computing side of things. I was training myself as I went along but I persuaded the general store manager that I was much more expert than I really was. The consequence of this was that he promoted me to a store-wide training job, getting managers and supervisors across the departments up to speed with computing. This went so well that when a personnel officer's job came up, I got it and then when the top human resources job become vacant I chose to go for that. I found I enjoyed the status I was building up and I liked the power that went with it. So here I am.

But you said, a moment ago, that it is 'pure accident' that you are in this job. And a few breaths later, you are telling me how you 'chose' to apply for the job. Can you explain this seeming contradiction to me?

Sorry about that. I suppose what was in my mind is that I originally wanted a career in marketing. This is what I hoped to specialise in on my degree course. So it's a sort of accident that I am now firmly in an HR career. I suppose that, on the other hand, there is consistency in that I am in a managerial sort of career. I wanted something that would give me seniority in an organisation – although I never thought of retailing as the industry I would end up in. And it is true that I enjoyed the human resources module I did in the second year at university – even if I failed it like all the others because I was enjoying myself too much pubbing and clubbing to do any academic work.

So why did you take the risk of not getting into a managerial career by not working at university?

Believe me, that is something I thought hard about at the time. In part, it was me sorting out who I was. You see my parents are in retailing and I was brought up to be a 'good hard-working Indian boy' who would eventually run the family business. And through my school years I accepted this. Well I more or less did. I worked enthusiastically in the family business whenever I had got my homework out of the way. I simply fitted into the business, like my older brothers, and did whatever my father asked me, whether it was delivering orders or sorting out the invoices. I didn't think of myself as cheap family labour. At home I was their dutiful Indian boy. At school I played that down and was just 'one of the lads' who were particularly interested in computers and computer games. Some of that group were Asian, others weren't. And it didn't matter. Asian identity was something for home. I was just another of the 'computer boys' at school. I sort of shifted my identity about across the two cultures I lived in. But I didn't really think about it at the time. I only started to think about all of this when I was at university. It was when I came home on the first vacation and found that I was expected to carry on the same as before. I started to see myself then as cheap family labour. I began to resent this and I got more and more awkward with my father and brothers – doing the minimum amount of work and refusing to take any kind of initiative at all. This all ended up in a big row and for the next few vacations I got work near the university, refusing to go home. I resolved never to have anything to do with retailing again. Apart from that, I did any work I could get, my main concern being to earn as much money as I could as fast as possible. I did labouring, worked in bars. I even did some horrible work in a chicken factory.

You just worked for money?

Exactly. The work was a means to an end.

And the end was?

Having a good time. And the money I made enabled me to carry on partying in term time too. I was sort of shaking off all those years of being the quiet conscientious boy. And I was also refusing the plan my parents had for me, as the first one in our family to go to university and, hence, the one who would eventually run the business (something I knew my elder brothers really resented).

But now you are a senior manager in a retailing business.

Funny isn't it? I am very career oriented now. I am making sure that I am learning about every aspect of this business so that I can eventually be a chief executive of a large retailing outfit. My parents have now accepted that I do not want to work in the family business. I think they are proud of what I have achieved and I suppose I want them to be even more proud of me when I really get to the top. My wife, who comes from a similar background, thinks similarly about her career as an accountant. I think my marriage, in fact, has been an important factor in my approach to career. Her family wanted to arrange a marriage for her and she had to fight them to marry me. So we have both had to make our way, and establish who we are, by sort of escaping from our families. So we are both making careers away from the Asian community. But, as we have both realised, we are still very much the products of the community and families that, in part, we turned away from. Yes, funny, isn't it. There are so many reasons for what you do, aren't there?

Ravi Barr's closing words rather neatly summarise the story he has told. But what is really interesting about his story is not just the large number, or even the variety, of the factors that have shaped his life and career. It is also the fascinating way that they interact with each other – home factors with work factors, family pressures with school priorities, ethnic influences with individual assertiveness, and so on. So complex is this interplay, in fact, that Ravi finds himself, rather paradoxically, talking of his career 'choices' since leaving university in terms of 'accident' one minute and 'choice' the next. This is not unusual when one interviews people about their work histories. The work biographies of most of us involve a complex interplay of choice and chance factors and when we report them to others we find ourselves, at certain points, drawing on all those stories in our culture which have the theme, 'Isn't it strange what things happen to people in life?'. And at other points in the narratives or biographies we present to people interviewing us, we draw on the discursive resource of the 'rational man or woman' who carefully plans a career to make the best use of their talents in the labour market. The 'either–or' dualism of choice *or* chance is not in fact helpful to understanding people's biographies. The two aspects of the duality do, however, interact with each other in different ways in different people's biographies. As we shall see in Chapter 10 (p. 442), the way we present that biography to employers or potential employers can have important consequences for recruitment and promotional decisions made by employers.

Ravi Barr's orientation to work is clearly tied up with his family and his ethnic background and with the process of managing his identity. He is making choices about his own life but those choices are very much made in the context of the structural situations in which he has found himself – whether these be the family and community structures into which he was born, or the structure of opportunities he later found himself in within the company for which he is now working. In different work situations in which he has found himself he has made different *implicit contracts* with the people employing him. When he first worked in the family firm he exchanged hard work and a willingness to be flexible for personal security and the social reward of belonging to a family and a community. Once he had left home and he felt that this reward was not what he was seeking, he was less willing to 'put in' so much effort or, as he points out, show so much initiative. The orientation to work and the implicit contract had changed, albeit with the same person and the same work situation. Ravi's changing concept of who he was and what he wanted from life led to a change in his work orientation. And when he sought employment while at university he thought of it in terms of a very simple trade – he wanted to maximise the money he could earn.

After the shock of having to leave university, Ravi approached his employment in the department store with a different kind of orientation. He was clearly willing to put more into that job than he had into the temporary jobs. And one of the rewards which was important in his understanding of the implicit contract with the company was the opportunity to work with computers. We can see then his orientation shifting further as he discovered his abilities in recruiting and training people. The ambition which then developed meant that the 'career potential' element of the reward side of Figure 4.2 was becoming more salient. Undoubtedly it was not replacing an interest in monetary reward, because we can presume that this was increasing at the same time, as were the rewards of status and power. We can see him trading a particular bundle of work inputs for a particular bundle of rewards. And this exchange is not just influenced by his relationship with the employing organisation. His current family life plays an important part in his emergent identity and his shifting work orientations. And this current family situation is itself related to his own and his wife's biographies. They are still working out their pasts as they work on the present and on their futures. Their exchanges with their present employers and with all the other people in their lives are indeed *strategic exchanges*. We each make strategic exchanges in our lives in our own ways.

Activity 4.2

Moving your attention away from Ravi Barr's story to your own, ask yourself the following questions.

- In what ways have both choice and chance played a part in your own unfolding work career or career ambitions?
- What different implicit contracts have you made in different work situations at various stages of your life? Use the employee input/employee reward boxes in Figure 4.2 to chart the perceived 'trades' you made in different jobs you have done.
- To what extent have you ever changed your orientation to work (and, of course, the way you perceived your implicit contract) within the same job? If you wish to be prompted on this question, you may choose to give a quick initial glance at what Sacha Boath has to say about how 'people change at work' in Case 4.2.

Varying and changing work orientations in a corporate affairs department
Case 4.2

Yes, you will hear several of the managers here refer to me and my department as Sacha and the Seven Dwarves. As Director of Corporate Affairs, I am the only woman in the company's top team and they like to tease me about being tall and fair-haired. That's OK, I can handle the banter and I suppose being compared to the fairy-tale Snow White is not really uncomplimentary. I do get bothered sometimes, though, that they are rather diminishing my team by referring to them as dwarves. Only one of them is really a small person, even if they are all shorter than me. In fact some of them have actually 'grown' in the job you might say. I think it's really interesting how people can change at work. Let me tell you about them; 'Smithy' Smith, 'Biffy' Currie, 'Sniffy' Gerardo, 'Snippy' Spedale, 'Chippy' Bliss, 'Iffy' Humphries and 'Sparky' Learmonth, as the managers call them.

Smithy, Biffy and Sniffy are my three public relations officers. Biffy and Sniffy are amazing cases of people who have changed. When I came here I was told they were simply miserable types. It was also said that they both had 'chips on their shoulders' because they had lost their jobs when the second of the town's papers closed down. They felt they were demeaning themselves by working in public relations. Both were well on the way to becoming alcoholics and they ruined their marriages, largely because of the drink. However, about a year ago there was this amazing change. In part, it was down to my giving them the most almighty shouting at – 'Shape up or ship out' is what I basically said. But it was also to do with some kind of conversion experience they had, as our Managing Director put it. They had both joined Alcoholics Anonymous and, at the same time, they discovered the delights of line dancing. Somehow the smartening up that went on with getting off the booze and their meeting women at the dancing sessions translated into their work. It was amazing. Almost overnight they changed from lazy and uninspired individuals who were in danger of letting the company down to smart and reliable characters who I can happily allow to speak for the company. Smithy, on the other hand, is somebody I increasingly can't trust. In her case, the change seems to have come about after moving in with a new partner, as opposed to losing a partner. She is my languages person and used to be brilliant at dealing with almost any issue where we needed to deal with Europe. It seems that her bloke has been getting resentful about her travelling abroad for us and this has led to her taking it out on all of us in the office. She's managed not to go abroad for six months now and the other day she rushed out of the office screaming, 'Oh, sod the

French'. One of my best people has become a complete liability for reasons which, it seems, have nothing to do with the company.

Changes at work do seem to be the source of the changes we've seen with Snippy, however. Her job is to monitor press coverage. She used to be the life and soul of the office. She would sit over there, snipping away at her press cuttings and joking with everybody who came into the office. But since we've rearranged the office and her desk is less central to what is going on, she seems to have completely dropped her role as the office wit. I shall have to rethink the office layout, I think. But, for some reason, she's recently taken up smoking and keeps disappearing to the smoking room across the road to have a cigarette. In the past, I could have spoken to her about that, but the way she is just now would make that difficult.

In some ways Snippy's social role in the office has been taken on by Iffy. She is my secretary, sorry PA – personal assistant. She used to be a total misery. She was a graduate trainee with the company. She said she didn't mind taking on a 'graduate secretary' role but she resented the fact that it was only female graduates who did that. They called her Iffy because she was always saying things like, 'If a man were asked to do that, he'd refuse.' So what's made the difference? I don't really know. The job title change might be a factor, but I don't think it was that important. And it might be that she became aware that I was never going to ask her to make me coffee or go out to buy flowers for me to give to my mother on Mother's Day (something she says happened to her before I came). Actually, I think it is simply that she and I have become good friends. We do meet socially but, at work, we really enjoy working together. There's no doubt that I am 'the boss', as anyone will tell you ('the blonde Tsarina', Iffy called me the other day, when I stormed into the office generally threatening murder all round). The simple truth is that Iffy enjoys working with someone she gets on with, and that has led her to take on more and more tasks which she then finds she really enjoys.

I wish I could bring about a similar change in Sparky. He runs the computing and IT side of the department – our web site and all that. When he was here first I think he felt that he was a pioneer and that he understood things none of us had a clue about. He was a cheerful chap to have around – a really sparky character in fact. It seems now that everything has settled down and his work is more routine, he is a bit bored. Consequently he is not helping people as much as he should be. He's well paid though and I think that he has got himself locked in here by the salary. He has taken on a mortgage on a new house recently and doesn't want to risk a job change. He's pretty secure too, given the relevance of his skills to our work. I can't see what promotional opportunities we can offer to 'turn him back on'. I'll have to look for some exciting new project.

Chippy is someone for whom everything is a new project. I have rarely seen anyone so positive about his job. He came to us from the maintenance department who 'redeployed' him when that operation was downsized. His resentment of moving into here was palpable. He thought he was simply going to be some sort of odd job man who would only occasionally use his carpentry skills when we needed a display preparing. However, once he realised that he could make the job an important one, by seeking opportunities to make exhibition stands and by being the key person at out-of-company presentations, he really changed. He regularly travels abroad now – which he had never done before, and I often think he has developed better public relations skills than some of the professionals. The job is very much what he has chosen to make it. After that first miserable couple of weeks here he just seemed to decide, 'Right, let's make something of this'. The MD – ever the joker himself – actually asked me the other day, 'Is that Chippy of yours still a chirpy chappy?'. Indeed he is.

These brief portraits painted by one manager of the staff in her department very effectively illustrate the foolishness of looking at the demeanour or the behaviour of any given person at work and concluding, 'Aha, that is the sort of person they are'. Although there will be certain consistencies which could be perceived over time in the lives and identities of each of these individuals, the orthodox psychology categories of 'personality type' hardly seem relevant to the complexities of what is going on in these seven lives and to the work orientations of 'Smithy' Smith, 'Biffy' Currie, 'Sniffy' Gerardo, 'Snippy' Spedale, 'Chippy' Bliss,' Iffy' Humphries and 'Sparky' Learmonth. The concepts of emergent identity, work orientation and implicit contract are far more helpful than any concept of personality type.

Activity 4.3

Carefully examine each of the individuals that Sacha Boath talks about and, using the model in Figure 4.2:

- note what factors appear to have led to their changed orientations;
- given that Sacha has only a partial picture of what has happened in each case, speculate about what other kinds of factor might also have come into play (i.e. things you might 'look into' if you were trying to do a research project on the orientations of people in this Corporate Affairs – or 'public relations' – department);
- try to think of any examples of people, other than yourself, whose work orientations appear to have changed during their employment within a particular job.

A complex multiplicity of factors seems to be relevant to the workplace identities and the work orientations of each of these people. Numerous factors influence how they see the implicit contract they have with their employer. Sacha Boath has clearly tried hard to understand each of these people and, indeed, she gets close to analysing how they might perceive the implicit contracts they have with her and the company. Notice, for example, the way in which she analyses how Sparky might be thinking about the rewards he is getting from the company: he has got security and good pay but he is not getting any intrinsic rewards or fulfilment from the job itself. He is bored. This might be compensated for by promotional opportunities, but that is not really a possibility. Sacha is therefore considering what she might do to give him more excitement in the job. She is not getting the work 'inputs' she wants, given what rewards she is offering. She therefore needs to act to get a better trade. And this takes us into that area of management often called 'motivation' and which, in Chapter 8 (pp. 315–24), we will be reconceptualising as a process in which managers manipulate the perceived implicit contracts of workers.

For the present, however, we simply want to give full recognition to the extent to which a person's identity is always *emergent*, their work orientation is always liable to change and their involvement at work has to be seen in the context of the strategic exchanges which are going on in their lives and biographies as a whole. And if we are going to look at people in this holistic way, then we have to recognise that they do not simply go to work to act as task-completing biological machines. The 'whole person' goes to work, as we recognised earlier.

And that means that they approach the organisation with feelings, preferences, beliefs and the whole range of human vulnerabilities, as well as the skills, aptitudes and willingness to follow instructions that the employing organisation is buying from them.

Feelings, emotions and the experience of stress

Work organisations are parts of an institutional pattern which has developed at a very recent stage in the overall evolution and history of the human species. This pattern is associated with *modernism* which, as we saw in Chapter 2 (p. 36), involves a concerted attempt to apply rational thinking to human activities and institutions in order to increase humans' control over their circumstances. The principles of *reason* and of *control* are thus central to the work of trying to shape modern organisations and, as we established earlier, the form which this reason takes is that of 'instrumental rationality', whereby calculated choices are made to find the best means for achieving given ends. People in modern organisations are not meant to perform work tasks in the way that they *feel* like doing at a particular moment. They are not meant to carry out tasks in a particular way because they *guess* that this is how to do it. And they are not meant to do a job in a particular way because that is the *traditional* way in which it has always been done. To act in these ways is to go against the principles of carefully, or scientifically, calculating the most efficient way of carrying out work tasks.

Max Weber, the key theorist of these matters, pointed out that this would mean that if modern organisations or 'bureaucracies' were to exist in a pure form, they would have no place for 'love, hatred and all purely personal, irrational and emotional elements which escape calculation' (Weber, 1978, p. 975). The key phrase here is 'which escape calculation'. Weber was identifying here the aspirations of those building and leading the large organisations of the modernising world and, as Albrow (1997) points out (in contradicting a common misreading of Weber), Weber was well aware that they were not seeking to *exclude* an emotional or affective dimension from organisational life. We might say that what they were seeking were ways of *harnessing* the 'humanness' and the emotional involvement of human labour. This was indeed the logic of the attention given to 'informal' aspects of organisational functioning in those classic 1930s studies by Roethlisberger and Dickson and by Barnard, which we looked at in Chapter 2 (pp. 61–2). Managers should pay heed to the 'sentiments' of workers in shaping factory activities, argued the former, while the latter put the management of 'informal activities' at the centre of the executive's job.

In effect, Barnard was recognising the need of organisational managers to appeal to employees' hearts and sentiments as well as to their minds. His social science influenced analysis of all of this, and the advocacy which follows from it, can itself be seen as part of what Weber recognised as a trend not to allow 'emotional elements' to 'escape calculation'. Emotions are all very well in the modern work organisation, in this view, but they must be kept under control and, wherever possible, harnessed to the ends being pursued by the organisation's controllers. Hatred for an enemy would probably be a managerially desirable emotion to be felt by soldiers in a modern army during a war. And passion for the product being sold by a commercial enterprise could be very welcome to those in charge of that enterprise. However, if either of these got 'out of hand' – beyond calculation and control – the soldiers might disastrously run amok and the over-passionate sales person might frighten away some of their customers.

It has been recognised in recent years that the bulk of management and organisational texts attend too little to the emotional side of organisational life and work involvement (see Further Reading on emotions and work, pp. 160–1). Where it is given recognition in standard texts, it is dealt with in an indirect, and often rather 'bloodless' way. Sometimes it is seen as a dimension of gaining employee compliance – rewarding people with *self-actualisation* or overcoming their *resistance to change* for example. At other times it becomes pertinent because of an interest in overcoming tendencies of individuals to break down through *stress* or the inclination of certain groups overenthusiastically to pursue *grievances*.

We can usefully reflect on why there has been little direct attention to the emotional aspects of working lives. The subjective states of the individuals whose feelings and emotions make up the 'emotional side of organisational life' are not easy to understand and, partly as a result of the ambiguity and unpredictability that such matters involve, people can readily become quite uncomfortable when trying to address them. It might also be the case that when we are working as researchers, or as thoughtful managers, in specific organisational situations, we feel uncomfortable about invading the privacy of the people we come across. We might ask whether we have the right to enquire too deeply into the emotional states and the private feelings of the people we meet in work situations. This would be a proper ethical question to ask. Yet if we want to understand the full complexities of organising and managing work, we need to attend to matters of feeling and emotion in the workplace. The ethnographic style of research, in which the researcher gets closely involved with the people living or working in the particular setting being studied, enables such factors to be looked at. An ethnographic episode which demonstrates the type of insight that can be gained in this way is that of Ken Steary's collision with his office desk (Case 4.3). At this stage we have not formally conceptualised the issues that arise in this broad area of the 'emotions and feelings'. This is deliberate. We will look at some events occurring in Ken Steary's hotel and then consider how we might bring some conceptual rigour to bear on them.

Activity 4.4

Read the researcher's conversation with Ken Steary in Case 4.3. Then:

- list all of the ways in which issues of emotion and feeling come into these events;

- identify any way in which those running this hotel organisation – represented in this story by the regional manager – appear to have taken account of the emotional dimension of what goes on in hotels.

Ken Steary laughs, cries and falls over

Case 4.3

You don't look good, Ken.
 I don't feel good, mate.
You look altogether stressed.
 Stress is supposed to be a mental thing, isn't it? Well, you see this black eye. That's stress for you. It's physical and it hurts. And I know what you think. You think that I am going to tell you that I got so stressed last night trying to manage this bloody hotel that I got into a fight with a customer. Well that isn't what happened.
Did a member of staff thump you, then?
 No. I didn't get into a fight with a member of staff. It was my office desk what did it.
I see.
 No you don't. I was at the end of my tether last night, stressed up, tired out and on the point of laughing and crying at the same time. But I am the manager and I am meant to be in control. I can neither afford to let the staff see me crack up nor let the hotel guests see me fall apart. So I went up to my office and drank myself stupid. And then I fell over, catching my eye on the corner of the desk. I thought I was doing really well, keeping up the façade of the man who is always in control – dealing with my pathetic grief in private. And now I've got to explain to everybody how I got the black eye. I've already told three different stories to explain it away. I am really losing the plot.
OK, tell me the plot then. What is the real story?
 The problems started yesterday with the visit from the Regional Manager. She comes round every month to look at 'the figures' with me and generally to keep me on my toes. I really hate her, the officious cow. She has a go at me for things that she couldn't do. She really likes to wind me up.
How do you mean?
 Well, yesterday, I started off in a good mood. I was feeling good because I knew the figures were OK. Our occupancy figures have been really excellent, the bar and restaurant turnovers are on the up and up and the staff turnover figures are slightly down. I've even got the wages tightly under control. But guess what? Did they thank me? Did they congratulate me? Did they hell. No, what I got from madam was, 'Region are perturbed about some complaints they have received.' They had got a couple of complaints about the sullen behaviour of my reception staff. I'd like to see her try to deal with a problem like that.
You recognise that this is a problem, then. I must admit that I was put off earlier by the rather surly manner of one of your barmen. I felt most unwelcome and would have walked out if I hadn't been meeting you.
 Don't you start. I thought you were my friend. But, yes, you are right. This is an issue that has been bothering me. I just didn't like the idea of my bosses sitting around their boardroom table tut tutting about poor old Ken Steary not being able to make his staff smile at the punters. And that cow of a regional manager wouldn't be able to make a drunk on his honeymoon smile. So who is she to lecture me?

But you accept that there is a problem?

Oh yes. And I could do with some help handling it. But who do I turn to? I am the boss here. And you can get very lonely, even in a big hotel full of people like this one was last night. I've got to show a smiling face to the world and my staff know damn well that they need to do the same. Even on my way up to my office last night I smiled at a grumpy guest who refused help with his suitcase and then complained that the steps on the stairs were too steep. 'What's wrong with using the lift, you stupid bastard?', I said under my breath as I felt my skin burning and my colour rising. But my expression was a picture of genuine sympathy. And since I've had this black eye, I have smiled a hundred times at one member of staff and one hotel guest after another.

But you can't get all of your staff to act in this way?

Most will, they know their jobs depend on the hotel doing well and that it won't do well if the guests are not treated hospitably. That doesn't seem unreasonable. And they have chosen to work in the hospitality industry, for God's sake. They are paid to be hospitable.

But are they paid to be actors?

Would you like a black eye too?

Matters of feeling and emotion come into this story from the beginning. One of the first things Ken says is that he does not *feel* good. He talks about how his black eye 'hurts' – suggesting that the abstract phenomenon he calls 'stress', itself 'hurts'. His reference to his hotel as 'this bloody hotel' is clearly emotionally loaded, as is his worry that one might infer that he had fought with a customer. He loads his account of his feelings the previous evening with terms like 'the end of my tether', 'tired out', 'crack up', 'fall apart', 'drank myself stupid', 'pathetic grief' and 'losing the plot'. The description of his 'laughing and crying at the same time' involves the use of a discursive resource commonly used in the wider culture to give a picture of somebody who is so out of control that they have gone beyond the cultural norm of crying to express sadness and laughing to express happiness. He talks of hating the Regional Manager and, twice, uses another common discursive resource which is applied to express strong antipathy to a woman, as does his ironic use of the term 'madam'. Positive feelings are expressed when Ken looks back to earlier the previous day when he 'felt good' and was, it seems, feeling that he deserved thanks and congratulations. These are aspects of the sort of reciprocity we referred to in Chapter 3 when discussing culture and social exchange (p. 81). His looking for these endorsements and the manager failing to provide them reveal significant *relational* aspects of the emotional temperature which built up for Ken. Also, the Regional Manager's use of language in saying that the 'region is perturbed' is interesting. She is mystifying exactly who is worried by *personifying* 'Region' (see above p. 50), something which, if Ken is reporting her verbatim, we might take to be slightly provocative. It implies that some power greater than any nameable human individual is looking down upon the insignificant figure of Mr Steary. The formality of the word 'perturbed' rather than the more obvious 'worried' has been taken by Ken, we can infer, as a further attempt to 'wind him up'.

The alleged 'sullenness' of the reception staff, and the researcher's mention of the 'surly manner' of a bar worker, are clearly matters of emotional interpretation made by customers of the apparent emotional state of these hotel employees. The researcher speaks of *feeling* unwelcome and Ken goes on in the conversation to paint a picture of a very emotional state he was in the previous night and the equally emotional state he is in at present with the use of one emotionally loaded expression after the other. He also makes a bitter joke about the Regional Manager's demeanour, one that has all sorts of sexual and sexist undertones (couldn't 'make a drunk on his honeymoon smile') and he even threatens the researcher with violence, even though (as it happened) he says it with a smile on his face, echoing back to the pathos of the earlier 'I thought you were my friend'.

This episode is packed with emotionality and it could be argued that an exaggerated picture of the role that feelings play in organisational life is being painted by the selection of an episode in which there has been a crisis in the life of one particular individual. There is some truth in this. But it can be argued that critical events like this simply reveal factors and issues that are present all the time but only come fully to the surface when circumstances arise in which the normal controls of social life are weakened and conventional courtesies are strained. For example, if the Regional Manager had been polite to Ken and thanked him for his good work before diplomatically raising the question of the customer complaints, there would still be emotional factors in play. The Regional Manager would have been taking Ken's feelings into account and he might have 'felt good' about being thanked and he might have appreciated the senior person's 'sharing' a managerial problem with him. This kind of social exchange process and the maintenance of reciprocity is so common or 'normal' in social and organisational life that we tend not to be consciously aware of it. It is when there is some breakdown in it that the presence of feelings and emotions in the work context become starkly apparent. They are, however, never absent.

The emotional issues raised by Ken Steary's tale go beyond ones of staff relationships. The issue that triggered Ken's distressing experience was one of how the organisation, as a business, relates to its customers. It does not apparently stay in business simply by selling food and renting beds to customers. It provides *hospitality* to its *guests*. The very tasks which are done 'in the organisation's name' (above p. 58) are ones with a strong emotional dimension. Ken is fully aware of this. And one can reasonably infer from his outburst, 'they have chosen to work in the hospitality industry, for God's sake', that a key source of frustration to him is the difficulty he is having in getting some of the staff to *engage emotionally* with their work, by acting in a friendly and smiling way towards 'guests'. We notice that he stresses how the Regional Manager would be unable do this. And we note that he emphasises how he is willing to 'make his face a picture of genuine sympathy', even when he is in a bad mood and is provoked by a 'stupid bastard' and 'grumpy guest'. A concept which we will use to look at the issues that arise here is that of *emotional labour*. But, before we can properly deploy that concept, we need to conceptualise the more general phenomena of emotion and feeling.

It has been possible in the above analysis to refer in a broad way to 'feelings and emotions' as if they were more or less the same thing. This is what we tend to do in everyday life. We talk about 'feeling happy' on one occasion, for example, and refer to the 'emotion' of happiness on another. It has been normal, in the history of human reflection, to link feelings and emotions. So why should we consider splitting them – distinguishing between the two? The only justification for doing this would be the pragmatist's one of developing our conceptual tools to enable us to analyse something more effectively than we would otherwise do, with a view to better informing our subsequent practices. On these grounds, it is useful to conceptualise feelings and emotions as separate, but closely linked, phenomena.

> ### Emotions and feelings *Concept*
>
> *Feelings* are sensations felt bodily which relate to a psychological state. *Emotions* are the way these sensations are made sense of with reference to culture, either privately or socially.

It is helpful to follow Fineman in separating *feelings* – the 'subjective experience' in which 'we are aware "in" ourselves of some bodily state, peturbation, or more diffuse psychological change' (Fineman, 1999, p. 546) from the more culturally mediated *emotions* with which they are associated. Fineman, however, treats emotions as *displays* of these feelings. He does this to enable him to distinguish between, say, the way someone might express the *emotion* of anger in a situation, by shouting and raging, while actually *feeling* pleasure in what they are doing. There is clearly an important distinction to be made here (to understand situations like the one Ken Steary was in when he *felt* angry with the grumpy customer while he *displayed* sympathy). However, it is felt more analytically useful here to say that the *feeling* was the physical sensation Ken describes when he says 'I felt my skin burning and my colour beginning to rise'. And the *emotion* is the cultural label of 'anger' that might be attached to this feeling when we try to make sense of it. The two are closely linked but the 'animal' sensation that Ken experienced does not automatically read across to the cultural interpretation of 'anger'. Ken himself, or somebody else hearing about his experience, might choose to interpret or 'construct' that experience as one of 'going mad', 'being disgusted', 'getting furious' or 'being appalled'.

The distinction between feeling and emotion, then, is a way of taking account of both the 'animal' and the 'cultural' aspects of our natures – our humanity. As we said earlier, with regard to instincts (pp. 81–2), everything in the human being, is culturally mediated. Animal 'things' are 'there in us', as indeed our body is ontologically 'there'. But they are always subject to processes of social construction, to cultural interpretation, to enactment. The situation is not as simple as, say, good *feelings* first being 'there', or being 'experienced', and then being *enacted* in a particular way as happiness, joy, contentment or whatever. To assume this is again to fall into the trap of the 'linear' type of psychology we rejected in the previous chapter (pp. 87–8). It might be possible, for example, for one to start off sad and then, with the cultural notion of happiness in mind, to lie back on a pile of comfortable cushions, smile to oneself and actually experience the sensation we label 'happiness'. It has been widely observed, in fact, that choosing to smile can make one 'feel happier' than one was before the smile appeared on our face.

We are getting ourselves involved here in matters which philosophers and psychologists have agonised over for centuries. Why should we trouble to engage with such matters? It is to sharpen our conceptual tool kit in order to come to terms with the issues that were raised in Ken Steary's story. If we are going to require people like Ken and his staff to perform in ways which involve emotional labour, then we need to understand the relationship between the feelings these people might have and the emotional face they are required to present to the world. What are we asking of people who we require to smile at – and 'make feel good' – hotel guests, airline passengers, hospital patients, shop customers and a multitude of other consumers of services in modern societies?

Emotional labour

Emotions and the way these are presented play a key part in all the exchanges we make with other human beings. We smile at a child to show our approval of its behaviour or we frown at a friend who fails to notice the new clothes we are wearing. This is an exchange, in the sense that we are suggesting certain emotions on our own part in order to elicit certain emotions in the other person, ones that will take the relationship forward in the way we wish it to go. This kind of emotional management, which characterises much of our private lives, is called *emotion work* by Hochschild (1985) and she contrasts it with *emotional labour*.

Emotional labour *Concept*

An element of work activity in which the worker is required to display certain emotions in order to complete work tasks in the way required by an employer.

Here, emotional work on the part of an organisational employee is carried out to further the interests of the employer who is buying their services. There is a close relationship between the emotion work which is a normal part of everybody's lives and emotional labour. In the workplace, one does 'emotion work' all the time, simply in order to relate to the other human beings with whom we come into contact. But this overlaps with those efforts that we feel obliged to make as part of our implicit contract with the employer. In dealing with other people at work we would generally be unaware of any tension between our 'natural' inclination to interact, say, in a warm and friendly way with colleagues or customers and what our employment entails. However, once our 'private self' (our self-identity as we are experiencing it at that moment) finds itself in some tension with our self as an 'organisational representative' (a manifestation of our social identity, as required of us by our employment) we are likely to experience discomfort. We tend, then, to become aware of that which we conceptualise as emotional labour. Such an awareness is reported by Ken Steary when he describes the friendly and sympathetic demeanour he presented to the grumpy guest. He felt obliged to behave in this way because of his understanding of his contract with the hotel company. As a hotel manager and a representative of the organisation he had to behave in this way. His private self, however, was silently addressing the customer as a 'stupid bastard'. He could not show this to the guest because to do so would be to break his implicit contract with the employer. And he believes some of his staff are doing precisely this. The reception staff who were complained of were forgetting, or ignoring, what Ken takes to be implicit in the agreement made between employees and employers in the *hospitality* industry: that employees should act hospitably.

A useful distinction that Hochschild makes when examining emotional labour is that between *surface acting* and *deep acting*. Ken Steary's behaviour was an example of surface acting, because he was aware that he was 'putting on a show'. He might be deceiving the guest, but he was not deceiving himself. With deep acting, the employee either 'works up' a feeling in themselves which fits with the emotion they are expressing in doing their job or, as Hochschild puts it, they train their imaginations to achieve the same effect. We see an example in some of the experiences of Cindy Sutor, a sex worker who is reflecting on her work and what it requires of her 'self'.

Activity 4.5

Cindy Sutor's work (Case 4.4) takes her towards the more extreme end of the 'emotional labour market'. Consider:

- how the concepts of *deep acting* and *surface acting* can be applied to Cindy's experiences;
- how the implicit contract she used to make with the clients or with the employer she now works for contains limits on what can be expected emotionally;
- having looked at this relatively extreme case of emotional labour, how many relatively 'normal' jobs can you think of which involve *emotional labour*;
- what elements of *emotional labour* there have been in any jobs you have done and to what extent (a) this involved deep and surface acting, (b) there were limits built into the implicit contract, as you perceived it, which helped in the managing of the emotional demands of the job.

Cindy sets the limits for emotional engagement in her work   Case 4.4

I have recently stopped working as a prostitute on my own account and I now do just five shifts a week for the sex phone line company. It pays less but it's safer. It's also different because I now just *talk* about what I actually used to have to *do*. But there are lots of similarities. In both kinds of work, you have got to protect your own idea of who you are. You must not sell your whole self. When I was working on the street I knew that I had to show a certain level of interest in the punter – but not too much. I'd say something like 'Come on, big boy', without really implying that I thought that he was a big boy. You train your clients to know what they are paying for. You show a certain amount of interest in the man, especially if you are hoping for repeat business, but what you don't do is show any kind of excitement and, certainly, absolutely no hint of passion. I'd demean myself if I let that happen. And if I felt myself getting interested I'd damn quickly shut that off. The only exception to this was when I got into the posh call girl game for a while. You get paid a lot more then. So you play it just a little more positively.

Working on the telephone line is really an acting job. You sometimes put on a sexy voice and tell the punter that you are dressed in a skimpy nightie. But, as you tell them this, you make sure you keep a blank face and you look down at the dirty old jeans you are wearing.

Sometimes, though, I get bored with this. If I then find myself talking to someone who sounds really nice I let myself imagine that he is someone that I would actually like to go out with. Then I close my eyes and let myself stop pretending. Sometimes I quite enjoy this, get genuinely excited even. It helps the shift go a bit faster. It's only daydreaming, though. But perhaps those punters do get a better deal – something more genuine. I doubt it though – a proportion of our calls are monitored by the management and I would not want that creep in the 'control room' to think I was giving more than I am being paid for.

As Cindy Sutor is engaged in activities which potentially have deep emotional significance yet which occur within a framework of instrumental economic transaction, she has to work hard to manage boundaries and to 'set limits'. The public or temporary social identity she is paid to adopt must not be allowed to take over her private self-identity. Such issues arise for workers in an increasing number and variety of occupations, ranging from the airline workers, to whose work Hochschild first applied the *emotional labour* concept, to sales staff, call centre workers, entertainers, medical workers, and the 'greeters' who welcome customers as they walk through the entrances of some supermarkets. The more work organisations attempt to develop internal cultures which follow the 'quality management' principles of treating fellow workers as 'internal customers', the more we will see a requirement for most employees to go beyond the 'emotion work' which is a normal and spontaneous part of all human exchange and to be monitored for the quality of the *emotional labour* they put in.

It might be argued that issues of this general kind have to be handled by all workers: protecting themselves from what has often been called the *alienation* of self or, in a more recent formulation, the 'corrosion of self' (Sennett, 1998). The notion of alienation is more a philosophical than a social scientific one and it adopts an *essentialist* view of the human individual, instead seeing 'humanness' *processually* as something which people 'work at' and 'achieve'. But the notion has played a major part in critiques of modern work institutions and the effects they have on the integrity of the human individual. It is consistent, however, with the process-relational recognition of the need of each human being to manage their identities. Identity has to be managed and a logic found or created which links people's self-identities and their social identities to keep them sane and capable of competently playing a part in social life.

> ### Alienation *Concept*
>
> The destruction of the integrity of the human self – a splitting of one part of a person's 'being' from another.

Cindy Sutor's management of identity involves a high degree of 'distancing' of her 'self' from her work and this means that much of her 'acting' is of a surface kind. However, she does talk of occasionally moving over into some 'deep acting' when she decides to use her imagination and let herself 'daydream'. But even that is circumscribed by the contractual setting in which she is operating – and by the constant reminder of this in the form of the monitoring manager in the 'control room'. Just as she did not want her prostitution clients to get more than they were paying for, she was not willing to exceed the 'inputs' she was making in her implicit contract with the phone line company. We can well imagine Ken Steary's unsmiling hotel workers in Case 4.3, in the same spirit, arguing that for the money they are paid they cannot be expected to put 'heart and soul' into their jobs. They cannot be expected to treat hotel guests in the way that they would treat guests in their own houses, any more than Cindy would treat her 'punters' as if they were lovers. We might not expect Ken, as a manager, to go along with such an argument. But if Ken were to point out that he always treats customers as if they were his personal guests, we can imagine his reception staff pointing out that Ken is much better rewarded than they are for continuously presenting a positive 'face' to customers. Implicit contracts are not only perceived differently by different parties to them. They are also frequently contested.

Stress, strain and distress

The stressed executive, falling apart under the strains of heavy responsibility, has been one of the clichés of modern life for some time. But this image is coming to be replaced by the one of employees of every kind afflicted with the pathology of *stress* in every corner of the pressured and increasingly competitive organisational world. We hear of people being 'off work with stress', in the same way that they might be off work with mumps or measles. But stress is not something that one 'has' in this way. The notion simply implies that someone is suffering in some way under the strains of their work situation to the extent that they are becoming unable to perform satisfactorily in that work. Stress is a reaction to circumstances and it can arise in situations other than work. A poor single parent with several energetic and demanding children could well find themselves approaching an emotional state where they no longer felt able to act as a parent is expected to act. A husband or wife, oppressed by the nature of their relationship with their spouse, could well find themselves emotionally unable to continue to act as a husband or wife is expected to behave. Similarly a teacher, office cleaner, social worker, factory worker or manager might reach a stage of emotional agitation within their work experiences in which they become incapable of fulfilling the tasks required of them.

Stress *Concept*

A sense of distress arising because of pressures experienced in certain social or economic circumstances that render the sufferer emotionally, and sometimes physically, incapable of continuing to behave in the ways expected of them in those circumstances.

What characterises the state of being 'stressed', in work or elsewhere, is clearly being in a position where the person *feels* they cannot continue to perform as they are expected (see Further Reading on work and stress, p. 161). It is a subjective state – it is not just a matter of being incapable. Someone who found that they simply did not have the patience to look after children, that they were no longer attracted to their spouse or that they were no longer physically strong enough to continue in their current job could *rationally decide* to abandon their children, leave their spouse or resign from their job. Stress – as the etymology of the word suggests – implies something oppressing, pressurising or 'drawing tight' around one. This leads to a feeling, a subjective state, in which one cannot tolerate these pressures. And that subjective state may be accompanied by one or more physical afflictions in which there is a breakdown of some part of the body. No sense can be made of the many experiences of stress if one persists with the Cartesian dualism which separates body and mind and tries to suggest that suffering has to be *either* in the body *or* 'just in the mind'.

While there is no denying the 'reality' of stress, as something which people experience and which can be manifested in physical symptoms, it is important to recognise that this reality is nevertheless one which involves processes of social construction (see above, pp. 56–8). People are making sense of their situation through the use of discursive resources which are available in their culture (pp. 102–5). In another place and time, a worker suffering from what we would nowadays label stress might simply be dismissed as a 'weak character' and a soldier who would, today, be recognised as undergoing stress might be shot at dawn as a coward. But to recognise the importance of processes of construction, interpretation or enactment in how stress is experienced and handled is not just a matter of how we are socially labelled. The sufferer from 'stress' will make sense of their situation in their own way, albeit in the context of the discursive resources which are available to them. Each individual will also be better or worse placed with regard to personal resources such as experience, physical strength, intelligence, intellectual ingenuity and a self-identity which entails their defining themselves, say, as a relatively robust or vulnerable person. They will also be better or worse placed with regard to friends, relatives or advisers to whom they can turn for advice and emotional support. All of these resources, cultural and personal (not that in the final analysis these can be separated – to decide that one is a 'fighter' rather than a 'quitter' is clearly both a personal and a discursive matter), are drawn upon to deal with whatever pressures, strains or 'stresses' are being experienced. Thus, in any workplace or occupational stress situation we choose to look at, we have to consider the interplay of two sets of factors: the *pressures of the work circumstances* and the psychological, emotional and *social resources of the worker* facing those circumstances.

Activity 4.6

Look at the experiences of Tim Dyke and Con Tessock in Case 4.5 and:

- note the ways in which the personal resources of the two individuals made a difference to the ways they experienced and dealt with the stress of handling the pressures of the work circumstances they faced;

- identify any work or organisational situation you have witnessed, experienced or can envisage in which different individuals react differently to the same potentially stressful situations, noting which factors you think were the most important in leading to these different reactions.

A tale of two deputies   Case 4.5

We were seen as a team over the several years we worked together as classroom teachers – Tim Dyke and Con Tessock, the dedicated teacher twins. Then, when the school got into trouble and they put the new Head Teacher in to sort it all out, it wasn't seen as strange that we were both appointed as deputy heads. I was to look after the lower school and Con the upper school. In some ways mine was the more difficult job because I had a higher proportion of disruptive pupils. By the time you reached the senior classes, which were Con's, the worst troublemakers had left. But we had both been pretty good at classroom control and we both had managed to get reasonable examination results with the sort of pupils which we had to handle. What I am saying is that we both started off the managerial stages of our careers similarly placed, similarly matched – not that there was any competitiveness between us, as far as I could see at the time anyway. So it's really interesting to try to work out why I am now about to become a head teacher and Con is a retired teacher at 48, 'put out to grass' on ill health retirement because he couldn't take the stress.

Because the school had been inspected and deemed by the inspectors to be an officially 'failing school', the local authority got rid of our old head teacher and put in Winnie Knowe with a brief to act as a 'superhead' and 'turn the school around'. So, from Winnie's arrival and the appointment of Con and myself as deputies, we were being constantly watched and monitored. We knew that everything we did was in order to get a clean bill of health when the Ofsted inspectors came back in. Every little success had therefore to be recorded, every little failure had to be explained and we had to write policy documents for every single aspect of school life – from a careers advice policy to a buildings maintenance policy. The workload was enormous, with all these tasks being piled on top of what was thrown at us by daily events in the school. Con and I seemed to cope well with this, not least because, as mates, we were able to work together. We had each other's shoulders to cry on, if we needed it. So far, so good. But, after a while Con started to get bad tempered with me and he increasingly failed to meet the deadlines we agreed to set each other. I first realised that things were really going wrong one day after he'd had a meeting with Winnie. He came into the staff room absolutely fuming. Winnie Knowe had failed to support a decision that Con had made about disciplining a girl who had been found with a pocket full of illegal pills. Not only had she not backed him, but Winnie had apologised to the girl's parents for the school not being 'sympathetic enough' to a girl 'going through a difficult time'. I couldn't blame Con for getting angry. What sort of time did Winnie think we were all having? I had got angry with the Head on a couple of occasions, for exactly the same reasons. She was clearly unwilling to back Con and me in any risks we took. When we were successful she used to take the credit, and when something went wrong, she blamed us.

Having a boss who does not back you when you are doing an already difficult job is a real strain, believe me. And not only was this made worse by her not giving us any kind of reward or thanks for good work done, she was always sneaking around asking the other staff about us. So, all of the time you felt you were being watched and that you would get slapped if you fell short. The stress of all this was made worse by the press, who seemed to be very keen to see us fail again. Anything negative they could get hold of, they would make a fuss about. You began to feel the whole world was against you. The kids in our school always were difficult. Con and I both knew that before we went there. But somehow the parents were now getting even more of a problem than they had been before. They had never been wonderfully supportive but, now, they seemed to take the attitude that we should sort out their kids all on our own. Disciplining these obstreperous teenagers was our job, they seemed to think. When we asked for their help they tended to look at us and say, 'Just because you are useless – a teacher in a failing school – don't expect us to do your job', and all that.

At times I thought the job was too much. At one point I came out in this rash. The doctor just laughed this off and told me that she knew it was just a stress symptom that I should 'shake off' – because she got exactly the same problem when she found her workload beginning to get too much for her. After that visit to the doctor, I decided that there wasn't much else I could do but will the rash to go away. That didn't work exactly, but once I got into the habit of a glass of good malt whisky every night, it slowly disappeared. Poor old Con, on the other hand, was down at the doctor's all the time. He developed an ulcer, which tended to make him even more evil tempered than he had already become. And he started to talk about a blood pressure problem too. With all of this he became more and more unpredictable, failing to turn up to meetings and one day he actually hit a pupil who, he said, had come out of a French lesson and called him 'Con the con'. It was his final downfall. So they got him out: a 'victim of the government, the Head Teacher and of stress' he said at the embarrassing leaving party we held for him.

Why, I ask myself, did I cope and my pal didn't? We were both able and confident teachers. We both had exactly the same stress problems at work. In a sense, I probably just made up my mind I was going to cope and realised that both of us couldn't go under. I sort of took responsibility for him as he started to break down. I needed to do that because I knew he was getting no support from his wife. She's a successful fashion designer who could not see how he couldn't deal with what she saw as the simple problems that face teachers. My wife, on the other hand, was once a teacher and she used to 'talk me down' some nights when I got home. And the kids used to take my mind off things. Con doesn't have kids, just a temperamental dog which is more unpredictable than our worst pupils. I thought at the time that Con had support from his parents, who are both ex-teachers, whereas my parents show no interest in my work. But I rather think, in retrospect, that his parents were just another source of pressure, always telling him what he might do in his job, without realising just how different a school like ours was from the old grammar schools they had taught in.

I also think that Con was starting to be troubled by his association with a notorious and rough school. 'Doesn't it damage your self esteem, having people know you work in such an awful place?', Con asked me one day. 'Self esteem, what's that?', I thought. On reflection I have come to the conclusion that I had no problems in this area. I had convinced myself that the world was a rough old place and that perhaps I was a bit of a hero taking on the challenge of working at the rougher end of the educational service. Con, on the other hand, convinced himself that things shouldn't be the way they are and that the world was somehow against him personally. 'The whole effing world, and this ulcer, is against me' he sobbed one day into his empty coffee mug, the one with the slogan 'A good teacher can make a world of difference' painted on it.

These two individuals involved in managing a large problem school were faced with considerable sources of stress. Not only did they have an enormous amount of work to do, at both the operational and the policy levels, but they also received very little support in the job. Even worse, they tended to get criticised from every quarter – by the head teacher, by journalists and by parents of pupils. Stress, as an emotional and physical reaction to these circumstances was something that Tim and Con both experienced. But Tim was better placed in terms of personal resources to manage the symptoms. Just at the physical level, it would seem that Tim was fortunate in that his body did not react as negatively as Con's did. But, we must be careful not to de-couple the physical and the emotional or mental aspects of human functioning in a Cartesian manner. We cannot assume that there was an initial physical difference between the two men. The mental state of each could itself have been a factor in the physical state that each found himself in, just as the physical state of each of them could have been a factor in their respective emergent mental and emotional states. However, it would seem that Tim was better placed than Con in terms of social and family resources, and the support and opportunity to relax that he could find at home.

On top of all of this, we can see Tim actively adopting a certain orientation towards his work which helped him manage his situation. He opted to define himself by applying a particular culturally available discursive resource to himself: the notion of a 'hero' who takes on a challenge. He also takes his relationship with Con into account in trying to explain his emergent orientation to events – suggesting that taking some responsibility for his friend was a factor in his adopting a positive stance towards the difficulties of their shared circumstances. Notice also that he adopts a positive characterisation of the school, as 'rough' as it was, as part of an educational *service*. And where Tim takes a stoic philosophical view of the world, seeing it as a generally 'rough place' that one has got to make the best of, Con adopts a different view of the world as one which 'ought' to be better than it is. Whereas Tim is willing to try to take control over circumstances, Con seems to be adopting an orientation in which he resigns himself to losing control, because the world is against him.

In looking at this case study in occupational stress and how individuals manage it, we must remember that we cannot read it as if we were actually seeing into the minds of these two individuals. Tim is creating an account of what happened, rather than neutrally 'reporting' it. He is constructing a plausible tale which helps make sense of things both for himself and for the researcher that he is speaking to. The only account we have of Con's experience is that which his old friend gives us, on the basis of what he remembers seeing and hearing. We might also note that Tim Dyke is taking part in the ongoing social construction process, whereby work researchers, and others, analyse the sort of events that happened here in terms of 'stress' factors and personal resources for 'managing stress'. Nevertheless, in pragmatist terms, there is value in using an analysis of this kind. It is invaluable in helping us to understand and, potentially, to manage stressful situations.

We are making use here of a process-relational style of analysis in which exchanges and reciprocities – positive ones and negative ones – are seen to play a part in the way two individuals manage their identities, their work and their lives. We have a framework that we can apply to situations of stress and stress management generally. It suggests that we should not regard stress as something that necessarily results from having either heavy responsibilities in our jobs or being faced with a heavy workload. The emotional and physical difficulties which we label 'stress' arise when the individual does not have the personal and social 'resources' to enable them to define the pressures of this responsibility or workload as *manageable*. Occupational stress, or *distress*, is avoided when the occupational or organisational circumstances are ones over which the individual feels they can assert control, rather than ones which will swamp them or lead to their 'breaking down'.

One of the ways in which stress at work can be handled is by having a home or family life that enables one to balance the stresses of work with the pleasures and recreation of home life. However, the growing problem of a 'long hours culture' in work organisations has made this increasingly unlikely for many professional and managerial employees – even if it were true in the first place that home life is the haven of peace and relaxation that we often would like it to be. In spite of employers claiming to be concerned with helping employees to find a 'work–life balance', organisational restructuring and the associated insecurities have increased the pressures on managers to spend long hours at work (Worrall and Cooper, 1999). For many people the stresses of family life and the stresses of work have come to be mutually reinforcing, leading to a situation when, as Hochschild (1997a and 1997b) has put it, 'work becomes home and home becomes work'.

One of the ways that people handle, or avoid, stress at work is to indulge in practices that we can characterise as acts of workplace mischief.

Workplace mischief and the organisational underlife

There are both 'official' and 'unofficial' aspects to the negotiated order of every organisation. It was shown in Chapter 2 (pp. 61–3) that, in different circumstances, unofficial or 'informal' practices can contribute either positively or negatively to the long-term survival of the organisation – towards officially approved ends, we might say. This applies to what we can call 'organisational mischief'.

Organisational mischief *Concept*

Activities occurring within the workplace that (a) according to the official structure, culture, rules and procedures of the organisation 'should not happen' and (b) contain an element of challenge to dominant modes of operating or to dominant interests in the organisation.

Although we are now focusing our attention on something explicitly called *mischief*, the same ambiguity arises with regard to its likely corporate effects. *Organisational mischief* is a category of unofficial workplace activity that involves some kind of challenge by organisational members to the dominant order of the enterprise (see Further Reading on deviance and misbehaviour in organisations, pp. 161–2). It clearly has the potential to undermine a dominant order or to thwart dominant interests. However, there are *unintended consequences* of mischievous actions just as there are unintended consequences of formal and official corporate initiatives (Chapter 2, pp. 63–73). This is illustrated by the story of the man who set fire to the premises where he worked as an extreme expression of the contempt he and his workmates felt for the company that employed them. After initial resentment at this act of sabotage, the senior management came to see it as an immense piece of good fortune. The building completely burned down, but it was old, inefficient and awkwardly located. New premises that were much better suited to strategic managerial priorities were built with the insurance money that the company received and a new, much more compliant, workforce was recruited to work on the new site. The challenge had misfired. An act of gross organisational mischief had the unintended consequence of reinforcing the order and the interests that it had been intended to undermine.

Much of the mischief that routinely occurs in the unofficial or informal *underlife* of an organisation challenges the dominant order much less directly, and often less deliberately, than was the case with the aggrieved arsonist. An employee might, for example, falsely claim that they were taking a day off work because they were ill when, in fact, they simply wanted to avoid the pressures of a typical Monday morning in their office. Such behaviour, especially if it becomes widespread or persistent, will have the effect of challenging organisational interests. The worker has prioritised their own interests over those of the employing organisation – in spite of the commitment they have made to the employer through their employment contract.

The *implicit contract* that employees make with employing organisations is the most useful starting point for any attempt to understand what is going on when people go absent from work, engage in sabotage, steal from the workplace, or 'misbehave' at work in any of the variety of other ways we will shortly be considering. A key element of the implicit contract between the employee and the employer is the employee 'input' of *compliance*, the acceptance of a degree of managerial control over the worker. This means that whenever someone joins an organisation as an employee they *surrender a degree of personal autonomy* but, as we have frequently observed, human beings do not readily give up control of their circumstances or their 'selves'. This is especially the case in modern democratic societies, where the concepts of human rights and the autonomy of the 'free citizen' are culturally significant and people are only willing to submit to the control of others to a very limited and closely circumscribed extent. When one takes a job, for a certain level of pay, job security, opportunity for fulfilment, and all the rest, one accepts that certain people, to a certain extent, may tell one what to do. Such an acceptance is typically loaded with reservation, reluctance and caution. Resistance to any attempted control that falls short of total legitimacy in the employee's eyes is to be expected in every workplace circumstance. And where that resistance cannot take the direct form of a straightforward refusal to comply – which often it cannot – we can expect the employee to seek one means or another to maintain their pride or otherwise protect their identity.

To defend their sense of 'self' and, in effect, to restore some balance to a threatened implicit contract, people engage in activities ranging from burning down their workplace to stealing a pencil from their desk; from circulating rude cartoons round an office to playing practical jokes on people. To point to this 'defence of self' aspect of such activity is not, however, to deny that people at work often joke with each other simply for the sake of enjoying a joke or take a pencil home simply because there is no one looking and the pencil from the telephone pad at home has worn out. However, this should not stop us recognising that there is often a further and a deeper significance to many of these acts – a significance that we must always take into account when trying to understand behaviour in organisations.

Many of the studies of workplace resistance to organisational control have focused on manual workers in industrial situations, and deep insights into the importance of acts of defiance and anti-authority cultural gestures have been gained by close studies of the experience of working class employment. It is unfortunate, however, when managerial workers are excluded from analyses of organisational mischief, as is done in the review of what they call 'organisational misbehaviour' by Ackroyd and Thompson (1999). Managers are themselves employees of organisations and the majority of them are subject to controls over their behaviour by more senior managers – controls that may be experienced by a manager as a 'threat to self' no less significant than the threat felt by a non-manager. Indeed the controls to which managers are subject can be far more sophisticated or even insidious than those experienced by more junior employees. Managers frequently invest more of their 'selves' in their work than do ordinary employees. Consequently, 'defence of self' gestures and acts of 'resistance' through mischief are to be seen from the top to the bottom of the organisational hierarchy. This is apparent in the case we will look at in Chapter 6 (Case 6.2, p. 219) where the later arrival and early departure of the senior manager Todd is not essentially different from that of an ordinary worker cutting short their working day. And the suspected discouraging of the visit by the police officer and the security consultant by the security manager is not essentially different from, say, a gym assistant in that organisation persuading a maintenance engineer not to repair an exercise machine that she does not like.

Mischief at any level of the organisation is likely to involve a mixture of the more 'psychological' *defence of self* and the more material pursuit of *self-interest*. A day 'illegally' taken off work may, for example, benefit a worker by giving them the satisfaction of upsetting a supervisor who has been overloading them with work. The worker's pride and sense of autonomy is thus defended and if they use that day to paint a room in their house, they also save the money they might otherwise have had to pay someone else. Their material self-interest has thus been served at the same time as they were protecting their sense of self-integrity and personal autonomy.

Some forms of mischief are relatively individualistic and involve just one person defending their sense of self, engaging in an act of personal resistance or otherwise furthering their personal interests. We might include here:

- *Spontaneous individual acts of absenteeism.* The shop worker staying away from work on the day that it is rumoured the company's 'mystery shopper' will be visiting the store to check up on the quality of service.
- *Inattentiveness through day-dreaming or chatting to work colleagues.* The counter staff in a council office failing to notice someone entering to pay their rent because they are too busy discussing rumours about their manager's private life; the police officer allocated to a particularly boring beat failing to notice a street crime because he is replaying in his mind the football match he watched the night before.
- *Minimal compliance with instructions.* The activities of the 'jobsworths' or 'bureaucratic personalities' we came across in Chapter 2 (p. 72); the warehouse labourer who was told to 'get those boxes moved out of the gangway before you go home' moving a pile of cardboard boxes containing fragile goods out into the yard so that heavy overnight rain destroys their contents.
- *Keeping information to oneself.* The maintaining of a strong sense of indispensability and 'being in control' by a bank's branch manager who gives staff only minimal information about the headquarters' guidelines to which the branch is meant to be working.
- *Bullying.* The regular tormenting of the weakest member of a work team by a supervisor who feels aggrieved at having to take orders from a manager who is 'half my age and barely out of college'.
- *Sexual harassment.* The repeated commenting on the sexual characteristics of women colleagues by a male employee who also pinned photographs of naked women to the wall above his desk and who only modified his behaviour when the women took to decorating another wall of the office with pictures of naked men.
- *Opportunistic pilfering or embezzlement.* The taking of a couple of new books from a library by a library assistant who feels that he is too poorly paid to

afford to buy books and who finds himself left alone to lock up a local library one evening; the regular siphoning-off of amounts of money by an accountant who finds that a particular very rich client rarely checks the figures with which they are provided.

- *The sabotaging or breaking of goods or equipment in a moment of individual frustration.* The throwing of a crate of bottled beer down the cellar stairs by a bar manager whose staff had failed to turn up for work, leaving him to cope with a rush of customers.
- *Using work premises or equipment for private purposes, both within and sometimes out of working hours.* The use of a production machine to make a toy for one's children; the photocopying at work of invitations to an employee's birthday party; the sending of flirtatious or aggressive personal e-mails to other employees.
- *The punishing of an awkward customer who has offended the worker.* The waiter who spits in the third plate of soup to be taken to a customer who has sent back a first plate of soup because it was too cold and a second plate of soup because it was too hot.
- *Leaving the organisation at an especially inconvenient time.* The university professor falling out with the faculty dean and resigning from their post so that their departure coincides with the beginning of the vital and difficult report-writing stage of a major research project which they have led and which only they fully understand.

All of these relatively individualistic pieces of mischief still have a social dimension. They all relate to problems in the employment 'trade' with the employing organisation. And it is likely that individual acts such as going absent from work will develop into a more general pattern of absenteeism, as more and more people see staying away from work as a defence against work overload. This possibility needs to be recognised when we identify some of the more social and group-oriented types of organisational mischief:

- *Acts of absenteeism or inconvenient resignation that accord with unofficial norms which have developed in an organisation or a sub-unit of an organisation.* The standard practice of people claiming to be ill when allocated to the shift in a restaurant when the most difficult customers tend to turn up.
- *The setting of group work-output norms that suit group members but are managerially defined as 'restrictions of output'.* The refusal of a group of machine operators in a garment factory to allow any of the group members to produce more than 15 garments per hour or fewer than 13 garments (because that is deemed a 'reasonable and fair' work rate by most of the group) in spite of the fact that the management want a higher output and indeed operate a bonus system that would give higher pay for higher output.
- *Organised fiddles.* The standard practice among staff in a public house of overcharging customers who are thought unlikely to check their change; shop staff giving extra change to customers to whom they are related.

- *'Dehumanising' or 'putting down' customers or clients – typically behind their backs but sometimes 'to their faces'.* The practice of referring to all customers as 'punters', 'marks' or 'Johns' rather than customers; the norm among motor mechanics in a garage of telling customers that the fault with their car is something different from what the customers say they believe it to be; the labelling by workers in a fish and chip shop of all customers into categories like FOBs (fat overeating slob), TLTCs (too lazy to cook) and SUBs (soaking up the beer).

- *Using work premises for group-sanctioned non-work purposes.* The use of a medical room by nightshift workers taking turns to snatch an illegal hour's sleep during the shift; the playing of competitive computer games involving several workers during office hours.

- *Workplace games.* The weekly competition between senior managers in a company to collect as many as possible management 'buzzwords' used by the managing director, both orally or in documents; the throwing of an item such as a chicken leg from worker to worker in a food factory whenever supervisors or managers are not looking.

- *Practical jokes, organised 'piss-takes' or 'wind-ups'.* The pinning of a large sheet of paper bearing the legend 'pompous bastard' to the back of a manager's jacket, unknown to him, before he shows a group of visitors around a new building; the nursing tutors in a hospital always ensuring that they send at least one member of each new intake of nurses to the medical stores to collect an item such as a 'bronchial tube' or a bottle of 'mild infarction'.

- *Organised bullying and harassment.* The persistent persecuting of black men and women workers in a textile factory, involving name-calling and the damaging of work in progress, by a group of white male maintenance workers whose supervisor not only encourages such behaviour but discriminates against men in his team who do not join in these practices by giving them fewer overtime opportunities and by allocating them to more than their fair share of unpleasant jobs.

- *The organised sabotaging of goods or equipment.* The regular damaging of an assembly line to give all the workers on it a break from machine-pacing; the deliberate overloading of an organisation's e-mail system by people widely and unnecessarily circulating copies of lengthy documents and large attachments.

- *The mobilising of groups to take sanctions against management as a means of resolving a grievance.* The decision of a group of design engineers, after taking a vote, to work on only one design at a time – this sanction to continue until the company brings the department up to its official full staff strength; the agreement by a group of van drivers that their union representative should tell management that no overtime will be worked until the pay is brought up to the level of a rival delivery service company; the refusal, after a brief lunchtime meeting, of all the departmental managers in a large retail store to attend meetings called by the general manager after the 6 p.m. closing time.

In each of these more group-oriented types of organisational mischief, we again see people protecting or advancing the material aspects of their implicit contract with the employer. The van drivers want more pay, for example, and are disrupting the overtime arrangements to achieve this. The cheating of drinkers in the public house is a means of maintaining a higher level of income than the employer provides in the pay packet. A certain level of pay – part legal, part illegal – has become part of the implicit contract associated with their employment, in effect. The machine operators who fix an output norm are also working to shape their implicit contract (as were the workers in the famous Bank Wiring Observation Room study at the Hawthorne plant reported by Roethlisberger and Dickson, 1939). There is, then, a degree of informal bargaining between employers and employees occurring in all of this misbehaviour. Does this mean we should reject the 'mischief' label, then? It does not. All of these behaviours are, to some degree, taken against the dominant order of the organisation. They constitute a refusal simply to accept the roles and rewards laid down for them by the employer. Just as with the more individualistic types of behaviour, these group-oriented actions have a 'defence of self' or protection of autonomy dimension for the members of the groups. This works in conjunction with the pursuit of shared material interests. Each member of the workgroup that has agreed its own definition of a 'fair day's work' can work with a sense that group membership protects them from managerial pressures. The food workers throwing food around the factory are ritually undermining the supervisors' control over their activities. The managers who mock their boss's pretentious language and the managers who refuse to attend their general managers' out-of-hours meetings, are expressing a degree of independence or distance from their senior managers. The strategies of independence that we see in all of these groups are not acts of rebellion or a fight for full autonomy. As part of their implicit contract with their employer, they submit to a certain amount of managerial control but what their collective misbehaviours are in effect saying to those in authority is 'This is who we are. So far and no further.'

Organisational employees who deal directly with customers or clients have an additional need to protect their personal identities and their sense of autonomy. It is not just the manager or supervisor who exerts pressures here on the worker to behave in a certain way. It is also the customer. In many aspects of service and retail work the worker is required to act like a servant. The emotional pressures that this can put on both the worker and the manager alike were looked at earlier and the problems of engaging in *emotional labour* were illustrated both by the hotel manager Ken Steary in Case 4.3 and the sex worker Cindy Sutor in Case 4.4. Some important psychic relief from the pressure to act subserviently is thus achieved by the rude labelling of clients in the chip shop and by the motor mechanics always claiming to know better than the motorists what is wrong with their vehicles. The notion of 'getting one's own back' on people who are put into the master or mistress role, vis-à-vis the service worker's role as servant, can take some very unpleasant forms. The ploy of the waiter who, behind the scenes, spits in the diner's food is a classic example of this, but repulsive as such behaviour may seem, it is far from uncommon in the food and drinks industry, at both the customer service end of the business and at the food processing stage. It is rare to find anybody who has worked in a food processing plant who cannot relate tales of people throwing rat droppings into food mixing machines, urinating into beer vats or tipping floor sweepings into hoppers of cereal. Outside the food industry, one hears similar reports of people chalking obscenities on the insides of the items of furniture they are making or leaving hidden parts of metal products insufficiently protected against rust. One hears of unspeakable things being done to dead bodies in hospitals or undertakers' workshops. All of these are human gestures of defiance and demonstrations of personal or group autonomy, however alienated or degraded a form of human expression we may deem them to be.

In the conversation about some of the examples of workplace mischief that they have come across as managers, Hazel Hopeman and Jenny Elgin recognise that there is 'something deeper' going on in what Jenny calls the 'underlife' of organisations.

Activity 4.7

Read the conversation in Case 4.6 between Hazel Hopeman, a manager in an airline, and Jenny Elgin, the manager of a supermarket, and:

- note down examples arising in this conversation of the various types of organisational mischief that we identified above (recognising that certain activities may straddle more than one category);
- think about any examples of organisational mischief that you have come across or heard about that you might have thrown into the conversation if you had joined Jenny and Hazel in their discussion;
- consider the extent to which Hazel and Jenny's attempts to make sense of (or 'theorise' about) these activities fit with the attempts to understand organisational mischief that have been made in this chapter so far.

Hazel and Jenny probe the organisational underworld — Case 4.6

What really started me thinking about these things was a strange experience I had one day when I was a victim of a practical joke organised by a couple of my departmental managers. I was walking around the shop doing my usual thing of smiling at everyone and having a friendly word with a customer here and a colleague there. One of the customers made a very strange comment. 'You don't look very sore to me', he said. I was puzzled, but carried on. Then one of the checkout operators said, 'You don't look sore to me Jenny.' Again, I said nothing. But when a customer who I'd helped with a query about Sunday opening hours asked me, with a rather enigmatic smile on her face, 'So what are you sore about, Miss Elgin?' I let my puzzlement show. 'Look at your badge, dear', the customer said. And when I looked at my 'Jenny Elgin, Store Manager' badge, I saw that it had been skilfully doctored to say 'Jenny Elgin, Sore Manager'.

I expect that did make you a 'sore manager'.

I was not pleased, I can tell you, Hazel. But I had been rather short tempered with my management team for more than a week. They knew I was having problems with my car and that I was getting tired of having to drive so far to work at this branch. 'Don't take it out on us', the grocery manager had said to me only the day before. He was very understanding. I don't think the others were. They were getting their message over to me another way.

And they were obviously having a good laugh too.

I am sure they were. But what occurred to me was that you always have to look for deeper meanings in these things. There are all sorts of things bubbling away, seething sometimes, beneath the surface – in the underlife of a business, if you like. I'm sure part of the context of 'the laugh' that my managers were having was the fact that I am the only woman manager in the store and that I am the only graduate manager they have ever had close contact with. They know I will be moving on in my career. But I doubt if any of them will. So they 'brought me down a bit'. I said nothing about what happened. But I've never forgotten about it.

I agree that you have to probe beneath the surface, as a manager, when you come across anything like this. One partly hilarious and partly very serious problem I had to deal with was the case of a cabin crew whose male and female members swapped clothes towards the end of a flight. When the passengers were disembarking, there were the cabin crew as usual, thanking passengers for flying with us and very politely wishing them well. But the women were in the men's trousers, and far more peculiarly, the two chaps were in dresses. As you can imagine, we got some complaints.

What was going on, Hazel?

In a way it didn't surprise me. As a management we are well aware of this issue of 'emotional labour' that researchers write about. The man who was behind the jape told me, 'Sometimes you've just got to burst out and be yourself.' 'Cross-dressing is being yourself?' I came back – incredulous. 'Well it is for me,' he said, winking at me in a very camp manner. I believed him. 'But what about the others?' I asked. 'Oh, they'd never done it before. But, you ask them, they all say that the laugh did them good.'

So who were they having a go at – the airline, the managers, the passengers?

Oh, I think all of these. And none of them at the same time. I don't think it is as direct or as specific as it was with the case of your managers 'having a go' about your irritability. I think it's all got to do with this 'underlife' that you talk about. All sorts of things are going on behind the scenes in every type of organisation, aren't they?

Yes, but I can't imagine that a lot can go on behind the scenes in an airliner. The cabin crew are on display most of the time, aren't they?

Absolutely right – and that's why I was very lenient with them.

And there must be little scope for them to engage in the sort of fiddles that we have to deal with in retailing.

Well, there is just one. The biggest fiddle in the past – one that used to give them a lot of satisfaction as well as being materially rewarding – was the fiddling of time.

Claiming more hours that they actually put in?

Exactly. But that's now gone with computerisation. The only scope they have to line their pockets and 'have one over the airline' at the same time is with regard to complementary alcohol. We can't know how many free drinks passengers have or have not accepted. So a good proportion of those drinks go home with the cabin crew. We are well aware of this. But, as I say, it's the only thing we are aware of. I'm sure it's much more complicated in your business?

It certainly is. We get everything from people hiding stock that they know is going to go down in price the next week to check-out staff keeping vouchers they should give to customers. I've caught staff eating food they have taken off the shelves and which will obviously never go past the till. You get people swapping the tickets on items so that they are scanned at a lower price than they should have been and colleagues giving discounts to friends who are not entitled to them. And a scam was recently discovered in which store managers in one region were getting builders retained by the business to build conservatories on their houses, and charge these to the company.

And do you get people deliberately causing damage?

How do you mean?

I was thinking about what goes on with the men who load and unload planes. They are largely young blokes who are young and very strong. You get the impression that they are very conscious of their masculinity. And I think that their very low status in the airport's pecking order is experienced as some kind of threat to this.

So what do they do?

Well, first, they are always fighting with each other. They have time on their hands when there's no plane to work on and, of course, they have quite a mixture of nationalities and ethnic backgrounds. It can be quite explosive. And when they are not knocking each other to pieces, they are prone to smashing up luggage or bits of freight.

Yes, I've only had a couple of fights to sort out in my career so far. But damage to goods is not uncommon. I had a disgruntled bloke regularly leaving stock out of refrigeration last year and we had a spate recently of staff damaging goods in order to get them reduced in price. There was also the time we caught one of the shelf stackers opening jars of peanut butter and scratching little smiley faces into the surface of the product. What amazed me was that we only received a handful of complaints from customers. Yet he must have contaminated scores of jars, from what we understand. It could have been very damaging for the business. But it didn't even get in the press.

You confined it to the store's 'underlife'?

Thank goodness, yes. The young man who did it apparently felt he was 'having a laugh' at the expense of shoppers who, he said, never bother to speak to him or even smile at him when he is filling shelves.

Oh this is something we are very aware of with our cabin crew. In their training we have to prepare them for ungrateful or rude passengers. They know the score and are generally very good.

Generally?

Well I suppose so. A story is told about one of our crews who got really sick of a man who was regularly rude to them. He was also very demanding. So, one day, they laced his coffee with a strong laxative. That really sorted the bloke out.

Do you think that really happened? I mean it sounds unlikely to me – given that the crew who did it would probably end up cleaning up any mess that got made.

True. But if the story is apocryphal, it is rather interesting, isn't it, that people still take pleasure in passing it on. It always gets a good laugh. It sort of helps keep the customer in their place, psychologically speaking.

Yes, that reminds me of a rather different story – a true one that happened here. But it also has that element of the employee putting a distance between themselves and customers. There was this very attractive young woman who used to shop in here. The male colleagues were always looking out for her coming into the store. Well it turned out that she did some modelling for one of those erotic magazines. When the blokes discovered this, they made sure they obtained plenty of copies of the pictures and passed them round all the staff – men and women alike. It meant that a lot of silly and unpleasant giggling went on whenever she came into the shop. It also led to a game among the lads of 'talent spotting', as they named it. I discovered that they were competing to identify likely models that they might contact a particular magazine about. Fortunately, the first woman who was approached, as far as I know, came straight to me. She was very good about it. But two of those young men no longer work for us!

If only we could get these young men – I'm thinking of our baggage handlers again – to leave their sexuality, and their problems with their masculinity, at home.

And women?

Yes, we ought to be fair here. But I think that the women cabin crew who work for us are all very discreet and sophisticated about how they relate to male passengers. There's no way they could – or, to be honest, we would want them to – leave their sexuality at home. But all sorts of trouble follows if sex does rear its beautiful head at work.

How do you mean?

I was thinking of the time that the airport security caught a couple of our employees having sexual intercourse on the altar of the airport chapel. It was after a party and the place was locked. But they had got a key and thought that no one would disturb them in that part of the building. They were both single and I don't think it even occurred to them that the tabletop they were using was meant to be an altar. But none of this stopped my boss from ordering me to sack both of them. I really had to fight him on this and, in the end, I refused to do it. What amazed me was how hot under the collar he got about the whole business. I mean it really upset him. I argued that there were no serious business or managerial implications whatsoever and that, at the most, it was a minor disciplinary matter. But he had a real problem with it.

I think it's the fear some managers feel about having the lid lifted on this 'underlife', as I call it. Some managers just don't want to acknowledge that people are a lot more than little robots. I think it's the idea that employees are flesh and blood that bothers them. I had a similar difficulty when I discovered that one of the office workers occasionally played this game of leaning out of her office window during her lunch break – the window is immediately above the shop entrance – and passing the time of day with customers. What they didn't know was that, while she was doing this, she was getting served from behind by her boyfriend.

What did you do about that?

Nothing. It was me who caught them. And I decided that their embarrassment at being caught 'at it' was punishment enough. I am utterly confident that they won't do it again. No damage was done. Nobody else knew about it. But when I related this story at a corporate training event, ages after the event, I found that several of the managers there were absolutely appalled. Several people regarded as an utter outrage what I thought was quite an amusing, and even touching, piece of mischief. 'It simply shouldn't have happened' one of them kept muttering. 'The workplace is no place for that sort of thing', another spluttered before walking out of the room.

What was their problem?

What indeed? But I always remember that phrase, 'The workplace is no place for that sort of thing'. If only it were that simple!

This conversation represents a good example of managers taking a step back from their everyday practice and reflecting on the significance of some of the activities that they come across, and indeed have to deal with at work. All of the activities about which they are comparing notes fit more or less with the categories of organisational mischief set out earlier. A series of *practical jokes* or 'wind-ups' make up perhaps the most significant category here. Such a joke is played on Jenny herself and Hazel reports jokes played on airline passengers both as a group (with the cross-dressing farewell) and on one particular passenger who was 'punished' with an unwanted laxative drink. These latter two pieces of mischief to some extent also fit into our category of *putting down customers* – something that would also apply to the 'talent-spotting' *workplace game* Jenny talks about. The same might apply to the office worker communicating to customers from her office window and enjoying the irony of the fact that she was taking certain pleasures they knew nothing of. However, this case, and that of the late night use of the airport chapel for lovemaking was an example of *the use of premises or equipment for private purposes* rather than for organisational ones. *Sabotage* occurs in the loading and unloading of aircraft at the airport and in the interfering with the peanut butter in the shop. We hear of *fiddles* occurring in the airline with regard to alcoholic drinks and both money and goods in the case of the shop.

Jenny and Hazel are doing more in their conversation than simply swapping stories about their respective work organisations. They appear to have a shared interest in making sense of the various examples of organisational mischief that they present to each other. They recognise a straightforward role that these activities play *at a surface level* in organisational members' lives. People enjoy the 'laugh' that follows from the practical joking. Service workers feel better for 'having a go' at or 'keeping in their place' both managers and customers. And employees 'line their pockets', as Hazel puts it, by engaging in fiddles at work. However, both women feel that there is something more significant about these activities, something going on *at a deeper level*. Jenny suggests that there are 'deeper meanings' to these activities and that there are all sorts of things 'bubbling away' or even 'seething' below the surface. Hazel seems to agree with this and takes on Jenny's notion of an organisational 'underlife'. And there is some interesting theoretical reflection that fits with this concept in her interpretation of the behaviour of the cross-dressing cabin crew members. She uses a notion of people 'bursting out and being themselves' to make sense of what was occurring here, thus seeing their gesture as a particularly positive form of the 'defence of self' aspect of much organisational mischief. She also connects the fighting and the sabotage that occurs among the young men who load and unload the aircraft with problems that she thinks they have with both their ethnic identities and their masculinity. In thinking about such 'deeper level' factors she is still aware that the behaviour also has a more 'surface level' function of relieving boredom between flights.

Sexuality, humour and the struggle for control

Jenny and Hazel both imply that the area of human sexuality may be one in which clues might be found about the deeper issues that organisational mischief relates to. They both speak of managers who 'had a problem' with the idea of sexual behaviour occurring at work. They were frightened, Jenny suggests, by the prospect of 'having the lid lifted' on the 'underlife' of the organisation. Both sexuality and humour appear to play a major part in the organisational underlife of the organisations that these two managers work in. Can we go more deeply into these matters to explore the full depths of the organisational underlife and what its significance might be in the lives of organisational managers and employees? This is quite a challenging question, and Activity 4.8 is an invitation to take it up.

Activity 4.8

Reread the conversation between Hazel and Jenny and:

- Consider why it might be that some of the managers that both Hazel and Jenny have come across seem to be especially troubled about sexual behaviour occurring in the workplace. Why do they consider the workplace to be 'no place for that sort of thing' do you think?

- Look back to the discussion of narratives and stories and how they can be seen as elements of human culture that help people to handle existential problems (pp. 99–102) and reflect on whether the 'laughs' that Hazel and Jenny talk about have a significance which fits with this kind of analysis. Does this workplace humour have a function that goes beyond simply providing 'fun at work' or the pleasure of 'getting one's own back' on certain people?

Jenny Elgin offers one explanation of why managers might be troubled by sexuality in the workplace. To lift the lid from the organisational underlife and contemplate its sexual dimension is to come to terms with 'the idea that employees are flesh and blood' (see Further Reading on sexuality in organisations, p. 163). This means accepting, Jenny thinks, the fact that 'people are a lot more than little robots'. Sexuality, this suggests, stands for the basic humanity – and the fundamental 'animality' we might say – of the people that managers might prefer to treat as cogs in the organisational machine. To be reminded that employees are living creatures with bodies, desires and libidinal drives might make some managers uncomfortable. It reminds them of how limited their capacity to control human beings is. For a manager to be reminded that employees are living animals with emotions and desires is to be reminded that one is being required to control the uncontrollable – to 'herd cats' (Chapter 1, p. 3). It is perhaps also discomforting because it reminds the manager of their own desires and the sexuality that they too are required to leave behind when they come to work. But sexuality, desire, and indeed the enjoyment of laughter, are not things that can be left behind when the human being goes to work, whether as a manager or as an ordinary employee. And they are behaviours that defy organisational control.

Work organisations are set up to be places where rational and instrumental behaviour occurs and where attention is to be focused on the completion of formal tasks. If there is to be love, it is to be love of work or love of the company. If there is to be passion, it is to be passion for the product or a passion for customer satisfaction. If there is to be desire, it is to be desire for the success of the organisation and a desire for the formal rewards of pay and security that are offered for contributing to that corporate success. For love, passion and desire to be directed to other than corporate ends is to threaten the managerial controls that are intended to achieve those ends. Any display of passion or desire on the part of organisational members for the bodies of other organisational members or for organisational clients is an especially powerful symbolic challenge to that control. We should not be surprised, therefore, that Jenny Elgin speaks of managers arguing emphatically that the workplace is 'no place for that sort of thing'. Indeed, most of us would see the point of their wanting to discourage shop workers spending time identifying which customers might be potential erotic magazine models or wanting to discourage office workers from having sexual intercourse at the window of their offices. However, Jenny and Hazel seem to be implying that a reasonable and sensitive manager would recognise that, while the sexuality of organisational employees may need to kept discreetly under control within the workplace, it is not something that can be completely suppressed. Sexuality may be expressed directly in the workplace through individuals courting each other or engaging in overtly sexual activities. Equally, it may be expressed indirectly through women expressing their femininity and men expressing their masculinity at work through the way they dress or through their style of relating to others. Either way, it is an aspect of the human spirit that will always present a possible challenge to managerial control.

Joking and humour can be seen, like sexuality, as expressions of the 'human spirit'. But humour, again like sex, is associated with pleasure rather than with work. Work organisations are meant to be serious places and not comedy clubs or sites for the pursuit of bodily pleasures. But both sex and humour are serious matters as well, it can be argued. This is partly because they are expressions of human 'spirit' and often express that spirit in the face of managerial attempts to harness human efforts to corporate ends. The office workers having sexual intercourse at the office window were not just finding an opportunity to express their love and desire for each other. They were also making a gesture of independence towards both their employer and the customers of the shop. The cabin crew cross-dressers can be seen as doing something similar with regard to the airline and to the passengers whom they had served. In each of these cases humour and sexuality were both involved in the expression of human autonomy. There was a serious aspect as well as a fun aspect to each of these two pieces of mischief. But the 'seriousness of humour' goes deeper than this (see Further Reading on humour in organisations, p. 162).

It might seem strange to talk about humour as a serious matter, but it can be understood as playing a seriously important role in the human construction of identities and the handling of existential anxieties. Earlier it was argued that narratives, stories, films, news stories, gossip and jokes all play a role in human culture of reassuring people in the face of the life's anxieties. It was pointed out how often these elements of culture lead us to contemplate the horrors of life – horrors ranging from being murdered or having an accident to a sexual partner's infidelity or the loss of one's job. Our engagement with fiction and non-fiction alike, with 'serious' stories as well as with comedy, frequently involves confronting the breakdown of order in our lives as we engage with the story we are reading or watching on a screen – before being reassuringly returned to order and reality as we close the book or leave the cinema. Humour, comedy and joking operate in a similar way. By making work-related jokes or transmitting funny stories about aspects of the work organisation, for instance, we challenge or question the normal order of the work organisation and its control apparatus – an order that is, however, left more or less intact after we have enjoyed 'the laugh' and returned to 'normal service'.

Activity 4.9

Look at the five 'messages from the underworld' (one picture and four documents) that have been collected from different work organisations and consider what role you think they might be playing in the lives of the employees of the organisations in which they were circulating.

Messages from the organisational underworld   Case 4.7

FIGURE 4.3 Our company was recently in a boat race with two of our competitors. Guess which boat was ours!

If you are unhappy

Once upon a time, there was a non-conforming swallow who decided not to fly south for the winter. However, soon the weather turned so cold that he reluctantly started to fly south. In a short time, ice began to form on his wings and he fell to earth in a barnyard, almost frozen. A cow passed by and crapped on the little swallow. The little bird thought it was the end. But, the manure warmed him and defrosted his wings. Warm and happy, able to breathe, he started to sing. Just then a large cat came by and, hearing the chirping, investigated the sounds. The cat cleared away the manure, found the chirping bird and promptly ate him.

There are three morals to this story. First, everyone who shits on you is not necessarily your enemy, second, everyone who gets you out of the shit is not necessarily your friend and, third, if you're warm and happy in a pile of shit, keep your mouth shut.

Job vacancy: Staffing and administration services sub-assistant

The pay is the market rate less 10% (but with a boredom compensation bonus).

We are a leading financial services company which is creeping into a very long period of unparalleled slow change.

If you are sure, predictable, pedantic and inflexible in your outlook, you could be just what we are looking for. Ideally aged exactly 42.5 years of age, a conservative dresser with at least 22 years' experience as the Personnel lady in a building society (or very similar environment) you are a play-it-safe procedure-follower who relishes plodding through long hours.

You will be administering pay and rations to our Head Office staff along with ensuring all paperwork is completed fully on staff movements.

Career prospects are excellent. Keep your nose clean and an increment each year can be yours. In as little as 15 years you could rise to be a Staff and Administration Services Assistant Officer with additional responsibility for sick pay.

Benefits are excellent: pay every month, holidays every year and your own desk and chair.

Interested applicants should apply in writing for a long application form from Major Gen. Horatio Flash-Blindly DSO (ret'd), Staffing and Administration Assistant Sub-General Manager, Newco Financial Services, Staid House, Oldtown.

We think we are an equal opportunities employer and believe this job would especially suit a nice lady.

In the beginning was the Plan

In the beginning was the Plan.
And then came the assumptions.
And the assumptions were without form.
And the Plan was completely without substance.
And darkness was upon the faces of the workers.
And they spake unto their Supervisors, saying
"It is a crock of crap and it stinketh".
And the Supervisors went unto the Section Heads and sayeth
"It is a pail of dung and none may abide the odour thereof".
And the Section Heads went unto their Managers and sayeth unto them
"It is a container of excrement and none may abide its strength".
And the Managers went unto their Directors and sayeth
"It contains that which aids plant growth and is very strong".
And the Managing Director went unto the Chairman, saying unto him
"It promoteth growth and is very powerful"
And the Chairman considered the Plan and sayeth unto the Board
"This powerful new Plan will actively promote the growth and efficiency of the Company".
And the Board looked upon the Plan.
And saw that it was good.
And the plan became policy.

Memorandum to all staff
From: the Board of Management
Subject: Retirement policy

As a result of the reduction of money budgeting for departmental areas, we are forced to cut down on the number of our personnel. Under the plan, older employees will be asked to go on early retirement, thus permitting the retention of younger people who represent our future.

Those being required to retire early may appeal to upper management. To make this possible there will be a Survey of Capabilities of Retired Early Workers (SCREW). The appeal process will be known as SHAFT (Scream to Higher Authority Following Termination). Under the terms of the new policy employees may be early retired once, SCREWED twice and SHAFTED as many times as the company deems appropriate.

If the employee follows the above procedures, he or she will be entitled to HERPES (Half Earnings for Retired Personnel's Early Severance). As HERPES is considered a benefit plan, any employee who has received HERPES will no long be SCREWED or SHAFTED by the company.

Management wishes to reassure the younger employees who remain on board, that the company will continue to see that they are well trained through our Special High Intensity Training known as SHIT. The company takes pride in the amount of SHIT our employees receive. We have given our employees more SHIT than any other company in the area. If any employee feels he or she does not receive enough SHIT on the job, see your immediate supervisor. Your supervisor is specially trained to make sure that you receive all the SHIT you can stand.

Each of these documents was widely circulated in the large organisations where they were collected by the researcher. The picture was collected in a hospital, the story of a swallow in a manufacturing company, the mock job advertisement in a building society, the 'In the beginning' text in a pharmaceutical company and the staff memorandum about early retirement in a retailing business. However, it is apparent that these same documents, sometimes in identical form, sometimes with local variations, can be found in one organisation after another. They circulate across societies, it would seem, as well as within organisations.

The documents mock or satirise aspects of the organisation and the way it is managed. They induce mirth by challenging the normal order of these organisations. The picture engages with the notion that the hospital has too many people giving orders (directing the boat), in relation to the numbers of people who are doing the real work (rowing the boat). The story of the swallow satirises those activities we have characterised as 'micropolitical' and implies that the workplace is a dangerous place in which it is difficult to know who is your friend and who is your enemy. The job advertisement apparently mocks the excessively bureaucratic nature of the building society and the poor career opportunities that staff are offered. Its satirical swipe at the employer's claim to be an equal opportunity employer suggests ignorance on the employer's part of the principles of equal opportunities (with the choice of the anachronistic and patronising term 'a nice lady'). It also portrays the management as hypocritical. Senior organisational managers seem to be the main target of 'In the beginning' piece and they are portrayed as plainly stupid, out of touch with common sense and prone to go along with any business nonsense as long as it can be dressed up in the language of planning, efficiency and growth. The workers and the section leaders can see that 'the plan' stinks. The managers, directors and the chairman, however, convince themselves that it is something worthwhile. And, with the retirement policy memorandum, another specific aspect of managerial language and discourse is mocked – the use of acronyms to give weight and importance to relatively routine managerial initiatives. But the document is, more seriously, an attack on what it implies are harsh, unfeeling and exploitative human resourcing policies being pursued by the company.

All of these documents, clearly intended to give employees 'a laugh', deal with serious matters that constitute threats both to employees and to the long-term survival of the organisations themselves (and hence, of course, to the job security of all employees). All comedy, as has been recognised by numerous theorists of humour from Aristotle onwards, deals with incongruity. It focuses upon the unexpected. It plays with the inappropriate. It turns normality on its head. The normal order of each of these organisations is made to look abnormal by being stretched and bent in the distorting mirror of the satirical document. This is exactly what was being done by the airline cabin crew exchanging clothes or by Jenny Elgin's colleagues altering her name badge. These documents and practical jokes distort normality so that we can laugh at and enjoy a temporary suspension of that normality before returning to our normal serious workplace demeanour and getting back to our work.

Workplace humour helps people adjust to aspects of work that they dislike or feel threatened by and it is always possible that some of the satirical intentions of comic interventions may be fulfilled. Mockery of individuals and practices can lead to changes in behaviour and procedures. But workplace humour and joking behaviour can be seen as playing a deeper role in people's lives too. It is part of the way we maintain our sanity. We often joke about the things that worry us most. At work for example, it is noticeable that people whose autonomy is most threatened by overbearing customers or managers will tend to make jokes about such customers or managers more often than those who do not experience such pressures. People whose jobs are the least secure tend to joke about 'getting the chop', 'getting the bullet' or receiving the 'little brown envelope' containing a redundancy notice than those who are relatively secure in their jobs. People doing the most dangerous jobs tend to be those who joke most about possible accidents. Those whose work in emergency services, hospitals and mortuaries involves them in matters of life and death, are the most prone to indulge in black humour and 'laugh in the face' of the death and mutilation that their jobs force them to confront. The joking here can be understood as a glimpse into the abyss. A glimpse into the abyss of disorder and madness, we might say, helps us retain our sanity in the light of the dangers that are seething down there and threatening to swallow us up. Much of our engagement with humour and comedy is like the tightrope walker in Figure 4.4 with his quick occasional glimpses down into the abyss over which he is walking.

To get across to the far side of the ravine, the tightrope walker must keep his eyes most of the time on the solid ground that he wants to reach. However, if he too casually or too confidently strides out in this direction, forgetting what horrors are seething beneath his feet, he is likely to slip from his rope. Equally,

FIGURE 4.4 Humour helps us over the existential abyss

though, if he looks down too intently into the cauldron below him, he will lose his balance and fall into the pit of horrors. When we move through our everyday lives, intent on our various life, work and family projects, we are like the tightrope walker looking to the solid ground that we wish to reach. But to remind ourselves of the precariousness of our situations, and to come to terms with everything that actually or potentially troubles us about the world, we glimpse into the abyss from time to time. We therefore laugh at the figure slipping over on the banana skin, we laugh at the stupidity of people from a neighbouring society, we laugh at the managers whose pretentiousness or incompetence threatens the security of our employment. Having laughed at what might otherwise frighten us into a loss of control in our lives (madness even), we return to our serious demeanour and travel onwards. When we bring sexuality and humour into the workplace, and when we indulge in the lavatory talk and sexually 'dirty' language of the 'underworld' documents reviewed earlier, we are reminding ourselves and those around us that we are not cogs in the corporate machine. We are demonstrating that we are also both creative human beings (who create jokes, write satires and make each other laugh) and recalcitrant biological animals (who copulate, excrete and refuse to be herded). Sexuality and humour thus play a part in the way each one of us struggles to control our lives and identity. It also plays its part, when it is mischievously brought into the workplace, in the struggle for control that goes on between people with varying degrees of power in the organisational pecking order.

We have concentrated in this chapter on various aspects of the informal and unofficial aspects of organisational life and looked at various challenges that are constantly being made to managerial efforts to shape and control work organisations. In the next chapter we turn to those aspects of the struggle for managerial control that are concerned with obtaining and maintaining 'human resources'.

Summary

In this chapter the following key points have been made:

- At the heart of the relationship between the employee and the employing organisation is an *implicit contract* whereby it is understood that the employee will make a particular set of contributions, at a particular level, to the organisation's work in return for a particular mix of rewards. This bargain has to be understood in light of both the life situation and projects of the employee and the strategic direction being followed by the organisation – it is thus central to the *strategic exchange* relationship between the individual and the organisation.

- The implicit contract, as it is understood by the employee, forms part of that employee's *orientation to work*, the meaning they attach to their employment and which influences the ways they act within that employment.

- Individuals' entry to work or to an organisation can be understood in terms of their *initial orientation to work*. This, however, is likely to change as both the organisational and the individual's circumstances (inside and outside work) change. The process of change continues as the individual's personal life and projects move on and as their employment career develops.

- Feelings and emotions play a central part in all work and organisational situations. They cannot be seen as incidental and peripheral to the rational task-based activities with which people are involved.

- In various kinds of work, service work and managerial work especially, there is an emotional dimension built into what is required of the worker. This *emotional labour* can be handled in different ways; by the worker choosing to engage in either 'deep' or 'surface' acting, for example.

- *Stress* is an emotionally related phenomenon. It involves an experience of distress which leads to an individual being incapable of performing the tasks that are required of them. It is not something that is inherent in either the individual or the work. It can only be understood by looking at how the circumstances of the individual interrelate with the organisational circumstances and pressures.

- People vary in how they cope with potentially stressing circumstances and the psychological, emotional and social resources that they can draw upon influence how well they cope.

- A variety of activities go on in every organisation which are not officially 'meant to happen' in the organisation. Examples of *organisational mischief* like fiddling, practical joking, sabotage and workplace sexual activity tend to challenge dominant modes of operating in organisations as well as helping people both to further and to defend their interests. They also enable people to protect their personal notions of 'self'. Managers and non-managers alike engage in organisational mischief.

- Sexuality and humour have a particular significance in the 'underlife' of the work organisation as they represent aspects of humanity (including the 'animal' aspects of humanity) that are especially unsusceptible to corporate or managerial control.

- Humour has a very important role in work situations in enabling people both to challenge and adjust to organisational controls and dominant interests. It also helps people control their lives generally and cope with the existential threats to sanity and a sense of order.

Recommended reading

The variety of ways in which matters of emotion arise within organisations is demonstrated by Steve Fineman in *Understanding Emotion at Work* (London: Sage, 2003) whilst David Wainwright and Michael Calnan provide a challengingly critical view of the way work stress has become such an important issue in recent times in their *Work Stress: The making of a modern epidemic* (Buckingham: Open University Press, 2002). The variety of forms of mischief that occurs in organisations is reflected upon by Steve Ackroyd and Paul Thompson in *Organisational Misbehaviour* (London: Sage, 1999) in a way which usefully complements the analysis in the present chapter. Humour plays a key part in this, as we have seen, and David Collinson shows us how attempts are increasingly being made in managerial circles to make humour 'work' for the organisation in his article, 'Managing humour' (*Journal of Management Studies*, 39(3): 269–288, 2002). And for more material on the role of sex in work and organisations see Jo Brewis and Steve Linstead's *Sex, Work and Sex Work: Eroticizing organization?* (London: Routledge, 2000).

Further reading

Further reading Work orientations, implicit and psychological contracts

Baldamus, W. (1961) *Efficiency and Effort*, London: Tavistock
Behrend, H. (1957) 'The effort bargain', *International Labor Relations Review*, 10: 503–515
Goldthorpe, J.H., Lockwood, D., Bechhofer, F. and Platt, J. (1968) *The Affluent Worker: Attitudes and behaviour*, Cambridge: Cambridge University Press
Guest, D. (1998) 'Is the psychological contract worth taking seriously?', *Journal of Organizational Behaviour*, 9: 649–664
Herriot, P., Manning, W.E.G. and Kidd, J.M. (1997) 'The content of the psychological contract', *British Journal of Management*, 8(2): 151–162
Kotter, J.P. (1973) 'The psychological contract', *California Management Review*, 15: 91–99
Levinson, H., Price, C., Munden, K. and Solley, C. (1966) *Men, Management and Mental Health*, Cambridge, MA: Harvard University Press
Noon, M. and Blyton, P. (2002) *The Realities of Work*, Basingstoke: Palgrave.
Robinson, S. and Rousseau, D.M. (1994) 'The psychological contract – not the exception but the norm', *Journal of Organisational Behavior*, 15(3): 245–259
Rousseau, D.M. (1995) *Psychological Contracts in Organisations: Understanding written and unwritten agreements*, Thousand Oaks, CA: Sage
Watson, T.J. (2003) *Sociology, Work and Industry*, Chapter 7, London: Routledge

Further reading Emotions and work

Albrow, M. (1997) *Do Organisations have feelings?*, London: Routledge
Damasio, A.R. (2000) *The Feeling of What Happened*, London: Heinemann
Fineman, S. (ed.) (1993) *Emotion in Organizations*, London: Sage
Fineman, S. (2003) *Understanding Emotion at Work*, London: Sage

Harré, R. and Finlay Jones, R. (eds) (1986) *The Social Construction of Emotions*, Oxford: Blackwell

Hochschild, A.R. (1985) *The Managed Heart: The commercialization of human feeling*, Berkeley, CA: University of California Press

Hopfl, H. and Linstead, S. (1993) 'Passion and performance: suffering and the carrying of organizational roles' in S. Fineman (ed.) *Emotion in Organizations*, London: Sage

Muchinsky, P.M. (2000) 'Emotions in the workplace: the neglect of organizational behaviour', *Journal of Organizational Behavior*, 21: 801–805

Putnam, L. and Mumby, D.K. (1993) 'Organizations, emotion and the myth of rationality' in S. Fineman (ed.) *Emotion in Organizations*, London: Sage

Taylor, S. (1998) 'Emotional labour and the new workplace' in P. Thompson and C. Warhurst (eds) *Workplaces of the Future*, London: Macmillan

Taylor, S. and Tylor, M. (2000) 'Emotional labour and sexual difference in the airline industry', *Work, Employment and Society*, 14(1): 77–95

Van Maanen, J. and Kunda, G. (1989) ' "Real feelings": emotional expression and organizational culture', *Research in Organizational Behavior*, 11: 43–103

Wouters, C. (1989) 'The sociology of emotions and flight attendants: Hochschild's "managed heart" ', *Theory, Culture and Society*, 6(1): 95–123

Further reading Work and stress

Cooper, C.L. (2000) *Theories of Organizational Stress*, Oxford: Oxford University Press

Cooper, C.L. and Sutherland, V.J. (1992) 'The stress of the executive lifestyle: trends in the 1990s', *Management Decision*, 30(6): 64–68

Cooper, C.L., Cooper, R.D. and Eaker, L. (1988) *Living With Stress*, Harmondsworth: Penguin

Newton, T., Handy, J. and Fineman, S. (eds) (1995) *Managing Stress: Emotion and power at work*, London: Sage

Wainwright, D. and Calnan, M. (2002) *Work Stress: The making of a modern epidemic*, Buckingham: Open University Press

Further reading Deviance and misbehaviour in organisations

Ackroyd, S. and Thompson, P. (1999) *Organisational Misbehaviour*, London: Sage

Adams, A. (1992) *Bullying at Work*, London: Virago

Collinson, D.L. (1992) *Managing the Shopfloor: Subjectivity, masculinity and workplace culture*, Berlin: de Gruyter

Collinson, D.L. (1994) 'Strategies of resistance: power, knowledge and subjectivity in the workplace' in J. Jermier, W. Nord and D. Knights (eds) *Resistance and Power in the Workplace*, London: Routledge

Dalton, M. (1948) 'The industrial rate buster', *Applied Anthropology*, 7(1): 5–23

Ditton, J. (1977a) *Part-time Crime: An ethnography of fiddling and pilferage*, London: Macmillan

Ditton, J. (1977b) 'Perks, pilferage and the fiddle: the historical structure of invisible wages', *Theory and Society*, 4(1): 39–71

Dubois, P. (1977) *Sabotage in Industry*, Harmondsworth: Penguin

Fine, G.A. (1988) 'Letting off steam: redefining a restaurant's work environment' in M.D. Moore and R.C. Snyder (eds) *Inside Organizations: Understanding the human dimension*, Newbury Park, CA: Sage, 119–128

Henry, S. (1987) *The Hidden Economy: The context and control of borderline crime*, Oxford: Martin Robertson

Jermier, J. (1988) 'Sabotage at work: the rational view', *The Sociology of Organisations*, 6: 101–134

Jermier, J., Knights, D. and Nord, W. (1994) *Resistance and Power in Organisations*, London: Routledge

Lee, D. (2000) 'An analysis of workplace bullying in the UK', *Personnel Review*, 29(5): 593–612

Mars, G. (1982) *Cheats at Work: An anthropology of workplace crime*, London: Counterpoint

Noon, M. and Delbridge, R. (1993) 'News from behind my hand: gossip in organisations', *Organisation Studies*, 14(1): 23–36

Punch, M. (1996) *Dirty Business: Exploring corporate misconduct: Analysis and cases*, London: Sage

Roy, D. (1952) 'Quota restriction and goldbricking in a machine shop', *American Journal of Sociology*, 57(5): 427–442

Roy, D. (1958) 'Banana time: job satisfaction and informal interaction', *Human Organisation*, 18(1): 158–161

Stockdale, M.S. (1996) *Sexual Harassment in the Workplace: Perspectives, frontiers and response strategies*, London: Sage

Thomas, A.M. and Kitzinger, C. (1994) 'It's just something that happens: the invisibility of sexual harassment in the workplace', *Gender, Work and Organisation*, 1(3): 151–161

Further reading Humour in organisations

Barsoux, J.-L. (1993) *Funny Business: Humour, management and business culture*, New York: Cassell

Boland, R.J. and Hoffman, R. (1983) 'Humour in a machine shop: an interpretation of symbolic action' in L.R. Pondy, P. Frost, G. Morgan and T. Dandridge (eds) (1983) *Organizational Symbolism*, Greenwich, CT: JAI Press

Bradney, P. (1957) 'The joking relationship in industry', *Human Relations*, 10(2): 179–187

Collinson, D.L. (1988) 'Engineering humour: masculinity, joking and conflict in shop floor relations', *Organization Studies*, 9(2): 181–199

Collinson, D.L. (2002) 'Managing humour', *Journal of Management Studies*, 39(3): 269–288

Davies, C. (1982) 'Ethnic jokes, moral values and social boundaries', *British Journal of Sociology*, 33(3): 383–403

Fox, S. (1990) 'The ethnography of humour and the problem of social reality', *Sociology*, 24(3): 431–446

Jacobson, H. (1997) *Seriously Funny: From the ridiculous to the sublime*, London: Viking

Linstead, S. (1985) 'Jokers wild: the importance of humour in the maintenance of organisational culture', *Sociological Review*, 33(4): 741–767

Mulkay, M. (1988) *On Humour*, Cambridge: Polity Press
Radcliffe-Brown, A.R. (1940) 'On joking relationships', *Africa*, 13: 195–210

Further reading Sexuality in organisations

Brewis, J. and Linstead, S. (2000) *Sex, Work and Sex Work: Eroticizing organization?*, London: Routledge
Burrell, G. (1992) 'Sex and organisations' in A.J. Mills and P. Tancred (eds) *Gendering Organisational Analysis*, London: Sage
Di Tomaso, N. (1989) 'Sexuality in the workplace: discrimination and harassment' in J. Hearn, D.L. Sheppard, P. Tancred-Sherrif and G. Burrell (eds) *The Sexuality of Organization*, London: Sage
Filby, M. (1992) 'The figures, the personality and the bums: service work and sexuality', *Work, Employment and Society*, 6(1): 23–42
Harlow, E., Hearn, J. and Parkin, W. (1992) 'Sexuality and social work organisations' in P. Carter, T. Jeffs and M. Smith (eds) *Changing Social Work and Welfare*, Buckingham: Open University Press
Hearn, J. and Parkin, W. (2001) *Gender, Sexuality and Violence in Organizations*, London: Sage
Roy, D. (1974) 'Sex in the factory: informal heterosexual relations between supervisors and workgroups' in C.D. Bryant (ed.) *Deviant Behavior*, Chicago, IL: Rand McNally

MANAGING AND MOTIVATING

CHAPTER 8

Managing, motivating, leading and tasking

Objectives

Having read this chapter and completed its associated activities, readers should be able to:

- Recognise that those aspects of the organisation of work at the level of basic task performance that are often treated as separate matters – motivation, leadership and job design – are better understood as closely related aspects of managerial task shaping and the winning of employee cooperation.

- See the advantages of considering organisational members' *orientations to work* and the *strategic exchanges* that occur in the context of the employment relationship rather than focus on people's general 'motivation to work'.

- Recognise the advantages of focusing on the managerial manipulation of employees' perceived *implicit contracts* rather than on managerial efforts to 'motivate' employees.

- Understand the extent to which there is negotiation and bargaining within the associated processes of 'motivation', 'leadership' and job design.

- Appreciate the importance of the *indulgency patterns* that arise – the implicit 'give-and-take' practices that can be observed in the relationships between workers and supervisors or managers.

- Appreciate that so-called 'process' theories of motivation like 'equity' and 'expectancy' theories nevertheless contain important insights that fit with the basic *strategic exchange* analysis developed in this chapter.

- Apply the concepts of *direct* and *indirect* managerial control attempts developed in the previous chapter to the *principles of work design* that have influenced the *job design practices* developed over the history of industrial capitalist economies.

- Understand how the application of different types of work design principles at different times can be related to the basic managerial problem of handling contradictions in the basic industrial and organisational system.

- Appreciate the ways in which values, choices and contingent circumstances influence the enactment of specific job designs – and are an element of the more general and strategic organisation-shaping processes that were identified in Chapter 7.

Linking motivation, leadership and job design

The organising and managing of work requires motivating organisational members to behave in certain ways, asking some organisational employees to play a more leading role than others in the workplace and deciding how tasks are to be allocated to people. The issues are always there and have to be tackled. However, it is important to avoid treating matters of motivating, leading and shaping tasks as separate and unconnected matters. This, however, is something that texts which treat 'motivation', 'leadership' and 'job design' as separate and discrete topics might encourage us to do. It is quite normal to find textbooks with separate chapters on 'motivation', 'leadership' and 'job design'. Yet ask any manager trying to direct the activities of an organisational section, department or function where the 'motivating' aspect of their work stops and 'leadership' starts. Even if they accepted the value of these concepts for understanding the work that they do, they would be hard pressed to explain how they differed in practice.

One might similarly ask any manager tackling issues of how tasks in an organisational department are going to be shaped and allocated whether this 'job design' work is simply a matter of the efficient sharing out of work tasks. No, they are likely to reply, a key consideration has to be how effectively different patterns of tasks and roles will 'motivate' or fail to motivate the people undertaking them. To choose whether, on the one hand, to ask employees to tackle the same simple task day in, day out or, on the other hand, to give each individual a variety of challenging tasks to do, requires giving thought to how those employees are likely to react in 'motivational' terms to such arrangements. If 'job designers' find themselves deciding to group people into work teams, it is unlikely to be long before they are talking about the need to design into the teamwork arrangements a role for a team *leader*. In practice, then, those matters that are typically treated as separate issues within orthodox managerial/academic discourses are closely interrelated.

The general meanings of the words that are used in this area would suggest this close interrelationship. When managers 'lead' people, our dictionaries suggest, they are getting people to follow or 'go along with them'. When they 'motivate' them, they are providing 'a stimulus to some kind of action'. These two things are clearly closely interrelated, and both are relevant to the work managers do when they design jobs – when they lay down the patterns of tasks that people are required to undertake. The cluster of tasks that any particular individual is asked to undertake will typically have been designed by managers to get their workers to 'go along with them' and to contain 'stimuli to action'. But managers do not do any of these things in their own departments or sections in isolation from what is going on more generally across the organisation in which they are involved. All of this motivating, leading and patterning of tasks happens in the context of the broader structural and cultural patterns that were looked at in Chapters 6 and 7. And, especially important, as we shall see, is the extent to which the structure and culture of the organisation tends towards the use of *direct* or *indirect* attempts to achieve managerial control. Managerial control is something that will never be completely achieved however hard managers work in *attempting* to achieve it. And the *productive cooperation* that managers are required to pursue will never be complete. Whatever productive cooperation is achieved has to be worked for. It has to be 'won'.

Motivating, leading and job designing are facets of this attempt to 'win cooperation' and they are often indistinguishable from each other in practice. We could say, though, that:

- when people speak of 'motivation' they tend to focus on the *people doing work tasks*;
- when people speak of 'leadership' they tend to focus on the *person trying to influence the carrying out of those tasks*;
- when people speak of 'job design' they tend to focus on the *tasks themselves* and in using the word 'design' are perhaps linking activities at the local level back to the way the organisation as a whole is structured, particularly in terms of either a *direct* or an *indirect* control emphasis.

In Chapter 5 attention was focused in Case 5.2 on Peter Brodie (pp. 177–8) as a manager who was working effectively to win the cooperation of a variety or people upon whom the long-term success of his enterprise depended. The focus there on the individual, however, brings to the fore the 'leadership' aspect of his managerial work. He was thus identified as an effective leader. This 'leadership' effectiveness cannot really be other than temporarily separated from the other aspects of what he was doing in his role as the chief executive of the charity he was shaping and running.

Motivation, leadership and job design need to be regarded as closely interrelated aspects of patterning of activities and understandings across the whole work organisation. And this means remembering that no manager works outside the basic structure and ethos of the organisation that employs them. The present chapter nevertheless tends to concentrate on activities at a more 'local' level within the organisation. It looks at those issues that are traditionally tackled under the traditional headings of motivation, leadership and work design as different facets of the overall processes that occur within task management practices and within the patterns of relationship, rivalry, adjustment and negotiated order that enable productive cooperation to occur to a level that allows the organisation to continue in existence into the future. The three Further Reading guides on leadership (Chapter 5, p. 196), motivation and work design (this chapter pp. 347–8) present material that is made available within the tradition of separating these aspects of managerial work from each other. The chapter itself, however, tries to minimise this kind of separation.

Earlier, we questioned the value of the social science concept of 'motivation' as a tool for analysing and understanding why people do what they do at work – or anywhere else for that matter. The problems with an emphasis on motives and motivation in understanding human behaviour were discussed in Chapter 3 (pp. 89–90). 'Motivation' was shown to be a concept that is rooted in systems-control thinking about human beings and their behaviour in which the person is seen as 'a little machine-like system in which goals or "motives" operate as a motor "powering" the human entity so that it behaves in a particular way' (p. 86).

The story of Grant Park and his coffee drinking activities was used in Chapter 3 to demonstrate that motives are not usefully seen as things that people 'have' which *precede* behaviour (in the modernist tradition of dualism and linear thinking) (pp. 88–9). Instead, it was argued, 'motives' have to be seen as social rather than purely individual phenomena – often acting as justifications for a piece of behaviour made after the event rather than as causal springs of action or 'triggers' of behaviours. What people do (whether it be to commit a murder or to work hard at a desk all day to please a boss) is an outcome of a multiplicity of factors going way beyond the straightforward fulfilling of motives or the meeting of needs. Whereas systems-control thinking sees human behaviours occurring as individuals who are *motivated* to fulfil *needs* and *wants*, process-relational thinking sees actions taking place 'in the light of interpretations made about the world, to *enact* whatever *projects* individuals who are undertaking *strategically* to shape their lives and to manage *existential challenges*' (Table 3.1, p. 94). Thus, if we want to understand what is 'motivating' a particular individual to behave in a particular way at work we would look at their overall *work orientation* – the meaning that they currently attach to their work (see Chapter 4, pp. 116–24). And this orientation has emerged in the light of their idea of 'who they are' (their identity) and 'where they are going in life' (their personal *strategic shaping*). It is also an aspect of how they are handling life's anxieties and the pressures of their circumstances – matters ranging from how their family is to be fed to ones of values and, say, of conscience about what one 'ought to be doing with one's life'.

From 'worker motivation' to work orientations and strategic exchange

What all of this implies is that we need to stop focusing on people's 'motives' and look at what people are thinking and doing within the broader context of the *strategic exchange* relationships between employing organisations and employees. People going to work in organisations are involved in strategically shaping their lives, and organisations themselves have to be shaped strategically to trade with a whole range of constituencies. Employers and employees come together in an exchange that helps both parties fulfil their respective strategies. And the 'strategy' of the employee can be understood as their basic *orientation to work*. This is something much more subtle, much more complex and much more dynamic than 'motives'.

Activity 8.1

Reread the stories of Ravi Barr (Case 4.1, p. 119) and Sacha and her corporate affairs department (Case 4.2, p. 122):

- to remind yourself of the extent to which people's orientation to work (their overall 'work motivation' as it might be called) varies at different times of their life and in different circumstances;

- to recognise that the efforts of managers and supervisors in the workplace to 'motivate' their staff are only one factor in the resulting 'motivational' state of those staff.

In considering these two stories and what they tell us about the variations that can exist between how people are oriented to (or 'motivated within') their work it readily becomes apparent that we tend to use the notion of motivation in two ways when we look at work behaviour and meaning, as is noted in Table 8.1.

In the story of Ravi Barr in Case 4.1 we notice how a variety of factors in his life experience and his changing notion of identity led to changes in how he was broadly oriented towards work at different times. This could be expressed in terms of how his 'motivation' varied from circumstance to circumstance. The

Table 8.1 Two ways in which we talk about 'motivation' in the work context

Motivation as *the factors leading a person to behave in a certain way at work* (this is similar to the *strategic exchange* notion of a person's orientation to work)	Motivation as *managerial action to influence the people's behaviour at work so they perform as managers require* (in *strategic exchange* terms, this entails managerial manipulation of the implicit contract to get people to behave in a way that leads to productive cooperation)
We say, for example, that a person's 'motivation' has changed when their orientation to work has shifted from one where they sought to maximise their cash return from the employer while showing little interest in the employer's business to one where they concentrate on making a conscientious input to developing the business with a view to building up to a high salary level later in their career	We often say that part of a manager's job is to 'motivate' their staff: find a way of getting them to act in a way that fits with organisational requirements. A manager might observe that the staff are primarily interested in short-term cash reward and prefer to be told exactly what to do. However, the manager decides that it is necessary for these staff to involve themselves in finding new ways of doing the job. The manager might therefore talk of 'motivating my people differently'. This might involve persuading them they will find taking more initiative within their jobs rewarding

term 'orientation' is preferred, however, because it suggests the relevance of a wider variety of factors influencing the way an individual thinks and behaves at work than something as simplistic as a set of 'motives'. It might be reasonable to use the notion of motive to label a simple interest in maximising one's income. However, it is less helpful when it comes to considering such matters as the way in which one expresses one's identity in one's work or the way one develops a working career to fit into a changing set of life priorities or circumstances. We can see the same problem when we look at the staff who work in Sacha Boath's public relations department in Case 4.2. The original 'poor motivation' of Biffy Currie and Sniffy Gerardo, for example, simply cannot be put down to something as simple as 'motives'. Their problems appear to Sacha to be related to problems of identity arising from the loss of their jobs as journalists. Complex problems of marital disharmony and alcoholism were related to this. But their changed work orientations (to a 'positive motivation', as some would put it) seem to have come from changes that they made in their private lives rather than from direct managerial efforts to 'motivate them'. Sacha does claim a part in this change by pointing to her threat to them that they would have to 'ship out' if they did not 'shape up'. For all we know this might have been crucial in getting both men to reconsider what they were doing with their lives, but it can hardly be recognised as a case of a manager 'motivating' a member of staff. Sacha has made a significant managerial intervention, it would seem, but it was an intervention rooted in a subtle consideration of a range of factors influencing the men's lives. It was also risky: the men could have been alienated even more from their work as public relations officers and descended even faster into personal and work troubles.

Trying to influence employees' work orientations is a much more complex matter than simply seeking to 'motivate' them by trying to 'meet their needs' – as much of the standard motivational thinking has it (and to which we will return shortly). One reason for this complexity is the fact, demonstrated in Ravi's case as well as in the case of Smithy (Sacha's third public relations officer), that work orientations are highly influenced by aspects of people's lives outside the workplace. This is not to say that organisational influences are not themselves of enormous importance. And here, what might seem at first sight like fairly simple changes can have considerable effects. Sacha tells us how Snippy Spedale's approach to her work and to relationships in the office have changed significantly since her desk was moved from a relatively central position in the room. The office rearrangement can be understood as a matter of change in job design – the pattern of tasks and work roles and how these relate to each other is inevitably changed whenever one changes the physical layout of a workplace, however minor this may be. But this has changed the 'reward' side of the perceived implicit contract at the heart of Snippy's work orientation. The pleasure of being at the centre of the office's social life and being able to joke with everybody that entered the office has gone away. And Sacha is thinking about how she can intervene in this. We can infer that she is considering trying to bring something of this back into the informal contract with Snippy when she tells us that she is going to have to 'rethink the office layout'.

Motivating and leading people through the manipulation of implicit contracts

By manipulating Snippy Spedale's work orientation, Sacha is, in orthodox terms, trying to 'remotivate' her. But equally one could say she is attempting this shift in orientation by engaging in some minor job redesign. One might even say she is displaying a degree of subtle 'leadership'. The same might be said of the case of Sparky Learmonth. Sacha recognises that his job has changed – it has become more routine and is thus less intrinsically satisfying for him. But Sparky is happy with his salary and his job security. Such are the complexities and the multiplicity of factors that come into the work orientation of any individual and the implicit contract between them and the employer. Sacha has considered manipulating this by promoting him but, given that this is not feasible, she is talking of finding 'some exciting new project' that will turn him on. Again we can ask whether what is going on here is 'motivation', 'job design' or 'leadership'. It is hard to separate these out. And it is unnecessary. It is more helpful simply to recognise that:

- managerial work involves getting employees to do things that they might not otherwise do;
- to do this managers have to understand the complexities of employees' work orientations;
- any attempt to change these must involve making some adjustment in the individuals' perceived implicit contract – the way employees understand the relationship between what they are 'putting in' to the job and what 'they are taking out' of the employment relationship;
- to change an implicit contract there is bound to be a degree of bargaining, but all negotiations over the 'employment trade' always relate to all the *strategic exchanges* which both the individual and the organisation are making and occur within a relationship involving power differences. The managers, as the employer's agents, with all the organisation's resources behind them, typically have a power advantage over the employees.

Manipulating employees' perceived implicit contract *Concept*

This is at the centre of all motivational, leadership and job design work done by managers. Tasks are shaped and rewards are offered as part of a bargaining process in which managers try to persuade employees to work in the way they want them to work.

All motivational, leadership and work design efforts made by managers attempt to influence employee behaviours by influencing the employee's perception or understanding of the contract that is at the heart of the relationship between the organisation and the worker. How people behave in the workplace is fundamentally

Table 8.2 An 'input–reward' representation of how employees perceive their implicit contract with the employing organisation

Employee input	Employee reward
• physical effort	• money
• mental effort	• job satisfaction
• initiative	• personal 'growth'
• responsibility	• social reward
• impairment – *fatigue, risk of injury etc.*	• security
• compliance – *acceptance of a degree of managerial control*	• power
	• status
	• career potential

influenced by their understanding of the 'employment deal' which, following the analysis provided in Chapter 4 (pp. 115–25), is represented in Table 8.2.

Managers, in 'leading' or getting workers to go along with them, in 'motivating' or giving them incentives to act in a certain way and in shaping their tasks are necessarily involved in complex processes of negotiation. Recognition of this is central to process-relational thinking. It is not just a matter of negotiating with workers what tasks they do or how much they are to be paid for doing those tasks. It is a negotiation over the basic 'realities' of the employment relationship. In the power relationship within which the employment relationship is always set ('if, in the end, you do not do what we ask, you will lose your job') the manager has to establish a pattern of workplace relations and understandings. Within this, the employees have to be persuaded that there is a fair and reasonable return for the efforts and initiatives that they make, the risks to health and mental well-being that they take, and the degree of managerial authority over them that they accept. That return will be a complex mix of monetary, psychological and social rewards. It will be a mix of so much pay, so much security, so much opportunity for career advancement, so much social 'standing' and so on, that makes a fair balance, in the employees' mind, with what is being asked of those employees by the employer.

Activity 8.2

Read the story that Dal Cross tells in Case 8.1 about the foundry yard gang and:

- use as many as possible of the elements or 'headings' in the model of the general 'implicit contract' identified in Table 8.2 to make sense of the yard gang's perceived implicit contract with their employer – the one that prevailed before Dal Cross arrived;

- consider what actions Dal might consider, in terms of manipulating the perceived implicit contract, to change the yard gang's way of working, and stop it being necessary to have a foreman or manager sitting in the office all day turning requests from across the site into direct orders to be given to the 'yardies'.

Dal Cross and the recalcitrant yard gang   Case 8.1

I think I learned everything I know about the management basics from that six months when I was put in charge of the people who do the outdoor work in our foundries. I had only been with the company for about 18 months and was coming towards the end of the management training programme. My final 'attachment', as they called them in those days, was to work with the foundry works manager. This man turned out to be quite different from what I expected. He was a highly qualified metallurgist and he prided himself on being an educated and cultivated individual who, at the same time, had a 'common touch' when it came to his relationships with foundry workers. I'll never forget the words he used when I went to see him to discuss the assignment he was going to give me. He said, 'I can give you a job which, if you succeed with it, will teach you all the basics about managing in this sort of business', and he then used this unforgettable phrase, 'I want you to sort out my recalcitrant yardies'. That night, as you might guess, I looked up the word recalcitrant in my dictionary. It said something like 'not susceptible to control or authority'. What was I taking on?

I had not, in those days, heard of Jamaican 'yardy' gangs and immediately recognised who he was talking about when he pointed out of the window at a couple of men who were slowly – incredibly slowly – sweeping up a section of the factory yard opposite the works manager's office. Their foreman was about to retire and I was to take over from him for a six-month period. The brief was to 'sort things out' and recommend to the works manager what should be done about a permanent replacement for the foreman who, the works manager said, he was 'damned glad to see the back of'. I have to admit that I was rather nervous about taking this on. But I had been complaining to the training manager that I wanted a 'real management assignment' in which I would not only learn about doing management but 'prove myself' as a manager. I'd asked for everything I was going to get, hadn't I?

The foundry site had been developing over 30 to 40 years and it had become a complex jungle of buildings and workshops with all sorts of alleyways leading off the twisting main road that ran through the site. The role of the dozen or so yardmen was to keep these ways clear, clean and safe. They were also responsible for moving materials and 'work in progress' about between buildings on the various motorised trucks and hand-pushed carts that they controlled. The responsibility for scrap handling was also theirs.

The work was very hard and often very dirty. One minute they were shifting foundry sand, the next minute carting heavy castings from the furnace room to the fettling shop and soon after that they were having to sweep floodwater away after a heavy rainstorm or shovel snow or ice off the roadways. The work could be dangerous, especially given the cramped areas they often worked in and the heavy and awkward material they sometimes had to handle. And there was a degree of responsibility with this work. Some of the moulds or patterns that they moved about were very fragile, as were some of the ceramic cores that they handled. One slip with these items and not only was money lost but the production schedule could be completely blown. On top of that, the scrap was often quite valuable and the security people were always anxious that no one with a criminal record or with criminal contacts should be in the gang. Scrap thieving can be quite a lucrative activity around engineering works, you know.

What was obvious to me from the moment I began meeting members of the gang was that they took no initiative whatsoever. They wouldn't even sweep up a broken beer bottle in the middle of the car park without being instructed to do so, I discovered. The foreman had insisted that no work be done unless it was under his instruction. Members of the gang had to do exactly what he told them. If any one of them disobeyed him they would find themselves spending a disproportionate amount of time cleaning lavatories. When I looked at the wages that the blokes got they seemed fairly reasonable to me. They compared well with other manual workers who did not have a skilled trade. It seemed that the relatively dangerous and physically uncomfortable aspects of the job were well compensated for by the fairly high security of employment that the job gave them. The foreman might have been a bossy so-and-so but he made sure that his blokes stayed in work if they went along with him. Nevertheless I was quite puzzled at first that they were willing to put up with the heaviness of the control that he exerted. But after a few days I realised that this was balanced by the space he gave them for 'having a laugh together', as they put it. He allowed them longer tea breaks than any other workers took and he turned a blind eye to their practice of 'taking it easy' for the last half-hour of each working day. I knew that other supervisors across the site resented all of this, both because it undermined their own authority with their workers and because they often found themselves unable to get things moved towards the end of a shift or when the yardies were finishing off their card game during a protracted tea break. But few complained too loudly to the yard foreman because he would 'punish' them by ensuring that their 'breakages' increased for a few days or by saying that he had no truck available to move their goods.

There seemed few satisfactions for the yardies in the tasks that they did but I think they nevertheless enjoyed coming to work. And although, in one sense, their status was low as an unskilled group who had some pretty unpleasant tasks to do, they did carry a certain perverse status among the workforce. This was because of the informal privileges they enjoyed as a result of their foreman's power to protect them from any disciplines that might come from another direction. Nobody, including the works manager, dared question what went on. Too much boat-rocking would follow from upsetting the yardies.

Some of the other supervisors used to call the foreman the 'yard führer' and one of them, who had an Italian background, simply called him 'Il Duce'. This name-calling was obviously more than a matter of people with a knowledge of languages using the German or the Italian word for 'leader'! And if I was going to follow my own beliefs about good leadership in my six months with these men, I was going to have to make some big changes. I had to run things the old way at first, however. If I hadn't, the foundry would have ground to a halt. No man was willing to move from the rest room until he had an instruction from me. When I suggested that they all surely knew 'what needed doing on a Monday morning if they thought about it', they responded that they 'were not paid to think'. That was the foreman's job. But after a couple of days sitting at the old foreman's desk receiving phone calls from around the site asking for a truck here, a lavatory cleaner there, a bin emptied somewhere else and an oil leak cleared up outside the main waxroom – and then despatching the appropriate yardy for that job – I was even more convinced that I had to change things.

The implicit contract between the company and the yard gang members, as Dal Cross understands it, is as complex as one we might find with any group of workers. On the employee 'input' side of the trade there is clearly a high level of physical effort required and the yardies subject themselves to a degree of 'impairment' by getting quite dirty and risking accidents in some of the dangerous conditions they meet. They do not appear to make much input by way of initiative taking, however, and the responsibilities they bear are of a relatively passive kind. They simply have to take care not to damage fragile items that they are moving about. But this is a heavier responsibility than it might at first sound, since damage to some of these goods could harm the overall performance of the foundry as a business operation. We might imagine, though, that the foreman himself would take formal responsibility for such damage, given that he exerts so much direct control over the yard gang's work.

The approach he takes to his job means that anyone working in his gang has to surrender a significant amount of personal autonomy while at work. For the rewards that they receive, these men have to submit to a high level of direction from a 'boss'.

The pay that the yardies received, Dal infers, was not an issue. Taken together with the other rewards, an acceptable balance between the two sides of the effort bargain had been struck. Security of employment was clearly a significant factor on the reward side. There appeared to Dal to be little reward in terms of job satisfaction, personal growth or career potential. But we can imagine that they felt some degree of power through their being identified with the power that the foreman himself had over other supervisors and managers. Dal certainly notes a degree of 'perverse' status coming from certain advantages that the yardies had over other foundry workers. They had a greater opportunity to enjoy leisure at work than any other group, for example. It can be inferred that these lengthy card-playing tea breaks and the winding-down time provided the yardies with a degree of 'social reward' in the workplace. It was a fairly distinctive factor going into the mix or balance of 'inputs' and 'outputs' that makes up the implicit contract of this particular group of workers with the employing organisation. It was at the core of their work orientation and is thus something that anybody would need to appreciate – Dal Cross included – who wanted to understand why the yardies thought and behaved in the way they did with regard to their work.

The implicit contract has just been referred to as a trade that goes on between employees and the employing organisation. But, of course, 'the organisation' is not literally a trader itself. The bargain that we say, in a shorthand way, 'the organisation' is making with its employees is in fact made in the organisation's name by the various managers, personnel recruitment staff and supervisors with whom the individual deals at different stages of their entry to and continuing involvement in the organisation. And where there is a manager or supervisor directly involved in shaping the everyday activities of any individual or group of individuals there will necessarily be a degree of day-to-day negotiation or *give and take* about what work is done and how and when it is done. The works manager clearly saw the yard gang as an especially 'recalcitrant' group – clearly thinking of the yardies and the foreman together as a group that had managed to get itself in some ways 'above the law' that applied to other groups under the works manager's authority. However, we could say that all employees – all human beings indeed – are recalcitrant to a degree (see the earlier discussion of this, pp. 2–3). Every manager, schoolteacher or parent knows that the employees, pupils or children formally 'under their control' will never follow every instruction that they are given or submit totally to every rule that is meant to shape their behaviour. There has to be a degree of 'give and take' which allows the person in authority to get 'some of their own way' in return for allowing those subject to that authority to 'get away' with infringing some of the rules which, if followed in every detail, would turn the individual into a puppet or a robot rather than a human being with free will and personal autonomy. Gouldner, in a classic study of factory life (1954), conceptualised as an *indulgency pattern* the tendency he saw for supervisors to 'turn a blind eye' to certain rule-breaking activities. The supervisors did this as part of an implicit understanding that the workers would, reciprocally, indulge the supervisors when they sought compliance over matters that the workers might reasonably refuse to go along with.

> ### Indulgency pattern *Concept*
>
> The ignoring by supervisors or managers of selected rule infringements by workers in return for those workers conceding to requests that, strictly speaking, they could refuse.

The joiners' shop ritual reported in Chapter 7 (in Table 7.2, p. 286) whereby the joiners always used the first 20 minutes of their shift to take an 'illegal tea break' while the supervisors deliberately kept their backs to the working areas for the same period of time is an example of a ritualised expression of an indulgency pattern. In this case a particularly assertive manual work group is ritually demonstrating that it only cooperates with 'management' on its own terms, and the supervisors are ritually displaying their acceptance of this. A more typical indulgency pattern, however, is one in which a manager ignores their staff taking an extra long lunch break once a week to do their shopping, in return for those employees complying with the occasional short notice request to do some overtime or to cover for another worker who has not turned up for work. The yard foreman clearly indulges his staff by allowing them to take long breaks and to stop working well before the official finishing time. This, we can reasonably infer, is a trade. It is a conceding of free time during working hours in return for the workers allowing the supervisor to have an unusually high level of task control over them.

It is clear that implicit contracts have some very subtle aspects to them. The very fact that they involve a range of formally unstated agreements makes the managerial 'motivational' task quite a subtle and challenging one. The manager is constantly bargaining with the people that in traditional 'organisation behaviour' terms they are said to be 'motivating' or 'leading'. And, given that managers are frequently required to take initiatives to make changes in work behaviour, they face the considerable challenge of having to renegotiate the ongoing work exchange or *contract* with the people whose behaviours they are trying to change. Dal Cross refers to his foundry assignment as a 'change management' one and he uses the analysis of the yard workers' work orientations and perceived implicit contract that we have just reviewed to make the changes he sees as necessary. And the *processes* that he engages in to negotiate these changes are ones where, once again, we see the overlapping of so-called motivational, leadership and job design initiatives.

Activity 8.3

Read Dal Cross's continuing story in Case 8.2 about his managerial experiences with the yard gang in the foundry and:

- using Table 8.2 again (p. 316), analyse the new implicit contract that makes possible Dal's re-organising of the yard gang;
- consider the extent to which Dal has made changes to 'job design' in setting up the modified 'site services' function;
- consider whether you can see a 'theory of leadership' behind Dal's working towards these changes;
- identify the extent to which it might be said that there is now a new 'indulgency pattern' within these 'site services' arrangements.

Leadership in practice and a 'triumph of change management' — Case 8.2

I had talked of 'proving myself' managerially by taking on this assignment with the foundry works manager and I knew that I was either going to fail miserably or that I was going to pull off a triumph of change management. I had been on a change management course and read all the stuff on choosing the 'right leadership style', motivating people, enriching jobs, empowering staff, quality circles and goodness knows what else. As I read through all this stuff again on the Monday evening after my first day with the yard gang, I struggled to make it all add up. I had to fall back on what I believed in about being a manager. When I had been interviewed for the management traineeship in the first place it seemed that I had said very much the right thing when I had argued that managers were going to have to initiate a lot of changes to make businesses successful in an increasingly competitive world. But managers would not be able to – nor should they morally – unilaterally impose these changes on the organisation's employees. The interviewing panel had been wary of my suggestion that this might involve negotiating work organisation changes with trade unions. But they warmed to my theme that managers and their staff had to 'work together' – with those being paid to be managers taking the lead – to find new ways of working that would give benefits to the organisation and the workers alike.

All these fine words came back to me on that Monday night. Although this was rather idealistic sounding, it did feel to me to be the only way I could *realistically* go about tackling the problem of the yard gang. The works manager was simply unwilling to allow the continuation of an operation led by a gang boss who bullied other managers and supervisors into a situation where they could neither question the level of service he gave them nor challenge the way he indulged his staff. What was clear to me was that I could not simply order the yardies to work differently and to start using their own initiative to provide the site with a fast and efficient service that didn't always have to be mediated by a gang boss.

Ever since my early reflections on what being a manager should mean, I knew that my preferred personal style of leadership would have to be one of establishing a relationship of trust with the men and then negotiating with them a new way of working. That Monday night I decided that I would 'give a lead' by proposing a working principle of 'providing a service to the site' and that this would entail treating people in the various foundry departments as 'internal customers'. I was fully aware that I could not simply foist these ideas onto the men as a cynical act of pushing management fads that I had heard about on a course. I was very tempted to use the 'empowerment' word in my discussion, for example. I think the word describes well what I wanted to do. But I thought that the pretentious overtones of this word would not go down well in the foundry context. If I was going to work with them in a trusting relationship I had to be subtle and establish with them that the 'new order' I had in mind would be one in which they would all be better off than under the old regime, in one way or another.

I called a meeting with all the men in their 'winding down' time on the Tuesday evening, promising overtime payment to cover time spent in this or subsequent meetings that might go beyond the end of the shift. I took time to listen to what each of the men felt about the good and the bad aspects of the job and I worked hard to get them to see where, as a bloke, I was 'coming from'. I think this worked out quite well, partly because I think I am quite good at presenting myself as a sincere sort of person. But it was equally because all of this was set within a promise that nobody would 'lose out' if they 'went along with me'. Pay would certainly not suffer and I would look into ways in which an 'improved service to the foundry' might lead to an improved pay level. As I pointed out, the company had a job evaluation scheme which would ensure that if they were to 'increase the thinking or initiative element' of their work then they should move to a higher pay band.

Above all, though, I argued that they would surely be much happier to be 'getting out from under the thumb' of the boss man who had pushed them around for so long. And surely it would be better to get proper job satisfaction from providing a service to people across the foundry that would be genuinely appreciated than to carry on taking whatever satisfaction they had been getting from long tea breaks and card games. Taking my managerial life into my hands – or so it felt at the time – I added to this that whatever pleasure they took in the 'fun time' that they had at work was surely undermined by the disgust that other workers felt at what they were 'getting away with'. A stony silence followed that particular input to the discussions. But I got out of the impasse that I had backed myself into by pointing out that if members of the new 'site services' department were to be given discretion over how they went about providing services then they would also obviously have to be given discretion over when they might need to rest or otherwise recover after carrying out a particularly onerous or exhausting task. All of this, I argued, would have to be part of the trust that would need to exist between the members of the department and whoever would be in charge of it.

I hope all of this doesn't sound too glib. It was all very hard work and I found myself fluctuating between elation and depression as I worked towards the new department that I wanted to establish. Without going into all the details, the 'gang' were now to be a 'team' who would meet each morning to allocate among themselves the areas in which each of them were to work through the day. Sections of the team would be allocated each day to an area of the foundry and the members of that section would themselves agree who would do what task – lavatory cleaning and bin clearing included – as the need for it arose within any given area of the site. I got the jobs upgraded and this was helped by a deal I did with the security department whereby the 'site services staff' carried out certain routine security tasks as part of their work. I also got the works manager to agree that it might be possible to appoint a team leader from within the group when I came to the end of my six months. I told the team that this was simply a possibility but that if any of them was interested in future promotion in the company they might like to talk to me about this idea. I felt it was important that the yard workers should have the incentive of personal development and a career available to them, just like elsewhere in the organisation. Site services, and everybody in it, were on the 'up and up', I was proud to say.

The new implicit contract does not involve any less physical effort or risk of impairment than the old one. The major changes are with regard to the increased degree of initiative that the men are being asked to show in organising their own work schedules and task allocations. This can be seen as an increased 'input'. Alongside this there is what might be seen as a reduced input: the removal of the old requirement to surrender a high degree of personal autonomy by submitting themselves to a foreman's tight and direct control. It is sometimes argued by managers in situations like this that the only change in reward that this requires is one that automatically follows from the workers being freed to take charge of their own working practices: the reward of increased job satisfaction. Such people argue that 'empowering' workers by giving them increased freedom to choose how to work is a reward in itself. However, it is far from unusual for employees to reject this line of bargaining. They are quite likely to respond in the way the yard workers did and raise the principle of 'being paid to think'. Employees are quite likely to observe that their 'empowerment' involves them taking on tasks that managers or supervisors previously carried out. They argue that taking on such work should be recognised with a higher rate of pay. Dal Cross is well aware of this type of argument, it would seem. Consequently he has sought ways of getting their pay increased: using the company's formal job evaluation scheme, one that incorporates the principle of paying for initiative and responsibility. To ensure that such an upgrading occurs he also adds a security guard dimension to their work. This has the potential tacitly to improve the status element of the reward side of the implicit contract. Dal also explicitly addresses the status issue by suggesting they will be better off without the rather questionable sort of status they gained by getting more leisure-in-work time than other employees.

Dal seems to be very aware that taking away the opportunity to enjoy unofficial social rewards in the extended tea breaks is not going to be easy. He therefore seeks to redefine it as implicitly a little shameful and unfair to other workers. It is not an untainted reward. But he goes even further to deal with this potentially tricky issue. In effect, he suggests his own version of the indulgency pattern that was part of the old regime. We can understand in this way his statement to the yard workers that they would 'obviously have to be given discretion over when they might need to rest or otherwise recover after carrying out a particularly onerous or exhausting task'. This offer is subtly connected to the principle of mutual trust that he speaks of as inherent in their generally increased discretion.

There is a lot of subtle 'motivational' work going on in the meetings of Dal and his staff and he shows considerable rhetorical skill in drawing on discursive resources like 'trust', 'service', 'internal customer' and 'team' to paint a very positive picture of the new world into which he wants to lead them. He was wary of using the discursive resource of 'empowerment', however. We might see this reluctance to use a possibly pretentious term as a reflection of Dal's skills of persuasion and leadership. He certainly seems to have worked out his own theory of leadership, one that incorporates a belief that one cannot impose changes on employees (or 'foist ideas' or 'management fads' on them). He sees negotiation as an important part of his 'personal style of leadership' and believes this should happen after establishing a trusting relationship with those with whom he is to negotiate. For Dal, this means allowing the men to get to know him personally and 'where he is coming from'. He also mentions taking time to listen to the views of the group before putting his ideas to them. To be a leader is nevertheless still a matter of initiating actions for Dal. He talks of 'giving a lead' by proposing the site service idea. However, that assertion of leadership is balanced with a clear recognition that is occurring within what is an essentially negotiated relationship of exchange – the employment bargain.

Dal is 'motivating' and 'leading' then, but he is also engaging is some significant job design work. By incorporating much of the foreman's old role into the work of the yard gang members themselves he is significantly redesigning the tasks away from the former *direct* control principles towards one in which control is much more *indirect*. Dal is not moving to a situation where the foundry management abandons control over the yard workers. It is asking them to control themselves, in the interests of the employing organisation as well as for their own benefit. He is utilising work design principles of *job enrichment*, *team-working* and the *semi-autonomous work group* (concepts we look at below, pp. 235–8). He does recognise, however, that the group might not satisfactorily work in an entirely 'leaderless' way when he ends his involvement with them in a few months' time. He therefore talks of the possibility of a team leader being appointed. And in talking of this he is making yet another adjustment to the implicit contract with the group – he is putting into the bargain for the first time a possibility of career advancement.

Equity, balance and expectancies in work orientations

Although it is now common for motivational theories that use ideas of equity or expectancy to be referred to as 'process theories' they go only a part of the way towards the full process-relational thinking that has been developed over the chapters of *Organising and Managing Work*. Their insights do parallel much of what has been said about orientations to work and implicit contracts however. An early process-oriented contribution to what has variously been referred to as 'balance', 'social comparison' or 'equity' theorising in this area was a classical study of American soldiers (Stouffer *et al.*, 1949). The researchers observed that there was a greater dissatisfaction with promotional opportunities in the Army Corps than in the Military Police. This was in spite of the fact that, objectively, there were better opportunities in the former part of the military than in the latter. The dissatisfactions and the 'de-motivating' influence of these were not the outcomes of what was objectively the case but arose out of the expectations of the people involved with regard to promotional opportunities. A general sense of unfairness had developed in large part as a result of individual soldiers comparing their own prospects with the way that others had been treated. Developments in this kind of thinking were pulled together into an 'equity theory of motivation' by Adams (1963, 1965). This sees people balancing what they put into their work with what they get out of it in the light of what they see other people putting in and taking out in similar situations.

> ### Equity or balance theories of work motivation *Concept*
>
> These theories show how work behaviour is influenced by how people perceive their situation after comparing their work/reward exchange (or 'implicit contract') with the employer to that of other members of the organisation.

The basic insight of so-called 'equity theory' is a vital one and it is wholly consistent with how the *work orientation* and *implicit contract* concepts have been used here. The central attention given in strategic exchange thinking to how people perceive or understand the contract they make with an employer is the same as in balance and equity thinking. The stress on how this perception involves comparisons with other people is implicit but clear in, for example the earlier reference to employees having to 'be persuaded that there is a fair and reasonable return' for everything that those employees 'put into' their work (p. 00). None of us can decide as to how 'fair or reasonable' we can regard anything that we are asked to do or anything that we are offered without making comparisons with other people and their circumstances.

Activity 8.4

Consider how far matters of 'equity', 'balance' or perceived fairness come into the stories Dal Cross in Case 8.2 (p. 321) and Campbell Toon in Case 1.3 (p. 23) have to tell us about:

- the way Dal first analyses the work orientations and perceived implicit contracts of the yard gang and, later, enters negotiations with the men;
- Campbell's attempts to increase the productivity of the packaging workers in his part of the factory by 'enriching' their jobs.

When Dal Cross was trying to make sense of the work orientations of the members of the yard gang in his early involvement with them he looked at the balance between what they were 'putting in' and 'getting out' – as far as he could understand it as an observer. He is explicit about the fact that he is talking at this stage about his perception of their perceptions, so to speak, when he says that their wages 'seemed fairly reasonable to me'. In effect he tries to put himself in their position, and makes the sort of comparison with others that he thinks that they would make – with 'other manual workers who did not have a skilled trade'. Some more subtle thinking along these lines is done as he goes on to look at what he calls the 'perverse status' that they enjoy in the foundry. This analysis emerges from his trying to make sense in 'balance' terms of the fact that the yardies get more free time for their own leisure during working hours than do other workers. All of these complexities are later taken into account during the bargaining that he enters into with the gang as he works to move them towards a new implicit contract. He tries to get them to redefine this 'privilege' by effectively suggesting that it is not really a reward at all.

Dal is well aware that worker perceptions of inputs and outputs have an important economic dimension. He appreciates that a pay increase is going to be vital in shifting the exchange relationship. It is interesting that the company's 'job evaluation' scheme that he makes use of is a device similar to that which many employers use to deal openly with matters of comparison and perceived fairness in wages or salaries paid to different groups within an organisation. Job evaluation schemes are used in deciding pay relativities in many work organisations. They use measurements of work 'inputs' and 'outputs' that are believed to be acceptable to everyone as the basis for pay comparisons. Such a scheme could also be a help to Cam Toon if he wishes to try again to redesign the work tasks of the members of his department. He reports how his workers were comparing the new tasks that they were doing with what they believe supervisors do. In principle, a job evaluation scheme would enable their new jobs to be measured, compared to the work that a supervisor typically does in similar areas of the organisation and a 'fair' wage for the new employment trade identified.

Expectancy theories of work motivation *Concept*

These theories show how work behaviour is influenced (a) by the particular wants and expectations which particular employees, in particular circumstances, bring to the organisation and (b) by the extent to which these are met by the employer.

The concept of *expectancy* has been utilised by various theorists to deal with these matters of employee perception or 'understanding'. The concept has played a central part in the turning away of motivation theorists from the focus on 'needs' towards use of the much more realistic 'wants' and expectations that employees bring to particular jobs. Instead of indulging in generalisations about the needs that human beings generally are said to bring to the workplace, it encourages managers to look at the specific work circumstances of whatever group of employees they are concerned with and at the specific expectations that they bring to their employment relationship with a particular employer. The 'expectancies' referred to by psychologists and motivation theorists like Vroom (1964) or Lawler (1971) correspond to some extent to the 'work orientations' notion that has emerged out of the industrial sociology tradition. We can draw out of expectancy thinking some highly commonsensical guidelines that can be applied to the various facets of work organisation and bear on the input–output bargain at the centre of the employment relationship management – from pay systems and promotional policies to job design and management style. For successful 'motivation' to occur several conditions have to be met.

- Employees must see that the effort they put in will, in fact, cause effective performance. It would be inappropriate for an individual output bonus to be paid to someone operating a machine that had a fixed rate or level of output, for example.
- Employees must see that appropriate performance will lead to their receiving the rewards claimed to be linked to them. Promotion would not be a good motivator, for example, if the individual either sees people being promoted for reasons other than effective performance or if they see cases of such performance failing to lead to promotion.
- The rewards available to employees must be ones in which they are actually interested – or can be persuaded to become interested in. The offer of the rewards of intrinsic job satisfaction (that Campbell Toon offered his staff, for example) or increased job status would be poor motivators for employees who simply wanted a quiet life at work in a secure job with a good level of pay to take home.
- Employees must have both the technical skills and knowledge to do the job.
- Employees must understand the broader implications of the role they are taking on – the sort of relationships they are expected to have with managers themselves and with other people in the organisation for example.

These practical managerial guidelines emerge from what textbooks label 'expectancy theories of motivation'. The theory behind these highly commonsensical recommendations is consistent with strategic exchange thinking and its emphasis on the interpretations and understandings that people bring to their employment. Expectancy thinking's focus is on the employees themselves, as we would expect from work emerging from the psychological tradition of 'motivational' theorising. In this respect, it is a more narrowly focused analysis than the strategic exchange one. Strategic exchange analysis is broader and deeper in its locating of managerial attempts to manipulate the implicit contract within both the social and cultural location and priorities of the employee and the strategic position and priorities of the employing organisation (whose exchanges with employees are just one resource exchange among many.

Strategic exchange analysis and the way it uses the concepts of work orientation and implicit contract is also broader (more fully process-relational we might say) than expectancy theory in its attention to the ongoing processes of negotiation and renegotiation that occur in the relationship between employers and employees. This is a relationship that exists within a political–economic context. And the nature of that context means that significant managerial efforts have to go into the constant handling of the basic tensions and contradictions that characterise the employment relationship in industrial capitalist societies. These tensions are always there in the background of every 'motivational' situation in the work organisation. Sometimes they are more obvious than at other times, however. They could be understood as manifesting themselves, for instance, when one of the two workers with whom Campbell Toon discusses the issue of whether or not 'money is a motivator' in Case 1.3 (p. 23) rejects the language of motivation and contextualises the proposed pay claim with the words, 'there's no way any factory worker is ever going to feel that they are paid enough'. Issues of social class and basic employer–employee conflicts are clearly playing a part here.

Work motivation, then, cannot be considered in isolation from a whole range of other issues that impinge on the negotiated relationship between the employing organisation and its employees. And there is no particular aspect of a manager's job that can be separated out from the rest of what they do as the 'motivational element' of their job. It has been clear throughout this chapter, not least in the reported managerial experiences of Dal Cross and Cam Toon, that to 'motivate' people (getting employees to do what they otherwise would not do) managers lead, build relationships, develop understandings, train people, devise promotional schemes and design jobs. Both Dal and Cam are, for example, engaged in a degree of job redesign work in their attempts to 'motivate' their staff to work more effectively. These were personal initiatives applying to their own departments. But, as was stressed earlier in the chapter, we cannot separate out what any manager does in their own department from the wider cultural and structural arrangements of the organisation as a whole. Each of these managers was attempting a move from a relatively *direct* approach to seeking managerial control to a relatively *indirect* one. In this, we can assume that they felt that such a move was not inconsistent with the broader cultural and structural trends in their companies. Broad considerations of job design are an important element in the strategic shaping of the organisation as a whole.

Direct and indirect control principles of work design

Organisational structures, and the task shaping and task allocation that is part of them, are very much 'emergent' phenomena – outcomes of the balance of managerial initiatives and employee acceptance. Process-relational thinking draws attention to the negotiated, political and emergent aspects of organisations. Organisations, as they emerge out of the processes of cooperation and conflict, rarely resemble their official managerial blueprint or organisation charts when we look at them in action. But this does not mean that managers are not continually working to design – or *re*design – the activities that are carried on in the organisation's name. To understand this, it is useful to look at certain work design principles that have played a part in shaping the practices of organisational managers throughout the history of the modern work organisation.

Work design/redesign principles — *Concept*

General principles about how narrow or broad the tasks associated with jobs should be and the extent to which jobholders should use discretion in carrying out those tasks.

Job design/redesign practices · Concept

The shaping of particular jobs, especially with regard to how narrow or broad the tasks associated with those jobs are and the extent to which jobholders exercise discretion in carrying out those tasks.

The terms 'job design' and 'work design' are often used interchangeably but, here, we will use them to represent two different but closely related ideas. The actual task pattern that emerges in any particular part of an organisation (the new version of the yard worker job introduced by Dal Cross in Case 8.2, for example) is referred to here as a matter of *job design* (or redesign). The broad principles that are drawn upon when designing or redesigning jobs are, however, referred to as *work design* principles. The former, then, are matters of actual practice and the latter matters of prescription or intent.

Work design is clearly something closely related to the broader structural and cultural 'design' of the organisation as a whole. It was argued in Chapter 7 that there is a basic choice that managers can make in trying to achieve managerial control through this design – through the shaping of the organisation as a whole. This is a choice between *direct* control attempts and *indirect* ones.

- An organisation leaning towards direct control principles would be a highly centralised one with a tightly bureaucratic structure and culture. There would be an emphasis on tight rules and closely prescribed procedures in which a relatively low level of psychological commitment would be sought from the employees. Because these arrangements imply that management is not putting a lot of trust in employees to do what is required of them of their own accord, a 'low trust' culture emerges in which relationships between employer and employees tend to be adversarial. Differences of interest between parties to the employment relationship thus become manifest and visible at a surface level.

- The organisation leaning more in the indirect control direction would be less centralised and have a loosely bureaucratic structure and culture. Rules would be relatively loose and procedures left flexible because employees would have discretion about how to carry out those tasks. They would, however, apply this discretion in a way that fitted with managerial requirements and the strategic priorities of the organisation because of their high level of psychological commitment to the organisation. This commitment is made possible, in turn, because of a culture of high trust between members of the organisation – one in which common or mutual interests between different parties to the employment relationship are emphasised. Differences of interest between parties to the employment bargain tend to remain below the surface of ongoing activities and are not expressed through overt confrontations.

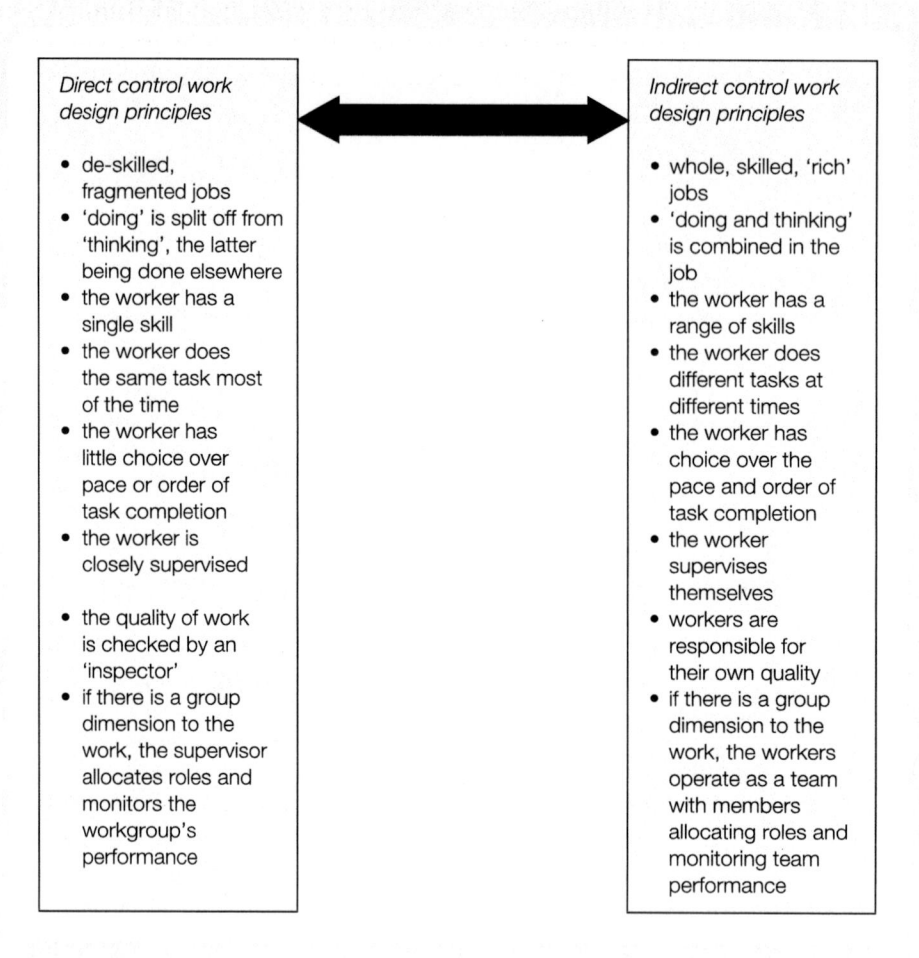

Direct control work design principles	Indirect control work design principles
• de-skilled, fragmented jobs • 'doing' is split off from 'thinking', the latter being done elsewhere • the worker has a single skill • the worker does the same task most of the time • the worker has little choice over pace or order of task completion • the worker is closely supervised • the quality of work is checked by an 'inspector' • if there is a group dimension to the work, the supervisor allocates roles and monitors the workgroup's performance	• whole, skilled, 'rich' jobs • 'doing and thinking' is combined in the job • the worker has a range of skills • the worker does different tasks at different times • the worker has choice over the pace and order of task completion • the worker supervises themselves • workers are responsible for their own quality • if there is a group dimension to the work, the workers operate as a team with members allocating roles and monitoring team performance

FIGURE 8.1 Direct and indirect control principles of work design

Within these two basic approaches to what we might call *organisational* design there are two basic sets of *work* design principles and these are outlined in Figure 8.1.

The two sets of work design principles outlined in Figure 8.1 are *ideal types* – constructs created by the social scientist to help make sense of the much more complex and potentially confusing picture that emerges when we go out into organisations to see what is happening 'on the ground' (as we saw with Weber's 'ideal type of bureaucracy' in Chapter 2, pp. 39–40). No actually observable job designs have ever fully followed the descriptions set out as two ends of the continuum in the diagram, and job designs can be found that are close to the basic work design principles set out in the two columns without following every element of the above characterisation. Within teamworking, to take an example from the 'indirect' side, it might be that the team allocates its own roles from day to day but is still subject to external monitoring of the resulting performance. Sometimes teamworking involves a 'team leader' who retains certain of the roles of the supervisor who plays an important role on the 'direct' side.

In practice, the actual job designs we are likely to come across in organisations will fall somewhere along the continuum outlined in Figure 8.1 and may even combine elements from both ends of it. The model is nevertheless valuable because it represents in a clear way the scope of choices open to managers when they embark on designing jobs in particular organisational settings. We might imagine some scheme like this having been in the minds of both Dal Cross and Campbell Toon when they set out to make changes in the designs of jobs for which they had managerial responsibilities. Both, as we noted earlier, were interested in making moves towards more *indirect* ways of controlling the work done in their departments. Each of these two managers were influenced by 'newer' work design ideas that they had come across. Dal tells us how he had been on a 'change management course' and amongst the 'stuff' that he had read was material on 'enriching jobs', 'empowering staff' and 'quality circles'. Cam refers to his 'classes on motivation', where one of the things he learned about was Herzberg's 'job enrichment principles'. Although these men mention different bits of 'management thinking', they do not closely follow any of the texts or manuals on any of these specific techniques. Instead, they pragmatically apply the basic principles that underlie all these specific innovations ('job enrichment', 'empowerment', 'quality circles', for example). These are the basic principles being characterised here as *indirect control* principles. Within these, Dal pragmatically devises his own form of 'teamworking', that in the longer run may or may not have a team leader role within it. Cam speaks of 'rearranging the jobs of my people so that there was more variety in their tasks'. He also tries to give them 'more freedom to choose how to do the work' by removing a level of supervision.

We shall shortly review some of the more significant managerial innovations and fashions that have been put forward in different guises and under different labels over the past half century. But it is more important to see what all of these have in common than to try to look for distinctions between, say, 'job enrichment', 'vertical task integration' and 'empowerment' or between 'semi-autonomous work groups' and 'teams'. Exactly that has been done here by clustering many of the features of these managerial innovations and identifying them as 'indirect control attempts' which, at the level of job design, are used to handle, in effect, the basic contradiction that all managerial work has to deal with. This is the contradiction whereby managers need to control what workers do while, at the same time, recognising that every managerial attempt at control is liable to be challenged. Organisational members, to varying degrees, will demand 'freedom' or autonomy in the workplace. But managers must make sure that this freedom is a freedom to do what, in the end, the managers want them to do. Loose control, in effect, is stronger than tight control. That is the basic principle of indirect control work design thinking.

Modernity, industrialism and the hesitant embracing of direct control work design

There is a powerful irony behind the fact that we typically treat the principles of *indirect* work design principles as managerial innovations, as 'new thinking', or in terms of progressive or enlightened management ideas. This is ironic because, in the larger historical scheme of things, it was the shift in industrialising societies towards *direct* forms of work control that was one of the fundamental innovations of the new industrial capitalist order. One has to take care not to romanticise the pre-industrial past but, generally speaking, the division of labour that operated in pre-industrial societies was a *social (or general) division of labour*.

> **Social or *general* division of labour** — *Concept*
>
> The allocation of work tasks across society, typically into occupations or trades.

The key work design principle was an occupational one: the working individual played their part in society as a farmer, brewer or shoemaker and would be expected to develop the cluster of skills that went with their particular craft or trade. They would be able to handle what work design experts later came to call 'whole tasks' – the planting, nurturing and harvesting of a crop or the production of a pair of shoes. In practice there were undoubtedly numerous people who did little more than sweep floors or carry trade workers' tools. However, something along the lines of what we have characterised as indirect work design principles were generally seen as desirable and at the centre of the pre-industrial social order. The rise of industrial capitalism, the growth of the institution of formal employment and the rationalising force of bureaucratisation saw a splitting down of many of the occupational roles within the old social division of labour into de-skilled jobs. There was now to be a *technical (or detailed) division of labour* whereby many work activities in factories and offices were split down so that individuals only did one specialised part of what had previously been the 'whole task' associated with an occupation.

> **Technical or *detailed* division of labour** — *Concept*
>
> The breaking down of 'whole' occupational roles into specialised and generally unskilled jobs.

We can envisage the seventeenth or eighteenth century violin maker working on each instrument all the way from the initial woodcarving stage to the varnishing and the adding of the bridge, pegs and strings. But we would find the typical worker in a modern violin factory only able to work the wood cutting machine, glue the front, sides and backs of the instrument together or varnish the violin when it reached the varnish shop. The work would have been de-skilled. Many more violins could be produced at a much higher rate of profit for the employer, but for this to occur, those with the expertise have to take on the role of instructing and monitoring the rest. The managers have to control the workers. Thinking is separated from doing (an important direct control design feature identified earlier in Figure 8.1) and the implications for human beings of this trend were recognised from the start. Adam Smith in his massively influential work *The Wealth of Nations* of 1776, in which the new industrial order was both chronicled and boosted further, provided an analysis of the splitting down of the process of making tacks ('pins' as he called them). This showed that if you fragmented the job of the craft pin maker, who was able to do every stage of pin making, so that each stage of the process became the specialised task of a different worker, a vastly greater number of pins could be produced per day. However, in an industrial order based on this principle, with all the increases of general wealth that would accompany it, these new specialised labourers would be serious 'losers'. 'Those who labour most get least', he observed. What he had in mind was what we might nowadays call the quality of their lives. Someone whose life 'is spent in performing a few simple operations', he observed has 'no occasion' to 'exert understanding' and hence 'becomes as ignorant as it is possible for a human creature to become'.

Smith's reservations about this aspect of modern industrialised labour have come forward and then retreated again at various times ever since he first expressed them. However, the growth of the de-skilling and direct control trend in the nineteenth century was significantly boosted by Charles Babbage (1832). Babbage powerfully demonstrated to employers just how much cheaper de-skilled labour was compared with skilled or craft-based labour. F.W. Taylor in the later part of the nineteenth century codified and systematised these direct control principles of work design and proselytised passionately for their introduction across the workshops of the fast growing industrial enterprises of that time (Taylor, 1911).

Scientific management (Taylorism) *Concept*

Work design principles that maximise the amount of discretion over task performance given to managerial experts, who calculate and precisely define how each job is to be carried out.

Taylor's so-called called *scientific management* entailed:

- managers and experts systematically or 'scientifically' analysing every work task;
- each job being fragmented to achieve the highest possible technical division of labour, on the basis of this analysis;

- the planning of work being separated from its execution;
- skill requirements and job-learning times being reduced to the minimum;
- materials handling by operators being minimised to avoid distraction from the worker's focal task;
- work performance being closely 'time-studied' and monitored;
- pay being tied directly to individual output to encourage each worker to maximise their efforts;
- the relationships between employers/managers and employees remaining formal and distant.

Although Taylor's principles were rarely followed in their entirety, the basic scientific management approach to work design was widely embraced in the industrial and industrialising world as it moved into the twentieth century. This included communist countries where one might have expected some resistance to what many saw as the de-humanisation of working people. But there was also controversy and resistance to the de-skilling and close control trend. We should perhaps note, however, that although Taylor can be seen as pointing to a way forward for large areas of industrial activity, his thinking was rooted in solving problems of workshops in the late nineteenth century American steel industry where much of the labour was unskilled and the workers unfamiliar with the English language. His system might have been more viable in that context than in others where workers might have expected more than monetary satisfactions from their employment. The same argument may apply to the innovations introduced into the car factories of Henry Ford where the 'robotising' of the worker implicit in Taylorism was extended by the placing of the worker on an assembly line. Ford was very conscious of the costs that could follow from treating workers in this way, however. He therefore departed radically from Taylorism in paying a fixed and relatively high wage and called for the worker to show a long-term loyalty to the employer and live a sober and responsible life fitting for a Ford worker. In this way, there was a shift away from the arm's-length type of employment relationship recommended by Taylor.

Fordism   *Concept*

A combining of mass production de-skilled job design in the industrial workplace with employment and state welfare policies that develop workers as both fit workers and willing consumers of the products of industry.

Ford, we might say, set out to manipulate the work orientation of the industrial worker in the more sophisticated way called for by the changing circumstances of the twentieth century. But his innovations also actively influenced the way employment and indeed whole economies and societies were to develop. He recognised that industrial workers could also become the consumers of the products they made. The implicit contract was now to be one which might be expressed by managers as, 'Work hard in our factories in the way we direct you and in return for that you will be well paid and will be able to afford to buy one of the cars you make. And the more cars you buy, the more work there will be – and the better off you will become.' Fordism thus goes way beyond work design. As Fordist work design practices spread in industrialised societies they were supported by the state, whose economic, welfare and educational policies were increasingly aimed at developing a healthy workforce who would also be the consumers of the products and services they produced.

At the same time that Fordism was spreading, attention was beginning to be paid to the arguments of Roethlisberger and Dickson (1939) and Elton Mayo (1933) arising from the research in the Hawthorne plant in Chicago. This research was said to show the importance to them of people's social involvement at work and it was alleged that employees worked more effectively when managers 'showed an interest' in them. These arguments kept alive in some managers' minds an awareness that employees' expectations at work were complex and would not necessarily be straightforwardly satisfied by monetary rewards alone. Such awareness did not detract, however, from general managerial recognition of the immense benefits to employers that Taylorism and Fordism offered by way of both cost efficiency and the tightness of managerial control. A widespread recognition of these benefits meant, and continues to mean, that a powerful de-skilling logic runs through many work design efforts across a multiplicity of different types of employment. As Marxian analysis suggests, the *labour process* in a society based on capitalist principles is one where de-skilling is frequently the option that most effectively enables the employer to exploit the labour power of their employees (Braverman, 1974).

Capitalist labour process *Concept*

In Marxian analysis this is the process whereby managers design, control and monitor work activities in order to extract surplus value from the labour activity of employees on behalf of the capital-owning class which employs them.

However, de-skilling always has its costs – as observers from Smith onwards had pointed out and as many managers themselves discovered. In some circumstances it was not the most effective way of utilising the efforts of employees (Friedman, 1977, Edwards, 1979).

Continuing doubts about de-skilled and tightly controlled work and the recognition of its inappropriateness to many work and labour market circumstances brings us back to Maslow and the significance we noted earlier of his recognition of the changing expectations that would be coming forward for workers in increasingly affluent sections of fast developing economies. As Cam Toon remembered from his management classes, Herzberg turned the Maslow principle into some specific job design practices: *job enrichment*.

> **Job enrichment** — *Concept*
>
> The expansion of the scope of jobs by such means as the re-integration of maintenance or inspection tasks; an extension of the work cycle; an increased degree of delegation of decision making by job holders.

Herzberg (1966) argued that what were frequently taken to be work incentives or 'motivators' – pay, good working conditions and good relationships with supervisors – were no longer motivators at all. They were, rather, 'hygiene factors' – conditions that had to be fulfilled before motivation would actually happen. And the rewards that would lead to this 'motivation' were ones such as achievement, recognition and, especially, the satisfaction coming from the job itself. Jobs should thus have more variety and responsibility built into them. Job enrichment would see the scope of jobs increased. The argument, in effect, was that managers should 'redesign' jobs along these lines to meet the rising expectations of modern employees.

But what about the social or group dimension of work design? The Hawthorne research referred to earlier (p. 12) had stressed the importance to employees of the social aspects of work and Maslow included 'social needs' in his scheme, albeit at a lower level than the rather idealised 'self-actualisation' notion that Herzberg tried to turn into something practicable. Mayo saw workers being 'tied into' the employing organisation via their location in meaningful groups of fellow workers. Maslow argued that people would look for social needs to be met at work once their lower level needs had been satisfied. However, other advantages of making groups or 'teams' central to work (re)design were stressed by British researchers working with the Tavistock Institute of Human Relations (Rice, 1958, Trist *et al.*, 1963). It was argued that work organisations should be regarded as *socio-technical systems*.

> **Socio-technical systems** — *Concept*
>
> An approach to work design in which the technical and the social/psychological aspects of the overall workplace are given equal weight and are designed at the same time to *take each other into account*.

The Tavistock researchers noted that, typically, the technical aspects of a work enterprise tended to be designed first: the buildings, hardware and the layout of both of these is 'blueprinted' first and a set of social arrangements then designed to slot into it. What would be more effective, the Tavistock writers argue, would be for the technical and the social components of the overall system to be designed simultaneously and for them to take each other into account.

Activity 8.5

Reread the story 'Walt and Roger develop a greenfield site' (Case 7.2, p. 262) and consider the extent to which it could be said that Roger is following socio-technical system principles in suggesting how he and Walt should go about designing both the physical/technical aspects of their new organisation and the social/cultural aspects.

Roger closely follows the principles that socio-technical thinking would suggest appropriate for both organisation and job design. He very effectively persuades Walt that organisation design should consider social and cultural factors, on the one hand, and technical and physical factors on the other hand, *at the same time* – the one taking the other into account. This would mean that when the 'system' is operating these two aspects of it – the 'socio' and the 'technical' – would *fit* with each other. Walt's approach of setting up the 'technical' aspect first and then 'adding people onto it' would lead to real difficulties once the site was operating, Roger persuaded him. At the level of job design, the same principles should be followed according to the Tavistock researchers. In setting up an office or workshop, the technical tasks (together with the desks or machines associated with the tasks) should be grouped together to form a logical 'whole task' that can then be performed by members of the group with minimal supervisory interference. We thus get a *semi-autonomous workgroup* in which a group of people possesses all the necessary skills and all the necessary equipment to manage themselves in, say, the assembly of a motor car. Or, we might see a group of staff take charge, as a team, of producing a company's in-house magazine. Members of the team would share out among themselves and jointly coordinate tasks ranging from the collection of stories to the assembling of the pages on a desktop publishing system.

Teamworking/semi-autonomous workgroups   *Concept*

The grouping of individual jobs to focus work activities on a *whole task*, with team members being fully trained and equipped so that they can be given discretion, as a group, over how the task is completed.

With this example of the 'self-managed' group of staff who produced their company's house magazine we see something that might be labelled 'a semi-autonomous workgroup' or put forward as an example either of 'teamworking' or 'high performance work design'. Labels change in the managerial world as fast as they do in the world of fashion clothing. Something close to what we see modern companies celebrate as highly innovative 'high performance teams' or 'cellular manufacture' might well have been seen in certain craft groups producing goods way back in the middle ages, albeit producing much simpler products or services. A detailed division of labour and tight direct control managerial supervision and surveillance has played a central part in the vast increases in wealth and welfare that industrial capitalism has brought about. But to de-skill and tightly control work task performance is to wield a double-edged sword. It can cut both ways: sometimes helping the managers of employing organisations to fulfil their agenda, sometimes hindering them because of the counterproductive 'de-motivating' or 'alienating' tendencies of de-skilled and directly controlled work.

Dilemmas and choices in shaping work tasks and gaining cooperation

Implicit in our review of changing work design principles and job design practices since the industrial revolution is a recognition that there may be circumstances in which certain work design principles are more successful, from a managerial point of view, than in others. For example, it is very likely that Taylor's scientific management practices would be more viable with the unskilled immigrant workers he came across in the nineteenth-century steel mills than they could ever be with well-educated and articulate workers in a modern aerospace company. Similarly, we are not too surprised to see principles very close to those articulated by Taylor proving satisfactory to the managers of a modern company hiring (and firing) relatively young and transient workers to serve hamburgers to a highly standardised recipe in fixed service format across the world (Ritzer, 1993, Royle, 2000). But we would be surprised to see the motivational and job design practices that prove profitable to the high street hamburger restaurant proving to be managerially successful in, say, a university or a city architect's department. There appear to be 'contingencies' that are relevant to managerial decision making in the job design area. These are the circumstances of the organisation, like its size, technology or environmental situation, which have a better 'fit' with certain types of organisational arrangement and culture than with others.

When we applied the contingency insight to general organisational arrangements earlier, it was emphasised that contingencies do not determine organisational arrangements. Managers take into account their interpretations of contingent circumstances when arguing about and negotiating what patterns of organisation they will work towards. So what are the contingent factors that might be relevant to managerial debate within any given organisation about the work design principles that are to be applied?

Activity 8.6

Review the model in Figure 7.4 'Choice and contingency in organisational shaping' (p. 275) and how this was explained in Chapter 7. How do you think the contingencies represented there might be built upon to bring out circumstantial factors directly relevant to job design issues?

The contingency of *organisational size* might be relevant to job design in that having a large number of employees increases the scope for making people's jobs more specialised, whether this is specialisation of the type that leads to the appointment of a company lawyer, say, or the de-skilling type of specialisation that fragments the job of a pin maker. However, the other two contingencies shown in the model are perhaps more significant – those of technology and environmental stability.

The organisation's *technology* is a key job design factor in two closely related ways. First, it defines the tasks that are to be done and the extent to which those tasks are amenable to fragmentation or de-skilling. The technology of brain surgery, for example, does not lend itself to a detailed division of labour in which a succession of single-skilled individuals take their turn at wielding different types of scalpel for different stages of an operation. The technology of high street hamburger cooking and serving, however, lends itself well to such an approach.

The nature of the *environment* within which the organisation operates is also immensely important. We saw in the last chapter that a fast-changing and highly competitive business environment, one that requires frequent innovative action on the part of employees to enable it to survive, finds an 'organic' or loose structure more appropriate to its situation than a tightly bureaucratic one. This clearly implies a need for job designs that do not involve the sort of tight prescription and standardisation that goes with direct control types of job design. There is a tendency therefore for managers to choose indirect control types of job design where there are environmental pressures requiring high levels of innovation or adaptability on the part of employees. There is an obvious incompatibility between asking people to apply high levels of discretion and innovation in their work and expecting them to take detailed orders from a manager and be continually checked up on by a supervisor.

A concept that is often used in this context is that of *flexibility*. It is frequently argued that a move towards indirect control job designs are necessary if workers are to perform flexibly so that an organisation can quickly change what it is doing to cope with competitive pressures. This, however, is only partly true. There are two types of flexibility that managers of organisations look for: flexibility for long-term adaptability and flexibility for short-term predictability.

Flexibility for long-term adaptability *Concept*

The ability to make rapid and effective innovations through the use of job designs and employment policies that encourage people to use their discretion and work in new ways for the sake of the organisation – as circumstances require.

This fits with *indirect control* work design principles and high-trust relationships.

Flexibility for short-term predictability *Concept*

The ability to make rapid changes through the use of job designs and employment policies that allow staff to be easily recruited and trained or easily laid off – as circumstances require.

This fits with *direct control* work design principles and low-trust relationships.

Sometimes organisations will have a predominant need for just one of these types of flexibility. A consultancy organisation would mainly need flexibility for long-term adaptability, for example, and would therefore tend to follow indirect control work design principles across the firm. An organisation in the sugar beet processing industry, with inevitably seasonal patterns of working, on the other hand, would need flexibility for short-term predictability. It would therefore find it more fitting to adopt predominantly direct control job designs. This would not only suit the seasonal need to hire at one time and fire at another; it would also fit with the generally low levels of skills required to apply the technology. And it would fit with the almost non-existent need to innovate and develop the product.

These two cases are relatively straightforward. But, in many organisations, managers find both types of flexibility are required. Sometimes one type of flexibility is relevant to one area of the organisation and the other to another area. This is a circumstance that will be considered later when we look at issues of how job design issues relate to overall issues of how an organisation is to be 'resourced' with inputs of human skill, knowledge and labour. Researchers on innovations in work design have frequently commented on the tendency for the managerial success of these initiatives at a local level to depend on whether or not they were supported by appropriate human resourcing policies at the level of the wider organisation (Buchanan and Preston, 1992). The possibility of organisations needing *dual human resourcing strategies* to cope with different types of flexibility being required in different parts of an organisation will be looked at in Chapter 10, (pp. 426–8).

Human resourcing policies inevitably have to cope with the fundamental contradiction that work design initiatives are always faced with. They must gain commitment and consent from the same employees that they need to 'exploit'. In recent decades of increasing international competition, we can see various employers desperately seeking new ways to handle this tension in order to stay in business – or rather to find new combinations of established work design principles. This has led to work design and human resourcing practices that incorporate novel mixtures of direct and indirect control principles. The *lean production* practices seen in the car industry are an example of this (Womack, Jones and Roos, 1990). 'Leanness' means that no time, effort, or resources are wasted and high psychological commitment to this ruthlessly tight regime is expected from a workforce that is expected to use its discretion in the spaces where this is allowed, always with the benefit of 'the customer' in mind.

Lean production *Concept*

The combining, typically within car assembly, of team working with automated technologies. Workers are required both to initiate 'continual improvements' in quality and to ensure that every task is got 'right first time' and completed to a demanding 'just-in-time' schedule.

A similar combining of direct and indirect control work design and human resourcing principles is seen with *business process re-engineering* (BPR) (Hammer and Champy, 1993; see Further Reading on work restructuring and re-engineering, p. 349). BPR has seen organisations across a range of industries restructured to focus on business *processes* (getting a product designed, manufactured and sold, say). This means turning away from an emphasis on business *functions* (where a design function focuses just on design, a manufacturing function focuses on production and a sales function concentrates just on selling, for example). A clear and integrated flow of processes is thus made possible by the use of advanced information technologies. Employees can be *empowered* and given new degrees of freedom to manage themselves in teams. They are no longer trapped in the separate boxes of functional organisation where managers, planners and schedulers have to direct and coordinate people's efforts to ensure that all the separate tasks and operations 'add up' to the provision of a successful product or service. The clearer logic of the basic process flow means that workers can 'make things add up' for themselves, as Roberto Auldearn's managing director put it when explaining the 'embracing of business process reengineering' at Dovecote Components in Case 8.3.

Business process re-engineering (BPR) — *Concept*

The restructuring of an organisation to focus on business processes rather than on business functions. Advanced management control information technologies are used together with team working and employee 'empowerment'.

Activity 8.7

Read Roberto Auldearn's account in Case 8.3 of how Dovecote Components 'embraced' business process re-engineering.

After looking back once again at the model set out in Figure 7.4 (p. 275), note the ways in which a part was played in this exercise in 'organisational shaping' by:

- contextual political, economic and cultural patterns;
- enacted contingencies;
- managerial values, goals and interests;
- managerial argument, negotiation and choice.

Consider the extent to which we are helped to make sense of this story by the notion of a basic contradiction whereby managers have to gain commitment and consent from the employees at the same time as they are required to exploit and manipulate them.

Re-engineering Dovecote Components   Case 8.3

Dovecote Components has been an important employer in this town for a long time. Most people around here just call it 'The Doocot'. For over 20 years now the workforce has been steadily falling as we have increased investment in newer technologies and found a whole lot of ways of making the work less labour intensive. Productivity was steadily rising over this period and, as a management, we felt freer to make changes without having to fight with trade unions over every little detail. Government policies were partly responsible for this, but the unions – indeed the workforce generally – recognised that we were struggling in an increasingly difficult and increasingly international market place. Almost every year would see some redundancies and there was not a great deal of argument about this. I think people regarded these job losses as a sort of unfortunate fact of life and I don't think they affected morale within the company to any real extent. But people did not realise just how difficult things were going to get as we saw the auto companies that bought our components increasingly looking across the whole global economy to source their production.

About five years ago we realised that we needed to make radical changes in the business. We had been developing our technologies incrementally over the years and had introduced at different times a variety of innovations ranging from quality improvement groups to cellular and team working. A lot of our production is now done on a just-in-time basis. Components go out of the door just a few hours before the car plant 200 miles away needs them to stick in its cars. It was becoming clear to us, however, that there were increasing numbers of other suppliers who could get their products to the factories just as promptly. And not only could they supply at significantly lower prices but several of them were much faster than us at developing and improving their products. Our customers were facing increasing global competition just as we were and were constantly looking to improve the quality and functionality of the components they put in their vehicles.

At the first executive meetings where we talked seriously about making radical changes I put forward a plan to set up a completely new 'Research, Design and Manufacturing Innovation' department. This would be a crack team that I would recruit by head hunting from my quite extensive contacts across the engineering world. It would combine product development and the improving of production methods – making sure we designed for ease of manufacture as well as to delight our customers. Immediately I suggested this I was shot down. The first bloke to 'have a go' didn't bother me. As a management accountant, our finance man was right to look critically at my plans and question how we could possibly afford this. But, like every one else, I knew that he personally disliked me and would attack anything I put forward. It was the MD, Jerry Penick, who really put the boot in however. This did bother me. In the first place, he said, 'there is certainly no way we can afford to do that'. And, 'secondly', he went on, 'your whole philosophy is out of date'. That made me wild. I ranted on about how advanced my 'design for manufacturing' ideas were and that I would easily get a job with one of our competitors if he had so little respect for me. In fact I did slam out of the meeting at one point. I think it was when the Manufacturing Director – a blinkered and territorially minded idiot if ever there was one – made it clear that he wasn't keen for me to get involved in manufacturing issues. The MD came and found me puffing a cigar in the directors' lavatory and persuaded me to go back into the meeting and hear his thoughts on 're-engineering the Doocot'.

It turned out that the consultants that Jerry had brought in six months earlier, 'just to look over things' as he told us, had in fact come up with this scheme to 're-engineer' the processes in Doocot 'from top to bottom'. 'We have got to jump out of our functional boxes and our obsession with departmental boundaries,' he said, looking directly at me and then at my manufacturing colleague. 'Everything has got to be stripped down to the basics and everyone will make their contribution to the basic processes of getting ideas quickly and efficiently through from the drawing board to the customer's delivery bay. The bloke on the drawing board will be as interested in that customer's needs as the driver of the delivery wagon will – or as I will.'

At this stage we were all looking at each other a little shocked. Most of us had heard of this 'business re-engineering' thing, but had not really related it to our situation. Molly, our marketing woman, ventured to say that all the re-engineering cases that she had come across had been more exercises in 'blood letting' and 'axing people as well as departments' than improving processes. 'Well', came back Jerry, 'I don't want any talk like that. But the re-engineering exercise will mean taking quite a big axe to our management structures. Levels will be taken out.' He accepted that 'delayering' and 'becoming leaner' would be painful. The consultants, together with a small senior management team, would 'look at everybody's job' and nobody 'whose job doesn't serve our core processes' would survive. This would be hard and it would 'hurt everybody involved', Jerry said. But those who survived would be much better off. It wasn't just that their jobs would be more secure. Their 'prospects with the firm' would also be better. Above all, people would benefit by being 'more empowered'. He explained that, at present, all the efforts that people put in and all the operations across the plant had to be 'made to add up' by managers, supervisors and other 'functionaries'. By taking a lot of these out, people would be given the satisfaction of 'adding it all up' for themselves. And, he added, by 'taking away all the managerial buffers that exist between the workforce and the market place' people will see the need to 'work hard, conscientiously and cooperatively *for the business and not for their department* because they will know that if they don't we all go under'.

The whole thing seemed sensible, if rather terrifying. For six months the 'Re-engineering Action Group' (RAG), comprising four senior managers and four consultants, were to work 'day and night' with Jerry to 'completely reshape the business'. The business was to be more 'focused' than at present and this basically meant making it smaller. 'We have got too big and unwieldy', Jerry argued, 'so we'll cut the less profitable lines and try to stay at a size where a smallish top management team can keep their eyes on everything.' There would be a major investment in ICT, with the savings made on labour costs more than covering the 'costs of the new computer systems'. The 'software and hardware that are available now for management control', he insisted, 'were sophisticated enough now to cover the work of all the people who will be leaving us – and more'.

So, all of this went ahead. I was lucky to be kept on. But both my Finance Director and Manufacturing Director colleagues – and enemies – got the push. I was on the RAG – the action group charged with 'implementing' the re-engineering. At first I felt privileged. But this feeling soon went. I began to realise quite early on that the whole thing was doomed from the start. We had embraced business process re-engineering in a big way. But we had embraced a monster. In principle, I thought, it was wise. It was harsh. But harsh measures were necessary. And all of those who stayed with the business would experience a much higher level of empowerment and involvement with the core processes of the enterprise. They would clearly benefit. But as we all quickly learned, it wasn't to happen like that, and it's so easy to see why, in retrospect.

In one voice, we were saying that people were to be empowered, to be trusted and were to have their 'energies' released to do 'really meaningful work'. But in another voice we were asking people to kneel down to have their heads chopped off. This is where the massive catch in the whole thing lay. On the one hand we were asking people to be empowered, to manage themselves and be committed to the business. The logic of de-layering was one of saying that an empowered and committed workforce could, in many respects, manage things better than managers could. But on the other hand, we were a group of managers and consultants acting as if we were mighty gods who knew better than anyone how things should be done.

As you can imagine, the whole thing was treated with deep suspicion and bitter hostility from the beginning. And that's just among the managers! We RAG members were treated with utter disdain and mistrust as hypocrites and axe wielders. Because nobody would cooperate with us or give us any information we could trust, we simply could not do the work we were meant to do. But how could we back down? Consequently we made lots of cuts and we reorganised the place from top to bottom without really knowing what we were doing. And, yes, the business has survived. But we are running it through a regime of terror with most of the best staff we had having moved out to other jobs. I give the business a couple more years at most. And I shall be out of here well before that. When you see me next time, I'll have flown the Doocot.

These events at Dovecote Components would not have come about if there had not been major changes in the global economy. The most important contextual pressure is the growth of competition from producers of motor components across the world and the combination of this with car manufacturers choosing to 'source' themselves from a global market place. Relevant nationally is the state's role in reducing the ability of trade unions to resist managerial initiatives. And, at the local level, there appears to be a degree of goodwill towards 'The Doocot'. This goodwill might have helped managers make incremental changes which involved loss of employment over the years. Equally, it is possible that a sense of betrayal of this goodwill may have increased the level of resentment towards management when it came to the radical cuts associated with the business process re-engineering initiative.

These contextual matters influenced the particular *contingencies* that Dovecote managers *enacted* (interpreted and acted with regard to). The instability of the increasingly competitive business environment is obviously the major contingent factor. Jerry Penick has also acted on the basis of his view of technological contingencies. He believes that significantly more effective 'management control' hardware and software is now available to the company, and he has views about the contingency of organisational size, arguing that Dovecote is 'too big and unwieldy'.

Although the big decisions about how to handle the company's difficulties have largely been made by Jerry Penick alone, arguments taking place between the senior managers seem to reflect different value positions and interests among them. Roberto himself puts forward a solution that fits with his personal area of expertise and it is a solution that would have increased his personal influence in the company, we can reasonably infer. It was obviously one that clashed with the interests of the Manufacturing Director, an 'enemy' of Roberto who, apparently, was very 'territorial'. This individual was keen to 'fight his corner' as was Roberto's other 'enemy', the Finance Director. It is difficult to separate the values and the personal interests of the protagonists to these arguments. But it would appear that the Marketing Director brought certain values of concern for human beings into the discussions. It would seem that Jerry, in speaking of the inevitability of 'hurting' some people in order to benefit others, has gone through some internal value debate.

It is Jerry's choice, as the most powerful actor within the management team, to adopt business process re-engineering. However, the resistance to the way this was implemented, especially from other managers across the company, turned out to be so great that the initiative was seriously undermined. What Jerry Penick appears not to have realised was that strategic management has to cope with – or 'manage' – the basic contradictions that underlie all employing organisations. The contradiction between the requirement that managers must exploit or 'use' employees as resources and the requirement that they must win commitment and consent from employees as human beings is badly mismanaged here. The Dovecote management is saying that the changes will benefit the 'survivors' of business process re-engineering. People should therefore commit themselves to the changes. But it is making it clear at the same time that, for the moment, every individual is being considered for possible removal from the firm. Roberto expresses this by referring to the company as speaking with two voices. In one voice, he says, it talks of trust and empowerment, but with the other voice it is effectively asking every individual to 'kneel down' to allow the management to cut off their heads, should the 'Re-engineering Action Group' not see them as fitting into the new, re-engineered scheme of things.

Many organisations have in recent years reacted to the sorts of pressure faced by Dovecote Components by adopting business process re-engineering. And, even by the accounts of leading proponents of the practice, many of these have achieved nothing like the dramatic changes expected. Given the radical nature of the initiative and the way it tends to bring to the surface major underlying tensions this is not surprising.

Matters of the basic structure of economies and of global economic change cannot be separated from managerial efforts to 'motivate' and 'lead' people within organisations or from the initiatives they take to design or 'redesign' jobs – whether they involve minor initiatives or larger radical ones like business process re-engineering (see Further reading on Work restructuring and re-engineering, p. 349). Nevertheless, at the level of the individual manager doing the everyday routine managerial tasks that are the responsibility of the majority of managers across the range of work organisations in both the commercial and the public service sectors these bigger issues may not be at the front of their minds. However, one of the purposes of the present book – in the spirit of critical thinking discussed in Chapter 1 – is to enable everyone involved in organisations to be aware of the relevance of these broader factors. And this is vital for thinking in a strategic manner about how any particular organisation relates to its environment. It is to this aspect of the organising and managing of work that Chapter 9 turns.

Summary

In this chapter the following key points have been made:

- What are often seen as separate 'topics' in the study of organisations and their management – 'motivation', 'leadership' and 'job/work design' – can better be seen as closely related to each other and, also, as closely tied into the wider structural and cultural features of the organisation in which they occur and as influenced by the whole way in which modern societies and economies are organised.

- It is more helpful to look at people's general *orientations to work* rather than to consider their 'work motivation'. A focus on orientations allows a wider range of relevant factors to be taken into account and makes us more aware of how people think about their work, and what they are prepared to do, and can change as circumstances change.

- The very notion of a 'theory of motivation' is a questionable and potentially unrealisable one. Such a theory would, in effect, be a theory of 'why people do what they do'. However, useful insights have been developed about the role of perceptions of 'equity' and the role of 'expectancies' in shaping work behaviour under the 'motivation theory' banner. These insights can be incorporated into a process-relational way of thinking.

- There are two main principles of *work design* – direct control and indirect control principles – which can be drawn on when managers engage in specific *job design* work. These two sets of principles, the first of which operates with a logic of de-skilling and the latter with a logic of 'enriching' jobs in skill and responsibility terms, have been applied in different ways at different times across the history of industrialised societies.

- The application of these principles, and how it varies with circumstances and the ways in which managers 'enact' contingent circumstances, can be understood in terms of managerial attempts to cope with the underlying contradictions in the organisation of work and employment in modern societies. Managers need to control and manipulate employees as resources and, at the same time, win a degree of consent and commitment to the enterprise from them as human beings. Problems that can arise with the recently popular managerial initiative of *business process re-engineering* can be understood in terms of managerial struggles to handle these fundamental tensions.

Recommended reading

On the very specific matter of motivation theories and how students relate to them, the Tony Watson study, 'Motivation: that's Maslow, isn't it' (*Management Learning* 27(4): 447–464, 1996; also in C. Grey and E. Antonacopoulu (eds) *Essential Reading in Management Learning*, London: Sage, 2004) can, its author hopes, be entertaining as well as challenging to current teaching and learing practices. And on the broader matter of the trends occurring in the way work is organised and tasks designed, perhaps the most effective way to get an overview is to look at and read selectively from *The Oxford Handbook of Work and Organization* edited by Steve Ackroyd, Rosemary Blatt, Paul Thompson and Pamela Tolbert (Oxford: Oxford University Press, 2004). Also valuable here is David Knights' and Darren McCabe's *Organization and Innovation: Guru schemes and American dreams* (Maidenhead: Open University Press, 2003).

Further reading

Further reading Motivation theories

Adams, J.S. (1963) 'Towards an understanding of inequity', *Journal of Abnormal and Social Psychology*, 67: 422–436

Adams, J.S. (1965) 'Inequity in social exchange' in L. Berkovitz (ed.) *Advances in Experimental Social Psychology, Vol. 2*, New York: Academic Press

Ambrose, M.L. and Kulik, C.T. (1999) 'Old friends, new faces: motivation research in the 1990s', *Journal of Management*, 25(3): 231–292

Carter, P. and Jackson, N. (1993) 'Modernism, postmodernism and motivation, or why expectancy theory failed to live up to expectation' in J. Hassard and M. Parker (eds) *Postmodernism and Organisations*, London: Sage

Maslow, A. (1943) 'A theory of human motivation', *Psychological Review*, 50: 37–96

Maslow, A. (1954) *Motivation and Personality*, New York; Harper and Row

Maslow, A. (1968) *Towards a Psychology of Being*, Princeton, NJ: Van Nostrand

McGregor, D.C. (1960) *The Human Side of Enterprise*, New York: McGraw-Hill

Rauschenberger, J., Schmitt, N. and Hunter, T.E. (1980) 'A test of the need hierarchy concept', *Administrative Science Quarterly*, 25(4): 654–670

Vroom, V.H. (1964) *Work and Motivation*, New York: Wiley

Watson, T.J. (1996) 'Motivation: that's Maslow, isn't it?', *Management Learning*, 27(4): 447–464

Further reading Work design, empowerment and teams

Babbage, C. (1832) *On the Economy of Machinery and Manufacture*, London: Charles Knight

Barker, J.R. (1993) 'Tightening the iron cage: concertive control in self-managing teams', *Administrative Science Quarterly*, 38: 408–437.

Barker, J.R. (1999) *The Discipline of Teamwork*, London: Sage

Becker, B. and Huselid, M. (1998) 'High performance work systems and firm performance: a synthesis of research and managerial implications', *Research in Personnel and Human Resources*, 16(1): 53–101

Belbin, M. (1993) *Team Roles at Work*, Oxford: Butterworth-Heinemann

Benders, J. and Van Hootegem, G. (1999) 'Teams and their context: moving the team discussion beyond existing dichotomies', *Journal of Management Studies*, 36(5): 609–628

Braverman, H. (1974) *Labor and Monopoly Capital*, New York: Monthly Review Press

Buchanan, D.A. (1994) 'Cellular manufacture and the role of teams' in J. Storey (ed.) *New Wave Manufacturing Strategies: Organisational and human resource management dimensions*, London: Paul Chapman, 204–225

Buchanan, D.A. (2000) 'An eager and enduring embrace: the ongoing rediscovery of teamworking as a management idea' in S. Procter and F. Mueller (eds) *Teamworking*, Basingstoke: Macmillan

Buchanan, D. and Preston, D. (1992) 'Life in the cell: supervision and teamwork in a "manufacturing systems engineering" environment', *Human Resource Management Journal*, 2(4): 55–76

Burawoy, M. (1979) *Manufacturing Consent: Changes in the labour process under monopoly capitalism*, Chicago, IL: Chicago University Press

Edwards, R. (1979) *Contested Terrain*, London: Heinemann

Friedman, A.L. (1977) *Industry and Labour*, London: Macmillan

Guzzo, R.A. and Dickson, M.W. (1998) 'Teams in organizations: recent research on performance and effectiveness', *Annual Review of Psychology*, 49: 307–338

Hackman, J.R. and Oldham, G.R. (1980) *Work Redesign*, New York: Addison Wesley

Hampton, M.M. (1999) 'Work groups' in Y. Gabriel (ed.) *Organizations in Depth*, London: Sage, 112–138

Harley, B. (2001) 'Team membership and the experience of work in Britain: an analysis of the WERS98 data', *Work, Employment and Society*, 15(4): 721–742

Herzberg, F. (1966) *Work and the Nature of Man*, Chicago, IL: World Publishing Co.

Marchington, M. (1992) *Managing the Team*, Oxford: Blackwell

Parker, S. and Wall, T. (1998) *Job and Work Design: Organizing work to promote well-being and effectiveness*, London: Sage

Pollert, A. (1988) 'Dismantling flexibility', *Capital and Class*, 34: 42–75

Pollert, A. (ed.) (1991) *Farewell to Flexibility?*, Oxford: Blackwell

Procter, S. and Ackroyd, S. (2001) 'Flexibility' in T. Redman and A. Wilkinson (eds) *Contemporary Human Resource Management*, Harlow: FT Prentice Hall

Procter, S. and Mueller, F. (eds) (2000) *Teamworking*, Basingstoke: Macmillan

Procter, S. and Mueller, F. (2000) 'Teamworking, strategy, structure, systems and culture' in S. Procter and F. Mueller (eds) *Teamworking*, Basingstoke: Macmillan, 3–24

Royle, T. (2000) *Working for McDonald's in Europe: The Unequal Struggle*, London: Routledge

Sinclair, A. (1992) 'The tyranny of team ideology', *Organization Studies*, 13(4): 611–626

Smith, A. (1974) *The Wealth of Nations*, Harmondsworth: Penguin (originally 1776)

Smith, C. and Thompson, P. (1998) 'Re-evaluating the labour process debate', *Economic and Industrial Democracy*, 19(4): 551–577

Taylor, F.W. (1911) *The Principles of Scientific Management*, New York: Harper

Trist, E.L., Higgin, G.W., Murray, H. and Pollock, A.B. (1963) *Organisational Choice*, London: Tavistock

Watson, T.J. (1986) *Management, Organisation and Employment Strategy*, London: Routledge

Watson, T.J. and Rosborough, J. (1999) 'Teamworking and the management of flexibility: local and social-structural tensions in high performance work design initiatives' in S. Procter and F. Mueller (eds) *Teamworking*, Basingstoke: Macmillan

Womack, J.P., Jones, D.J. and Roos, D. (1990) *The Machine that Changed the World*, New York: Rawson

Wood, S. and Albanese, M. (1995) 'Can we speak of high commitment management on the shop floor?', *Journal of Management Studies*, 32(2): 215–247

Further reading Work restructuring and re-engineering

Ackroyd, S., Batt, R., Thompson, P. and Tolbert, P.S. (eds) (2004) *The Oxford Handbook of Work and Organization*, Oxford: Oxford University Press

Buchanan, D.A. (1997) 'The limitations and opportunities of business process re-engineering in a politicised organizational climate', *Human Relations*, 50(1): 51–72

Burke, R. and Cooper, C.L. (2000) *The Organization in Crisis: Downsizing, restructuring and privatisation*, Oxford: Blackwell

Champy, J. (1996) *Reengineering Management: The mandate for new leadership*, New York: Harper Business

Davenport, T. (1993) *Process Innovation: Reengineering work through information technology*, Boston, MA: Harvard Business School Press

Grey, C. and Mitev, N. (1995) 'Reengineering organizations: a critical appraisal', *Personnel Review*, 24(1): 6–18

Grint, K. and Willcocks, L. (1995) 'Business process re-engineering in theory and practice: business Paradise regained?', *New Technology: Work and Employment*, 10(2): 99–108

Hammer, M. and Champy, J. (1993) *Reengineering the Corporation*, London: Nicholas Brealey

Hammer, M. and Stanton, S. (1995) *The Reengineering Revolution: A handbook*, New York: Harper Business Press

Knights, D. and McCabe, D. (2003) *Organization and Innovation: Guru schemes and American dreams*, Maidenhead: Open University Press

Knights, D. and Willmott, H. (eds) (2000) *The Reengineering Revolution: Critical studies of corporate change*, London: Sage

Redman, T. and Wilkinson, A. (2001) 'Downsizing' in T. Redman and A. Wilkinson (eds) *Contemporary Human Resource Management*, Harlow: FT Prentice Hall

Storey, J. (ed.) (1993) *New Wave Manufacturing Strategies*, London: Chapman

Wilkinson, A. and Willmott, H. (eds) (1995) *Making Quality Critical: New perspectives on organizational change*, London: Routledge

Wilkinson, A., Redman, T., Snape, E. and Marchington, M. (1998) *Managing with Total Quality Management: Theory and practice*, Basingstoke, Macmillan

Willmott, H. (1994) Business process re-engineering and human resource management, *Personnel Review*, 23(3): 34–46

Willmott, H. (1995) 'The odd couple?: re-engineering business processes; managing human relations', *New Technology; Work and Employment*, 10(2): 89–98

WORKING TOGETHER – TEAM WORKING

6 WORK GROUPS AND TEAMS

Groups and teams are a major feature of organisational life. The work organisation and its sub-units are made up of groups of people. Most activities of the organisation require at least some degree of co-ordination through the operation of groups and teamwork. An understanding of the nature of groups is vital if the manager is to influence the behaviour of people in the work situation. Attention should be given to the analysis of behaviour of individuals in group situations and to their effective performance. The manager needs to be aware of the interactions and operation of work groups and teams.

Learning outcomes

After completing this chapter you should be able to:

- explain the meaning and importance of work groups and teams;
- distinguish between groups and teams, and between formal and informal groups;
- explain the main reasons for the formation of groups and teams;
- examine factors which influence group cohesiveness and performance;
- analyse the nature of role relationships and role conflict;
- detail member roles, and group functions and interactions;
- review the importance of, and influences on, successful teamwork.

Critical reflection

'People value their individuality and enjoy the right of self-expression. Membership of a group means giving up some of that personal identity. The real skill of management is therefore to make full use of people's individuality for the mutual benefit of the group as a whole.'

If you were a manager how would you attempt to achieve this balance?

THE MEANING AND IMPORTANCE OF GROUPS AND TEAMS

Work is a group-based activity and if the organisation is to function effectively it requires collaboration and co-operation among its members. **Groups** are an essential feature of any organisation. Individuals seldom work in isolation from others. Although there is no single accepted definition, most people will readily understand what constitutes a group. The essential feature is that its members regard themselves as belonging to the group. A popular definition defines the group in psychological terms as:

> *any number of people who (1) interact with one another; (2) are psychologically aware of one another; and (3) perceive themselves to be a group.*[1]

Another useful way of defining a work group is a collection of people who share most, if not all, of the following characteristics:

- a definable membership;
- group consciousness;
- a sense of shared purpose;
- interdependence;
- interaction;
- ability to act in a unitary manner.[2]

Groups are a characteristic of all social situations and almost everyone in an organisation will be a member of one or more groups. The working of groups and the influence they exert over their membership is an essential feature of human behaviour and of organisational performance. Members of a group must co-operate in order for work to be carried out, and managers themselves will work within these groups. People in groups influence each other in many ways and groups may develop their own hierarchies and leaders. Group pressures can have a major influence over the behaviour of individual members and their work performance.

DIFFERENCES BETWEEN GROUPS AND TEAMS

The use of the word 'teams' has become increasingly fashionable in recent years. *Crainer* refers to the use of 'teamworking' as a side effect of increasing concentration on working across functional divides and fits neatly with the trend towards empowerment. However, despite the extensive literature about teams and teamworking, the basic dynamics of teamworking often remain clouded and uncertain.

> *Teams occur when a number of people have a common goal and recognise that their personal success is dependent on the success of others. They are all interdependent. In practice, this means that in most teams people will contribute individual skills many of which will be different. It also means that the full tensions and counter-balance of human behaviour will need to be demonstrated in the team.*[3]

In common usage and literature, including to some extent in this book, there is a tendency for the terms 'groups' and 'teams' to be used interchangeably. It is not easy to distinguish clearly between a group and a team. According to *ACAS*: 'the term "team" is used loosely to describe many different groupings and a variety of labels are given to the types of teams. It is doubtful whether any definitions of types of teams would be universally acceptable.'[4]

According to *Holpp*, while many people are still paying homage to teams, teamwork, empowerment and self-management, others have become disillusioned. Holpp poses the question: What are teams? 'It's a simple enough question, but one that's seldom asked. We all think we know intuitively what teams are. Guess again. Here are some questions to help define team configurations.'

- Are teams going to be natural work groups, or project-and-task oriented?
- Will they be self-managed or directed?

- How many people will be on the teams; who's in charge?
- How will the teams fit into the organisation's structure if it shows only boxes and not circles or other new organisational forms?

Holpp also poses the question: Why do you want teams?

> If teams are just a convenient way to group under one manager a lot of people who used to work for several downsized supervisors, don't bother. But if teams can truly take ownership of work areas and provide the kind of up-close knowledge that's unavailable elsewhere, then full speed ahead.[5]

Teamwork a fashionable term

Cane suggests that organisations are sometimes unsure whether they have teams or simply groups of people working together.

> It is certainly true to say that any group of people who do not know they are a team cannot be one. To become a team, a group of individuals needs to have a strong common purpose and to work towards that purpose rather than individually. They need also to believe that they will achieve more by co-operation than working individually.[6]

Whereas all teams are, by definition, groups, it does not necessarily follow that all groups are teams.

Belbin points out that to the extent that teamwork was becoming a fashionable term, it began to replace the more usual reference to groups and every activity was now being described as 'teamwork'. He questions whether it matters whether one is talking about groups or teams and maintains that the confusion in vocabulary should be addressed if the principles of good teamwork are to be retained. Belbin suggests there are several factors that characterise the difference between groups and teams (*see* Figure 6.1). The best differentiator is size: groups can comprise any number of people, but teams are smaller with a membership between (ideally) four and six. The quintessential feature of a small, well-balanced team is that leadership is shared or rotates whereas large groups typically throw up solo leaders.[7]

While acknowledging the work of Belbin it appears that the term 'group' is often used in a more general sense and 'team' in a more specific context. We continue to refer to 'group' or 'team' according to the particular focus of attention and the vocabulary of the quoted authors.

Figure 6.1 Differences between a team and a group

	Team	Group
Size	Limited	Medium or large
Selection	Crucial	Immaterial
Leadership	Shared or rotating	Solo
Perception	Mutual knowledge understanding	Focus on leader
Style	Role spread co-ordination	Convergence conformism
Spirit	Dynamic interaction	Togetherness persecution of opponents

Source: Belbin, R. M. *Beyond the Team*, Butterworth-Heinemann (2000). Copyright © 2000. Reproduced with permission from Elsevier Ltd.

Another possible distinction is based on the development and maturity of the 'group'. For example, in terms of Tuckman's model (discussed later in this chapter), not until a group proceeds beyond the stages of forming, norming and storming and successfully reaches the performing stage does it become a team.

GROUP VALUES AND NORMS

The classical approach to organisation and management tended to ignore the importance of groups and the social factors at work. The ideas of people such as F. W. Taylor popularised the concept of the 'rabble hypothesis' and the assumption that people carried out their work, and could be motivated, as solitary individuals unaffected by others. The human relations approach, however (discussed in Chapter 2), gave recognition to the work organisation as a social organisation and to the importance of the group, and group values and norms, in influencing behaviour at work.

One experiment involved the observation of a group of 14 men working in the bank wiring room. The men formed their own sub-groups or cliques, with natural leaders emerging with the consent of the members. Despite a financial incentive scheme where workers could receive more money the more work they did, the group decided on 6,000 units a day as a fair level of output. This was well below the level they were capable of producing. Group pressures on individual workers were stronger than financial incentives offered by management.

Informal social relations

The group developed its own pattern of informal social relations and codes and practices ('norms') of what constituted proper group behaviour.

- **Not to be a 'rate buster'** – not to produce at too high a rate of output compared with other members or to exceed the production restriction of the group.
- **Not to be a 'chiseller'** – not to shirk production or to produce at too low a rate of output compared with other members of the group.
- **Not to be a 'squealer'** – not to say anything to the supervisor or management which might be harmful to other members of the group.
- **Not to be 'officious'** – people with authority over members of the group, for example inspectors, should not take advantage of their seniority or maintain a social distance from the group.

The group had their own system of sanctions including sarcasm, damaging completed work, hiding tools, playing tricks on the inspectors and ostracising those members who did not conform with the **group norms**. Threats of physical violence were also made and the group developed a system of punishing offenders by 'binging', which involved striking someone a fairly hard blow on the upper part of the arm. This process of binging also became a recognised method of controlling conflict within the group.

According to *Riches*, one way to improve team performance is to establish agreed norms or rules for how the team is to operate and rigorously stick to them. Norms could address the obligations of individual members to the team, how it will assess its performance, how it will work together, what motivation systems will be used, how it will relate to customers, and the mechanisms to facilitate an honest exchange about the team norms and behaviour.[8]

FORMAL AND INFORMAL GROUPS

Groups are deliberately planned and created by management as part of the formal organisation structure. However, groups will also arise from social processes and the informal organisation.

The informal organisation arises from the interaction of people working within the organisation and the development of groups with their own relationships and norms of behaviour, irrespective of those defined within the formal structure. This leads to a major distinction between formal and informal groups.

Formal groups

Groups are formed as a consequence of the pattern of organisation structure and arrangements for the division of work, for example, the grouping together of common activities into sections. Groups may result from the nature of technology employed and the way in which work is carried out, for example the bringing together of a number of people to carry out a sequence of operations on an assembly line. Groups may also develop when a number of people of the same level or status within the organisation see themselves as a group, for example, departmental heads of an industrial organisation or chief officers of a local authority. **Formal groups** are created to achieve specific organisational objectives and are concerned with the **co-ordination of work activities**. People are brought together on the basis of defined roles within the structure of the organisation. The nature of the tasks to be undertaken is a predominant feature of the formal group. Goals are identified by management, and certain rules, relationships and norms of behaviour established.

Formal groups tend to be relatively permanent, although there may be changes in actual membership. However, temporary formal groups may also be created by management, for example, the use of project teams in a matrix organisation. Formal work groups can be differentiated in a number of ways, for example on the basis of membership, the task to be performed, the nature of technology, or position within the organisation structure.

Virtuoso teams

Boynton and Fischer draw attention to '**virtuoso teams**' that are formed specifically for big change in organisations. They are comprised of individual superstars or virtuosos with a single clear, ambitious mandate and are not intended to remain together over multiple initiatives or projects. Virtuoso teams require a special kind of leadership and to be managed in a manner that unleashes the maximum contribution from each individual superstar. Although most organisations rarely form such teams, they are required for radical change opportunities that represent a significant departure from prior practice and/or how an organisation conducts its business. Examples of big changes that represented a virtuoso team are the Manhattan Project, Thomas Edison's inventory factory and Roald Amundsen's polar expedition.[9]

Informal groups

The formal structure of the organisation, and system of role relationships, rules and procedures, will always be augmented by interpretation and development at the informal level. **Informal groups** are based more on personal relationships and agreement of group members than on defined role relationships. They serve to satisfy psychological and social needs not related necessarily to the tasks to be undertaken. Groups may devise ways of attempting to satisfy members' affiliation and other social motivations lacking in the work situation. Membership of informal groups can cut across the formal structure. They may comprise individuals from different parts of the organisation and/or from different levels of the organisation, both vertically and diagonally, as well as from the same horizontal level. An informal group could also be the same as the formal group, or it might comprise a part only of the formal group (*see* Figure 6.2).

Members of an informal group may appoint their own leader who exercises authority by the consent of the members themselves. The informal leader may be chosen as the person who reflects the attitudes and values of the members, helps to resolve conflict, leads the group in satisfying its goals, or liaises with management or other people outside the group.

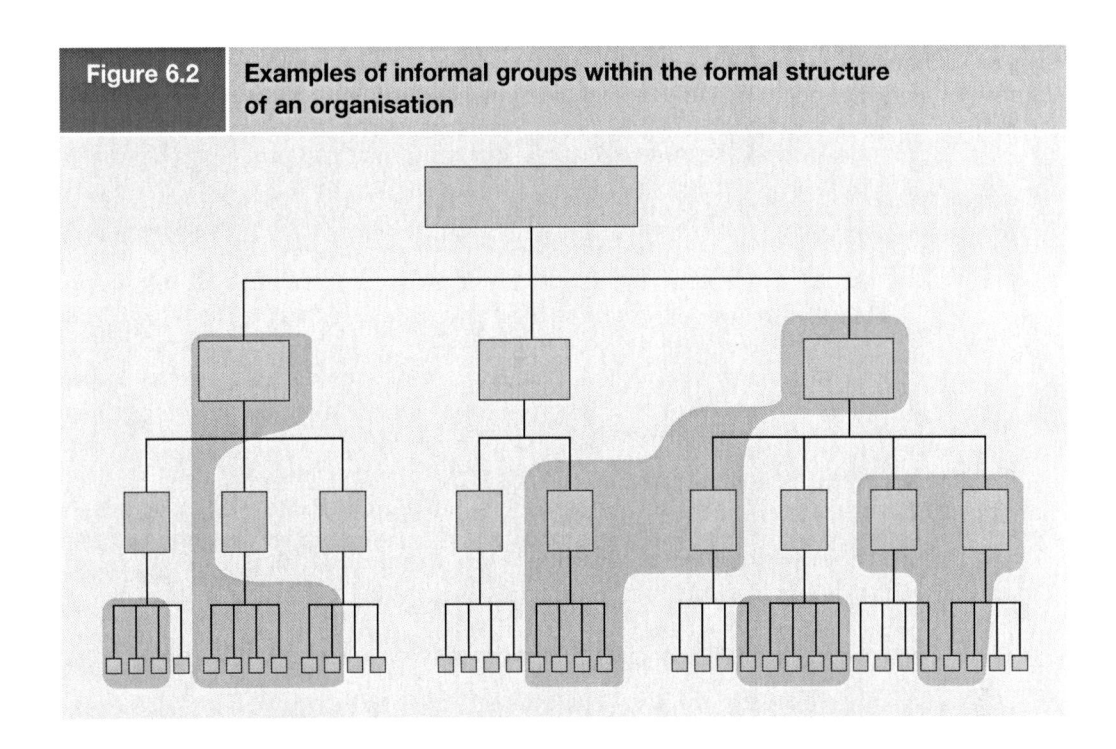

| Figure 6.2 | Examples of informal groups within the formal structure of an organisation |

The informal leader may often change according to the particular situation facing the group. Although not usually the case, it is possible for the informal leader to be the same person as the formal leader appointed officially by management.

Major functions of informal groups

Lysons suggests four main reasons for informal groups.

- **The perpetuation of the informal group 'culture'.** Culture in this context means a set of values, norms and beliefs which form a guide to group acceptance and group behaviour. Unless you broadly subscribe to the group culture, you will not belong and will be an 'outsider' or 'isolate'.
- **The maintenance of a communication system.** Groups want all the information that affects their welfare, either negatively or positively. If groups are not apprised of policies and motives behind actions, they will seek to tap into formal communication channels and spread information among group members.
- **The implementation of social control.** Conformity to group culture is enforced by such techniques as ridicule, ostracism and violence. This is illustrated, for example, by the enforcement of group norms in the bank wiring room discussed above.
- **The provision of interest and fun in work life.** Many jobs are monotonous and fail to hold workers' attention. Work may also offer few prospects. Workers may try to compensate by interpersonal relations provided by the group and in such activities as time-wasting by talking, gambling, practical joking and drinking.[10]

> We humans are a gregarious lot. We like to gather together and establish our own social networks, which are often the real key to creativity and innovation in organisations . . . But many managers are unaware that seemingly pointless social networking does in fact play a crucial part in the way people interact with each other and get work done.
>
> Sue Law, 'Beyond the Water Cooler'[11]

An example of informal groups

A lack of direction and clear information flow within the formal structure can give rise to uncertainty and suspicion. In the absence of specific knowledge, the grapevine takes on an important role, rumours start and the informal part of the organisation is highlighted, often with negative results. A typical example concerned an industrial organisation in a highly competitive market and experiencing a drop in sales. Two top managers had suddenly lost their jobs without any apparent explanation and there were board meetings seemingly every other day. Although there was no specific information or statements from top management, the general feeling among the staff was that whatever was about to happen was most unlikely to be good news.

At lunchtime three junior members of staff, one female and two male, each from different departments, were having a chat. With a half smile the female member said to the others that she could well be seeing a lot more of both or at least one of them before long. She said that she had heard, unofficially, from her manager that the department was about to be awarded a very profitable order. She surmised that other departments, which she had also heard had lost their parts of the same contracts and not had many orders recently, would have to integrate into the successful department with the possible loss of certain jobs. The other two members both believed this and talked about it within their own departments as if it were a fact. The result? Even more uncertainty throughout the organisation, increased gloom and distraction from the task. In fact, no such integration did take place, only a minor restructuring of the organisation with no direct loss of jobs other than through voluntary early retirement. However, it proved very difficult for top management to effectively quash the rumour and restore trust and morale.

REASONS FOR FORMATION OF GROUPS OR TEAMS

Individuals will form into groups or teams, both formal and informal, for a number of reasons.

- **Certain tasks can be performed only through the combined efforts of a number of individuals working together**. The variety of experience and expertise among members provides a synergetic effect that can be applied to the increasingly complex problems of modern organisations.
- **Collusion between members** in order to modify formal working arrangements more to their liking – for example, by sharing or rotating unpopular tasks. Membership therefore provides the individual with opportunities for initiative and creativity.
- **Companionship and a source of mutual understanding and support from colleagues**. This can help in solving work problems and also to militate against stressful or demanding working conditions.
- **Membership provides the individual with a sense of belonging**. It provides a feeling of identity and the chance to acquire role recognition and status within the group or team. (See the discussion on social identity theory later in this chapter.)
- **Guidelines on generally acceptable behaviour**. It helps to clarify ambiguous situations such as the extent to which official rules and regulations are expected to be adhered to in practice, the rules of the game and what is seen as the correct actual behaviour. The informal organisation may put pressure on members to resist demands from management on such matters as higher output or changes in working methods. Allegiance to the group or team can serve as a means of control over individual behaviour and individuals who contravene the norms are disciplined – for example, the process of 'binging' in the bank wiring room, mentioned above.
- **Protection for its membership**. Group or team members collaborate to protect their interests from outside pressures or threats.

Individuals have varying expectations of the benefits from group membership, relating to both work performance and social processes. However, working in groups may mean that members spend too much time talking among themselves rather than doing. Groups may also compete against each other in a non-productive manner. It is a question of balance. It is important, therefore, that the manager understands the reasons for the formation of groups and is able to recognise likely advantageous or adverse consequences for the organisation.

GROUP COHESIVENESS AND PERFORMANCE

Social interaction is a natural feature of human behaviour, but ensuring harmonious working relationships and effective teamwork is not an easy task. The manager's main concern is that members of a work group co-operate in order to achieve the results expected of them. Co-operation among members is likely to be greater in a united, cohesive group. Membership of a cohesive group can be a rewarding experience for the individual, can contribute to the promotion of morale and aid the release of creativity and energy. Members of a high-morale group are more likely to think of themselves as a group and work together effectively. Strong and cohesive work groups can, therefore, have beneficial effects for the organisation. There are many factors which affect group cohesiveness and performance that can be summarised under four broad headings, as shown in Figure 6.3.

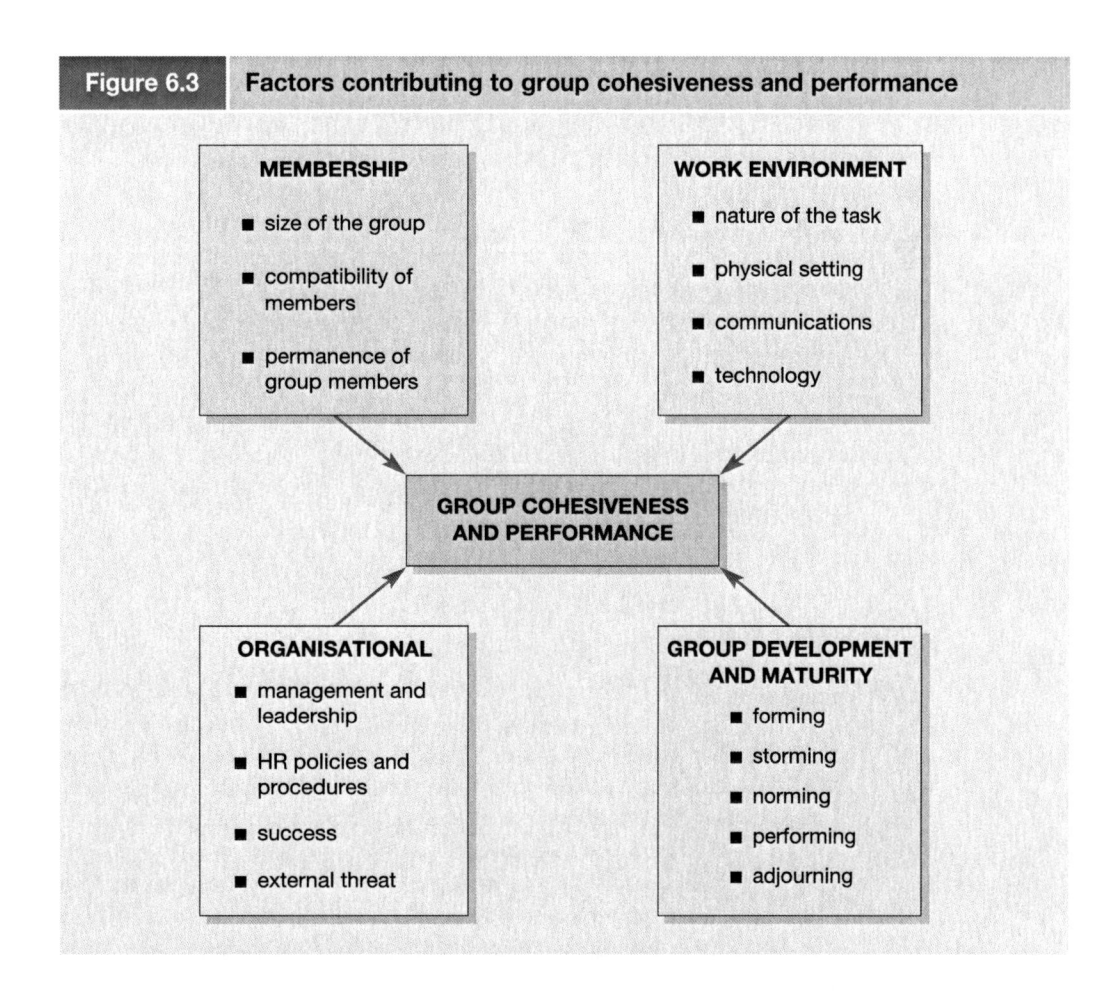

Figure 6.3 Factors contributing to group cohesiveness and performance

MEMBERSHIP
- size of the group
- compatibility of members
- permanence of group members

WORK ENVIRONMENT
- nature of the task
- physical setting
- communications
- technology

GROUP COHESIVENESS AND PERFORMANCE

ORGANISATIONAL
- management and leadership
- HR policies and procedures
- success
- external threat

GROUP DEVELOPMENT AND MATURITY
- forming
- storming
- norming
- performing
- adjourning

MEMBERSHIP

Size of the group

As a group increases in size, problems arise with communications and co-ordination. Large groups are more difficult to handle and require a higher level of supervision. Absenteeism also tends to be higher in larger groups. When a group becomes too large it may split into smaller units and friction may develop between the sub-groups.

It is difficult to put a precise figure on the ideal size of a work group and there are many conflicting studies and reports. Much will depend upon other variables, but it seems to be generally accepted that cohesiveness becomes more difficult to achieve when a group exceeds 10–12 members.[12] Beyond this size the group tends to split into sub-groups. A figure of between five and seven is often quoted as an apparent optimum size for full participation within the group. Many readers will be familiar with the classic 1957 movie *Twelve Angry Men* in which one juror persuades the other 11 to change their minds over a murder verdict. This drew attention to a range of intra-group conflicts and the difficulty in groups of more than ten people attempting to reach consensus.

Cane asks the question: how many people should be in a team?

> *The answers from different organisations as to what is the perfect number vary from between four and fifteen depending on a whole range of variables. Fifteen is about the maximum number of people anyone can communicate with without having to raise their voice significantly and any less than four has a restriction in the amount of creativity and variety that can be produced. It is interesting to note that these figures range between the maximum and minimum numbers of sports teams – perhaps less of a coincidence than it seems.*[13]

Compatibility of the members

The more homogeneous the group in terms of such features as shared backgrounds, interests, attitudes and values of its members, the easier it is usually to promote cohesiveness. Variations in other individual differences, such as the personality or skills of members, may serve to complement each other and help make for a cohesive group. However, such differences may be the cause of disruption and conflict. Conflict can also arise in a homogeneous group where members are in competition with each other. Individual incentive payment schemes, for example, may be a source of conflict.

Permanence of group members

Group spirit and relationships take time to develop. Cohesiveness is more likely when members of a group are together for a reasonable length of time and changes occur only slowly. A frequent turnover of members is likely to have an adverse effect on morale and on the cohesiveness of the group.

WORK ENVIRONMENT

The nature of the task

Where workers are involved in similar work, share a common task or face the same problems, this may assist cohesiveness. The nature of the task may serve to bring people together when it is necessary for them to communicate and interact regularly with each other in the performance of their duties – for example, members of a research and development team. Even if members of a group normally work at different locations they may still experience a feeling of cohesiveness if the nature of the task requires frequent communication and interaction – for example, security guards patrolling separate areas who need to check with each other on a regular basis. However, where the task demands a series of relatively separate operations or discrete activities – for example, on a machine-paced assembly line – it is more difficult to develop cohesiveness. Individuals may have interactions with colleagues on either side of them, but little opportunity to develop a common group feeling.

Physical setting

Where members of a group work in the same location or in close physical proximity to each other, this will generally help cohesiveness. However, this is not always the case. For example, in large open-plan offices staff often tend to segregate themselves from colleagues and create barriers through the strategic siting of such items as filing cabinets, bookcases or indoor plants. The size of the office and the number of staff in it are, of course, important considerations in this case. Isolation from other groups of workers will also tend to build cohesiveness. This often applies to a smaller number of workers on a night shift.

Communications

The more easily members can communicate freely with each other, the greater the likelihood of group cohesiveness. Communications are affected by the work environment, by the nature of the task and by technology. For example, difficulties in communication can arise with production systems where workers are stationed continuously at a particular point with limited freedom of movement. Even when opportunities exist for interaction with colleagues, physical conditions may limit effective communication. For example, the technological layout and high level of noise with some assembly line work can limit contact between workers. Restrictions on opportunities for social interaction can hamper internal group unity. Adams points out that a major reason why getting a team to work well is such a challenge in large organisations.

Technology

We can see that the nature of technology and the manner in which work is carried out have an important effect on cohesiveness and relate closely to the nature of the task, physical setting and communications. Where the nature of the work process involves a craft or skill-based 'technology' there is a higher likelihood of group cohesiveness. However, with machine-paced assembly line work it is more difficult to develop cohesiveness. Technology also has wider implications for the operation and behaviour of groups and therefore is considered in a separate section later.

ORGANISATIONAL

Management and leadership

Teams tend to be a mirror image of their leaders. The form of management and style of leadership adopted will influence the relationship between the group and the organisation and are major determinants of group cohesiveness. In general terms, cohesiveness will be affected by such things as the manner in which the manager gives guidance and encouragement to the group, offers help and support, provides opportunities for participation, attempts to resolve conflicts and gives attention to both employee relations and task problems.

McKenna and Maister draw attention to the importance of the group leader establishing a level of trust among the group by helping them understand the behaviours that build trust. 'The job of the group leader is to encourage people to earn the trust of others in their group and then show them how it can translate into greater commitment, greater creativity, greater professional satisfaction, and better performance.'[14] *Farrell* makes the point that managers are ultimately responsible for creating a balance in the workplace and should take the lead in setting standards of behaviour in teams.[15]

HR policies and procedures

Harmony and cohesiveness within the group are more likely to be achieved if HR policies and procedures are well developed and perceived to be equitable, with fair treatment for all members. Attention should be given to the effects that appraisal systems, discipline, promotion and rewards, and opportunities for personal development have on members of the group.

Success

The more successful the group, the more cohesive it is likely to be, and cohesive groups are more likely to be successful. Success is usually a strong motivational influence on the level of work performance. Success or reward as a positive motivator can be perceived by group members in a number of ways, for example the satisfactory completion of a task through co-operative action, praise from management, a feeling of high status, achievement in competition with other groups, benefits gained, such as high wage payments from a group bonus incentive scheme.

External threat

Cohesiveness may be enhanced by members co-operating with one another when faced with a common external threat, such as changes in their method of work or the appointment of a new manager. Even if the threat is subsequently removed, the group may continue to have a greater degree of cohesiveness than before the threat arose. Conflict between groups will also tend to increase the cohesiveness of each group and the boundaries of the group become drawn more clearly.

GROUP DEVELOPMENT AND MATURITY

The degree of cohesiveness is affected also by the manner in which groups progress through the various stages of development and maturity before getting down to the real tasks in hand. This process can take time and is often traumatic for the members. *Bass and Ryterband* identify four distinct stages in group development:

- mutual acceptance and membership;
- communication and decision-making;
- motivation and productivity; and
- control and organisation.[16]

An alternative, and more popular, model by *Tuckman* identifies five main successive stages of group development and relationships: **forming, storming, norming, performing** and **adjourning**.[17]

- **Stage 1 – forming**. The initial formation of the group and the bringing together of a number of individuals who identify, tentatively, the purpose of the group, its composition and terms of reference. At this stage consideration is given to hierarchical structure of the group, pattern of leadership, individual roles and responsibilities, and codes of conduct. There is likely to be considerable anxiety as members attempt to create an impression, to test each other and to establish their personal identity within the group.
- **Stage 2 – storming**. As members of the group get to know each other better they will put forward their views more openly and forcefully. Disagreements will be expressed and challenges offered on the nature of the task and arrangements made in the earlier stage of development. This may lead to conflict and hostility. The storming stage is important because, if successful, there will be discussions on reforming arrangements for the working and operation of the group, and agreement on more meaningful structures and procedures.
- **Stage 3 – norming**. As conflict and hostility start to be controlled, members of the group will establish guidelines and standards and develop their own norms of acceptable behaviour. The norming stage is important in establishing the need for members to co-operate in order to plan, agree standards of performance and fulfil the purpose of the group.

- **Stage 4 – performing.** When the group has progressed successfully through the three earlier stages of development it will have created structure and cohesiveness to work effectively as a team. At this stage the group can concentrate on the attainment of its purpose and performance of the common task is likely to be at its most effective.
- **Stage 5 – adjourning.** This refers to the adjourning or disbanding of the group because of, for example, completion of the task, members leaving the organisation or moving on to other tasks. Some members may feel a compelling sense of loss at the end of a major or lengthy group project and their return to independence is characterised by sadness and anxiety. Managers may need to prepare for future group tasks and engendering team effort.

Another writer suggests that new groups go through the following stages:

- the polite stage;
- the why are we here, what are we doing stage;
- the power stage, which dominant will emerge;
- the constructive stage when sharing begins; and
- the unity stage – this often takes weeks, eating together, talking together.[18]

Creative leadership and group development

In an examination of creative leadership and team effectiveness, *Rickards and Moger* propose a modification to the Tuckman model and suggest a two-barrier model of group development. Creative leadership is suggested as producing new routines or protocols designed as **benign structures** which help teams progress through the first barrier at Tuckman's **storm** stage (a behavioural barrier), and beyond a second barrier at the norm stage (a norm-breaking barrier). From empirical studies of small groups and project teams Rickards and Moger put forward two challenges to the prevailing model of team development.

(i) Weak teams posed the question 'what is happening if a team fails to develop beyond the storm stage'?
(ii) The exceptional teams posed the question 'what happens if a team breaks out of the performance norms developed'?

The suggestion is that the teams are differentiated by two barriers to performance. The weak barrier is behavioural and defeated a minority of teams; the strong barrier was a block to creativity or innovation, and defeated the majority of those teams who passed through the weak barrier. The two-barrier model provides a starting point for exploring the impact and influence of a team leader on the performance of teams. Rickards and Moger suggest seven factors through which a leader might influence effective team development:

- building a platform of understanding;
- creating a shared vision;
- a creative climate;
- a commitment to idea ownership;
- resilience to setbacks;
- developing networking skills; and
- learning from experience.[19]

> ### Critical reflection
>
> 'Given the obvious importance of social networks and interpersonal relationships for both the morale and job satisfaction of staff and their levels of work performance, the main focus in the study of organisational behaviour should be on the operations and management of the informal organisation.'
>
> *Can you present a counter-argument to this contention?*

SOCIAL IDENTITY THEORY

Within work organisations there will be a number of different but overlapping groups representing a variety of functions, departments, occupations, technologies, project teams, locations or hierarchical levels. Organisational effectiveness will be dependent upon the extent to which these groups co-operate together, but often the different groupings are part of a network of complex relationships resulting in competitiveness and conflict. A feature of the importance and significance of group membership is the concept of social identity theory. *Tajifel and Turner* originally developed the idea of **social identity theory** as a means of understanding the psychological basis of intergroup discrimination.[20] Individuals are perceived as having not just one 'personal self' but a number of several 'selves' derived from different social contexts and membership of groups.

Because of the need for a clear sense of personal identity, the groups or social categories with which we associate are an integral part of our self-concept (social identity). A natural process of human interaction is social categorisation, by which we classify both ourselves and other people through reference to our own social identity. For example, membership of high status groups can increase a person's perceived self-esteem. According to *Guirdham* 'self-categorisation is the process that transforms a number of individuals into a group'.[21] *See* Figure 6.4.

Haslam refers to the relationship between individuals and groups in an understanding of organisational behaviour, and argues that:

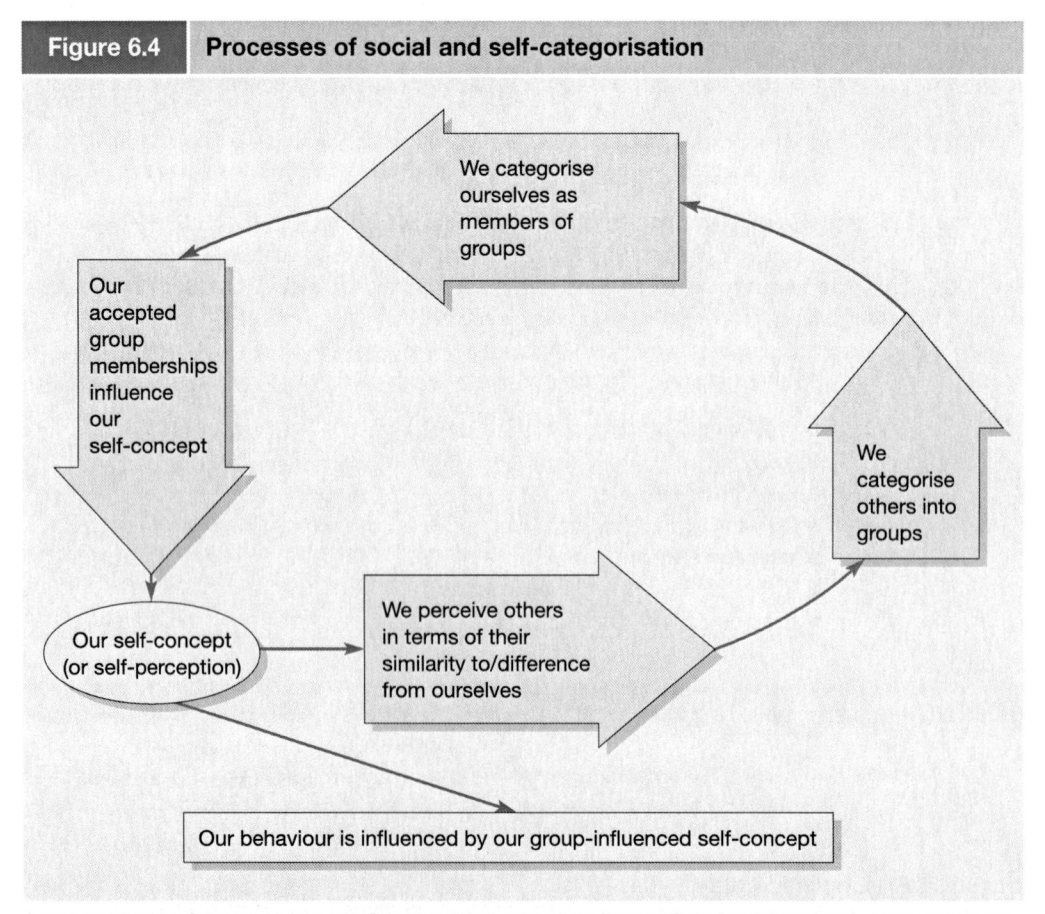

Figure 6.4 Processes of social and self-categorisation

- We categorise ourselves as members of groups
- Our accepted group memberships influence our self-concept
- Our self-concept (or self-perception)
- We perceive others in terms of their similarity to/difference from ourselves
- We categorise others into groups
- Our behaviour is influenced by our group-influenced self-concept

Source: Adapted from Guirdham, M. *Interactive Behaviour at Work*, third edition, Financial Times Prentice Hall (2002), p. 119. Reproduced with permission of Pearson Education Ltd., © Pearson Education Limited 2002.

> in order to understand perception and interaction in organizational contexts we must do more than just study the psychology of individuals as **individuals**. Instead, we need to understand how social interaction is bound up with individuals' **social identities** – their definition of themselves in terms of group memberships.[22]

We identify ourselves in terms of membership of certain social groupings and differentiate ourselves from other social groupings. This leads to minimising differences between members of our own groupings (in-group) and maximising differences from other groupings (out-groups). Over time, the sense of shared identity with the in-group increases a feeling of what is right and proper and highlights differences from the out-groups.[23] As a result, this reinforces both social identity with our own category and the projection of negative perceptions and stereotypes towards out-groups. Stereotyping can lead to shared attitudes to out-groups and to increased conflict amongst work groups. Tajfel and Turner suggest that the mere act of individuals categorising themselves as group members lead them to exhibit in-group favouritism. *Hewstone* et al. suggest that even without realising it, we tend usually to favour the groupings we belong to more than denigrate out-groups. Successful intergroup bias enhances self-esteem.[24]

POTENTIAL DISADVANTAGES OF STRONG, COHESIVE GROUPS

If the manager is to develop effective work groups, attention should be given to those factors that influence the creation of group identity and cohesiveness. This may result in greater interaction between members, mutual help and social satisfaction, lower turnover and absenteeism, and often higher production.[25] However, strong and cohesive groups also present potential disadvantages for management. Cohesive groups do not necessarily produce a higher level of output. Performance varies with the extent to which the group accepts or rejects the goals of the organisation. Furthermore, with a very high level of cohesiveness and attention to social activities, there may even be a fall in output. The level of production is likely to conform to a standard acceptable as a norm by the group. It may be remembered that in the bank wiring room experiment of the Hawthorne studies, group norms imposed a restriction on the workers' level of output.

Once a group has become fully developed and created cohesiveness, it is more difficult for the manager successfully to change the attitudes and behaviour of the group. It is important that the manager should attempt to influence the group during the norming stage when members are establishing guidelines and standards and their own norms of acceptable behaviour. When a group has become fully developed and established its own culture it is more difficult to change the attitudes and behaviour of its members.

Intergroup conflict

Strong, cohesive groups may develop a critical or even hostile attitude towards people outside the group or members of other groups. This can be the case, for example, when group cohesiveness is based on common status, qualifications, technical expertise or professional standing. Group cohesiveness may result in lack of co-operation with, or opposition to, non-members. As a result, resentment and intergroup conflict may arise to the detriment of the organisation as a whole. (Recall the discussion on social identity theory, above.) In order to help prevent, or overcome, unconstructive intergroup conflict, the manager should attempt to stimulate a high level of communication and interaction between the groups and to maintain harmony. Rotation of members among different groups should be encouraged.

Yet, intergroup rivalry may be deliberately encouraged as a means of building stronger within-group cohesiveness. The idea being that a competitive element may help to promote unity within a group. However, intergroup rivalry and competition need to be handled carefully. The manager should attempt to avoid the development of 'win–lose' situations.

Emphasis should be placed on overall objectives of the organisation and on superordinate goals. These are goals over and above the issues at conflict and which, if they are to be achieved, require the co-operation of the competing groups.

CHARACTERISTICS OF AN EFFECTIVE WORK GROUP

The characteristics of an effective work group are not always easy to isolate clearly. The underlying feature is a spirit of co-operation in which members work well together as a united team and with harmonious and supportive relationships. This may be evidenced when members of a group exhibit:

- a belief in shared aims and objectives;
- a sense of commitment to the group;
- acceptance of group values and norms;
- a feeling of mutual trust and dependency;
- full participation by all members and decision-making by consensus;
- a free flow of information and communications;
- the open expression of feelings and disagreements;
- the resolution of conflict by the members themselves;
- a lower level of staff turnover, absenteeism, accidents, errors and complaints.

However, as *Brooks* points out, as teams operate at the higher order of group dynamics this list is arguably more reflective of 'effective **work teams** rather than work groups and this is how it should be – these are teams not groups'.[26]

The effects of technology

Technology is clearly a major influence on the pattern of group operation and behaviour. The work organisation may limit the opportunities for social interaction and the extent to which individuals are able to identify themselves as members of a cohesive work group. This in turn can have possible adverse effects on attitudes to work and the level of job satisfaction. In many assembly line production systems, for example, relationships between individual workers are determined by the nature of the task, the extent to which individual jobs are specified and the time cycle of operations.

ACAS draws attention to technological advances and how new technology enables production to be tailored quickly to customer requirements, often on an individual basis.

> *Mass production techniques, where jobs are broken down into simple tasks, are not suitable for the new customer focused manufacturing nor the expectations of an educated workforce. Organisations need workers to be more flexible, to co-operate with other workers, supervisors and managers throughout the organisation, to operate sophisticated technology and to be more adaptable. In addition, the sheer complexity of operations in industry, commerce and the services places them beyond the expertise and control of any one individual. In these circumstances some form of teamwork becomes not just desirable but essential.*[27]

Impact of information technology

The impact of information technology demands new patterns of work organisation and affects the formation and structure of groups. It will influence where and how people interact. Movement away from large-scale, centralised organisation to smaller working units can help create an environment in which workers may relate more easily to each other. Improvements in telecommunications mean, on one hand, that support staff need no longer be located within the main production unit. On the other hand, modern methods of communication mean that individuals may work more on their own, from their homes, shared offices or hotels, or work more with machines than with other people.[28]

VIRTUAL TEAMS

The combination of increasing globalisation and widespread developments in information communications and technology has given greater emphasis to the opportunities for, and need of, **virtual teams**. Instead of face-to-face proximity, virtual teams are a collection of people who are geographically separated but still work together closely. The primary interaction among members is by some electronic information and communication process. This enables organisations to function away from traditional working hours and the physical availability of staff. Computer-based information systems and increased wireless connectivity further the opportunities for virtual working. By their very nature, virtual teams are likely to be largely self-managed.

According to *Hall*, the virtual team is a potential future compromise between fully fledged teams and well-managed groups.

> *I am watching the rise of this idea with interest but am sceptical that it will actually create a 'third way'. Real teams can only be forged in the crucible of personal interaction: videoconferences and Net communications are still poor substitutes for this. Of course, once a team has formed it can use these media, as members will know each other well, but that's not the important bit. It's the forming, norming and storming that make a team.*[29]

Management and communication skills

However, *Parker* highlights that remote working may also have an impact on the social aspects of organisational working with an increasing feeling of isolation.

> *Remote teamworking is not simply a matter of ensuring staff have access to a laptop and telephone line, and assuming that they will be able to continue with their work. The management and communication skills that this new working culture requires are also key to success.*[30]

A similar point is made by *Norval* who maintains that many remote workers can feel isolated and that the organisation is ignoring them, and this can affect their motivation. Without the visual sense and informal communications within the office, managers need to make a more conscious effort to build rapport and to rethink their management style.[31]

Symons considers one advantage of virtual teamworking using asynchronous media is the clarity and richness of contributions when respondents are removed from the urgency of immediate interaction, and this can be particularly relevant in cross-cultural groups. However, as the leader cannot influence by their physical presence, and as hierarchies fade online, managing dispersed teams requires a range of subtly different leadership skills. It is important to develop mutual trust, a democratic approach of shared control and decision-making, and to adopt the role and style of a coach. 'The leader has to establish and maintain "credit" with the group, as "position power" has little or no currency in virtual working.'[32]

Organising the virtual team

Garrett maintains that collaborating with other people in different cities or countries is not always a successful arrangement and lists the following to help organise the virtual team:

- **Say hello** – the most successful teams spend time during their formation period face-to-face getting to know each other.
- **Build trust** – to hold the team together so that you can depend on other team members and feel comfortable opening up to them.
- **Recruit with care** – people who can communicate in the right way at the right time are more likely to be successful in virtual teams.
- **Don't rely on email** – the written word is easily misunderstood so supplement its use with other forms of communication.

- **Encourage dissent** – without face-to-face meetings people become reluctant to speak out but a healthy organisation needs people to speak out and challenge leaders and each other.
- **Use technology thoughtfully** – used badly, sophisticated tools can be a disaster and people need to be trained to use the technology not simply have it imposed on them.
- **Measure outcomes** – focus on the outcomes rather than time management, find a personal way to appraise performance, rather than email, and hold regular chats with members.
- **Do say** – 'By proactively creating virtual teams we can go where talent is, extend our reach and work more efficiently.'
- **Don't say** – 'We call them a virtual team because they're not quite the real thing.'[33]

Cultural diversity

One reason for the growth in virtual teams is because of increasing globalisation and team members working and living in different countries. This gives rise to potential difficulties of cultural diversity. As *Francesco and Gold* point out:

> *The more culturally diverse the members, the more difficult it is to manage a virtual team. Cultural diversity, which will be increasingly common, adds to the complexity of managing virtual teams because different values, customs, and traditions require more leadership under conditions that reduce the ability to use direct leadership.*[34]

And according to *Murray*, although virtual working presents some unexpected benefits, if managing diversity in the workplace is a tough task for business leaders, the challenges of keeping executives from different backgrounds working together in various parts of the world is even more difficult. Virtual working does not eradicate the sort of cultural misunderstandings that can arise in a face-to-face situation.

> *Cultural or behavioural differences that can manifest themselves in face-to-face working situations can be exacerbated in virtual teamworking, particularly when the group has members from different backgrounds.*[35]

ROLE RELATIONSHIPS

In order that the organisation can achieve its goals and objectives, the work of individual members must be linked into coherent patterns of activities and relationships. This is achieved through the 'role structure' of the organisation.

A **'role'** is the expected pattern of behaviours associated with members occupying a particular position within the structure of the organisation. It also describes how a person perceives their own situation. The concept of 'role' is important to the functioning of groups and for an understanding of group processes and behaviour. It is through role differentiation that the structure of the work group and relationships among its members are established. Some form of structure is necessary for teamwork and co-operation. The concept of roles helps to clarify the structure and to define the pattern of complex relationships within the group.

The formal organisational relationships (line, functional, staff or lateral) – discussed in Chapter 9 – can be seen as forms of role relationships. These individual authority relationships determine the pattern of interaction with other roles.

The role, or roles, that the individual plays within the group is influenced by a combination of:

- **situational factors**, such as the requirements of the task, the style of leadership, position in the communication network; and
- **personal factors** such as values, attitudes, motivation, ability and personality.

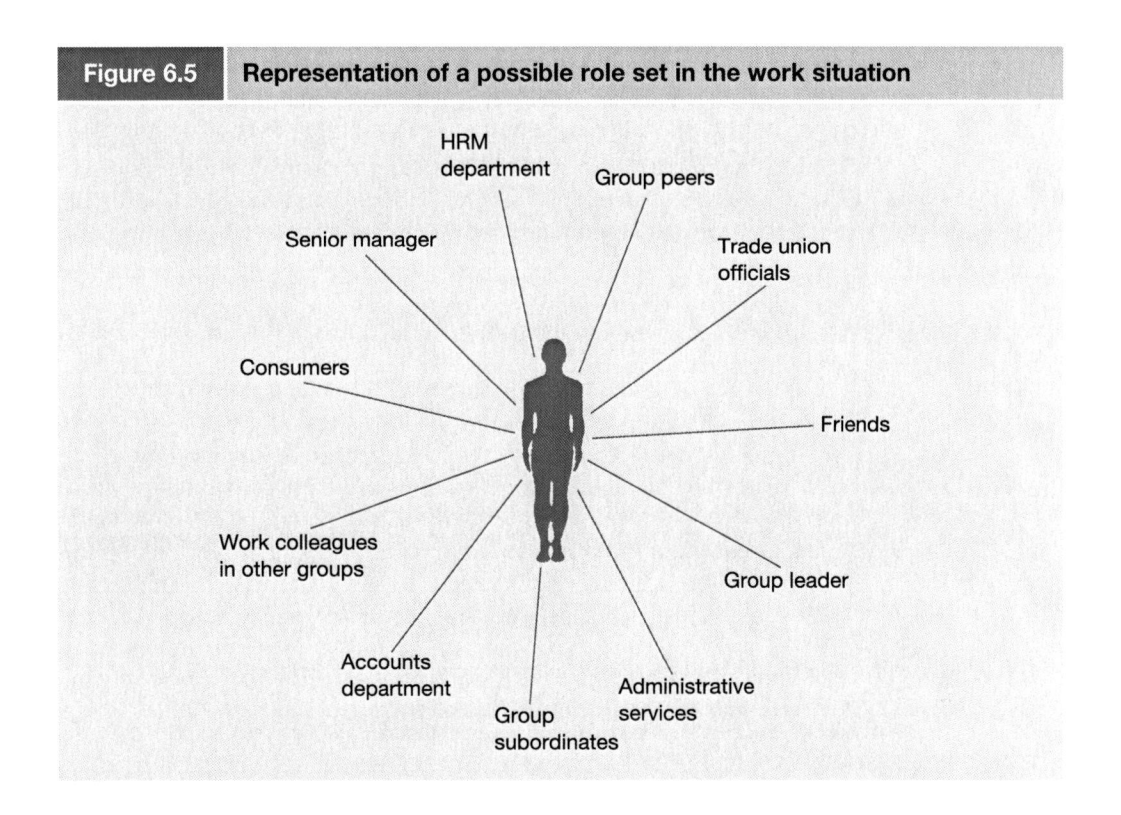

Figure 6.5 Representation of a possible role set in the work situation

Labels around central figure: HRM department, Group peers, Senior manager, Trade union officials, Consumers, Friends, Work colleagues in other groups, Group leader, Accounts department, Group subordinates, Administrative services

The role that a person plays in one work group may be quite different from the role that person plays in other work groups. However, everyone within a group is expected to behave in a particular manner and to fulfil certain role expectations.

A person's role-set

In addition to the role relationships with members of their own group – peers, superiors, subordinates – the individual will have a number of role-related relationships with outsiders – for example, members of other work groups, trade union officials, suppliers, consumers. This is a person's '**role-set**'. The role-set comprises the range of associations or contacts with whom the individual has meaningful interactions in connection with the performance of their role (see Figure 6.5).

Role incongruence

An important feature of role relationship is the concept of '**role incongruence**'. This arises when a member of staff is perceived as having a high and responsible position in one respect but a low standing in another respect. Difficulties with role incongruence can arise from the nature of groupings and formal relationships within the structure of the organisation. There are a number of work-related relationships such as doctor and nurse, chef and waiter, senior manager and personal assistant which can give rise to a potential imbalance of authority and responsibility.

Difficulties with role incongruence can also arise in line-staff relationships: for instance, a relatively junior member of the HR department informing a senior departmental manager that a certain proposed action is contrary to the policies of the organisation. Another example with staff relationships is where a person establishes themselves in the role of 'gatekeeper' to the boss[36] – for instance, where a comparatively junior personal assistant passes on the manager's instructions to one of the manager's more senior subordinates or where the personal assistant attempts to block a more senior member of staff having access to the manager.

Role expectations

Many **role expectations** are prescribed formally and indicate what the person is expected to do and their duties and obligations. Formal role prescriptions provide guidelines for expected behaviours and may be more prevalent in a 'mechanistic' organisation. Examples are written contracts of employment, rules and regulations, standing orders, policy decisions, job descriptions, or directives from superiors. Formal role expectations may also be derived clearly from the nature of the task. They may, in part at least, be defined legally, for example under the Health and Safety at Work Act, or as with the obligations of a company secretary under the Companies Acts, or the responsibilities of a district auditor under the Local Government Acts.

Not all role expectations are prescribed formally, however. There will be certain patterns of behaviour that although not specified formally will nonetheless be expected of members. These informal role expectations may be imposed by the group itself or at least communicated to a person by other members of the group. Examples include general conduct, mutual support to co-members, attitudes towards superiors, means of communicating, dress and appearance. Members may not always be consciously aware of these informal expectations yet they still serve as important determinants of behaviour. Under this heading could be included the concept of a psychological contract which was discussed in Chapter 1.

Some members may have the opportunity to determine their own role expectations, where, for example, formal expectations are specified loosely or only in very general terms. Opportunities for **self-established roles** are more likely in senior positions, but also occur within certain professional, technical or scientific groups, for example senior research staff, or where there is a demand for creativity or artistic flair, for example head chefs. Such opportunities may be greater within an 'organic' organisation and will also be influenced by the style of leadership adopted – for example, where a *laissez-faire* approach is adopted.

Critical reflection

'Self-interest and opportunism are natural features of human behaviour and will always take preference over the demands and best interests of the group or teamwork.'

How would you present a counter point of view? How far are you prepared to put the interests of a work group before your own interests?

ROLE CONFLICT

Patterns of behaviour result from both the role and the personality. The concept of role focuses attention on aspects of behaviour existing independently of an individual's personality. **Role conflict** arises from inadequate or inappropriate role definition and needs to be distinguished from personality clashes. These arise from incompatibility between two or more people as individuals even though their roles may be defined clearly and understood fully. In practice, the manner in which a person actually behaves may not be consistent with their expected pattern of behaviours. This inconsistency may be a result of role conflict. Role conflict as a generic term can include:

- role incompatibility;
- role ambiguity;
- role overload;
- role underload.

These are all problem areas associated with the creation of role expectations (*see* Figure 6.6).

Figure 6.6 Role relationships and conflicts

```
                        ROLE EXPECTATIONS
                    ↙          ↓          ↘
              Informal      Formal      Self-established
                    ↘          ↓          ↙
                   Expected pattern of behaviours

    ROLE CONFLICT                              Role perception
    Role incompatibility                       Role motivation
    Role ambiguity          →   [person]   ←   Role capability
    Role overload
    Role underload                             Role sanctions

                    Role stress
                           ↓
               ACTUAL PATTERN OF BEHAVIOURS
```

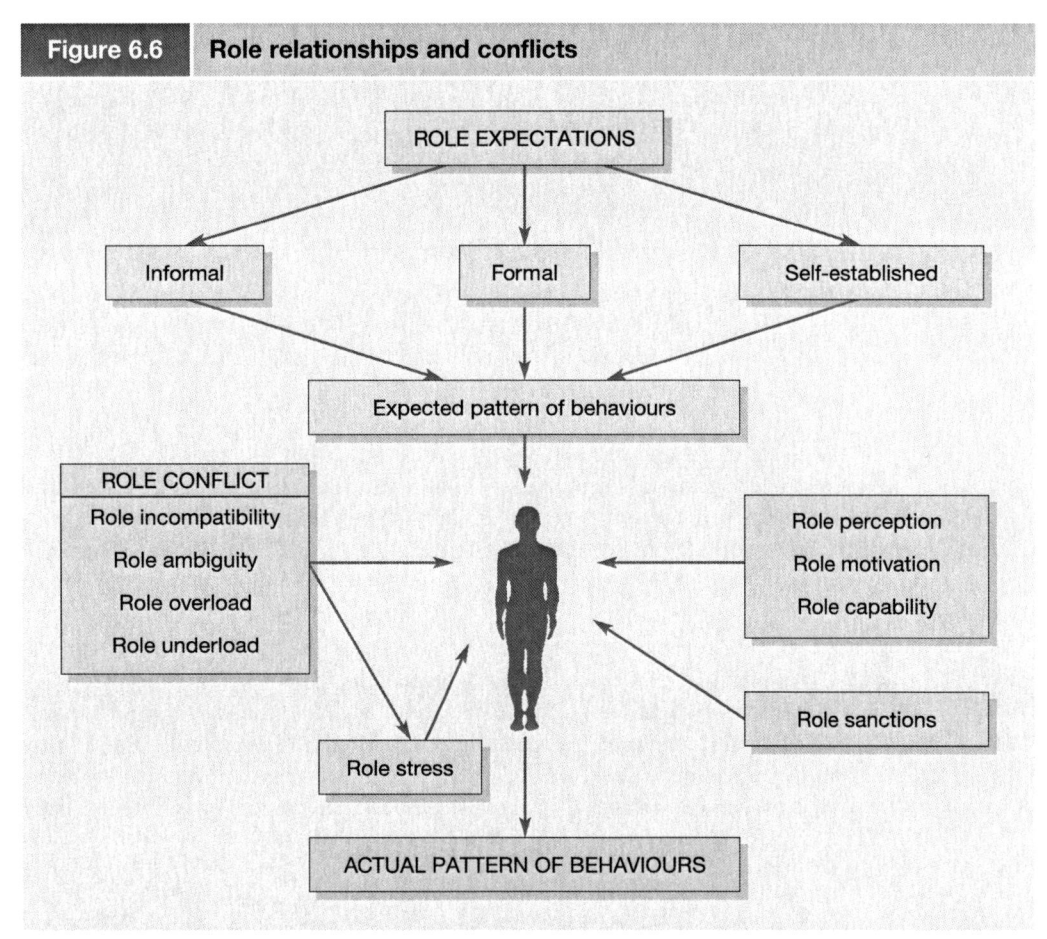

Source: Adapted from Miner, J. B. *Management Theory*, Macmillan (1971), p. 47.

- **Role incompatibility** arises when a person faces a situation in which simultaneous different or contradictory expectations create inconsistency. Compliance with one set of expectations makes it difficult or impossible to comply with other expectations. The two role expectations are in conflict. A typical example concerns the person 'in the middle', such as the supervisor or section head, who faces opposing expectations from workers and from management. Another example might be the situation of a manager who believes in a relaxed, participative style of behaviour more in keeping with a Theory Y approach, but whose superior believes in a Theory X approach and expects the manager to adopt a more formal and directive style of behaviour.
- **Role ambiguity** occurs when there is lack of clarity as to the precise requirements of the role and the person is unsure what to do. The person's perception of their role may differ from the expectations of others. This implies that insufficient information is available for the adequate performance of the role. Role ambiguity may result from a lack of formally prescribed expectations. It is likely to arise in large, diverse groups or at times of constant change. Uncertainty often relates to such matters as the method of performing tasks, the extent of the person's authority and responsibility, standards of work, and the evaluation and appraisal of performance.
- **Role overload** is when a person faces too many separate roles or too great a variety of expectations. The person is unable to meet satisfactorily all expectations and some must be neglected in order to satisfy others. This leads to a conflict of priority. Some writers distinguish between role overload and work overload. Role overload is seen in terms of the total role-set and implies that the person has too many separate roles to handle. Where there are too many expectations of a single role – that is, a problem of quantity – this is work overload.

- **Role underload** can arise when the prescribed role expectations fall short of the person's perception of their role. The person may feel their role is not demanding enough and that they have the capacity to undertake a larger or more varied role, or an increased number of roles. Role underload may arise, for example, when a new member of staff is first appointed or from the initial effects of empowerment.

Role conflict and matrix organisation

Problems of role conflict can often arise from the matrix form of organisation (discussed in Chapter 9) and, for example, from the use of flexible project teams. Where staff are assigned temporarily, and perhaps on a part-time basis, from other groups this creates a two-way flow of authority and responsibility.

Unless role differentiations are defined clearly this can result in conflicting expectations from the manager of the person's own functional grouping and from the manager of the project team (role incompatibility). It can also lead to uncertainty about the exact requirements of the part the person is expected to play as a member of the project team (role ambiguity). The combinations of expectations from both managers may also result in role overload.

Role stress

Role conflict can result in role stress. Although a certain amount of stress may **arguably** be seen as a good thing, and especially at managerial level helps to bring out a high level of performance, it is also potentially very harmful. Stress is a source of tension, frustration and dissatisfaction. It can lead to difficulties in communication and interpersonal relationships and can affect morale, effectiveness at work and health. There are a number of ways in which management might attempt to avoid or reduce role conflict and the possibilities of role stress.

- Increase specification and clarity of prescribed role expectations, for example through written statements on objectives and policy, use of manuals and set procedures, introduction of appropriate rules, and detailed job descriptions. However, such measures may be resented by staff. They may restrict the opportunity for independent action and personal development, giving rise to even more role conflict.
- Improved recruitment and selection and the careful matching of abilities, motivation, interests and personalities to the demands of a particular role.
- Attention to induction and socialisation programmes, job training and retraining, staff development and career progression plans.
- Medical examinations and health screening to give early indications of potential stress-related problems.
- The creation of new roles or assimilation of existing roles. The reallocation or restructuring of tasks and responsibilities. The clarification of priorities, and the elimination or downgrading of minor roles.
- Giving advance notice and explanation of what is likely to happen, for example of an expected, additional heavy workload which must be completed urgently. Where possible and appropriate provide an opportunity for practice or experience.
- Attention to factors which may help improve group structure and group cohesiveness, and help overcome intergroup conflict.
- Review of organisation structure, information flow and communication networks, for example members of staff being answerable to more than one superior.

Other influences on behaviour

Even if there is an absence of role conflict and role stress, a person's actual behaviour may still be inconsistent with their expected pattern of behaviours. *Miner* gives three reasons that may account for this disparity.[37]

- The person does not perceive their job in the way the role prescriptions specify. This is a form of role ambiguity, but may arise not because the role prescriptions themselves are unclear but because the person misunderstands or distorts them.
- Motivation is lacking and the person does not want to behave in the way prescribed.
- The person does not have the capabilities – knowledge, mental ability or physical skills – required to behave in the way the role prescriptions specify.

Application of sanctions

Organisations apply a number of both positive and negative sanctions as inducements for members to contribute and behave in accordance with their prescribed roles. Typical examples are: an increase in salary or wages; promotion; a sideways or downwards move in the organisation structure; the threat of dismissal.

There are also a number of less direct sanctions that may be adopted. These include the size of office or work area, the allocation of unpopular tasks, giving opportunities for paid overtime work, level of supervision or empowerment, the amount of information given or the extent of consultation, granting or withholding privileges.

Role sanctions may also be applied through the operation of the informal organisation. Members of the group may impose their own sanctions and discipline individuals who contravene the norms of the group or expected standards of behaviour.

THE IMPORTANCE OF TEAMWORK

How people behave and perform as members of a group is as important as their behaviour or performance as individuals. Harmonious working relationships and good teamwork help make for a high level of staff morale and work performance. Effective teamwork is an essential element of modern management practices such as empowerment, quality circles and total quality management, and how groups manage change. Teamwork is important in any organisation but may be especially significant in service industries, such as hospitality organisations where there is a direct effect on customer satisfaction.[38]

According to ACAS, teams have been around for as long as anyone can remember and there can be few organisations that have not used the term in one sense or another. In a general sense, people talk of teamwork when they want to emphasise the virtues of co-operation and the need to make use of the various strengths of employees. Using the term more specifically, teamworking involves a reorganisation of the way work is carried out. Teamwork can increase competitiveness by:

- improving productivity;
- improving quality and encouraging innovation;
- taking advantage of the opportunities provided by technological advances;
- improving employee motivation and commitment.[39]

The general movement towards flatter structures of organisation, wider spans of control and reducing layers of middle management, together with increasing empowerment of employees, all involve greater emphasis on the importance of teamworking. 'There's no doubt that effective teamwork is crucial to an organisation's efforts to perform better, faster and more profitably than their competitors.'[40]

This view on the importance of teamwork is supported by *Adams*.

> *The point is that teamwork is not an option for a successful organisation; it is a necessity. Teamwork can lead to achievement, creativity and energy levels that someone working alone, or perhaps with just one other person, could hardly imagine.*[41]

Skills of effective teamworking

According to *Guirdham*, the growth of teamwork has led to the increased interest in interface skills at work.

> More and more tasks of contemporary organisations, particularly those in high technology and service businesses, require teamwork. Taskforces, project teams and committees are key elements in the modern workplace. Teamwork depends not just on technical competence of the individuals composing the team, but on their ability to 'gel'. To work well together, the team members must have more than just team spirit. They also need collaborative skills – they must be able to support one another and to handle conflict in such a way that it becomes constructive rather than destructive.[42]

A similar point is made by *Ashmos and Nathan*: 'The use of teams has expanded dramatically in response to competitive challenges. In fact, one of the most common skills required by new work practices is the ability to work as a team.'[43]

De Rond and Holland draw an interesting comparison between an analysis of the team dynamics among Oxford and Cambridge boat race crews and managing high performance teams in the workplace.[44] Compared with the boat race crews, not all business teams have such clear and unchangeable objective, they cannot cherry-pick membership, there is less physical training, and it is more difficult to isolate individual contributions. Nevertheless, de Rond and Holland draw a number of parallels between crews and teams including, both require a superb sense of co-ordination; are composed of intelligent individuals impatient of jargon or management talk; co-operation and competition co-exist in a necessary, but socially often awkward, relationship; and both suffer from the Ringelmann Effect (the inverse relationship between team membership and individual effort). The Ringelmann effect is discussed later in this chapter.

> To build good teams you need a wide pool of staff with different talents to draw upon . . . Good managers should delight in the diversity and excellence of their staff and know that one of their main jobs is to manage the problems that come with any diverse group of talented people. In any group of talented people you will naturally get interpersonal tensions. It is important that you show you respect all the different skills and personalities in your team.[45]

Critical reflection

'Teamworking is no more than a fashionable term used by management to give workers an exaggerated feeling of importance and empowerment. In reality an emphasis on teamworking is only likely to lead to more work, less freedom and even closer control from other team members.'

How far do you agree with this comment? What is your personal experience of teamworking?

INTERACTIONS AMONG MEMBERS

If groups are to be successful and perform effectively, there must be a spirit of unity and co-operation. In the previous chapter we mentioned that how people behave and perform as members of a group is as important as their behaviour or performance as individuals, and drew attention to the importance of effective teamwork. The main focus of attention in this chapter is the actual roles, behaviours and performance of people working in groups or teams. Once again, however, we should be aware of the tendency for the terms 'groups' and 'teams' to be used interchangeably. Members of a group must work well together as a team. As *Crainer* reminds us, in most teams people will contribute individual skills, many of which will be different. However, referring to the work of *Obeng*,[46] Crainer points out that it is not enough to have a rag-bag collection of individual skills.

> The various behaviors of the team members must mesh together in order to achieve objectives. For people to work successfully in teams, you need people to behave in certain ways. You need some people

to concentrate on the task at hand (doers). You need some people to provide specialist knowledge (knowers) and some to solve problems as they arise (solvers). You need some people to make sure that it is going as well as it can and that the whole team is contributing fully (checkers). And you need some people to make sure that the team is operating as a cohesive social unit (carers).[47]

Co-operation and interactions

As ACAS points out:

In a general sense people talk of teamwork when they want to emphasise the virtues of co-operation and the need to make use of the various strengths of employees . . . To remain competitive organisations need to make optimum use of equipment and people if they are to thrive or even survive.[48]

In order to understand the functions and processes of a group, it is necessary to understand what happens when people meet; the actions and behaviour of individual members; the parts people play; the patterns of interactions and forces within the group; and influences on individual and group performance. According to *Guirdham*, for example:

Many of the concepts that have helped us understand interactive behaviour in work relationships are also needed for understanding it in groups, including role behaviour, norms and co-operation, competition, conflict and conflict resolution. Most of what there is to understand about group work applies equally to both decision-making groups and teams but there are some further issues particular to the two different kinds of groups. There is, however, no suggestion that teams do not have to solve problems![49]

BELBIN'S TEAM-ROLES

One of the most popular and widely used analyses of individual roles within a work group or team is that developed by *Meredith Belbin*. Following years of research and empirical study, Belbin concludes that groups composed entirely of clever people, or of people with similar personalities, display a number of negative results and lack creativity. The most consistently successful groups comprise a range of roles undertaken by various members. The constitution of the group itself is an important variable in its success.[50] Initially, Belbin identified eight useful types of contribution – or team-roles.

A **team-role** is described as a pattern of behaviour, characteristic of the way in which one team member interacts with another whose performance serves to facilitate the progress of the team as a whole. In a follow-up publication, Belbin discusses the continual evolution of team-roles, which differ in a few respects from those originally identified and adds a ninth role.[51] Strength of contribution in any one role is commonly associated with particular weaknesses. These are called allowable weaknesses. Members are seldom strong in all nine team-roles. A description of the evolved nine team-roles is given in Table 6.1.

The types of people identified are useful team members and form a comprehensive list. These are the key team-roles and the primary characters for successful teams. Creative teams require a balance of all these roles and comprise members who have characteristics complementary to each other. 'No one's perfect, but a team can be.' Belbin claims that good examples of each type would prove adequate for any challenge, although not all types are necessarily needed. Other members may be welcome for their personal qualities, for example a sense of humour, but experience suggests there is no other team-role that it would be useful to add.

Back-up team-roles

The most consistently successful teams were 'mixed' with a balance of team-roles. The role that a person undertakes in a group is not fixed and may change according to circumstances. Individuals may have a 'back-up team-role' with which they have some affinity other than

Table 6.1 Belbin's evolved nine team-roles

Roles and descriptions	Team-role contribution	Allowable weaknesses
Plant	Creative, imaginative, unorthodox. Solves difficult problems.	Ignores details. Too preoccupied to communicate effectively.
Resource investigator	Extrovert, enthusiastic, communicative. Explores opportunities. Develops contacts.	Over-optimistic. Loses interest once initial enthusiasm has passed.
Co-ordinator	Mature, confident, a good chairperson. Clarifies goals, promotes decision-making. Delegates well.	Can be seen as manipulative. Offloads personal work.
Shaper	Challenging, dynamic, thrives on pressure. Has the drive and courage to overcome obstacles.	Can provoke others. Hurts people's feelings.
Monitor–Evaluator	Sober, strategic and discerning. Sees all options. Judges accurately.	Lacks drive and ability to inspire others.
Teamworker	Co-operative, mild, perceptive and diplomatic. Listens, builds, averts friction.	Indecisive in crunch situations.
Implementer	Disciplined, reliable, conservative and efficient. Turns ideas into practical actions.	Somewhat inflexible. Slow to respond to new possibilities.
Completer	Painstaking, conscientious, anxious. Searches out errors and omissions. Delivers on time.	Inclined to worry unduly. Reluctant to delegate.
Specialist	Single-minded, self-sharing, dedicated. Provides knowledge and skills in rare supply.	Contributes on only a narrow front. Dwells on technicalities.

Source: Belbin, R. M., *Team Roles at Work*, Butterworth-Heinemann (a division of Reed Elsevier UK Ltd) and Belbin Associates (1993) p. 23. Reproduced with permission.

their primary team-role. If certain roles were missing members would call upon their back-up roles. Team-roles differ from what Belbin calls 'functional-roles'. These are the roles that members of a team perform in terms of the specifically technical demands placed upon them. Team members are typically chosen for functional roles on the basis of experience and not personal characteristics or aptitudes.

Belbin has developed a Self-Perception Inventory designed to provide members of a group with a simple means of assessing their best team-roles.

The value of Belbin's team-roles inventory

Despite possible doubts about the value of Belbin's Self-Perception Inventory, it remains a popular means of examining and comparing team-roles. For example, in order to explore whether local government managers were distinctively different from the model of private sector management, *Arroba and Wedgwood-Oppenheim* compared samples of the two groups of managers and Belbin's key team-roles. There were noticeable similarities between the two groups, with the noticeable exception of the marked difference between private sector managers and local government officers in the score for teamworkers and the team-roles they preferred to adopt. The individual characteristics of managers in the two sectors differed. The data implied that local government officers were committed to organisational objectives and dedicated to task achievement, but the low score for teamworkers suggested the high commitment to organisational tasks was not supplemented by a concern for interpersonal processes. In local government, the drive and enthusiasm and emphasis on task were exaggerated, while attention to idea generation and productive interpersonal relationships was less marked.[52]

Team roles among UK managers

Using Belbin's model, *Fisher* et al. undertook a study of the distribution of team roles among managers. Over the past 15 years many layers of management have been removed and the gap in people to lead and motivate has increasingly been filled by the creation of multitudes of teams. The participants of the study were 1441 male and 355 female managers, all with some management experience. All had completed a personality questionnaire and were candidates short-listed for a range of management positions in both the private and public sectors. The study analysed data supplied by ASE/NFER Publishing Company and results were then compared with the Belbin model. The data broadly agreed with the Belbin model. The authors conclude that as much is still unknown about teams, it is reassuring that further support has been found for the popular Belbin team-role model. There are several unresolved problems with teamworking but these might lie more with practices in staff recruitment than in team theory.[53]

PATTERNS OF COMMUNICATION

The level of interaction among members of a group or team is influenced by the structuring of channels of communication. Laboratory research by *Bavelas*[54] and subsequent studies by other researchers such as *Leavitt*[55] have resulted in the design of a series of communication networks. These networks were based on groups of five members engaged in a number of problem-solving tasks. Members were permitted to communicate with each other by written notes only and not everyone was always free to communicate with everyone else.

There are five main types of communication networks – wheel, circle, all-channel, Y and chains (*see* Figure 6.7).

- **The wheel**, also sometimes known as the star, is the most **centralised network**. This network is most efficient for simple tasks. Problems are solved more quickly with fewer mistakes and with fewer information flows. However, as the problems become more complex and demands on the link person increase, effectiveness suffers. The link person is at the centre of the network and acts as the focus of activities and information flows and the co-ordinator of group tasks. The central person is perceived as leader of the group and experiences a high level of satisfaction. However, for members on the periphery, the wheel is the least satisfying network.
- **The circle** is a more **decentralised network**. Overall it is less efficient. The group is unorganised, with low leadership predictability. Performance tends to be slow and erratic. However, the circle is quicker than the wheel in solving complex problems and also copes more efficiently with change or new tasks. The circle network is most satisfying for all the members. Decision-making is likely to involve some degree of participation.
- **The all-channel (or comcon) network** is a decentralised network that involves full discussion and participation. This network appears to work best where a high level of interaction is required among all the members in order to solve complex problems. Leadership predictability is very low. There is a fairly high level of satisfaction for members. The all-channel network may not stand up well under pressure, in which case it will either disintegrate or reform into a wheel network.
- **A 'Y' or chain network** might be appropriate for more simple problem-solving tasks, requiring little interaction among members. These networks are more centralised, with information flows along a predetermined channel. Leadership predictability is high to moderate. There is a low to moderate level of satisfaction for members.

Figure 6.7 Communication networks

Wheel

Circle

All-Channel (or Comcon)

Y

Chains

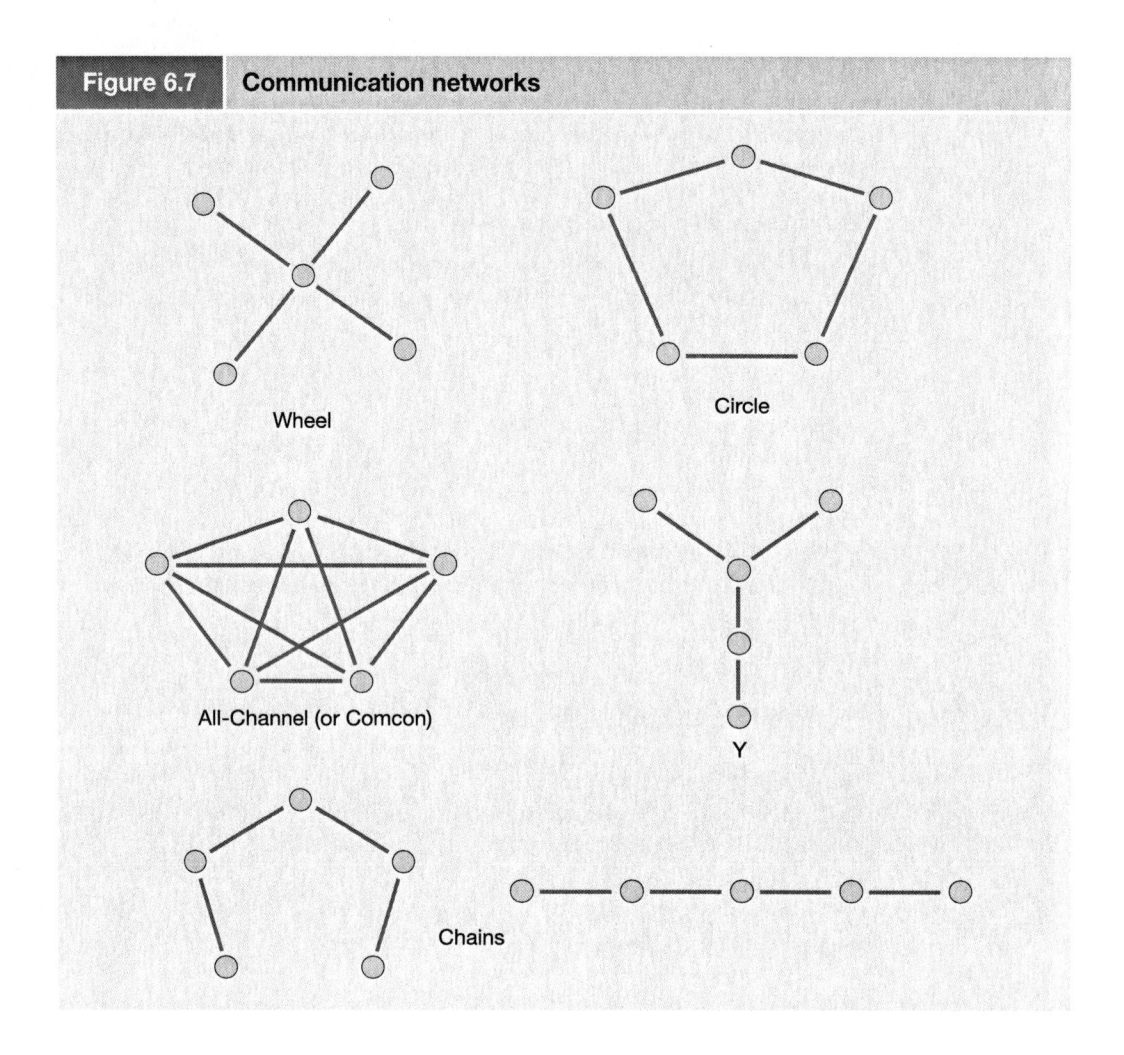

The relationship between centralised and decentralised networks and performance of the group is outlined in Figure 6.8.

Implications for the manager

Despite the obvious artificiality and limitations of these communication network studies, they do have certain implications for the manager. Knowledge of the findings may be applied to influence the patterns of communication in meetings and committees. They also provide a reasonable representation of the situations that might apply in large organisations. It will be interesting for the manager to observe the patterns of communication adopted by different groups in different situations. The manager can also note how communication networks change over time and how they relate to the performance of the group.

No one network is likely to be effective for a range of given problems. The studies draw attention to the part of the manager's job that is to ensure the most appropriate communication network for the performance of a given task. Problems which require a high level of interaction among members of the group may not be handled efficiently if there are inadequate channels of communication or sharing of information. The choice of a particular communication network may involve trade-offs between the performance of the work group and the satisfaction of its members.

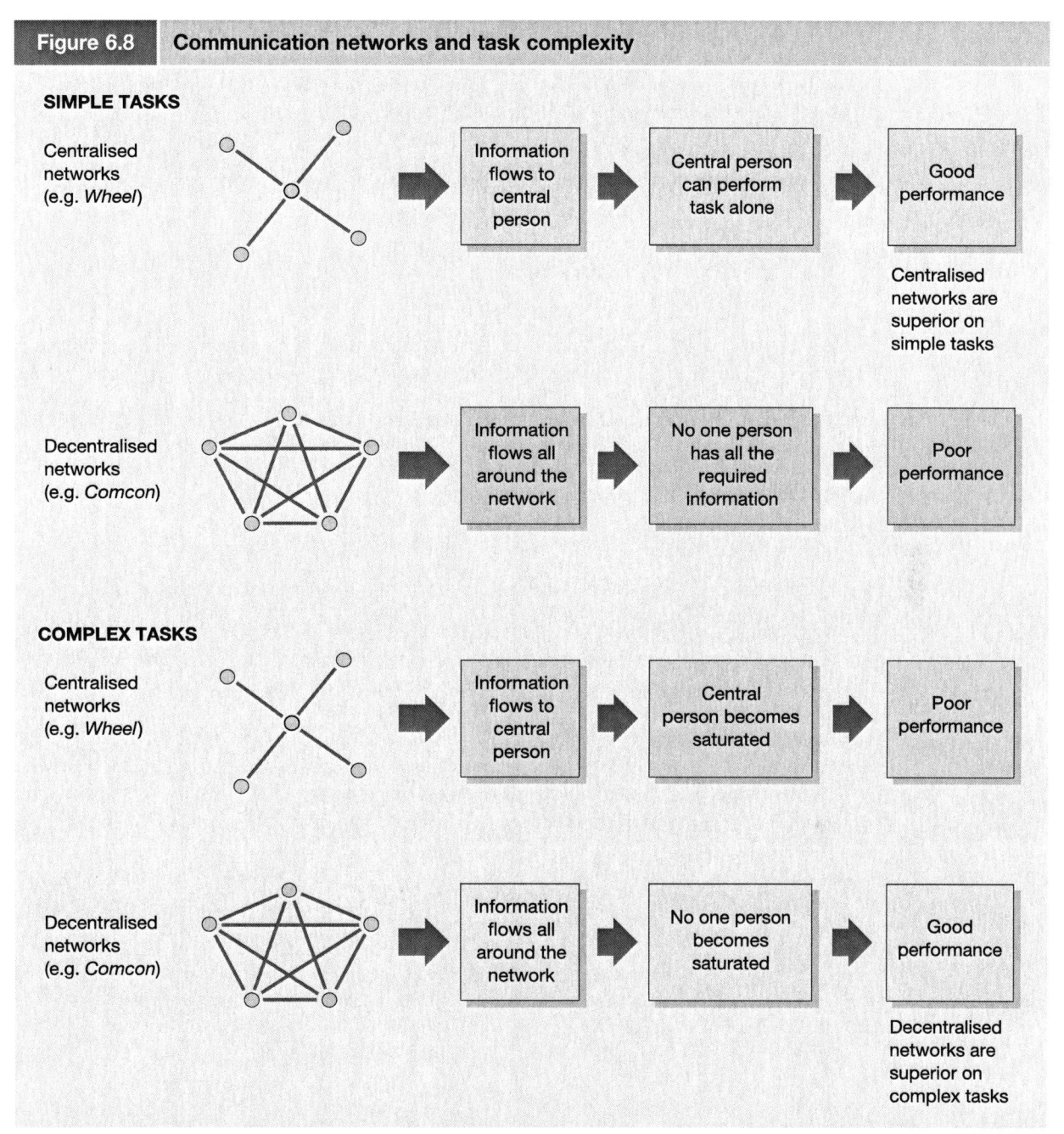

Figure 6.8 Communication networks and task complexity

SIMPLE TASKS

Centralised networks (e.g. *Wheel*) → Information flows to central person → Central person can perform task alone → Good performance

Centralised networks are superior on simple tasks

Decentralised networks (e.g. *Comcon*) → Information flows all around the network → No one person has all the required information → Poor performance

COMPLEX TASKS

Centralised networks (e.g. *Wheel*) → Information flows to central person → Central person becomes saturated → Poor performance

Decentralised networks (e.g. *Comcon*) → Information flows all around the network → No one person becomes saturated → Good performance

Decentralised networks are superior on complex tasks

Source: Greenberg, J. and Baron, R. A. *Behavior in Organizations*, sixth edition, Prentice Hall Inc. (1995), p. 306. Reproduced with permission from Pearson Education Inc.

Task and maintenance functions

If the group is to be effective, then, whatever its structure or the pattern of interrelationships among members, there are two main sets of functions or processes that must be undertaken – **task functions** and **maintenance functions**.

- **Task functions** are directed towards problem-solving, the accomplishment of the tasks of the group and the achievement of its goals. Most of the task-oriented behaviour will be concerned with 'production' activities or the exchange and evaluation of ideas and information.

- **Maintenance functions** are concerned with the emotional life of the group and directed towards building and maintaining the group as an effective working unit. Most of the maintenance-oriented behaviour will be concerned with relationships among members, giving encouragement and support, maintaining cohesiveness and the resolution of conflict.

Task and maintenance functions may be performed either by the group leader or by members. Ultimately it is the leader's responsibility to ensure that both sets of functions are carried out and the right balance is achieved between them. The appropriate combination of task-oriented behaviour and maintenance-oriented behaviour is essential to the success and continuity of the group.

In addition to these two types of behaviour, members of a group may say or do something in attempting to satisfy some personal need or goal. The display of behaviour in this way is termed **self-oriented behaviour**. This gives a classification of three main types of functional behaviour that can be exhibited by individual members of a group: **task-oriented, maintenance-oriented** and **self-oriented**.

Classification of member roles

A popular system for the classification of member roles in the study of group behaviour is that devised originally by *Benne and Sheats*.[56] The description of member roles performed in well-functioning groups is classified into three broad headings: **group task roles, group building and maintenance roles** and **individual roles**.

- **Group task roles**. These assume that the task of the group is to select, define and solve common problems. For example, initiator-contributor, opinion seeker, co-ordinator, evaluator, recorder. Any of the roles may be performed by the various members or the group leader.
- **Group building and maintenance roles**. The analysis of member functions is oriented towards activities which build group-centred attitudes or maintain group-centred behaviour. For example, encourager, gatekeeper, standard setter, group commentator. Contributions may involve a number of roles and members or the leader may perform each of these.
- **Individual roles**. These are directed towards the satisfaction of personal needs. Their purpose is not related either to group task or to the group functioning. For example, aggressor, blocker, dominator, help-seeker.

In order to help improve the performance of the organisation it is necessary to understand the nature of human relationships and what goes on when groups of people meet. Working in a group is likely to be both a psychologically rewarding, and a potentially demanding experience for the individual. Group performance and the satisfaction derived by individuals are influenced by the interactions among members of the group. As an example of this, Figure 6.9 gives an unsolicited commentary from five final-year business studies degree students after completing a group-based assignment.

Critical reflection

'The nature of the hierarchical structure and inevitable role conflicts, power struggles, politics and personality clashes means that individuals will usually complete a task more quickly and effectively than a group or team.'

To what extent do you think this is fair comment? What has been your own experience?

> **Figure 6.9**   Unsolicited commentary from students after group-based assignment
>
> **WHAT WE FEEL WE HAVE LEARNT FROM WORKING IN A GROUP**
>
> 1. 'We learned that we had to listen to everybody's points of view and take these into consideration.'
> 2. 'We found that we had to be prepared to make certain sacrifices and adopted a democratic decision process. However, if an individual felt very strongly about a specific point and persisted with a valid argument then this had to be included.'
> 3. 'We often felt frustrated.'
> 4. 'It was time-consuming and difficult to schedule meetings due to differences in timetables and preferences in working hours.'
> 5. 'We learned that it is good to pool resources because this increased the overall standard of the piece of work. We feel this was only because we all set high personal standards and expected these from our fellow group members. We learnt that it is possible to work in other less productive groups where individual levels of achievement may decrease.'
> 6. 'We learned that it is better to work in a smaller and not a larger group, as there is a tendency for individual ideas to be diluted.'
> 7. 'Groups formed on the basis of friendship are not as effective as groups formed with work as the major influence. The former tend to be unproductive.'
> 8. 'We found that it was good to get positive response, encouragement and feedback from team members. Likewise, it was demotivating to receive a negative response.'
> 9. 'We learned a lot about our individual personalities.'
> 10. 'We benefited from sharing personal experiences from our industrial placements.'
> 11. 'It is important to separate work and personal relationships.'

INDIVIDUAL COMPARED WITH GROUP OR TEAM PERFORMANCE

It is, however, difficult to draw any firm conclusions from a comparison between individual and group or team performance. An example of this can be seen from a consideration of decision-making. Certain groups, such as committees, may be concerned more specifically with decision-making, but all groups must make some decisions. Group decision-making can be costly and time-consuming.

One particular feature of group versus individual performance is the concept of social loafing and the 'Ringelmann effect', which is the tendency for individuals to expend less effort when working as a member of a group than as an individual. A German psychologist, *Ringelmann*, compared the results of individual and group performance on a rope-pulling task. Workers were asked to pull as hard as they could on a rope, performing the task first individually and then with others in groups of varying size. A meter measured the strength of each pull. Although the total amount of force did increase with the size of the work group, the effort expended by each individual member decreased with the result that the total group effort was less than the expected sum of the individual contributions.[57]

According to *Hall*, there is a danger of elevating teams into a 'silver bullet' – a magic solution to all business problems.

> *It is not that I don't think teams work. They clearly do and it would be difficult to run an organisation of any size if you couldn't create and manage a team . . . The truth is that teams are not always the right answer to a problem. Often a well-briefed and well-managed group of individuals will do a task fine . . . A further point is that some very skilled individuals are not good team players.*[58]

However, the general feeling appears to be that the collective power of a group outshines individual performance.[59] 'Even though individuals working on their own are capable of phenomenal ingenuity, working together as a team can produce astounding results and a better decision.'[60] *Guirdham* believes that:

> *Compared with individuals, groups can make objectively better decisions to which people feel more commitment, while teams can perform functions and carry out projects better and more efficiently. This can only happen, however, if the people have the special skills and abilities needed.*[61]

One might expect, therefore, a higher standard of decision-making to result from group discussion. However, on the one hand, there is the danger of compromise and decisions being made in line with the 'highest common view' and, on the other hand, there is the phenomenon of the so-called **risky-shift**.

The risky-shift phenomenon

This suggests that instead of the group taking fewer risks and making safer or more conservative decisions, the reverse is often the case. Pressures for conformity means there is a tendency for groups to make more risky decisions than would individual members of the group on their own. Studies suggest that people working in groups generally advocate more risky alternatives than if they were making an individual decision on the same problem.[62]

Presumably, this is because members do not feel the same sense of responsibility for group decisions or their outcomes. 'A decision which is everyone's is the responsibility of no one.' Other explanations offered for the risky-shift phenomenon include:

1 People inclined to take risks are more influential in group discussions than more conservative people.
2 Risk-taking is regarded as a desirable cultural characteristic that is more likely to be expressed in a social situation such as group working.[63]

However, groups do appear to work well in the evaluation of ideas and to be more effective than individuals for problem-solving tasks requiring a range of knowledge and expertise. From a review of the research *Shaw* suggests that evidence supports the view that groups produce more solutions and better solutions to problems than do individuals.[64]

'Groupthink'

The effectiveness of group behaviour and performance can be adversely affected by the idea of **'groupthink'**. From an examination of some well-known government policy-making groups, *Janis* concluded that decisions can be characterised by groupthink which he defines as 'a deterioration of mental efficiency, reality testing, and moral judgment that results from in-group pressures'.[65] Groupthink results in the propensity for the group to just drift along. It is a generalised feature and can be apparent in any organisational situation where groups are relied upon to make important decisions.

Janis identifies a number of specific symptoms of groupthink:

1 There is an illusion of invulnerability with excessive optimism and risk-taking.
2 The discounting or discrediting of negative feedback that contradicts group consensus results in rationalisation in order to explain away any disagreeable information.
3 An unquestioned belief in the inherent morality of the group which leads members to be convinced of the logical correctness of what it is doing and to ignore ethical or moral consequences of decisions.
4 The group's desire to maintain consensus can lead to negative stereotyping of opponents or people outside the group, or to the acceptance of change.
5 There is pressure on individual members to conform and reach consensus so that minority or unpopular ideas may be suppressed.
6 Each member of the group may impose self-censorship in order to suppress their own objectives, or personal doubts or disagreements.

7 As a result of self-censorship, there is an illusion of unanimity with a lack of expressed dissent and a false sense of unity.
8 In the unlikely event of dissent or contrary information, this will give rise to the emergence of 'mind guards' who act as filters, guarding group leaders, deflecting opposition and applying pressure on deviants.

According to *Hambrick*:

Groupthink tends to occur when group members have very similar experiences and frame of references, particularly when they have relatively long tenures in the group. A company head who dislikes conflict or who punishes dissenters also creates the conditions for groupthink.[66]

Some commentators referred to groupthink as a feature of the perceived lack of decisive leadership and action associated with the economic depression in late 2008.

BRAINSTORMING

A **brainstorming** approach (sometimes now referred to as '**thought showers**' or 'cloud bursting' in order not to offend people with disorders such as epilepsy) involves the group adopting a 'freewheeling' attitude and generating as many ideas as possible, the more wild or apparently far-fetched the better.[67] As an illustrative exercise a group may be asked to generate as many and varied possible uses as they can for, for example, a man or woman's leather belt. Brainstorming is based on encouraging members to suspend judgement, the assumption that creative thinking is achieved best by encouraging the natural inclinations of group members, and the rapid production and free association of ideas. The quantity of ideas will lead to quality of ideas.

There are a number of basic procedures for brainstorming:

- It is based on maximum freedom of expression with a totally relaxed and informal approach.
- The initial emphasis is on the quantity of ideas generated, not the quality of ideas.
- No individual ideas are criticised or rejected at this stage, however wild or fanciful they may appear.
- A group size of between six and ten members is recommended.
- Members are encouraged to elaborate or build on ideas expressed by others and to bounce suggestions off one another.
- There is no comment on or evaluation of any particular idea until all ideas have been generated.
- There is need for good reporting of all the ideas either in writing and/or by tape or video recording.

An interesting and popular exercise to help illustrate the suspension of initial perceived barriers and the encouragement of creative thinking is given in Figure 6.10. This exercise may also be used to compare individual and group/team-based performance. Your tutor will provide the (or least one) answer. There may be others that the author is unaware of!

Effectiveness of brainstorming groups

One might reasonably expect that members of a brainstorming group would produce more creative problem-solving ideas than if the same members worked alone as individuals. Availability of time is an important factor. Over a longer period of time the group may produce more ideas through brainstorming than individuals could. Perhaps surprisingly, however, there appears to be doubt about the effectiveness of brainstorming groups over an individual working under the same conditions. Nevertheless, brainstorming still appears to have many advocates and is a popular activity for staff development programmes. Despite the rather negative view of nominal group brainstorming, we should recognise the importance of innovation for successful organisational performance.[68]

Figure 6.10　An example of creative thinking

The task is to see if it is possible to touch each of the nine spots using only four straight, interconnected lines.

SENSITIVITY TRAINING

Interest in the study of group process and behaviour has led to the development of group dynamics and a range of group training methods aimed at increasing group effectiveness through improving social interaction skills. A central feature of group dynamics is **sensitivity training**, in which members of a group direct attention to the understanding of their own behaviour and to perceiving themselves as others see them. The objectives are usually stated as:

- to increase sensitivity (the ability to perceive accurately how others react to oneself);
- diagnostic ability (the skill of assessing behavioural relationships between others and reasons for such behaviour); and
- behavioural flexibility or action skill (the ability to relate one's behaviour to the requirements of the situation).

The Johari window

A simple framework for looking at self-insight, which is used frequently to help individuals in the sensitivity training process, is the '**Johari window**' (*see* Figure 6.11). This classifies behaviour in matrix form between what is known–unknown to self and what is known–unknown to others.[69] A central feature of the **T-group** is reduction of the individual's 'hidden' behaviour through self-disclosure and reduction of the 'blind' behaviour through feedback from others.

- **Hidden behaviour** is that which the individual wishes to conceal from, or not to communicate to, other group members. It is part of the private self. An important role of the group is to establish whether members conceal too much, or too little, about themselves from other members.
- **The blind area** (that is behaviour known to others but unknown to self) includes mannerisms, gestures and tone of voice and represents behaviour of the impact of which on others the individual is unaware. This is sometimes referred to as the 'bad breath' area.

Members must establish an atmosphere of openness and trust in order that hidden and blind behaviours are reduced and the public behaviour enhanced.

BUILDING SUCCESSFUL TEAMS

Whatever the debate about a comparison between individual and group or team performance, or self-managed groups, effective teamworking is of increasing importance in modern organisations. This demands that the manager must be aware of, and pay attention to, a number of interrelated factors, including:

Figure 6.11 The Johari window

```
                    Behaviour ─────────→ Behaviour
                    known to self         unknown to self
Behaviour known
to others
               ┌──────────────┬──────────────┐
               │   PUBLIC     │    BLIND     │
               ├──────────────┼──────────────┤
               │   HIDDEN     │   UNKNOWN    │
               └──────────────┴──────────────┘
Behaviour unknown
to others
```

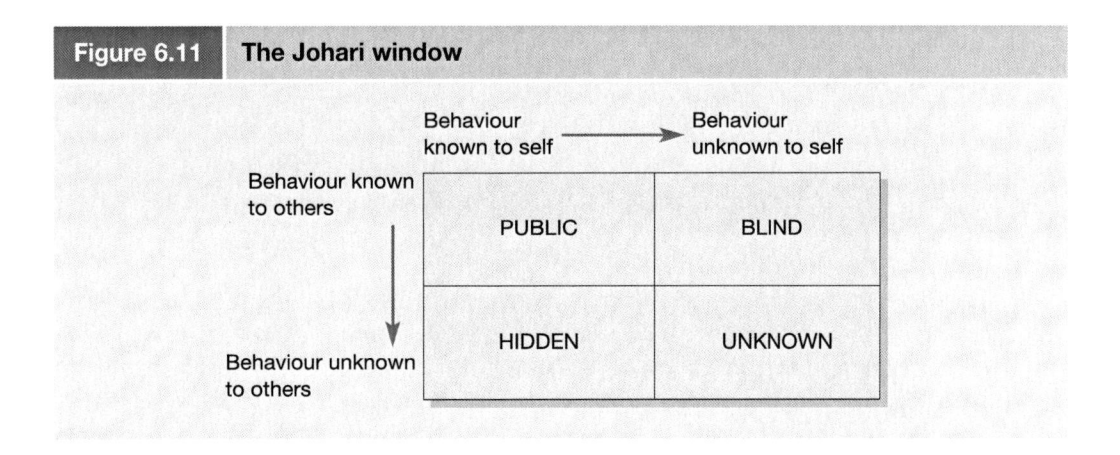

- clarification of objectives and available resources;
- organisational processes and the clarification of roles;
- empowerment, decision-making and channels of communication;
- patterns of interaction, and attention to both task and maintenance functions;
- social processes and the informal organisation;
- management systems and style of leadership;
- training and development.

The effectiveness of the team will also be influenced by the tasks to be undertaken, the nature of technology and the organisational environment. Ultimately, however, the performance of the team will be determined very largely by the characteristics of its members. The nature of group personality means that what works well for one team may not work well for an apparently similar team in the organisation.

We know everyone is different. When selecting people for your team, the most important thing to look for is ones who are decent, honest, bright and capable. You will find that good people will naturally work together as a team, will interrelate well and will want each other to succeed. And while I'm on the subject of teams, don't send people off on those terrible outward-bound weekends. Have a party instead.[70]

As *Wilson* points out, for example, although teamworking, like most management ideas, is very simple, nevertheless this simplicity conceals a great challenge.

The principles of teamworking may be easily understood, but the task of installing it can be quite daunting. Introducing teamworking is not a straightforward grafting job, the simple matter of adding a new idea to those already in place. It is about making a fundamental change in the way people work. Every teamworking application is different. Each organisation, department and individual group is faced with unique problems and in some situations it is more about getting rid of old ways of doing things than injecting new ones.[71]

A concept map of effective work groups is set out in Figure 6.12.

Skills for successful teamwork

The increasing need for collaboration and teamwork together with recognition for the individual has highlighted the need for attention to social skills and effective relationships between people. If people are not working together they are essentially a collection of individuals. *Douglas* refers to the importance of helping people to master the so-called 'soft' skills:

Figure 6.12 Concept map of effective work groups

EFFECTIVE WORK GROUPS

- GROUP EFFECTIVENESS
- FACTORS INFLUENCING GROUP EFFECTIVENESS
- BENEFITS OF EFFECTIVE WORKGROUPS

BENEFITS
- INDIVIDUAL
- ORGANISATION

ORGANISATION
- Individual contributions when taken together can result in a greater level of achievement (synergy)
- Groups can often work better at problem-solving than can individuals
- The employees can see more clearly that they are undertaking a process of employee involvement in the organisation
- Decisions become collectively shared, leading to easier implementation
- Communication channels become less fragmented and more efficient
- Conflict resolution is more often handled at the work group level

GROUP EFFECTIVENESS
Groups are effective when:
- The group achieves the target set
  - on time
  - to acceptable quality standards
  - within budget

AND
- the group members achieve personal rewards including
  - recognition of effort by other group members
  - recognition by the organisation
  - encouragement in their efforts

MANAGEMENT
- TEAM COMPOSITION

OVERALL MANAGEMENT
Management needs to deal with the following aspects:
- Setting appropriate team tasks
- Choosing team members carefully, having regard to:
  - individual skills
  - personality
  - availability, if a potential team member works on more than one project
  - the correct balance of skills
- Providing appropriate support
  - information
  - resources
  - such training as may be needed
  - opportunities for the team to build itself before and during the project
  - arrangements to monitor and inform the team over the project period

TEAM COMPOSITION AND ROLES (after BELBIN)
- LEADER.................... Co-ordinates the team activity
- SHAPER.................... Ensures the team attends to the task
- PLANT...................... Source of ideas
- EVALUATOR............. Examines and dissects ideas
- RESOURCE INVESTIGATOR....... Seeks resources inside and outside the team
- COMPANY WORKER....... Schedules tasks and activities
- FINISHER................. Ties up loose ends
- TEAM WORKER......... Backs up the team and maintains social relationships

IT IS ONLY IN LARGE TEAMS THAT EACH ROLE IS CARRIED BY ONE PERSON – MORE USUALLY, MORE THAN ONE ROLE IS HELD BY EACH INDIVIDUAL. CARE SHOULD BE TAKEN THAT ROLES DO NOT CONFLICT

INDIVIDUAL
Individual needs can be satisfied by:
- providing support
- maintaining morale
- having a small group to identify with
- efforts being more easily recognised
- enhanced mental security
- a feeling of protection

NOTE THAT NOT ALL EMPLOYEES WORK HAPPILY AS MEMBERS OF TEAMS. ORGANISATIONS NEWLY ADOPTING A PROJECT TEAM-BASED APPROACH NEED TO TAKE INTO ACCOUNT WORKING PREFERENCES OF EXISTING EMPLOYEES

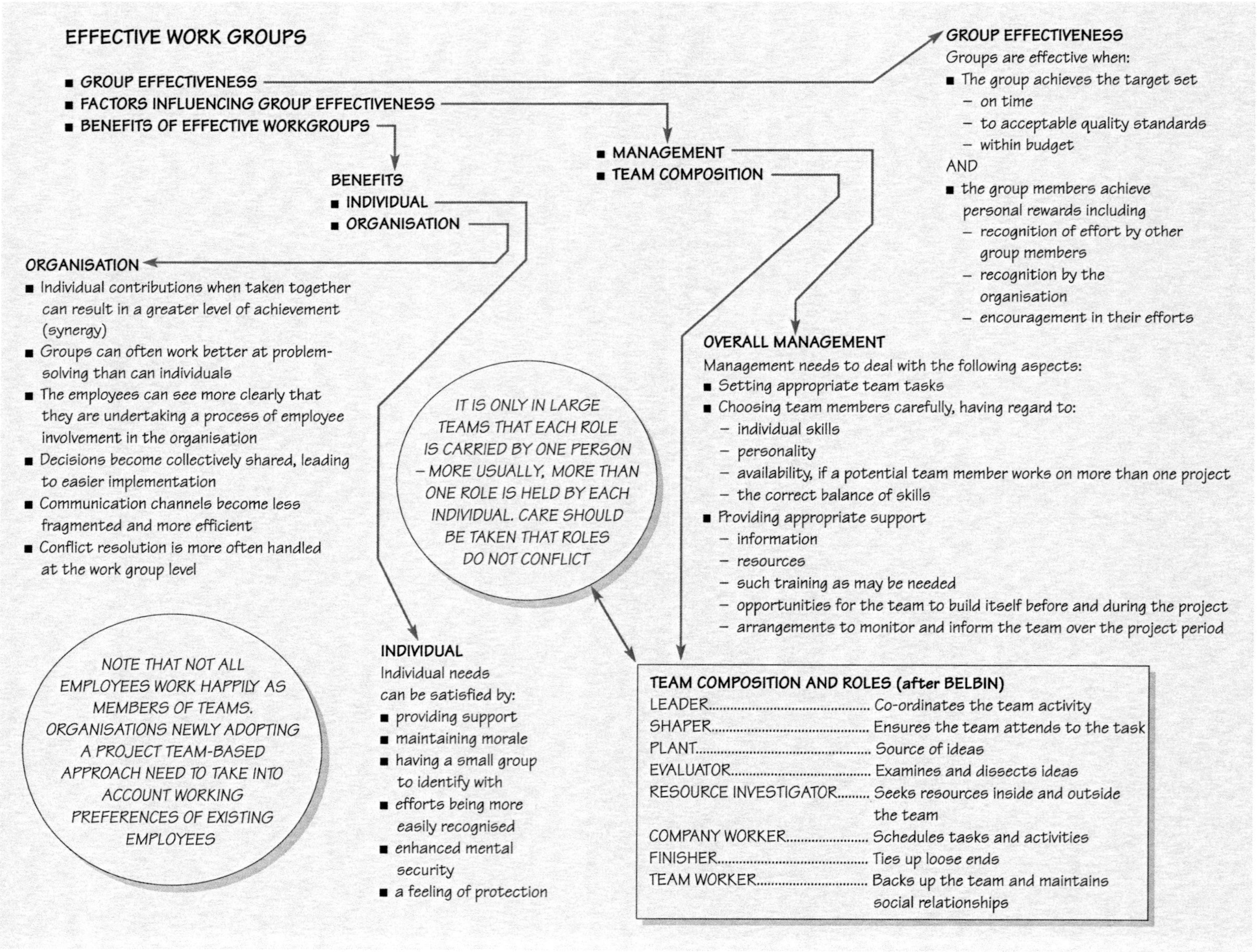

Source: Copyright © 2008 The Virtual Learning Materials Workshop. Reproduced with permission.

Organisations in most sectors – and especially in ones that are particularly demanding from a scientific or technical point of view – are operating in environments where collaboration, teamwork, and an awareness of the commercial consequences and implications of technical research are as important as scientific and technical skills themselves. Personnel with scientific and technical skills significantly disproportionate to their 'people' skills – by which I primarily mean people management capabilities and the knowledge of how to work with maximum effectiveness as part of a team – are increasingly unlikely to be as much of an asset to their organisation as they ought to be.[72]

However, Douglas points out that as we all interact with people to a greater or lesser extent in our everyday lives, there is a tendency to assume that people management skills are merely an extension of our natural abilities. In fact, people management skills are the more difficult and rare type of skill, but to a large extent they can be learned.

The role of emotional intelligence

Landale refers to the importance of emotional intelligence, discussed in Chapter 3, for effective team performance and to a research study by Yale University that found teams with high levels of EI outperformed teams with low levels of EI by a margin of two to one. However, individual high EI does not automatically translate into a high EI team and an extra set of skills is needed such as inclusive and collaborative working, being open to new opportunities, adaptability to change, and direct and honest communications.[73]

Critical reflection

'All this discussion about group membership and building successful teams is very interesting and sounds fine in the classroom. But it ignores the reality of the work environment for example with managing groups of workers in a restaurant kitchen, on a production assembly line, in a gay pub, or with professionals such as lecturers, doctors or lawyers.'

What are your views?

SYNOPSIS

■ Work is a group-based activity, and groups and teams are a major feature of human behaviour and work organisation. Harmonious working relationships and good teamwork help make for a high level of staff morale and organisational performance. There are two main types of groups at work, formal and informal.

■ Formal groups are deliberately planned and created by management as part of the organisation structure and to achieve specific organisational objectives. Informal groups are based on personal relationships and serve to satisfy members' psychological and social needs.

■ Factors that affect group cohesiveness can be considered under the broad headings of membership, work environment, organisational factors, and group development and maturity. An important and significant feature of group membership is social identity theory.

■ Membership of strong and cohesive groups can be a rewarding experience for the individual and have beneficial effects for the organisation. There are, however, potential disadvantages of strong, cohesive groups and the manager should attempt to prevent unconstructive intergroup conflict.

■ The combination of increasing globalisation and widespread developments in information communications and technology has given greater emphasis to the opportunities for, and need of, virtual teams. Members are geographically separated but still need to work together closely.

■ Inadequate or inappropriate role definition can result in role conflict, including role incompatibility, role ambiguity, role overload and role underload. It is important that the manager makes every effort to minimise role conflict and the causes of role stress.

- It is difficult to draw any firm comparison between individual and group or team performance. The effectiveness of group behaviour can be affected by the risky-shift phenomenon, the idea of groupthink and arguably a brainstorming approach.

- The effectiveness of the group/team will be influenced by the style of management, tasks to be undertaken, nature of technology and organisational environment. Ultimately, however, success will be determined very largely by the characteristics and behaviour of their members.

REVIEW AND DISCUSSION QUESTIONS

1. What is a group? Explain the importance and influence of group values and norms and give practical examples from within your own organisation.
2. How would you distinguish between a 'group' and a 'team'? To what extent do you believe the distinction has practical significance for managers?
3. Distinguish between formal and informal groups and provide your own supporting examples. What functions do informal groups serve in an organisation?
4. Identify different stages in group development and maturity. What other factors influence the cohesiveness of work groups? Give examples by reference to a work group to which you belong.
5. Discuss critically the advantages and disadvantages of virtual teams and how you believe they are likely to develop in the future.
6. What is meant by the role structure of an organisation? Construct a diagram that shows your own role-set within a work situation. Give examples of informal role expectations to which you are, or have been, a party.
7. Assess critically the likely standard of individual compared with group or team performance. Explain what is meant by (a) the risky-shift phenomenon, (b) groupthink and (c) brainstorming.
8. Detail fully the main factors to be considered in a review of effective teamworking.

MANAGEMENT IN THE NEWS

Dragon boat racing on the Thames

Dominic Bliss

A pain is spreading down my arm. Twenty of us, seated in 10 rows, two to a bench, are paddling furiously aboard a 40ft dragon boat. It is a disconcerting, not to mention exhausting, experience. As we plough down the Thames in London's Royal Albert Dock, we take orders from a helmsman and keep time to a drum. It's almost as if we're slaves in a galley, except we're supposed to be doing this for fun. I'm racing with the Thames Dragon Boat Club, and I'm quickly learning that perfectly synchronised paddling is the key to survival. Without it there's no way to generate speed through the water.

'Watch the strokes at the front of the boat and keep in time with them,' shouts team coach Liam Keane, seated beside me in the boat. 'Ideally, we want everyone's paddles entering and exiting the water at exactly the same time. You could have

Is dragon boat racing the truest of all team sports? Tight teamwork and simple technique make dragon boat racing the perfect corporate team sport.

20 enormous beefcakes powering a dragon boat, but if they're not paddling in time with each other, they won't be effective.'

'When people first start this sport, they just go for power,' Keane adds. 'But you need to get into a team mentality. Get your timing locked in and feel the rhythm of the boat.' His voice starts to waver as the helmsman suddenly barks out the orders to increase the pace, at which the 10-year-old drummer, Amy, seated at the prow, ups the tempo accordingly. We've reached 65 strokes a minute, which is close to race pace. My arms and shoulders are beginning to protest as the lactic acid builds up, and my heart pumps wildly. Although each paddling action is identical, one has to concentrate hard to get the timing and the angle of entry into and out of the water just right.

On more than a few occasions I catch a crab and splash the right ear of the female paddler in front of me with ice-cold water. In due course I get my own dousing courtesy of the chap sitting behind me, who is also a beginner. There's neither the time nor the spare breath to apologise. I'm told later that we achieved a top speed of about 8 knots. With a full crew of experienced paddlers in a race situation, this might reach 9 knots. The tight teamwork required and the simple technique make dragon boating the perfect corporate team sport. 'Anybody can do this,' Keane stresses. 'You can put a bunch of novices into a boat and within 10 minutes they're paddling. You couldn't do that with rowing because it's more of a fine art. They might end up capsizing the boat.'

Paul Coster, the club chairman, insists that dragon boating is the truest of all team sports. 'The camaraderie is so important,' he says. 'We train together, we race together, we get drunk together. That's why lots of companies do this. It's great for team-building.' Back on the water, our practice is beginning to pay off. Suddenly we all lock into the same rhythm – 20 paddlers in perfect unison. It almost feels as if we've ceased to be separate athletes and have joined forces into a single entity, like a shoal of fish or a flock of birds. And for a blissful moment, I forget the pain.

Source: Adapted from Dominic Bliss, 'Dragon boat racing on the Thames', *Financial Times*, 4 April 2009. Copyright © 2009 The Financial Times Limited, reproduced with permission.

Discussion questions

1 Using the model at Figure 6.1 to structure your answer, explain why dragon boat racing can be a useful means of turning groups into teams.

2 What can we learn from the article about the importance of the 'informal' aspects of organisations? What problems could the informal group or organisation cause for managers in an organisation with a highly diverse workforce?

ASSIGNMENT 1

Recall your experience of a work group or team with which you are familiar and comment critically on:

1 the extent to which members were clear about the goals of the group, what they were expected to achieve, and how their performance would be evaluated;

2 the diversity of group membership, and significances of diversity for the operations and success of the group; and

3 what *exactly* made the group effective or fall apart?

ASSIGNMENT 2

Working in small self-selecting teams you are required to design and present an 'ice-breaker' exercise as a fun way to help groups of new students (or other new members or delegates) to get to know and interact with each other. The exercise should be:

simple, easy to understand and undertake, entertaining, something to which all members of the team/group can contribute, and that can be completed within 30 minutes.

Your tutor will be asked to decide which team has come up with the most novel, engaging and appropriate exercise.

If possible, attempt to employ the chosen exercise in a real-life situation. How successful was the exercise?

CASE STUDY

Top Gear

First aired in 1977 as an essentially factual programme about cars and road safety, *Top Gear* has been on the BBC national schedules since 1978. The 2008–09 season achieved record viewing figures of between 7–7.5m (around 25 per cent of audience share) with its blend of car review, driving news and comment, liberally interspersed with stunts, challenges and unlikely races. These have become a centrepiece of the show; memorable items include the increasingly desperate attempts to 'kill' a Toyota Hilux, a drive across the desert in Botswana in used cars, and a race up (and back down) a mountain between an Audi and a speed climber.[74] The team's propensity for 'mucking about' gives the distinct impression that Richmal Crompton's William and the Outlaws have got older and become TV presenters.

Jeremy Clarkson and *Top Gear* have become almost synonymous. His style of presentation coupled with outspoken, politically incorrect and often outrageous views boosted viewing figures. His reviews can be ecstatic as well as wholly dismissive. Despite regular criticism from road safety campaigners, environmentalists, and public transport organisations together with a range of individual complaints from Stonewall (the gay and lesbian pressure group) Headway (a brain injury charity) and the RNIB amongst others, Clarkson remains the main draw of the programme. Public opinion is divided as to whether he is clever and obnoxious or simply obnoxious – in either case he is self-assured, funny, occasionally bad tempered, and never averse to a bit of cheating if it means he gets to win. He also knows a great deal about cars.

James May was an established journalist when he joined the show. He appears slightly more 'posh', erudite and cultured than avowed 'petrolheads' Clarkson and Hammond, and thus a butt of their jokes. He was nicknamed 'Captain Slow' for his careful driving style, combined with a preference for classic vehicles over the sporty machines favoured by the others. In the show's challenges, where the presenters are often required to adapt or alter a vehicle to serve some other purpose, he is careful, organised (he keeps tools clean and neatly arranged) and thoughtful. Where Clarkson and Hammond are likely to improvise or go for the spectacular, May plans and pays attention to the minor details. In news pieces he is usually the one to show a fascination with technicalities and the 'boring' facts and figures.[75] In addition to presenting *Top Gear*, May writes a regular motoring column, has published a number of books and made documentaries on various scientific subjects including the moon landings.

In 2002, Richard Hammond arrived from a job presenting *Motorweek*. Generally seen as the most likeable and good humoured member of the team, his happy enthusiasm coupled with his size earned him the nickname 'Hamster'. He often finds himself between the abrasive Clarkson and the obsessive, sometimes tetchy, May, and seems to act as a buffer between the two. His popularity became evident when, on 20 September 2006, he had a catastrophic accident whilst test driving a jet powered car for the series. Airlifted to Leeds General Infirmary, he was initially reported as having significant brain injury.[76] Fears that the Hamster would not fully recover were allayed when he left hospital a matter of weeks after the crash. He made a remarkably speedy return to the show in February 2007 to huge acclaim, and his status as the petrolhead with a heart of gold was affirmed when he adopted and restored the battered Opel Kadett (named Oliver) in which he had driven across Botswana for series 10.

The show's 'tame racing driver' – the unidentified automaton in the white jumpsuit and helmet, is the subject of regular speculation and much press hype.

What makes a team tick? Top Gear's Jezza, Captain Slow, the Hamster and the Stig blend of personalities make for the best jobs in telly.

Source: Nils Jorgensen/Rex Features

His contribution to the show is to provide consistent, high-level technical and driving expertise for the speed trials of featured vehicles, and to tutor the 'star' who attempts a fast lap of the *Top Gear* track each week. He occasionally participates in challenges; memorably attempting to cross London by public transport in a race with a speedboat (Clarkson), a bicycle (Hammond) and a Mercedes (May).[77]

The executive producer of the show, Andy Wilman, is just as important a member of the team as the presenters. He is generally credited, along with Clarkson, with re-launching the show in 2001 and creating the formula which pushed it back up the ratings. His contributions included the idea of the studio audience, the *Top Gear* race track and the features which make it entertaining even for those without an obsessive interest in cars. He views the team spirit which prevails in the show as crucial to its success:

It's taken us three, maybe four yours to get the show to this level of comfort. The presenters just muck about – it's obvious that they're at ease, even when they get niggly with each other.[78]

Top Gear has both admirers and critics in large numbers. It is accused of political bias, the glorification of speed,[79] macho bigotry, political incorrectness and sexism. The only female petrolhead to have appeared on the show is Sabine Schmitz,[80] who beat Clarkson's fastest time round the Nürburgring in a Jaguar S-type by 47 seconds at her first attempt.[81] Yet one of Wilman's treasured moments was not on screen at all; it was when the team visited British troops in Afghanistan for three days before Christmas 2007.

For three days they shook hands, signed autographs and did their best to spread a bit of cheer to lads who wouldn't be with their families at Santa time, and the reaction of the soldiers was humbling.[82]

Your tasks

1 Analyse the main team members using Belbin's team roles as a framework. Which roles do the members appear to fit? Note: One person may have both a main role and a backup role. Are there any significant components missing?

2 *Top Gear* is criticised for being all male and exhibiting 'laddish' behaviour. Do you think the BBC should add a woman to the team? Explain the reasoning for your answer.

The Botswana trip from series 10 can be accessed via the *Top Gear* website http://www.topgear.com/uk/videos/botswana-1 and http://www.topgear.com/uk/videos/botswana-2

The Vietnamese trip from series 12 can be accessed via the *Top Gear* website http://www.topgear.com/uk/videos/vietnam-pt-1#/uk/videos-by-category?VideoCategory=TheBigFilms&Page=2 and http://www.topgear.com/uk/videos/vietnam-pt-2#/uk/videos-by-category?VideoCategory=TheBigFilms&Page=2

The American trip from series 12 can be accessed via the *Top Gear* website http://www.topgear.com/uk/videos/team-america-2-part-1 also http://www.topgear.com/uk/videos/team-america-2-part-2#/uk/videos-by-category?VideoCategory=TheBigFilms&Page=1 and http://www.topgear.com/uk/videos/team-america-2-part-3#/uk/videos-by-category?VideoCategory=TheBigFilms&Page=2

NOTES AND REFERENCES

1 Schein, E. H. *Organizational Psychology*, third edition, Prentice Hall (1988), p. 145.
2 Adair, J. *Effective Teambuilding*, Gower (1986).
3 Crainer, S. *Key Management Ideas: Thinkers that Changed the Management World*, third edition, Financial Times Prentice Hall (1998), p. 237.
4 'Teamwork: Success Through People' Advisory Booklet, ACAS, October 2007, p. 24.
5 Holpp, L. 'Teams: It's All in the Planning', *Training & Development*, vol. 51, no. 4, April 1997, pp. 44–7.
6 Cane, S. *Kaizen Strategies for Winning Through People*, Pitman Publishing (1996), p. 116.
7 Belbin, R. M. *Beyond the Team*, Butterworth-Heinemann (2000).
8 Riches, A. 'Emotionally Intelligent Teams', Organisational Change & Leadership Development, www.anneriches.com.au, accessed 11 March 2003.
9 Boynton, A. and Fischer B. *Virtuoso Teams: Lessons From Teams that Changed their Worlds*, Financial Times Prentice Hall (2005).
10 Lysons, K. 'Organisational Analysis', Supplement to *The British Journal of Administrative Management*, no. 18, March/April 1997.
11 Law, S. 'Beyond the Water Cooler', *Professional Manager*, January 2005, pp. 26–8.

12. See, for example: Jay, A. *Corporation Man*, Penguin (1975). In an amusing historical account of the development of different forms of groups, Jay suggests that ten is the basic size of human grouping.
13. Cane, S. *Kaizen Strategies for Winning Through People*, Pitman Publishing (1996), p. 131.
14. McKenna, P. J. and Maister, D. H. 'Building Team Trust', *Consulting to Management*, vol. 13, no. 4, December 2002, pp. 51–3.
15. Farrell, E. 'Take the Lead in Setting Standards of Behaviour in your Team', *Professional Manager*, vol. 19, no. 1, January 2009, p. 14.
16. Bass, B. M. and Ryterband, E. C. *Organizational Psychology*, second edition, Allyn & Bacon (1979).
17. Tuckman, B. W. 'Development Sequence in Small Groups', *Psychological Bulletin*, vol. 63, 1965, pp. 384–99; and Tuckman, B. W. and Jensen, M. C. 'Stages of Small Group Development Revised', *Group and Organizational Studies*, vol. 2, no. 3, 1977, pp. 419–27.
18. Cited in Green, J. 'Are Your Teams and Groups at Work Successful?', *Administrator*, December 1993, p. 12.
19. Rickards, T. and Moger, S. 'Creative Leadership and Team Effectiveness: Empirical Evidence for a Two Barrier Model of Team Development', Working paper presented at *The Advanced Seminar Series, University of Upsalla, Sweden*, 3 March 2009. See also, Rickards, T. and Moger, S. 'Creative Leadership Processes in Project Team Development: An Alternative to Tuckman's Stage Model?' *British Journal of Management*, Part 4, 2000, pp. 273–83.
20. Tajfel, H. and Turner, J. C. 'The Social Identity Theory of Inter-Group Behaviour' in Worchel, S. and Austin, L. W., (eds) *Psychology of Intergroup Relations*, Nelson-Hall (1986), pp. 7–24.
21. Guirdham, M. *Interactive Behaviour at Work*, third edition, Financial Times Prentice Hall (2002), p. 118.
22. Haslam, S. A., *Psychology in Organizations: The Social Identity Approach*, second edition, Sage Publications (2004), p. 17.
23. See, for example Flynn, F. J., Chatman, J. A. and Spataro, S. E., 'Getting to Know You: The Influence of Personality on Impressions and Performance of Demographically Different People in Organizations', *Administrative Science Quarterly*, vol. 46, 2001, pp. 414–42.
24. Hewstone, M., Ruibin, M. and Willis, H. 'Intergroup Bias', *Annual Review of Psychology*, vol. 53, 2002, pp. 575–604.
25. Argyle, M. *The Social Psychology of Work*, second edition, Penguin (1989).
26. Brooks, I. *Organisational Behaviour: Individuals, Groups and Organisation*, third edition, Financial Times Prentice Hall (2006) p. 99.
27. 'Teamwork: Success Through People', Advisory Booklet, ACAS, October 2007, p. 8.
28. See, for example: Kinsman, F. 'The Virtual Office and the Flexible Organisation', *Administrator*, April 1994, pp. 31–2; and Chowdhury, S. *Management 21C*. Financial Times Prentice Hall (2000).
29. Hall, P. 'Team Solutions Need Not Be the Organisational Norm', *Professional Manager*, July 2001, p. 45.
30. Parker, C. 'Remote Control – a Case Study', *Manager, The British Journal of Administrative Management*, March/April 2002, p. 30.
31. Norval, D. in conversation with Law, S. 'Beyond the Water Cooler', *Professional Manager*, January 2005, pp. 26–8.
32. Symons, J. 'Taking Virtual Team Control', *Professional Manager*, vol. 12, no. 2, March 2003, p. 37.
33. Garrett, A. 'Crash Course in Managing a Virtual Team', *Management Today*, September 2007, p. 20.
34. Francesco, A. M. and Gold, B. A. *International Organizational Behavior*, second edition, Pearson Prentice Hall (2005), p. 118.
35. Murray, S. 'Virtual Teams: Global Harmony is their Dream', *Financial Times*, 11 May 2005.
36. See, for example: Lerner, P. M. 'Beware the Gatekeeper', *Amtrak Express*, July/August 1994, pp. 14–17.
37. Miner, J. B. *Management Theory*, Macmillan (1971).
38. See, for example: Mullins, L. J. *Hospitality Management and Organisational Behaviour*, fourth edition, Longman (2001).
39. 'Teamwork: Success Through People', Advisory Booklet, ACAS, October 2007, p. 6.
40. Lucas, E. 'And the Winner is Everyone', *Professional Manager*, January 2001, p. 10.
41. Adams, S. 'A-class Teams Achieve A-class Results', *Manager, The British Journal of Administrative Management*, Autumn 2008, p. 21.
42. Guirdham, M. *Interactive Behaviour at Work*, third edition, Financial Times Prentice Hall (2002), p. 12.
43. Ashmos, D. P. and Nathan, M. L. 'Team Sense-Making: A Mental Model for Navigating Uncharted Territories', *Journal of Managerial Issues*, vol. 14, no. 2, Summer 2002, p. 198.
44. De Rond, M. and Holland, D. 'Pulling Together', *Professional Manager*, vol. 17, no. 5, September 2008, pp. 30–2.
45. Peeling, N. *Brilliant Manager: What the Best Managers Know, Do and Say*, Pearson Prentice Hall (2005), pp. 129–30.
46. Obeng, E. *All Change*, Pitman Publishing (1994).
47. Crainer, S. *Key Management Ideas: Thinkers that Changed the Management World*, third edition, Financial Times Prentice Hall (1998), p. 238.
48. 'Teamwork: Success Through People', Advisory Booklet, ACAS, October 2007, pp. 4–6.
49. Guirdham, M. *Interactive Behaviour at Work*, third edition, Financial Times Prentice Hall (2002), p. 463.
50. Belbin, R. M. *Management Teams: Why They Succeed or Fail*, Butterworth-Heinemann (1981).
51. Belbin, R. M. *Team Roles at Work*, Butterworth-Heinemann (1993).
52. Arroba, T. and Wedgwood-Oppenheim, F. 'Do Senior Managers Differ in The Public and Private Sector? An Examination of Team-Role Preferences', *Journal of Managerial Psychology*, vol. 9, no.1, 1994, pp. 13–16.
53. Fisher, S. G., Hunter, T. A. and Macrosson, W. D. K. 'The Distribution of Belbin Team Roles among UK Managers', *Personnel Review*, vol. 29, no. 2, 2000, pp. 124–40.
54. Bavelas, A. 'A Mathematical Model for Group Structures', *Applied Anthropology*, vol. 7, 1948, pp. 19–30, and Bavelas, A. 'Communication Patterns in Task-Oriented Groups', in Lasswell, H. N. and Lerner, D. (eds) *The Policy Sciences*, Stanford University Press (1951).
55. Leavitt, H. J. 'Some Effects of Certain Communication Patterns on Group Performance', *Journal of Abnormal and Social Psychology*, vol. 46, 1951, pp. 38–50. See also: Leavitt, H. J. *Managerial Psychology*, fourth edition, University of Chicago Press (1978).
56. Benne, K. D. and Sheats, P. 'Functional Roles of Group Members', *Journal of Social Issues*, vol. 4, 1948, pp. 41–9.
57. Kravitz, D. A. and Martin, B. 'Ringlemann Rediscovered: The Original Article', *Journal of Personality and Social Psychology*, May 1986, pp. 936–41.

58 Hall, P. 'Team Solutions Need Not Be the Organisational Norm', *Professional Manager*, July 2001, p. 45.
59 See, for example: Blanchard, K. and Bowles, S. *High Five: None of Us is as Smart as All of Us*, HarperCollins Business (2001).
60 Stanley, T. J. 'The Challenge of Managing a High-Performance Team', *SuperVision*, vol. 63, no. 7, July 2002, pp. 10–12.
61 Guirdham, M. *Interactive Behaviour at Work*, third edition, Financial Times Prentice Hall (2002), p. 498.
62 Kogan, N. and Wallach, M. A. 'Risk-Taking as a Function of the Situation, the Person and the Group', in Newcomb, T. M. (ed.) *New Directions in Psychology III*, Holt, Rinehart & Winston (1967).
63 For a comprehensive review of the 'risky-shift' phenomenon, see, for example: Clarke, R. D. 'Group Induced Shift Towards Risk: A Critical Appraisal', *Psychological Bulletin*, vol. 76, 1971, pp. 251–70. See also: Vecchio, R. P. *Organizational Behavior*, third edition, Harcourt Brace & Company (1995).
64 Shaw, M. E. *Group Dynamics*, McGraw-Hill (1976).
65 Janis, J. L. *Victims of Groupthink*, Houghton Mifflin (1972) and Janis, J. L. *Groupthink*, second edition, Houghton Mifflin (1982).
66 Hambrick, D. 'Putting the Team into Top Management', in Pickford, J. (ed.), *Financial Times Mastering Management 2.0*, Financial Times Prentice Hall (2001), p. 289.
67 Osborn, A. F. Applied Imagination: Principles and Procedures of Creative Thinking, Scribner's (1963).
68 See, for example: Waterman, R. *The Frontiers of Excellence*, Nicholas Brearley (1994).
69 Luft, J. *Group Processes: An Introduction to Group Dynamics*, second edition, National Press (1970). (The term 'Johari window' was derived from a combination of the first names of the original authors, Joseph Luft and Harry Ingham.)
70 Robinson (Sir) Gerry *I'll Show Them Who's Boss*, BBC Books (2004), p. 183.
71 Wilson, J. 'Building Teams – with Attitude', *Professional Manager*, September 1998, p. 13.
72 Douglas, M. 'Why Soft Skills Are an Essential Part of the Hard World of Business', *Manager, The British Journal of Administrative Management*, New Year 2003, pp. 34–5.
73 Landale, A. 'Must have EQ', *Manager: The British Journal of Administrative Management*, February/March 2007, p. 24.
74 Many of these can be enjoyed at the show's website, www.bbc.co.uk/topgear/videos, accessed 7 August 2009.
75 For instance, in the final show of the 13th series May and Clarkson had to devise an advert for the VW Scirocco; May's involved information about the vehicle's performance and a suggestion that it would have been the choice of major ecclesiastic figures from history; Clarkson's version was based on explosions and the invasion of Poland.
76 BBC news website 2006 'TV host seriously hurt in crash' 21 September 2006. http://news.bbc.co.uk/1/hi/england/north_yorkshire/5365676.stm, accessed 7 August 2009.
77 You can find out who won at http://www.topgear.com/uk/videos/london-calling, accessed 7 August 2009.
78 Warman, M. 'How *Top Gear* Drove its Way into Our Hearts' *Daily Telegraph* 2 November 2007. http://www.telegraph.co.uk/news/features/3634534/How-Top-Gear-drove-its-way-into-our-hearts.html, accessed 8 August 2009.
79 Moran, J. 2009 'The Myth of *Top Gear*' *The Guardian*, 10 June 2008. http://www.guardian.co.uk/commentisfree/2008/jun/10/automotive.bbc, accessed 8 August 2009.
80 The German racing driver and presenter of a German motoring programme, D-Motor.
81 She later got within 9 seconds of beating his Jaguar time in a Ford Transit van.
82 Wilman, A. 2009 '*Top Gear* producer gives inside story on *Top Gear*', The Times Online, 21 June 2009. http://www.timesonline.co.uk/tol/driving/features/article6536786.ece?token=null&offset=0&page=1, accessed 7 August 2009.

HRM AS A CONCEPT

CHAPTER 10

Organising and managing human resources

Objectives

Having read this chapter and completed its associated activities, readers should be able to:

- See the value of regarding the 'human resources' which organisations require for long-term survival not as people but as the efforts and capabilities that an organisation requires to be able to function in both the short and the long term.

- Recognise that human resourcing and employment issues in organisations, while requiring specialist expertise in their management, are nevertheless activities in which all managers are inevitably involved.

- Put into context the alleged 'rise of HRM', noting the considerable ambiguities and conceptual inadequacies associated with the 'HRM' notion.

- Understand the centrality to organisational strategy making of human resourcing issues and appreciate the inadequacy of treating HR strategy as something that follows from or 'serves' the main corporate or business strategy.

- Relate the day-to-day issues of organisational human resourcing to basic dilemmas and tensions that have to be managed when employing people within industrial capitalist societies and economies.

- See how human resource management plays a particularly strategic role in employing organisations because it necessarily applies to employment issues (a) a corporate rather than a sectional focus and (b) a long-term rather than an immediate or short-term focus.

- Appreciate the distinctive tensions and ambiguities facing HR specialists in their relationships with other departments and managers.

- Recognise that the basic choice between *direct* and *indirect* efforts to achieve managerial control identified in Chapter 8 is central to strategic human resourcing choices and relates to the choice between *low commitment* and *high commitment* HR strategies – a choice which is influenced by how problematic employee constituencies are perceived to be for the organisation's future.

- Come to terms with the fact that employees are not unchanging entities, units of labour or 'human resources' that can be selected, recruited controlled and processed, as some HR thinking tends to assume.

Organisational human resources and the employment relationship

Human resourcing and employment issues are utterly central to the existence of work organisations. They not only affect the employment experience of every single member of an organisation, they also pervade every aspect of organisational management. This is not to argue that human resourcing work is more important than finance, production or service delivery, say, as a facet of organisational management. Activities in all of these areas are vital to an organisation's performance and long-term survival. The difference with human resourcing matters is that they tend to arise with regard to every other aspect of managerial work. It is possible for most members of management to leave specialists in these areas to handle the main tasks of marketing, accounting or production. The same is not possible with regard to human resourcing matters however. Most people in managerial positions will have some responsibility for other employees. They thus necessarily get involved in the selection of staff to work in their departments as well as with the training, payment, deployment, appraisal, career development, welfare, grievances, discipline and possible redundancy of these employees. Expert support is likely to be required in all of these areas, and managers with corporate HR responsibilities will almost inevitably impose constraints on local managerial discretion. Human resourcing responsibilities, to varying degrees, will form part of the work of most managers in modern organisations, however. Even where a manager does not have direct responsibility for other employees, they will still be unable to distance themselves entirely from matters of employment relationships – not least because they are employees themselves with an interest in their own rewards, career development and future deployment.

A frequently heard cliché says that 'people management' is a concern of every manager in an organisation. Is this the argument that is being advanced here? It is not – at least not in these terms. In Chapter 1 it was argued that it is unhelpful to frame managerial work in terms of 'managing people'. This was because such a notion is morally questionable and because the expectation that anyone can actually 'manage people' is utterly unrealistic. The recalcitrance or unmanageability of human beings is one of the very factors that make human resourcing issues so central to organisational strategy making. This point will be developed later in this chapter. But in talking of 'human resourcing' or 'human resource management' are we not adopting a position that is even more morally dubious than what is implied in talk of 'people management'? The answer to this question would most certainly be yes – if we were using the term 'human resources' to mean 'human beings'. To speak of people as human resources, let alone to *relate* to people in such a dehumanising way, is surely to adopt a stance little different from that of slave traders and slave owners. To treat people as means to ends instead of treating them as free and autonomous citizens of a democracy would be to abandon some of the key principles that modern societies are allegedly based upon. Yet people's *services* are acquired by employing organisations in industrial capitalist societies and are exploited to serve ends other than those of the employees themselves. In slavery it was people themselves who were bought and sold. Under capitalism it is people's labour – the work that they can do for an organisation – that is bought and sold. In recognition of this, we need a concept of human resources that avoids treating people as 'resources' while recognising that people bring with them into the employment relationship with a work organisation efforts, skills and capacities which are indeed treated as resources and which managers do try to 'manage'.

Human resources — *Concept*

The efforts, knowledge, capabilities and committed behaviours which people contribute to a work organisation as part of an employment exchange (or a more temporary labour engagement) and which are managerially utilised to complete tasks and enable the organisation to continue its existence into the future.

A key dimension, then, of the overall managerial task in a work organisation is that which concerns itself with obtaining, developing and from time to time dispensing with 'human resources' in this sense and maintaining the basic pattern of employment relationships which make the utilisation of these resources possible. This takes us towards a notion of *human resource management*.

'HRM': an ambiguous and confusing term?

Before we can develop further a useful notion of *human resource management*, we have to come to terms with the rather messy situation that currently exists whereby the term 'human resource management' is used in a confusing variety of ways. This can cause considerable confusion in the study of human resourcing aspects of organisations and the changing ways in which employment issues are being managed.

The term 'HRM' tends to be used in three ways:

- to refer to an academic area of study which brings together what were previously the separate topic areas of personnel management, industrial relations

HRM as a concept 229

Table 10.1 A summary of how much academic writing on HRM tends to contrast an aspired-to 'new' HRM with the 'personnel management' which it rejects

Key features aspired to for the 'new' HRM	Alleged characteristics of personnel management rejected by the 'new' HRM
HRM takes on a strategic emphasis and a strong business or 'bottom-line awareness'	Personnel management is said to have an operational emphasis and simply involve itself in 'servicing' the organisation with a supply of suitable and compliant staff
HRM concentrates on building harmonious and reciprocal relationships with employees	Personnel management is said to concentrate on managing conflicts with employees
With HRM, employment and resourcing issues become the concern of all managers	Personnel management was said to keep employment and resourcing issues as its own specialist concern
HRM specialists work as 'business partners' with other managers (in so far as HR specialists are retained, rather than their expertise being outsourced or 'bought in' from consultants)	Personnel managers are said to relate to other managers sometimes by advising them on employee issues and, at other times, by policing them to ensure compliance with corporate personnel policies and procedures
HRM develops a personal and high commitment relationship between the employer and each individual employee	Personnel management is said to find it acceptable to have either a low commitment arm's-length relationship with each individual employee or to relate to employees 'collectively' through the intermediary of a trade union
HRM is associated with a high-trust organisational culture making significant use of team working and other 'indirect control' devices that make close supervision, detailed procedures and strict hierarchies unnecessary	Personnel management is said to be associated with lower trust relationships with employees, more 'direct' management controls and relatively bureaucratic structures and procedures

and aspects of 'organisational behaviour' such as motivation, leadership and work design;

- to refer to all those aspects of managerial work that deal with employees (sometimes used interchangeably with 'people management');
- to refer to those activities that were once referred to as *personnel management* ones but which are said to justify a re-labelling as 'HRM' when they take on the features identified in the left-hand column of Table 10.1. In this usage, 'HRM' is a new approach to handling human resourcing and employment issues in organisations.

These alleged differences between something called 'HRM' and something called 'personnel management' are ones that have been put forward by academic writers trying to identify possible trends in how human resourcing and employment management issues are dealt with in work organisations (see Storey, 1992, Legge, 1995 and Further Reading on HRM, the academic literature, p. 445). The labelling of these two approaches as 'HRM' on the one hand and as 'personnel management' on the other has been entirely a choice of academics. In the world of personnel management practice, many practitioners were moving in this alleged 'HRM' direction long before academic observers chose to apply the HRM label to such shifts of emphasis. It is important to recognise, however, that the trend within work organisations to replace the 'Personnel' title with 'HR' is not necessarily connected to the alleged move from personnel practices to 'HRM' practices within organisations. Many personnel departments have indeed been renamed as HR departments but this has largely been a matter of adopting a title that is more fashionable and which is felt to sound more hard-headed or businesslike than 'personnel'. It is only marginally connected to the academic distinction between HRM and personnel management.

Unfortunately much academic work jumps back and forth between two uses of the HRM label. Sometimes it uses the term HRM to refer to human resourcing and employment management work generally as we are doing here. At other times it uses the label to refer only to a particular human resourcing and employment management approach – one which we will here be characterising as 'high commitment HRM'. Let us, for now, examine the nature of HRM as a broad phenomenon which occurs in every work organisation, whether it be large or small, socially progressive or reactionary, and whether or not it possesses a formalised 'HR' function.

Human resource management

It was argued in Chapter 2 that systems-control assumptions about work organisations usefully draw attention to patterns of cooperation and how different elements of organisations link to each other. They nevertheless tend to avert attention from all the 'conflicts, arguments, debates, ambiguities and sheer guesswork that characterises the *process* and *relationships* that what we might call "real" managerial practice has to cope with all of the time' (p. 52). Systems-control perspective tends to work with a notion of overall organisational goals, implying through this that organisations are more 'unitary' and have a level of overall consensus about purposes and priorities than has ever been observed in practice. A great deal of HRM writing has a strong unitary flavour of this kind (Watson, 2004, 2006). Process-relational perspective, on the other hand, gives full weight to the multiplicity of goals and priorities that exist within every organisation. It recognises that differences of interest and clashes of individual and group priorities have constantly to be coped with – or managed. It also recognises the centrality of *power* and *micropolitical* activities to the way organisational order is negotiated and it acknowledges the significance of various types of *organisational mischief* to organisational functioning. What is required is a notion of *human resource management* that acknowledges the pluralistic, messy, ambiguous and inevitably conflict-ridden nature of work organisations.

A notion of HRM that is consistent with a process-relational framing of organisational realities would be one that recognises that managerial work involves attempts to achieve as much productive cooperation and unity of purpose as is sensibly possible in any given organisation. It also recognises that this is only ever partially achievable and that HRM work, in every aspect, has to handle ambiguities, tensions and conflicts. It will never find panaceas or 'best practices' that will overcome dissent and turn every organisation into a happy family or a unified team. Instead it will engage in a constant struggle to 'manage conflicts', to persuade, put pressure upon and negotiate with employees – making deals and shaping implicit contracts that will enable work tasks to be performed in a way that helps the organisation continue into the future.

In this spirit we can put forward a formal definition of HRM.

Human resource management *Concept*

That part of managerial work which is concerned with acquiring, developing and dispensing with the efforts, skills and capabilities of an organisation's workforce and maintaining organisational relationships within which these human resources can be utilised to enable the organisation to continue into the future.

This conception of HRM is essentially strategic in its emphasis on enabling the utilising of employee efforts and capabilities to bring about long-term organisational survival. It incorporates those activities that have always been associated with personnel management, including the recruiting of employees and their training and development. It also acknowledges something that is rarely mentioned in formal definitions of either personnel or human resource management – the fact that a significant element of personnel and HR work has for some decades been the ending of employment relationships with employees, especially through redundancies. The *relational* and *exchange* elements of human resourcing work are acknowledged in the reference to the maintaining of employment relationships. This recognises two important human resourcing tasks: the seeking of compliance, commitment and productive cooperation on the one hand and the handling of conflicts, arguments and employee 'misbehaviours' on the other.

Something that is kept open in the above conception of human resource management is the question of who does this 'HRM work'. The same procedure is being followed here as was followed with regard to 'management' in Chapter 5. Three dimensions of 'management' were identified in Table 5.3 (p. 167): the function of *management* (which has to be carried out regardless of whether a few or many of the organisations employees are directly involved in it); the activity of *managing* (actions taken to achieve the function of managing or shaping the organisation); the formal role of *manager* (which becomes necessary when size or complexity of operations requires a division of labour between managers and others who focus on carrying out direct work tasks). Table 10.2 identifies three equivalent dimensions of HRM.

A whole range of processes and activities are carried out in work organisations to fulfil the strategic function of human resource management, as Table 10.2 shows. All of the human resourcing activities identified in the table are meant to ensure that the organisation has both the human skills and capabilities and the degree of social coherence necessary for its continuation into the

> **Table 10.2 Three dimensions of human resource management**
>
> **Human resource management** as a *function* is that part of managerial work which is concerned with acquiring, developing and dispensing with the efforts, skills and capabilities of an organisation's workforce and maintaining organisational relationships within which these human resources can be utilised to enable the organisation to continue into the future
>
> ---
>
> **Human resourcing** as an *activity* is the range of actions that fulfil the HRM function:
>
> - monitoring current and likely future staffing requirements to enable some programming of future human resourcing efforts
> - collecting and making available for managerial decision making information on employees, employee capabilities and the deployment of both of these
> - selecting and recruiting employees
> - hiring labour from agencies and sub-contractors (as an alternative to creating an employment relationship with these providers of labour)
> - dispensing with employees whose services are no longer required or who are otherwise deemed incapable of fulfilling tasks required of them
> - training, and developing employee capabilities
> - consulting, communicating and negotiating with representatives of organised labour (trade unions or professional associations) over whatever conditions or details of employment may have become subject to collective bargaining
> - communicating and consulting with employees and employee groupings over employment matters without the intermediaries of trade union representatives
> - fixing levels of and administering wages, salaries, fringe benefits and other rewards or 'compensation package' elements
> - establishing and ensuring compliance with policies on health and safety, sickness and absenteeism, discipline, fair and equal opportunities – both to maintain the health and goodwill of employees themselves and to ensure compliance with legal requirements
>
> ---
>
> **Human resourcing (HR) practitioners** occupying a *formal role* are employed in a personnel or HR department to ensure that the human resourcing activities necessary for long-term organisational continuation are carried out, directly through their own efforts and indirectly through their involvement (both enabling and constraining) with other managers

future. Involved in many of these activities will inevitably be processes of competition, conflict and the wielding of power – all of which can as readily lead to confusion, breakdown and corporate failure as it can help the work organisation 'hold together' and function as a reasonably cooperative enterprise. The challenge faced by those concerned with human resourcing and employment management is enormous, as will be stressed in the consideration of the underlying strategic significance of human resourcing to which we now turn. Once this has been looked at, we will return to the issue of the relationship between human resourcing specialists and other managers with whom they have to work to fulfil the basic HRM function. As Table 10.2 implies – with its reference to there being both an enabling and a constraining role here – this is by no means a straightforward and always harmonious relationship.

The essentially strategic nature of human resourcing

It was argued earlier that human resourcing and employment issues are 'utterly central to the existence of organisations' and that they 'pervade every aspect of organisational management' (p. 403). Subsequently HRM was said to be 'essentially strategic in its emphasis on enabling the utilising of employee efforts and capabilities to bring about long-term organisational survival' (p. 407). One inference that could be drawn from this wording is that we are *analytically* privileging the organisation and its survival over the human beings that are involved in it. Perhaps such a position could be defended on the grounds that it is possible to see an organisation continuing in existence over time in spite of the fact that it has had a complete turnover in the personnel involved in it. However, it is possible to counter this with the recognition that without the human beings that are involved with an organisation at any particular point in time that organisation would not exist at all. We are back to the centrality of human resourcing and employment issues to the existence of the organisation and to three particular aspects of this centrality:

- the centrality of human resourcing issues to *processes* of organisational strategy making;
- the role of human resourcing in handling *tensions and contradictions* that underlie the whole employment relationship in industrial capitalist societies;
- the role of the human resourcing function in maintaining *corporate integration* and capabilities to ensure *long-term* organisational viability.

The centrality of human resourcing issues to processes of organisational strategy making

One frequently hears business leaders and senior managers claim that 'our people are our most important asset'. This wording can readily be criticised as dehumanising employees by treating them as means to ends ('assets' being little different from 'resources'). However, if we generously assume that the word 'people' is simply being used as convenient shorthand for human efforts, skills and capabilities, then perhaps we can acknowledge these words as signalling recognition by those employers that their enterprises are dependent upon the skills and efforts of the people they employ. In fact, we might infer that top managers are coming to recognise that without the people whom they employ – themselves included – the organisation simply would not exist. Yet much of the systems-control thinking that still dominates managerial thinking and a lot of academic writing in this area fails to represent the relationship between general corporate strategies and human resourcing strategies in accordance with this important insight. It treats the human resourcing strategy as something that follows from, supports or serves a main corporate strategy. Malcolm Lossie raises some of the practical issues that can arise from this in Case 10.1.

Activity 10.1

Consider, first, what you think is the most appropriate relationship to exist in an organisation between the shaping of the main corporate or business strategy on the one hand and a human resourcing strategy (in the sense of the general way in which the organisation deals with employment and human resourcing matters) on the other. Consider whether human resourcing strategies are best understood as subordinate to overall corporate strategies, or as equal in significance to them. Then read the conversation with Malcolm Lossie in Case 10.1 and consider whether you are still happy with your original view in the light of what this HR director has to say.

Malcolm Lossie plays it canny — Case 10.1

It took my predecessor as HR director years and years to get a seat on the main board of this company. He fought like mad to get the right even to listen to what the top men were saying about the direction the business should take. But, just before I took over from him, he told me that he rarely found himself able to speak up about HR matters, even when, in his view, they were key to business decisions that were being made.

And is this different for you now?

After three years in the job, I'd say that I am just beginning to make my voice heard. But it is an uphill struggle. And if I get just one thing wrong, I shall lose every bit of the limited credibility that I have built up.

Yet I thought that you were recruited here precisely because you had credibility – in fact I've heard it said that you were headhunted because they knew that HR issues were vitally important to where the company was going. And they apparently thought that you were one of the few people who was good enough.

Yes, that fits with what I was told. But when it comes to it, there is one attitude that dominates. This is the attitude that engineering issues combined with financial considerations are the most important strategically.

Strategic discussions – board level discussions generally – get little beyond that. The board members would prefer it if they could just follow their engineering instincts about strategic directions – you know, pursue those projects that are the most exciting in engineering terms on the assumption that the world will buy the wonderful things that they produce. That's how it once was, I am told. But they have learned that they must temper this approach with recognition of the financial 'realities' that they must work within. Sometimes I think it would be too much to ask of them, that they should treat human resourcing matters alongside engineering and financial matters. I remember so well one occasion when I got quite forceful and pointed out that a decision that they were moving towards would involve a wave of redundancies. This, coming straight on top of an earlier headcount reduction programme, could have a very destructive effect on morale and recruitment to growing areas of the business, I warned. I was immediately shot down by one of the most powerful non-executive directors. 'You can't let the tail wag the dog, young man,' he said, in the most patronising tones I have ever heard. 'If we make the right business decision then it is up to you to make it work in HR terms.' The Chairman was much more gentle but suggested that the board thought that they had recruited in me the best HR man available precisely because some very tricky employment issues were likely to arise from the way they were going to change the business.

So do you accept their definition of the HR role in corporate strategy?

No. I don't.

Sure. But I was looking earlier at your HR mission statement and that is full of stuff about a 'business driven' approach to HR and 'ensuring that the business aims' of the company are 'met through HR policies that are seen as fair, consistent . . .'

Just a minute.

This does sound like the business dog very clearly wagging the HR tail.

Hang on. Get behind the rhetoric. I admit that I am using the language that is preferred along the [directors'] corridor here. I've got to play along with them if I am going to get to where I need to be. It's, you know, 'softly, softly, catchee thief'. I am playing it canny. I know that I have got to talk this language of the 'business coming first' and of the point of HR being to 'help achieve business goals'. But my thinking goes beyond this.

Please go on.

I've got a simple picture in my mind. I see the human resources here as the starting point of our strategic considerations – not as the means of doing whatever suits the shareholders. Now let me make it clear, I am not saying that all the business things we do should be for the sake of the company's employees. But this company is the bundle of brilliant engineering talent that has made it a world leader. The starting point for any strategic discussion has therefore got to be the bundle of core competences that we possess. This is what I am getting my fellow directors to recognise, one by one. As I said to our head of design the other day, 'Where do these brilliant engineering ideas that our future depends on come from in the first place? They come from our human resources.' 'I'd never thought of it like that before,' he replied.

Isn't that a bit abstract though?

It's anything but abstract. It is vital that I get my colleagues to think in this way if I am going to make a proper professional contribution to securing the long-term future of this firm. The danger at the moment is that they are looking at separate projects, one at a time. They are inclined to say to me, 'We're starting to work on such and such – so get recruiting a hundred of these and fifty of those. Oh and we are going to run down x and y, so you can lose the people there. Get the accounting chappies to make sure the costs and savings balance out.' No consideration is given to what projects might come along in the future – or indeed where those projects are going to come from – if we try to operate a hire and fire approach in the labour market we are talking about. This is the market for the world's best engineers. So that's what I am working on: getting them to see the human resources as the starting point for strategic thinking and as the source of the efforts that will provide a future for the business. This is all very practical. It is anything but abstract. I recognise that I will continue to recruit in certain areas and lose people in other areas and that, year on year, I will reduce the overall headcount. But I want to do this within a framework of building a secure core of committed engineering and managerial talent that can innovate and take risks and bring home the bacon for another hundred years.

Malcolm Lossie is giving very hard-headed arguments here for refusing to make human resourcing strategies subservient to general corporate strategy concerns. In effect, he claims that by treating the set of human resources that currently make up the organisation as of equal importance to issues of future corporate performance, a better corporate performance is likely to be achieved in the long run. He recognises that a successful corporate strategy and business performance is not just dependent on the human resources that employees supply in the form of willing and cooperative labour but is also dependent on the human resources of creativity and inventiveness. In this sense, he argues, human resources are the starting point for strategic thinking. They are not

A systems-control view (HR strategy making as subsidiary to organisational strategy making)	A process-relational view (HR strategy making as integral to organisational strategy making)
Corporate strategy making ⟹ HR strategy making	Corporate strategy making ⇄ HR strategy making

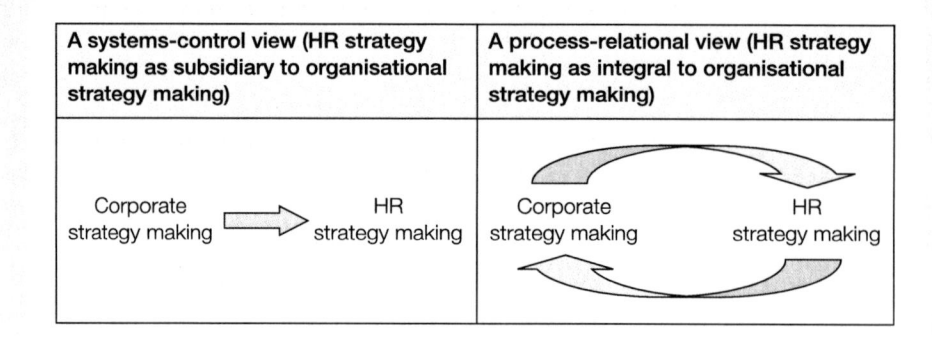

FIGURE 10.1 Systems-control and process-relational ways of framing the relationship between corporate and HR strategy making

something that managerial strategic ingenuity (a 'human resource' itself of course) simply looks to an HR director to supply, like so many nuts and bolts, to help fulfil a corporate strategy. This systems-control view of the relationship between corporate and HR strategy making is a linear one which sees human resource strategy making as a subsidiary or servant of corporate strategy making. It is represented on the left-hand side of Figure 10.1 whereas the more processual sort of relationship that Malcolm encourages us to take is represented on the right-hand side. Here there is a continuous interplay between these two aspects of strategy making and they can be seen as having equal importance.

Human resourcing and the handling of tensions and contradictions underlying the employment relationship

A basic challenge facing the management of every employing organisation is that of managers having to *gain some control over*, *shape* and *exploit* the human resources of labour, skill and capability brought to them by employees. This is necessary for the enterprise to continue in existence. The challenge is a vast one because these 'resources' can only be obtained and utilised through making exchange relationships with human beings – with people who have minds, wills and identities of their own. To gain access to the *human resources* they want, they have to deal with *human beings*. These human beings will inevitably want to make use of the organisation for their own particular purposes (money income, social status, job interest and all the rest) just as much as the organisation wants to make use of them.

There is thus a basic tension that has to be handled. This is a tension, we might say, between the need for organisational managements to have malleable and controllable human resources of effort, skill and capability continually available to them and the basic recalcitrance or sense of independence inherent in the human beings who are the providers of these resources. This profoundly significant tension, which puts pressure on every aspect of managerial work generally and human resourcing work specifically, is not just one that arises at the level of work organisations. It arises in some key principles of the type of economy and society of which all modern work organisations are components. This is the *industrial capitalist* type of political economy that dominates the twenty-first century world, and at the heart of this way of organising economic and social life is the *employment and rational organisation of free labour*. What we have here is a combination of three principles that are essential elements of *modernity* (Chapter 2, pp. 35–7) and which differentiate modern industrial capitalist societies from, say, feudal or tribal societies. They are:

- The principle of *employment* whereby workers sell some of their capacity to work and apply skills and capabilities to an employer (as opposed, say, to the serf working for a lord as a duty inherent in a feudal type of order or a slave working for the person who owns them).

- The principle of the formally rational *bureaucratic work organisation* whereby work activities are located in a technical division of labour, based on rational calculative 'design work' by expert managers, and a hierarchical control structure (as opposed, say, to people carrying out work along lines traditionally associated with the trade or occupation of which they are a part).

- The principle of *free labour* whereby each citizen has the legal freedom (or 'democratic right') to choose with whom to make an employment contract and to end that exchange relationship whenever it suits them (as opposed, say, to their being tied into a particular work situation by feudal bonds or by an owner–slave property relationship).

These underlying principles of the modern industrialised society have worked together effectively enough to make this type of social and economic order the dominant one in the contemporary world. In systems terms, it is a system that works. (Although we should never forget that while it has 'worked' to give massive increases in human welfare and democratic freedom it has also made possible some of the most systematic tyrannies and murderous wars of all times.) However, there are contradictory tensions within this way of organising society and economy. In the eyes of the most powerful critic of this system, Karl Marx, these contradictions were such that, in the long run, capitalist societies were bound to collapse. History so far, however, has shown that these contradictions have been *managed* to avoid such a collapse and it is possible to see the human resourcing component of the management of industrial capitalist work organisations as functioning to manage these contradictions. It by no means does this on its own. It performs such a role alongside a whole range of general state provisions and initiatives, in education, health and welfare provisions and employment legislation, for example.

The basic contradiction that human resource management helps to 'manage' is that between the principle of *controlling* human activity, which is inherent in the institutions of employment and rational organisation of work, and the principles of *freedom*, *choice* and *autonomy* that are implicit in the institution of free labour. The citizens of industrial capitalist societies are thus given democratic rights, which define them as people who have a right to influence their own destinies and to choose with whom to seek employment. Once in employment, though, they find themselves subject to controls imposed both by bureaucratic rules and by 'bosses' who have authority over them in the managerial hierarchy of the organisation in which they have chosen to work. Members of modern societies are encouraged to be free thinking, mobile, assertive individuals vigorously pursuing their own and their families' interests. At the same time, however, they are encouraged to be loyal and obedient citizens and employees. The continuous tension between these two aspects of modern life is one that, we might say, is 'built in' to the sort of societies in which an increasing proportion of people in the modern world live. And at the 'local' level of each employing work organisation, it is a tension with which managers continually have to deal. They strive to achieve a degree of *control* over employees' activities while at the same time having to accept that they must win employees' *willing consent* to work cooperatively in the way required of them.

This analysis has knowingly and deliberately been provided in terms that derive from the tradition of systems thinking about human social arrangements. There has been an implicit use of a notion of both the industrial capitalist society and the modern work organisation as *systems* whose various components or organising principles can both function well together, keeping the 'system' going, or come into tension with each other threatening the collapse of that system. Further, it could be argued that 'HRM' has been treated here as a subsystem of organisational and societal systems that performs the function of handling disintegrative tendencies and thus avoiding the collapse of the system. An analogy that suggests itself is one of HRM functioning within work organisations in the same way that the regulator or the safety valve on a steam engine avoids a steam driven machine from blowing up. This analogy, for all its crudity, offers a useful insight.

It is in the spirit of trying to develop insights into the deeper or societal implications of human resource management that the basic systems analogy has been used here. It is not being suggested that societies and organisations *are* systems constructed out of sub-systems that sometimes function to achieve system integration and sometimes fail to function and bring about disintegration or disequilibrium. But it is suggested that the use of such mechanistic analogies can help us temporarily to simplify the immense complexities we confront when we try to generalise about large-scale social and economic arrangements – and thus help generate worthwhile insights. We have therefore looked at social orders and organisations for the moment *as if* they were systems. We have to remember that this is simply a device for making sense of the vast complexities of the human initiatives, conflicts, ambiguities, successes and failures in which we have to struggle to see any kind of pattern. It was accepted in Chapter 2 that *systems-control* ways of framing organisations have value in drawing our attention to certain 'system-like' characteristics of organisational life. But the importance was stressed of going beyond systems thinking and looking at the *processes* and ongoing *relationships* that occur within the very limiting 'black box' that systems analysis works with (p. 274). The insight that HRM has a conflict management or a systems integrating *function* needs to be combined with consideration of particular activities, processes and relationships like those in which we saw Malcolm Lossie involving himself earlier in Case 10.1. Similarly Inva Gordon's arguments in Case 10.3 (which we will come to later, pp. 430–3) for adopting more 'indirect control' or high commitment human resourcing measures in the Viewfield call centre organisation can be connected to the notion of HRM 'functioning' to manage more effectively certain potentially disintegrative tensions.

The necessarily corporate and long-term focus of HRM

The managerial function of HRM, to which HR specialists and other managers alike contribute, handles basic work and employment tensions and contradictions in a way that gives human resourcing work a centrally strategic significance. Regardless of who carries it out, human resourcing work plays an important *general* role in ensuring that the organisation is able to continue into the future. It does this by trying to balance the managerial need to gain a certain amount of control over employees with recognition that people do not readily submit themselves to such control. There are, however, two more *specific* strategic human resourcing roles, both clearly related to this more general role, which can perhaps only be performed satisfactorily by a corporate HR department. These are:

- *Maintaining corporate integration*. Meeting the need constantly to monitor and influence the comparative treatment of employees across an organisation of any size or complexity to ensure that there is a sufficiently strong general perception of fair treatment and justice across the organisation to prevent a level of conflict, resentment or legal challenge that might damagingly undermine the level of productive cooperation necessary for the organisation's long-term future or might damage its reputation in the labour markets it draws upon.
- *Human resourcing for the future*. Meeting the need to encourage departmental or functional managers with shorter-term and more specific task responsibilities to look beyond the immediate pressures of their day-to-day situation to consider the pattern of skills, capabilities and commitments that the organisation requires for the longer term.

Activity 10.2

In the light of these two suggested corporate HR roles, consider what particular issues within the range of human resourcing activities (listed in the human resourcing activities section of Table 10.2) might require the existence of a corporate HR department in an organisation of any size. Then read Jack Avoch's justifications in Case 10.2 for retaining a corporate HR department that he put to Jean-Yves, the new Chief Executive at Gollachers.

Jack fights his corner

Case 10.2

When Jean-Yves took over as Chief Executive last year, one of his very first meetings was with me. I had this strange feeling as I went up to his office that, as the recently appointed head of HR, I was either going to be given a key role in the company's future or he was going to say goodbye to me. I was right to be anxious. He told me how much he admired what he had heard about my achievements and how he particularly liked the fact that I had seriously reduced the influence of the company's trade unions as well as having got most of the managers 'turned on to HR issues'. It had occurred to him, however, that the next logical step was for the managers across the organisation to take responsibility for the HR in their own areas and for my HR department to be wound up. He put this in terms of 'really empowering managers' and 'making them accountable for their own actions with regard to how they treat people'. He assured me that his mind wasn't made up on the matter but he also put it to me that 'the logic of this is unassailable, isn't it?' He then asked me whether I believed in 'managers' right to manage?' I was rather thrown by this but felt I had to reply that I did. 'So, if this shouldn't be challenged by trade unions and the like, then surely it shouldn't be challenged any more by a corporate HR department.'

I could see the trap I had walked into. When the unions were powerful here, everybody saw a role for a strong personnel or HR department to negotiate with them. They also saw the need to make sure that we didn't get managers making local agreements with their union reps that would lead to comparability claims across the company which would cost the company dear (something that apparently happened several times in the past). What I now needed to do, to fight my corner and defend the people in my HR department, was to persuade Jean-Yves that managers across the organisation simply could not be left to cover every aspect of HR. They would always tend to prioritise local, departmental and immediate issues rather than corporate and long-term ones.

'With the best will in the world', I put it to Jean-Yves, 'you can't expect managers not to give priority to whatever HR issues are most urgent in their own area at any given time. This is the case even if they are very business oriented and strategically aware, as most of our managers are.' I didn't believe what I was saying here, actually, but I knew I would get nowhere if I implied to Jean-Yves that a lot of the managers simply could not be trusted to act in any interest other than that of their own little empire. 'In spite of the unions no longer being the main channel for grievances, this means that it is vital that someone keeps an eye on the whole playing field and ensures that we don't get people in one area being paid more than people in another for similar work.' I told Jean-Yves some stories of recent events that illustrated the problems here. One was the case of a department who organised their own flexi-time arrangements without involving HR. People in three other departments in that building soon decided that they would like to work in this more flexible way, but their managers argued that the work there was different and that they couldn't cope with other than a 9 to 5 arrangement. I pointed out, in the first place, that the manager should not have done that without involving HR. And, in the second place, I observed that if my department had not been there to sort out the rows that blew up, it would have to have been the Chief Executive who would have needed to 'waste her time' dealing with it.

This last bit seemed to make Jean-Yves think. I also told him about a recent industrial tribunal that had given the company a lot of bad publicity and set back one of our recruitment exercises. I said that this arose because a manager had dismissed an employee without reference to HR and that, again, if we weren't there constantly monitoring this kind of thing, there would be a lot more such tribunals. Just one of these 'every now and again' is damaging for the firm I argued. 'And indeed for the chief executive's own reputation,' I dared to add. 'Tell me more,' he went on, looking quite worried now. 'Think of it like this,' I said. 'These things are bound to happen from time to time even if your managers are really sensitive about good employment practice and all the highly complicated employment legislation. But who would have to go into court to speak for the company, if you didn't have a HR director?', I asked him. And I answered my own question before he had time to. 'It would be down to the chief executive again I am afraid.'

I went on to point out the various corporate initiatives I was currently working on. One of these was an improved graduate recruitment programme. Another was a human resource information system which would be centrally run but which would 'considerably help empower managers by making available to them everything from their staff's training records and holiday entitlements to labour turnover figures and salary details. 'Who else but an HR department could do these things?', I asked him. And I asked whether he wanted every manager going out and finding his or her own graduates, for example. Jean-Yves started to fight back by arguing that a number of the things that we did could be 'outsourced' or done by consultants. Our annual staff attitude survey was one he pointed to here. 'But what about our very significant work on monitoring current competencies and future skill needs?', I came back at him. 'Left to their own devices, most of our managers are rather unwilling to divert their staff from current tasks in hand to develop the skills they are going to need in the future. But we currently keep them on their toes on this and press them to what we call "investing in the future through HR development".' You just cannot expect managers, with the departmental and delivery pressures they face every day to look to the long term in this way, without 'being prompted by someone who has this longer-term vision', I insisted.

'Speaking of long-term vision,' Jean-Yves said, standing up and pointing out of his window, 'a lot of restructuring needs to be done across Gollochers.' 'Indeed, I would expect you to be thinking that way,' I commented, feeling my confidence growing by the second. He continued, 'I can see that we are going to be recruiting staff to certain areas at the same time as we are losing people from others – although there might be some scope for redeployment of people if we do this skilfully.' I nodded, and smiled, 'That's not an easy thing to do.'

'Do you think we can do it?', he asked. 'I have done it before', I explained, 'and my staff . . .'. He cut me off, 'I know what you are going to say. No need. I'll come and see you and your people tomorrow and we'll get the job started.'

Jack appears to have been successful in persuading Jean-Yves to retain a corporate HR department and, indeed, to use Jack and his department to help him restructure Gollochers, though Jack had to work hard to 'fight his corner'. Jean-Yves had clear and well thought out reasons for dispensing with the HR department. It was not a matter of his ignoring the importance of the human resourcing function or, it would appear, having received bad reports about Jack himself. On the contrary, he speaks of the good things he had heard about Jack's achievements. And he could be seen as wanting to strengthen the overall human resourcing *function* (as opposed to *department*), rather than diminishing it. Jean-Yves speaks of making managers more involved in HR issues by getting them to 'take responsibility for how they treat people', and he implies that the existence of a formal HR department tends to constrain managers in this respect. It undermines, he suggests, their 'right to manage'. Jack's response to this is a shrewd one. He carefully avoids being too critical of managers but he suggests that 'with the best will in the world' and with all their 'departmental and delivery pressures' managers could not be expected to pay sufficient attention to broad corporate matters or to the long-term human resourcing needs of the business. He talks of the difficulty they are bound to have in looking at 'the whole playing field' or in considering what human resources will be needed for the longer-term future – unless they are prompted by someone like Jack and his colleagues.

Jack uses a variety of illustrations to support his argument for a corporate HR department – an element of the organisation's overall management that can prompt others to think corporately and long term about employment matters. The first one is the pay issue and the implication of his few words here is that dangerous perceptions of unfairness could arise if someone was not 'keeping an eye' on what people in different areas were being paid for work of equivalent value. The specific example of one department independently initiating flexible working times is then used to illustrate the sort of problem that can arise. The negative effects of the company having to defend itself in an industrial tribunal are then pointed out. This damages both the organisation's and the chief executive's reputation, might harm recruitment and can take up a lot of management time, Jack suggests. A corporate HR department would presumably avoid this happening too often and would handle such problems if and when they arose. Jack then turns to the implied inefficiencies and inconsistencies that might arise if each department took on the graduate recruitment work currently done by corporate HR and he stresses how departmental managers would benefit from the sort of human resource information system that can only be run corporately. Jack finally wins his case by letting Jean-Yves work out for himself that the very priority that he has set for himself as chief executive – the 'restructuring' of Gollochers – could not really be achieved without HR help at the corporate level. Jack clearly wants Jean-Yves to recognise that with HR devolved to managers across the various operational areas of the company there would be an enormous problem of managing the recruitment of staff for some areas while people were being dismissed from other parts of the company. All of that could be made more acceptable to a workforce, it is implied, if redeployment of people across the areas is made possible. And the inevitable inference that follows from this is that only a corporate HR department could manage this process. Jack and his corporate HR department survive, having established their indispensability to Jean-Yves as a strategically important unit that can play a key role in supporting the HR aspects of his own strategic work.

Running through the story that Jack Avoch tells is the suggestion that relationships between HR specialists and other managers are not simple or straightforward. Jean-Yves seems to be alluding to certain tensions between the two when he brackets HR departments with trade unions as putting limits on managers' 'right to manage'. And implicit in the corporate HR role that Jack argues for is a notion of HR sometimes *supporting* and *enabling* managers (with the HR information system, for example, or on graduate recruitment) but at other times *constraining* them (on how they pay people, settle their working hours, deal with employment law and training matters for example). While Jack Avoch might want to persuade us that there are likely to be unmanageable problems without a corporate HR department, it is clear that the existence of a formal HR presence can, in itself, create problems.

HR specialists and other managers: tensions and ambiguities

When the three main elements of HRM were identified earlier in Table 10.2, it was recognised that human resourcing activities are likely to be carried out by a mixture of human resourcing specialists and other managers. If we look at the role played by those people who are employed in personnel or HR departments we will see that there are four dimensions to their work:

- They carry out specialised administrative tasks relating to human resourcing (from keeping personnel records to placing job advertisements).
- They work with other managers to support them in the fulfilment of human resourcing activities that affect the departments or functions of those managers. This entails, for example, helping managers select, recruit, develop and reward staff that are needed for the department to carry out its tasks and help the department dispense with the services of employees when they are no longer required. This implies a service or *enabling* relationship between HR and other managers.
- They monitor the activities of managers to ensure that they comply with corporate human resourcing policies and procedures necessary to prevent organisational disintegration. This entails, for example, preventing managers from making decisions that have damaging repercussions for other managers (especially on pay and other rewards where perceptions of unfairness across areas can arise), ensuring that managers comply with employment legislation, negotiated agreements with trade unions and with corporate policies on such matters as equal opportunities, disciplinary procedures, communication and consultation. This implies a 'policing' or *constraining* relationship between HR and other managers.
- They monitor the activities of other managers to ensure that they are acquiring and developing human resources that are necessary for the long-term future, as well as for the present. This implies both an *enabling* and a *constraining* relationship between HR and other managers.

This combination of roles creates considerable problems (see Further Reading on HR and other managers, p. 445). Somehow, HR departments have *both* to serve or enable managers *and* to control and constrain them. This creates a considerable ambiguity in managers' eyes – often confusing them in practice about whether the personnel or HR department is primarily there to help them in their work or to hinder them. The uncomfortable truth is that both of these tend to be the case, from the point of view of managers concentrating on the priorities of their own department and the immediate pressures faced by their department. The result of this is that in many work organisations there is a tense and ambivalent relationship between HR managers and others. On the one hand, the manager is often dependent upon and appreciative of the help that the HR specialists give. But, on the other hand, they come to resent the limits that are put on their actions and decisions by the HR specialists' insistence that the manager complies with certain corporate or legal requirements. This compliance simply makes the manager's day-to-day life more difficult.

On top of these ambiguities are further ones deriving from the history of personnel management. One half of personnel management's historical roots are in a relatively *tender* or *caring* tradition of employee welfare and industrial social work and the other half of its roots are in a relatively *tough* and *controlling* tradition of labour management and collective bargaining with trade unions. The willingness of personnel specialists in recent years to replace the 'Personnel' title with a 'Human Resources' one can partly be understood as an attempt to play down the welfare and caring dimension of this history. Nevertheless, it is unlikely that employee expectations that personnel or HR departments can and should show a caring face towards employees will go away. The caring/controlling set of historical ambiguities with regard to the HR department tends to remain alongside the ambiguities created by the dual role of HR as both a service to and a constraint upon the line or departmental manager.

HR specialists are typically confronted with the considerable challenge of presenting themselves to the workforce generally as a caring department, concerned with justice and the fair treatment of employees while, at the same time, they must present themselves to corporate management as a department concerned with controlling and exploiting the efforts and capabilities of employees. Simultaneously, they have to present themselves to line or departmental managers as providing a supportive, enabling and empowering service while, to corporate management, they promise to monitor, control and constrain managers so that they do not prioritise their departmental interests with regard to employees over corporate and longer-term strategic concerns.

These ambiguities and tensions are bound to have considerable implications for the way strategic human resourcing is carried out in practice. As we shall now see, there are certain circumstances in which employee groups are more problematic to management than they are in others and the extent to which employee constituencies are perceived as problematic for the organisation's future is likely to be a key influence on the type of human resourcing strategy which emerges. Such a perception tends to put pressure on managers to choose relatively *high commitment* human resourcing strategies. Should the workforce be seen, on the other hand, as less of a problem with regard to the organisation's future, then there is less pressure on managers to choose this more complex and potentially costly approach. A *low commitment* human resourcing strategy, in such circumstances, is more likely to be selected. Such processes of HR strategic choice are not simple or straightforward, however. Ambiguity and differences of value, understanding and interest are always present when strategic choices are made.

Choices and constraints in human resource strategy making

It was clearly established in earlier chapters that managerial choices about general strategic direction and about the type of structure, culture and job design that are adopted are influenced by a combination of organisational circumstances (or 'contingencies') and managerial interests, values and preferences. No organisational strategy, structure, culture or pattern of work design comes about as a direct consequence, however, of circumstances or contingencies in the way systems-control oriented 'contingency theory' implies. The state of a national or global economy, the market situation of a particular organisation or its size or technological nature does not *determine* what sort of strategy, culture or structure an organisation has. As our earlier analysis recognised (Chapter 7, pp. 272–82), contingencies such as those of organisational environment, size and technology do have important implications for the way in which any organisation is shaped.

The influence of these factors is always mediated by the way managers interpret and *enact* them, and these interpretations of organisational circumstances are taken into managerial decision-making arguments, discussions and debates. It is in this context of interpretation, argument and micropolitical contest that decisions emerge that lead to actions which, when taken together over a period of time, reveal a strategic pattern. This analysis can now be brought forward from its earlier application to how organisations are 'shaped' to our present concern with how human resourcing strategies emerge.

Human resourcing strategy *Concept*

The general direction followed by an organisation in how it secures, develops, utilises and, from time to time, dispenses with human resources of effort, skill and capability to enable it to continue into the long term.

The way human resourcing strategy is conceptualised here is fully in accord with the concepts of organisational strategy and strategy making developed in Chapter 9. It attempts to go beyond much of the standard thinking on strategic HRM (Watson, 2004; see also Further Reading on strategic HRM, pp. 446–7) A human resourcing strategy is not looked at as a plan, or as a dimension of a corporate Strategic plan. Instead, it is treated as the general pattern that emerges over time as the managers of an organisation seek to supply the organisation with the human resources – in the sense of human efforts, skills and capabilities – that it needs to go forward into a long-term future. To help us see some patterning in the complex mixture of human resourcing activities and procedures that exists in each employing organisation we can utilise a continuum upon which any particular organisation's human resourcing strategy can be placed. The positions at the ends of this continuum are those of a *low commitment* HR strategy at one end and a *high commitment* HR strategy at the other.

- A *low commitment HR strategy* could be characterised as a 'hire and fire' one, in which labour is acquired at the point when it is immediately needed and the employee is allocated to tasks for which they need very little training, with the employment being terminated as soon as those tasks have been completed. The relationship between employer and employee is very much a calculatingly instrumental one and contact between managers and workers very much at 'arm's-length'.

- A *high commitment HR strategy* can be identified where the employer seeks a much closer relationship with employees and wants them to become psychologically or emotionally involved with the enterprise. The employer is likely to offer employees opportunities for personal and career development within their employment, which is expected to continue over a longer-term period and potentially to cover a variety of different tasks.

It should immediately become apparent that this continuum of HR strategies has a close relationship with the indirect control/direct control continuum that was used in Chapter 7 to consider managerial choices about 'organisational shaping'. It is therefore possible to extend the model that was used in Chapter 7 to incorporate those direct/indirect control options into the choice that is made between high and low commitment human resourcing strategies. This recognises that low commitment human resourcing strategies are typically manifested in large part through the use of direct control management practices and procedures, whereas high commitment strategies are expressed in large part through the use of indirect attempts to achieve managerial control. Figure 10.2 is a version of the model introduced in Chapter 7 (Figure 7.4, p. 275) which has been extended to bring together the notions, on the one hand, of low commitment employment relationships with direct managerial controls and, on the other hand, high commitment employment relationships with indirect management controls.

The basic claim here is that, all things being equal, a low commitment type of human resourcing strategy is likely to be more appropriate to a situation where employees are not a major source of uncertainty for an employer than one where they create strategic uncertainty. An organisation is not likely to require a highly participative and strong commitment set of arrangements if it has a simple technology and a relatively straightforward business environment that allows it to employ easily obtainable and replaceable employees, for example. However, if an organisation's management sees that its future would be uncertain without meeting the much higher demands that are likely to follow from employing a highly skilled or educated workforce to operate a complex technology or deal with an especially tricky business environment – a workforce that is not easy to obtain or replace – it is much more likely to consider a high commitment set of employment conditions and work arrangements. This is necessary to encourage those people both to stay with the organisation and creatively and flexibly apply themselves to undertaking complex tasks. Note, however, that this proposition was made with the qualification 'all things being equal'. They are not equal, of course.

Managerial values and interests also come into the equation, as do the interpretive processes whereby managers decide how problematic the labour force is, in terms of the organisation's future. It is possible for managers to decide that their social values make them prefer higher commitment employment practices

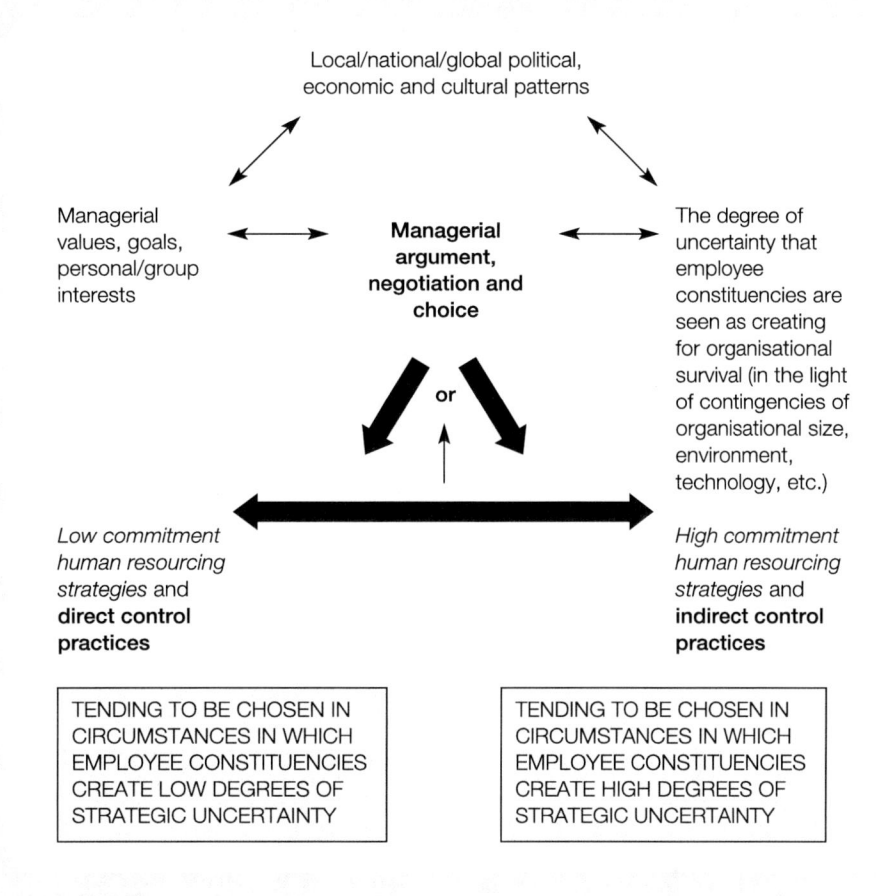

FIGURE 10.2 Contingency and choice in human resourcing strategy

in principle. This, however, would tend to create cost problems – making their labour costs higher than competing employers who were more willing to adopt a simpler hire and fire policy. By the same token, a set of HR strategy makers who disagreed in principle with high commitment practices and indirect management controls, but who employed highly skilled or educated people in a tight labour market would have difficulty retaining staff. In practice, then, there is likely to be interplay between managerial value preferences and perceptions of contingent circumstances making employees more or less strategically problematic (uncertainty creating). And, given that the individuals within any strategy-making management group are likely to vary in their personal interests, values and priorities, we can expect to see strategic choices emerging out of processes of argument and debate. This was very apparent with regard to some human resourcing issues which arose in the Motoline case in Chapter 7 (and to which we will return below). We will also see this kind of process occurring with the case of the Viewfield call centre company, shortly.

Before we do this we must, first, look in more detail at the range of practices and arrangements that tend to be associated with the two ends of the continuum shown in Figure 10.2. Table 10.3 does this by identifying a range of direct–indirect control options that are available with regard to several areas of the organisation and its management that we have considered in earlier chapters – strategy-making practices, culture, structure and work design – together with a number of further areas of organisational management. The table suggests a very inclusive and wide-ranging notion of what human resourcing strategy is about. This is wholly consistent with our conceptualising of human resourcing strategy as the general direction followed by an organisation in how it secures, develops, utilises and dispenses with human resources of effort, skill and capability to enable it to continue into the long term. Such a perspective invites us to see human resourcing strategy as the basic manner or style in which people's work capacities are utilised across every aspect of an organisation. Choices about this manner or style relate to issues ranging from how strategy making is conducted in the organisation down to the way an HR or personnel department is staffed. At the level of strategy making, for example, a low commitment/indirect control approach only utilises the strategic thinking of a minority of those employed as managers – the very senior managers and their specialist strategic advisers. At the opposite end of the continuum, a high commitment/indirect control approach involves many more people in strategic activities – all managers are seen as having relevant competence in this area. And, with regard to the staffing of an HR department, the former approach tends to treat personnel work as something that can only be done by specialists. The latter style, however, takes a broader view of the capacities of both HR and non-HR managers by suggesting both that their work can to some extent be 'integrated' and that both sets of managers, in certain circumstances, can work in the other's area of activity.

Many of the options identified at the high commitment/indirect control end of the continuum should perhaps be seen as *aspirations* rather than as 'options' in the strict sense of the term. A number of these options here have been advocated as generally desirable by the *total quality management* movement (Wilkinson *et al.*, 1998) and the virtues of other practices falling at this end of the continuum have been extolled by those wanting to prescribe 'best practice' in areas ranging from work design and pay systems to human resource development. In spite of all this advocacy, however, managers themselves are likely to be aware that these are aspirations that are never likely to be fully realised in practice. They may wish to move towards a culture where more of the values that people within the organisation hold are 'shared' ones. However, it is unlikely that anyone with any familiarity with the world of work is likely to think that it is realistic to achieve an organisational culture in which everyone holds the same values.

The same point applies to the aspiration in the area of employment relations towards 'mutual' relationships rather than adversarial ones and negotiations in which both sides always 'win'. It is by no means unrealistic to seek some movement in this direction, as trade unions have tended to acknowledge in calling

Table 10.3 General organisational and managerial options and aspirations related to the basic high commitment/low commitment HRM choice

	General organisational *direct control* options associated with *low commitment HRM* (where human resources tend to create low levels of uncertainty for managers)	General organisational *indirect control* options associated with *high commitment HRM* (where human resources tend to create high levels of uncertainty for managers)
Strategy making	• performed by top management, possibly with the aid of strategy experts	• top management provide 'vision' or 'strategic intent' and develop strategy through interaction with other levels
Culture	• rule based • emphasis on authority • task focus • mistakes punished	• shared values • emphasis on problem solving • customer focus • learning from mistakes
Structure	• layered hierarchy • top-down influence • centralisation • mechanistically bureaucratic (rigid)	• flat hierarchy • mutual (top-down/bottom-up) influence • decentralisation/devolution • organically bureaucratic (flexible)
Work/job design	• de-skilled, fragmented jobs • doing/thinking split • individual has single skill • direct control of individual by supervisor	• whole, enriched jobs • doing/thinking combined • individual multi-skilled • indirect control within semi-autonomous teams
Performance expectations	• objectives met to minimum level • external controls • external inspection • pass quality acceptable	• objectives 'stretch' and develop people • self controls • self/peer inspection • continuous improvement in quality sought
Rewards	• pay may be varied to give individual incentives • individual pay linked to job evaluation	• pay may be varied to give group performance • individual pay linked to skills, 'mastery'
Communication	• management seek and give information • information used for sectional advantage • business information given on 'need to know' basis	• two-way communication initiated by any party • information shared for general advantage • business information widely shared
Employment relations	• adversarial • collective • win/lose • trade unions tolerated as inconvenient constraints • OR unions used as convenient intermediaries between managers and employees	• mutual • individual • win/win • unions avoided OR unions increasingly by-passed in the hope of their eventual withering away • OR unions involved in *partnership relations* with employers to give a 'voice' to employees in working towards employment security, innovative work practices, fair rewards and investment in training
Employee development	• training for specific purposes • emphasis on courses • appraisal emphasises managerial setting and monitoring of objectives • focus on job	• training to develop employees' skills and competence • continuous learning emphasis • appraisal emphasises negotiated setting and monitoring of objectives • focus on career
HR/personnel department	• marginal, and restricted to 'welfare' and employment administrative tasks • reactive and *ad hoc* • staffed by personnel specialists	• integrated into management, and working as 'partners' with other managers • proactive and strategic • staff interchange with the 'line' or other functions

for employers and trade unions to work together in *partnership relations* to the advantage of corporate and employee interests alike. However, the notion that conflicts between the goals and interests of the multiplicity of parties involved in an organisation can ever be totally overcome is utterly unrealistic. In fact, the very existence of trade unions and the institution of collective bargaining recognises differences of interest between employers and employees – interests that these arrangements are intended to manage. And, although trade unions and collective bargaining have become less significant in work organisations in many countries in recent times, they have by no means disappeared. This is recognised in Table 10.3 and the possibility for a continuing trade union role within a high commitment type of HR strategy – one which stresses 'partnership' between employer and employee interests – is included (see Bacon, 2001).

Activity 10.3

The direction in which Mick Moy and Joy Petty were trying to take Motoline (Chapter 7, p. 277) can be understood as one towards a high commitment type of HR strategy. Reread 'Getting on track at Motoline' and:

- use Table 10.3 to note the various ways in which the new management regime was moving towards a high commitment and indirect control approach;

- observe how Mick's personal values and background affected his attitude towards trade unions;

- consider how realistic you think Mick is being in considering what might be characterised as a 'partnership' relationship with trade unions in the new Motoline.

Flexibility and dual human resourcing strategies

We have seen that the basic human resourcing style of an organisation can be understood in terms of whether it leans towards an employment style involving *high commitment relationships* between employer and employees and utilises indirect attempts at managerial control of activities or leans towards an employment style involving *low commitment relationships* utilising direct managerial control practices. It is possible, however, that managers in certain organisational situations might want to apply different human resourcing strategies to different parts of their organisation. Why would they do this? To put it at its simplest, it is done in recognition of the fact that the workers who do certain work tasks can be related to in ways that are less costly than others. In economic terms, the *transaction costs* of going to the market for labour in the lower skilled or more peripheral areas of activity are lower than they would be if that labour were employed or incorporated within the bureaucratic hierarchy of the enterprise (see Rowlinson, 1997 on the application of this type of economic thinking to organisations). In circumstances like these, then, organisations might be found to operate a *dual human resourcing strategy*.

Dual human resourcing strategy *Concept*

A dual human resourcing strategy exists where an organisation applies (a) a high commitment ('relationship') HR strategy involving a long-term employment relationship to core workers and managers and (b) a low commitment ('transactional') HR strategy to more peripheral suppliers of labour (sometimes involving an employment relationship, sometimes involving a market relationship).

The flexible firm *Concept*

An organisational pattern in which an organisation seeks some of its human resourcing from a *core workforce* whose members are given employment security, high rewards and skill enhancement opportunities in return for a willingness to adapt and innovate and a *peripheral* workforce whose members are given more specific tasks and less commitment to continuing employment or skill enhancement.

Organisations following a dual HR strategy are adopting features of what has been identified as the *flexible firm* (Atkinson, 1985). The dual HR strategy or 'flexible firm' principle is by no means a new one. It has been used since early industrial times. It even existed during the latter part of the twentieth century when *Fordism* was at its height (Chapter 8) and when it appeared that the standard form of work career for most people was becoming one of lifetime employment with a commercial organisation or a public bureaucracy. Its most obvious presence – as today – was in project-oriented industries like building and civil engineering, where organisations had very different requirements for labour at different stages of the projects they undertook. Thus, one source of 'human resourcing' would be labourers, craft workers and technical experts who would be 'bought in' as required. The other source would be the organisation's own employees who were felt to be necessary to integrate activities over time and give continuity to the organisation's development. Also, many organisations through most of the twentieth century had some elements of this dual human resourcing approach *within* its employed workforce, in the form of a differentiation between 'works' and 'staff'. Here the latter employees generally had superior terms and conditions of employment, and, typically, were expected to be 'closer' to management than the former. A higher degree of commitment was sought from these staff members who, however junior they might be, were, in principle at least, on the bureaucratic career ladder – which 'works' employees were not.

With changing social values, the growth of service work and the reduced significance of differences between manual work and office work, employers have tended to abandon the works–staff distinction and have *harmonised* employment terms and conditions across labour categories. The trend is towards the dual human resourcing principles being applied to those who are, on the one hand, a potentially long-term *employed* group and, on the other hand, a short-time *hired* group. The first exception is where, in terms of the model in Figure 10.2, organisations find themselves with relatively stable markets and simple technologies in which a low commitment direct-control employment strategy is viable (the workforce not being a source of strategic uncertainty for the management). The second exception – where the circumstances will often overlap with those of the first – is in sectors, like certain parts of the hospitality industry, where there are people willing to take on short-term employment. These might be younger people still involved in education or people with family responsibilities who can only manage a partial and perhaps intermittent relationship with employment. Such people are willing to be casually employed because they are only seeking a short-term involvement and this matches the short-term requirement of the employer.

The short-term/long-term distinction is vital to understanding the dual human resourcing approach to achieving flexibility. Managers tend to look for the two different types of flexibility explained in Chapter 8 (p. 339):

- flexibility to meet short-term *adjustment* needs which calls for an ability to bring in and dispense with labour and human expertise as markets fluctuate or as projects begin and end;
- flexibility to meet long-term *adaptability* needs which calls for human commitment and expertise from a core of employees who will willingly and enthusiastically make innovations and actively adapt their practices to ensure that the organisation continues into the long term.

A *transactional* or *market* HR sub-strategy will thus meet the flexibility for short-term adjustment requirement and the *relationship* or *employment* HR sub-strategy will meet the flexibility for long-term adaptability need. And the relative emphasis given to each of the two human resourcing approaches is likely to vary with organisational circumstances. A project-oriented organisation (ship or oil-rig building or civil engineering perhaps) regularly needing to adjust to meet changing demands might give greater emphasis towards a *transactional* (market) approach, for example. An organisation developing and producing high technology consumer products might, on the other hand, use a greater proportion of labour engaged on a *relationship* (employment) basis. In each case, nevertheless, the fact that both types of flexibility are likely to be required in an increasingly competitive economic context means that most organisations will use both means of acquiring human resources of skill, knowledge and labour.

HR strategy making in practice

The strategic options identified earlier in Table 10.3 are based on thinking and practices covered in literatures on HRM, strategic management, labour market analysis, change management, total quality management and various other attempts at giving managerial advice and selling panaceas for managerial inadequacies. What has been avoided here, however, is any labelling of the two basic styles, the 'high commitment' and the 'low commitment' approaches, as 'old' and 'new' or as 'bad practice' and 'best practice'. This would be to play down the relevance of contingent factors – the extent to which different organisational circumstances may fit better with some types of organisational or managerial practice rather than others. Many readers will nevertheless want to apply value judgements to these alternatives, whether this derives from their own notion of what they believe 'works best' or what they feel about the right and wrong way to 'treat people at work'. This is precisely what happens in the managerial 'arguments, negotiations and choices' processes at the centre of the model in Figure 10.2. One manager in a particular organisation may argue, for example, that it is morally wrong to use labour as a short-term means to business ends – because it involves people's identities and their livelihoods and denies them the security that any employee in a modern society should have a right to. He might be persuaded, though, by another manager that such a low commitment employment strategy is the one that is most likely to be successful and to justify this he might point to certain organisational circumstances or contingencies. He might observe that the organisation has a very simple technology, faces very seasonal business demands and enjoys a plentiful supply of job applicants who appear to be happy to accept unskilled work with no long-term future. He is pointing out, in other words, that the employee constituencies in his organisation are not particularly problematic: they do not, in strategic exchange terms, create a great deal of uncertainty for those running the organisation, with regard to its overall strategic direction.

Activity 10.4

Read Inva Gordon's account in Case 10.3 of human resource strategy making at Viewfields and, using Figure 10.2 as an analytical guide, identify the factors that led to a shift in strategic emphasis, noting:

- changing contextual factors at the local or national level;

- the extent to which employees were perceived by the Viewfield management team to be increasingly strategically 'problematic' – in the sense of creating uncertainties for the organisation's continuation and in the light of changing contingencies (i.e. perceived organisational circumstances);

- the interests, values and goals of members of the management group that influenced how they acted with regard to these contingent and contextual factors ('enacted' them);

- how all these things got mixed together in the managerial arguments or negotiations that occurred – considering in particular any of the factors discussed earlier about the tensions that can arise between HR and other managers.

'Viewfields, how can I help you?' — Case 10.3

It was about a year ago I recognised that I was really going to have to assert myself if I was going to do my HR job properly here at Viewfields. Sandy Viewfield had recruited me as a personnel officer when I was only about a year out of university. I know he was impressed with me but he had it mind that I would be a quiet and compliant recruiter of staff who would very efficiently work the human resourcing machine for him – getting people in when he needed them, making sure that no employment laws were broken and getting rid of people when they were no longer wanted. He seemed happy to appoint a woman to the job, given that he believed that 'people work' was particularly 'suitable for a female' (especially since a lot of the staff were women and Sandy found women 'a bit unpredictable and difficult to understand').

Sandy had left a big telecoms company to set up the call centre business. He had risen from an engineering job up to regional manager level and he brought with him several other people with mainly telephone engineering backgrounds. The accountant, Wesley Nigg, came from a telephone systems manufacturing company. He now calls himself the Finance Director and he, together with Sandy, Maddy Dornoch – the Marketing Director – and myself form the senior management group. Sandy uses the word 'strategy' all the time and he likes to think of himself as the great strategist. He talks like this, anyway, always reminding us that he had 'the vision' to set up a business that will stay at the 'cutting edge of call centre technology'. And, yes, by 'technology' he tends to mean the hardware and the computer software that is used. People are just the add-ons that, regretfully, he has to use to work this kit. I am convinced that, in the long run, he thinks that there will be sufficiently intelligent machines available that he won't have to employ operators. For the present, however, he has to have several hundred people working for him on the several dozen accounts that we currently have. As these numbers have grown and as 'personnel problems' have increased in number and frequency he has had to turn to me more and more. It was only after I had proved to him that I was indispensable by rescuing him from what might have been a very damaging court case over a severe harassment affair, did he let me call myself 'HR director' and allow me to play a regular part in senior management meetings. Maddy is in rather a similar position. Sandy is socially unskilled, to put it politely, and he managed to lose several of our best accounts simply by being rude to the people who were bringing him business. That is the main reason he reluctantly decided to get in a marketing expert – or rather let me find someone to take on this role. He didn't like the idea of bringing another woman into the management group. But Maddy was obviously so good that he did the right thing and appointed her. 'Yes, she's clearly the best man for the job.' he commented to me after the interviews, demonstrating his less than sophisticated grasp of HR principles!

I am pleased to have a women colleague in the management group. But it worries me at the same time. We end up with women-versus-men sorts of argument all too often. Sandy and Wesley act like stereotypical engineers and accountants and Maddy and I have to play the 'but people matter' line every time. I am sure that Sandy and Wesley resisted a number of the employment innovations that I have made, with Maddy's full support, more than they would have done had either of us been men. I once accused them of being prejudiced against the managerial arguments that Maddy and I were putting forward just because we were women. This was at a meeting that was turning from the intended company policy review into a seriously unpleasant row. Wesley, however, said that he was resisting our ideas purely on cost grounds. And Sandy said that it was much more a matter of his worrying about our 'general naïvety' about human beings as opposed to any specifically 'female naïvety'.

So what were these issues? They were actually rather fundamental ones about the nature of our business as well as about how we treated our employees. Maddy argued that what we primarily sold to our client companies was a 'human service' – a 'warm and helpful interface between their businesses and the people who wanted to deal with those businesses over the telephone'. I argued that we needed to think about our staff as the key to making this possible. It wasn't the quality of the telephone systems we used that would guarantee us a future, any more than it was the software or the quality of the 'scripts' that Maddy's marketing staff were so good at writing and putting in the operators' hands. It was the ability and the willingness of staff to convince the people who called up that they wanted to please and help them. 'Until you can buy robots that sound like warm and intelligent human beings', I told Sandy that night, 'you are going to have to learn to treat the operators in such a way that they feel committed to the company and are willing to use their initiative to give the callers the quality of service that they – and the client businesses who trust us to represent them – are looking for.'

It was quite fortunate that my mention of robots rather amused Sandy. It might well have angered him if I had spoken less carefully and had seriously implied that he was only capable of relating to machines (which, privately, I sometimes think to be true). In HR work you have got to be subtle and skilled if you are going to get your way. If you start trying to tell managing directors of companies that they are getting it wrong, without being very subtle about it, you are finished – especially if they are men and you are a woman. You've still got to tell them some hard truths, but you tread carefully. You use all the charm and subtlety you can muster to convince them that, unless they listen to you, their business might come unstuck. And we were coming unstuck at Viewfields.

When Viewfields started up it was all very straightforward from Sandy's point of view. He set up the equipment in a rented building on the edge of town and simply advertised in the local paper for staff. There wasn't a lot of competition at that time. Sandy was definitely ahead of the game in the call centre business. He had several big clients and unemployment was high across the region. This meant that he had a plentiful supply of labour, and it was compliant and easily controllable labour too. The technology makes it easy for supervisors to keep a check on the number of calls each operator is handling. It is also easy for them to check that the operators are both following their script and are speaking in a pleasant and helpful manner. Anyone who fell short was simply replaced by the next person in the queue for jobs. The pay was not too bad but there were few rest breaks and there was very limited variety in the work that each person did. Sandy's view was that once a person had 'mastered' a particular script and learned what was expected of them on that client's behalf then time should not be wasted getting them to learn to handle callers on another account. He and Wesley also got very cross if it appeared that operators were going out of their way to be helpful to callers. In fact, it was their harassing a couple of employees who were accused of this that led to the court case that made Sandy and Wesley recognise that they were not the most skilled at handling people issues.

Times have changed a lot since those early days, as reluctant as Sandy and Wesley were to admit it. The labour market is now much tighter and we have to rely a lot on students who do not take readily to supervisors who bully them or to being instructed in every detail of what they are to say to callers. About a year ago our labour turnover and absence levels were becoming so bad that we were struggling to keep the phones manned. Recruitment costs, Wesley said, were unacceptably high and Maddy warned that several clients were threatening to end their contracts if the number of complaints they were receiving about our staff being brusque and offhand did not reduce significantly. 'They are complaining about staff speaking like robots,' Maddy reported – and the irony of this was not lost on Sandy. 'What are we going to do, then?' he asked me. 'What is our HR strategy going to be?'

I explained that we had to take a generally different approach to our staff if the business was going to have a healthy future. Given that we were limited by the standard sort of technology that most call centres use, we could not change things radically – fundamentally upskilling the basic jobs we offer, for example. But we could look for ways of both making people feel less dissatisfied with the work they had to do and also making them feel that the company was one worth staying with and being committed to. The first thing I got accepted was that we would improve some of the basic workplace facilities like the quality of the rest rooms. To my surprise, Wesley said that he could find money to build a small gymnasium for staff to use. Sandy laughed at this, pointing out to us that Wesley had for a long time said that he personally wanted to find a gym to use. But Wesley argued that this kind of thing should be enough to make people prefer to work for Viewfields rather than for any of our rivals, none of which had this kind of facility. I told Wesley that these were just 'hygiene' factors, in motivational terms, and that we had to look for more significant changes relating to the work itself.

When I said that what I had in mind were such things as allowing operators to adapt the basic scripts to suit their personal style, both Sandy and Wesley got very uncomfortable. And when I suggested that we set up development opportunities for staff to learn how to write scripts themselves, by allowing them an hour a week to work with marketing staff, they wanted to end the meeting. Wesley went into a long lecture about unit labour costs, or something of the kind, and Sandy said that it would give us a messy and unmanageable division of labour. 'We can't afford to confuse people about where their place is in the system', he said, 'and it will put supervisors into an impossible position when they are trying to monitor calls – how will they know whether an operator is doing the job properly and efficiently if there isn't a defined script and strictly allocated minutes?' 'Oh, I was envisaging getting rid of a separate supervisor's role and allowing operator teams to allocate one of themselves to the monitoring desk each week, with a view to that individual looking for ways of helping colleagues improve their performance, rather than keeping the old system where supervisors basically used the monitoring equipment to police the operators.'

When I went a step beyond this and suggested that we move to a largely internal promotional system and that we recruit all operators as people who can potentially move upwards, eventually having their own client accounts to manage, Wesley lost his temper and told Sandy that he should never have employed a soft-headed and totally unrealistic 'personnel type' like me. He left the meeting and Maddy and I spent the next two hours working on Sandy. He told us that this sounded like revolutionary talk to him. Yet he was willing to give consideration to what was being said because, he claimed, he 'had enough vision to see that this was as much a marketing development as a soppy HR one'. Without Maddy pointing out that it was a 'hard-headed business case' that was being put to him, I don't think we would have got anywhere with my ideas. But Sandy did invite us to develop these ideas further and he promised that he would try to 'bring Wesley round', if we could persuade them that, not only would these ideas overcome some of the 'people problems' that we currently had, but that they would significantly help the business grow.

After several months of argument I got all of this accepted. In fact, the current HR practices go even further than I originally envisaged. The teams not only choose the person to cover the developmental/monitoring role each week, they also organise their own cover for sick colleagues, altering their own shifts to make sure the work is covered. And it would appear that most of the recruitment that we have done recently has been of people introduced by current employees. Each employee, if they want it, can have an hour's 'personal development time' to work with marketing staff or, if they wish, to work on the self-help and distance learning packages that we have on the computers in the 'development room' that was built as an extension to the staff rest area. I've been especially pleased to see that team members are happy to 'trade' development time within the teams. People who are not career-oriented swap their weekly development allowance for time off with people who do want more than an hour a week to develop their career potential.

All of this was hard fought for, I must stress. The company is a much more morally acceptable place to work in, from my personal point of view. But this has only come about because there was a significant business case to put for changing the HR strategy in this way. Having said that, the business case was not one that was immediately obvious to either Sandy or Wesley. Without the hard work put in by Maddy and me to get the men to think differently, little would have changed. Perhaps if the staffing problems had got really out of hand, they might have shifted their ground. But I have no doubt that any changes that Sandy and Wesley would have been capable of making on their own initiatives would have been nothing more than minimal – and would not have helped Viewfields survive in the long term. Wesley is still sceptical and constantly complains about the salary costs, in spite of the fact that the rate of our business growth and our growing popularity with both clients and employees gives the company the 'leading edge' position that Sandy is so keen to maintain. As Sandy points out to Wesley, the profits that are being made 'fully justify the higher labour costs'. I suppose the four of us operate quite effectively as a management team but I sometimes wonder how much easier it would all be if business arguments were not always mixed up with the tensions that are always there because Maddy and I are women, are younger than the other two and have not got what Sandy calls a 'proper grounding in telecoms technology' or what Wesley refers to as 'a decent financial education'. This is all nonsense of course – but I long ago realised that, in management, you have to deal with the irrational in people as much as with the rational. Perhaps it all adds to the fun of the job. But I think, as I said to Maddy the other day, that the real reward that I get from seeing our HR strategy in practice is when I hear an operator say to a caller 'how can I help you?' and I get the impression that they really mean it.

The final statement that Inva Gordon makes about the sincerity of an operator's offer of help to callers is perhaps rather revealing about her personal values – something also implied by her reference to Viewfields as a more 'morally acceptable place to work'. She brings ethical and caring concerns to her work. Yet we can also imagine Sandy Viewfield, or even Wesley Nigg, taking pleasure in hearing operator's speaking to callers in a seemingly sincere manner, but Sandy and Wesley, we might guess, would be far less concerned than Inva about whether the operators were *actually* sincere in what they said (whether they were engaging in *deep* rather than *surface acting* – see Chapter 4, p. 132). What would matter to them would be that the operators' performances were likely to be 'good for the business'. In spite of the considerable difference of priority and value between the members of Viewfield's strategic management team, a distinctive change had occurred in the HR strategy. This had come about in the light of both varying values among these four individuals and the changing circumstances, or contingencies, faced by the organisation. The 'managerial argument, negotiation and choice' put at the centre of Figure 10.2 was influenced, as the model suggests, by:

- national and local economic and cultural factors – the changing levels of unemployment for example;
- managerial values, goals and interests – these varying from Sandy's ambitions to run a 'leading edge company' and Inva's ethical concerns to Wesley's interest in having a gym available for his own use and the attitudes each of them had towards age and gender;
- the managerially perceived increase in uncertainty being created for the organisation's future by employee constituencies – reflected in absence, labour turnover, recruitment costs and, above all, in the poor level of work performance that was losing Viewfields business. The key contingency behind this was the one of the changing business environment – a higher level of competition in both the main call centre market and in the local labour market.

The managerial choice that emerged from this decision-making *garbage can* (Chapter 6, pp. 215–21) involved shifting along the continuum shown in

Figure 10.2 in the direction of a *high commitment human resourcing strategy* accompanied by a related shift in the direction of indirect control practices (team working, emphasis on promotions within an internal labour market, etc.). There was no question of a radical shift to a wholly different type of employment practice or a sudden embracing of HR 'best practices'. Instead there was a pragmatic shift in managerial approach resulting from a combination of *choice* and *circumstance*, a combination that took its particular form as a result of processes of argument, challenge and debate and as a result of the specific mix of knowledge, insight, ignorance and prejudice to be found within the group of managers making the shift. The changed contingencies affecting the organisation meant that the main employee constituency was being experienced by managers as more problematic than it was before. The newer human resourcing strategy made a better fit with the organisation's circumstances – a higher commitment and indirect control type of strategy was more appropriate to a situation in which employees were becoming a greater source of strategic uncertainty than they had previously been.

This improved 'fit' between organisational circumstances and human resourcing strategy did not come about automatically – it was chosen by the company's managers. But it was a choice that emerged only after considerable argument, debate and conflict over values. It was also made in an atmosphere of interpersonal tension and in the light of differences of gender, age and occupational background among the group of managers making the strategic choice. Also playing a part in this was a tension between Inva as an HR specialist, on the one side, and Sandy and Wesley on the other. Sandy and Wesley were suspicious of the proposals being developed by Inva, seeing them as naïve and as perhaps too people oriented or 'caring'. Maddy's support for this was respected but it too was taken less seriously than it might have been, early on, probably because of her gender, work background and relative youth. Inva and Maddy, however, would no doubt have argued that they were the more business and strategically oriented ones, in the long-term sense, because they could see the necessity of adopting a higher HR strategy if the organisation was going to perform well into the long term.

Human resource decision making does not just occur with regard to the sort of strategic matters that Inva Gordon and her colleagues were tackling. Decisions are made from day to day about which potential employee to recruit, which employees to allocate to which task, which employee to promote, discipline or dismiss. Operational decisions and choices like these are made every day, and they are just as liable to be influenced by ambiguity and differences of interest as are the more strategic types of decision that we have just been looking at.

Selection, choice and discrimination in human resourcing

Human resourcing involves ensuring that work organisations have the necessary human skills, knowledge and capabilities that can be turned into work efforts which will enable the organisation to continue into the future. In practice, this means that decisions regularly have to be made about specific human individuals and about how they are to be treated within a potential or an actual employment relationship. Human resourcing decisions about recruitment and selection, allocation of tasks and rewards, promotions, dismissals and redundancies are routinely made in employing organisations, typically through the combined efforts of human resourcing or personnel specialists and managers who have a more direct authority relationship with the employee. The concern is with getting the 'right person' for a post, a reward, a punishment or a redundancy notice.

Selecting the 'right person' in all of these areas of human resourcing work is, generally speaking, a matter of achieving a decision that is right in two senses. First, the decision needs to be 'right' in the sense that the person selected is the most appropriate one to do a particular job, say, or to go on a particular training course. Second, the decision needs to be 'right' in that it is seen to be broadly fair and acceptable to whatever individuals, groups or authorities that might take an interest in that decision. At the simpler level, this second criterion means that neither the individual employee themselves nor any other employee or manager is likely to be left with a grievance that might lead them to behave in an organisationally disruptive way following the decision. At a more complex level, it means that the decision should neither contribute to a general atmosphere of injustice or low trust within the organisation nor lead to legal actions against the organisation because the employer can be shown to have unfairly treated or discriminated against an employee in a manner which has been deemed to be illegal in that society – with regard, say, to that employee's gender or race.

For these various reasons, there is considerable pressure on human resourcing decision makers to make the 'right decision'. A 'wrong decision' can be very costly in a financial sense as well as highly damaging to an organisation's general performance or public reputation. Personnel specialists have therefore been increasingly pressured to find ways of making managers feel confident that they are making the best possible choices when they make selection decisions about employees – when they discriminate between one person and another as a potential employee or a candidate for reallocation, promotion, reward, punishment or dismissal. Discrimination between one person and another is at the heart of all of these processes. And discrimination means making human judgements that always and inevitably have an ethical dimension to them. To treat one person one way and another person another way inevitably raises questions of justice, fairness, right and wrong. This is something that often makes managers feel uncomfortable – as does the ambiguity and unpredictability inevitably accompanying decisions about human beings and how they are going to behave in the future.

It is perhaps instructive that the term 'discrimination' is widely applied in the employment context only to what might be termed socially unacceptable choices. The notion that there could be a non-discriminatory selection is clearly nonsense (to choose or select is, by definition, to discriminate). Yet it is almost as if managers are trying to convince themselves that they are not discriminating at all and a lot of personnel or human resourcing practice over the years has appeared to support such a possibility. Attempts have thus been made to develop a *rationalistic and bureaucratic personnel management technology* that not only removes ethical uneasiness from personnel decision making but also plays down the ambiguity and unpredictability that is inevitably associated with judgements made by some human beings about others. Managers have wanted to be equipped with an efficient and neutral set of procedures and technologies which can measure and calculate an employee's, or a potential employee's, appropriateness for treatment of one kind or another (recruitment, promotion, etc.).

It would be foolish to criticise managers, inside and outside HR departments, for trying to devise procedures that enable the best possible person to be chosen for any particular role or treatment or for trying to make that choice in a way that will be deemed to be legal and regarded as generally fair by all concerned. However, there is a considerable danger of managers having too much faith in the ethical neutrality and the predictive powers of human resourcing or personnel techniques and procedures. As we will shortly hear Francesca Carrbridge argue with regard to selection decisions generally, 'At the end of the day a manager must recognise that a choice of one person rather than another involves basic human judgement, intuition and trusting to good fortune. You've got to keep these basic human judgements under control with personnel procedures that try to keep things fair and balanced. But all the selection techniques, personality tests and equal opportunity procedures in the world cannot replace simple human guesswork, a trust in one's "gut feel" and the subjective feeling that you are being as fair as possible when you choose Mrs X rather than Mr Y.'

Activity 10.5

Read what Francesca Carrbridge has to say in Case 10.4 about the difference between her approach to employment decision making and that of her predecessor, Dag Dunearn, and try to identify the different sets of assumptions, or styles of 'framing' reality, which each of them tends adopt with regard to:

- the nature of work organisations;
- the nature of human beings.

To do this, it should be helpful to draw on the distinction between systems-control and process-relational thinking that has been used throughout previous chapters and is summarised in Table 1.4 (p. 30), having been introduced, with regard to work organisations in Chapter 2, p. 30, and with regard to human beings in Chapter 3, p. 94.

Francesca dismantles the people-processing sausage machine — Case 10.4

I noticed, Francesca, that you very much played down the importance of the personality tests that your staff had carried out when it came to the final discussions at the end of today's appointment process.

Yes, I prefer to pay as little attention as possible to personality test results.

Which raises the question of why you use these tests, doesn't it?

Of course it does. When I first came into HR work, I used to argue vehemently against their use. I felt that they were a form of pseudo-science that managers might use as a sort of crutch. I feared that test results and 'advice from psychologists' might discourage managers from standing on their own two feet and making basic human judgements that they would have to stand by and cope with once the decision had been made. I didn't want to let managers believe that there is such a thing as the 'right person', let alone someone with the 'right personality' for any particular post. I did a psychology degree myself and was very aware of how poor a predictor of future job performance research shows these things to be. I did my degree dissertation on this at university and what struck me most strongly was not just the poor predictive power of these tests but the point that several writers made about how a person's job performance is much more likely to be influenced by how they are treated once they are in a job than by so-called personality attributes that they bring to the job. That's a pretty powerful thought, isn't it?

Yes, it is. Perhaps we can come back to it.

I just want to stress the importance of managers realising that a selection decision involves a fallible human choice – it is not the outcome of a magic personnel technique. I want them to take responsibility for their decisions. This is really important because it is often how they subsequently deal with the person once they are appointed that makes that appointment a successful or an unsuccessful one.

I see. But you still haven't explained why as HR director here you spend time and money on occupational testing, something you appear to be against on principle.

I don't oppose all kinds of occupational testing. I'm very happy to use tests which check that people actually have the aptitudes that we are looking for in certain employees. I wouldn't employ an assembly worker who has to manipulate tiny electronic parts who could not pass a standard manual dexterity test any more than I'd take on an office trainee who could not pass a basic literacy test, a sales worker who could not pass a verbal reasoning test or someone to work in our pay office here who failed a numeracy test.

Your problem is with personality tests, then?

It is. Or rather it was. What I recognised after a while was that managers in selection processes did not generally come to rely on test results to anything like the extent that I feared. The tendency that I have observed across many organisations, and years of experience, is that they only take notice of what the testers say when it tends to confirm what their own judgement is telling them. Contrary indications are just ignored.

So why bother with them?

I decided after fighting several battles, especially with a couple of chief executives I worked with, that it wasn't worth it. To put it simply, it appears to make a lot of senior managers feel better if they think that something sort of 'scientific' has gone on somewhere within the selection process. I think it plays a sort of symbolic role for a lot of managers – it is a talisman that makes them feel better about the rather chancy thing they are doing when they are making a decision to appoint, say, someone on £50,000 a year whose later underperformance could cause major difficulties. Recruitment and selection – let alone promotion and deployment decisions – involve a great deal of guesswork. They are very much a gamble, much of the time. And managers are often queasy about this. They feel better if certain procedures have been followed that appear to have something rational or objective about them. I've come to live with this – as long as it does not involve managers denying their responsibility for the decisions they have made, as I just explained. I've therefore become tolerant of the practice of using some personality testing. I'd much prefer to save time and money and drop them though.

Is cost the only problem you have with these tests now?

Oh, I still don't like them. But I admit my predecessor here put me off them. I think I associate testing with his general way of doing HR, or personnel, work.

This is the man you replaced?

Dag Dunearn was a testing maniac. I used to have major battles with him, as his deputy. He used all sorts of tests, some that are relatively uncontroversial as well as some of the more marginal ones, like graphology, to screen out certain applicants for jobs – rejecting them before the managers whose area the job was in had even got to see their applications. Imagine that: you don't even get to have your application put in front of a departmental manager, let alone get an interview, because some charlatan retained by a personnel manager says your handwriting indicates that you are an unreliable person.

But your problems with his approach went further than this?

Indeed. We just didn't see the world in the same way, let alone how you should do personnel work. In the end, the other top managers decided he had to go. He was simply too inflexible, bureaucratic and officious. So I got his job and I think I am well respected. I do put limits on managers' freedom to manoeuvre – over matters like equal opportunities and other areas where employment legislation affects us. And I am fairly bureaucratic in areas where you need to be bureaucratic – over things like accurate employee records and managers following proper procedures in areas like health and safety, discipline, induction, appraisal and all that. But managers generally understand why these things have to be done and realise that I am happy to see all sorts of innovation and experimentation occurring as long as the basic and necessary procedures are followed.

How was it before you took over then?

Dag took what I call a sausage machine approach to HR. He saw the organisation as a big system that ran on sausages. The job of the personnel department, as it was called then, was to act as a sausage machine, producing sausages of the right size and the right type at the right time for each job that had to be done. I don't think he could tell the difference between sausage making and people processing. He would make sure that the organisation contained the right proportion of sausages with black skins and the designated number of disabled sausages, as well as maintaining what he deemed was a correct balance between male and female sausages – if you'll excuse the analogy here. He believed there was a formula for choosing the 'right' person for every job. Every person, just like a sausage, had a fixed set of properties and the job of personnel was to calculate what sort of characteristics were required for every job in the organisation – and then the right sausage would be served up for that post. Do you follow me?

I'm not sure – you are stretching the analogy a bit. Give me an example.

Well, what I had in mind was the way that, whenever there was a vacancy, no action would be taken by the personnel department even to advertise it until the manager concerned had produced a meticulous job description, accompanied by a detailed person specification which would set out in detail exactly what sort of person (I nearly said sausage) that they wanted the personnel department to find for them.

And the problem with this?

Dag saw the organisation's job structure as a much more fixed thing than it is in practice. Managers often said to me that they would be happy to consider a variety of different candidates, with various different strengths, for appointment to an area where there was a vacancy. If they found someone generally useful, then they could adapt the job to fit the person. This went totally against Dag's view of organisations as machines that require human cogs to make them run. He saw his job as getting exactly the right human cog for every little piece of the organisational machine. I remember an argument I had with him over this. He told me that I misunderstood professional personnel management – the basis of which was to make sure that round pegs were found for round holes and square pegs for square holes. It was totally ridiculous, in his view, to go changing the shapes of the 'organisational holes' to make sure that whatever pegs you might chance upon would fit into them. It seems like quite a good idea to me, however.

He was rather mechanistic, you are saying?

Yes, and it was very counterproductive. The business was increasingly requiring flexible and adaptive workers who would themselves influence the jobs they would do once recruited. And Dag was standing in the way of this. His efforts over equal opportunities were equally counterproductive. On several occasions, for example, he held up important selection or promotion interviews for months, until he could get a list of candidates that he deemed to have a reasonable race and gender balance.

The means were getting in the way of the ends for which they were devised, you could say.

Exactly.

And you avoid this happening?

As far as I can. I am passionately concerned about fairness and equal opportunities. But if I were to get obsessed with setting up checks and controls in these areas, like Dag did, it would take us back to a situation where working towards gender and ethnic diversity would simply have a bad name with managers. And they would do everything they could to get round equal opportunity measures wherever they could. My approach is to get managers to believe in the spirit and principle of fairness and equality. It may sound idealistic but I prefer to see the organisation as a sort of moral community – a place in which people can more or less trust each other. That's what I work towards anyway. People are not fixed quantities or objects, like sausages, and I think that if they are encouraged to work together in a good atmosphere they will both develop themselves, as individuals, and change the organisation so that it can cope better with all the changes that are being thrown at it.

So you are much more open and flexible about processes like selection and recruitment?

Indeed, but not only that. Management is not just a technical matter, in my view. When you go through an interviewing process, for example, you are both trying to get to know the candidates, as human beings, and enabling them to get to know you as an employer with a certain culture and set of cultural values. The process is a sort of negotiation between the potential employee and the potential employer. You, as a recruiter, cannot really know what any of these people is really going to be like if you take them on. And they cannot be too sure of just what it is going to be like working for you. So there is a process of weighing each other up. This involves a great deal of ambiguity and awareness that some people are simply more skilled at presenting themselves to a prospective employer than others (from the completing of the application form to what they both mention and avoid mentioning in an interview). And what this all adds up to is that managers have to deploy the basic human skills of eliciting helpful responses from people and judging the likelihood of one person being a better bet for the organisation than another.

That's how you get the right people for the organisation?

No. The 'right person', as you put it, would be the one who you could guarantee would do the job as required. That is just not possible. It is, as I've just said, a matter of who is 'the better bet'. As I was stressing earlier, some of the most important determinants of how well someone does the job (whatever the job turns out to be like, once they start doing it) are ones that arise after the appointment of the individual. How a person is treated once recruited is surely just as important as the recruitment and selection process that brought them into the organisation. On various occasions I have seen what looked like the perfect appointment turning out to be a disaster because the person's abilities were either misused or under used, once appointed. And by the same token, I've seen some potentially high-risk appointments turning out to be great successes because the managers involved worked hard to use the recruits' talents to the best effect. I want managers to recognise all of this and not see HR as a source of administrative and psychological black magic that can find them the 'right person' for every job.

You want managers to make their own judgements and take on their own risks?

Yes, supported by whatever expertise we have to offer in HR. At the end of the day a manager must recognise that a choice of one person rather than another involves basic human judgement, intuition and trusting to good fortune. You've got to keep these basic human judgements under control with personnel procedures that try to keep things fair and balanced. But all the selection techniques, personality tests and equal opportunity procedures in the world cannot replace simple human guesswork, a trust in one's 'gut feel' and the subjective feeling that you are being as fair as possible when you choose Mrs X rather than Mr Y.

It is apparent from what Francesca Carrbridge says that she is sensitive to the tensions we identified earlier as typically, if not inevitably, existing between HR and other managers. She manages those tensions by allowing managers flexibility and the chance to innovate, as long as they conform with the basic principles that she lays down to fulfil the HR role of maintaining the organisational workforce as a whole (equal opportunities, compliance with legislation, induction and appraisal procedures, etc.). Her predecessor, Dag Dunearn, on the other hand, exacerbated those tensions by dictating to managers and treating them in an inflexible and officious way. This led to his downfall, it would appear, which Francesca relates to his view of the nature of work organisations. She talks of his view of the organisation as a big machine that requires appropriate employees in the same way that a machine requires cogs. This fits with what we have called a systems-control way of 'framing' organisations. It sees the structure of jobs in the organisation as something that is pre-decided in the organisational design – thus making it possible for the personnel department to ask a departmental manager for a precise 'job description' accompanied by a clear 'person specification'. The candidate who fits that specification – with this 'fit' being measured wherever possible by the use of neutral and objective tests – is judged to be the 'right person for the job'. This suggests that Dag sees human beings, and not just organisations, in systems-control terms. Each human being 'has' a particular personality or an otherwise similarly fixed set of characteristics – ones that they will carry forward into their subsequent appointment or promotion, regardless of the circumstances in which they find themselves after that appointment.

Francesca scorns this 'sausage machine' approach to HR. Her analogy is a little forced at times but it gives a clear indication of what she has tried to move away from in her regime. She sees the organisation more as a human community, she explains, in which human and fallible judgements are made about employees and prospective employees. The organisation is a much more ambiguous place and every decision has its moral implications, she suggests. The selecting of people is part of a *process*, which continues long after the actual appointment decision is made. It is not part of a sausage-making system. Managers have to take responsibility for their judgements, not just acknowledging the fallibility of their choice making but accepting responsibility for making the appointment a success after it has been made. All of this suggests a process-relational way of 'framing' both organisations and people. The organisation is seen as a more flexible and negotiable set of arrangements than a

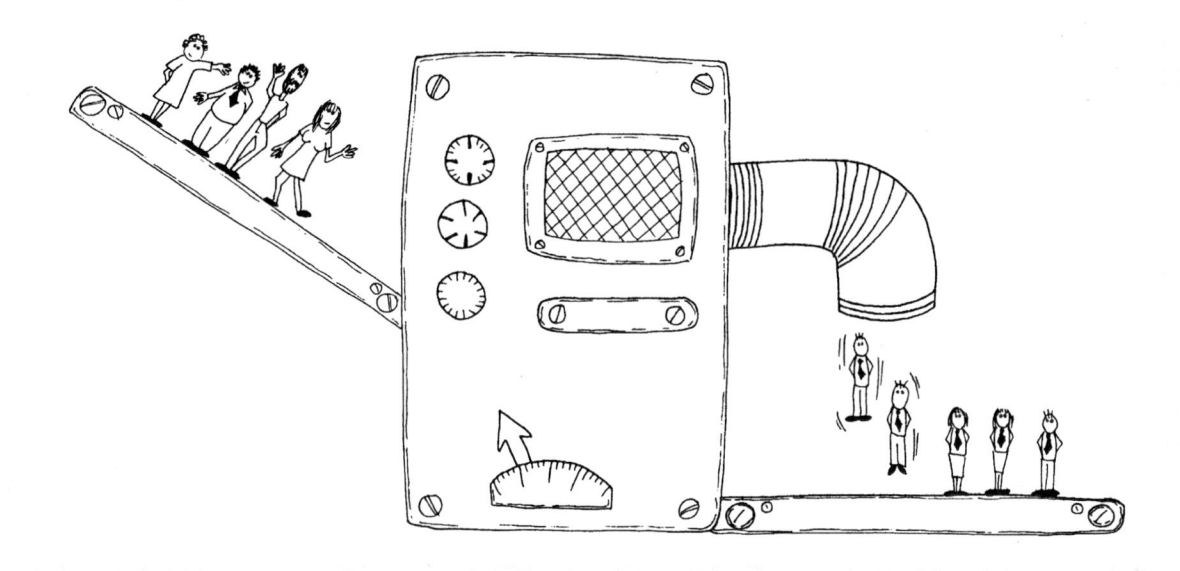

FIGURE 10.3 The people-processing sausage machine

systems-control approach would point to. This makes it possible for managers to consider selecting a generally appropriate candidate for an appointment and for the task structure and way of working to be modified once that person becomes involved in it. But Francesca not only avoids regarding the organisation as a fixed entity. She also sees human beings as adaptable – and not as a fixed set of attributes or personality characteristics. How they behave in the organisation is a matter of the processes that they become involved in and the set of relationships in which they play a part.

A process-relational framing of the 'people processing' aspect of human resourcing is one that locates choices over such matters as recruitment, promotion, appraisal or deployment within the employment relationship between employees and the employing organisation. The organisation does not itself, in any direct sense, employ people, of course. Managers do this in the organisation's name, and managers are fallible human beings working within bounded rationality and with their judgements shaped by personal beliefs and prejudices as well as by personal and group interests. In effect, the HR selection processes in which managers engage are bargaining processes (see Newell, 2004 and Further Reading on 'people processing' aspects of HRM, p. 447) – albeit bargaining processes in which the parties are rarely equals. They are processes within which an implicit contract is created between employer and employee, an often vague and ambiguous contract that is subject to all sorts of change when the individual finds themselves in the post for which they were selected. Also, their *orientation to work* becomes subject to changes both within and outside the work setting (Chapter 4, pp. 115–24). Bargaining is also quite likely to go on between the managers taking part in the selection process themselves. Most HR decisions are made within the sort of 'garbage can' process we examined earlier (Chapter 6, pp. 215–21) with a variety of different managerial and personal views and interests coming into play and contributing to the overall *negotiated order* (Chapter 2, pp. 59–65) of the organisation. And, just as any selection decision is influenced by how the managerial selectors operate, it will clearly also be influenced by how the employee or respective employee presents themselves. A shrewd candidate for a job, a promotion or a posting will tell credible and appealing stories about themselves and who they are and what they can do, drawing on appropriate *discursive resources* to impress selectors. We saw his very clearly with Mike Kilrock in Case 3.4 (p. 103), and his drawing on discourses of *leadership, entrepreneurship* and *professionalism* to win himself a promotion in his funeral directing organisation.

We do not know how successful Mike Kilrock was in his bid for promotion. Whenever a candidate for selection presents themselves to selectors, they take a risk. They cannot know how their presentation of self and the story they construct about themselves will be received. In the same way, the managers who choose or reject such a candidate cannot know with any certainty that the outcome will be the best one that they could have made. They too are taking a risk.

'At the end of the day', to borrow Francesca Carrbridge's expression from Case 10.4 in the present chapter, managerial skills are very much ones of making basic human judgements, shrewd guesses and bargains that will contribute to a greater or a lesser extent to the long-term performance of the organisation that employs them. This analysis applies to human resourcing and other aspects of organisational and managerial work alike.

Summary

In this chapter the following key points have been made:

- It is both unrealistic and morally dubious to regard human beings themselves as 'human resources'. It is more appropriate to treat *human resources* as the human efforts, skills and capabilities that an organisation requires to be able to operate into the long term.

- Human resourcing issues affect every employee in a work organisation – managers and non-managers alike. And, within management, involvement in human resourcing matters is necessarily a concern of both human resourcing specialists and non-HR managers.

- Human Resource Management (HRM) is a term that is used in a confusing variety of ways. It was largely developed as a concept by academic observers trying to detect significant changes in employment practices. Particular confusion has been caused by academic writers' attempts to differentiate 'HRM' from 'personnel management'. Such a differentiation is only very loosely connected to a trend among practitioners to re-label personnel departments as Human Resources (HR) departments.

- Human resource strategy making is central to broader practices of strategy making in employing organisations and the common tendency to see it as following from – or serving – the main business strategy of an organisation can be misleading. It is more helpful to see it as *both* following from and contributing to the main process of corporate strategy making.

- The human resourcing function of modern work organisations can be understood, in part, as helping to cope with some basic tensions or contradictions inherent in industrial capitalist ways of organising economies and societies. In particular, it has to handle the difficulties caused by the fact that although people are taught to think of themselves as free choice-making citizens in such societies, they are nevertheless subjected to supervisory and managerial control at work. Managerial ways have to be found of both allowing a certain amount of discretion to employees and finding ways of exerting a degree of control over them. The involvement of HR functions in both the 'care' and the 'control' of employees and their concern with both 'welfare' and 'efficiency' reflects this.

- The HR role in organisations is a particularly strategic one because it tends to take on responsibilities for maintaining integration of the workforce at a corporate level and for looking at longer-term employment issues that departmental managers are less likely to be concerned with. This contributes to the tensions and conflicts that often arise between HR specialists and other managers.

- Human resourcing strategies vary from organisation to organisation with some being closer to a *high commitment* pattern of arrangements and practices and others closer to a *low commitment* pattern. The pattern emerging in any particular organisation will be the outcome of various managerial preferences and values on the one hand and certain managerially interpreted contingent or circumstantial factors on the other. All things being equal, a high commitment type of employment strategy will tend to be adopted when managers perceive the employee constituencies to be strategically problematic, in the sense of creating uncertainties for long-term continuation. This might result, for example, from a highly skilled or educated level of workforce being required to operate a relatively complex technology. This would lead employees to place high demands on the employer in terms of both intrinsic and extrinsic rewards. When employee constituencies are much less problematic, on the other hand, and are less able to make strong demands on the employer, for example, there are cost and efficiency pressures on managers to adopt a *low commitment* type of HR strategy.

- The *high* or *low commitment* HR strategic option is closely related to a whole set of other options: ones in areas ranging from job design and pay systems to strategy-making procedures and cultural patterns. In all of these areas an *indirect control* approach will be associated with a *high commitment* HR strategy and direct control approach associated with a *low commitment* HR strategy.

- In certain circumstances, organisations may adopt a dual human resourcing strategy, applying different types of strategy to different parts of the overall workforce.

- Human resourcing decisions involving the selection of individuals in areas such as recruitment, promotion, reward, deployment and dismissal are made every day in work organisations. There has been a tendency for a rational and calculative *personnel technology* to be applied to these choices. This involves strongly bureaucratic procedures and the heavy use of such devices as psychological tests. Such a technology is intended to help select individuals in a way that will be deemed efficient, acceptable and fair. However, it tends to become restrictive and counterproductive. Its use can be associated with a systems-control way of thinking about work organisations and people. A more realistic process-relational way of thinking indicates that selection and discrimination processes are highly ambiguous and are dependent on basic human processes of judgement, guesswork, chance taking, debate and negotiation. Selection and HR choice processes in general are better seen as parts of broader and more continuous processes of bargaining and adjustment in which both organisational arrangements and human beings themselves change and adapt within the ongoing negotiated order of the organisation.

Recommended reading

A rigorous critique of how HRM tends to be studied, together with a research-based case study which illustrates an alternative and more 'critical' approach to the subject tying in closely with the material in the present Chapter 10 is to be found in Tony Watson, 'Human resource management and critical social science analysis' (*Journal of Management Studies*, 41(3): 447–467, 2004). But to get an appreciation of the various different facets of contemporary HR or employment management practices it is helpful to read selectively from edited texts such as those by Tom Redman and Adrian Wilkinson, *Contemporary Human Resource Management* (Harlow: FT Prentice Hall, 2003) or John Leopold, Lynette Harris and Tony Watson, *The Strategic Management of Human Resources* (London: FT Prentice Hall, 2005) or Peter Boxall, John Purcell and Patrick Wright (eds), *The Oxford Handbook of Human Resource Management* (Oxford: Oxford University Press, 2006). For those with a special interest in the strategic aspects of HR then Peter Boxall and John Purcell's *Strategy and Human Resource Management* (Basingstoke: Palgrave, 2003) is recommended. And for those wanting to understand trends in employment relations (or 'industrial relations') Peter Ackers and Adrian Wilkinson's *Understanding Work and Employment* (Oxford: Oxford University Press, 2003) is suggested.

Further reading

Further reading HRM, the academic literature

Beech, N. (1998), 'Literature review: rhetoric and discourse in HRM', *Management Learning*, 29(1): 110–113

Beer, M., Spector, B., Lawrence, P.R., Mill, Q.D. and Walton, R.E. (1984) *Managing Human Assets*, Boston, MA: Harvard Business School Press

Guest, D. (1989) 'Personnel and HRM: can you tell the difference?', *Personnel Management*, January: 48–51

Guest, D. (1990) 'Human resource management and the American Dream', *Journal of Management Studies*, 27(4): 377–397

Hart, T.J. (1993) 'HRM – time to exorcize the militant tendency', *Employee Relations*, 15(3): 29–36

Kamoche, K. (2001) *Understanding Human Resource Management*, Buckingham: Open University Press

Legge, K. (2004) *Human Resource Management: Rhetorics and realities*, Basingstoke: Palgrave

Mabey, C., Skinner, D. and Clark, T. (eds) (1998) *Experiencing Human Resource Management*, London: Sage

Marchington, M. and Grugulis, I. (2000). ' "Best practice" human resource management: perfect opportunity or dangerous illusion?', *International Journal of Human Resource Management*, 11(4): 905–925

Noon, M. (1992) 'HRM: A map, model or theory?' in P. Blyton and P. Turnbull (eds) *Reassessing Human Resource Management*, London: Sage

Redman, T. and Wilkinson, A. (eds) *Contemporary Human Resource Management*, Harlow: FT Prentice Hall

Steyaert, C. and Janssens, M. (1999) 'Human and inhuman resource management: saving the subject of HRM', *Organization*, 6(2): 181–198

Storey, J. (1992) *Developments in the Management of Human Resources*, Oxford: Basil Blackwell

Storey, J. (ed.) (2001) *Human Resource Management: A critical text, 2nd edition*, London: Thomson Learning

Watson, T.J. (1995) 'In search of HRM: beyond the rhetoric and reality distinction or the dog that didn't bark', *Personnel Review*, 24(4): 6–16

Watson, T.J. (2004) 'Human resource management and critical social science analysis', *Journal of Management Studies*, 41(3): 447–467

Watson, T.J. and Watson, D.H. (1999) 'Human resourcing in practice: managing employment issues in the university', *Journal of Management Studies*, 36(4): 483–504

Further reading HR and other managers

Caldwell, R. (2003) 'The changing roles of personnel managers: old ambiguities, new uncertainties', *Journal of Management Studies*, 40(4): 983–1004

Gennard, J. and Kelly, J. (1994) 'Human resource management: the views of personnel directors', *Human Resource Management Journal*, 5(1): 15–32

Guest, D. and King, Z. (2004) 'Power, innovation and problem-solving: the personnel manager's three steps to heaven', *Journal of Management Studies*, 41(3): 401–423

Legge, K. (1993) 'The role of personnel specialists: centrality or marginalization?' in J. Clark (ed.) *Human Resource Management and Technical Change*, London: Sage, 20–42

Purcell, J. (2001) 'Personnel and human resource managers: power, prestige and potential', *Human Resource Management Journal*, 11(3): 3–4

Torrington, D. (1998) 'Crisis and opportunity in HRM: the challenge for the personnel function' in P. Sparrow and M. Marchington (eds) *Human Resource Management: The new agenda*, London: FT Pitman

Torrington, D. and Hall, L. (1996) 'Chasing the rainbow: how seeking status through strategy misses the point for the personnel function', *Employee Relations*, 18(6): 79–96

Tyson, S. and Fell, A. (1986) *Evaluating the Personnel Function*, London: Hutchinson

Watson, D.H. (1988) *Managers of Discontent: Trade union officers and industrial relations managers*, London: Routledge

Watson, T.J. (1977) *The Personnel Managers*, London: Routledge

Watson, T.J (2001) 'Speaking professionally – occupational anxiety and discursive ingenuity among human resourcing specialists' in S. Whitehead and M. Dent (eds) *Managing Professional Identities*, London: Routledge

Further reading Strategic HRM

Boxall, P. (1996) 'The strategic HRM debate and the resource-based view of the firm', *Human Resource Management Journal*, 6(3): 59–75

Devanna, M.A., Fombrun, C.J. and Tichy, N.M. (1984) 'A framework for strategic human resource management' in C. Fombrun, N.M. Tichy and M.A. Devanna (eds) *Strategic Human Resource Management*, Chichester: Wiley

Fombrun, C., Tichy, N.M. and Devanna, M.A. (eds) (1984) *Strategic Human Resource Management*, New York: Wiley

Gratton, L., Hope Hailey, V., Stiles P. and Truss, C. (1999) *Strategic Human Resource Management*, Oxford: Oxford University Press

Jacques, R. (1999) 'Developing a tactical approach to engaging with "strategic" HRM', *Organization*, 6(2): 199–222

Kamoche, K. (1994) 'A critique and a proposed reformulation of strategic human resource management', *Human Resource Management Journal*, 4(4): 29–47

Kamoche, K. (1996) 'Strategic human resource management within resource capability view of the firm', *Journal of Management Studies*, 33(2): 213–233

Mabey, C., Salaman, G. and Storey, J. (1998) *Strategic Human Resource Management*, 2nd edition, Oxford: Blackwell

Procter, S.J., Rowlinson, M., McArdle, L., Hassard, J. and Forrester, P. (1994) 'Flexibility, politics and strategy: in defence of the model of the flexible firm', *Work, Employment and Society*, 8(2): 221–242

Purcell, J. (1995) 'Corporate strategy and its link with human resource management strategy' in J. Storey (ed.) *Human Resource Management: A critical text*, London: Routledge

Sánchez-Runde, C. (2001) 'Strategic human resource management and the new employment relationships: a research review and agenda' in J. Gual and

J.E. Ricart (eds) *Strategy, Organization and the Changing Nature of Work*, Cheltenham: Elgar

Schuler, R.S., Jackson, S.E. and Storey, J. (2001) 'HRM and its link with strategic management' in J. Storey (ed.), *Human Resource Management: A critical text*, 2nd edition, London: Thomson Learning

Watson, T.J. (2004) 'Organisations, strategies and human resourcing' in J. Leopold, L. Harris and T.J. Watson (eds) *The Strategic Management of Human Resources*, London: FT Prentice Hall, 6–33

Further reading 'People processing' aspects of HRM

Anderson, N. and Ostroff, C. (1997) 'Selection as socialization' in N. Anderson and P. Herriot (eds) *International Handbook of Selection and Assessment*, Chichester: Wiley

Campbell, J. and Knapp, D. (eds) (2001) *Exploring the Limits in Personnel Selection and Classification*, Mahwah, NJ: Lawrence Erlbaum Associates

Cooper D. and Robertson, I.T. (1995) *The Psychology of Personnel Selection*, London: Routledge

Dipboye, R. (1992) *Selection Interviews: Process perspectives*, Cincinnati, OH: South Western

Judge, T.A. and Cable, D.M. (1997) 'Applicant personality, organizational culture and organization attraction', *Personnel Psychology*, 50: 359–394

McDaniel, M.A., Whetzel, D.L., Schmidt, F.L. and Maurer, S.D. (1994) 'The validity of the employment interviews: a comprehensive review and meta analysis', *Journal of Applied Psychology*, 79: 599–616

Newell, S. (2004) 'Assessment, selection and evaluation' in J. Leopold, L. Harris and T.J. Watson (eds) *The Strategic Management of Human Resources*, London: FT Prentice Hall, 140–177

Newell, S. and Shackleton, V. (2001) 'Selection and assessment as an interactive decision–action process' in T. Redman and A. Wilkinson (eds) *Contemporary Human Resource Management*, Harlow: FT Prentice Hall

Newton, T. and Findlay, P. (1996) 'Playing God? The performance of appraisal', *Human Resource Management Journal*, 6(3): 42–58

Silverman, D. and Jones, J. (1976) *Organisational Work: The language of grading and the grading of language*, London: Macmillan

Townley, B. (1989) 'Selection and appraisal: reconstituting social relations?' in J. Storey (ed.) *New Perspectives on HRM*, London: Routledge

Townley, B. (1993) 'Performance appraisal and the emergence of management', *Journal of Management Studies*, 3(2): 221–238

Semester 2
PROCESSES AND PRACTICES

ENTERING THE WORKPLACE: SELECTION AND ASSESSMENT

Chapter 4
SELECTION
Dora Scholarios

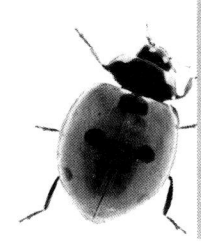

Introduction

'Best-practice' employee selection is usually associated with the 'psychometric' model. This recommends rigorously developed psychometric tests, performance-based or work simulation methods, and the use of multiple methods of assessment, all designed to accurately measure candidates' knowledge, skills, abilities, personality and attitudes.

This view has dominated literature on selection. Its popularity is no doubt due to its emphasis on objectivity, meritocracy and efficiency, which are all evident in the story of selection, and indeed the emergence of HRM, over the last century. Industrialisation and mass manpower planning during the early twentieth century required a systematic way of matching the attributes of individuals to the requirements of jobs, and early psychological research on understanding and scaling individual differences (for example, the work of Alfred Binet or Raymond Cattell in the field of education) provided tools for military and commercial organisations faced with this massive scale problem of person–job fit. These early assessment efforts became gradually refined to show how organisations of all types could gain from systematic selection methods. By the 1980s, it had become a core element of competitive strategy, and an essential part of an organisation's strategic capability for adapting to competition (Hamel and Prahalad 1989). Systematic selection is now regarded as one of the critical functions of HRM, essential for achieving key organisational outcomes (Storey 2007), and a core component of what has been called a high-commitment or high-performance management approach to HRM (Marchington and Wilkinson 2005; Pfeffer 1998).

This chapter begins with a review of the principles of the psychometric model and the range of assessment methods available to organisations that follow this model. The chapter then considers whether organisations have adopted these methods. This leads to a more sceptical account of sophisticated selection, and the possibility of alternative paradigms which move away from a techniques-driven approach. Three alternatives are covered: a 'best fit' approach; an 'interactive action-oriented' perspective (Newell 2006); and a discourse view, which describes selection as a contested, rather than rational, process, muddied by multiple possible interpretations and interests. We conclude by examining what these alternative paradigms imply for selection practice and for HRM.

A brief overview of psychometric quality

How do we identify people with knowledge, skill, ability and the personality to perform well at a set of tasks we call a job? Even more difficult, how do we do this before we have ever seen that person perform on the job? (Ployhart et al. 2006, p.10)

It is this latter task which gives the psychometric model its alias as the 'prediction' or 'predictivist' paradigm and takes up the majority of space in most textbooks on the subject of selection. Decisions whether to hire someone are usually based on their performance on a test assessing their suitability for the job – hence the prediction – but how do we make sure this test does what it is intended to do? Four standards are used to make this evaluation (more detail on each can be found in any textbook account of selection; e.g. Schmitt and Chan 1998; Searle 2003a).

1. The method of assessment must be *reliable*; i.e. accurate and free from contamination. Reliable methods have high physical fidelity with job performance itself, are standardised across applicants, have some degree of imposed structure, and show consistency across multiple assessors. Work samples or simulations, which measure performance on a structured task reflecting behaviours used in the job, are likely to have high reliability. Interviews are generally thought to have low reliability, although the use of panels, rather than individual decision makers, and structure and standardisation, like question-response scoring, have been shown to increase their reliability (McFarland *et al.* 2004).

2. Selection methods must also be *valid* – relevant for the work behaviours they are meant to predict. At minimum, to be valid, assessment must be designed around a systematic job analysis and person specification for the job, and be reliable. For example, introducing structure into interviews also enhances their validity (Schmidt and Zimmerman 2004). A valid method, though, should also show an association between scores on the assessment tool and desired job behaviours. This is often expressed as a correlation coefficient – known as a criterion-related validity coefficient – representing the relationship between scores on the predictor (or proposed selection method) and scores on a criterion (or proxy measure) of job performance. This correlation coefficient can range from 0 (chance prediction or no relationship) to 1.0 (perfect prediction). Table 4.1 summarises what values are considered to be low, moderate or high predictive validity coefficients for a range of selection methods.

3. *Subgroup predictive validity* should be the same for different applicant groups, such as men and women; i.e. the selection method should treat all groups the same. Members of one subgroup should not be selected disproportionately more or less often than members of another. The example of cognitive ability testing illustrates perfectly the trade-offs between predictive validity and different subgroup prediction. Psychometric tests which measure general cognitive ability (also known as general intelligence) provide the best predictors of future success in the workplace regardless of the specific job, with validity coefficients in the region of .60 (Schmidt and Hunter 1998). However, some minority groups, particularly blacks and Hispanics, tend to score lower as a group on such tests, even though the tests themselves are not inherently unfair. As a result of this differential predictive validity, the US federal government has encouraged the search for alternatives to cognitive ability testing for hiring purposes in order to minimise adverse impact against historically and socially disadvantaged groups.

4. The selection method should have high *utility* for the organisation. This usually takes into account cost and potential return on investment so that methods with high validity which are not expensive to develop or administer will have higher utility. This also is affected by the hiring context; for example, the number of applications received for a job opening and the proportion of these who will be hired (the selection ratio).

The 'what' and 'how' of selection

Each of these four psychometric standards is concerned with how we s... assessment tools, or selection methods, for determining people's suitability for jo... evant is what underlying individual characteristics we wish to capture with these meth... a range of methods (the 'how') could be used to tap into a single underlying construct (t... 'what'). In this sense, application forms, interviews and psychometric tests could all be used to measure personality, but with varying degrees of psychometric rigour.

One useful framework distinguishes between cognitive, non-cognitive and performance-based individual differences. Cognitive characteristics reflect intellectual processes, academic achievements and knowledge; non-cognitive characteristics include personality traits, motivation, past experience and qualifications; and performance-based characteristics refer to more hands-on behavioural examples of job performance. Each of these constructs represents the 'what' to be measured; the selection technique used to do this represents the 'how'.

Table 4.1 brings together the psychometric standards and three types of individual differences to classify various selection methods. The table also indicates the general findings from research on user acceptability with respect to these methods, an issue to which we return later in the chapter. We discuss only some of these selection methods here. An important point to note from the discussion and Table 4.1 is that performance-based selection methods generally have higher reliability/validity, lower subgroup differences in predictive validity and higher user acceptability, all of which has resulted in their increasing popularity.

Table 4.1 The psychometric quality of alternative selection methods

Selection method	Predictive validity	Subgroup differences (race/gender)	Utility	User acceptability
Cognitive				
Ability/aptitude test	High	Large/small	High	Moderate
Achievement/job knowledge test	High	Moderate/small	High	Favourable
Non-cognitive				
Personality test	Low/moderate	Small/small	Moderate	Unfavourable
Biographical information	Moderate	Small/small	Moderate	Unfavourable
Experience	Moderate	Small/small	Low	Moderate
Performance-based				
Work sample	Moderate/high	Small-moderate/small	Moderate	Favourable
Interview – unstructured	Low	Small/small	Moderate	Low
Interview – structured	High	Small/small	Moderate	Moderate
Situational judgement test	Moderate	Moderate/small	High	Favourable

Source: Adapted from Ployhart et al. 2006 (Table 7.3) and Schmidt and Hunter 1998

Notes: Descriptors for criterion-related validity coefficients are based on the following accepted ranges: 0.10 = low; 0.20 = moderate; 0.30 and above = high

COGNITIVE ABILITY

Psychometric tests are standardised instruments designed to measure individual differences, most commonly cognitive ability or aptitude, achievement or personality. Although there is some blurring between cognitive ability and aptitude, measures of ability focus more on current levels of skill in specific areas, such as arithmetic or verbal ability, while aptitude refers to one's potential to learn or acquire skill, regardless of past experience, and is often associated with a broader measure of intelligence. Ability may underlie aptitude – high logical reasoning ability may be required for computer programming aptitude – which shows how aptitudes may be targeted at specific occupational areas (consider how an aptitude for making inferences from numerical data contributes to performance in financial services occupations). Tests of achievement include school examinations, typing tests or statutory professional examinations; e.g. for accountancy certification or where public safety may be at risk, as in the use of firefighting equipment or electrical safety.

During the 1980s, there was a flurry of influential research centred on tests of general cognitive ability (referred to as g), which include both ability and aptitude. Most test batteries measuring g consist of tests of numerical, verbal, reasoning and spatial ability, and emphasise future potential for learning or adapting to new situations. Research shows that tests of g provide the best way of predicting performance differences between job applicants in any type of job, with potentially high returns on investment (utility) for organisations. Using the statistical techniques of meta-analysis to aggregate across validity studies, g has been found to be a strong predictor of diverse measures of job success, including supervisory ratings, production quantity and quality, and training performance (e.g. Hunter and Hunter 1984). More recently, this has been shown to hold across different employment and cultural contexts. For example, Bertua *et al.* (2005) showed high validity for a range of UK jobs, and Salgado *et al.* (2003) did the same for 10 European Commission countries.

Current thinking on the structure of ability distinguishes between tests which measure fluid intelligence, representing general reasoning ability across situations, and crystallised intelligence, which represents a culturally specific view of intelligence which develops as a result of specific experiences (Carroll 1993). An example of how these tests are being used by graduate employers as a way of measuring fluid intelligence, and hence future potential, is described in Box 4.1. Today, over 70 specialised ability tests are available as aids to decision makers.

Box 4.1 HRM in practice

Psychometric testing in graduate jobs

The most recent survey of UK blue-chip graduate employers by the Association of Graduate Recruiters (2007) shows that psychometric testing is being used as a way of dealing with the oversupply of graduates qualifying with first or upper second class degrees; in the UK, this was thought to be 57 per cent in 2007. Although a 2:1 degree is still thought to be the 'gold standard' and used as a minimum requirement by 64 per cent of employers, university degrees of variable quality mean that qualifications alone are becoming less effective for initial screening. Blue-chip companies are increasingly using tests of numeracy, logical reasoning, literacy and verbal reasoning, which recruiters believe differentiate graduates with the highest potential.

That is not to say that *g* is now uncontroversially the psychometric test of choice in employment contexts. There are several areas of resistance. Firstly, performance on a test does not necessarily reflect intelligence or the test-taker's best possible performance, but may depend on whether the individual is interested in doing well, where they focus their attention and how much effort they expend. This leads to the distinction between typical and maximal performance. Rather than focusing on predicting someone's maximal behaviour, like most tests of cognitive ability, some argue that we should focus on finding out how a person typically performs a task in the actual job environment (Klehe and Anderson 2005). Later sections in this chapter consider the role of personality tests as one way of predicting typical behaviour.

A second development is in tests measuring different kinds of 'intelligence'. This includes dimensions of creative and emotional intelligence which cannot be captured by linguistically-based psychometric tests, but which some now argue affect many aspects of work performance (Weisinger 1998). Tacit knowledge, which represents practical knowledge of 'how' to do a job and is inferred from experience rather than academically acquired, has also received attention, especially in non-routine and unstructured jobs, such as management (Sternberg *et al.* 1995). Tacit knowledge also underlies the increasing use of situational judgement tests, which we consider later under performance-based methods.

Finally, as shown in Table 4.1, cognitive ability testing suffers from high subgroup differences in predictive validity; i.e. it has adverse impact on members of minority racial groups. Even though the reliability, validity and utility of cognitive ability testing have all been shown – that is, they are free from any bias – their use is a liability to employers who are concerned with maintaining a diverse workforce. Different applicant groups, for example Caucasian, Hispanic, Asian and African Americans, tend to score differently on these tests, which can lead to substantially different hiring rates, especially as organisations become more selective (i.e. hire fewer applicants or increase their cut scores on selection methods). In the US, federal law has battled with the issue of minority group preference in hiring and university entrance admissions and whether selection procedures should be race-neutral or race-conscious (see, for example, Kravitz 2008).

Internationally, the debate has tended to recommend careful design and validation of tests for particular groups (men/women, racial/cultural groups) to provide norm-referenced testing. If we remember the culturally specific element of intelligence (crystallised intelligence), though, we might question whether Western-designed tests are appropriate for other cultures' understanding of ability. Many multinational organisations face such issues when selecting staff who can work in any part of the world. There are interesting, unresolved dilemmas here with respect to culture-free and valid testing, as articulated by Searle (2003a, p.189). Should we aim for generic measures which tap into fluid (cultural-neutral) intelligence, or should we acknowledge the importance of cultural differences in what abilities are valued and develop different tests for different parts of the world? Another alternative may be that multinationals devise their own tests, which are valid for predicting performance in specific roles which transcend geographical boundaries.

PERSONALITY

Personality is a non-cognitive characteristic. With respect to the value of personality tests, there is continuing debate about fakeability, generally low predictive validity (Table 4.1), and even about the very existence of such a thing as personality (see, for example, Dilchert *et al.* 2006). Despite this, there has been a resurgence of interest focused especially on the Five Factor Model or the 'Big Five' dimensions. This claims that personality differences between people can be explained by five dimensions – extraversion, conscientiousness, agreeableness, neuroticism or emotional stability, and openness to experience (Costa and McCrae 1992). One of these in particular – conscientiousness – has emerged as a valid predictor of many aspects of work performance. This combines hard work, thoroughness, self-control and dependability, and is shown to have higher validity when used to predict pro-social aspects of work performance (also known as discretionary behaviour), such as altruism and (inversely) turnover or theft (Salgado 2002).

The most recent summaries conclude that personality tests are valid and useful when developers pay attention to possible moderators, such as social desirability effects or the specific task contexts which are being predicted (Viswesvaran *et al.* 2007). For instance, there are a number of studies showing that the dimensions of extraversion, agreeableness and neuroticism predict customer service behaviours but that in sales environments (closing a deal, for example), agreeableness may be a disadvantage (Liao and Chuang 2004).

Another application is in the use of personality tests to predict team performance. The aggregated score of team members on some of the Big Five personality dimensions, including the score of team leaders, is related to how well the team works together. Personality explains findings that homogeneous groups are more cohesive, while those which are heterogeneous are better at problem solving (Moynihan and Peterson 2004).

Ones *et al.* (2007) summarised the findings from accumulated validity studies and showed that the Big Five personality dimensions predict performance best for customer service, sales and managerial occupations. Although faking is a possibility, well-designed personality tests are most useful when used in combination with other information about the person and for specific work contexts. They also have lower adverse impact on women or racial minority groups than cognitive ability tests, which is one reason given for their increased use alongside other methods (Shackleton and Newell 1997).

Despite these developments, the debate about the role of personality testing in selection has continued, with prominent researchers arguing from both sides of the fence. The most recent exchange occurred over two 2007 issues of the prestigious journal *Personnel Psychology* (see Morgeson *et al.* 2007; Ones *et al.* 2007; Tett and Christiansen 2007).

Newer types of measures based on personality and other non-cognitive psychological constructs are also emerging. Two deserve mention here. First, emotional intelligence describes an individual's personal and social competence in managing their own and others' emotions, and is thought to be especially suited to predicting performance in roles requiring interpersonal interaction and leadership qualities (Zeidner *et al.* 2004). A second development is in the use of personality traits to form compound traits which are essentially custom-made personality measures based on combinations of traits designed to predict job-relevant behaviour in a specific context. These offer higher levels of predictive validity. Integrity, for example, which is often rated by employers as one of the most important employee characteristics, is made up of measures of hostility, impulsiveness, trust and dutifulness; these have been used to predict dishonest behaviour with high validity. Other compound scales have been designed for predicting customer service, stress tolerance, violence and managerial potential (see Ones *et al.* 2005).

BIOGRAPHICAL INFORMATION

Another non-cognitive characteristic is biographical information or biodata, where applicants describe retrospectively their past experience and work history. The assumption is that performance on past jobs predicts how someone will behave in future job situations, as it reflects underlying personal competencies such as attitudes or motivation. Application forms designed to collect biodata tend to be used by the majority of organisations as their initial screening device, and are now commonly found online (Hill and Barber 2005).

In general, biodata has moderate to high predictive validity for predicting tenure and performance (Reilly and Chao 1982). 'Hard', verifiable items, such as success in educational or occupational pursuits, tend to be more valid than 'soft' items related to values or aspirations, which are liable to faking (Lautenschlager 1994). Selectors must also avoid using information haphazardly without consideration of the important qualities to be judged for the job opening. The general principle behind making biodata job-relevant involves a process called 'criterion keying' – linking responses to each item with either high- and low-performing groups of employees and being able to specify what responses are the most desirable. Furnham (1997), for example, explains that items which showed an applicant's emphasis on financial responsibility, early family responsibility and stability were all good differentiators of good and bad insurance salesmen.

Instruments known as weighted application blanks or biographical information blanks make the weighting of important items more objective and may reduce adverse impact against protected groups (Chapman and Webster 2003). However, focusing on past accomplishments is clearly suited only to those with experience, which excludes much of the youth applicant pool. This is one reason why many graduate recruitment schemes are designed with a view to focusing on personal competencies rather than experience. Similarly, many organisations use qualifications as a way of screening out a large number of applicants, for example by increasing the minimum level of qualifications required, from non-degree to degree. However, the requirement of a university degree may bear no relation to the knowledge, skills, abilities and personality characteristics actually required to do the job. For similar reasons, recent legislation addressing age and disability discrimination in the UK would place any items from which this information could be inferred (e.g. age) at risk of legal challenge; i.e. the selection method would adversely impact particular subgroups, such as older or disabled applicants. Practices such as only accepting candidates who are 'first jobbers' or those who have graduated within a restricted number of years, which can be inferred from biodata, would all be considered discriminatory.

PERFORMANCE-BASED METHODS

The third type of individual difference targeted by selection methods is performance itself. Performance-based tests and simulations focus on replicating a set of behaviours required on the job rather than an underlying psychological characteristic. The focus is on measuring present performance in order to predict future performance, although methods taking this approach can reflect varying degrees of complexity and physical fidelity to the actual tasks to be performed on the job, as shown in Table 4.1.

Work samples or job simulations are samples of the job, so represent 'high-fidelity' methods which focus primarily on assessing current skills and performance of actual tasks – what a person can actually do rather than what they 'know'. Unsurprisingly, compared to cognitive and non-cognitive measures, these methods have higher validity and less adverse impact for non-traditional candidates (e.g. women, minority ethnic groups) (Schmitt and Mills 2001). Users, including managers and candidates, are generally more favourable towards performance-based methods. Selectors tend to pay more attention to observed behavioural information about a candidate than self-report data derived from personality or biodata, and candidates benefit from a realistic preview of the job itself. In a direct comparison of the psychometric qualities of a job simulation versus cognitive test for selecting insurance agents, Schmitt (2003) showed that while the simulation had lower validity (.36 versus .46 for the cognitive test), a higher proportion of capable minority individuals were selected using the simulation. Box 4.2 outlines the role simulation which was developed by Schmitt for these customer service agents.

Situational judgement tests have been called 'low-fidelity' simulations or 'white collar work samples' (Muchinsky 1986). These typically ask applicants to select from several possible behavioural responses for a question about a work situation. This is essentially a test of judgement, which emerged originally as a measure of tacit knowledge or knowledge acquired through experience to complete everyday tasks. As there is no absolute correct answer, responses may vary depending on how the questions are designed, revealing some uncertainty about what is actually being measured. Ployhart and Erhart (2003) showed that asking

Box 4.2: HRM in practice

Increasing realism through performance-based methods

Job simulations

Schmitt (2003) describes a role-play simulation which replicates a typical day in the life of a service representative at an insurance company. Typical tasks were questions from customers about insurance rates and the various coverage options and products available to current or potential customers. A computer program first provided candidates with information about the company, how they should handle customer calls, and how to use several computerised databases to obtain information for customers. The candidates also had access to a policy-and-procedures manual and reference charts. Candidates had 30 minutes to review the material and to examine an abbreviated version of the customer database. The assessment began when two trained assessors made a series of 11 customer calls to the applicants. To respond appropriately to these calls, the applicants needed to draw together the information available to them, including the computerised databases, so that they could provide appropriate answers to the 'customer' queries. The assessors each used detailed scripts and took turns in playing the role of customer with the candidates. The assessor who was not role-playing listened to the conversation and took detailed notes.

Situational judgement tests

Lievens and Coetsier (2002) describe a video-based physician–patient situational judgement test for medical school admissions in Belgium. Scripts were written and verified by subject matter experts (professors) based on the identification of critical incidents, and videos were filmed with semi-professional actors, with the involvement of experienced physicians. In a follow-up study (Lievens *et al.* 2005), this test was shown to have validity for predicting medical school performance where interpersonal skill was important (e.g. situations involving patient interaction).

Situational interview

Maurer (2006) describes an engineering company's interview of technically qualified applicants for entry-level jobs. The aim of the interview was to assess their tendency to act in ways that 'fit' expected actions in critical job situations consistent with the values, goals and culture of the organisation and the work group. Incumbent project engineers created the following project management dilemma and rating criteria using a behaviourally anchored five-point scale:

> Suppose that you are in charge of a large-scale equipment installation project that must be completed on time to avoid significant penalties for exceeding the expected due date. The six-month-long project is now about 75 per cent completed and your PERT analysis indicates that, at best, it will be finished about two or three days ahead of schedule. However, an installation supervisor who works for you has just informed you that there may be a delay in material delivery that could add 7–10 working days to the project. What would you do to deal with this situation?

> 1 = Poor. Ignore the situation since it is only a potential problem. Be prepared to deal with it when/if you hear that the delay is actually going to occur.
>
> 3 = Acceptable. Tell the supervisor that you expect him or her to deal with the problem. Remind the supervisor of the completion date and make it clear that you expect it to be met and that you want to be kept appraised of the situation.
>
> 5 = Excellent. Meet with the supervisor ASAP to determine the exact nature of the potential problem and formulate a plan for preventing or dealing with it. Set a follow-up procedure to make sure that the plan is being carried out.

The two points without specific anchors (i.e. the 2 and 4 points on the scale) would be used to evaluate answers that do not conform with all parts of the behavioural anchors. For instance, a response such as, 'Since it is not yet a problem, I would simply tell the supervisor to deal with it' would be a level 2 response since it contains parts of both the 1 and 3 anchors but does not comply with the full text of either.

people what they 'would do' in a certain situation tended to tap behavioural intentions, personality and past behaviour; asking what they 'should do' tapped job knowledge and cognitive ability. It may also be that 'would do' questions are more open to response distortion or faking – this remains an unresolved issue. Nevertheless, they have generally high validity, low subgroup differences, distinctiveness from other measures of past experience and job knowledge, and benefit from evolving delivery formats. New developments allowing multimedia, such as video-based clips, are better able to portray dilemmas or conflict encounters. As these become more powerful in representing the 'reality' of work, they may be able to increase fidelity for the assessment of judgement, prioritisation, decision making or diagnostic skills (Olson-Buchanan and Drasgow 2005) (see Box 4.2 for some examples).

Finally, structured interviews involve situational or behaviourally based assessments. The vast literature on the use of interviews for recruitment and selection highlights its various roles; e.g. as a way of selling the organisation to applicants or to prescreen applicants on minimum requirements. While the former involves a considerable amount of negotiation and subjective interaction – something we return to later in the chapter – the latter is based on simple, verifiable questions and is now frequently carried out by telephone. When interviews are used to assess more complex individual qualities, such as personality, knowledge, social skills or values which may or may not fit with the organisation, the need for reliable, valid techniques becomes much more apparent.

In short, structured interviews show high predictive validity (Table 4.1). Some examples of how structure can be introduced are by using a critical-incident-based job analysis for designing the questions, using multiple, trained interviewers and raters, minimising any use of prior information, such as applicant test scores, or limiting follow-up, prompting or elaboration.

With respect to our current interest in assessing performance, the use of questions based on hypothetical situations (situational interviews), past behaviour or experience (behavioural interviews) or direct job knowledge questions (either knowledge of facts or of procedures) provide the greatest potential in terms of psychometric quality (see Box 4.2 for an example). Like situational judgement tests, these do not directly measure an applicant's ability to do the job so they have lower fidelity to the job than work samples or simulations. Interview questions are usually tied to specific competencies which have been identified in the job analysis, however, and this emphasis on job relevance has been found to allow assessors to focus more on knowledge, skills, abilities and other qualities more directly linked to actual performance rather than relying on inferences about underlying characteristics. Structured interviews are not correlated with cognitive ability or personality tests, so it has been argued that companies can significantly enhance the validity of their selection methods by adding a structured interview to their hiring process (Huffcutt and Youngcourt 2007).

MIXED APPROACHES

The emphasis on behaviour is also visible in the competency movement. Competencies are transferable personal qualities, such as teamworking or business awareness, which draw from a range of skills, abilities, traits, job knowledge, experience and other qualities needed to perform a job effectively. Service-orientation for example, includes personality characteristics such as courtesy, consideration and tact (Hogan *et al.* 1984) but also behaviours displayed towards customers and colleagues during the service delivery process (Baydoun *et al.* 2001). The focus here is on behavioural outputs – individuals' achievements or what they should be able to do. In theory, therefore, different combinations of underlying psychological characteristics may achieve the same outputs (i.e. display competence in the job), which is why the focus is more on performance than the underlying cognitive or non-cognitive construct.

Of growing interest are 'future-oriented' behavioural competencies which go beyond immediate person–job fit. A typical example is in the selection of managers with leadership potential. Financial services firm HBOS uses a single behavioural competency framework based on 'leadership commitment' to guide selection across 18 different graduate schemes (e.g. HR, finance, IT, actuarial, corporate banking) and a range of methods, including online application forms, numerical and verbal reasoning tests, a telephone interview and teamwork and business scenario exercises (*People Management,* 4 October 2007).

Finally, an amalgam of many of these approaches is reflected in assessment centres which focus on a series of situational exercises designed to reveal various behaviourally based performance dimensions (Thornton and Mueller-Hanson 2004). As they use multiple methods, multiple assessors and systematic scoring procedures for integrating candidate data, they are thought to provide good validity for many occupations. They have high favourability both with managers and candidates because of their face validity (their appearance of measuring job-related factors), and the range of exercises ensures lower adverse impact against under-represented groups. Some concern has been expressed about what assessment centres are actually measuring, despite the formalised systems and scoring. One critical account of graduate assessment centres describes a high degree of active, impression management by candidates, especially by those who are identified as 'stars' (the most employable candidates on paper), or the 'players' who were able to produce 'flashes of the appropriate behavioural competencies' (Brown and Hesketh, 2004, p.173). There was also inevitable subjectivity on the part of assessors whose evaluations of candidates might be based not on the objective test scores, but on performance in coffee breaks or even opinions formed when 'watching from afar'. From a more psychometric slant, careful attention to how assessors are trained and how they conduct their final evaluations, as well as to the design of the exercises themselves, is essential for improving reliability and maximising the potential validity of this approach (Lievens and Klimoski 2001). Given their high cost, though, they are likely to have utility only for the highest skilled, and more valuable, potential employees; for example, managers or professionals.

Summary of trends

From the review so far, we can detect several important trends in selection practice which build on the four indicators of psychometric quality.

- *More reliable and valid assessment tools.* This can be achieved, for example, by: conducting detailed job analyses, introducing structure and standardisation, training assessors, carrying out validation studies, and making more use of statistical aggregation and correction techniques, like meta-analysis, across validity studies to increase the precision of the prediction task (for a review see Sackett and Lievens 2008). Advances in these areas have resulted in increased confidence in the validity of many selection methods.

- *Greater use of high validity/low adverse impact assessment tools.* As seen in Table 4.1, biodata, structured behavioural and situational interviewing, situational judgement tests, work samples and assessment centres have lower differential subgroup validity; i.e. they are less likely to adversely impact non-traditional applicant groups. Many selection processes use multiple methods in order to increase validity and lower adverse impact. For an example applied to call centre agents which combines biodata, psychometric cognitive or non-cognitive tests, and situational judgement tests see Konradt *et al.* (2003).

- *Increasing importance of assessing non-cognitive qualities.* Across all types of jobs, interest has grown in a wider spectrum of behaviours, such as organisational citizenship or adaptability. The challenge has been to design valid tools to target these qualities. Some personality tests have been shown to be good predictors of this type of behaviour, and situational interviews can be designed to assess behaviours such as helping colleagues or volunteering (Latham and Skarlicki 1995).

- *Increasing use of bespoke simulations.* These provide valid behavioural indicators of qualities relevant to a particular job or organisation, along with low adverse impact and high user acceptability. These organisationally specific approaches reflect a growing strategic orientation which links selection to wider competencies, not just job-specific skills, which are essential for ensuring competitive advantage and dealing with strategic pressures, such as restructuring. Searle (2003a) argues:

    > the use of these tools reflects an increasing sophistication and confidence among human resource professionals, who see the adoption of more complex and rigorous assessment and development practices as demonstrating this professional group's pivotal place in helping to shape organizations for the future. (p.226)

- *Online delivery of assessment.* This affects psychometric quality in various ways. Thirty per cent of UK organisations, and more among multinationals, report that they use online selection in some form (CIPD 2007), citing benefits like reaching a wider applicant pool, testing at a distance, and being able to confirm personality profiles usually gained through the 'gut-feel' of the interview (*People Management,* October 2007). Predictive validity and positive applicant reactions have been reported (Bartram 2000), especially for high-fidelity situational and behavioural assessments of performance, although questions remain about security, equality of access, and the quality of applicants (Anderson 2003).

What do organisations actually do?

Psychometric principles of good practice in the design and administration of tests are endorsed by professional psychological and HR associations in various countries. Whether employers pay heed to these recommendations, though, can be pieced together from various studies. Two of the most recent surveys of practice in the UK are summarised in Table 4.2. Consistent with past surveys across different countries (e.g. Ryan *et al.* 1999), the CIPD 2007 survey showed continuing reliance on interviews (generally a low-validity method), but over half of UK organisations (63 per cent) structured these around competency-based questions, which indicates a move towards questions based on systematic job analysis. The figures for psychometric tests of ability and personality show that three-quarters of companies use these in some way, and 18–29 per cent use them frequently. Leading

Table 4.2 Selection methods used by UK employers

CIPD Recruitment, Retention and Turnover Survey 2007[a]	Frequently use	Use in some way
Interviews (general/biographical/based on CV)	77	92
Structured interviews (panel)	58	88
Competency-based interviews	63	86
Tests for specific skills	29	80
General ability tests	26	72
Literacy and/or numeracy tests	25	70
Personality/aptitude tests	18	56
References	17	45
Assessment centres	16	47
Group exercise (e.g. role playing)	10	46
Online tests	9	30

Workplace Employment Relations Survey 2004[b]	Ever/routinely use performance/competency tests?	Use informal methods to fill vacancy
SME (private, <250 employees in UK)	40	79
Large enterprise (private, 250+ employees in UK)	50	76
Public sector	70	44
Managers/senior officials	39	68
Professionals	25	50
Associate professional/technical	19	50
Administrative/secretarial	41	40
Skilled trades	14	75
Caring, leisure, personal services	10	67
Sales/customer service	16	73
Process, plant, machine operatives	11	80
Routine unskilled	12	75

Note: 'Informal methods' include direct approaches to candidates, speculative applications, referrals and word of mouth.

[a] n=905 [b] Workplaces with more than 10 employees; n=2024 managers (see Kersley et al. 2006).

companies are more likely to use personality tests, for example 40 per cent of Fortune 100 companies, all of the top 100 in the UK (Rothstein and Goffin 2006) and those with more professional/managerial vacancies (Wolf and Jenkins 2006). Beagrie (2005) estimates that two-thirds of medium–large organisations use some type of psychometric test. Other studies show that 20 per cent of US companies use tests of cognitive ability, less than in the UK (Salgado and Anderson 2002), which is thought to be a sign of their low user acceptability and associated legal problems.

The WERS 2004 survey showed that performance-based and competency tests were used at some point by 70 per cent of public sector organisations compared to 50 per cent and 40 per cent of private sector large enterprises and SMEs, respectively. When asked if they were routinely used for particular occupations, these were most likely for managerial and administrative/secretarial positions. This may reflect the use of personal competency methods for management (e.g. application forms or interviews designed to assess leadership qualities or business awareness) and work samples/achievement tests for administrative/secretarial positions (e.g. for clerical tasks, or data manipulation). Wolf and Jenkins (2006) suggest that their use is more common in organisations which do more to ensure that recruitment and hiring practices are non-discriminatory and encourage diversity, a feature which is generally found in the public sector.

Also notable from Table 4.2 is the strong reliance on informal methods, such as responding to speculative applications and word of mouth. This was less likely in the public sector and for managerial/professional positions, but even here approximately half of all respondents admitted filling vacancies in this way. Informality was most likely in lower-skilled, elementary occupations.

Taking this evidence together, informal selection methods appear to dominate in most organisations, but there is some indication that larger organisations with a dedicated HR function, and especially those in the public sector, are more likely to adopt a psychometric approach, especially for managerial or skilled/technical positions.

Explaining practice

Selection is more than the application of assessment techniques. It is now accepted that selection can be thought of from at least three other perspectives which take into account the organisational and social hiring context (see also Iles 1999): (1) selection as 'best fit' for the organisation (as opposed to a normative, 'best practice' model); (2) selection as an interactive decision process involving multiple stakeholders; and (3) selection as discourse, where power and interests dominate what happens more than the validity and utility of assessment methods.

(1) SELECTION AS 'BEST FIT': THE ORGANISATION'S PERSPECTIVE

In the study of HRM generally, there is often an assumption of similar needs across sectors, organisations, occupations and even countries, which leads to 'best practice' guidelines, such as those of the psychometric model. These guidelines, however, are formulated almost completely in a vacuum. Valid methods are held always to have high utility, but this assumes a low selection ratio (i.e. a low number hired relative to the number of applicants), that the cost of poor selection is high (as it may be in a top management or skilled position), and that the top performers can always be selected (i.e. the 'best' actually accept the job offer). The reality of staffing is that these conditions are not always met.

Table 4.3 summarises a range of factors which shape selection practice. These are organised using Klehe's (2004) distinction between economic and social pressures as a way of illustrating the effects of the wider context of selection decisions and allow us to make predictions about when sophisticated (i.e. strategic/psychometric) approaches are likely to be adopted.

With respect to economic pressures, the higher the initial cost and development required, and the more dependent the organisation is on the approval of owners concerned with short-term financial impact, the less likely it will be to adopt sophisticated methods. Short-term resource considerations (e.g. the cost of more structured behavioural interviewing, training inexperienced assessors, relieving managers for multi-method assessment days, or evaluating procedures) often outweigh the longer-term potential returns. This is why competency-based methods are more common for managers (Table 4.2). Similarly, the fewer applicants the organisation has to choose from and the more dependent it is on filling the vacant post quickly, the less likely the organisation is to invest heavily in its selection procedure. This may be the position of many SMEs (as shown in Table 4.2), organisations located in suburban or rural areas, or sectors where there is high demand for key skills and skills shortages. The informality of unsolicited correspondence and face-to-face contact may be a more rational option for attracting suitable candidates where there is a small pool of qualified applicants or where the position must be filled quickly.

Social pressures are divided into two types in Table 4.3: legislative/institutional and stakeholder pressure. We consider the role of stakeholders in the next section. For now, it is

Table 4.3 Factors influencing selection practice and decisions

Economic pressures

Short-term financial impact
- Skills supply and labour market tightness
- Patterns of employment and turnover
- Organisation size
- Life cycle of the organisation
- Long-term versus short-term performance orientation
- Ownership (multinational, single owner, shareholder pressures)
- Presence of HR
- Experience/training of selectors
- Time resource constraints

Long-term financial impact
- High skill (managerial/professional) occupations/vacancies
- Career potential of position (internal labour markets, investment in training)
- Competition and rate of change
- Market segment/differentiation strategy
- Organisation values

Social pressures

Legislative/institutional
- Regulatory environment
- Visibility/accountability of organisation
- National culture
- Entry standards/statutory requirements

Other stakeholders
- Users
- Applicants
- Industry/profession
- Test developers

possible to identify the direct effects of employment legislation on hiring practice. Employers are increasingly required by law in many countries to pay attention to psychometric principles. Public sector organisations are especially affected. In an examination of 400 Canadian federal selection discrimination cases, Terpstra and Kethley (2002) showed that the government sector was more likely to have had litigation brought against it than any other sector. This kind of accountability and risk encourages the use of multiple methods, greater standardisation, and monitoring of selection procedures in order to ensure diversity (Jewson and Mason 1986; Pearn 1993) – a finding which is supported by the data in Table 4.2. US federal legislation also goes further in placing a burden on employers to justify the job-relatedness of all selection measures, and this is one of the reasons why psychometric testing is used more in some European countries (the UK, Spain and Portugal) than in the US (Salgado *et al.* 2003). UK employers, conversely to those in the US, perceive the rigour of a testing approach as a 'precautionary measure' which can protect them from legal challenge (Wolf and Jenkins 2006).

In other ways, though, the institutional context in Europe, Australia and Asia is more restrictive in terms of labour relations, with greater reliance on recruitment from educational systems or internal labour markets. Huo *et al.* (2002) speculated that a greater focus on individual candidate fit with cultural values in Australia was related to a recent tradition of joint consultation practice between employees and employers at the level of the enterprise.

In Box 4.3, we use this framework to illustrate the pressures faced in three different industry examples – hotels, construction companies and voluntary sector organisations. In these

Box 4.3: HRM in practice

Selection in three sectors

Economic pressures	Selection	Social pressures
Hotels		
Labour market (competition, shortages) *Short-term pressures to fill vacancies* (casualisation, high turnover) *Market segmentation* (chain, deluxe) *Resource pressures* (only chains have centralised HR/train selectors)	*Short-termist approach* Informal methods targeted at local transient labour market/unpredictability *Longer-term approach* Strategic alignment (high-quality localised approach, combines standardisation with informal networks) Emphasis on staff retention, permanent positions, person–culture fit	*Applicant perceptions* (low pay, poor prospects, antisocial hours, hard work, isolated locations)
Construction (manual and skilled/technical workers)		
Workflow (project-/network-based, local site decentralisation, flexibility due to design/supply variations) *Project ownership* (network of subcontractors and professionals, local focus) *Labour market* (skill shortages, limited training, competency-based skill certification, voluntary) *Resources* (working to contract, time, cost) *Change* (rapid technological change, changing markets, multiskilling)	Larger firms more formalised ('skills identity card', HR functions) Local variation even where formalised procedures existed (procedures called 'raindances') Strong emphasis on probationary days (work simulations) and site-manager local networks (time-served on other jobs) After technical ability, value honesty, conscientiousness, adaptability	*Applicant perceptions* (dangerous work, masculine culture, antisocial hours) *Industry* (Construction Industry Training Board common accreditation) *Customers* (pressures for improved quality, cost reduction) *Firm-specific demands* (work against industry standards) *Site-manager* (autonomous at local level) *Legislation* (Health and Safety)
Voluntary sector (front-line care and social services)		
Resources (insecure funding, 'full cost recovery' problematic, increased scope due to work transition from public services, increasing need to staff new business processes and functions) *Labour market* (competition with private/public sector, shortage of high skill/graduates) *High attrition/turnover* (unrealistic expectations)	Person–organisation fit essential Social process/attraction strategies (ensure value congruence, provide applicant power/choices, realistic job/organisation previews) Need for rebranding to attract wider applicant pool (flexible working, work–life balance, satisfaction, 'altruism payoff', underutilised graduates)	*Applicant perceptions* (uncompetitive salaries, insecurity, high emotional demands, women's work, need value-based high commitment, skills underused) *Public perception* (unprofessional, voluntary (unpaid), not a career, need for greater transparency)

Sources: Lockyer and Scholarios 2004, 2007; Nickson *et al.* 2008

situations, cost, time, and recruitment crises may be more salient than reliability and validity (Johns 1993; Muchinsky 2004). We return to these examples again in the next section.

(2) SELECTION AS AN INTERACTIVE DECISION PROCESS

Social pressures can also originate from other stakeholders in the hiring process. This includes the selectors (managers, HR) who implement the procedures, institutional bodies which set guidelines for entry into occupations or exert influence over assessment (e.g. professional associations), and applicants themselves. Searle (2003b) has argued that, with the growing use of online testing, test developers, whose interests are quite distinct from those of organisations and applicants, have become an increasingly powerful stakeholder because of the access they have to the results of testing processes. From this perspective, hiring is not just about the organisation choosing the right assessment tools for its needs, but involves an interactive process of information exchange and negotiation – a series of 'social episodes' (Herriot 1989) – between the organisation and its wider environment. This impacts two general areas.

How methods are perceived by stakeholders

In Table 4.1, we introduced the idea of user acceptability as a counterweight to the psychometric ideals of reliability and validity. This refers to whether the method is perceived as credible, and hence whether managers or practitioners will actually use it, as well as how it is perceived by the candidates who are exposed to it. Performance-based methods are more favourable as users can clearly see the relevance of the assessment for the job itself. This means these methods are more likely to be adopted and used appropriately than less transparent, psychometric tests.

The participation of users in the development of selection methods is also important. Millmore (2003), in his exploration of what makes recruitment and selection strategic, talks about the involvement of multiple stakeholders as equal partners in the process and the involvement of all levels of management and peers in the design of the process (e.g. defining person specifications, panel interviews). This should lead to greater consensus about the qualities being sought and hence more reliable assessment.

Applicants, too, should be considered equal partners. Schuler (1993) argued that applicants have the right to be treated with dignity, provided with information about what is expected of them and on their performance, and involved in the process by providing their consent and even their own input. Millmore suggested providing, at least, information packs and feedback on performance at all stages of the selection process. Candidates should also have their privacy respected, for example in questions asked in application forms or interviews, and the right to appeal against decisions which they think are unfair. This introduces the idea of perceptions of fair treatment, or what is sometimes called procedural justice (Cropanzano and Wright 2003). Some suggestions to improve fairness perceptions are to use a combination of methods, or modify how tests are administered. In general, research on applicant perceptions of fairness has shown that, consistently, across Europe, North America and Asia, the rankings for the most to least favourable methods are: (1) interviews, (2) CVs, (3) work sample tests, (4) biographical information, (5) written ability tests, (6) personal references, (7) personality tests, (8) honesty/integrity tests, (9) personal contacts and (10) graphology (Anderson and Witvliet 2008).

Going even further than this, some would argue that individuals entering a position should be able to influence the job demands rather than being fitted for the job requirements, thus making selection a truly two-way process. Work sample tests, for example, tend to imply that there is agreement about a single correct way to perform the job; however, candidates could be given freedom to demonstrate other ways of performing the job successfully rather

> ### Box 4.4: HRM in practice
>
> **Has the power shifted to graduates?**
>
> A study by Reed Consulting (2007) found that 22 per cent of 2,500 graduates surveyed refused a job offer because they were unhappy with an organisation's recruitment process. Sixty-six per cent of job applicants did not receive a response – making potential talent feel disregarded and devalued – and this was especially the case in the financial services sector which receives high volumes of applications. Companies run the risk of losing qualified candidates to competitor organisations. The study also found that:
>
> - more than one-third of UK graduates avoid products and services offered by a company that disappointed them in the recruitment process;
> - 90 per cent of dissatisfied candidates tell family and friends about their bad experiences, with serious implications for damaging both the consumer and employer brand;
> - failure to respond to a recruitment hotline phone call in 30 seconds results in 29 per cent of applicants hanging up.
>
> Purcell *et al.* (2002) showed that, as a way of dealing with skill shortages, leading employers were doing more to attract non-traditional graduates. As well as identifying skills and competencies for specific jobs, they also
>
> - encouraged underrepresented groups to apply;
> - actively sold themselves as equal opportunities employers;
> - established expectations at the recruitment stage (culture, career opportunities);
> - offered work experience to allow graduates to make choices;
> - responded to the diversity of the workforce with work–life balance flexibility.

than confined to the taken-for-granted views which are demanded by the psychometric approach (Searle 2003a, p.233).

The important point in all of these arguments is that applicant exposure to the assessment method influences important outcomes – whether qualified applicants maintain interest in the job for which they are applying, whether they decide to continue to the next stage of assessment, whether they accept the job if offered or even whether the method has 'negative psychological effects', such as lowering self-esteem (Anderson and Goltsi 2006, p.237). Box 4.4 illustrates how applicant perceptions have impacted graduate recruitment.

How applicants perceive the job or organisation

As we saw in Chapter 3 on recruitment, negative impressions may be caused by uninformative websites; disinterested recruiters; long, complicated application processes; or any message which communicates undesirable images of the employer brand (Van Hoye and Lievens 2005). The early stages of selection can be used to build identification with the organisation and encourage only those who see a match with the values of the organisation to remain in the application process. In an example from a police force in an American Midwest city, the interview stage provided a realistic preview of the job and prompted some candidates to withdraw from the process (Ployhart *et al.* 2002). Of most relevance to organisations is how potential applicants perceive 'fit' between their own goals and what is offered by the job, including issues such as pay, working conditions, organisational values and reputation, and career options.

This is important for several reasons. Firstly, if some applicant groups withdraw from the process more frequently than others, then potentially qualified candidates who are required to meet skill gaps are excluded. This seems to be the case for graduates who are not pursuing voluntary sector jobs vacancies because of the perceptions of what the jobs offer (see Box 4.3).

Secondly, this exclusion may adversely impact members of minority groups, such as women or blacks. These applicants withdrew disproportionately from the American police selection process indicated above. This also harms diversity staffing targets, an issue of some concern to police forces in many parts of the world who consider being representative of the community as essential to good policing.

Finally, in some employment situations, the balance of power lies with applicants rather than the organisation; for instance, Box 4.4 illustrates the competition to attract the brightest gradates. An example of this was shown in Box 4.3 where it was shown that the voluntary sector suffers recruitment difficulties because it competes with both the private and public sector for specialists and graduates. In another example, the hospitality industry is often portrayed as being in competition with higher-paying, 'cleaner', more flexible, temporary, part-time work offered by the likes of the call centre industry. Tackling negative perceptions of potential applicants and the use of informal methods of selection may be better practice in these situations. Of course, problems of inequality, bias and limits on diversity which are associated with informality still have to be recognised.

A further purpose of selection is to build relationships between the organisation and future employees. The interview has high social validity for both managers and candidates as it allows two-way communication and a richer environment for both to establish congruence or person–organisation 'fit'. Roe and van den Berg's (2003) survey suggested that European employers prefer interviews for this reason. In a similar vein, British Telecom replaced external assessors with their own managers in the final interviews at their graduate assessment centre in order to 'interface with the candidates themselves' (*The Guardian,* 19 January 2008).

One last consequence of paying attention to social processes in selection is their 'socialisation impact' (Anderson 2001). Methods which allow both parties to establish 'fit' will lead to employees who are more likely to be satisfied in their jobs, more committed to the goals of the organisation, and less likely to leave. A clear application of this is provided by the voluntary sector example in Box 4.4. Thus, as well as establishing hurdles, selection informs, attracts and increases the commitment of applicants to the job and organisation as the relationship progresses.

(3) SELECTION AS DISCOURSE

A more radical view is that selection is a process which cannot easily be reduced to the quality of assessment tools and rational decision making. The reference to discourse relates to the idea that there are many different ways of talking about (i.e. describing and understanding) selection. The choice of which discourse we focus on at a particular point in time will vary; for example, some may value meritocracy and hence use a discourse which focuses on developing neutral assessment techniques which are reliable and valid (a psychometric discourse), while others are more concerned with mutual respect, treating applicants in an ethical way and building relationships of trust (a social process or decision-interactive discourse). These two examples, in fact, are often used to describe the quite different dominant discourses which guide actual selection practice in North America versus Europe, respectively (de Wolff 1993). These selection discourses have become accepted by the culture as a result of societal values and guiding principles, established for example through legislation. Other discourses also may develop within organisations, clusters of organisations or professions as a result of other powerful forces. This may explain why 'blue-chip' multinational companies, which project themselves as global market leaders or 'good employers', often lead the way in adopting the most sophisticated, expensive and psychometrically sound selection systems, in order to be seen to comply with 'good practice' as presented by respected external bodies (e.g. those promoting equal opportunities legislation or human resource professionalism). This view goes as far as to argue that selection discourses, such as strict psychometric measurement, can be used as a way of making the management of people more explicitly controllable, e.g. to further particular interests (Townley 1989).

We use two examples here to illustrate this perspective and how it challenges the psychometric model (see also Iles 1999). The first questions whether job suitability can be objectively reduced to an agreed set of individual knowledge, skills, abilities and traits.

The 'good' firefighter In one of the author's research studies, the qualities of a firefighter were mused over by the Fire Service's personnel officer. They have to be able to put up with long periods of monotony and boredom but can suddenly be faced with emotional and harrowing situations. In many ways, the job is now so procedural that things rarely go wrong (e.g. virtual reality of many of the city's buildings means that firefighters no longer enter smoke-filled buildings without knowing where they are going). In fact, they have to be able to follow instructions without questioning orders in what can be a militaristic culture. At the same time, they are looking for general ability and the ability to think strategically. As well as basic physical ability and practical tests, assessors are looking for evidence of person–culture fit (prior knowledge of the service, commitment to a career and serving the community), all of which is assessed through self-report questions on an application form (e.g. why do you want to become a firefighter?) and interviews with senior officers. How can this complexity of demands be reduced to behaviours appropriate for every situation? Assessors often cannot agree on the suitability of candidates, and use other shortcuts, such as appearance, to justify their decisions, even though they all go through assessor training. 'State of the art' for firefighter selection recommends a combination of cognitive/mechanical and interpersonal/emotional skills tests (Blair and Hornick 2005), but this 'all rounder' view may just be the latest construction of the 'good' firefighter, which contrasts to earlier beliefs that firefighters should be the 'bravest and strongest' (shown through physical ability), 'smartest' (cognitive testing), or have the 'right' person profile (personality testing). Some may argue that this is just another discourse of what is 'acceptable', reflecting society, and the historical and cultural influences of those who draw up the person specifications and make final decisions. The effects of this are illustrated in a study of a similar profession, police work, which showed how good performance is constructed in terms of a 'masculine crime fighting' discourse (as opposed to an equally valid service discourse which privileges skills associated with femininity) and prevents potentially qualified women from applying. (Dick and Nadin 2006)

The second example raises the question whether formalisation and legislation can ever eliminate the inherent subjectivity of hiring decisions. This challenges the assumption of the rational assessor.

Graduate assessment centres Despite multiple assessors and careful exercise design, assessment centres have been portrayed as 'politically charged contexts', 'largely uncontrollable and permeated with problems of meaning', and a 'conspiracy of distortion' between assessors who rank subjectively while hiding behind a 'façade of systematic and scientific professionalism' (Knights and Raffo 1990, p.37). Brown and Hesketh's (2004) analysis of attempts to measure 'soft' competencies at graduate assessment centres showed that even after training on diversity issues, assessors were still inclined to resort to first impressions or compare people to the existing management in the company. In 'washing-up sessions' some opinions held more sway than others (e.g. a particularly negative view of how one candidate described what she gained from her gap year) and simplistic heuristics were used to organise the information from each exercise about the candidates. Candidates were labelled 'stars', 'geeks', 'razors' and 'safe bets'. Value was attached to 'appearance, accent and appropriate behaviour' (p.161), tending to favour the social capital possessed by Oxbridge candidates, while finding ways to match these to the 'objectively defined' behavioural indicators.

Conclusions and implications for HRM

There has been a recent frenzy of activity to develop the most valid assessment tool for predicting a diverse range of work behaviours, with 'best practice' showing a gradual shift towards holistic assessments encompassing a mix of measures of cognitive, non-cognitive and performance qualities. The move to performance-based methods, with their lower adverse impact against underrepresented groups, is particularly notable, as this seems to have accommodated the trend towards diversity as a strategic direction, whether among large private multinationals or the more publicly accountable government sectors.

Beyond this, though, different ways of understanding selection have also gained strength. These expand on the non-rational, unplanned, informal, social and power bases of selection, leading to an alternative language for evaluating the outcomes of any hiring process. Diverse contexts dictate alternative logics from that of prediction or formality, suggesting more of a 'best fit' approach than a normative one. For instance, the employee attributes required may shift alongside an organisation's strategic goals, and firms facing staffing problems will shape their selection strategies in ways which they consider will attract the 'right type' of employees or enhance employee retention. The 'best practice' model of selection offered by the psychometric model assumes that the number of applicants exceeds the positions available, and that the best applicants will always accept the jobs they are offered. This is clearly not the case.

Selection can also be judged in terms of the quality of the social exchange between organisations and other stakeholders. The treatment of applicants, their perceptions and attitudes, take on a more important role in ensuring they find the job and organisation attractive and whether person–organisation 'fit' is achieved. Also important is the way that selection techniques are used to further interests which often are only tenuously linked to the psychometric paradigm's aspirations of objectivity and fairness. Each of these perspectives – 'best fit', social process and discourse – highlights the deficiencies of the psychometric model for achieving a comprehensive understanding of all aspects of the selection problem (cf. Herriot 1993; Iles 1999).

Within HRM, selection has been viewed as a core function essential for achieving key organisational outcomes; high performance, low levels of absenteeism and turnover, and high employee well-being and commitment have all been linked with 'selective hiring' (Storey 2007). As argued in several HRM texts (Legge 2005), however, the reality of strategic integration and practice seldom has matched the rhetoric, and this seems equally as applicable to the adoption of 'best practice' selection. Based on 'best fit' perspectives, expensive testing and bespoke assessment may be reserved for higher-value core employees that organisations wish to retain or those at senior levels (Kwiatkowski 2003).

From the psychometric perspective, HR professionals (or those responsible for selection) should serve a monitoring function, ensuring that assessment methods are designed appropriately with a view to current legislation and practice developments and that relevant performance criteria (broad as well as job-specific) are used. Methods should be reappraised often and based on more frequent and focused validation programmes, although all this assumes that HR and HR issues are afforded an appropriate status and influence within the organisation. Social process perspectives may add to this the need to ensure that all stakeholders' views are accommodated in the design if not implementation of the assessment, and that selectors are encouraged to think of the applicant groups they wish to attract as potentially powerful decision makers with their own views about the attractiveness of the organisation and the job. The increased devolution of HR functions to line managers may also suggest the need for an additional level of support in managing the complexities of the process (Whittaker and Marchington 2003), although in many organisations, such as SMEs, this is rarely available. Nevertheless, these issues become particularly crucial if we acknowledge the discourse perspective's warnings of how persistent subjectivity, vested interests and less politically neutral forces are able to obstruct the ideal of creating meritocratic selection systems.

CASE STUDIES

Methods designed to reveal a service or sales orientation now form the basis of many hiring processes used in call centres. Baldry *et al.* (2007) described the following call centre selection processes.

CASE STUDY 4.1

Moneyflow

Dora Scholarios

One call centre in the financial services sector, Moneyflow, dedicated 3 hours 20 minutes to each candidate for the position of customer adviser. At the time of this example, there was a vibrant employment market in the area and this call centre was competing against 15 other companies for qualified staff. The demand for staff was high, as many of those recruited often left after the two days' training. Recruitment consultants were used to pre-select candidates for the company to interview. This recruitment agency was chosen because, in comparison to other agencies used, it seemed to understand the business and skill specifications required by the company and provide higher-quality candidates.

Stages of selection

1. A general register of candidates was developed (few active call centre workers were available, given the buoyant employment situation for call centre work in the area).
2. Ads were placed locally and nationally, including in universities. Local ads for part-time work were aimed at encouraging returners to work.
3. Candidates were asked to complete work history, details of present employment, and a financial planning questionnaire (to eliminate credit risks). The company designed and validated a self-assessment application form for the call centre adviser role based on work profiling and critical incident methods. This captured five customer-oriented competencies (customer focus, fact finding, relating to customers, convincing, oral communication) and two related to contextual performance (independent facilitation, job dedication) (see Bywater and Green 2005). It also acted as a realistic job preview to inform candidates of the sales component of the job and act as a self-selection tool.

4. Skills testing: tests of visual accuracy; spelling; key depressions; arithmetic; and alphanumeric skill. All these were provided by the company to the agency.
5. Interview (20–30 minutes) based on CV/work history. Sales skills were explored further in the interview.
6. Telephone role play: 'You are a CA in a travel service . . .' Looking for questioning and listening skills as well as selling/additional sales.
7. Recruitment consultants sent a list of pre-selected candidates to the company to select for a 1 hour interview with two team leaders. Depending on need, the agencies often put all candidates forward for interview without pre-selection.

Questions

1. What underlying psychological characteristics are being assessed at each stage?
2. Based on the information provided in Table 4.1, what do you think the overall psychometric quality of such a procedure might be? Take into account what you know about the criterion of successful performance for call centre agents, the use of both recruitment agencies and team leaders to carry out the assessment, and the wider labour market context of the call centre.
3. Is user acceptability an important factor in this selection process?

CASE STUDY 4.2

Thejobshop

Dora Scholarios

Thejobshop is a growing city-based, multi-business outsourced call centre, which operates on behalf of 15 external clients. Outsourcing is attractive to organisations which do not have any call centre expertise and has the advantage of being able to set up a call centre in a very short period of time. Pay also tends to be lower in an outsourced call centre. The staffing numbers involved in a contract can range from approximately 200 to 3. There is some variation, though, in the extent to which client businesses retain autonomy over their operations. At the one extreme are 'co-sourcing' accounts, notably in the high-value operations, where the business retains greater controls over the service provided. These provide operators with distinct e-mail addresses and corporate slogans. At the other extreme are lower-value accounts where Thejobshop completely manages the operations on behalf of the client.

These differences are reflected in how selection is managed. Thejobshop tries to keep the clients out of the selection process as much as possible as they feel they know what they are looking for, although some, like the blue-chip IT company, are more hands-on and want to shape the type of person employed to match their culture. Carco (a luxury car sales business) wants 'tans and teeth' and 'young happy and shiny' people, even though most of their customer base is older and would prefer someone older to speak to. They make regular visits on site.

The operations manager said:

We perhaps show the client a half dozen who we feel are right and let them comment. We're looking for 'basic core competencies', although we try to tailor them for each set of interviews, for each individual client. We give clients the opportunity to give us details of the competencies they are looking for. For example, we asked drinks supplier DrinksNow to supply us with a list of the competencies they were looking for. They gave us a piece of A4 with a list of eight points, that's all. A new financial sector client has identified their target customer group as 95 per cent female and mostly over the age of 35. They want the customer service agents to reflect this. The match between client, product and agent tends to happen naturally.

Agencies are used to prescreen on keyboard skills (paste and copy, data entry) and basic numerical and literacy skills because of the need to find people quickly, 60 people within days. If Thejobshop is given a few weeks' notice they place their own adverts in the press and control the process. This is preferable as agencies often are less discriminating and just want 'bums on seats to get their cut'. They also tend to prefer people with previous call centre experience as they will be aware of the shift systems and nature of the work, so it won't be a shock.

CASE STUDY 4.3

Entcomm

Dora Scholarios

Entcomm, located in a small ex-industrial town near Glasgow, provides telecommunications and entertainment services for a large US multinational company. The call centre handles inquiries, billing, payments, new accounts and repairs maintenance. During a recent period of high-volume recruitment for 150 customer service adviser (CSA) posts it has found difficulties finding flexible staff. They advertise in local further education colleges and universities, and especially target training courses in IT for women returners and over-50s. This addresses the problem of employing young part-timers (high turnover) while achieving some flexibility in staffing to cover fluctuations in business. The vacancies are for 12–20 hours per week (4–6 hours per shift), in some cases finishing at 12.45am, and the starting pay is £6 per hour.

There is a friend and family recruitment scheme where the employee receives £300 for a full-time member of staff found acceptable. Referrals still have to pass the tests, though. The first filtering comes from a tele-screen interview which gives an initial indication of whether the prospective CSA has the required telephone manner and whether the shift preferences are compatible with the business needs. Keyboard skills are tested at this stage, followed by two role-play exercises. These will involve one difficult customer (who may shout and scream) and one technical issue from a customer.

This procedure is outsourced to an agency who receive £350 per CSA they supply for the next stages of selection. The final interview is competency-based and conducted by team leaders and HR. A lot of emphasis here is put on why the recruits find this an attractive job, e.g. entertainment sector, no cold calling. The interviews also include questions about coping with stressful situations building on the role-play simulation. Existing employees talk about how they cope with difficult situations, and some are better than others. Jenny, an agent in her early twenties, commented 'screaming customers I can cope with . . . one day though it was a really patronising customer and it just threw me completely . . . it was just the straw that broke the camel's back – I actually got up off the seat one day and I threw a booklet'.

Cathy, who is in her fifties, was more resilient. 'I can let a customer scream away and let them rattle on until they are finished and then say now I'll help you . . . it's just my experience I suppose.'

Questions

1. Examine the economic and social pressure impacting selection in both Thejobshop and Entcomm. (Use the framework provided in Box 4.3.)
2. Explain the 'balance of power' in the selection process between employers, candidates and other stakeholders in each of the call centres.
3. Do these call centres operate a selection process which follows the psychometric process? Explain your answer.
4. What would the discourse perspective say about the definition of the competent call centre employee in the three call centres (Moneyflow, Thejobshop and Entcomm)? How does this affect the process and outcomes of selection?

Bibliography

Anderson, N. (2001) 'Towards a theory of socialization impact. Selection as pre-entry socialization', *International Journal of Selection and Assessment*, Vol.9, Nos.1/2, pp.84–91.

Anderson, N. (2003) 'Applicant and recruiter reactions to new technology in selection: a critical review and agenda for future research', *International Journal of Selection and Assessment*, Vol.11, pp.121–36.

Anderson, N. and Goltsi, V. (2006) 'Negative psychological effects of selection methods: construct formulation and an empirical investigation into an assessment center', *International Journal of Selection and Assessment*, Vol.14, No.3, pp.236–55.

Anderson, N. and Witvliet, C. (2008) 'Fairness reactions to personnel selection methods: an international comparison between the Netherlands, the United States, France, Spain, Portugal, and Singapore', *International Journal of Selection and Assessment*, Vol.16, No.1, pp.1–13.

Association of Graduate Recruiters (2007) *The AGR Graduate Recruitment Survey 2007: Summer Review*, available at www.agr.org.uk

Baldry, C., Bain, P., Taylor, P. and Hyman, J. (2007) *The Meaning of Work in the New Economy*, Basingstoke: Palgrave Macmillan.

Bartram, D. (2000) 'Internet recruitment and selection: kissing frogs to find princes', *International Journal of Selection and Assessment*, Vol.8, pp.261–74.

Baydoun, R., Rose, D. and Emperado, T. (2001) 'Measuring customer service orientation: an examination of the validity of the customer service profile', *Journal of Business and Psychology*, Vol.15, No.4, pp.605–20.

Beagrie, S. (2005) 'How to excel at psychometric assessments', *Personnel Today*, 25 March, p.25.

Bertua, C., Anderson, N. and Salgado, J. (2005) 'The predictive validity of cognitive ability tests: a UK meta-analysis', *Journal of Occupational and Organizational Psychology*, Vol.78, No.3, pp.387–409.

Blair, M.D. and Hornick, C.W. (2005) 'Fire selection in the new millennium', Paper presented at the 29th Annual Conference of the International Public Management Association Assessment Council, Orlando, FL.

Brown, P. and Hesketh, A. (2004) *The Mismanagement of Talent*, Oxford: Oxford University Press.

Bywater, J. and Green, V. (2005) 'Can scorable application forms predict task and contextual performance in call centre work?', *Selection and Development Review*, Vol.20, No.6.

Carroll, J.B. (1993) *Human Cognitive Abilities: A Survey of Factor-Analytic Studies*, Cambridge: University of Cambridge Press.

Chapman, D.S. and Webster, J. (2003) 'The use of technologies in the recruiting, screening, and selection processes for job candidates', *International Journal of Selection and Assessment*, Vol.11, Nos.2–3, pp.113–120.

CIPD (2007) *Recruitment, Retention and Turnover Survey*, London: Chartered Institute of Personnel and Development.

Costa, P.T., Jr. and McCrae, R.R. (1992) 'Normal personality assessment in clinical practice: the NEO Personality Inventory', *Psychological Assessment*, Vol.4, pp.5–13.

Cropanzano, R. and Wright, T.A. (2003) 'Procedural justice and organizational staffing: a tale of two paradigms', *Human Resource Management Review*, Vol.13, pp.7–39.

Dick, P. and Nadin, S. (2006) 'Reproducing gender inequalities? A critique of realist assumptions underpinning personnel selection research and practice', *Journal of Occupational and Organizational Psychology*, Vol.79, No.3, pp.481–98.

Dilchert, S., Ones, D. S., Viswesvaran, C. and Deller, J. (2006) 'Response distortion in personality measurement: born to deceive, yet capable of providing valid assessments?' *Psychology Science*, Vol.48, pp.209–25.

Furnham, A. (1997) *The Psychology of Behaviour of Work*, Hove: Psychology Press.

Hamel, G. and Prahalad, C.K. (1989) 'Strategic intent', *Harvard Business Review*, pp.63–74.

Herriot, P. (1989) 'Selection as a social process', in M. Smith and I.T. Robertson (eds) *Advances in Selection and Assessment*, Chichester: Wiley, pp.171–78.

Herriot, P. (1993) 'Commentary: a paradigm bursting at the seams', *Journal of Organizational Behavior*, Vol.14, pp.371–75.

Hill, D. and Barber, L. (2005) *Is graduate recruitment meeting business needs?* Web audit, Institute for Employment Studies.

Hogan, R.T., Hogan, J. and Busch, A. (1984) 'How to measure service orientation', *Journal of Applied Psychology*, Vol.69, No.1, pp.167–73.

Huffcutt, A.I. and Youngcourt, S.S. (2007) 'Employment interviews', in D. Whetzel and G. Wheaton (eds), *Applied Measurement: Industrial Psychology in Human Resources Management*, New Jersey: Lawrence Earlbaum, pp.181–200.

Hunter, J.E. and Hunter, R.F. (1984) 'Validity and utility of alternative predictors of job performance', *Psychological Bulletin*, Vol.96, pp.72–98.

Huo, Y.P., Huang, H.G. and Napier, N.K. (2002) 'Divergence or convergence. A cross-national comparison of personnel practices', *Human Resource Management Journal*, Vol.41, No.1, pp.31–44.

Iles, P. (1999) *Managing Staff Selection and Assessment*, Milton Keynes: Open University Press.

Jewson, N. and Mason, D. (1986) 'The theory and practice of equal opportunities policies: liberal and radical approaches', *Sociological Review*, Vol.34, No.2, pp.307–24.

Johns, G. (1993) 'Constraints on the adoption of psychology-based personnel practices: lessons from organizational innovation', *Personnel Psychology*, Vol.46, No.3, pp.569–92.

Kersley, B., Alpin, C., Forth, J., Bryson, A., Bewley, H., Dix, G. and Oxenbridge, S. (2006) *Inside the Workplace: Findings from the 2004 Workplace Employment Relations Survey*, London: Routledge.

Klehe, U. (2004) 'Choosing how to choose. Institutional pressures affecting the adoption of personnel selection procedures', *International Journal of Selection and Assessment*, Vol.12, No.4, pp.327–42.

Klehe, U.-C. and Anderson, N. (2005) 'The prediction of typical and maximum performance', in A. Evers, O. Smit-Voskuijl and N. Anderson (eds) *Handbook of Personnel Selection*, Oxford: Blackwell.

Knights, D. and Raffo, C. (1990). 'Milkround professionalism in personnel recruitment: myth or reality?' *Personnel Review*, Vol.19, No.1, pp.28–37.

Konradt, U., Hertel, G. and Joder, K. (2003) 'Web-based assessment of call center agents: development and validation of a computerized instrument', *International Journal of Selection and Assessment*, Vol.11, Nos.2–3, pp.184–93.

Kravitz D.A. (2008) 'The diversity-validity dilemma: beyond selection – the role of affirmative action', *Personnel Psychology*, Vol.61, pp.173–93.

Kwiatkowski, R. (2003) 'Devolving HR responsibility to the line: threat, opportunity or partnership?', *Journal of Managerial Psychology*, Vol.18, No.5, pp.245–61.

Latham, G.P. and Skarlicki, D.P. (1995) 'Criterion-related validity of the situational and patterned behavior description interviews with organizational citizenship behavior', *Human Performance*, Vol.8, pp.67–80.

Lautenschlager, G.J. (1994) 'Accuracy and faking of background data', in G.S. Stokes, M.D. Mumford and W.A. Owens (eds) *Biodata Handbook*, Palo Alto, CA: Consulting Psychologists Press, pp.391–419.

Legge, K. (2005) *Human Resource Management: Rhetorics and Realities*, Basingstoke: Palgrave Macmillan.

Liao, H. and Chuang, A. (2004) 'A multilevel investigation of factors influencing employee service performance and customer outcomes', *Academy of Management Journal*, Vol.47, pp.41–58.

Lievens, F. and Coetsier, P. (2002) 'Situational tests in student selection: an examination of predictive validity, adverse impact, and construct validity', *International Journal of Selection and Assessment*, Vol.10, No.4, pp.245–57.

Lievens, F. and Klimoski, R.J. (2001) 'Understanding the assessment centre process: where are we now?', *International Review of Industrial and Organizational Psychology*, Vol.16, pp.246–86.

Lievens, F., Buyse, T. and Sackett, P.R. (2005) 'The operational validity of a video-based situational judgment test for medical college admissions: illustrating the importance of matching predictor and criterion construct domains', *Journal of Applied Psychology*, Vol.90, No.3, pp.442–52.

Lockyer, C.J. and Scholarios, D.M. (2004) 'Selecting hotel staff: why best practice doesn't always work', *International Journal of Contemporary Hospitality Management*, Vol.16, No.2, pp.125–35.

Lockyer, C. and Scholarios, D. (2007) 'The "raindance" of selection in construction: rationality as ritual and the logic of informality', *Personnel Review*, Vol.36, No.4, pp.528–48.

Marchington, M. and Wilkinson, A. (2005) *Human Resource Management at Work: People Management and Development*, London: CIPD.

Maurer, S.D. (2006) 'Using situational interviews to assess engineering applicant fit to work group job and organizational requirements', *Engineering Management Journal*, 1 September.

McFarland, L.A., Ryan, A.M., Sacco, J.M. and Kriska, S.D. (2004) 'Examination of structured interview ratings across time: the effects of applicant race, rater race, and panel composition', *Journal of Management*, Vol.30, pp.435–52.

Millmore, M. (2003) 'Just how extensive is the practice of strategic recruitment and selection?' *The Irish Journal of Management*, Vol.24, No.1, p.87.

Morgeson, F.P., Campion, M.A., Dipboye, R.L., Hollenbeck, J.R., Murphy, K. and Schmitt, N. (2007) 'Reconsidering the use of personality tests in personnel selection contexts', *Personnel Psychology*, Vol.60, No.3, pp.683–729.

Moynihan, L.M. and Peterson, R.S. (2004) 'The role of personality in group processes', in B. Schneider and D.B. Smith (eds) *Personality and Organizations*, Mahwah, NJ: Erlbaum, pp.317–45.

Muchinsky, P.M. (1986) 'Personnel selection methods', in C. Cooper and I. Robertson (eds) *International Review of Industrial and Organizational Psychology*, New York: Wiley.

Muchinsky, P.M. (2004) 'When the psychometrics of test development meets organizational realities: a conceptual framework for organizational change, examples, and recommendations', *Personnel Psychology*, Vol.57, pp.175–209.

Newell, S. (2006) 'Selection and assessment', in T. Redman and A. Wilkinson (eds) *Contemporary HRM* (2nd edn), London: Pearson Education, pp.65–98.

Nickson, D., Warhurst, C., Hurrell, S. and Dutton, E. (2008) 'A job to believe in: recruitment in the Scottish voluntary sector', *Human Resource Management Journal*, Vol.18, No.1, pp.18–33.

Olson-Buchanan, J.B. and Drasgow, F. (2005) 'Multimedia situational judgment tests: the medium creates the message', in J.A. Weekly and R.E. Ployhart (eds) *Situational Judgment Tests: Theory, Measurement*, London: Routledge, pp.253–78.

Ones, D., Viswesvaran, C. and Dilchert, S. (2005) 'Personality at work: raising awareness and correcting misconceptions', *Human Performance*, Vol.18, pp.389–404.

Ones, D., Dilchert, S., Viswesvaran, C. and Judge, T.A. (2007) 'In support of personality assessment in organizational settings', *Personnel Psychology*, Vol.60, No.4, pp.995–1027.

Pearn, M. (1993) 'Fairness in selection and assessment: a European perspective', in H. Schuler, J.L. Farr and M. Smith (eds) *Personnel Selection and Assessment: Individual and Organizational Perspectives*, Hillsdale, NJ: Lawrence Erlbaum.

Pfeffer, J. (1998) *The Human Equation. Building Profits by Putting People First*, Boston, MA: Harvard Business School Press.

Ployhart, R.E. and Erhart, M.G. (2003) 'Be careful what you ask for: effects of response instructions and the construct validity and reliability of situational judgment tests', *International Journal of Selection and Assessment*, Vol.11, No.1, pp.1–16.

Ployhart, R.E., McFarland, L.A. and Ryan, A.M. (2002) 'Examining applicants' attributions for withdrawal from a selection procedure', *Journal of Applied Social Psychology*, Vol.32, No.11, pp.2228–52.

Ployhart, R.E., Schneider, B. and Schmitt, N. (2006) *Staffing Organizations. Contemporary Practice and Theory*, Mahwah, NJ: Lawrence Erlbaum.

Purcell, K., Rowley, G. and Morley, M. (2002) *Recruiting from a Wider Spectrum of Graduates*, May, London: Council for Industry and Higher Education.

Reed Consulting (2007) *Candidates as Customer: Changing Attitudes to Recruitment.* London: Reed Consulting.

Reilly, R.R. and Chao, G.T. (1982) 'Validity and fairness of some alternative employee selection procedures', *Personnel Psychology*, Vol.35, No.1, pp.1–62.

Roe, R. and van den Berg, P. (2003) 'Selection in Europe: context, developments and research agenda', *European Journal of Work and Organizational Psychology*, Vol.12, No.3, pp.257–87.

Rothstein, M.G. and Goffin, R.D. (2006) 'The use of personality measures in personnel selection: what does current research support?', *Human Resource Management Review*, Vol.16, No.2, pp.155–80.

Ryan, A.M., McFarland, L., Baron, H. and Page, R. (1999) 'An international look at selection practices: nation and culture as explanations for variability in practice', *Personnel Psychology*, Vol.52, pp.359–94.

Sackett, P.R. and Lievens, F. (2008) 'Personnel selection', *Annual Review of Psychology*, Vol.59, pp.419–50.

Salgado, J.F. (2002) 'The Big Five personality dimensions and counterproductive behaviors', *International Journal of Selection and Assessment*, Vol.10, Nos.1 & 2, pp.17–125.

Salgado, J.F. and Anderson, N.R. (2002) 'Cognitive and GMA testing in the European Community: issues and evidence', *Human Performance*, Vol.15, pp.75–96.

Salgado, J.F., Anderson, N., Moscoso, S., Bertua, C. and De Fruyt, F. (2003) 'International validity generalization of GMA and cognitive abilities: a European Community meta-analysis', *Personnel Psychology*, Vol.56, No.3, pp.573–605.

Schmidt, F.L. and Hunter, J.E. (1998) 'The validity and utility of selection methods in personnel psychology: practical and theoretical implications of 85 years of research findings', *Psychological Bulletin*, Vol.124, No.2, pp.262–74.

Schmidt, F. and Zimmerman, R.D. (2004) 'A counterintuitive hypothesis about employment interview validity and some supporting evidence', *Journal of Applied Psychology*, Vol.89, No.3, pp.553–61.

Schmitt, N. (2003) 'Employee selection: how simulations change the picture for minority groups', *Cornell Hospitality Quarterly*, Vol.44, pp.25–32.

Schmitt, N. and Chan, D. (1998) *Personnel Selection. A Theoretical Approach*, London: Sage.

Schmitt, N. and Mills, A. (2001) 'Traditional tests and job simulations: minority and majority performance and test validities', *Journal of Applied Psychology*, Vol.86, No.3, pp.451–58.

Schuler, H. (1993) 'Social validity of selection situations: a concept and some empirical results', in H. Schuler, J.L. Farr and M. Smith (eds), *Personnel Selection and Assessment: Individual and Organizational Perspectives*, Hillsdale: Lawrence Erlbaum Associates, pp.11–26.

Searle, R.H. (2003a) *Selection and Recruitment. A Critical Text*, Milton Keynes: The Open University.

Searle, R.H. (2003b) 'Organizational justice in e-recruiting: issues and controversies', *Surveillance and Society*, Vol.1, No.2, pp.227–31.

Shackleton, V. and Newell, S. (1997) 'International assessment and selection', in N. Anderson and P. Herriot (eds) *International Handbook of Selection and Assessmant*, London: John Wiley & Sons.

Sternberg, R.J., Wagner, R.K., Williams, W.M. and Horvarth, J.A. (1995) 'Testing common sense', *American Psychologist*, Vol.50, No.11, pp.912–27.

Storey, J. (2007) 'Human resource management today: an assessment', in J. Storey (ed.) *Human Resource Management: A Critical Text* (3rd edn), London: Routledge.

Terpstra, D.E. and Kethley, R.B. (2002) 'Organizations' relative degree of exposure to selection discrimination litigation', *Public Personnel Management*, Vol.31, No.3, pp.277.

Tett, R.P. and Christiansen, N.D. (2007) Personality tests at the crossroads: a response to Morgeson, Campion, Dipboye, Hollenbeck, Murphy, and Schmitt', *Personnel Psychology*, Vol.60, No.4, pp.967–93.

Thornton, G.C., III, and Mueller-Hanson, R.A. (2004) *Developing Organizational Simulations: A Guide for Practitioners and Students*, Mahwah, NJ: Lawrence Erlbaum.

Townley, B. (1989) 'Selection and appraisal: reconstituting "social relations"?', in J. Storey (ed.) *New Perspectives on Human Resource Management*, London: Routledge, pp.92–108.

Van Hoye, G. and Lievens, F. (2005) 'Recruitment-related information sources and organizational attractiveness: can something be done about negative publicity?', *International Journal of Selection and Assessment*, Vol.13, No.3, pp.179–87.

Viswesvaran, C., Deller, J. and Ones, D.S. (2007) 'Personality measures in personnel selection', *International Journal of Selection and Assessment*, Vol.15, No.3, pp.354–58.

Weisinger, H. (1998) *Emotional Intelligence at Work*, San Francisco: Jossey-Bass.

Whittaker, S. and Marchington, M. (2003) 'Devolving HR responsibility to the line: threat, opportunity or partnership?', *Employee Relations*, Vol.25, No.3, pp.245–61.

Wolf, A. and Jenkins, A. (2006) 'Explaining greater test use for selection: the role of HR professionals in a world of expanded regulation', *Human Resource Management Journal*, Vol.16, No.2, pp.193–213.

de Wolff, C.J. (1993) 'The prediction paradigm', in H. Schuler, J.L. Farr and M. Smith (eds) *Personnel Selection and Assessment: Individual and Organizational Perspectives*, Hillsdale, NJ: Lawrence Erlbaum.

Zeidner, M., Matthews, G. and Roberts, R.D. (2004) 'Emotional intelligence in the workplace: a critical review', *Applied Psychology: An International Review*, Vol.53, No.3, pp.371–99.

GETTING ON:
THE DEVELOPMENT OF
THE HUMAN RESOURCE

LEARNING AND DEVELOPMENT

THE OBJECTIVES OF THIS CHAPTER ARE TO:

1 Explore four perspectives on the nature of learning and consider the implications that each has for development provision and support

2 Explain the role of behavioural competencies in learning and development

3 Review some of the practical characteristics of learning and development

4 Explain the various methods of addressing learning and development needs

5 Investigate the nature of evaluation in this context

There has been a considerable shift in the way that individual development is understood and characterised. We have moved from identifying training needs to identifying learning needs, the implication being that development is owned by the learner with the need rather than by the trainer seeking to satisfy that need. This also has implications for who identifies the needs and the way that those needs are met. Current thinking suggests that needs are best developed by a partnership between the individual and the organisation, and that the methods of meeting these needs are not limited only to formal courses, but to a wide range of on-the-job development methods and distance/e-learning approaches. While a partnership approach is considered ideal the phrase 'self-development' is an important one in our development lexicon, indicating the growing emphasis on individuals having ownership of and taking responsibility for their own development. There has also been a shift in the type of skills that are the focus of development activity from an interest in technical skills to the development of personal skills, self-management and attitudes. Lastly, while the focus on development for the current job remains high, there is greater pressure for development which is also future oriented. These shifts reflect the changes that we have already discussed in terms of global competition, fast and continuous change and the need for individuals to develop their employability in an increasingly uncertain world.

THE NATURE OF LEARNING

For the purpose of this text we consider the result of learning to be changed or new behaviour resulting from new or reinterpreted knowledge that has been derived from an external or internal experience. There are broadly four theoretical approaches or perspectives to understanding the nature of learning, and the training and development that organisations carry out reflect the explicit or implicit acceptance of one or more perspectives. We will look at each perspective, in the evolutionary order in which they became important. There is no right or wrong theory – each has strengths and weaknesses.

The **behaviourist** perspective is the earliest which, reflecting the label, concentrates on changes in observable behaviour. Experiments with animals formed the foundation of this theory, for example the work of Skinner, Watson and Pavlov. Researchers sought to associate rewards with certain behaviours in order to increase the display of that behaviour. The relevance of this for organisations today may be seen for example in telesales training where employees are taught to follow a script and calls are listened to, to ensure that the script is followed. Reward or punishment follows depending on behaviour. Trainers are not interested in what is going on in the heads of employees, they merely want them to follow the routine to be learned. This approach has also been used for a range of interpersonal skills training. One American company, for example plays video sequences to trainees portraying the 'correct' way to carry out, say, a return to work interview. Trainees then practise copying what they have seen and are given cue cards to use when carrying out that particular interpersonal event. The problems with the perspective are that it is overtly manipulative, simplistic and limited. It may produce only temporary changes in behaviour and increase cynicism.

Cognitive approaches are based on an information-processing perspective and are more concerned with what goes on in the learner's head. This is a more technical perspective and maps out the stages of learning, such as: expectancy to learn (motivation); attention and perception required; experience is coded (meaning is derived); meaning is stored in long-term memory; meaning is retrieved when needed; learning is applied; feedback is received (which may supply reinforcement). The strengths of this perspective are that it stresses the importance of learner motivation and individual needs, it recognises that the individual has some control over what is learned and it identifies feedback as an important aspect of learning. The weaknesses are that it assumes learning is neutral and unproblematic and it is a purely rational approach that ignores emotion. From this perspective useful development activities would be seen as formal courses offering models and ideas with lots of back-up paperwork. Activities to improve learning motivation are also important, for example helping employees to recognise their own development needs and providing rewards for skills development. Mechanisms for providing feedback to employees are also key.

The third perspective is based on **social learning theory,** in other words learning is a social activity and this is based on our needs as humans to fit in with others. In organisations this happens to some extent naturally as we learn to fit in with things such as dress codes, behaviour in meetings and so on. Fitting in means that we can be accepted as successful in the organisation, but it is not necessary that we internalise and believe in these codes. Organisations often use role models, mentors and peer support, and 'buddies', to intensify our natural will to fit in. The disadvantages of this perspective are that it ignores the role of choice for the individual and it is based, to some extent, on a masquerade.

The **constructivist** perspective is a development of the information-processing perspective, but does not regard learning as a neutral process: it is our perception of our experiences that counts; there is no 'objective' view. This perspective accepts that in our dealings with the world we create 'meaning structures' in our heads and these are based on our past experiences and personality. New information and potential learning need to fit with these meaning structures in some way, which means that a similar new experience will be understood differently by different people. We tend to pay attention to things which fit with our meaning structures and ignore or avoid things that do not fit. As humans we are also capable of constructing and reconstructing our meaning structures without any new experiences. These meaning structures are mainly unconscious and therefore we are not aware of the structures which constrain our learning. We are generally unaware of how valid our meaning sets are, and they are deeply held and difficult to change. Making these structures explicit enables us to challenge them and to start to change them. This perspective recognises that learning is a very personal and potentially threatening process. We develop mechanisms to protect ourselves from this threat, and thus protect ourselves from learning. The implication of this is that learning support needs to encourage introspection and reflection, and providing the perspectives of others (for example as in 360-degree feedback, outdoor courses or relocations) may assist in this process.

PRACTICAL CHARACTERISTICS OF LEARNING AND DEVELOPMENT

Learning from experience

A significant amount of work has been done which helps us understand how managers, and others, learn from their experiences. Kolb *et al.* (1984) argue that it is useful to combine the characteristics of learning, which is usually regarded as passive, with those

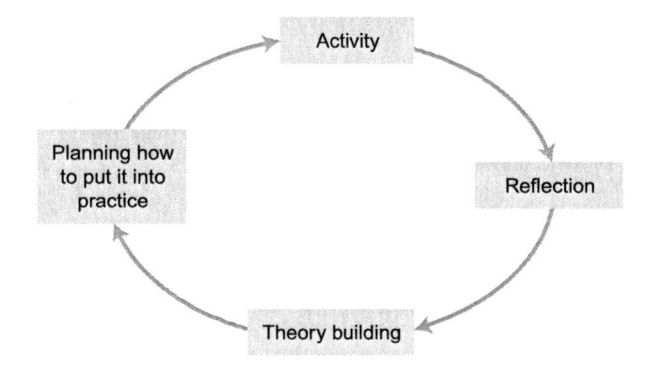

Figure 18.1 The learning cycle

of problem solving, which is usually regarded as active. From this combination Kolb *et al.* developed a four-stage learning cycle, which was further developed by Honey and Mumford (1989).

The four stages, based on the work of both groups of researchers, are shown in Figure 18.1.

WINDOW ON PRACTICE

Gwen is a management trainer in a large organisation running a number of in-house management courses. She has just moved into this position from her role as section leader in the research department; the move was seen as a career development activity in order to strengthen her managerial skills.

Gwen is working with her manager to learn from her experiences. Here is an extract from her learning diary based on the learning cycle:

Activity – I've had a go at running three sessions on my own now, doing the input and handling the questions.

Reflection – I find the input much easier than handling questions. When I'm asked a question and answer it I have the feeling that they're not convinced by my reply and I feel awkward that we seem to finish the session hanging in mid-air. I would like to be able to encourage more open discussion.

Theory building – If I give an answer to a question it closes off debate by the fact that I have 'pronounced' what is 'right'. If I want them to discuss I have to avoid giving my views at first.

Planning practice – When I am asked a question rather than answering it I will say to the group: 'What does anyone think about that?' or 'What do you think?' (to the individual who asked) or 'What are the possibilities here?' I will keep encouraging them to respond to each other and reinforce where necessary, or help them change tack by asking another question.

Each of these four stages of the learning cycle is critical to effective learning, but few people are strong at each stage and it is helpful to understand where our strengths and weaknesses lie. Honey and Mumford designed a questionnaire to achieve this which identified individuals' learning styles as 'activist', 'reflector', 'theorist' and 'pragmatist', and explain that:

- **Activists** learn best from 'having a go', and trying something out without necessarily preparing. They would be enthusiastic about role-play exercises and keen to take risks in the real environment.
- **Reflectors** are much better at listening and observing. They are effective at reflecting on their own and others' experiences and good at analysing what happened and why.
- **Theorists'** strengths are in building a concept or a theory on the basis of their analysis. They are good at integrating different pieces of information, and building models of the way things operate. They may choose to start their learning by reading around a topic.
- **Pragmatists** are keen to use whatever they learn and will always work out how they can apply it in a real situation. They will plan how to put it into practice. They will value information/ideas they are given only if they can see how to relate them to practical tasks they need to do.

Understanding how individuals learn from experience underpins all learning, but is particularly relevant in encouraging self-development activities. Understanding our strengths and weaknesses enables us to choose learning activities which suit our style, and gives us the opportunity to decide to strengthen a particularly weak learning stage of our learning cycle. While Honey and Mumford adopt this dual approach, Kolb firmly maintains that learners *must* become deeply competent at all stages of the cycle. There has been considerable attention to the issue of matching and mismatching styles with development activities and the matching and mismatching of trainer learning style with learner learning style.

ACTIVITY 18.1

1. If you have not already done so obtain the Honey and Mumford questionnaire and work out your learning style(s).
2. Select your weakest style and try to identify two different learning activities which fit with this style, but that you would normally avoid.
3. Seek opportunities for trying out these learning activities. If you practise these activities on a regular basis this should help you strengthen the style you are working on.
4. Log your experiences and in particular what you have learned about these 'new' learning activities.

Table 18.1 Planned and emergent learning

Learner type	Planned learning score	Emergent learning score
Sage	High	High
Warrior	High	Low
Adventurer	Low	High
Sleeper	Low	Low

Source: Adapted from D. Megginson (1994) 'Planned and emergent learning: A framework and a method', *Executive Development*, Vol. 7, No. 6, pp. 29–32.

Planned and emergent learning

From a different, but compatible, perspective, David Megginson characterises learners by the extent to which they plan the direction of their learning and implement this (planned learning), and the extent to which they are able to learn from opportunistic learning experiences (emergent learning). Megginson (1994) suggests that strengths and weaknesses in these two areas will influence the way individuals react to self-development. These two characteristics are not mutually exclusive, and Megginson combines them to identify four learning types, as shown in Table 18.1.

Warriors are those who are strong at planning what they want to learn and how, but are less strong at learning from experiences they had not anticipated. They have a clear focus on what they want to learn and pursue this persistently. On the other hand Adventurers respond to and learn from opportunities that come along unexpectedly, they are curious and flexible. However, they tend not to plan and create opportunities for themselves. Sages are strong on both characteristics, and Sleepers display little of either characteristic at present. To be most effective in self-development activities learners need to make maximum use of both planned and emergent learning. For a further explanation of this model also *see* Megginson and Whitaker (1996/2007).

ACTIVITY 18.2

Consider your development over the past year: do you feel that your strengths are in planning your learning or in learning opportunistically?

Choose your weaker approach, and identify how you could strengthen this.

Identifying learning and training needs

The 'systematic training cycle' was developed to help organisations move away from ad hoc non-evaluated training, and replace it with an orderly sequence of training activities, but this approach has been less prominent of late. Harrison (2009) contests that such a cycle is not necessarily the most appropriate to use as it falls far short of the messy world of practice, and does not focus adequately on learning. In spite of this the cycle does retain some value, and we describe an adaptation of such a model to make it more applicable to today's environment. The model is set within an external environment and

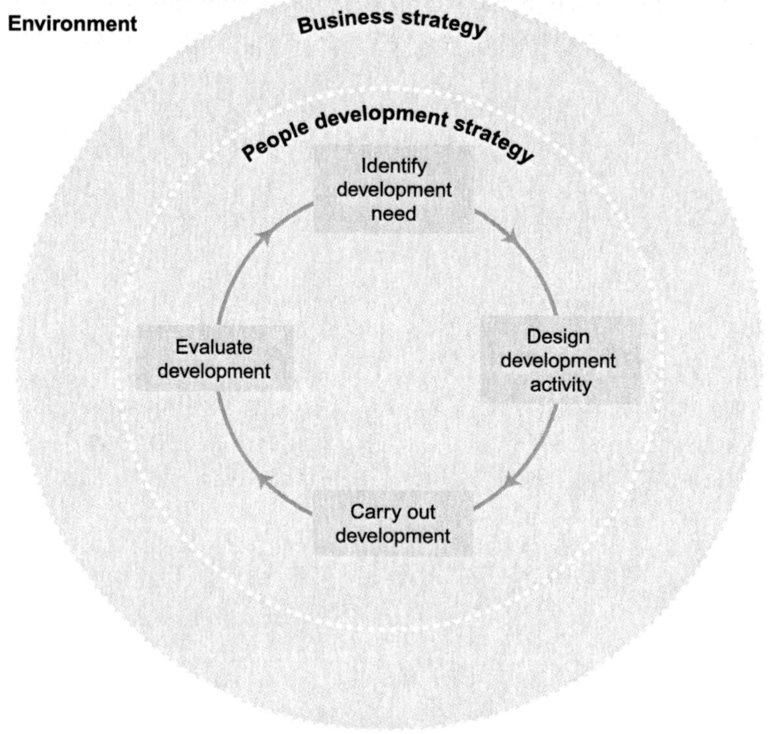
Environment
Business strategy
People development strategy
Identify development need
Design development activity
Carry out development
Evaluate development

Figure 18.2 A systematic model of learning and training

within an organisation strategy and an HR development strategy. Even if some of these elements are not made explicit, they will exist implicitly. Note that the boundary lines are dotted, not continuous. This indicates that the boundaries are permeable and overlapping. The internal part of the model reflects a systematic approach to learning and to training. Learning needs may be identified by the individual, by the organisation or in partnership, and this applies to each of the following steps in the circle. This dual involvement is probably the biggest change from traditional models where the steps were owned by the organisation, usually the trainers, and the individual was considered to be the subject of the exercise rather than a participant in it, or the owner of it. The model that we offer does not exclude this approach where appropriate, but is intended to be viewed in a more flexible way. The model is shown in Figure 18.2.

There are various approaches to analysing needs, the two most traditional being a problem-centred approach and matching the individual's competency profile with that for the job that person is filling. The problem-centred approach focuses on any performance problems or difficulties, and explores whether these are due to a lack of skills and, if so, which. The profile comparison approach takes a much broader view and is perhaps most useful when an individual, or group of individuals, are new to a job. This latter approach is also useful because strategic priorities change and new skills are required of employees, as the nature of their job changes, even though they are still officially in the same role with the same job title. We discuss competencies in the following section. When a gap has been identified, by whatever method, the development required needs to be phrased in terms of a learning objective, before the next stage of the cycle, planning and designing the development, can be undertaken. For example, when a gap or need has been identified around team leadership, appropriate learning objectives may be that learners, by the end of the development, will be able 'to ask appropriate questions at the outset of a team activity to ascertain relevant skills and experience, and to check understanding of the task' or 'to review a team activity by involving all members in that review'.

> **ACTIVITY 18.3**
>
> Write learning objectives for the following individuals who are experiencing problems in their performance:
>
> 1 Tina, who always dominates meetings, and neglects the contribution of others.
> 2 Brian, who has never carried out a selection interview before, and is very unsure of how to go about this.
> 3 Mark, who feels he has lots of contributions to make at meetings, but never actually says anything.
> 4 Sara, who can never get to meetings on time.

The planning and design of learning will be influenced by the learning objectives and also by the HR development strategy, which for example may contain a vision of who should be involved in training and development activities, and the emphasis on approaches such as self-development and e-learning. Once planning and design have been specified the course, or coaching or e-learning activity, can commence, and should be subject to ongoing monitoring and evaluated at an appropriate time in the future to assess how behaviour and performance have changed.

BEHAVIOURAL COMPETENCIES

Characteristics of behavioural competencies

Boyatzis (2008) in a development of his previous work defines a competency as an ability or capability expressed in a range of related behaviours attached to 'intent'. He uses the example of a range of listening and questioning behaviours which may be attached to the underlying intent of genuinely being interested in the other person's views. This competency might be described as 'understanding the other person'. But he does warn us that there may be other intents for such behaviours! Boyatzis maintains his position that a competency is: 'an underlying characteristic of a person which results in effective and/or superior performance in a job' (Boyatzis 1982: 21), and in 2008 identifies three major groups of competencies relating to emotional intelligence; social intelligence; and cognitive intelligence.

Boyatzis originally developed a common competency framework for managers but subsequently tailor-made competency frameworks have come thick and fast from the training and development specialists, and most large companies have produced such a framework. Most frameworks have clusters of competencies, like the Boyatzis model, and to each of the competencies within the cluster a list of behavioural indicators is usually attached. Some frameworks include level definitions encapsulating the simplicity or sophistication of the way that the competency is displayed while others include positive and negative behaviours in relation to a competency, as shown in the following two Windows on practice.

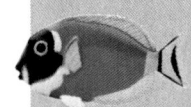

WINDOW ON PRACTICE

An example of behavioural skills with level definitions from Connexions

Working with others

The ability to work constructively within a group/team environment

Level definitions	Examples of actions demonstrated at each level
Stage Three – Contributes to organisational success by defining, planning and implementing strategies for the future and building strategic relationships and alliances – Manages and allocates available resources, including financial, capital and people to best meet current and future requirements (2 of 4)	– Is able to recognise opportunities for organisation-wide networking – Develops and maintains strategic partnerships and alliances – Understands the strategic implications of working within different cultures (3 of 4)
Stage Two – Able to transfer knowledge – Challenges procedures – Develops best practice – Provides leadership to others (4 of 6)	– Builds confidence in others to take further responsibility – Provides constructive feedback to others on performance and impact on others – Maximises networking opportunities (3 of 7)
Stage One – Uses information to improve systems – Regularly acts on own initiative – Takes responsibility for own actions and decisions	– Understands team goals and objectives and works proactively for team success – Shares knowledge, skills and experience openly and honestly – Volunteers to work in projects or sub-committees – Helps others to achieve goals (4 of 10)
Foundation stage – Takes responsibility for own actions and decisions – Understands fundamental principles and applications – Refers to others for guidance – Follows procedures and processes	– Responsive, open and friendly in manner – Considers and relates well to all kinds of people – Personally enthusiastic, positive and approachable – Owns up to responsibility, even if mistakes happen – resilient (4 of 9)

Source: Connexions Cheshire and Warrington, but a national framework.

WINDOW ON PRACTICE

A sample competency from the Police Force

Respect for Race and Diversity – A

Behaviour category

Considers and shows respect for the opinions, circumstances and feelings of colleagues and members of the public, no matter what their race, religion, position, background, circumstances, status or appearance.

Understands other people's views and takes them into account. Is tactful and diplomatic when dealing with people, treating them with dignity and respect at all times. Understands and is sensitive to social, cultural and racial differences.

Positive indicators

- Sees issues from other people's viewpoints
- Is polite and patient when dealing with people, treating them with respect and dignity
- Shows understanding and sensitivity to people's problems, vulnerabilities and needs
- Makes people feel valued by listening to and supporting their needs and interests
- Understands what offends and adapts own actions accordingly
- Respects confidentiality wherever appropriate

(this is a selection from a full list of 13)

Negative indicators

- Does not consider other people's feelings
- Does not encourage people to talk about personal issues
- Makes situations worse with inappropriate remarks, language or behaviour
- Is thoughtless and tactless when dealing with people
- Is dismissive and impatient with people
- Does not respect confidentiality
- Uses humour inappropriately

(this is a selection from a full list of 11)

Source: Police (Cheshire Constabulary). However, these are national competencies.

Case 18.1 on this book's companion website at **www.pearsoned.co.uk/torrington** concentrates on Goleman's emotional intelligence competencies which we discussed in Chapter 13 on leadership.

Advantages of behavioural competencies

Behavioural competencies are often seen as a means of expressing what is valued by the organisation as well as what characteristics have been seen to result in superior performance. In addition they are seen to provide a critical mechanism for the integration of human resource practices which is considered essential to a strategic approach to HR. Thus, once a competency framework has been researched and designed it can be used in recruitment, selection, training, performance management and reward (see, for example, IDS 2008). In this way employees are given consistent messages about what is valued and what is expected of them, and as not all competencies are equally developable it gives good direction as to which competencies need to be selected for in new employees. Westminster City Council, for example, has introduced a competency framework (CIPD 2006) which Tony Reynolds, Organisation Development Manager, describes as 'a golden thread running through the people management process' (p. 12); he also says that 'they are the behaviours we want to recruit, develop, manage and reward' (p. 12). However, in practice this link is often weak; for example Abraham and his colleagues (2001) found organisations willing to identify a set of managerial competencies that described a successful manager, but did not place a corresponding emphasis on including these competencies in their performance appraisal. A further advantage of competency frameworks is that, as they can be expressed as behaviours, they are more easily measurable, and thus can be used explicitly in all HR processes. This means, for example, that in a development centre, assessors can be trained in how to observe a long list of behaviours. In the centre itself each assessor can then check the behaviours of the candidates under observation to record how many times that particular behaviour is displayed.

Problematic aspects of behavioural competencies

Criticisms of the approach have been focused around the complex process required to research the appropriate competencies for the organisation, and perhaps more importantly, the fact that such competencies, due to the research process itself, will be inevitably backward looking rather than future oriented. Hayes *et al.* (2000) also note that a competency framework may not include every aspect that is critical to superior performance, and also that while one set of competencies may result in high performance this does not necessarily mean that such performance may not be achieved via a different set of competencies. Whiddett and Kandola (2000) similarly argue that processes *solely* based on competencies are flawed and that a wider perspective needs to be taken. Without the wider perspective the scope for encouraging and using diversity may be diminished. In terms of performance management they also highlight that changes in behaviour may be due to factors other than competencies, and this, of course, has implications for development. We also need to remember that a person's behaviour is not necessarily consistent, and may be affected by the environment and the situation, and Boyatzis (2009) does suggest that it is important to identify the 'tipping point' which identifies how often the relevant behaviours need to be displayed. Salaman and Taylor (2002) suggest that there are five inherent weaknesses where organisations limit themselves to a behavioural competency approach for managers including: marginalisation of the cultural, social and organisational context, the fact that such frameworks emphasise a narrow set of behaviours and attitudes with a lack of emphasis on the long-term processes of management development, and that competencies are founded on the questionable assumption that managers behave rationally and are achievement driven.

> **ACTIVITY 18.4**
>
> Research the use of behavioural competencies in your own organisation (if they are used), or one with which you are familiar.
>
> 1 What are the advantages of their use?
> 2 What are the disadvantages?
> 3 Compare views, if you can, from members of the HR function, line managers elsewhere, and other professionals.

METHODS OF LEARNING AND DEVELOPMENT

Off-job methods: education and training courses

Educational courses undertaken during a career are frequently done on a part-time basis leading to a diploma or master's degree with a management or business label, and/or qualification for a professional body. It is considered that such courses provide value for both the employer and the participant – and MBA study is a popular route. For advantages of such a course for the employee *see*, for example, Baruch and Leeming (2001). An alternative approach to qualification is the NVQ route which we discussed in the previous chapter, which is more closely tied to on-job experiences and not concerned with 'education'.

In addition there are consultancy courses. Varying from a half-day to several weeks in length, they are run by consultants or professional bodies for all comers. They have the advantage that they bring together people from varying occupational backgrounds and are not, therefore, as introspective as in-house courses and are popular for topical issues. They are, however, often relatively expensive and superficial, despite their value as sources of industrial folklore, by which we mean the swapping of experiences among course members.

The most valuable courses of this type are those that concentrate on specific skills or knowledge, such as developing time management, interviewing or disciplinary skills, or being introduced to a new national initiative. This short-course approach is probably the only way for individuals to come to terms with some new development, such as a change in legislation, because they need not only to find an interpretation of the development, but also to share views and reactions with fellow employees to ensure that their own feelings are not idiosyncratic or perverse.

In-house courses are often similar in nature to consultancy courses, and are sometimes run with the benefit of some external expertise. In-house courses can be particularly useful if the training needs to relate to specific organisational procedures and structures, or if it is geared to encouraging employees to work more effectively together in the organisational environment. The drawbacks of in-house courses are that they suffer from a lack of breadth of content, and there is no possibility of learning from people in other organisations.

Alternatively, there are outdoor-type courses (sometimes known as Outward Bound, after the organisation that pioneered them). Outdoor courses attempt to develop skills involved in working with and through others, and aim to increase self-awareness and self-confidence through a variety of experiences, including outdoor physical challenges. Courses like these continue to be increasingly used, and their differential value is assumed to hinge on their separation from the political, organisational environment. A natural, challenging and different environment is assumed to encourage individuals to forsake political strategising, act as their raw selves and be more open to new ideas, but the idea of providing a de-politicised environment is perhaps a naive hope rather than a reality. Learning experiences based on drama are increasingly popular; in these participants are engaged in improvisation through role play and exercises. For a fascinating insight into the variety of forms this may take *see* Monks *et al.* (2001). There are other forms of simulation and experiential learning in addition to role play, such as games and computer simulations, virtual worlds, and mock-up worlds which take place away from the job as shown in the Window on practice.

WINDOW ON PRACTICE

Fake station offers real training

London Underground has designed a mock tube station called West Ashfield, as reported by Stevens (2010) which is used to prepare staff for real-life situations before they go out into the field. It is being used to train drivers, gate operators and apprentices and also to provide retraining when staff are moved to new areas.

The station will also be used by police, fire and ambulance services who will be trained alongside London Underground staff in preparation for emergency situations such as mass evacuations, and people falling under trains.

Previously this training would have been done on a Sunday and required the closing of a real tube station. London Underground recognises the importance of hands-on experience in developing staff confidence and with simulation it can expose staff to the pressures they will experience in the real workplace.

Virtual building sites

Based on experiences in the Netherlands a new construction training centre has been opened in Coventry designed to use computer technology to create virtual construction sites with the aim of improving the people management skills of site workers. Participants use a control stick to 'work' on a 12-metre high panoramic screen. Actors are used to present scenarios for the trainees to deal with and supervisors can observe via cameras. Balfour Beatty is intending to use the site for management, people and communication skills, particularly for site managers, and the company's training manager believes that it will provide higher-value training as it is specific and highly relevant to their day-to-day work.

Sources: Stevens, M. (2010) 'Fake Station offers real training', *People Management*, 28 January, p. 12.
Phillips, L. (2009b) '"Virtual building sites" at new training centre', *People Management*, 4 June, p. 10.

One of the major concerns with these different types of off-job courses and activities is the difficulty of ensuring transfer of learning back to the workplace. As part of their research on the contribution of off-job courses to managers Longenecker and Ariss (2002) asked managers what helped them retain what they had learned and transfer it to the workplace. Developing goals/plans for implementing new skills was most frequently identified. In addition managers said that it helped to review materials immediately after the programme; be actively involved in the learning itself; make a report to peers/superiors on what they had learned; review material and development plans with their mentor/manager; and include development goals in performance reviews. It is generally agreed that a supportive climate helps transfer (for example line manager interest and involvement) and Nielsen (2009) found that collaborative activities on return to the workplace aided trainees in transferring their course-based learning to the workplace. Santos and Stewart (2003), for example, found that transfer was more likely if reward such as promotion or pay was attached to developmental behaviour change, and also where there was a helpful management climate in terms of pre- and post-course briefings and activities.

WINDOW ON PRACTICE

Experiential activities

Brockett (2006) explains how EDF Energy aims to improve customer service via experiential course activities for engineers, dispatch and call-centre workers. During the course participants play the roles of guests at a sixtieth birthday party. Cake, music and decorations accompany this. Half-way through the party there is a surprise power cut represented by a blackout and audio recording of family members becoming distressed and stumbling about in the dark. The aim was to let course members experience what their customers experience when they have a power cut so that they can better understand the effect that it has on people's lives. Performance improvements followed in terms of repair times, accuracy of estimated repair times and increase in commendations letters from the public. This suggests that an experience, especially in the shoes of the customer, can have a powerful impact on employee perceptions and behaviours.

Phillips (2006) provides an example of BUPA care staff in a retirement home. As part of a 'Personal Best' programme aimed at improving customer service staff took the role of residents so as to see life through their customers' eyes. So, for example, they were fed puréed food and were hoisted in a mechanical sling from a chair into a bed. As a result staff behaviour towards residents has changed, for example explaining the hoisting procedure to residents and doing it more slowly.

Sources: Brockett, J. (2006) 'Energy firm gets party vibe', *People Management*, Vol. 12, No. 10, 18 May, p. 12; Phillips, L. (2006) 'BUPA Stars', *People Management*, Vol. 12, No. 22, 9 November, pp. 30–2.

Learning on the job

Manager coaching and other internal and external coaching

The line manager's role in learning and development has increased with the devolution of HR tasks. Coaching is an informal approach to individual development based on a close relationship between the individual and one other person, either internal or external to the organisation. The coach is often the immediate manager, who is experienced in the task, but there is increasing use of external coaches, especially for more senior managers, or specially trained internal coaches, and 'coaching' has become very much a professional occupation with its own code of ethical practice. We will look at this in more detail, but first we explore the coaching role of the line manager.

The manager as coach helps trainees to develop by giving them the opportunity to perform an increasing range of tasks, and by helping them to learn from their experiences. Managers work to improve the trainee's performance by asking searching questions, actively listening, discussion, exhortation, encouragement, understanding, counselling and providing information and honest feedback. The manager coach is usually in a position to create development opportunities for the trainee when this is appropriate. For example, a line manager can delegate attendance at a meeting, or allow a trainee to deputise, where this is appropriate to the individual's development needs. Alternatively a line manager can create the opportunity for a trainee to join a working party or can arrange a brief secondment to another department. Coaches can share 'inside' information with the individual being coached to help him or her understand the political context in which the individual is working. For example, they are able to explain who will have most influence on a decision that will be made, or future plans for restructuring within a department.

Skilled coaches can adapt their style to suit the individual they are coaching, from highly directive at one end of the scale to non-directive at the other. The needed style may change over time, as the trainee gains more confidence and experience. IDS (2009) found that a good coach is one who had a genuine interest in the coachees; believes that everyone is capable of more and focuses on potential rather than past performance; knows that the coach does not have all the answers; believes a person's past is no indication of his or her future; understands that an open, supportive and mutual relationship is required for effective coaching; understands that results may be short or long term and believes they should build awareness, responsibility and self-belief. A variety of barriers to coaching have been identified including performance pressures and a feeling that the role was not valued, but Anderson (2009) found that time pressures, lack of confidence to deal with difficult people and organisational culture were key. IDS (2006a) suggests that in view of the emphasis in coaching on honest self-reflection, there will be barriers in organisations where the culture is not one of openness and honesty. They also point out that coaching has been seen as a remedial tool but that it probably has more to offer as a development opportunity for turning good performers into excellent ones.

There has been an increasing trend to broaden the concept of coaching in terms of both content and who carries out the coaching. Many organisations are now providing or arranging intensive training for designated internal coaches who operate broadly in the organisation, just in a coaching role. This is quite different from the basic training line managers are likely to receive. External executive coaching is often provided by consultancies and specialist coaching organisations. IDS (2009) provides an excellent range of case studies demonstrating the different ways in which organisations are using coaching. Various forms of coaching may include career coaching, performance coaching, skills coaching, business coaching and life coaching. Given the increasing professionalisation of coaching it is not surprising that the quality of the coaching experience is receiving attention. Supervision of practice is increasingly being used in a way that is similar to supervision for counsellors, which involves regular meetings with a more experienced practitioner to explore their client relationships and reflect on practice. A CIPD study carried out by the Bath Consultancy Group (Arney 2006) found that nearly half the coaches received regular supervision, and that supervision was a fast growing practice. There are as yet no industry guidelines on required supervision but Mahony (2009) suggests that one hour's supervision to between 8 and 15 hours' coaching practice is a typical ratio. Such individual supervision is carried out with a mind to client confidentiality; however there is also a growing trend for group supervision of coaches and also for organisations wanting to collect common themes discussed in coaching sessions as these can be used to inform organisational thinking (Arney 2006). Both these approaches put client confidentiality at greater risk.

WINDOW ON PRACTICE

Group supervision at PricewaterhouseCoopers

Group supervision has been used for internal coaches for some time and involves sessions of three hours every month led by an external facilitator with experience of coaching supervision and a background in psychology or psychotherapy.

Coaches present a case, with the emphasis on the work of the coach and the coaching relationship rather than the individual client. In order to protect confidentiality real names are not disclosed. It is an opportunity for an individual coach to get reactions from others about their own practice, and also to reflect on approaches that others take. So the aim is to encourage constant learning and reflection, through making one's work open to scrutiny.

Source: Summarised from E. Arney (2006) 'Insider's Guide', *People Management*, Vol. 12, No. 23, 23 November, pp. 40–2.

Coaching at the Medical Research Council (MRC) and Unilever

Hall (2006) reports on the arrangement that external coaching company 'Laughing Phoenix' has made with the Medical Research Council (MRC) which involves coaching the 30 most senior HR professionals. One of the conditions of the agreement was that the company would feed back recurring themes to the MRC so that they could align coaching with the wider business picture. Unilever has contacted internal coaches regularly to 'harvest some of the intelligence they had gathered from their clients', again keen to pick up recurring themes, helping the organisation know which areas to tackle and help the coaches understand the context of their work.

Source: Hall, L. (2006) 'Inside Job', *People Management*, Vol. 12, No. 16, 10 August, pp. 34–6.

The emphasis on coaching is underlined by the CIPD journal, *Coaching at Work*, and the development of the institute's coaching standards; more than two-thirds of the organisations responding to the CIPD *Learning and Development Survey* used coaching in their organisations (CIPD 2009). Concerns for quality are being addressed, for example by a kitemarking scheme for coaching and mentoring qualifications, launched by the European Coaching and Mentoring Council (*see* **www.emccouncil.org**), and the British Psychological Society now has a specialist interest group focused on coaching. Web case 18.2 is on coaching at this book's companion website, **www.pearsoned.co.uk/torrington**.

Mentoring

Mentoring offers a wide range of advantages for the development of the mentee or protégé, coaching as described above being just one of the possible benefits of the relationship. The mentor may occasionally be the individual's immediate manager, but usually it is a more senior manager in the same or a different function. Kram (1983) identifies two broad functions of mentoring, the first of which is the career function, including those aspects of the relationship that primarily enhance career advancement, such as exposure and visibility and sponsorship. The second is the psychosocial function, which includes those aspects of the relationship that primarily enhance a sense of competence, clarity of identity and effectiveness in the managerial role. Mentoring for women managers currently has a high profile (*see*, for example, Ehrich 2008 and Maxwell 2009). More generally Fowler and O'Gorman (2005), on the basis of research with both mentors and mentees, describe eight individual mentoring functions which are: personal and emotional guidance; coaching; advocacy; career development facilitation; role modelling; strategies and systems advice; learning facilitation; and friendship. There is evidence that mentoring does benefit both parties, and Broadbridge (1999) suggests that mentors can gain through recognition from peers, increased job satisfaction, rejuvenation, admiration and self-satisfaction. Indeed reciprocity is expected in a mentoring relationship and there is evidence both mentor and mentee can make claims on each other (Oglensky 2008). The drawbacks to mentoring that were revealed in Broadbridge's research include the risk of over-reliance, the danger of picking up bad habits, the fact that the protégé may be alienated from other sources of expertise and the sense of loss experienced when a mentor leaves. In addition, the difficulty of dealing with conflicting views in such an unequal relationship was identified. Perceived benefits, however, considerably outweighed any drawbacks. There is a danger of assuming that mentoring is unquestionably good and Oglensky (2008) notes that mentoring can be a source of stress, conflict and dysfunction.

Managers are also seen as responsible for developing talent, and while a mentor/protégé relationship might not naturally occur, mentorship may be encouraged or formalised. For example, there are systems where all new graduates are attached to a mentor as soon as they join the organisation. The difficulties of establishing a formal programme include the potential mismatch of individuals, unreal expectations on both sides and the time and effort involved.

> **WINDOW ON PRACTICE**
>
> **Reverse mentoring**
>
> Dell, the computer company, has begun a new mentoring programme where male senior executives are mentored by female middle managers with the aims of giving the male bosses an insight into the challenges that women face in the organisation and also of helping more women gain senior jobs.
>
> Source: Phillips, L. (2009b) 'Dell to roll out "reverse mentoring"', *People Management*, 22 October, p. 12.
>
> **Mentoring at Fifteen**
>
> Liam Black, Director of Fifteen (Jamie Oliver's project to turn disadvantaged youngsters into cooks), initiated a structured programme to turn six members of staff into qualified mentors able to support the more vulnerable youngsters to aid retention. The staff are from different companies run by Oliver and are not directly working with the youngsters. The six are working towards a Certificate in Workplace Mentoring from the Oxford School of Coaching and Mentoring (accredited by Oxford Brookes University), which is suitably tailored to their work-based needs. The programme is a six-month blended learning package and the mentors will work with the youngsters setting goals, developing coping strategies and building their often non-existent self-esteem.
>
> Cottee, P. (2006) 'Oliver's Army', *People Management*, Vol. 12, No. 19, 28 September, pp. 44–5.

Web case 18.3 is on mentoring at this book's companion website, **www.pearsoned.co.uk/torrington**.

Peer relationships

Although mentor-protégé relationships have been shown to be related to high levels of career success, not all developing individuals have access to such a relationship, and even formal schemes are often reserved for specific groups such as new graduate entrants. Supportive peer relationships at work are potentially more widely available to the individual and offer a number of benefits for the development of both parties. The benefits that are available depend on the nature of the peer relationship, and Kram and Isabella (1985) have identified three groups of peer relationships, which are differentiated by their primary development functions. These can be expressed on a continuum from 'information peer', based primarily on information sharing, through 'collegial peer', based on career strategising, giving job-related feedback and friendship, to 'special peer', based on emotional support, personal feedback, friendship and confirmation. Most of us benefit from one or a number of peer relationships at work but often we do not readily appreciate their contribution towards our development. Peer relationships most often develop on an informal basis and provide mutual support. Some organisations, however, formally appoint an existing employee to provide such support to a new member of staff through their first 12–18 months in the organisation. These relationships may, of course, continue beyond the initial period. The name for the appointed employee will vary from organisation to organisation, and sometimes the word 'buddy', 'coach' or 'mentor' is used – which can be confusing! The skills and qualities sought in peer providers are likely to include accessibility, empathy, organisational experience and proven task skills.

> **ACTIVITY 18.5**
>
> Consider each significant peer relationship that you have at work. Where does each fit on the continuum of relationships described above, and what contributions does it make towards your development?
>
> If you are in full-time education consider the contribution that each of your relationships (whether at university, home or work) has to your development.

Self-development

Natural learning is learning that takes place on the job and results from an individual's everyday experience of the tasks to be undertaken. Natural learning is even more difficult to investigate than coaching, mentoring or peer relationships, and yet the way in which we learn from everyday experiences, and our level of awareness of this, is very important for our development. To some extent self-development may be seen as a conscious effort to gain the most from natural learning in a job, and to use the learning cycle as a framework. Self-development can be focused in specific skills development, but often extends to attitude development and personal growth.

> **ACTIVITY 18.6**
>
> The video *Groundhog Day* can be viewed as a journey of self-development. Watch the video and answer the following questions:
>
> - How did Phil's attitudes change and how was this reflected in his behaviour?
> - What do you think Phil learned?
> - How did he learn it?
> - Why is personal development so difficult?

The emphasis in self-development is that each individual is responsible for, and can plan, his or her own development, although he or she may need to seek help when working on some issues. Self-development involves individuals in analysing their strengths, weaknesses and the way in which they learn, primarily by means of questionnaires and feedback from others. This analysis may initially begin on a self-development course, or with the help of a facilitator, but would then be continued by the individual back on the job. From this analysis individuals, perhaps with some help at first, plan their development goals and the way in which they will achieve them, primarily through development opportunities within the job. When individuals consciously work on self-development they use the learning cycle in a more explicit way than in natural learning. They are also in a better position to seek appropriate opportunities and help, in their learning, from their manager.

Many of the activities included in self-development are based on observation, collecting further feedback about the way they operate, experimenting with different approaches and in particular reviewing what has happened, why and what they have learned. Self-development, however, is not a quick fix as it requires a long-term approach and careful planning and, attention needs to be paid to how the self-development process is to be supported. Extensive induction into the process is important as is an explanation of the theoretical underpinning, appropriate skill development, preparation for peer feedback, and further support in tracking progress.

Self-development groups

Typically, in self-development groups a group of individuals are involved in a series of meetings where they jointly discuss their personal development, organisational issues and/or individual work problems. Groups may begin operating with a leader who is a process expert, not a content expert, and who therefore acts as a facilitator rather than, but not to the complete exclusion of, a source of information. The group itself is the primary source of information and may operate without outside help as its members' process skills develop. The content and timings of the meetings can be very flexible, although meetings will require a significant level of energy and commitment if they are to operate well. It is important that the members understand what everyone hopes to get out of the group, the role of the facilitator (if there is one), the processes and rules that the group will operate by and how they agree to interact.

Learning logs

Learning logs are a mechanism for learning retrospectively as they encourage a disciplined approach to learning from opportunistic events. The log may be focused around one particular activity and is usually designed to encourage the writer to explain what happened, how he or she has reflected on this, what conclusions he or she has made and what future learning actions he or she wishes to make. Alternatively logs can be used in the form of a daily or weekly diary.

ACTIVITY 18.7

Identify a management skills area that you need to develop. (You may find it particularly helpful to choose an interpersonal area, for example, assertiveness, influencing others, presentation, being more sociable, contributing to meetings, helping others.)

Keep a learning diary over the next few weeks, logging anything that is relevant to your development area. Use the framework which Gwen used in a previous example (see Window on practice box at the beginning of this chapter).

At the end of the period review what you have learned in your development area and also what you have learned about the learning cycle.

Learning contracts

There is increasing use of learning contracts, sometimes used within more formalised self-development groups; on other management courses; as part of a mentoring or coaching relationship; or in working towards a competency-based qualification. These contracts are a formal commitment by the learner to work towards a specified learning goal, with an identification of how the goal might be achieved. They thus promote a proactive approach to learning. Boak (1991) has produced a very helpful guide to the use of such contracts and suggests that they should include:

- an overall development goal
- specific objectives in terms of skills and knowledge
- activities to be undertaken
- resources required
- a method of assessment of learning

The value that individuals gain from learning contracts is dependent on their choosing to participate, their identification of the relevant goal and the importance and value they ascribe to achieving it. Only with commitment will a learning contract be effective, because ultimately it is down to the individual learner manager to make it happen.

WINDOW ON PRACTICE

David wanted to improve his influencing skills and has sent the following draft learning contract to his manager for discussion:

Goal
To improve my influencing skills with both peers and more senior managers.

Specific objectives
- To prepare for influencing situations.
- To try to understand better the perspective of the other.
- To identify the interpersonal skills required – probably active listening, reflecting, summarising, stating my needs, collaboration (but maybe more).
- To be able to identify that I have had more influence in decisions made.

Activities
- Watch a recommended DVD on influencing skills.
- Re-read my notes from the interpersonal skills course I attended.
- Watch how others in my department go about influencing.
- Ask other people (supportive ones) how they go about it.

- Identify possible influencing situations in advance, and plan for what I want and what might happen.
- Reflect back on what happened, and work out how to do better next time.
- Ask for feedback.

Resources

- DVD.
- Notes.
- The support of others.

Assessment

- I could ask for feedback from colleagues and my manager.
- My own assessment may be helpful.
- Make a log over time of decisions made and my originally preferred outcome.

E-learning and blended learning

E-learning can be defined as 'learning that is delivered, enabled or mediated by electronic technology' (Sloman and Rolph 2003: 1), and by 2009 (CIPD 2009) 42 per cent of organisations reported expanding their use of e-learning, but there remained 26 per cent of organisations where e-learning was not used at all. E-learning covers a wide variety of approaches from using CD-roms to use of the company intranet and the Internet. More sophisticated approaches do not confine e-learning to interactive learning at a distance. Increasingly, synchronous learning is used where all participants log on at the same time, with a tutor or facilitator being available online. Individuals can progress through material alone or network with others to complete a task and use chatrooms and have a dialogue with the tutor. Videoconferencing can also be used to bring participants together at the same time. For example, some MBAs have been delivered via videoconferencing rather than classroom-based teaching. Web 2.0 interactive technology has also widened the possibilities, as we demonstrated in Chapter 16.

The advantages of e-learning are that:

- Learning can often take place at a convenient time, for example when the job is less busy meaning that it is less disruptive
- Learning does not usually have to be planned in and can be used opportunistically as time becomes available
- Learning does not have to take place during working hours
- E-learning can be cost effective when delivering a unit to a large number of employees
- Modules or units can be completed when topics are relevant to job demands, rather than according to schedule determined by others

- When a learning need is identified development via e-learning can take place immediately rather than waiting for a slot on a course
- Large numbers of employees can all be trained at the same time, for example where there is a new product launch, rather than waiting for a slot on a course
- E-learning means that the training delivered is always consistent and not dependent on tutor or manager skills
- Learners can take as long as they need to progress rather than being constrained by a timetable that applies to all
- The material produced for e-learning is sustainable and easy to update and can be customised
- E-learning can encompass virtual reality in training, for example preparing employees to deal with dangerous situations where it would be inappropriate to rely solely on learning on the job

Hammond (2001), for example, describes the case of Cisio which is constantly launching new IT-based products. The company has moved from 90 per cent classroom-based training for its sales representative to 80 per cent online training so that the large numbers of representatives can experience training immediately the product is launched. Channel 4 (Cooper 2001) has a strategy to replace much of its classroom teaching activity with interactive learning, and the London Emergency Services are using virtual reality training to prepare employees for emergency events, as in the London Underground example (Stevens 2010) on page 404 of this chapter.

Progress however has been modest despite high expectations. One of the reasons for this is that while organisations are often enthusiastic there has been much evidence of employees being unwilling to use e-learning. E-learning can be a solitary activity and is often very dependent on individual self-discipline, and there are some learners who will simply find that an interactive computer-based learning unit does not compare with the conviviality and action associated with attending a course. Thus motivation dwindles unless there is other support to encourage learners to complete the units they need. Computer literacy is another barrier for many employees. At one level this may be basic computer skills, but more sophisticated packages involving synchronous learning and joint learner tasks, bulletin boards and group/tutor dialogues can also be very difficult for many employees who have good everyday computer skills and they will need time to learn how particular packages work and how to use the facilities. If the right preparation and support are not made available employees can easily be put off by one difficult experience in which they found they could not keep up with the rest of the synchronous learning group. In some organisations access to the appropriate equipment was a problem for those employees who did not have a personal computer on their desks. There is evidence that some initial concerns were perhaps unfounded. For example in the Indian banking sector Mittal (2008) found that older age did not compromise the effectiveness of e-learning and nor did a lower job level.

There was much initial euphoria about what e-learning could contribute but increasingly it has been recognised that motivating learners is critical and most organisations now have much more realistic expectations of what e-learning can achieve, and often have to improve and re-launch e-learning solutions before they bed in. The support provided may well be critical, as may the way that such methods are introduced and used.

> **WINDOW ON PRACTICE**
>
> **A different slant on e-learning**
>
> Virtual Reality has been around for many years in the gaming world but it is only recently that learning and development professionals have begun to grasp the potential that this technology has to offer.
>
> For example 'Second Life'™ produced by Linden, is a site that can be used just for fun, but also for learning and development. In this 'second life' world an individual creates a virtual persona, called an avatar, and engages with other avatars, involving themselves in making and selling things, education, discussion groups and so on as in the real world.
>
> Organisations that use it as a vehicle for people development may have a custom version of the world built for them, sometimes creating their office, store or campus so that learners experience a virtual world which mirrors their real one.
>
> Virtual worlds can be used to give individuals experience of trying out new skills, learning new ideas and making mistakes. There is the potential for individuals to 'meet' and engage with others in ways that would be difficult in the real world. One way that the virtual worlds can be used for people development is for there to be a 'scripted' approach. This means that some of the avatars are controlled to create situations which can then be discussed afterwards. 'Open access' (that is not scripted) learning may also be used, for example for team exercises where teams address a challenge and are given feedback, just as on an 'outdoor' team training event.
>
> Sources: www.secondlife.com; CIPD (2008) 'Virtual worlds and learning: using Second Life at Duke Corporate Education', CIPD case study from www.cipd.co.uk; Syedain, H. (2008) 'Out of this world', *People Management*, Vol. 14, No. 8, 17 April, pp. 20–3.

The difficulties experienced with e-learning have focused some organisations on understanding where e-learning fits with other approaches to learning and using it in ways that provide the most value. For example e-learning can be very effectively used before a face-to-face course to do pre-work so that for example all attendees are starting from a roughly similar knowledge base. In this case those employees who have the knowledge base already can be exempt, while e-learning enables the others to get up to speed before the course begins. Similarly e-learning can be used effectively for course briefings and general preparation, such as the completion and analysis of pre-course questionnaires and other pre-work which saves time at the beginning of the event itself.

At the end of a course e-learning can be used for refreshers, for self-checking of understanding and planning how to apply the learning gained on the course. Similarly e-learning can be used in combination with manager coaching. This has led to the term 'blended learning' which is often used to indicate the blending of e-learning with face-to-face learning experiences, while others use it more broadly to indicate 'a range of ways that e-learning can be delivered when combined with multiple additional routes that support and facilitate learning' (Sloman and Rolph 2003: 6).

Blended learning is increasingly used to indicate a blend of any approaches to learning, and there is evidence that learning and training now involve a much wider range of activities (CIPD 2006); for example Pickard (2006) reports on the blended learning approach at the Department for Work and Pensions which integrates self-managed learning, coaching and e-learning.

In conclusion, e-learning has a critical role to play but it would be dangerous to see it as the answer to all learning needs and the future of learning and development at work. Its value is best exploited where it is the most appropriate approach to meeting key development needs, such as preparing for dangerous tasks by using virtual reality, and where it can be combined with other learning activities to ensure a more complete learning experience and where it particularly suits the learning style of the individual learner.

> **WINDOW ON PRACTICE**
>
> **Julie Scumming at AXA**
>
> Clarke (2006) recounts a very inventive learning experience at AXA, highly job based and involving a variety of activities. The exercise started with a Christmas card from a fictitious employee Julie Scumming. Posters followed announcing her arrival and then her fictitious husband entered the offices, shouting. After this there were diary entries on the intranet from both Julie and her boss which staff began to follow, and picked up the story that Julie was a devout Christian who felt she was being discriminated against and bullied by her boss and peers. Dummy tabloid articles were circulated, a stand-up row in the canteen was performed by actors. Sticky notes were put on computers saying not to get 'stuck like Julie', and an advent calendar counted down the days to the main event which was a tribunal hearing for managers. When the tribunal panel retired to consider their verdict actors acted out scenes which had led up to the tribunal. Meanwhile employees could log on to discussion forums to express their views about the case, and there was a poll about the anticipated results. Involvement in all of this was voluntary but many staff participated. The objective was to raise awareness about discrimination issues. Responses to questionnaires after the event demonstrated that managers were more aware of religious discrimination issues.
>
> Source: Clarke, E. (2006) 'Julie Diligent', *People Management*, Vol. 12, No. 14, 13 July, pp. 32–43.

EVALUATION OF TRAINING AND DEVELOPMENT

One of the most nebulous and unsatisfactory aspects of the training job is evaluating its effectiveness, yet it is becoming more necessary to demonstrate value for money. While Campbell (2006) estimates that employer, public and individual spend on workforce training and development in the UK nears £30 billion each year, Phelps (2002) suggests there is no satisfactory return on investment calculation to prove its value, and that we remain unsure whether training breeds success or success breeds training. Evaluation is straightforward when the output of the training is clear to see, such as reducing the number of dispatch errors in a warehouse or increasing someone's typing speed. It is more difficult to evaluate the success of a management training course or a programme of social skills development, but the fact that it is difficult is not enough to prevent it being done. Cunningham (2007), however, suggests that there is a danger that trainers and developers become too focused on trying to prove return on investment, and he works with an organisation where the focus of evaluation is for the trainees to present to their sponsors/managers their assessment of value that they and the organisation have gained from their learning.

A familiar method of evaluation is the post-course questionnaire, which course members complete on the final day by answering vague questions that require them to assess aspects of the course using only such general terms as 'good', 'very good' or 'outstanding'. The drawbacks with such questionnaires are, first, that there is a powerful halo effect, as the course will have been, at the very least, a welcome break from routine and there will probably have been some attractive fringe benefits such as staying in a comfortable hotel and enjoying rich food. Second, the questionnaire tends to evaluate the course and not the learning, so that the person attending the course is assessing the quality of the tutors and the visual aids, instead of being directed to examine what has been learned.

Hamblin (1974), in a much-quoted work, identified five levels of evaluation: (1) evaluating the training, as in the post-course questionnaire above; (2) evaluating the learning, in terms of how the trainee now behaves; (3) evaluating changes in job performance; (4) evaluating changes in organisation performance; and (5) evaluating changes in the wider contribution that the organisation now makes. Perhaps the most well-referenced approach to evaluation is Kirkpatrick (1959) who suggested four levels of evaluation, somewhat similar to Hamblin: (1) reaction level; (2) learning level (have the learning objectives been met?); (3) behaviour (how has the individual's behaviour changed after returning to the job?); and (4) results and impact on the bottom line (what is the impact of training on performance?).

Measuring performance effectiveness after a learning intervention involves identifying changes in behaviour, knowledge, skills and attitudes and it is important that the criteria for evaluation are built into development activities from the very beginning, and not tagged on at the end. Lingham and his co-researchers (2006) provide a good example of how this can be done in practice. They describe an action research project where evaluation was built in from the outset and involved collaboration between organisational leaders, trainers, participants and evaluators. A four-phase approach was used:

- Phase 1: Design of training programme (organisational leaders, trainers and evaluators agree design and methods to obtain feedback from participants after the initial runs of the training programme).
- Phase 2: Launch and evaluation of initial programme (training conducted and agreed methods used to collect participants' views).
- Phase 3: Feedback and design of evaluation instrument (organisational leaders, trainers and evaluators meet to review feedback and field notes and adapt the training programme where necessary. A survey instrument designed for evaluation of future iterations of the programme).
- Phase 4: Ongoing training and evaluation (training programme conducted with new design/content, evaluation survey used and results fed back into Phase 3.

(adapted from Lingham *et al.* 2006)

SUMMARY PROPOSITIONS

18.1 There are four perspectives on learning: behaviourist, cognitive, social and constructivist. Each has different implications for the approach taken to training and development.

18.2 The emphasis has moved from training to learning, with individuals taking ownership of their own learning needs. To be effective learners we need to understand the nature of learning and our own strengths and weaknesses.

18.3 Behavioural competencies are useful for identifying learning needs and assessing learning progress.

18.4 The emphasis on formal development programmes is declining in favour of greater interest in approaches to on-the-job development, such as coaching, mentoring, peer relationships and self-development.

18.5 There has been an upsurge of interest in e-learning. However, the extent to which employees take advantage of such opportunities will be affected by the context and the support available. E-learning is increasingly being blended with other forms of learning.

18.6 Evaluation of development is critical but difficult. It is most effective when built into the design of the development activity rather than tagged on at the end.

GENERAL DISCUSSION TOPICS

1 If learning is an individual process, why is so much training done in groups? What are the implications of moving towards more individualised learning?

2 Discuss the view that the role of the trainer/facilitator is critically important in the effectiveness of a training programme.

FURTHER READING

CIPD (2009) *E-learning Progress and Prospect: A CIPD factsheet.* London: CIPD.
A useful summary of types of e-learning, measures of take-up to date and guidance on implementation.

Neilsen, A. and Norrekit, H. (2009) 'A discourse analysis of the disciplinary power of management coaching', *Society and Business Review*, Vol. 4, No. 3, pp. 202–14.
This is a fascinating and thought-provoking review of the literature on coaching from the point of view of control. The article finds that there are two approaches to coaching: employee coaching which seems to involve action control and direct monitoring; and executive coaching which appears to involve the control of the spirit as well as results and achievements and the authors argue that this acts as a constraint of the individual's self-realisation project. They conclude that coaching can be a stronger disciplining technique than control by targets/numbers.

Passmore, J. (ed.) (2006) *Excellence in Coaching: The industry guide*. London: Kogan Page.
A combination of contributions from both academics and practitioners provides expertise in a range of areas relevant to coaching.

Slotte, V. and Herbert, A. (2008) 'Engaging workers in simulation-based e-learning', *Journal of Workplace Learning*, Vol. 20, No. 3, pp. 165–80.
This is a lovely example of how simulation-based e-learning and face-to-face methods can be combined. The authors explain how this approach was used in a bookstore to develop customer service skills. The simulation package presented scenarios of different types of difficult customer and staff initially worked with a live coach to facilitate their discussions of how to approach each situation, and offer concepts where appropriate. They found this thought provoking and their discussions continued after the end of the one-day initial programme. Later they continued to use the simulation programme with virtual coaching from 'Esko' who gave continuous feedback. Some said they preferred this mechanical feedback to their responses to different scenarios in that it felt safer to try out alternatives and make mistakes.

REFERENCES

Abraham, S., Karns, L., Shaw, K. and Mena, M. (2001) 'Managerial competencies and the managerial appraisal process', *Journal of Management Development*, Vol. 20, No. 10, pp. 842–52.

Anderson, V. (2009) 'Research: line manager as coach', *People Management*, 21 May, p. 42.

Arney, E. (2006) 'Insider's Guide', *People Management*, Vol. 12, No. 23, pp. 40–2.

Baruch, Y. and Leeming, A. (2001) 'The added value of MBA studies: graduates' perceptions', *Personnel Review*, Vol. 30, No. 5, pp. 589–601.

Boak, G. (1991) *Developing Managerial Competencies. The management learning contract approach*. London: Pitman.

Boyatzis, R. (1982) *The Competent Manager*. New York: John Wiley.

Boyatzis, R. (2008) 'Guest Editorial: competencies in the 21st century', *Journal of Management Development*, Vol. 27, No. 1, pp. 5–12.

Boyatzis, R. (2009) 'Guest editorial: competencies as a behavioural approach to emotional intelligence', *Journal of Management Development*, Vol. 28, No. 9, pp. 749–70.

Broadbridge, A. (1999) 'Mentoring in retailing: a tool for success?', *Personnel Review*, Vol. 28, No. 4.

Brockett, J. (2006) 'Energy firm gets party vibe', *People Management*, Vol. 12, No. 10, p. 12.

Campbell, M. (2006) 'Demonstrating the value of learning, training and development', in *Latest Trends in Learning, Training and Development: Reflections on the 2006 Learning and Development Survey*. London: CIPD.

Carroll, S. and Gillen, D. (2001) 'Exploring the teaching function of the managerial role', *Journal of Management Development*, Vol. 21, No. 5, pp. 330–42.

CIPD (2006) *Learning and Development: Annual Survey 2006*. London: CIPD.

CIPD (2008) 'Virtual worlds and learning: using Second Life™ at Duke Corporate Education', CIPD case study from **www.cipd.co.uk**.

CIPD (2009) *Learning and Development Annual Survey, 2009*. London: CIPD.

Clarke, E. (2006) 'Julie diligent', *People Management*, Vol. 12, No. 14, 13 July, pp. 32–43.

Cooper, C. (2001) 'Connect four', *People Management*, February.

Cottee, P. (2006) 'Oliver's army', *People Management*, Vol. 12, No. 19, 28 September, pp. 44–5.

Cunningham, I. (2007) 'Viewpoint: sorting out evaluation of learning and development: making it easier for ourselves', *Development and Learning in Organisations*, Vol. 21, No. 5, pp. 4–6.

Ehrich, L. (2008) 'Mentoring and women managers: another look at the field', *Gender in Management: An International Journal*, Vol. 23, No. 7, pp. 469–83.

Fowler, J. and O'Gorman, J. (2005) 'Mentoring functions: a contemporary view of the perceptions of mentees and mentors', *British Journal of Management*, Vol. 16, pp. 51–7.

Hall, L. (2006) 'Inside job', *People Management*, Vol. 12, No. 16, pp. 34–6.

Hamblin, A.C. (1974) *Evaluation and Control of Training*. Maidenhead: McGraw-Hill.

Hammond, D. (2001) 'Reality bytes', *People Management*, January.

Harrison, R. (2009) *Learning and Development*, 5th edn. London: CIPD.

Hayes, J., Rose-Quirie, A. and Allinson, C. (2000) 'Senior managers' perceptions of the competencies they require for effective performance: implications for training and development', *Personnel Review*, Vol. 29, No. 1, pp. 92–105.

Honey, P. and Mumford, A. (1989) *A Manual of Learning Opportunities*. Maidenhead: Peter Honey.

IDS (2006a) *Coaching in the Workplace*. HR Studies No. 831, October. London: IDS.

IDS (2006b) *E-Learning*. HR Studies No. 818. London: IDS.

IDS (2008) *Competency Frameworks*. HR Study No. 865, March. London: IDS.

IDS (2009) *Coaching and Mentoring*. HR Study No. 897, July. London: IDS.

Kirkpatrick, D. (1959) 'Techniques for evaluating training programs', *Journal of the American Society of Training Directors*, Vol. 13, pp. 3–26.

Kolb, D.A., Rubin, I.M. and McIntyre, J.M. (1984) *Organization Psychology*, 4th edn. Englewood Cliffs: Prentice-Hall.

Kram, K.E. (1983) 'Phases of the mentor relationship', *Academy of Management Journal*, Vol. 26, No. 4, pp. 608–25.

Kram, K.E. and Isabella, L.A. (1985) 'Mentoring alternatives: the role of peer relationships in career development', *Academy of Management Journal*, Vol. 28, No. 1, pp. 110–32.

Lingham, T., Richley, B. and Rezania, D. (2006) 'An evaluation system for training programs: a case study using a four-phase approach', *Career Development International*, Vol. 11, No. 4, pp. 334–51.

Longenecker, C. and Ariss, S. (2002) 'Creating competitive advantage through effective management education', *Personnel Review*, Vol. 21, No. 9, pp. 640–54.

Mahony, D. (2009) 'Coaches need supervision too', *People Management*, 24 September, p. 33.

Maxwell, G. (2009) 'Mentoring for enhancing females' career development: the bank job', *Equal Opportunities International*, Vol. 28, No. 7, pp. 561–76.

Megginson, D. (1994) 'Planned and emergent learning: a framework and a method', *Executive Development*, Vol. 7, No. 6, pp. 29–32.

Megginson, D. and Whitaker, V. (1996/2007) *Cultivating Self-development*. London: IPD.

Mittal, M. (2008) 'Evaluating perceptions on effectiveness of e-learning programs in Indian banks: identifying areas for improvement', *Development and Learning in Organisations*, Vol. 22, No. 2, pp. 12–14.

Monks, K., Barker, P. and Mhanachain, A. (2001) 'Drama as an opportunity for learning and development', *Personnel Review*, Vol. 20, No. 5, pp. 414–23.

Nielsen, K. (2009) 'A collaborative perspective on learning transfer', *Journal of Workplace Learning*, Vol. 21, No. 1, pp. 58–70.

Oglensky, B. (2008) 'The ambivalent dynamics of loyalty in mentorship', *Development and Learning in Organisations*, Vol. 61, No. 3, pp. 419–49.

Phelps, M. (2002) 'Blind faith', *People Management*, Vol. 8, No. 9, p. 51.

Phillips, L. (2006) 'BUPA stars', *People Management*, Vol. 12, No. 22, pp. 30–2.

Phillips, L. (2009a) '"Virtual building sites" at new training centre', *People Management*, 29 January, p. 10.

Phillips, L. (2009b) 'Dell to roll out "reverse mentoring"', *People Management*, 22 October, p. 12.

Pickard, J. (2006) 'Suits ewe', *People Management*, Vol. 12, No. 12, pp. 36–7.

Prickett, R. (1997) 'Screen savers', *People Management*, 26 June, pp. 36–8.

Salaman, G. and Taylor, S. (2002) 'Competency's consequences: changing the character of managerial work', paper presented at the ESRC Critical Management Studies Seminar: Managerial Work. Cambridge: The Judge Institute of Management.

Santos, A. and Stewart, M. (2003) 'Employee perceptions and their influence on training effectiveness', *Human Resource Management Journal*, Vol. 13, No. 1, pp. 27–45.

Sloman, M. and Rolph, J. (2003) *E-learning: The learning curve – The change agenda*. London: CIPD.

Smethurst, S. (2006) 'Staying power', *People Management*, Vol. 12, No. 7, pp. 34–6.

Stevens, M. (2010) 'Fake station offers real training', *People Management*, 28 January, p. 12.

Syedain, H. (2008) 'Out of this world', *People Management*, Vol. 14, No. 8, pp. 20–3.

Whiddett, S. and Kandola, B. (2000) 'Fit for the job?', *People Management*, 25 May, pp. 30–4.

JUST DESSERTS – REWARDING AND PERFORMING

Chapter 13

Employee reward

Amanda Thompson and Alan J. Ryan

Objectives

- To present the historical and theoretical foundations underpinning contemporary employee reward practice.
- To define employee reward and identify the key components of reward.
- To explore the concept of reward management and the benefits and difficulties associated with introducing a strategic approach to reward.
- To consider key employee reward choices facing organisations.
- To explore the economic and legal context for reward and the implications for employee reward practice.
- To identify the internal/organisational factors affecting organisational approaches to reward and the influence of sector.
- To consider key choices and emergent trends in terms of establishing pay levels, designing pay structures and determining criteria for pay progression.

Introduction

This chapter identifies and discusses developments in employee reward and considers the practical ways in which reward management can be used, as part of a suite of human resource practices, to elicit employee engagement and drive individual and organisational performance. The chapter traces the historical path of reward, focusing initially on the nature of the wage–effort bargain and previous, somewhat limited approaches to reward, revolving principally around the key construct of pay. The chapter then moves to identify and explore the meaning of reward in the contemporary setting, focusing upon reward as a potential strategic lever which can be used by organisations to orient individuals and teams in the direction of business goals and values. The overarching themes of the remainder of the chapter concern the economic and legal environment for reward and the challenges associated with designing a reward strategy that is affordable, equitable and relevant. Embedded within these themes, emphasis is placed on pragmatic reward choices and dilemmas experienced by organisations in the twenty-first century, including decisions about the relative importance of internal equity and external pay comparability, the role of job evaluation, the factors which tend to be influential in shaping the reward 'mix', where to pitch pay and how to design pay structures and manage pay progression.

The historical and theoretical foundations of employee reward

We now outline and examine the extent to which human resource management (HRM) has developed current practical and theoretical issues surrounding the management of reward systems within modern organisations. A critical element of these discussions is the management of structures and strategies. This chapter introduces the notion of reward(s) as a central function in the development of a strategic role for HR functionaries and offers some explanation of the objectives of current reward management structures, strategies and systems.

'There's only one reason we come here – the money' has not been an unusual comment heard from employees in all organisations since the period of industrialisation. Such comments echo the nature of the employment relationship as a reward/effort bargain (Chapter 11). Whether openly, covertly, personally or collectively, we all become involved in the resolution of this bargain at some time during our working life. This chapter discusses how management have resolved and continue to resolve their problem of converting the labour potential, obtained by their transactions in the labour market, into the labour performance they desire; simply securing the required effort levels without rewarding at levels detrimental to the generation of sufficient profit. In this sense we view reward as a core function for HR managers and rewards as composed of more than the mere 'notes' in the pay packet. Terms such as 'pay', 'compensation' and 'remuneration' are all recognisable expressions, but as we argue below 'reward' is something qualitatively different in that the issues covered encompass both financial and non-financial benefits.

The development of reward systems

As a distinctive concern for managerial functionaries, the topic of reward is a recent addition, indeed it is fair to say that reward management has often been viewed as the 'poor relation'. Within the early labour management literature, it was discussed in terms of the management of figures and procedures (Urwick, 1958; Yates, 1937). Such discussions clearly view 'reward' as solely a matter of financial benefits (wage/effort) rather than including consideration of the non-financial benefits. We can argue from this initial analysis that during the development of a 'factory-based' system, in the late nineteenth/early twentieth centuries, it appears wage, rather than effort, was the central concern. Further that this period was accompanied by a system within which owners frequently found difficulty in securing consistent levels of control of the effort side of the bargain (Hinton, 1986; Lovell, 1977; Zeitlin, 1983). Employees, who were until that time self-controlled and in many respects driven by subsistence needs, had worked in small 'cottage' industries within which the product of labour was owned by the producers (workers themselves; notably in regard to the skilled artisans) and they worked only as hard as necessary in order to meet their subsistence needs. As Anthony suggests, 'A great deal of the ideology of work is directed at getting men [sic] to take work seriously when they know that it is a joke' (1977: 5).

Owners found that getting workers to keep regular hours and to commit the effort owners considered to constitute 'a fair day's work' was problematic. In response to this dilemma they employed the 'butty' system of wage management. Under this system, owners committed a specific level of investment to a selected group of workers (normally skilled artisans) who then hired labour on 'spot contracts' by the day. The major problem for the owners with this system was that these 'subcontractors' had control over the effort/reward bargain and were able to enrich themselves at the expense of the owners. The owners enjoyed little or no control over the process of production so the system was economically inefficient and failed to deliver the returns (rents/profits) required or more importantly the returns that were possible from the process of industrialisation.

From this group of 'favoured' workers, along with the introduction of some university graduates there grew a new management cadre. This was a slow process, Gospel notes that generally, in UK industry, this group (management, technical and clerical) amounted to only 8.6 per cent of the workforce in most manufacturing organisations by the start of the First World War (1992: 17). It can be further argued that even within these organisations the development of a dedicated, specialised managerial function was uneven and patchy. These changes did little to address the problems associated with the wage/effort bargain, meaning productivity was below optimum levels. A key component in these problems was that they were underpinned by the actuality that 'the managers' brain was still under the workers' cap', or more precisely that these new managers rarely possessed the skills or knowledge of the production process held by the workers. This led to lower than optimum levels of production and reduced profits, a system F.W. Taylor described as 'systematic soldiering'. This activity was engaged in by workers, according to Taylor, 'with the deliberate object of keeping their employers ignorant of how fast work can be done' (Taylor, 1964: 74). From his observations Taylor took the view that workers acting in this manner were merely behaving as 'economically rational actors' desiring their own best interests. It was clear therefore that management needed to take the reins of the production process and reclaim their right to determine the outcome of the wage/effort bargain.

Taylor, as the so-called 'father of scientific management', developed a system of measuring work, which assisted the process of reclaiming managerial rights. Jobs were broken down into specific elements which could then be timed and rated, whilst in the process, returning the determination of the speed of work to management and allowing for the development of pay systems which reflected, however crudely, performance. This scientific system devised by Taylor became the basis of countless pay systems operating effectively alongside the routinisation and deskilling of work which is often associated with scientific management within the literature (see, for example, Braverman, 1974; Burawoy, 1985; Hill, 1981; Littler, 1982, 1985; Thompson, 1983; Wood, 1982). Whilst this allowed management to reassert their control over the level of outputs, to relocate the managers' brain under their own hats and hence the determination of the wage/effort bargain, it did generate problems in relation to managerial attempts to convince workers to take work seriously. In straightforward terms we can suggest that the 'measured-work' techniques advocated by adherents of Taylorism further separated conception from execution and led to feelings of alienation. Alienation can be defined as 'various social or psychological evils which are characterized by a harmful separation, disruption or fragmentation which sunders things that properly belong together' (Wood, 2000: 24); in our terms that means the separation of workers from that which they produce. Blauner (1964) argued that such an objective state is created as an offshoot of the subjective feelings of separation which workers experience under modern production systems. These feelings and their outcomes can be briefly outlined in the following manner:

- *Powerlessness*: the inability to exert control over work processes.
- *Meaninglessness*: the lack of a sense of purpose as employees only concentrated on a narrowly defined and repetitive task and therefore could not relate their role to the overall production process and end product.
- *'Self-estrangement'*: the failure to become involved in work as a mode of self-expression.
- *Isolation*: the lack of sense of belonging (adapted from Blauner, 1964).

Although scientific management originated at the beginning of the twentieth century, its legacy has lived on in many areas. Similar experiences have been reported in the design of work in service industries and call centres (Ritzer, 1997, 2000; Taylor and Bain, 1999; Taylor and Bain, 2001; Callaghan and Thompson, 2001). The solution to this problem has been sought, following Taylor's notion of man as an economic actor, by the introduction of various reward systems and mechanisms, the core objectives of which were originally to operationalise effective control over the wage/effort bargain and later with current systems to alleviate the feelings of alienation and generate commitment to organisational goals.

In this regard it is possible to argue that such reward systems are not designed in the 'perfect world' that some commentators have imagined. Rather they are controlled by various external and internal stimuli and operate within a complex landscape. These incentives or pressures can be broken down and identified in simple terms which highlight some of the more complex debates we address within this chapter. In no particular order, we can see that they include the ability of the organisation to pay, which in the current times of financial restraint and turbulence is greatly reduced. To this we can add the bargaining strength – both internally and more widely – of trades unions. Whilst the decline in trade union membership alongside the rise in non-union forms of representation (Dundon and Rollinson, 2004; Gollan 2007), and the increased importance of small firms (Marlow *et al.*, 2005) especially within the private sector, may have weakened such power there are still sectors within the economy where organisations have to make a judgement about the residual power available to trade unions. Such residual power is also a dynamic force behind moves to maintain differentials in line with existing custom and practice. A further element in this consideration is the wider increase in the 'cost of living' which places strains on both the employer and the employees. This is not ameliorated by the recent period of rapid technological change which has influenced labour markets and available skills patterns. Whilst organisational and technological change may have increased productivity, and hence arguably created increased profits, employers must decide what percentage of such increases can be used to develop wage systems which reflect current effort (see the discussion below on new pay). These pressures have been crystallised into three main features which affect the quantity given:

- labour market pressures – supply and demand;
- product markets – competition and demand;
- organisational factors – sector, technology and size (Milkovitch and Newman, 1996).

These consideration lead to a discussion of the extent to which employers can develop, design, and control reward systems in an ever-changing (some would say globalised) economy.

Design and debates

Whilst this chapter often discusses reward systems in a manner which appears to offer a chronological explanation, we would note that the development of a 'new' system does not indicate the total removal of other older mechanisms. Evidence suggests that in many modern organisations we continue to find both 'old' and 'new' pay systems operating in tandem, delivering control on different levels for various groups of workers (Armstrong and Brown, 2006; Armstrong and Stephens, 2005).

In terms of the types of reward mechanism applied, we can note the application of a number of different mechanisms based on 'time worked'. Time rates are mechanisms whereby reward is related to the number of hours worked and are often applied to manual workers in the form of hourly rates and non-manual workers by the application of monthly or annual salaries. In the past, these rates were set in a number of ways which relied on the power of employers to unilaterally lay down the appropriate amount, by statutory enactment, or by collective bargaining. Employer discretion has been limited in a number of ways by the introduction of statutory rules and regulations ranging from the Truck Acts, enacted in the mid nineteenth century which required payment in cash – an attempt to prevent the misuse by employers of 'factory shop vouchers' – to the 1891 Fair Wages Resolution which obliged employers on local or national government projects to pay the standard/recognised rate for a job. Both of these measures, along with the Wage Councils, which were first established in 1909, were modified or repealed in the 1980s – with the Agricultural Wages Board, due in part to employer support, being the only survivor. More recently the government has put in place the National Minimum Wage Act (1999) which sets hourly rates across the whole economy for various groups of workers – primarily manual workers. These rates were set following meetings of the Low Pay Commission and graduated according to the age of the worker concerned.

A criticism of time-based mechanisms is that they are often related to historic rather than current value, and can result in discrimination, demarcation disputes and a sense of injustice. Such time-related mechanisms are often based on the notion of a pay hierarchy in which groups of jobs/skills are banded. Although widely applied basic versions of these instruments are poor in terms of relating wage to current effort; often rewarding effort which has been applied externally (gaining a recognised skill) and is inappropriate to current tasks. The advantages of these systems are that management can control wage costs by

(a) limiting the access to various grades in the hierarchy;

(b) by limiting the range of the grade (say 4 per cent top to bottom); and

(c) demonstrating they are fair in relation to agreed procedures.

The problems created are not necessarily with the pay hierarchy system per se but with the manner in which skills relating to specific grades are defined; solutions must then address the structure, strategy and rationale of the reward system rather than the application of such mechanisms.

Bowey and Lupton (1973) developed a scheme for highlighting the manner in which such hierarchies are built and sustained. They argued that five factors are in play when selecting, deciding the location of each job within the hierarchy. These were:

- skill;
- responsibility;
- mental effort;
- physical effort; and
- working conditions (Bowey and Lupton 1973).

Using these factors it is possible to identify similarities between jobs rather, than is the case with standard job evaluation schemes, differences. Following the identification of these similarities it is possible to locate various jobs within the pay hierarchy. What is more difficult is to translate this identification into a pay structure due to the various allocation or availability of the elements which make up an individual pay packet. Most conspicuous are the differences in the elements which are included in the individual pay packet at each level. So, for example, elements such as overtime, shift premium, individual bonus payments and other special allowances, lead to increased earnings for some groups but not others. It is possible, in part, to explain the gender differences in earnings by reference to these elements. Hellerstein and Newmark (2006) argue that the difference in directly observable reward maybe be founded on either productivity differences or pure (taste-based) discrimination. In adopting this residual wage approach to wage discrimination they suggest it is possible to estimate the true level of taste-based wage difference – whether looking at ethnicity, gender, age, disability or other forms of discrimination. (See discussion on equal pay below.)

Conboy (1976) noted that the key advantage of these time-based instruments is that both parties have a clear idea of the 'wage' element of the bargain. For management the problem is that these mechanisms do not give any clear indication of the 'effort' element of the bargain. This has led to time rate instruments being complicated by the addition of 'performance' elements, often in the form of 'piece-rates' or other complex 'bonus' calculations in an attempt to determine acceptable effort levels (e.g. predetermined motion time systems and measured-day-work). The traditional form of such schemes can be demonstrated using the diagram shown in Figure 13.1.

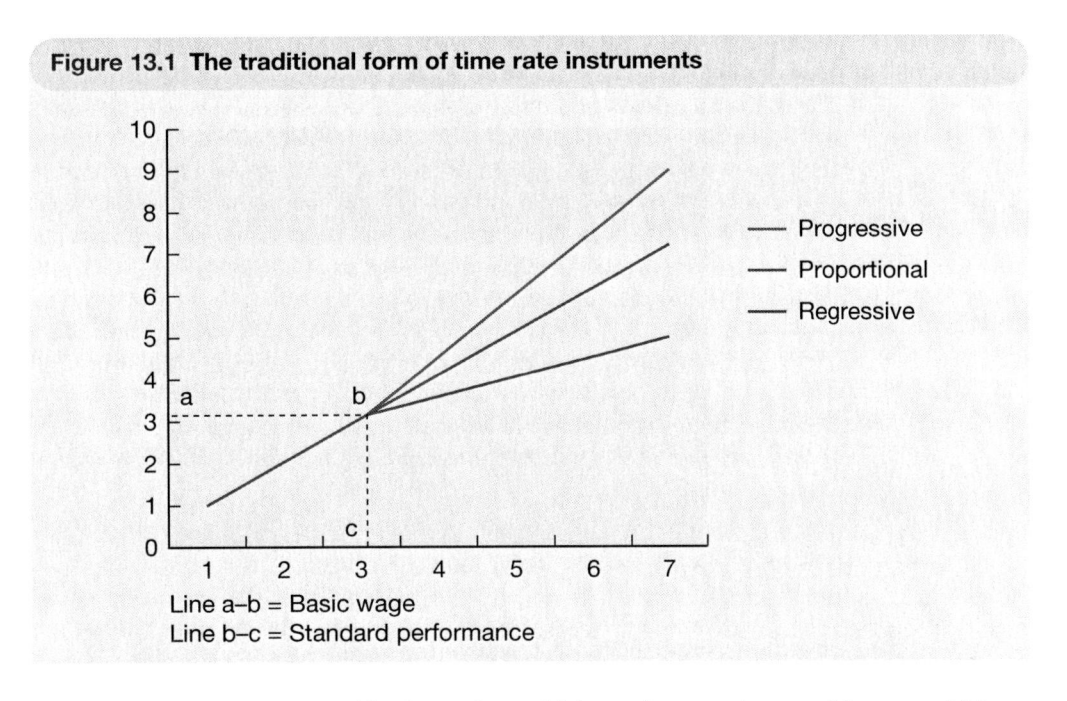

Figure 13.1 The traditional form of time rate instruments

```
10
 9
 8
 7 ─── Progressive
 6 ─── Proportional
 5 ─── Regressive
 4
 3  a         b
 2
 1
 0
    1  2  3  4  5  6  7
       c
```

Line a–b = Basic wage
Line b–c = Standard performance

Many schemes give guaranteed basic earnings which are then supplemented in ways which we can class as proportional (wages increase in direct relationship to output), progressive (wages increase more than output) or regressive (wages increase at a slower rate than output).

An important element in this discussion regards the manner in which the 'base' element is decided. We have become familiar with the notion of a National Minimum Wage, which sets the minimum rate for specified groups; outwith this scheme, organisations need some mechanisms by which to assign values to various roles within the organisation. Traditional mechanisms (and in a slightly modified manner 'new pay' systems) have related to hierarchy calculations or simplistic forms of job evaluation scheme. A job evaluation scheme operates by allocating values to each of a series of elements (e.g. skill or responsibility) and then measuring each 'job' in order to arrive at an agreed 'score'. The scores are then placed on the pay spine in relation to accepted criteria. These criteria will be formed by the interaction of two sets of relativities. Scores will need to reflect 'external relativities', by which we mean the situation that appears to hold in relation to external markets and environmental conditions, and 'internal relativities', meaning an appearance of fairness in relation to other jobs/roles within the organisation. In the basic form, these schemes introduce us to the notion of reward packages under which different elements can be rewarded in various ways. However, these schemes fell out of favour in some respects because they are seen to 'pay-the-job' rather than 'pay-the-worker', and as such were difficult to relate to individual performance (see the discussion below).

Time-based pay is clearly the simplest form of wage payment system, easily understood by both parties; it allows the development of 'overtime' payments for work completed in addition to the contracted hours in any given period and formed the basis of the creation of systems classed as payment by results (PBR). Early PBR schemes were time based in that they used the time accumulated by the pace of work as a percentage of the time allowed to form a foundation for the calculation of performance payments. So, in a simple form, if a task is timed to take 8 minutes but is completed in 6 then there is a saving of 25 per cent, but the increase in performance is 33⅓ per cent in that if the job is completed in 6 minutes then the 2 minutes left is equal to a third of the new job time. From the employers point of view therefore paying a 25 per cent bonus leaves a surplus per piece of 8⅓ per cent. This adds to the perceived advantages of this style of PBR linked to hierarchical reward systems by providing increased worker effort because they see the resultant higher pay within weeks and higher output.

During the twentieth century such structures/systems were widely used within British industry in an attempt to increase productivity. However, they are associated with a number of detrimental effects and disadvantages. Often the rates were negotiated following a work-measurement exercise which led to discontent and disillusionment. Too often operators can find easy ways around the rate in order to secure high earnings without the expected higher performance; these routes around the scheme often resulted in a reduced level of quality – in part because workers felt under pressure to produce and in part because quality and speed do not always combine. Further, by leaving the production levels in the hands of the workers it undermines managerial attempts to secure control and, indeed, may even be said to have resulted in both a loss of managerial prerogative and the abrogation of managerial roles. As these rates were often set within tightly defined employer/trade union collective agreements they encouraged the increased – notably during the 1950s–1970s – of local shop agreements which resulted in considerable 'wage drift' during a period of economic restraint. Many of these problems are to some extent mirrored in the bonus schemes within the financial sector in the twenty-first century.

We can conclude then that such payment by results systems, whilst originally crude, developed alongside the more extensive division of labour achieved by the increasing use and application of technology, ergonomics (pseudo-scientific work measurement) and mechanical production methods. These early techniques can be easily applied to such divided work because of four basic characteristics of such work:

- short job cycles;
- high manual content (which, using sophisticated ergonomic processes, can be measured);
- batch production (with repeated orders/processes);
- no marked fluctuations in required outputs (adapted from Conboy, 1976).

The simplistic assumptions underlying these and other PBR systems are twofold. First, workers are motivated to increase performance (work harder) by money, and second, any increases in output will result in equivalent increases in wages. The schemes are intended to be self-financing and designed to reduce 'wasteful activity' in that they can be used to redesign the labour process. Whilst such schemes now enjoy less popularity than they have in previous decades, there is still evidence that they are used in relation to specific groups of workers.

Hierarchy schemes in general continue to find favour especially amongst salaried staff. A key element of such schemes is the practice of incremental progression. Such schemes operate on the simple premise that advancing years of service result in additional reward because of loyalty or greater experience. Whilst they have recently been challenged – on the basis that they discriminate on the grounds of age – they continue to form a foundation for the solution of the labour problem for many organisations.

> **STOP and think**
>
> *To what extent do you think the solutions to the labour problem suggested so far reflect management's inability to clearly determine the 'effort' side of the bargain?*

Having set out the basic framework within which the wage/effort bargain can be viewed, we now move on to consider developments that are more recent. In the discussion that follows we move from an analysis of solutions to the labour problem founded on the cash nexus to a series of arguments which indicate more complex and considered solutions.

Employee reward

The subject of reward is vast and continually evolving, in short it has been described as a 'bundle of returns offered in exchange for a cluster of employee contributions' (Bloom and Milkovich, 1996: 25). This is a rather loose definition and sheds little light on what form 'returns' might take or what contribution employees might make to reap such returns. Usefully, the definition does, however, capture the multiplicity of returns and possible employee contributions, suggesting that reward comprises a blend of offerings and that employees' contributions can be numerous and eclectic.

The notion of a *range* of different forms of return in exchange for employee contributions of various types signals a departure from a narrow focus upon wages and effort. Wages or monetary return for the effort expended by employees, as charted in the opening part of this chapter, remain central to the employment relationship; however, the advent of the concept of reward, and more pointedly reward management, prompts organisations to consider the differing ways in which employees positively impact the organisation via a range of contributions (not restricted to effort) and how best to signify organisational appreciation. The practice of reward veers away from a single dimensional focus on wages and instead encompasses a plethora of financial and non-financial returns employees might potentially receive in exchange for favourable contributions to the organisation. In terms of employee contributions to the organisation, effort becomes but one input amongst many potential offerings, indeed its value to the organisation may well be considered less important and less attractive than other employee behaviours, for example, measureable *outcome-related* contributions. It is clear thus that reward is a more inclusive term than wages or payment and that it is used to denote a diverse range of devices at the organisation's disposal to recognise the role individuals and teams play in the operation of, and ultimate success of the business. Reward steps beyond the perimeters of compensation, remuneration and benefits terminology where emphasis is placed on pay and other settlements which carry a monetary value to a new plane in which almost anything could be construed as a return to employees for exhibiting desirable behaviour, from a cash bonus or health care benefit to employee involvement in decision making, increased role responsibility, autonomy, access to more interesting work and other factors relating to the nature of the work itself and the environment in which it is carried out.

Components of reward

As indicated above, reward comprises several elements, extending beyond base pay thus presenting employers with a number of complex decisions. The first of these is which components to include in the reward package and the associated rationale for inclusion or rejection. Further decisions entail whether to permit employees a degree of choice in the reward 'mix' so that they can, for example, sacrifice salary in exchange for benefits or indeed choose from a menu of benefits to a defined value or cash limit. In addition, employers have fundamental decisions to make concerning whether the reward offering will be standardised and universal (applied to all employees) or tailored and status/seniority related (Marchington and Wilkinson, 2008). Such decisions will be influenced by the nature of the external operating environment, the behaviour of competitors and a range of internal organisational factors; these key determinants of the features of organisational reward systems will be explored later within the chapter.

For all workers, base pay forms the starting point in the reward package. The term is used to denote the hourly rate, wage or annual salary employees are paid for the work they do based either upon some measure of job size or some aspect of the person, for example, qualifications, skill set or demonstrable competencies. Base pay is a critical component as it is used as the anchor rate for calculating redundancy payment entitlement, sick pay, pension level in a final salary scheme, overtime rates, as applicable, and other such employee rights. Base pay might be set deliberately low if, for example, commissions can be earned in excess and the organisation is keen to incentivise sales activity, base pay might also be suppressed where benefits are generous and so the overall worth of the reward bundle is considered to be commensurate with market rates. As is detailed later, however, the introduction of the National Minimum Wage (NMW) in April 1999 imposed minimum limits on base pay in an attempt to curb the problem of low pay in the economy, as a result employers are now obliged to adhere to minimum rates and review pay in accordance with changes in the NMW rates. The level of base pay awarded to employees and movement in base pay can be individually negotiated between managers and employees, unilaterally determined by owners/management, the subject of collective bargaining with relevant trades unions recognised within the industry and /or organisation or as occurs in some cases, set by National Pay Review Bodies.

Over and above base pay, further decisions may be made concerning supplementary payments attributable to skill or performance, for example, and other additions such as overtime, danger or dirt money, shift premium, bonuses or commissions. Dominant reward terminology refers to supplementary payments which are consolidated into base pay as forms of contingent pay and those that are non-consolidated as elements of variable pay (Armstrong, 2002). In practice, both forms of pay described are event- and/or behaviour-dependent and therefore not an assured, regular form of payment. Variable pay in particular is sometimes described as 'at risk' pay by being non-consolidated employees are compelled to repeat activities and behaviours to trigger variable pay in each subsequent business period and so secure a consistent level of reward. In addition, employees are disadvantaged in the sense that base pay, the driver of other entitlements, remains unaffected by variable pay, regardless of how frequently variable pay is awarded or what portion of total salary variable pay comprises. The combination of base pay plus variable pay and/or contingent pay represents total earnings and is reflected in the employee pay advice slip, yet entitlement to employee benefits enables the employee to accumulate additional remuneration. Employee benefits, sometimes called 'perks' (perquisites) or fringe benefits carry a financial value or afford the recipient tax advantages which result in a net financial gain, however in contrast to earnings, benefits are often presented in non-cash form. Where benefits are particularly generous and constitute a substantial component of the reward package they tend to be identified in job advertisements to indicate the total financial value of the role to potential applicants (see Box 13.1).

Benefits can be classified as *immediate, deferred or contingent*. Employees derive value from immediate benefits instantaneously, such benefits might include the provision of a company car, a laptop computer, discounts, expensed mobile phone or subsidised meals. Where benefits are deferred their value accrues and has a future rather than present value to the employee, a clear example of such a benefit is a pension plan or share scheme. Contingent benefits are

Box 13.1

West Midlands Fire Service

HR Officer (Employee Relations)

Salary: £25,146–£26,706 per annum + relocation + benefits

Royal Mail

HR Business Partners

South East/South West and Home Counties

Salary up to £60,000 per annum + benefits to include car allowance and bonus

Trafford College

Director of Human Resources

£54k plus contributory pension scheme

Source: People Management, 15, 2, January 2009.

those that are triggered in certain circumstances, for example sick pay schemes, paternity and maternity pay and leave arrangements. Rather than deferring to the aforementioned classification, Wright (2004: 182) prefers to consider benefits in four distinct groupings:

- *Personal, security and health benefits*: for example, pension, company sick pay scheme, life cover, medical insurance, loans.
- *Job-, status- or seniority-related benefits*: for example, company car, holiday leave beyond statutory minimum, sabbaticals.
- *Family friendly benefits*: for example, childcare or eldercare facilities, nursery vouchers, enhanced maternity/paternity/parental leave arrangements.
- *Social or 'goodwill' or lifestyle benefits*: for example, subsidised canteen, gym/sports facilities, discounts, ironing collection/dry cleaning.

Benefits can be voluntary, affording employees the choice whether to 'opt in' and use them according to their personal needs and financial position. Should employees elect to purchase benefits such as childcare vouchers, cycle-to-work scheme loan, life cover or pension contributions, arrangements tend to be set up for deductions to occur at source, this can attract tax advantages for the employee, for example, where childcare assistance is purchased. The 'Advantages' benefits package operated by DHL Logistics is typical of voluntary benefit schemes. It incorporates the company's Voyager pension scheme, childcare savings via the 'Care-4' scheme, Denplan dental care, AXA PPP healthcare and a range of leisure, health, motoring and financial discounts and offers. Details of the scheme are presented in a booklet distributed to all employees and staff take up is encouraged. To promote the scheme, further value illustrations are available to demonstrate to individual employees the total worth of the benefits should they choose to make use of 'Advantages'. A recent CIPD survey reports that voluntary benefit schemes are in use in 27 per cent of organisations (CIPD, 2008a). In other organisations benefits are universal, in other words provided to all and regarded as 'perks' of the job. This is in direct contrast to status or seniority-related benefits, which employees only qualify for if they have accrued the requisite number of year's service or are employed at or beyond a prescribed grade or level. Flexible benefit schemes or 'cafeteria benefits', so named because of the choices presented to employees, have been around for a number of years in some organisations, however, data depicting the prevalence of such schemes would suggest a degree of employer reticence. Of all the organisations surveyed by the CIPD (2008a) just 13 per cent operated flexible benefits and a further 12 per cent indicated plans to introduce such a scheme. Flexible schemes were present in 22 per cent of organisations with over 5000 staff, possibly indicating that larger workplaces are more likely to be able to resource a system of flexible benefits, both financially and logistically. Earlier data (Employee Benefits, 2003) estimated adoption of flexible benefits in around 8 per cent of organisations, again suggesting that this mode of providing employee benefits enjoys relatively narrow appeal. The basic premise of a flexible or cafeteria benefits scheme is that employees can spend up to a points limit or cash total, purchasing benefits from a defined menu. Cafeteria schemes may comprise fixed (inflexible, core) benefits and flexible ones (a so-called 'core plus' scheme) or offer complete freedom of choice to the maximum cash value/points value. In other schemes pre-packaged sets of benefits may be on offer to employees; these schemes are referred to as modularised benefits (Wright, 2004: 207).

It is difficult to generalise the provision of benefits as part of the overall reward package and predict the types of benefits any one organisation will deem appropriate to adopt. The impetus for providing benefits can be viewed from a number of perspectives:

- Do organisations see benefits as a way of compensating for lower pay or do higher pay and generous benefits tend to co-exist as part of a deliberate strategy aimed at attracting and retaining staff?
- Do employers select benefits in the belief that they will motivate employees and instil a greater sense of loyalty and commitment?

- Is benefit provision enhanced by employers where trade unions lobby successfully to expand the reward package on behalf of their members?
- Are benefits a mechanism for employer branding, the costs of which some organisations are prepared to bear? (Wright, 2009.)

The answers to these questions are intricate and beyond the scope of this chapter. We do know, however, that whilst employee benefits in themselves are a fairly steadfast feature of reward in the UK, recent years have witnessed some shifts in the types of benefits more commonly provided by employers. Wright (2009: 175) detects 'cutbacks in the most costly benefits and at the same time a growth in low-cost lifestyle and voluntary benefits'. She attributes such trends to the dual influences of the changing composition of the labour force (particularly the influx of mothers) and the need for employers to be economically prudent and focus on value for money as competition intensifies. These trends would seem to be reflected to some extent in the benefits top-ten (see Table 13.1), particularly in the list of benefits most commonly provided to all employees.

Non-financial reward

Whilst the components of reward identified and discussed so far have a financial basis, reward can also be non-financial, or relational (Brown and Armstrong, 1999), for example praise, thanks, opportunities to develop skills and recognition awards such as 'employee of

Table 13.1 Top ten employer-provided benefits by provision

Provided to all employees	Provision dependent on grade/seniority	Part of a flexible benefit scheme only
Training and career development (71%)	Mobile phone (business use) (58%)	Dental insurance (9%)
25 days' or more paid leave (67%)*	Car allowance (50%)	Childcare vouchers (6%)
Tea/coffee/cold drinks (free) (62%)	Company car (49%)	Critical illness insurance (5%)
Christmas party/lunch (free) (62%)	Private medical insurance (32%)	Cycle-to-work scheme loan (5%)
On-site car parking (60%)	Relocation assistance (25%)	Health screening (5%)
Childcare vouchers (56%)	Fuel allowance (21%)	Private medical insurance (5%)
Life assurance (51%)	25 days' or more paid leave (20%)*	Healthcare cash plans (4%)
Eyecare vouchers (46%)	On-site car parking (14%)	Permanent health insurance (3%)
Enhanced maternity/paternity leave (43%)	Permanent health insurance (13%)	Life assurance (3%)
Employee assistance programmes (42%)	Health screening (12%)	Gym (on-site or membership) (2%)

Percentage of respondents in brackets.
*Excludes statutory leave.

Source: from *Reward Management: A CIPD Survey*, CIPD (2009) p. 13, with the permission of the publisher, the Chartered Institute of Personnel and Development, London (www.cipd.co.uk).

the month', 'going the extra mile' and service awards. Awards are often publicly acknowledged in ceremonies and/or in company newsletters and notice boards thus communicating to the wider workforce the employee behaviours the organisation values and is prepared to reward. Non-financial rewards also include the general quality of working life (QWL), for example the work environment, flexibility, work-life balance, managerial style/attitude, job-role autonomy and responsibility plus opportunities for employee involvement and employee voice; collectively these factors might be termed the work 'experience'. Definitions of non-financial rewards are bound up with the concept of total reward described below, emphasising the potential benefits to be derived from considering reward in the broadest of senses. As Perkins and White conclude (2008: 315),

> definitions of non-financial reward are multi-faceted and often complex, requiring dissection of the elements to facilitate detailed cost–benefit analysis while simultaneously seeking to promote 'holistic employment experience' value greater than the sum of the parts.

Total reward

In recent years there has been interest in the notion of managing rewards such that the various components are carefully crafted together to support one another and so maximise the satisfaction employees experience in the course of, and as a result of their employment. This approach is the essence of a total rewards process (Armstrong and Murlis, 1998). WorldatWork (2000) loosely describe total rewards as all of the employer's available tools that may be used to attract, retain, motivate and satisfy employees, encompassing every single investment that an organisation makes in its people, and everything employees value in the employment relationship. The components of total rewards are succinctly presented in the model shown in Figure 13.2.

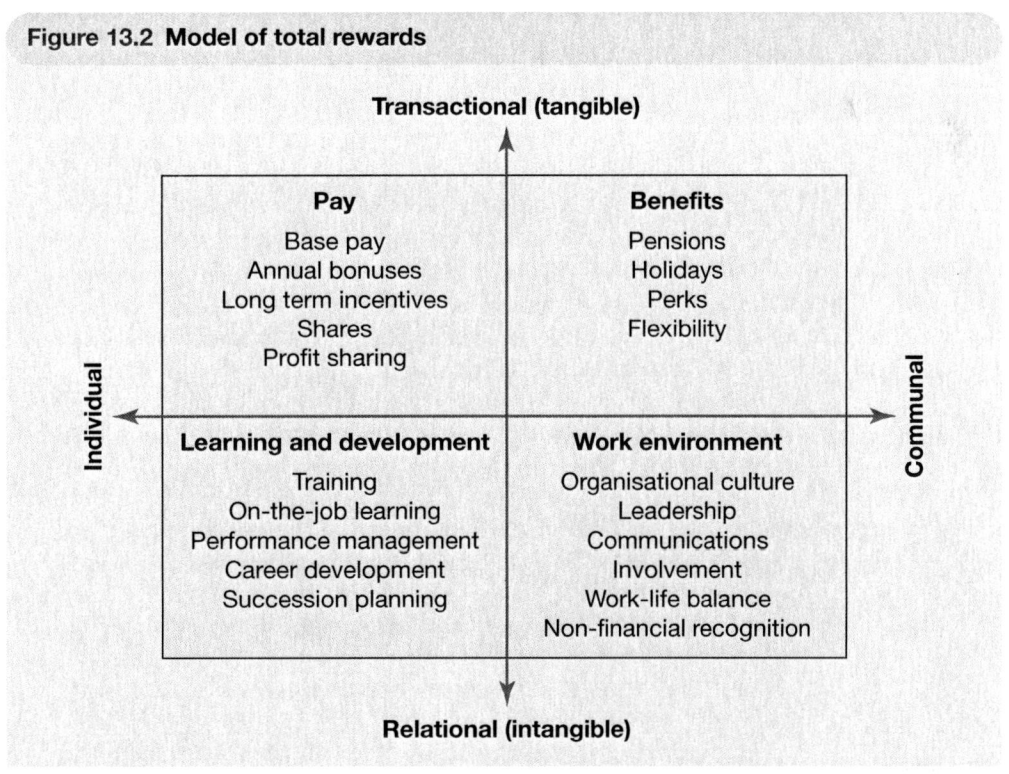

Figure 13.2 Model of total rewards

Transactional (tangible)

Pay	**Benefits**
Base pay	Pensions
Annual bonuses	Holidays
Long term incentives	Perks
Shares	Flexibility
Profit sharing	

Individual ←→ Communal

Learning and development	**Work environment**
Training	Organisational culture
On-the-job learning	Leadership
Performance management	Communications
Career development	Involvement
Succession planning	Work-life balance
	Non-financial recognition

Relational (intangible)

Source: Brown and Armstrong (1999: 81).

Thompson and Milsome (2001) insist that the concept of total rewards is necessarily holistic and integrative, it should also provide an approach to reward in the organisation which augurs well with the business objectives and desired organisational culture and as such is conflated with strategic approaches to reward. In addition, it is people centred, customised, distinctive (offering support to a unique employer brand) and it is evolutionary, in the sense that it is developed incrementally as opposed to the product of drastic, sudden change. A total rewards approach is reputed to offer potential for organisations striving to reduce costs, heighten visibility in a tight labour market, recruit and retain successfully, increase flexibility and improve productivity (Armstrong, 2002: 10) and so would certainly seem to 'tick the boxes' for contemporary organisations. In practice however, the latest CIPD Reward Survey (CIPD, 2009a) reports that only one fifth of organisations claim to have implemented total rewards while a further 22 per cent plan to introduce it during 2009. It could perhaps be deduced from these findings that a total rewards approach is somewhat elusive and difficult for employers to establish.

Reward management and the emergence of strategic approaches to reward

The term 'reward management' was first used in 1988 by Armstrong and Murlis to denote the development of a new field or collective set of activities to emerge within the arena of HRM. The new term recognised that static techniques, principally concerned with salary administration, were fast giving way to a more dynamic approach emphasising the use of pay (and other rewards) in a flexible and innovative way with the aim of improving individual, team and organisational performance. The activity 'reward management', has been described as encompassing not only the development, maintenance, communication, and evaluation of reward processes, but also concerned with the development of appropriate organisational cultures, underpinning core values and increasing the commitment and motivation of employees (Armstrong and Murlis, 1998).

It is, however, widely considered that the most effective approaches to reward are based upon careful consideration of an underlying philosophy and strategy that corresponds to overall business strategy (Taylor, 2008; Storey, 1992; Lawler, 1990). In accordance with this belief, the mantra follows that organisations should seek to ensure that the philosophy behind their approach to reward is in keeping with the organisation's values and beliefs and that reward strategy supports the achievement of wider corporate objectives; indeed this is part of the total rewards approach referred to earlier and strongly conveyed in the rhetoric of 'new pay' or 'strategic pay' purported by American writers Lawler (1990, 1995, 2000) and Schuster and Zingheim (1992). The precise function reward has to play in advancing organisational objectives, however, is unclear. Early models of strategic HRM such as the Harvard model (Beer *et al.*, 1984) placed reward centrally as an integral HR activity and Storey (1992) identified reward as a 'key strategic lever'. Resource-based models too suggest pay acts as an important lever and can support a firm in achieving sustained competitive advantage. Kessler (2001), however, still needs to be convinced that there is sound evidence based upon credible methodologies that reward contributes to business performance and leads to sustained competitive advantage. There must also be a degree of reservation about the ease with which reward strategy can be matched seamlessly with business strategy and the extent to which employees will respond as intended to reward mechanisms designed to elicit certain desired behavioural patterns (Lewis, 2006).

Despite these doubts it appears to have become established orthodoxy that a strategic approach to reward can be used to leverage the kinds of employee behaviours that contribute to business goals (Marchington and Wilkinson, 2008). Proponents of strategic reward suggest it is possible for reward strategies, intentionally or otherwise, to signal what the organisation considers important and what it clearly does not value. For example, reward strategies that rest on service-related salary increments are likely to convey messages that the organisation values loyalty and long tenure above all else whereas the use of competence-related pay would suggest a need for employees to develop and demonstrate core competences and job-specific competences. Table 13.2 seeks to demonstrate a number of aligned relationships between the key thrust of business strategy and the direction of reward strategy.

Table 13.2 Examples of alignment: reward strategy and business strategy

Business strategy	Reward strategy
Achieve value added by improving employee motivation and commitment	Introduce or improve performance pay plans – individual, team, gain sharing
Achieve added value by improving performance/productivity	Introduce or improve performance pay plans and performance management processes
Achieve competitive advantage by developing and making best use of distinctive core competencies	Introduce competence-related pay
Achieve competitive advantage by technological development	Introduce competence-related or skills-based pay
Achieve competitive advantage by delivering better value and quality to customers	Recognise and reward individuals and teams for meeting/exceeding customer service and quality standards/targets
Achieve competitive advantage by developing the capacity of the business to respond quickly and flexibly to new opportunities	Provide rewards for multi-skilling and job flexibility. Develop more flexible pay structures (eg. broad-banding)
Achieve competitive advantage by attracting, developing and retaining high-quality employees	Ensure rates of pay are competitive. Reward people for developing their competencies and careers (for example, using the scope made possible in a broad-banded grading structure)

Source: from *Reward srategy: How to develop a reward strategy. A CIPD Practical Tool*, CIPD (CIPD 2005) http://www.cipd.co.uk/subjects/pay/general/tools.htm?IsSrchRes=1, with the permission of the publisher, the Chartered Institute of Personnel and Development, London (www.cipd.co.uk).

STOP and think

*What messages does the reward strategy in your own organisation convey? Are these the messages that the organisation **intends** to convey?*

Reward strategy in practice

Latest CIPD survey information (CIPD, 2009a) illustrates that 26 per cent of the sample acknowledges the existence of a reward strategy within their organisations while a further 24 per cent plan to adopt one in 2009. These figures seem to show a retraction when compared with the same survey a year and indeed two years earlier (CIPD, 2007, 2008a). In 2008, 33 per cent of respondents claimed to have a reward strategy, in 2007 the corresponding figure was 35 per cent with a further 40 per cent of respondents planning to introduce one in the course of 2007, the 2008 findings would suggest that this was not something they did in fact manage to do! The 2009 survey ponders whether the falling portion of respondents claiming to have a reward strategy could be attributed to some organisations perhaps questioning whether they had a reward strategy in the first place, a kind of crisis of confidence, or whether some employers did have a strategy but have recently had to relinquish it due to the fragility of the economic climate (CIPD, 2009a: 6). Of those organisations claiming to have a reward strategy, 85 per cent maintain that implementing their reward strategy has been difficult at times. The survey shows that overall the main inhibitors to the effective operation of the reward strategy are budgetary constraints/pressures, line managers' skills and abilities, line management attitudes and staff attitudes, although respondents from different sectors report notably different barriers to success.

Concerns over the ability of organisations to mount strategic approaches to reward are not new. In research conducted by the Institute for Employment Studies, Bevan (2000: 2) commented that having a reward strategy sounded like a 'tall order'. To be successful, he argues, reward strategy is supposed to be downstream from business strategy and reinforce business goals, drive performance improvements within the business, deliver cultural and behavioural change, integrate horizontally with other HR practices and keep pay budgets under control, so 'little wonder that so many employers under-perform in the design and delivery of a truly strategic approach to reward – if such a thing exists' (2000: 2). The same IES research (Bevan, 2000) detected ten common mistakes responsible for contributing to the under achievement of many reward strategies. The errors revolve around design or delivery and are summarised in Table 13.3.

Table 13.3 Reward strategy: ten common mistakes (Bevan, 2000)

1	Starting at the end	Trying to emulate the reward system used by competitors without recognising unique organisational drivers and what the business strategy requires
2	Having no success criteria	Failing to think through the underpinning reward philosophy and objectives and what success might look like so little idea whether the reward strategy is performing
3	Trusting the business strategy	Problems with the business strategy, for example failure to articulate it clearly and the chance that business strategy changes faster than reward is able to follow
4	Equating complexity with flexibility	Trying to build over-elaborate reward systems in an attempt to appeal to a diverse workforce, this can have the effect of confusing employees such that they fail to see a clear line of sight between performance and reward
5	Confusing speed with haste	Trying to rush in new reward systems, potentially damaging employee relations and harming the culture of the organisation
6	Focus on excellence	Focusing reward on excellence in the minority as opposed to encouraging performance improvements among the majority
7	Ignoring pay architecture	Getting weighed down in detail, for example wrangles over performance markings, rather than paying proper attention to pay structures and frameworks used to facilitate reward decisions
8	Failing to get real 'buy-in'	Failing to get full commitment from senior managers and line managers
9	Having too much faith in line managers	Relying on the skills and abilities of line managers to make difficult reward decisions without the necessary training and support
10	Failing to integrate reward with other strands of HR	Lack of logic between reward processes and systems and other HR practices, this can be due to a variety of reasons including conflicting process goals, process ownership issues and timing

Source: Bevan (2000: 3)

> **STOP and think**
>
> *Do you recognise any of the above mistakes in your own organisation's efforts to design and implement a reward strategy capable of supporting and reinforcing strategic business objectives?*
>
> *Which mistakes have occurred and how might they be rectified?*

Key reward choices

Whilst accepting the notion of aligning reward to business strategy to optimise the utility of reward mechanisms a number of key, value-laden choices must be made in the process. Marchington and Wilkinson (2008: 464) suggest that there are five essential reward decisions an organisation needs to draw consensus on:

- what to pay for, job size, time, performance, skills/qualifications or some other person-centred attribute or behaviour;
- whether to place primary focus on internal equity when determining pay or be more concerned with external benchmarks;
- whether to operate a centralised or decentralised approach to reward or a hybrid with some central control and a degree of localised latitude;
- whether to build hierarchy into the reward system such that there are seniority or status related rewards or to devise a harmonised, single-status approach;
- the precise nature of the reward 'mix'.

Getting these decisions right is critical if reward is to reinforce the strategic direction of the organisation. Similarly, the decisions made need to be ones most likely to motivate individuals to orient their actions and behaviours towards business goals. This is demanding for any organisation given that motivation is individualised and complex. Thought needs to be invested in considering the extent to which different rewards are capable of motivating employees, the value of intrinsic and extrinsic motivation to employees, the role of pay in motivating people and the importance of equity in reward systems and reward management practices.

Motivation theory offers useful insight and can help guide the design and management of reward processes. Notably amongst the many theories of motivation, Herzberg's 'Two-Factor Theory' (Herzberg, 1966) suggests that pay is a *hygiene* factor rather than a motivator and so in itself it is unlikely to motivate. Herzberg contends that pay needs to be adequate to prevent dissatisfaction but other factors induce a motivational state such as responsibility and autonomy. This is, indeed, a salutary message particularly to those organisations that attempt to use pay or the prospect of financial rewards as an incentive for greater output, better quality or other outcomes they determine to be desirable.

Process theories of motivation such as 'Expectancy Theory' (Vroom, 1982) attempt to explain the internal thought processes that instil a motivational state. Expectancy theory offers us the insight that employee motivation is the result of a complex set of decisions and assumptions made by the individual. For an employee to be motivated and therefore to expend effort, the rewards on offer have to be something that the individual values (hold 'valence'), hence the importance of the reward 'mix. In addition, the individual must have belief that the rewards are achievable. An appreciation of expectancy theory encourages organisations to construct a clear 'line of sight' so that employees are in no doubt what it is they need to do in order to gain the rewards offered. If there is ambiguity or partiality disturbing the line of sight individuals are likely to be de-motivated, even if the potential rewards hold personal valence.

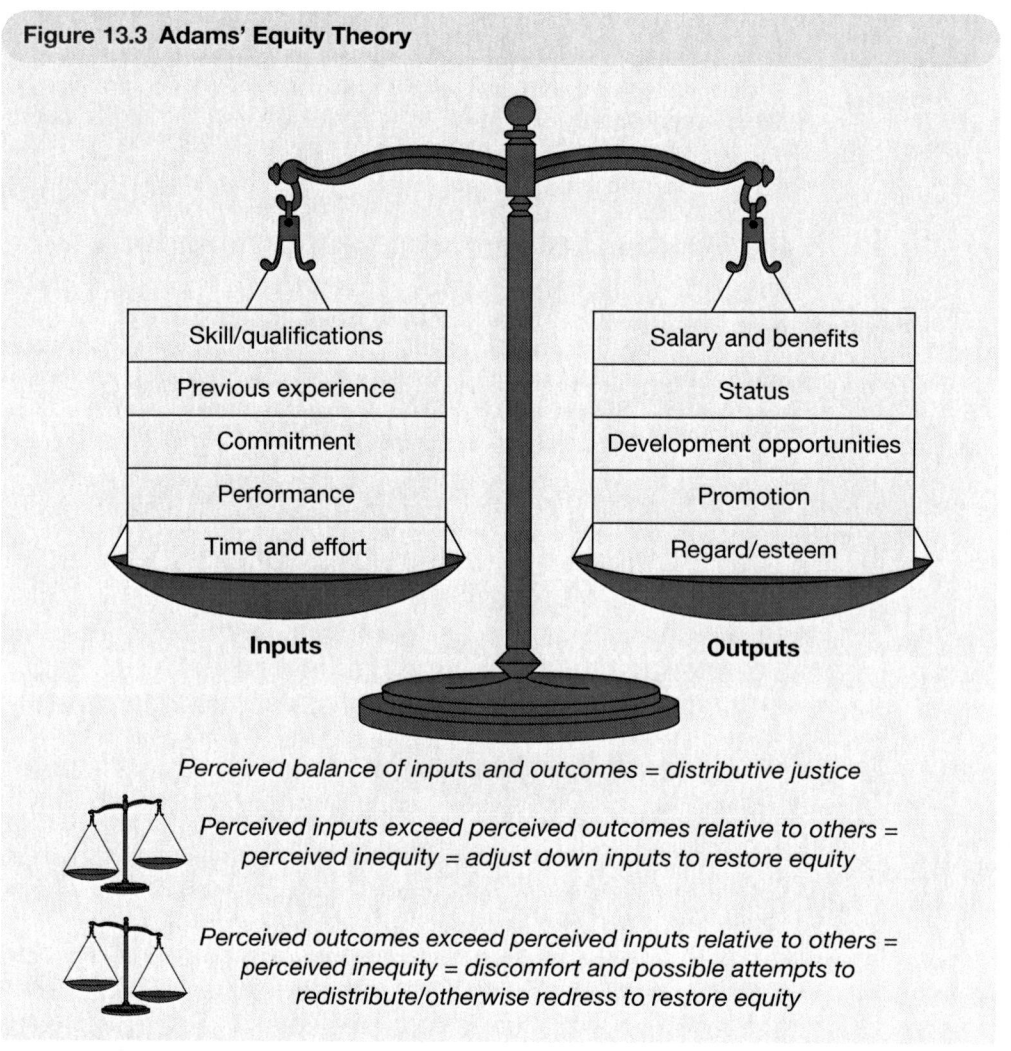

Figure 13.3 Adams' Equity Theory

Inputs:
- Skill/qualifications
- Previous experience
- Commitment
- Performance
- Time and effort

Outputs:
- Salary and benefits
- Status
- Development opportunities
- Promotion
- Regard/esteem

Perceived balance of inputs and outcomes = distributive justice

Perceived inputs exceed perceived outcomes relative to others = perceived inequity = adjust down inputs to restore equity

Perceived outcomes exceed perceived inputs relative to others = perceived inequity = discomfort and possible attempts to redistribute/otherwise redress to restore equity

Source: Adams (1965)

Finally, Adams' 'Equity Theory' (Adams, 1965) prompts organisations to consider the perceived fairness of rewards and their application. Adams suggests that employees will compare the rewards they receive (outputs) in return for their effort, skill, qualifications, time and other contributions (inputs). Employees will be motivated where they perceive 'distributive justice' and de-motivated where they perceive inequity. Employees may seek to adjust their inputs when they perceive inequity. Using the subliminal messages inherent in Adams' theory, organisations would be advised to take steps to ensure that their reward systems are fair, consistently applied and sufficiently transparent so that employees can see for themselves how reward decisions are determined (see Figure 13.3).

Factors influencing organisational approaches to reward practice and pay determination

An organisation's approach to reward generally, and to pay determination, will be shaped both by factors in the external environment within which it operates and an array of internal firm-specific characteristics, namely the nature of the business, the size of operation, organisational structure and culture, types of employees, jobs and technology, management and ownership and so forth. Each of the reward choices Marchington and Wilkinson (2008) posit in the segment above cascade a range of further ancillary choices thus creating the potential for multiple models of reward practice. Because of this it is difficult to generalise about approaches to reward and impossible to be prescriptive. More safely, an organisation's approach to developing a reward strategy ought to start from the standpoint 'what makes sense for this organisation?' (Wright, 2004: 8) whilst subsuming relevant knowledge relating to the internal and external factors influencing choice. In this segment of the chapter we briefly discuss the key factors in the external and internal environment that shape and influence organisational approaches to reward.

The economic climate

This chapter has already alluded to some of the ways in which the economic environment might influence reward, notably the way in which employers are likely to switch to less costly benefits in tougher economic conditions, and the way in which employers can reduce risk and financial burden by making more extensive use of variable pay. The economic context is an important determinant of pay levels and a barometer for future trends. In setting pay levels, employers cannot help but be influenced by the market rates for jobs. As Kessler (2007: 167) remarks 'organisations cannot survive if they fail to pay competitive labour market rates to attract employees with the skills needed to provide a service or manufacture a product'. Of course, there is no such thing as a single market rate for a job, rather several rates or a zone of discretion, the spread of which is influenced by the supply of and demand of labour, geographical factors and the actions of employers competing for labour. In tight labour markets, where competition for resources is intensive and supply is low, market rates are driven higher, affecting the price employers have to pay to attract adequate resources. Economic activity rates and unemployment indicators are thus key factors influencing pay levels. In addition, for most organisations the rate of growth in the economy is a critical benchmark for the salary review process and impacts upon organisations' ability to pay. According to the IRS (2008) employers use various measures of inflation to guide pay increases, of these the Retail Prices Index (RPI) is the most popular measure with more than eight in ten employers (81.7 per cent) saying they would refer to this measure during forthcoming pay reviews. In an economic downturn there is evidence to suggest that employers tighten their belts where pay is concerned and look to minimise or avoid pay increases. Cotton (2009) suggests that in the current climate of an economy in recession and mounting insolvencies, workers are not optimistic that they will receive a pay rise during 2009.

The legal context for reward

Since the rise of industrialisation there have been numerous legal interventions into the realm of reward management. These have ranged from the Truck Acts of the nineteenth century, which were designed to ensure skilled workers were paid in cash, through to more recent interventions in terms of minimum wage regulation. These demonstrate the ways in which legal regulation can be seen to shape reward practices. Statutory regulation has been in place in the United Kingdom for some 30 years which was intended to ensure pay equity in gender terms. More recently, legislation has been implemented to regulate pay at the lower extreme of the labour market, to impose minimum holiday entitlement and a restraint on working hours. Here we briefly discuss in turn the ways in which the Equal Pay Act 1970, The National Minimum Wage Regulations 1999 and the Working Time Directive 1998 constrain and influence employee reward practices.

The Equal Pay Act 1970 (EqPA)

> Labor market discrimination occurs when groups of workers with equal average productivity are paid different average wages.
> (Baldwin and Johnson 2006: 122)

Equal Pay regulations have a history founded in the Convention on Equal Pay approved by the International Labour Organisation in 1950–51, a regulation that had antecedents within the Treaty of Versailles in 1919, if not before (Jamieson, 1999). In the UK the EqPA was enacted as part of the move towards membership of the European Economic Community (now the EU) in the early 1970s. Employers were allowed five years' 'grace' to voluntarily adjust and to permit them to get their reward structures in order before the legislation came into force in 1975. Broadly, the legislation is designed to grant everyone the right to equal terms and conditions of employment in situations where they do the same work as a colleague of the opposite sex. Over the ensuing period this has been widened by the application of European Law to the extent that the UK has modified its laws (see the Employment Act 2002 s 42 for example) to include in this group colleagues of the opposite sex who do work that has been rated as equivalent under a job evaluation scheme or where it can be proved by other mechanisms that the work is of equal value. The manner in which this is achieved is to imply into all contracts of employment an 'equality clause', which has the consequence of requiring the employer not to treat persons of different genders less favourably simply on the basis of gender. In spite of this legislation, there still exist very significant inconsistencies between men's and women's pay. It does not matter whether wages are measured hourly or weekly, women currently receive approximately 83 per cent of the full-time male average, whilst in part-time work 'almost 50 per cent of women who work part-time earn nearer 60 per cent' of their average for their male counterparts (McColgan, 2008: 401). As McColgan (2008) notes, bringing equal pay claims is a sluggish, unwieldy and costly process, especially as the government refuses to go along with the development of class actions and shows even less willingness to implement legislation which places a positive obligation on employers to eliminate pay discrimination.

In spite of this lack of legislative backing to pursue equal pay, some employers seek to address such inequality within their reward structures. This can be achieved by the introduction of a number of reward polices and practices such as:

- ensuring employees reach the top of a given scale within a reasonable timescale;
- setting targets for all staff to reach pay points within a specific timescale;
- setting competency *and* experience criteria for each pay point;
- shortening the scales;
- reducing the number and range of performance measures (Equality and Human Rights Commission, 2009).

As Fredman (2008) suggests, the fact that the current difference in gender-related pay is down to 12.6 per cent when measured using the median figure (rather than the usual mean which rates it at 17.2 per cent) following 34 years of equal pay legislation gives no reason for satisfaction. Indeed, the change in the mechanisms for calculation merely masks the continuing inability of some groups to secure equality of treatment especially where 'the median part-time gender pay gap was a scandalous 39.1% in 2007' (Fredman 2008: 193). The continuing gap indicates the need for a more complex response which addresses both government and employer unwillingness and the narrow coverage of the current legislation.

> **STOP and think**
>
> *Whilst some inroads have been made, to what extent do you think the continued reliance upon the three requirements for equal pay claims (same or equivalent establishment, same employer and equal work) continue to limit the progress towards equal pay?*
>
> *Consider an organisation of which you are aware and indicate mechanisms they could institute in order to address inequalities in terms and conditions.*

National Minimum Wage Regulations 1999

The regulation of wages is a central debate within the realm of 'worker protection, globalization, development and poverty reduction' (Evain, 2008: 20). These were put in place in order to develop the dual goals of fairness and efficiency. As the report of the Low Pay Commission suggested it can be argued that low wages lead to a malevolent cluster which comprises low morale, low performance and low productivity. The introduction of a national minimum wage is said to have benefited some 1.3 million workers (Low Pay Commission, 2001). Many of those affected worked in organisations where pay setting was inexact and did not recognise the need for formal systems, further the new wage levels benefited women more than men due to inequality and the extent of part-time work amongst women. The UK currently has three rates covering those over compulsory school age but under 18, those aged between 18 and 21 and those aged 22 and above. The rates are changed in October each year and from 2008 they were £3.53, £4.77 and £5.73 respectively. As with the Wage Council rates before them these rates are poorly policed and many small employers, especially those in the service sector, avoid enforcement (Arrowsmith and Gilman, 2005). Arrowsmith and Gilman argue that in such small firms 'Pay levels reflect not only economic, product and labour market factors but also the informality of internal pay structures' (2005: 169). As we note below, such indeterminacy and informality support existing pay bias, as it is often based on pre-determined skill patterns, time worked and length of service.

The level within the UK is set at above the equivalent of US$1,000 per month (in the period 2006–07) which locates the UK within the top 18 per cent of countries where such a minimum is set (Evain, 2008) and within a group of industrialised countries where the rate is set other than by government alone. Evain (2008) notes more than 100 countries in membership of the International Labour Organisation (ILO), which have ratified the Minimum Wage Fixing Convention 1970 (No 131), either enact minimum wage legislation, set such rates following the recommendation of a specialised body, or through collective bargaining. World-wide, the average range of minimum rates vary from US$30 in Africa, US$75 in many Asian countries, US$480 in Eastern Europe and Latin America to the US$1,000 or above in the majority of industrialised countries. These rates reflect national, regional, sectored and/or global imperatives and satisfy many competitive pressures. By removing wage calculation out of competition organisations can, in domestic and global settings, strive for alternative means of differentiation in terms of product or service. The issue then becomes the enforcement mechanism, Eyraud and Saget (2005) suggest that these regulations are often poorly enforced leading to a continued decline in working conditions across the globe. The extent to which the legislation in the UK is enforced, and the individualised mechanisms for enforcement, tend to support the view that whilst the existence of such regulation is designed to ensure a high level of protection, the continued avoidance of such rules as indicated by Arrowsmith and Gilman (2005) is wide spread.

> **STOP and think**
>
> *Minimum wage legislation is said to advance a wide range of policy goals.*
>
> What do you think such goals might be and how effectively does the current UK regulation achieve these goals?

Working Time Regulations 1998

Placing limits on working hours is an essential activity in the quest for worker protection and ensuring the health and safety of those at work. In the current climate it has also become a touchstone of the movement towards securing a sustainable work-life balance. In terms of the latter, there are two discourses which each have a separate focus. These uses of the concept cover the *personal control of time* on the one hand and the notion of *workplace flexibility* on the other (see Humbert and Lewis, 2008). In terms of the reward agenda, we concentrate primarily on the latter in that we are seeking solutions to the question of providing options for people with a work place focus who also enjoy non-work (chiefly family) commitments. In that respect the Working Time Regulations (1998) [WTR] offer some attempt to balance the demands of the employer with the needs of family life by placing limits on a range of working time issues. At a glance the key provisions are:

- maximum 48-hour working week for many groups;
- An average eight-hour shift in each 24-hour period for night workers;
- A rest break after six consecutive hours' work;
- Rest periods of 11 continuous hours daily and 35 continuous hours weekly; and
- A minimum of 5.6 weeks' leave per annum.

The UK regulations have their basis in the EU Directive (93/104/EC), which is said to have introduced the new principle of 'humanisation' into EU social regulations, under which employers should be required to take into account the general principle of adapting work and wage in order to alleviate monotonous work and work at a pre-determined rate. The fact that the UK has implemented the directive subject to a number of derogations does not alter the fact that reward managers need to consider the effects of the regulations. That the Employment Appeals Tribunal (EAT) could in a recent case (*Corps of Commissionaires Management Ltd* v *Hughes* [2008] EAT|196|08) hold that the rest break is only triggered after six hours and not multiples thereof, is a simple indication of the minimalist approach of the UK government and the reluctance of management to extend the protection within the UK. During 2009 elements of the EU Directive relating to the definition of 'working time' – notably in relation to 'on-call' time and junior doctors – will come into force and change the options for UK reward managers. The development of 24/7 production and 'rolling shifts' has not been unduly limited by the daily or weekly rest periods due to the availability of opt-outs, however, as these opt-outs are withdrawn it will present fresh challenges for reward managers in the UK.

World-wide most members of the ILO have some form of regulation on working time. In a recent survey (Evain, 2008), attention is drawn to the fact that working time regulation was the subject of the very first ILO convention (Convention 1: 1919) and that the topic has been a major regulatory concern since that date. The general rule, where a normal hourly figure is placed on the working week, is that the figure of 40 or less is applied. In the UK we have no universal normal working limit because the WTR exclude 'professional workers' and/or workers who are not paid in relation to time. The latter group includes many clerical workers, most managers and almost all professional workers. This limitation is not unique to the UK as it can be found in some 24 per cent of industrialised countries. A key result of such exceptions has been the development of 'extreme work' hours most of which are unpaid. It is reported that managers in the UK work the longest hours in Europe, with 42 per cent working in excess of 60 hours a week; this phenomenon runs alongside evidence that work has also intensified (Burke and Cooper, 2008). Hewlett and Luce (2006) describe the amalgamation of these two factors, in the work of 'high earners', as the basis for the creation of 'extreme work'. Such work is portrayed as combining elements such as:

- unpredictable workflow;
- fast pace under tight deadlines;
- scope of responsibility that amounts to more than one job;

- work-related events outside regular working hours;
- availability to clients and/or more senior managers 24/7;
- large amounts of travel;
- large (and increasing) number of direct reports;
- physical presence at the workplace on average at least 10 hours a day (adapted from Hewlett and Luce, 2006).

For reward managers, these elements present few problems because they tend to either describe the role chosen and adopted by the individual or take place within the terms of the existing contract of employment. As such, they are rewarded by existing reward structures including PBR or other personalised reward agreements. In their survey of US business managers and professionals, Hewlett and Luce found that 91 per cent cited unpredictability as a key pressure point whilst 86 per cent also included increased pace within tight deadlines, 66% included work-related events outside normal hours and 61 per cent 24/7 client demands (2006: 54). Perhaps the words of the eighteenth-century washer-woman Mary Collier better fit modern managers and professionals both male and female;

> Our toil and labour daily so extreme,
> that we have hardly ever the time to dream.
>
> (Quoted in Thompson 1991: 81)

From this discussion we can begin to see that legislative activity, whilst a key source for elements which influence reward structures, are not the only, nor perhaps the most important, influences.

Internal/organisational factors and the influence of sector

In addition to reflecting factors in the external environment, organisations' chosen approach to reward will be shaped by the idiosyncratic nature of the firm and sector-specific factors. There are no hard and fast rules, so the full plethora of reward choices is theoretically at the disposal of the organisation. As far as its capabilities stretch, the organisation must develop an approach to reward that is compliant, cost-effective and capable of attracting, retaining and motivating employees commensurate with the needs of the business. It is beyond the boundaries of this chapter to discuss in detail the complex configurations of reward and corresponding internal drivers that are likely to be significant in each case. Instead, a more general stance is adopted, which notes some of the discernable differences between reward practices according to workplace characteristics such as ownership/sector, unionisation and workplace size. We return to these themes in the final part of the chapter, where contemporary trends in pay and reward practices are discussed against rhetoric of heightened strategic use of reward.

Large-scale surveys such as the Workplace Employment Relations Survey (WERS) (Kersley *et al.*, 2006) and the CIPD Annual Reward Survey allow changes and trends in employee reward practice to be tracked over time; they also provide a snapshot of employee reward practices at the time of the survey. CIPD research provides analysis by firm size (number of employees), firm sector (manufacturing and production, private sector services, voluntary sector and public services) and by occupation (senior management, middle/first-line management, technical/professional and clerical/manual), whilst WERS provides further industry breakdown and in addition, considers the variance between reward practices in unionised and non-unionised workplaces and foreign-owned and UK-owned workplaces. A sample of observations is drawn from WERS 2004 (Kersley *et al.*, 2006) and the latest CIPD survey (2009a) and shown in Table 13.4.

Table 13.4 Trends in reward practice

Reward strategy	• The incidence of reward strategy shows little variance by sector but does appear to be more closely correlated to workplace size – 48 per cent of respondents in workplaces of 5000+ employees reported the existence of reward strategy compared with 20 per cent of repondents where there were between 50 and 249 employees
Pay structures	• In the public sector and to a lesser extent in the voluntary sector, employers are far more likely to us pay spines • The most common approach to pay structures taking all sectors into account is the use of individual pay rates/ranges and spot salaries although there are variations by sector and by occupation • Broad-banding is most prevalent in manufacturing and production • Most senior managers are paid according to individual pay rates/ranges/spot salaries as are most clerical and manual workers
Pay progression	• The CIPD report that the most common approach to pay progression is to use a combination of factors (combined approach) in contrast to a single factor such as length of service, skills or individual performance • Combination approaches are more common in manufacturing and production and private sector services than they are in the voluntary sector and public services • Where combination approaches are used, the most common combination in the public sector is individual performance and length of service, individual performance is the most popular factor across all sectors, market rates feature strongly in the private sector and competency is more typical in the voluntary sector
Pay/salary determination	• Market rates are shown to be more important in determining salaries in private sector firms • In the public sector collective bargaining was the dominant form of pay setting • In the private sector, the percentage of employees with pay set through collective bargaining was much higher in foreign-owned workplaces than in UK-owned workplaces • Clerical and manual staff are more likely to be covered by collective bargaining arrangements than managerial staff • The views of the owner/managing director are more likely to be a factor in setting salary levels in small firms than in large organisations (CIPD, 2009a) • Pay set by management where this is the sole method of pay determination is a growing phenomenon in private sector workplaces (43 per cent of private sector workplaces in 2004 compared with 32 per cent in 1998) (Kersley et al., 2006) • Job evaluation processes are more likely to underscore salary determination in the public sector and voluntary sectors than in the private sector • Job evaluation is more likely to be used by large employers than small employers • Public sector organisations are far more likely to have conducted an equal pay reviews (EPR) to audit internal pay equity than private sector employers

Pay determination – internal or external focus?

As the final segment of Table 13.4 demonstrates, a key decision when setting levels of pay is whether to place emphasis on comparability with the external market or internal equity. The lure of the external market would appear to be more compelling for private sector organisations, whereas the greater use of tools such as job evaluation and the Equal Pay Review process in the public sector suggests internal equity is more paramount here. Ultimately, however, any approach must try and reconcile the need to keep pace with external market rates with due concern for internal equity.

Job evaluation has come in for criticism in recent years for being excessively paperwork-driven and costly and too rigid to be of value to organisations trying to be adaptable and flexible in the face of intensive competitive pressures. The notion of conceiving tightly defined job descriptions, of the kind needed for traditional job evaluation schemes is also heralded in some quarters as incompatible with flatter organisational structures and associated desire to create flexible ways of rewarding employees. Job evaluation consequently is supposed to have withered away, at least from mainstream use. On the contrary, IDS (2000) suggest that much of the criticism directed at job evaluation is unsupported by hard empirical evidence and that in practice organisations are showing signs of using it to complement broad-banding and in conjunction with role profiling and competencies. Brown and Dive (2009: 29) would appear to agree,

> By evolving to meet the needs of organisations for more fluid structures, more market- and person-driven pay and more talented leaders – as well as performing its traditional function as a foundation for fair pay management – job evaluation seems to be securing its place in the HR professional's toolkit for the foreseeable future.

Typically, job evaluation schemes attempt to fairly address issues of internal comparability in terms of pay. Job evaluation is defined as 'the process of assessing the relative size of jobs within an organisation' (Armstrong and Murlis, 1998: 81). The term 'size' in this context means the value of the job to the organisation.

Armstrong and Murlis identify the defining characteristics of job evaluation (JE) as:

- A *judgemental process*: always (to some extent) reliant on the exercise of judgement in interpreting facts and situations and applying these to decisions about the relative 'size' of jobs.
- An *analytical process*: it is about making informed judgements based upon an analytical process of gathering facts about jobs (based on job analysis techniques).
- A *structured process*: a framework is provided to help evaluators make consistent and rational decisions.
- A *job-centred process*: JE focuses on jobs, not on the people doing them and/or how well they do them. This aspect has clearly raised questions about the value of JE to organisations that adopt a person-based approach as opposed to job-based approach to reward.

Job evaluation is therefore, not a 'perfect' determinant of job relativities. As we can see, it relies to some extent on subjective judgements and it may present some challenges in contemporary workplaces where there is likely to be greater fluidity in job roles.

Devising pay structures

Whether or not organisations engage systematically with the process of job evaluation or take a stronger lead from benchmarking salaries in the external market without recourse to job evaluation techniques, most would agree with Armstrong (2002: 204), that 'pay structures are needed to provide a logically-designed framework within which equitable, fair and consistent reward policies can be implemented'. Perkins and White (2008: 98) argue that grading structures are 'the core building blocks of any organisation's human resource management system, not just for pay but often for conditions of service and career development as well'. The degree of sophistication characterising the design of pay structures in organisations can vary considerably according to firm size, sector and occupational group. For example, smaller firms are generally less likely to operate formal pay structures especially during the formative stages of the business, relying perhaps instead on management discretion to set individual rates of pay for employees (Perkins and White, 2008). However, research in small and medium-sized organisations (SMEs) would indicate that as small firms grow, an informal approach to HRM becomes less tenable (Barrett and Mayson, 2007; Barrett *et al*., 2008; Mazzarol, 2003); it is at this point that SMEs are likely to begin to inject greater levels of formalisation across a range of human resource practices, including reward. Further, the 2009 CIPD Reward Survey points to sectoral differences and occupational differences.

Responses indicate that pay spines with fixed incremental points are common at all levels in the public sector, while individual pay rates or ranges, which allow for greater flexibility, are more prevalent in the private sector. By occupation, senior managers are most likely to be subject to individual pay rates or ranges.

According to Armstrong (2002: 203) a pay structure:

- defines the different levels of pay for jobs or groups of jobs by reference to their relative internal value as established by job evaluation, to external relativities as established by market rate surveys and, where appropriate, to negotiated rates for the job;
- except in the case of 'spot rates', provides scope for pay progression in accordance with performance, skill, contribution or service;
- contains an organisation's pay ranges for jobs grouped into grades, individual jobs or job families; or pay scales for jobs slotted into a pay spine; or the spot rates for individual jobs where there is no scope for progression.

In essence, a pay structure defines the rate, or range of the payment rate, for jobs within the organisational structure. Whilst this might sound a relatively simple task, there are a number of design choices to be made:

- Should the organisation establish spot rates for individual jobs or devise a more complex structure or series of pay structures?
- How many pay structures are necessary?
- What types of pay structures are suitable?
- If a grading structure is deemed appropriate, how many grades should there be; how wide should each grade or band be; and how close should grade differentials be?

Further decisions must subsequently be made about 'whether, or on what basis, employees will progress through the pay structure' (Perkins and White, 2008: 152).

General design features

As a rule, pay structures need to be flexible enough to accommodate change in the organisation or in the external market and sufficiently clear for individuals to understand where in the structure they are placed and how pay progression is achieved. Spot rates, as referred to in Armstrong's definition above, are set rates of base pay for individual jobs, independent to one another and not tied to a scale or range. Where there is a spot rate for a job, all employees incumbent in the role are paid the same base rate for the job; this may be supplemented by forms of variable pay such as overtime and shift premium or attendance bonus. Spot rates tend to preside in manufacturing and warehouse/distribution centres and in other forms of manual work (Armstrong, 2002). It is difficult to regard a series of spot rates as a pay structure per se, however, spot rates can be customised to personify typical features of a pay structure, for example a mini-series of spot rates (generally referred to as an individual pay range) could be assigned to a role such that there is scope to pay a lesser training or learning rate to individuals new to the role, a target spot rate for a fully competent employee and a further (higher) rate to recognise superior skill, experience or performance. In other circumstances, organisations may elect to manage spot rates in such a way as to incentivise consistently high levels of output, this might be attempted in a somewhat punitive fashion, by dropping lower performing employees to a less favourable spot rate until such a time as higher productivity is resumed.

Whilst, as illustrated, a degree of tailoring is possible, spot rates do not readily offer scope for pay progression; rather they supply a series of detached job rates. Such an approach may be eminently suitable where jobs are fairly static in nature and career development opportunities and expectations are limited. In contrast grading, pay spines and job families, more aptly fit the description of a framework for the enactment of pay policy, in addition, they offer options for pay progression, through the spine, grade or family of jobs based upon length of service or other criterion best suited to the organisation's strategic business objectives.

A single structure or several structures?

An organisation may be able to design and implement a single pay structure to incorporate the entire range of jobs (or the vast majority of jobs) across the organisation, alternatively two or more structures may be in place to assimilate different groups of roles represented within the organisation (for example, a manual pay scale and an office and managerial salary structure). In recent years, both the National Health Service (NHS) and the Higher Education (HE) sector have untaken extensive pay reform, underpinned by job evaluation to develop single pay structures. The NHS scheme, 'Agenda for Change', succeeded in introducing a single national pay scale for NHS hospital employees (with the exception of doctors and consultants), similarly the National Framework Agreement in Higher Education has created a single pay spine for support staff and academic staff in HE institutions.

> **STOP and think**
>
> *What benefits do you think hospitals and universities are likely to derive from the formulation of single pay structures in their respective organisations?*

Pay spines

A pay spine is a series of fixed incremental salary points reflecting all jobs from the highest paid through to the lowest paid incorporated in the structure. Incremental points may increase at an evenly distributed rate throughout the spine, for example each increment might be set 2.5 per cent above the next from the bottom to the top of the structure. Alternatively, increments might be wider at higher levels in the organisation (Armstrong, 2002). Pay spines are common in the public services sector including education, health, local government and the police service (Perkins and White, 2008). In these work environments, pay grades are superimposed upon the pay spine to form a structure in which a series of increments apply within each grade. Employees' annual salaries are typically automatically raised to the next incremental point on the basis of length of service, this either occurs on an individual basis, triggered by the anniversary of the employee joining the organisation or collectively at a fixed date in the calendar. Except in extreme cases of poor performance, where an increment might be withheld or where progression 'gateways' have to be crossed, employees continue to receive automatic annual increments (and possibly accelerated increments awarded according to performance criteria) until such a time as they reach the top point in the grade. Pay progression thereafter, in the form of increments, is contingent on the employee gaining promotion to a higher grade. In some organisations further additional discretionary points may be available beyond the upper limit of the grade boundary, reserved for those employees who have performed exceptionally throughout the year or those who have made a special contribution. In public services, where pay spines are prevalent, uplift to the pay spine is the subject of national pay bargaining between trade unions and employers; where a cost of living percentage increase in pay is agreed the incremental scale is adjusted upwards accordingly. Pay spines offer employees a degree of pay progression certainty and give employers certainty in terms of total salary expenditure, but may be perceived as bureaucratic and excessively rigid.

> **STOP and think**
>
> *Try to think of other potential benefits and disadvantages associated with pay spines.*

Graded pay structures

Aside from the use of a central pay spine, organisations opting for a formal pay structure are likely to use some form of grading. The general principles of a pay-grading structure are that jobs are grouped together into grades or bands, often according to some measure of job size. Graded structures require firms to determine how many grades or bands to build into the structure, the width of each grade ('bandwidth'), the degree of overlap to configure between grades and the size of grade differentials to apply throughout the structure. Jobs should be grouped together such that a distinction can be made between the characteristics of the jobs in different grades and the grade hierarchy should broadly take account of the organisational hierarchy. Additionally, there should be a significant step in demands on job holders in the next highest grade such that salary differentials can be suitably justified (www.e-reward.co.uk, January 2007).

Narrow-graded pay structures

Narrow-graded pay structures, or 'traditional' graded structures as they are sometimes referred to, comprise a large number of grades, typically ten or more with jobs of broadly equivalent worth slotted into each of the grades (Armstrong, 2002). As the name would suggest, the width of each grade within the structure ('bandwidth') is narrow, perhaps amounting to a range where the upper salary limit of the grade is anywhere between 20 per cent and 50 per cent higher than the lower salary limit (www.e-reward.co.uk, January 2007). Salary differentials between pay ranges are invariably around 20 per cent (Armstrong, 2002), calculated with reference to the grade mid-point. There is usually an overlap between ranges, which can be as high as 50 per cent (www.e-reward.co.uk, January 2007). The purpose of an overlap is to provide the employer with the scope to recognise and reward a highly experienced and/or qualified employee at the top of a grade more generously than someone who is still in the learning curve zone of the next higher grade (see Figure 13.4). Ultimately, however, the individual placed in the higher grade has greater scope for salary progression. He/she will be able to move closer towards, and eventually, beyond the target rate for a fully competent employee within the grade, contingent upon on satisfying the criteria for pay progression used by the organisation.

For illustrative purposes Figure 13.5 shows a single narrow grade with a bandwidth of 40 per cent, while Figure 13.6 shows an extract of a narrow graded pay structure where the bandwidth is 40 per cent throughout the structure, a grade overlap of 20 per cent is applied and the differential between grades is set at 20 per cent.

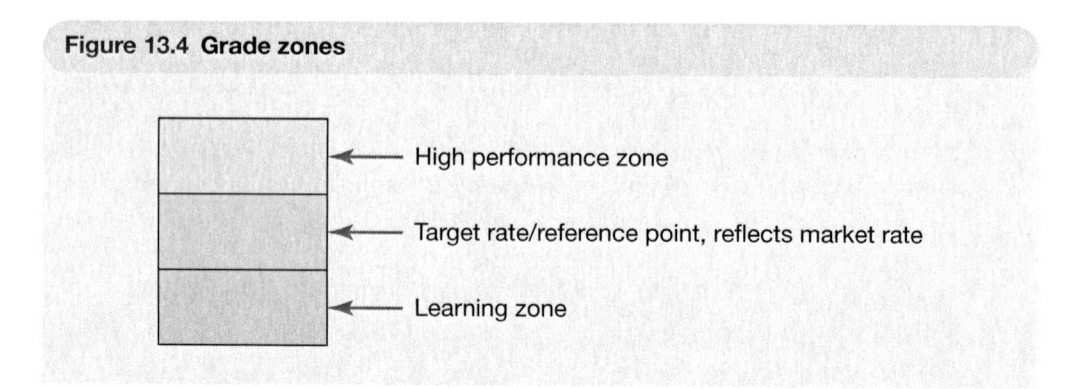

Figure 13.4 Grade zones

- High performance zone
- Target rate/reference point, reflects market rate
- Learning zone

Figure 13.5 Narrow salary grade (40 per cent bandwidth)

£28,000 ← Upper level salary

£24,000 ← *Midpoint* (aligned to market rates, lower, median or upper quartile)

£20,000 ← Lower level salary

Figure 13.6 Extract of narrow-graded pay structure

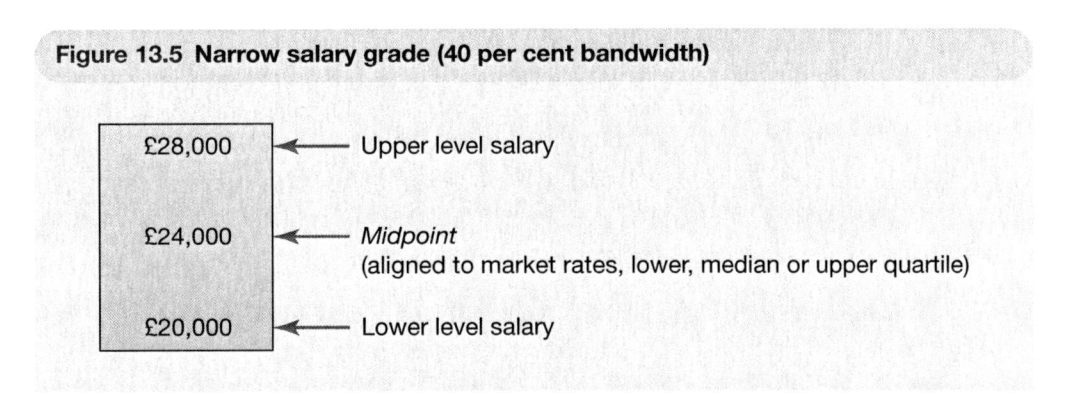

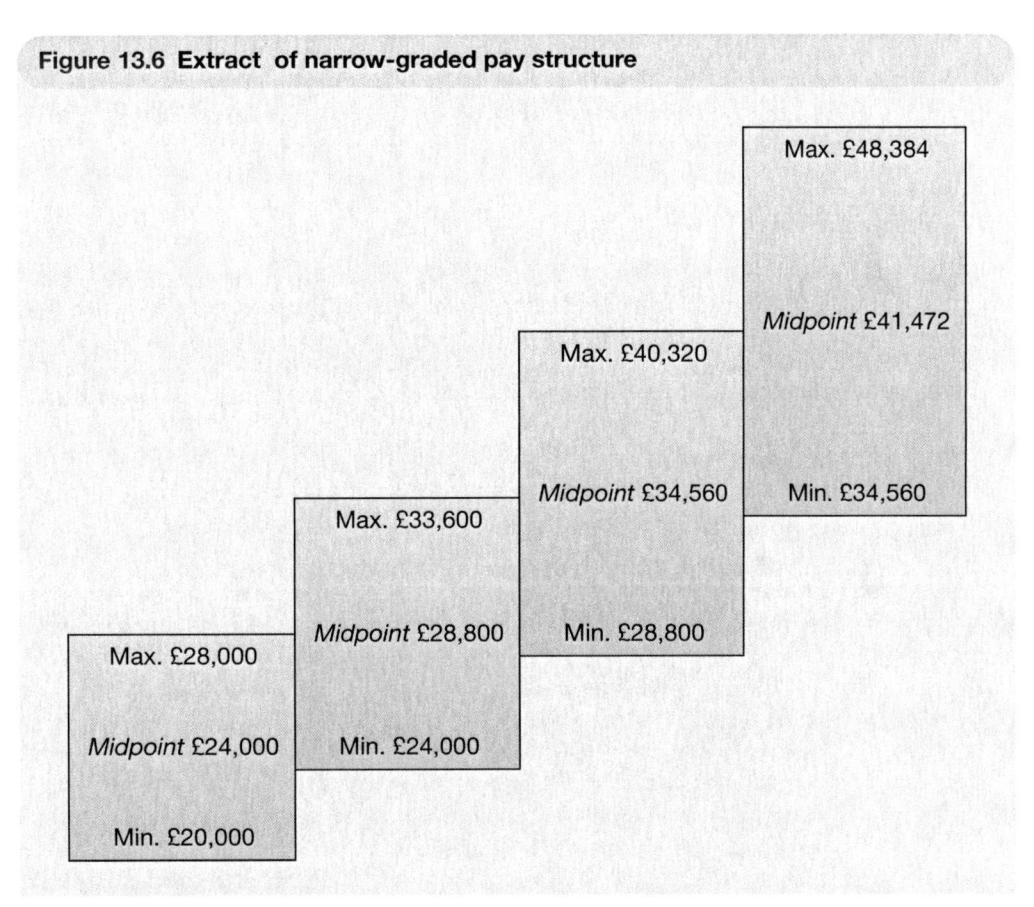

Max. £28,000
Midpoint £24,000
Min. £20,000

Max. £33,600
Midpoint £28,800
Min. £24,000

Max. £40,320
Midpoint £34,560
Min. £28,800

Max. £48,384
Midpoint £41,472
Min. £34,560

It is practice to identify a reference point or target rate in each grade which is the rate for a fully competent individual who is completely qualified and experienced to execute the job to the required standard. This target rate is frequently, but not always, the *midpoint* in the range, aligned to market rates for similar jobs and set in accordance with the organisation's pay stance (upper, median or lower quartile), (www.e-reward.co.uk, January 2007). Analysis seems to show that among private sector service employers, the target rate does tend to be the mid-point in the range, whereas in the public sector the target rate is close to the top of the range. In the manufacturing and production sectors and across the voluntary sector employers are broadly divided as to whether the target salary is at the mid-point or towards the top end of the pay band (CIPD, 2009b).

Broad-banded pay structures

In contrast to a narrow-graded pay structure, a broad-banded structure involves the use of a small number of pay bands, usually just four or five (Armstrong, 2002), each with a bandwidth of between 70 and 100 per cent (Perkins and White, 2008). The broader salary range attached to bands in the structure gives employers greater flexibility than is possible in a narrow-graded structure and is arguably more suitable for use in flatter organisations where employee development and career progression is not inextricably linked to vertical movement through the hierarchy. Flatter organisations tend to develop a more flexible outlook as far as careers are concerned, promoting lateral career development and 'zig-zag' careers. Whilst narrow grades might inhibit such moves, broad bands allow employers to recognise and reward non-vertical career movement and role growth. For this reason broad-banded pay structures are sometimes labelled career-based structures (CIPD, 2000). The CIPD (2000) is keen to point out, however, that some organisations claiming to have made the transition to a broad-banded structure have simply collapsed several narrow grades into fewer wider grades and crucially failed to re-position their own and their workforce's perceptions in terms of career development and salary progression. The CIPD suggests pay structures of this type ought to be called broad-*graded* because of their attachment to the vertical progression mentality more closely associated with narrow-grading structures, the CIPD also offers the less flattering term 'fat-graded' to describe such structures.

A further feature of true broad-banded pay structures is that they afford employers greater latitude in establishing starting salaries and so the opportunity to pay more to attract suitably qualified and experienced staff to 'hard to fill' positions. Whilst this facility might be perceived useful, especially in tight labour markets, the opportunity to place an employee on a salary anywhere within the wide range between the band minimum and maximum gives managers the discretion to apply individual differentiation and therein license to cloud any notion of transparency (IDS, 2006). Where this is the case, broad-banding would appear to heighten the risk of an equal pay claim whilst simultaneously loosening the employer's rein on the pay budget, potentially leading to higher reward costs. So can pay levels be managed fairly and cost-consciously within a broad-banded pay structure?

Managing pay within a broad-banded pay structure

Perkins and White (2008) suggest employers have indeed been anxious about the potential for untrammelled pay progression as a result of wide pay bands. In an effort to curb costs and manage pay more systematically within a broad-banded structure, some organisations have sought to mark out zones within bands to indicate the expected salary range for particular roles. The salary level reflected in the zone is likely be arrived at by benchmarking with comparators in the external market. Similarly, a series of target rates for particular jobs in the band could be identified and superimposed upon the band to denote the market rate for a fully competent individual performing in the job. Further, a series of bars or gateways can be etched into the band to serve as thresholds. To cross a threshold and thereby access the higher salary zone beyond the bar, job holders might be required to demonstrate defined competency levels or reach particular standards of performance. These methods of managing pay within a broad-banded pay structure would appear to improve transparency and provide a surer basis for ensuring equal pay for work of equal value. The role for job evaluation in establishing a hierarchy of jobs within a broad-banded structure is also more apparent where zones or target rates for roles are incorporated.

> **STOP and think**
>
> - Is there a grading structure within your organisation?
> - How many grades/bands exist within your own organisation?
>
> | Number of bands | Senior executives | Managerial/professional | Staff /manual |
> |---|---|---|---|
> | 3 or less | ☐ | ☐ | ☐ |
> | 4–5 | ☐ | ☐ | ☐ |
> | 6–9 | ☐ | ☐ | ☐ |
> | 10+ | ☐ | ☐ | ☐ |
>
> - Would you classify your own organisation's pay structure as **broad-graded, broad-banded** or **traditional (narrow-graded)**?
> - What advantages and disadvantages are associated with the pay structure in place within your own organisation?

Job families

Finally, pay structures can be characterised wholly or partially by the use of job family structures, or labour market structures as they are sometimes called. Armstrong (2002: 206) maintains that

> a job family structure consists of separate grade or pay structures for jobs which are related through the activities carried out and the basic skills used, but are differentiated by the level of responsibility, skill or competence required.

There may be six to eight levels within each job family, representing the range of jobs in the family from lower ranking jobs through to higher ranking posts (CIPD, 2008b). In essence, this approach to devising pay structures treats different occupations or functions separately and results in a series of pay ladders for different sets of jobs. Alternatively, a single job family structure could co-exist with a main stream pay structure in an organisation where the family of jobs concerned cannot easily be assimilated in the mainstream structure without giving rise to anomalies. In practice, job family pay structures are beneficial where an organisation needs to recruit to job roles within a particular occupational group and there is fierce competition in the labour market forcing the price of wages up. A job family pay structure allows the organisation to align to the external market more closely and so improve its chances of attracting and retaining adequate resources (CIPD, 2008b).

Pay progression

As Wright (2004: 78) argues 'there is little point in organisations having elaborate pay structures unless they are offering employees some progression opportunities for their pay *within* the pay structure' (original emphasis). A number of means are at the organisation's disposal to manage employees' movement within the salary structure, indeed, the way in which this is done in different types of organisations tends to vary far more than actual levels of wages and salaries (Perkins and White, 2008). *How* organisations pay portrays their stance on reward and is in many ways a more strategic decision than *how much* to pay. Where a strategic approach to reward is manifest, methods of pay progression will be informed by a clear notion of the organisation's values and strategic imperatives such that the 'right' individuals are recognised and rewarded for the 'right' behaviours. As was suggested earlier in this chapter, strategic approaches to reward are not universally applied, and even where they are, weaknesses and difficulties often mire best efforts. Where pay progression is concerned sometimes pragmatic decisions, underscored by the lack of resources and expertise to design and manage more elaborate pay progression mechanisms, drive organisations to apply blanket solutions such as automatic annual increments linked to employee service and across-the-board percentage pay increases. Indeed, for some organisations, and the stakeholders involved in the particular employment relationship, annual service-related increments and unified pay awards may signify equity, parity and transparency and therefore be viewed more positively than other means of salary progression.

However, whilst service-related pay progression rewards the build-up of expertise in the job and may help employers with retention, it risks signalling to employees that longevity of service is more important than the quality and/or quality of the work undertaken and the manner in which work is conducted. Similarly, universal pay increases, resulting in the same pay award to everyone regardless of their contribution, fail to take into account other factors that might justifiably be used to determine the speed and scale of individual salary progression. Service-related increments are a traditional method of pay progression in the public sector, but they are less frequently used by private sector employers who tend to prefer mechanisms that reward other factors such as performance, competence and skill (CIPD, 2008c). Similarly the 2009 CIPD Reward Survey shows that the use of collective bargaining, resulting in the same percentage pay increase for represented groups of employees, is far more prevalent in the public sector than it is in private sector and voluntary sector organisations.

In contrast, a number of alternative means of managing salary progression are available including:

Individual performance-related pay (PRP)

PRP links individual pay progression with employee performance. The basic notion of individual PRP is that the promise of rewards contingent on performance will incentivise employees to perform optimally thus raising individual performance and leading to improved levels of organisational performance. Within a PRP scheme, employee performance is typically assessed against pre-set targets or pre-agreed objectives often at appraisal time, although a separate pay review meeting could be used to determine a PRP increase. PRP payments may be consolidated into base pay or paid as a bonus (variable pay). PRP schemes ebb and flow in popularity and have been the subject of much controversial debate in the reward literature. In particular the supposed causal link between PRP and performance or productivity has been heavily questioned (Thompson, 1992; Marsden and Richardson, 1994; Kessler and Purcell, 1992). Indeed, rather than glowing accolades heralding the benefits of PRP, much attention has been drawn to the potential negative ramifications associated with using it. Reservations tend to revolve around the following issues:

- PRP schemes operate on the basis that employees will be motivated by money whereas motivational theories suggest money is not the only motivator, or even necessarily an effective motivator.
- The size of the 'pay pot' and how to divide this appropriately commensurate with individual performance achievements.
- Problems associated with measuring performance in a fair and objective manner.
- The ability of managers to manage the award of PRP; to make, communicate and justify difficult and potentially divisive reward decisions.
- Potential for pay discrimination/bias.
- Potential harm to efforts to engender team-work as individual PRP encourages employees to focus on their own performance targets or objectives without concern for the greater good of the team, department or wider organisation.
- Focus on output/outcomes, but not the means used to accomplish performance outcomes.

Further, Kessler and Purcell (1992) argue that linking assessments of performance to pay can induce tunnel vision whereby employees concentrate on those aspects of their job that trigger pay increases and ignore other parts of their job role. They also suggest that the limitations of the pay pot may mean that even employees with positive appraisal ratings only receive relatively small pay-outs that fail to measure up to the 'felt-fair' principle. In view of the criticisms individual PRP has attracted, the CIPD (2008c) indicates that some employers are moving towards a broader concept of contribution-related pay which not only measures outcomes but takes into account how employees achieved the performance outcome. Pay schemes related to contribution propose a more holistic view of individual performance taking into account processes and behaviour.

Contribution-related pay

As indicated above, interest in contribution-related pay is partly prompted by concern that individual performance-related pay takes too narrow an interpretation of performance by focusing upon outcomes in isolation. Organisations expressing a preference for contribution-related pay signal an interest in how the results are achieved as well as the results themselves. Indeed, the way in which employees conduct their work and the attitudes and behaviours they display may have been identified by such organisations as a critical factor in securing competitive advantage, so to try to match pay to softer measures of behaviours as well as harder results data would seem to indicate an attempt to design a pay progression mechanism that places due emphasis on strategic fit. Armstrong (2002: 309) defines contribution-related pay as 'a process for making pay decisions which are based on assessments of both the outcomes of the work carried out by individuals and the level of skill and competence which have influenced these outcomes'. It is thus an attempt at a mixed, blended or hybrid method incorporating the ethos of performance-related pay and competence based pay. It means paying for results (outcomes) and competence, for past performance and potential for future success (see Figure 13.7).

The mechanisms used to pay for contribution can vary considerably. Recognising that contribution-related pay incorporates multi-dimensional measures, some organisations reward the acquisition and display of required competencies in base pay, and reward results achieved with an unconsolidated bonus (variable pay) whilst others arrive at a composite increase in base pay taking into account both competence and results pay-outs (Brown and Armstrong, 1999).

Competence-related pay

Competence-related pay, used alone as means of pay progression, adopts a relatively narrow focus akin to the use of individual performance-related pay, however, emphasis is placed on employees' input to the job, rather than performance or output. The aim of competence-related pay is to encourage and reward the development of particular competencies desired by the organisation; it amounts to a method of paying employees for *the ability to* perform as opposed to paying *for* performance (Armstrong, 2002). Perkins and White (2008: 176) comment that 'whereas individual performance related pay can appear to be simply a punitive system to

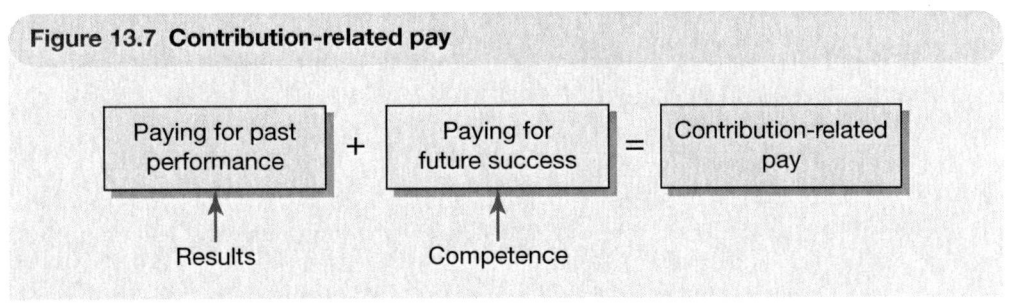

Figure 13.7 Contribution-related pay

Paying for past performance (Results) + Paying for future success (Competence) = Contribution-related pay

Source: Adapted from Brown and Armstrong (1999: 137).

Table 13.5 The advantages and disadvantages of competence-related pay

Advantages	Disadvantages
• Encourages competence development • Fits de-layered organisations by facilitating lateral career moves • Helps to integrate role and organisational core competencies • Forms part of an integrated, competence-based approach to people management • Delivers message that competence is important	• Relies on appropriate, relevant and agreed competence profiles • Assessment of competence levels may be difficult • Might pay for irrelevant competencies • Links to pay may be arbitrary • Costs may escalate if inappropriate or unused competencies are rewarded

Source: from *Employee Reward*, 3rd ed., CIPD (Armstrong, M. 2002) p. 306, with the permission of the publisher, the Chartered Institute of Personnel and Development, London (www.cipd.co.uk).

penalise workers, competency-based systems can in contrast appear positive for employees' own career development'. The introduction of competence-based pay requires a competency framework to be in place and means for measuring individual competence levels to be agreed and understood by managers and employees alike. Table 13.5 summarises the advantages and disadvantages of competence-related pay.

> Skills based pay provides employees with a direct link between their pay progression and the skills they have required and can use effectively. (Armstrong, 2002: 314)

Skills-based pay

Skills-based pay is sometimes referred to as 'pay for knowledge' or 'knowledge-based pay' (Perkins and White, 2008: 181). The aim of skills-based pay is to encourage employees to acquire additional skills, units of skill or specific qualifications that are deemed important to meet business needs. Skills-based pay might be closely tied to NVQs (National Vocational Qualifications) and the units and levels of qualifications set out in modular qualification frameworks of this type, alternatively the organisation may identify discernable skills or blocks of skills and arrange these in a hierarchy to indicate progressive skill levels. Marchington and Wilkinson (2008) identify both constraints and benefits in the use of skills-based pay. They argue that in order for skills-based pay to aid the efficiency and effectiveness of the organisation, thorough skills-needs analysis needs to be conducted to ensure only those skills critical to business success are encouraged and rewarded. Further, the organisation must pledge a clear commitment to training to underpin the scheme. Finally, whilst skills-based pay is likely to encourage a desire for upward mobility and thirst for skills acquisition amongst workers, care must be taken to ensure that only skills used are paid for, otherwise costs will escalate and the organisation will fail to profit. In addition to costs concerns, Armstrong (2002) suggests employees may become frustrated and de-motivated once they exhaust the skills hierarchy and pay progression grinds to a halt.

Team-based pay

Team rewards involve linking pay increases or a portion of individuals' pay increase to an assessment of performance at team rather than at an individual level. Team-based pay is essentially a variant of individual performance-related pay, designed to reinforce collaborative working and team results. Pay for the achievement of team objectives or targets can be distributed as a fixed sum to all team members or can be calculated as a percentage of base salary (Armstrong, 2002). Armstrong and Murlis (1998: 395) contest that 'the case for team pay looks good in theory but there are some formidable disadvantages':

- its effectiveness relies on the existence of well-defined and mature teams;
- distinguishing individual team members' contributions to the team could be problematic;
- it can be difficult to develop fair and objective methods for measuring team outcomes;
- team rivalry may develop;
- organisational flexibility may be hampered in the sense that employees in high-performing, well-rewarded teams might be unwilling to change roles;
- high performers in low-achieving teams may feel unduly penalised and dissatisfied.

Pay progression based on measures of organisational performance

Finally, there are a three main ways in which individuals' pay can be linked to organisational performance, namely gain-sharing, profit-related pay and share-ownership schemes. The general premise of all three schemes is that by linking pay to organisational performance, employees will be encouraged to focus on value-added activities and will identify more closely with the goals of the organisation. Where the organisation is successful as a result of employees' efforts and contributions, due rewards are passed to employees either in the form of a consolidated payment, a cash one-off payment (unconsolidated, variable pay) or the issue of company shares, and hence a financial stake in the organisation, where the preferred method of linking pay to organisational performance is a share-ownership scheme. Briefly, gain-sharing schemes apply a formula to award individuals a share of the financial gains made by the organisation as a result of improvements in quality, productivity enhancements or cost reduction strategies assisted by employees. Profit-related pay or profit-sharing, on the other hand, typically rewards employees with a slice of the company profits generated over and above a pre-specified profit target or level. The level of payouts varies between 2 and 3 per cent of salary and 10 per cent and more (Armstrong 2002: 356). CIPD data (2009a) would suggest that pay progression based on organisational performance is used as part of the pay progression criterion in around a half of all private sector organisations but that its use in the voluntary sector and in the public sector is limited.

Trends in reward practice – towards a strategic approach or more traditionalism?

Since the early 1990s 'new pay' enthusiasts (Lawler, 1990, 1995, 2000; Schuster and Zingheim, 1992) have consistently promoted the efficacy of transforming pay and reward such that it serves as a more effective driver of organisational performance. In essence, 'new pay' or 'dynamic pay' (Flannery et al., 1996) advocate a far more managerialist view of the design and application of reward tools, resonating with the acclaimed superiority of strategic approaches to reward and the notion of 'total rewards'. Its key ingredients include a greater helping of variable pay, a move away from rigid payment structures to fluid and flexible ones, pay centred on the person not on the job, pay progression dependent on performance, competence, skills, contribution or some other form of contingent pay and a shift away from collectivism to individualism in reward. Such practices are considered to offer the organisation greater agility to reward individual employees commensurate with the impact they make upon critical business objectives and greater control over the pay budget. In this final part of the chapter, we discuss the extent to which organisations in the UK appear to echo the new pay rhetoric by marking out the support of business goals as the supreme priority governing reward objectives and throwing out traditional pay practices in favour of the new.

As we have learned throughout this chapter, there are a multitude of ways to do reward. At the same time, there is a strong tide running through business text books, the HR practitioner press and the professional body, persuading organisations that the right way to do reward is to align it with business strategy. Much of the evidence would suggest that despite the pressure to make the link to business strategy few have grasped the nettle firmly. Indeed, the 2009 CIPD Reward Survey indicates a smaller proportion of respondents with a reward strategy in place than the year before and no more enthusiasm to devise one in the year ahead. The CIPD attributes the drop to the current economic turmoil but their reward adviser, Charles Cotton, considers this foolhardy, 'I believe that during these difficult times it becomes even more important for practitioners to determine whether their reward practices support the objectives of the business' (2009a: 35).

Whilst there might be loose attachment to fully fledged reward strategy, there is evidence that elements of 'new pay' are permeating reward practices, particularly in the private sector. Here we see greater use of broad-banded pay structures, greater reference to market rates when determining salary levels and a higher propensity to use more varied and individualised methods of pay progression, 'Only in the public sector and the not for profit sector is seniority-based pay still the most common form of progression' (Perkins and White, 2008: 193). The decline of collective bargaining in the private sector and the rise in performance-related pay would also seem to indicate that a managerial agenda of individualism and greater use of contingent pay in place of uniform rates for jobs is winning through (Kersley *et al.*, 2006). In contrast, much of the public sector, at least in non-managerial roles, remains riddled with traditionalism.

Summary

This chapter began by outlining seven key objectives and these are revisited here.

- Historically, the area of HRM that we now recognise and understand as employee reward, majorly concerned wages and payment systems and the ways in which these could be used to exert control over both sides of the wage/effort bargain, enlarge the area of managerial control and so maximise organisational profitability.

- Contemporaneously, employee reward is defined more broadly to include base pay, variable pay, benefits and non-financial rewards.

- Reward is now recognised by many employers as a key strategic lever which can be used to mould and direct employee behaviour such that it supports and reinforces business goals. Strategic approaches to reward emphasise the importance of matching reward systems and practices to corporate strategy and integrating reward such that it complements other HR policies and practices. Debates persist, however, as to the precise contribution reward can make to business performance and doubts are cast on the ability of employers to design and implement reward strategy effectively.

- There are no right and wrong approaches to employee reward, rather, a myriad of choices are available to organisations. Key choices entail whether to pay for the person or pay for the job, whether to centralise or decentralise reward decision making, whether to place primary focus on internal equity when determining pay or be more concerned with external benchmarks, whether to build hierarchy into the reward system such that there are seniority or status related rewards or to devise a harmonised, single-status approach and how to determine the precise nature of the reward 'mix'.

- Reward decisions are influenced by a range of factors in the external operating environment. In particular, the economic climate affects employers' ability to pay and it guides organisations in determining salary levels/size of the pay review. The legal framework surrounding reward is designed to protect the low paid, set standards for hours of work and holiday entitlement and to ensure equal pay for work of equal value.

- In practice, approaches to reward are influenced by the size and nature of the organisation, the presence of trade unions, ownership/sector and types of workers employed
- Notable differences emerge between the public sector and private sector in terms of favoured methods for establishing pay levels, the design of pay structures and the criteria for pay progression.
- Despite the rhetoric of 'new pay' and the resounding case for strategic approaches to reward, traditionalism remains pervasive alongside experimentation with the new.

Case study

Changes to reward and recognition at KCLSU

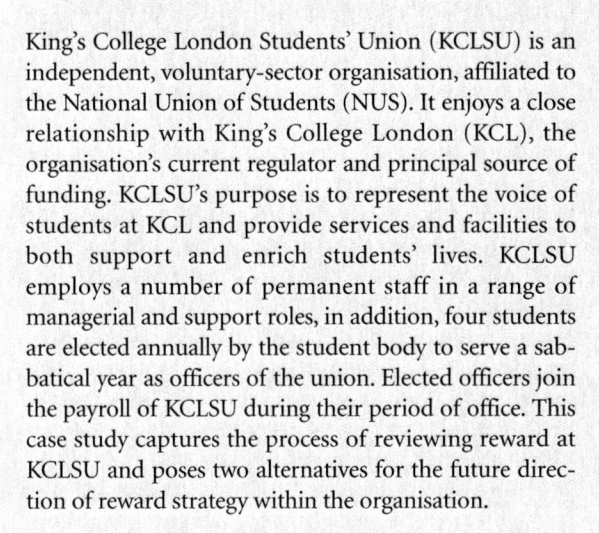

King's College London Students' Union (KCLSU) is an independent, voluntary-sector organisation, affiliated to the National Union of Students (NUS). It enjoys a close relationship with King's College London (KCL), the organisation's current regulator and principal source of funding. KCLSU's purpose is to represent the voice of students at KCL and provide services and facilities to both support and enrich students' lives. KCLSU employs a number of permanent staff in a range of managerial and support roles, in addition, four students are elected annually by the student body to serve a sabbatical year as officers of the union. Elected officers join the payroll of KCLSU during their period of office. This case study captures the process of reviewing reward at KCLSU and poses two alternatives for the future direction of reward strategy within the organisation.

Background

Pay structures and reward strategy at KCLSU need to be reviewed for three main reasons:

- KCLSU currently uses the pay structure in place at King's College London (KCL), an arrangement that has persisted for many years. Along with much of the higher education sector, KCL is currently undergoing a process of modernisation within its pay structures and the current structure is in the process of being phased out. KCLSU is unsure whether the new KCL pay framework will be appropriate for adoption in the students' union. Also, a reconsideration of the logic of KCLSU sharing the KCL pay structure is timely as the organisation is on the brink of becoming regulated by the Charity Commission, rather than the college, and subject to more diversified funding.
- The recognition that there is a need for a modern pay structure to reflect the values of KCLSU, such as contribution and development, and the fact that KCLSU is a modern, forward thinking organisation
- KCLSU needs to be a competitive employer within the voluntary sector, this is essential for staff recruitment and retention purposes

Current system

As indicated above, KCLSU currently utilises the pay scales and process in operation at KCL. The current pay structure is based on the following criteria:

- Several pay spines exist for different grades of staff within the college. KCLSU currently uses two of the existing KCL pay spines: 'Academic and related', which is used primarily for the senior management team and 'Clerical and related' for all other staff.
- The pay spines are divided into overlapping grades; each grade has up to nine increments including discretionary increments at the top of each of grade.
- Individual salary progression is via automatic annual increment to the top of a grade.
- A cost of living increase is awarded annually in August (usually in the region of 3 per cent).
- Discretionary increments are subject to authorisation by a staff member's line manager, historically these have been awarded without question and there is an expectation in place that they will be granted.
- Once a staff member has reached the top of their grade, a proposal for progression to the next grade can be submitted to the HR Committee, who will make a decision as to whether progression will be authorised or not. Currently, the President, Chief Executive and Human Resources Manager sit on the HR Committee.
- If progression to the next grade is not authorised, the staff member will stay at the top of their current grade. The HR Committee will automatically review their salary annually.
- Salaries for new staff members are determined through comparison with existing roles.

This system has a number of inherent problems.

Case study continued

Issues with the current system

There are a number of significant issues with the current pay structure:

- *Progression*: currently, progression through the grades and the award of annual increments is primarily automatic and based on length of service rather than individual contribution. Several staff members will reach the upper limit of their current grade or scale within the next 12–18 months.
- *CEO remuneration*: the KCL pay scales have historically proved unsuitable for the remuneration of the KCLSU Chief Executive due to their upper limits. Therefore KCLSU has developed its own scale for this post and advises the KCL payroll for pay-processing purposes.
- *Benchmarking*: historically benchmarking has only taken place within the students' union sector and not against charity, not-for-profit or public sector equivalents. Increasingly, staff are being attracted to public sector/charity roles as opposed to staying with the students' union world. A recent salary benchmarking exercise drawing information from *Charity Rewards 2005/2006: A Comprehensive National Survey of Pay and Benefits in the Voluntary Sector*[1] has highlighted that current KCLSU salaries may be uncompetitive within the voluntary sector, especially at junior and middle management level i.e. 42 per cent of staff. In fact, the current upper limits of the salary ranges for KCLSU middle and junior managers are below the lower quartile for the charity sector. Taking a wider view, all the upper limits of the current salary ranges are below the median for the charity sector with the exception of the Skilled Manual and Specialist Clerical roles, where the upper limit of the salary range sits £617 above the median. All the lower limits of the current salary ranges are below the lower quartile for the sector, except that for Skilled Manual and Specialist Clerical roles. Elected officer remuneration is typically below that of graduate entrants.
- *Pay and performance*: the KCL pay scales have no latitude for relating pay to performance; there is no reward for good performance other than discretionary rises; there is no organisational imperative added to personal performance. The pay structure has no 'bonus' mechanism.

Observations and developments

KCL pay and modernisation programme

The pay and modernisation programme is KCL's response to the National Framework Agreement (NFA), which focuses on modernising pay within the Higher Education sector. The guiding principles of the programme are those of equal pay for work of equal value and consistency of grading.

- The programme also aims to harmonise terms and conditions of employment for all job roles within the college.
- The new pay structure will focus on rewarding individual contribution; progression will be linked to satisfactory performance and tied into a new appraisal scheme.
- Individual contribution will be measured by both performance (outputs) and competence (inputs).
- The new pay structure will provide the ability to make annual additional payments for rewarding outstanding individual performance.
- The new pay structure will use a single set of pay grades for all staff. Position of a role on the pay spine is to be determined by a single job evaluation scheme. The scheme in use is HERA (Higher Education Role Analysis).
- There are five job families of associated job roles, which are designed to aid job evaluation and underpin career paths.

Considerations – stay with KCL or 'go it alone'?

KCL has indicated that KCLSU is welcome to assimilate to the new KCL pay structure and continue to use college payroll services, however, KCLSU is unsure whether continuing to mirror KCL's pay structures and philosophy will adequately reflect and support the competencies and values KCLSU is striving to embed. KCLSU is also concerned that the issues it currently experiences as a result of adopting KCL's reward framework will prevail with the new, modernised version.

KCLSU want to adopt a reward strategy capable of harnessing the skills and enthusiasm of KCLSU staff to provide a fantastic service to students at KCL, through a clear and sustainable link between reward and achievement. In particular they are keen to ensure that the new approach will:

- provide the flexibility to respond to different demands in a way that is simple, clear and free from bureaucracy, recognising that different parts of the business have different needs;
- provide predictable or guaranteed earnings that give financial certainty, but with the opportunity to reflect upon business success, and reward people for the passion or creativity that contributes to that success;

Case study continued

- value people for what they do and how they do it, so that KCLSU delivers on its promises and makes a difference to the quality of student life at KCL;
- act as an effective magnet to attract good people, recognising the need for a steady influx of fresh thinking and new approaches, alongside the development of existing talent;
- support KCLSU values and reward employees for living KCLSU values (see Table).

KCLSU values

Value	Examples of how this might be demonstrated
Making sure every person in the organisation matters	• Communicates openly and honestly, always giving consideration to the views and feelings of others • Listens to others, questions when unclear to ensure mutual understanding and allows for discussion • Gives and receive feedback sensitively creating an environment where issues can be discussed constructively • Acts as a team player, actively supports team and organisation objectives • Demonstrates cross-organisational understanding • Shows respect and consideration for the needs of others, and the context within which they work • Demonstrates an understanding of the value of diversity, and the strengths and skills of others
Focusing on our students	• Has a clear understanding of role, and how it relates to the team's and KCLSU's objectives • Demonstrates dedication and enthusiasm towards students • Represents KCLSU positively to students • Seeks and acts upon feedback from both students and internal/external sources.
Continually striving to improve	• Is focused on meeting and exceeding objectives • Is prepared to ask for support from colleagues/line manager when required, to help meet objectives • Sets challenging targets that encourage personal development • Committed to innovation, developing new ideas and solutions • Demonstrates adaptability, flexibility, and a willingness to experiment • When required is entrepreneurial and willing to take appropriate risks
Not being complacent, overcoming unnecessary bureaucracy	• Actively seeks and shares information for the benefit of themselves, team and KCLSU • Seeks to develop effective and efficient ways of working at individual, team and organisational level • Sees mistakes as an opportunity to learn and encourages others to think in the same way
Being confident of our role	• Promotes positive understanding of the aims of KCLSU • Acts as a role model inspiring, supporting, motivating and encouraging others • Raises awareness and understanding of issues affecting students • Values the contribution of others, and recognises and celebrates others' achievements
Managing people well	• Articulates a clear vision for staff; establishes clear aims and objectives for individuals and teams • Ensures that every team member has a clear understanding of their role and how it relates to KCLSU's objectives • Manages individuals and teams consistently, objectively and fairly • Carries out constructive performance reviews with team members • Encourages colleagues to continue their professional development • Listens to feedback and forms recommendations to improve service, develop ideas and deal with issues • Helps develop a culture in which people are valued and able to reach their full potential

1. Croner Reward 2005.

Source: KCLSU

Case study continued

Questions

1. Critically assess the degree to which KCL's pay and modernisation programme is likely to address the issues and concerns KCLSU currently experiences as a result of using the KCL pay framework
2. Consider the benefits and risks associated with KCLSU 'going it alone'.
3. Identify the immediate and on-going/longer-term resource implications for KCLSU if the organisation decides to break away from the KCL pay framework and supporting infrastructure.
4. Using your knowledge and understanding of reward options identify and justify a set of preliminary proposals for a KCLSU 'tailor-made' reward strategy.

References and further reading

Adams, J. (1965) 'Inequity and social exchange' in L. Berkowitz (ed.) *Advances in Experimental Social Psychology 2*, New York: Academic Press, pp. 267–96.

Anthony, P.D. (1977) *The Ideology of Work*. London: Tavistock Publications.

Armstrong, M. (2002) *Employee Reward*, 3rd edn. London: CIPD.

Armstrong, M. and Brown, D. (2006) *Strategic Reward*. London: Kogan Page.

Armstrong, M. and Murlis, H. (1998) *Reward Management; A Handbook of Remuneration Strategy and Practice*. London: Kogan Page.

Armstrong, M. and Stephens, T. (2005) *A Handbook of Employee Reward Management and Practice*. London: Kogan Page.

Armstrong, M., Cummins, A., Hastings, S. and Wood, W. (2003) *Job Evaluation: A Guide to Achieving Equal Pay*. London: Kogan Page.

Arrowsmith, J. and Gilman, M. (2005) 'Small firms and the national minimum wage' in S. Marlow, D. Patton and M. Ram (eds) *Managing Labour in Small Firms*. London: Routledge, pp. 159–77.

Baldwin, M. and Johnson, W. (2006) 'A critical review of studies of discrimination against workers with disabilities' in W. Rodgers III (ed.) *Handbook on the Economics of Discrimination*. Gloucester: Edward Elgar, pp. 119–60.

Barrett, R. and Mayson, S. (2007) 'Human resource management in growing small firms', *Journal of Small Business and Enterprise Development*, 14, 2, 307–20.

Barrett, R., Mayson, S. and Warriner, M. (2008) 'The relationship between small firm growth and HRM practices' in R. Barrett and S. Mayson (eds) *International Handbook of Entrepreneurship and HRM*. Cheltenham: Edward Elgar, pp. 186–204.

Beer, M. (1984) *Managing Human Assets*. New York: Free Press.

Beer, M., Spector, B., Lawrence, P., Mills, D. and Walton, R. (1984) *Human Resource Management; A General Manager's Perspective*. New York: Free Press.

Bevan, S. (2000) *Reward Strategy: 10 Common Mistakes*. London: Institute for Employment Studies.

Blauner, R. (1964) *Alienation and Freedom: The Factory Worker and his Industry*. Chicago, IL: University of Chicago Press.

Bloom, M.C. and Milkovich, G. (1996) 'Issues in managerial compensation research' in C.L. Cooper and D.M. Rousseau (eds) *Trends in Organizational Behavior*, Vol. 3. Chichester: John Wiley, pp. 23–47.

Bowey, A. and Lupton, T. (1973) *Job and Pay Comparisons*. Aldershot: Gower.

Braverman, H. (1974) *Labour and Monopoly Capital: The Degradation of Work in the Twentieth Century*. London: Monthly Review Press.

Brown, D. and Armstrong, M. (1999) *Paying for Contribution; Real Performance-Related Pay Strategies*. London: Kogan Page.

Brown, D. and Dive, B. (2009) 'Level-pegging'. *People Management*, 15 January: 26–29.

Burawoy, M. (1985) *The Politics of Production*. London: Verso.

Burke, R. and Cooper, C. (2008) *The Long Work Hours Culture: Causes, Consequences and Choices*. Bingley: Emerald.

Callaghan, G. and Thompson, P. (2001) 'Edwards revisited; technical control and call centres' 22 *Economic and Industrial Democracy*, 22: 13–40.

CIPD (2000) *A Study of Broad-banded and Job Family Pay Structures*. CIPD Report. London: CIPD.

CIPD (2003) *Total Reward*. Research Summary. London: CIPD.

CIPD (2005) *Reward Strategy: How to Develop a Reward Strategy. A CIPD Practical Tool*. London: CIPD.

CIPD (2007) *Reward Management*. A CIPD Survey. London: CIPD.

CIPD (2008a) *Reward Management*. A CIPD Survey. London: CIPD.

CIPD (2008b) *Market Pricing; Approaches and Considerations*. CIPD Factsheet. London: CIPD.

CIPD (2008c) *Pay Progression*. CIPD Factsheet. London: CIPD.

CIPD (2009a) *Reward Management*. CIPD Survey. London: CIPD.

CIPD (2009b) *Pay and Reward: An Overview*. CIPD Factsheet. London: CIPD.

Conboy, B. (1976) *Pay at Work*. London: Arrow Books.

Cotton, C. (2009) 'Workers gloomy about their pay prospects', *Impact: Quarterly update on CIPD Policy and Research*, 26: 18–19.

Druker, J. and White, G. (2009) 'Introduction' in G. White and J. Druker (eds) *Reward Management: A Critical Text*. Abingdon: Routledge, pp. 1–22.

Dundon T. and Rollinson, D. (2004) *Employment Relations in Small Firms*. London: Routledge.

Employee Benefits/MX Financial Solutions (2003) 'Flexible Benefits Research 2003', *Employee Benefits*, April: 4–9.

Equality and Human Rights Commission (2009) www.equalityandhumanrights.org.

e-Reward (2007) *Graded Pay Structures*, factsheet. www.e-reward.co.uk.

Evain, E. (2008) *Working Conditions Laws 2006–2007*. Geneva: ILO.

Eyraud, F. and Saget, C. (2005) *The Fundamentals of Minimum Wage Fixing*. Geneva: ILO.

Flannery, T.P., Hafrichter, D.A. and Platten, P.E. (1996) *People, Performance and Pay*. New York: The Free Press.

Fredman, S. (2008) 'Reforming equal pay laws', 37 *Industrial Law Journal 193*.

Fudge, J. and Owens, R. (2006) *Precarious Work, Women and the New Economy*. Oxford: Hart Publishing.

Gollan, P. (2007) *Employee Representation in Non-Union Firms*. London: Sage.

Gospel, H. (1992) *Markets, Firms and the Management of Labour in Modern Britain*. Cambridge: Cambridge University Press.

Heery, E. (2000) 'The new pay: risk and representation at work' in D. Winstanley and J. Woodall (eds) *Ethical Issues in Contemporary Human Resource Management*. Basingstoke: Palgrave, pp. 172–88.

Hellerstein, J. and Newmark, D. (2006) 'Using matched employer-employee data to study labor market discrimination' in W. Rodgers III (ed.) *Handbook on the Economics of Discrimination*. Gloucester: Edward Elgar, pp. 29–60.

Herzberg, F. (1966) *Work and the Nature of Man*. Cleveland, OH: World Publishing.

Hewlett, S. and Luce, C. (2006) 'Extreme jobs: the dangerous allure of the 70-hour work week', *Harvard Business Review*, (December): 49.

Hill, S. (1981) *Competition and Control at Work*. London: Heinemann.

Hinton, J. (1986) *Labour and Socialism*. London: Wheatsheaf Books.

Humbert A.L. and Lewis, S. (2008) 'I have no life other than work – long working hours, blurred boundaries and family life' in R. Burke and C. Cooper *The Long Work Hours Culture: Causes, Consequences and Choices*. Bingley: Emerald, pp. 159–82.

IDS (2000) 'Job evaluation', *Incomes Data Services StudyPlus*; Autumn.

IDS (2002) 'Kingsmill recommends a package of measures to address the gender pay gap', *Incomes Data Services Report 848*, January: 4–5.

IDS (2006) *Developments in Occupational Pay Differentiation. A Research Report of the Office for Manpower Economics*, October 2006. London: Incomes Data Services.

IRS (2003) 'Employers value job evaluation', *IRS Employment Review 790 /Employment Trends*, 19 December: 9–16.

IRS (2008) 'Survey of pay prospects'.

Jamieson, S. (1999) 'Equal Pay' in A. Morris and T. O'Donnell (eds) *Feminist Perspectives on Employment Law*. London: Cavendish, pp. 223–40.

Kersley, B., Alpin, C., Forth, J., Bryson, A., Bewley, H., Dix, G. and Oxenbridge, S. (2006) *Inside the Workplace: Findings from the 2004 Workplace Employment Relations Survey*. Abingdon: Routledge.

Kessler, I. (2001) 'Reward system choices' in J. Storey (ed.) *Human Resource Management: A Critical Text*, 2nd edn. London: Thomson Learning, pp. 206–31.

Kessler, I. (2007) 'Reward choices: strategy and equity' in J. Storey, (ed.) *Human Resource Management: A Critical Text*, 3rd edn. London: Thomson Learning, pp. 159–76.

Kessler, I. and Purcell, J. (1992) 'Performance related pay; objectives and application'. *Human Resource Management Journal*, 2, 3, Spring: 16–33.

Kohn, A. (1993) 'Why incentive plans cannot work', *Harvard Business Review*, September–October: 54–62.

Lawler, E. (1990) *Strategic Pay*. San Francisco, CA: Jossey-Bass.

Lawler, E. (1995). 'The new pay; a strategic approach', *Compensation and Benefits Review*, July/August: 46–54.

Lawler, E. (2000) 'Pay and strategy; new thinking for the new millennium', *Compensation and Benefits Review*, January/February: 7–12.

Lewis, P. (2006) 'Reward management' in T. Redman and A. Wilkinson (eds) *Contemporary Human Resource Management*, 2nd edn. London: FT/Pearson, pp. 126–52.

Littler, C. (1982) *The Development of the Labour Process in Capitalist Societies*. London: Heinemann.

Littler, C. (ed.) (1985) *The Experience of Work*. Aldershot: Gower.

Lovell, J. (1977) *British Trade Unions 1875–1933*. London: MacMillan.

Low Pay Commision (2001) *1st Report of the Low Pay Commission*. London: HMSO.

Marchington, M. and Wilkinson, A. (2008) *HRM at Work; People Management and Development*, 4th edn. London: CIPD.

Marlow, S., Patton, D. and Ram, M. (2005) *Managing Labour in Small Firms*. London: Routledge.

Marsden, D. and Richardson, R. (1994) 'Performing for pay? The effects of "merit pay" in a public service', *British Journal of Industrial Relations*, June: 243–61.

Mazzarol, T. (2003) 'A model of small business HR growth management', *International Journal of Entrepreneurial Behaviour and Research*, 9: 27–49.

McCann, D. (2005) *Working Time Laws: A Global Perspective*. Geneva: ILO.

McColgan, A. (2008) 'Equal pay' in P. Cane and J. Conaghan, *The New Oxford Companion to Law*. Oxford: Oxford University Press, pp. 401–02.

Milkovitch, G. and Newman, J. (1996) *Compensation*, 5th edn. Burr Ridge: Irwin.

Murlis, H. (2004) 'Managing rewards' in D. Rees and G. McBain (eds) *People Management: Challenges and Opportunities*. Basingstoke: Palgrave, pp. 152–70.

Perkins, S.J. and White, G. (2008) *Employee Reward: Alternatives, Consequences and Contexts*. London: CIPD.

Pfeffer, J. (1998) 'Six dangerous myths about pay', *Harvard Business Review*, May–June: 108–21.

Ritzer, G. (1997) *The McDonaldization Theory*. London: Sage.

Ritzer, G. (2000) *The McDonaldization of Society*. London: Sage.

Schuster, J. and Zingheim, P. (1992) *The New Pay: Linking Employee and Organisational Performance*. New York: Lexington Books.

Storey, J. (1992) *Developments in the Management of Human Resources*. Oxford: Blackwell.

Taylor, F.W. (1964) *Scientific Management*. New York: Harper & Row.

Taylor, P. and Bain, P. (1999) 'An assembly line in the head' *Industrial Relations Journal*, 30: 101–17.

Taylor, P. and Bain, P. (2001) 'Trade unions, workers rights and the frontier of control in UK call centres', *Economic and Industrial Democracy*, 22: 29–41.

Taylor, S (2008) *People Resourcing*, 4th edn. London: CIPD.

Thompson E.P. (1991) 'Time, work-discipline and Industrial Capitalism' in E.P. Thompson *Customs in Common*. Harmondsworth: Penguin, pp. 68–92.

Thompson, M. (1992) 'Pay and performance; the employer experience', *Institute of Manpower Studies*. Report No. 218, London.

Thompson, M. (2009) 'Salary progression systems' in G. White and J. Druker (eds) *Reward Management; A Critical Text*. Abingdon: Routledge, pp. 120–47.

Thompson, P. (1983) *The Nature of Work*. London: Macmillian.

Thompson, P. and Milsome. S. (2001) *Reward Determination in the UK*. Research Report, London: CIPD.

Urwick, L. (1958) *Personnel Management in Perspective*. Oxford: Oxford University Press.

Vroom, V. (1982) *Work and Motivation*. New York: John Wiley.

White, G. (2009) 'Determining pay' in G. White and J. Druker (eds) *Reward Management: A Critical Text*. Abingdon: Routledge, pp. 23–48.

Wood, A.W. (2000) 'Alienation' in *Concise Routledge Encyclopedia of Philosophy*. London: Routledge, p. 24.

Wood, S. (ed.) (1982) *The Degradation of Work?* London: Hutchinson.

WorldatWork (2000) *Total Rewards: From Strategy To Implementations*. Scottsdale, AZ: WorldatWork.

Wright, A. (2004) *Employee Reward in Context*. London: CIPD.

Wright, A. (2009) 'Benefits' in G. White and J. Druker (eds) *Reward Management: A Critical Text*. Abingdon: Routledge, pp. 174–91.

Yates, M.L. (1937) *Wages and Labour Conditions in British Engineering*. Cambridge.

Zeitlin, J. (1983) 'The labour strategies of British engineering employers 1890–1922' in H. Gospel and C. Littler, *Managerial Strategies & Industrial Relations*. Aldershot: Gower, pp. 25–54.

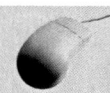

For multiple-choice questions, exercises and annotated weblinks related to this topic, visit **www.pearsoned.co.uk/mymanagementlab**.

EMPLOYMENT RELATIONS –
CONTROL, CONFLICT AND COMMITMENT

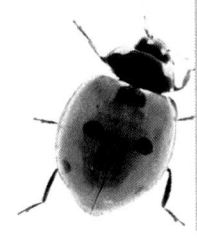

Chapter 8
INDUSTRIAL RELATIONS
Nicolas Bacon

Introduction

The purpose of this chapter is to outline some of the key contemporary developments in industrial relations issues and consider the implications. The term 'industrial relations' when broadly defined encompasses the study of all aspects of the employment relationship (see Heery *et al.* 2008, p.2); more narrowly defined, it has traditionally focused on those areas of the employment relationship in which managers deal with the representatives of employees rather than managing employees directly as individuals (Edwards 1995). The main parties to the employment relationship and the key actors are workers and workers' organisations (usually trade unions), employers and managers, and also the state. These actors create rules to regulate work, covering such issues as wages and working hours (termed 'substantive rules') and how to bargain, consult and resolve disputes over issues (termed 'procedural rules'). Whether substantive or procedural rules are set unilaterally by employers, the extent to which the state decides to intervene and regulate employment, and the role of workers and trade unions in the process of establishing rules, are among the central industrial relations issues explored in this chapter. Employers set rules to try to maximise efficiency, but other actors in the employment relationship may feel that employers often make choices that do not maximise efficiency, and that the decisions managers make may therefore damage organisational performance and threaten the terms and conditions of employees. In addition, workers and the state are also interested in the fairness of employment outcomes and seek to influence employer policies on a range of issues, such as what constitutes a fair day's work for a fair day's pay and the distribution of pay between different workers and between workers and managers, and to ensure equal opportunities for employees. As a result, industrial relations are often subject to joint regulation between employers and trade unions. Joint regulation of employer practices therefore requires employee participation in decision making and it is appropriate to start by considering how managers react to this challenge to their authority.

Management approaches to industrial relations

The suggestion that trade unions or the state should intervene, or intervene more, in regulating employment provokes a strong response in many employers and managers, many of whom prefer to make employment decisions unilaterally. Employers and managers responding in this way hold a set of assumptions about the right to manage (frequently termed the management prerogative) and the rights of workers, unions and the state to intervene in employment relations (Budd and Bhave 2008). These assumptions held by managers are the mixture of a complex blend of experiences, predispositions, learned behaviour and prejudice and are influenced and reinforced by incentives for managers either to act just in the interests of shareholders or to balance the interests of a broader range of stakeholders. The assumptions held by managers are termed 'frames of reference', (Fox 1966, p.1974) which describe managers' often deeply held assumptions towards a labour force and the rights of workers, trade unions or the state to influence management decisions. Three separate frames of reference can be identified: unitarism, pluralism and radical. A manager with one frame of reference will differ from a manager with an alternative frame of reference in terms of their beliefs about the nature of organisations, the role of conflict and the task of managing employees. Managers holding a unitarist frame of reference believe that the natural state of organisations is one of harmony and cooperation. All employees are thought to be in the same team, pulling together for the common goal of organisational success. The employee relations task of management is to prevent conflict arising from misunderstandings that result if they fail to adequately communicate organisational goals to employees. Any remaining conflicts are attributed to mischief created by troublemakers. A pluralist frame of reference recognises that organisations contain a variety of sectional groups who legitimately seek to express divergent interests. The resulting conflict is inevitable and the task of managers is to establish a system of structures and procedures in which conflict is institutionalised and a negotiated order is established. The radical critique of pluralism is not, strictly speaking, a frame of reference for understanding management views of the employment relationship. It draws upon Marxism and explains workplace conflict within a broader historical and social context and places a stress upon the unequal power struggle of opposing social classes.

There are no simple methods to assess whether most managers hold one frame of reference or another – indeed, they usually hold a complex set of ideas rather than falling neatly into a single and possibly oversimplistic frame of reference, and of course managers may hold different views in different countries. In Britain at least, most managers oppose sharing power with unions and prefer managerial unilateralism, express a preference for flexible labour markets and oppose government involvement in wage setting (Poole et al. 2005). As trade union power has declined, managers oppose state involvement in industrial relations issues, although this is not always the case, as managers in the past have supported state intervention to control the power of trade unions. Managers have, however, become less hostile to unions as union power has declined; for example, managers currently see less of a need for the state to intervene to restrict union power (Poole et al. 2005)

Answers to another question frequently posed to managers indicate that a majority of workplace managers do not have a single frame of reference. In the 2004 Workplace Employment Relations Survey (WERS04), most managers directly responsible for industrial relations issues in Britain (62 per cent) were 'neutral' about union membership, whereas 21 per cent were 'in favour', with 17 per cent 'not in favour' of union membership by employees in their workplace (Kersley et al. 2006, pp.112–13). However, when the same managers are asked more explicitly whether they prefer to manage employees directly or through unions then unitarist preferences emerge. For example, 79 per cent of all managers surveyed agreed with the statement 'we would rather consult directly with employees than with unions', increasing to 82 per cent of public sector managers and 88 per cent of managers in small workplaces with fewer than 50 employees (Kersley et al. 2006, p.50). Consequently, management approaches to industrial relations are often characterised as mixing and matching unitarist and pluralist beliefs (Edwards et al. 1998). Many managers hold such views because it reflects the reality of employees' need for representation to protect their interests from employers, or an acceptance that in some industries unions are powerful and employees will only regard rules as legitimate if employees and their representatives participate in management decisions. In some organisations, unitarist managers also actively seek to deter employees from joining trade unions, whereas pluralist managers in some cases in contrast encourage employees to join unions. Encouraging or deterring employees from joining unions appears to be important as employers' attitudes towards unions are significantly associated with union presence in the workplace (Kersley et al. 2006, p.114) and union membership across Europe (Schnabel and Wagner 2007) and no doubt outside Europe.

Frames of reference are also important because they underlie the broader management style adopted in organisations towards the workforce. The approach taken to industrial relations is often linked to broader work organisation and human resource management issues. It is common therefore to link managers' approach to industrial relations with a more general management style towards employees that also affects work organisation and human resource management practices (Fox 1974; Purcell and Sisson 1983; Purcell and Ahlstrand 1994; Storey and Bacon 1993; for a review see Bacon 2008). Later in this chapter we will describe the decline of joint regulation. An important question is whether employers have adopted a unitarist approach to industrial relations in order to facilitate high-performance work practices to improve organisational performance by developing employee commitment (Bacon 2003). Or, in contrast, do managers avoid unions in order to improve organisational performance by reducing employment costs and seeking to exercise greater control over employees? Before we look at this, however, employers cannot devise effective industrial relations approaches without carefully considering the views of their employees, and it is to employee views that we now turn.

Why employees join unions

A widespread criticism of management during the 1960s and 1970s, a point which still holds today, is that employees may not feel that everyone shares the same goals in their workplace and they may reject a unitarist perspective. In many, if not most, workplaces employees talk of 'us' and describe managers as 'them', believing that there are two sides with partially conflicting interests (Clegg 1979). Thus, many employees subscribe to a pluralist perspective and feel that workers and managers are on different sides with separate interests, rather than feeling that working for an organisation is like playing for a football team where all groups supporting a club are on the same side and pursuing a common goal (Ramsey 1975).

As many employees feel they have different interests from employers, they often join trade unions. Trade unions have approximately 320 million members worldwide, which amounts to between one-fifth and one-quarter of the global labour force (Visser 2003). Significant variation exists between countries. For instance, Russia, Ukraine and Belarus (58 per cent) and China (42 per cent) have high rates of union membership; around one-quarter (26 per cent) of European workers are union members; whereas a smaller proportion of workers in North America (13 per cent) and Asia (10 per cent) belong to unions. It is therefore important that employers understand why employees join trade unions.

Employees join unions for a wide range of reasons (Schnabel 2003, p.19). They may join a union because they feel dissatisfied with their work situation (termed the frustration-aggression thesis), joining a union may bring benefits such as higher wages that outweigh the costs of membership (a rational choice explanation), or employees may be encouraged to join by the traditions and opinions of their work group (an interactionist explanation). In a study across 18 EU countries, in addition to the strong effects of employers' attitudes in the workplace mentioned earlier to explain whether union members are present in the workplace, the probability of union membership is also affected by workplace characteristics, personal characteristics and an individual's attitudes (Schnabel and Wagner 2007). The types of workplace, the personal characteristics of the labour force and individual attitudes may of course vary between countries and alongside other factors help explain national differences in levels of union membership. State support for unions, the union role in social insurance schemes and of course national political history are also important to explain differences in national levels of union

Table 8.1 The reasons employees give for joining unions

Support if I had a problem at work	72%
Improved pay and conditions	36%
Because I believe in trade unions	16%
Free legal advice	15%
Most people at work are members	14%

Source: Waddington and Whitston 1997, p.521

membership. To illustrate in more detail, some of the factors identified in the study of 18 EU countries just mentioned were important in a survey of almost 11,000 union members in the UK (Waddington and Whitston 1997). In the UK survey employees revealed that they continued to join unions for collective protection and to improve their terms and conditions (Table 8.1). These findings are in line with studies suggesting that workers' perceptions of 'them' and 'us' are still strong, even though managers over the past 20 years have attempted to improve industrial relations through a wide range of initiatives described in other chapters in this book (see Coupland *et al.* 2005; D'Art and Turner 1999; Kelly and Kelly 1991).

The decline of joint regulation

The degree of joint regulation of industrial relations is not of course fixed but changes in response to global and national economic, social and political pressures. In a majority of countries union membership has fallen over the past 20 years, especially in Europe and North America. Increased market competition, for example, has reduced the willingness of employers to recognise and negotiate with trade unions in many, but not all, countries (Brown 2008). Table 8.2 shows the extent of decline in union density – the proportion of employees who are union members – in 20 OECD countries. In different European regions and in liberal market economies, union density has declined, although it has declined only marginally in northern Europe (Denmark, Finland, Norway and Sweden) and has declined most steeply in liberal market economies (Australia, Canada, Ireland, New Zealand, the UK and the US).

Declining union density is only one indication of joint regulation and it is also important to consider trends in collective bargaining coverage – the proportion of employees whose terms and conditions of employment are set by collective bargaining. Reflecting the comments made above about unionisation reflecting national economic and political differences, Table 8.3 shows that the most dramatic decline in collective bargaining coverage has occurred in liberal market economies (Australia, Canada, New Zealand, the UK and the US). Among central European countries collective bargaining coverage has remained stable (Austria and

Table 8.2 Average union density (%) and density change in 20 OECD countries, 1980–2000

Region	1980	1990	2000	Change 1980–2000
Northern Europe	71.5	71.5	71	−0.5
Mainland Europe	35	25	22	−12.8
Central Europe	42	36	32	−10.6
Liberal market economies	47	38	26	−20.7

Source: Hamann and Kelly 2008, p.138

Table 8.3 Average percentage of employees covered by collective bargaining in 20 OECD countries, 1980–2000

Region	1980	1990	2000	Change 1980–2000
Northern Europe	78	78	83	+5
Mainland Europe	73	78	83	+8
Central Europe	77	77	75	−2.5
Liberal market economies	55	47	36	−18.4

Source: Hamann and Kelly 2008, p.139

Belgium), declined (Germany and Switzerland) and increased in the Netherlands. In mainland Europe it has increased (France, Greece, Italy, Portugal and Spain), as it has in northern Europe.

Within each group of countries and within each country joint regulation has probably not declined at a uniform rate. However, in liberal market economies the steep decline of joint regulation appears to have affected all industrial sectors, if not evenly. If we consider a third indicator of joint regulation, union recognition, in the UK for example, the number of workplaces recognising unions declined between 1980 and 2004 in all sectors but the decline was modest in the public sector compared to the private sector (Table 8.4).

What are the main reasons for the decline in joint regulation? Focusing on liberal market economies, because this is where the decline is most evident, and using the UK as an example, the decline in union recognition in the UK since the 1980s is mainly due to the failure of unions to organise workers and gain recognition for collective bargaining in new firms and new workplaces (Machin 2000). Responding to heightened competitive pressures, managers have proved reluctant to recognise unions for fear of higher wages, and unions have found it difficult to recruit the growing numbers of female and service sector workers. As the number of large manufacturing plants and manual workers declined, the traditional habitat for the UK's system of industrial relations based on adversarial collective bargaining was disappearing (Millward *et al.* 1992). During the 1990s, these factors accounted for three-quarters of the decline in collective bargaining, although, in addition, managers in unionised workplaces were less likely to continue ongoing collective bargaining arrangements, with about one quarter of the decline in the 1990s explained by abandoning collective bargaining in ongoing workplaces (Charlwood 2007).

Trade union influence appears even lower than suggested by current levels of union recognition when we consider the scope and depth of joint consultation and bargaining. It is difficult to assess the extent to which managers rely upon collective agreements with trade

Table 8.4 Average percentage of workplaces with 25+ employees recognising unions, 1980–2004

	1980	1984	1990	1998	2004
Manufacturing	65	56	44	28	37
Private services	41	44	36	23	20
Public sector	94	99	87	87	88
All	64	66	53	42	39

Source: Blanchflower *et al.* 2007, p.288

unions in workplaces. Although formal collective agreements may include procedural arrangements for continued union influence in the workplace (Dunn and Wright 1994) managers have increasingly exercised their prerogative to make important changes unilaterally, particularly in working methods (Geary 1995). This suggests that although many employers retain agreements with unions, collective agreements have been hollowed out and in workplaces where union representatives are present only a modest level of joint regulation occurs. On average in British workplaces with recognised unions, for example, across seven different bargaining issues, employers report negotiating with union representatives in 10 per cent of workplaces, consult in 36 per cent, inform union representatives in 20 per cent, and neither negotiate, consult nor inform in 28 per cent of workplaces (Brown and Nash 2008). Managers in many workplaces appear to regard certain HR issues as off-limits to union representatives and do not even provide information on these issues to unions. As a consequence, trade union influence in many workplaces has 'withered on the vine', and where union representatives remain in place this resembles a unionised approach to industrial relations which in fact is little more than a 'hollow shell' (Hyman 1997).

Employers deny unions influence because they seek greater freedom to choose employment practices. From the mid-1980s, employers certainly appeared to exercise an increasing degree of strategic choice in redesigning employment practices as unions made significant concessions to employer demands. The strategic choice theory of industrial relations marked a paradigm shift from unions making demands and employers conceding to those demands, to managers, rather than unions, becoming the central industrial relations actor in liberal market economies such as the US, and making demands to which unions had to accede (Strauss 1984). At the core of strategic choice theory in industrial relations is the assumption that managers 'have discretion over their decisions; that is, where environmental constraints do not severely curtail the parties' choice of alternatives' (Kochan *et al.* 1984, p.21). However, declining union influence does not necessarily increase employer freedom of choice, for two reasons. First, the state has increasingly intervened to regulate employment practices to compensate for the decline of joint regulation between employers and unions (Piore and Safford 2006). To give one example, as unions are not able to easily organise workplaces with the lowest levels of pay, the British government introduced a national minimum wage and statutory recognition procedure for trade unions, both long-established features of US industrial relations. Second, intensive market forces have reduced employer discretion in employment practices in many instances. If all employers are, for example, forced to marginalise trade unions because they have to reduce employment costs then this is hardly a strategic choice but a market imperative (Lewin 1987: for a broader review see Bacon 2008). Whether employers have exercised significant levels of strategic choice in industrial relations or not, the implications of declining union influence are dramatic and tell us much about employer motives.

The implications of declining joint regulation

Trade unions have a range of beneficial effects, including forcing managers to improve human resource management practices (the 'shock effect' of unions requiring an improvement in management); increasing employee voice in the workplace to express the interests of employees, redistribution of outcomes and promoting equal opportunities (the 'sword of justice' effect); and increasing job satisfaction and reducing labour turnover. Union effects appear to have reduced remarkably in recent years; on some issues unions now appear to have no discernible effects and in other cases the effects only apply in specific circumstances (see Brown 2008, p.123). The long-term implications of the decline in joint regulation are potentially far-reaching.

According to the collective voice/institutional response model of unionism (Freeman and Medoff 1984), unions express employees' views and have an impact on managers greater than the views expressed by individual employees, which are frequently ignored by managers. With this collective voice unions seek to raise employee wages and bargain for a range of beneficial policies for members, such as greater training. As a result, unionised workers traditionally received higher wages compared to non-unionised workers (the union wage premium) and, as described earlier, employees act rationally in joining unions for higher wages that outweigh the costs of membership. At a time when unions are less powerful, employers correspondingly are less likely to recognise and work with unions in order to remove union pressure to provide improved terms and conditions. As a result, the union wage premium comparing the wages of unionised and non-unionised workers during a period of union weakness has reduced overtime (Blanchflower and Bryson 2003). Nevertheless, in 2005 the union wage premium in Britain was 10 per cent of gross hourly earnings (Bryson and Forth 2008). Trade unions also have a second important effect on wages by narrowing the pay distribution in attempting a fair redistribution of reward. It is therefore not surprising that declining unionisation results in increasing wage inequality (Charlwood 2007) and the salaries of executive directors and managers have risen exponentially as unions have been less able to increase members' wages.

Moving beyond wages, declining unionisation has also affected training provision and the ability of unions to raise training levels. Trade unions raise training levels in a variety of ways. Unions bargain directly for more training, increase wages so employers have to train employees in order for employees to contribute more and offset higher wages, and in expressing and seeking to resolve employee grievances, unions reduce employee turnover, thereby extending the period in which employers benefit from training investments. The positive union effect on training is also in decline. Whereas training was higher in unionised workplaces throughout the 1980s and 1990s in Britain, by 2004 unionised workplaces in the private sector no longer provided more training than non-unionised workplaces in the private sector, and the union training premium in the public sector was weak (Hoque and Bacon 2008). Even where unions have prioritised training (see the discussion of union learning representatives later in this chapter), and employers negotiated and bargained with union representatives over training, there is little evidence that employers respond to this pressure. In Britain at least, trade unions are currently not able to raise training levels above those provided in non-union workplaces in the private sector.

Trade unions also fulfil a 'sword of justice' role in promoting fairness and equality in the workplace and this may also have been harmed by the decline of joint regulation (Metcalf 2004). Unionised workplaces report more family-friendly policies and are more likely to have an equal opportunities policy (Noon and Hoque 2001; Walsh 2007). For example in Britain, whereas 63 per cent of non-union workplaces had an equal opportunities policy in 2004, 96 per cent of unionised workplaces had such a policy (Kersley *et al.* 2006, p.238). In the absence of union pressure and the willingness of employers to respond to this pressure, employers are less likely to adopt family-friendly and equal opportunities policies.

As the evidence reviewed so far suggests, unions are associated with many positive employment practices in the workplace, although employers are increasingly unresponsive to union pressure. There is also evidence that employers seek to offset the higher costs associated with unionisation by saving on employment costs elsewhere. For example, White (2005) reports that unionised compared to non-union workplaces not only report more high-performance work practices, fringe benefits and family-friendly practices, but unionised workplaces also report high levels of labour-cost-cutting policies such as reducing staffing levels, outsourcing and delayering management hierarchies. This suggests that where unions encourage managers to adopt expensive productivity-enhancing HR practices, employers look to reduce other employment costs by reducing staffing levels or employing staff on inferior terms and conditions through contractors.

Earlier in this chapter the declining influence of unions on employer policy was shown by the significant number of unionised workplaces in which managers did not negotiate, consult or inform union representatives on key employment issues. Recent evidence suggests that trade unions are no longer as effective in raising the concerns of their members because managers are increasingly less willing to listen to concerns expressed through union representatives and prefer to deal with individual employees. Trade unions rely on the logic of collective action – expressing the collective voice of employees has more influence than an employee acting alone. Managers appear increasingly unresponsive to union voice, with evidence that unions are no longer able to shock employers into better practices to raise productivity (Bryson *et al.* 2006). Trade unions find it increasingly difficult to resolve workplace grievances with unresponsive employers, and as a result find it increasingly difficult to increase the levels of satisfaction employees experience in their jobs. Guest and Conway (2004), for example, report that union members compared to non-union members report lower levels of job satisfaction, consistent with the suggestion that management unresponsiveness to union-expressed grievances and demands constrains union voice and increases the levels of dissatisfaction among union members. This is a worrying finding because job satisfaction is associated with turnover, and reduced turnover increases the incentive for employers to invest in commitment-enhancing human resource management practices, as the period over which they benefit from such investments is greater if fewer staff exit. Employer unresponsiveness to trade unions is gradually shutting off the productivity-enhancing impacts of trade unions.

Employers feel justified in avoiding unions or being unresponsive to pressure from recognised unions because unions may damage productivity by exercising monopoly power to defend restrictive work practices and raise wage costs above market rates. These issues have been extensively debated by labour economists without clear resolution one way or the other. Metcalf (2004), summarising the data on the productivity effects of unions, the impact of unions on financial performance and the probability of firm closure, notes that there is no difference in the productivity, financial performance or likelihood of closure of union and non-union workplaces. It certainly seems likely that at a time of union weakness, any union impact on productivity is minimal, whether the impact is positive or negative. The declining impact of unions has, however, affected their ability to encourage employers to adopt sophisticated human resource management practices, improve employee terms and conditions, and raise job satisfaction levels at work. The joint regulation of industrial relations has certainly declined but what does this mean for the increasing number of workers who find themselves in non-union workplaces, and how effectively are the interests of non-union workers represented?

Non-union workplaces

According to one estimate, the majority of UK workplaces had become non-union by 1995 (Cully and Woodland 1996). In the classic account by Fox (1974), to maintain a non-union status managers enforce management prerogative by coercive power to justify a unitarist ideology. Managers have often used a wide-ranging web of defences against unionisation that in their more extreme variants in the US include 'sweet stuff' to make management policies more acceptable to employees, 'fear stuff' to discourage union joining and 'evil stuff' to demonise unions (Roy 1980). Managers holding a unitarist frame of reference may adopt quite different approaches (Purcell and Ahlstrand 1994): a 'sophisticated human relations' approach requires investment in staff development and use of a wide range of human resource management policies to substitute for the services unions provide for members (a union substitution approach or 'sweet stuff'); a 'paternalist' approach seeks to build the loyalty and commitment of staff through consideration for employee welfare ('sweet stuff'); and a 'bleak house' strategy involves minimising labour costs and aggressively avoiding union recruitment ('fear stuff' and 'evil stuff').

Several key commentators in the late 1980s predicted a growth in the non-union 'sophisticated human relations' approach (Sisson 1989). A non-union environment appeared well suited to the demands of developing committed and flexible employees, as demonstrated by several large non-union US multinationals such as IBM, Hewlett Packard and Mars (Foulkes 1980; Kochan et al. 1986). For example, IBM had combined corporate success, a positive employee relations climate of low conflict, low labour turnover and long service, with good pay and conditions. In addition, the company provided procedures to fulfil many of the functions met by unions, including a complex array of alternative procedures (a no-redundancy policy, single status, equal opportunities policies, merit pay and performance assessments), a strong emphasis on internal communications and a grievance system. Most employees working at an IBM plant in the UK studied by Dickson et al. (1988) were positively attached to the individualistic ethos of the company and perceived little need for union protection. In the case of 'Comco', explored by Cressey et al. (1985), employees also identified strongly with the company and enjoyed 'greater benefits' and 'less disciplinary pressure'. Scott (1994) outlined a slightly different 'golden handcuffs' approach whereby employees in a chocolate works received good terms and conditions in return for accepting a high rate of effort and strict rules.

Despite this evidence, non-union companies with a sophisticated approach to managing employees appear to remain the exception. A study of high-tech companies in the southeast of England, where we might expect companies to reproduce the IBM non-union model, uncovered little evidence of sophisticated HRM, with companies either opportunistically avoiding unions or adopting the style of 'benevolent autocracies' (McLoughlin and Gourlay 1994). Furthermore, the assumed benefits of a 'sophisticated human relations' approach may be illusory. Blyton and Turnbull (2004) suggest that Marks & Spencer, so often held up as an exemplar non-union company, simultaneously pursued a 'union substitution' strategy in retail outlets while forcing suppliers into a cost minimisation approach. In another example, a steel plant that had introduced apparently exemplary human resource and work organisation practices subsequently derecognised trade unions, with employees reporting that managers insisted on attitudinal compliance, work intensification and the suppression of any counterbalancing trade union activity (Bacon 1999). It is also striking that among these cases, IBM lost its pre-eminence in its sector, Marks & Spencer now sources from Asian suppliers, leading to the closure of many UK suppliers, and the steel plant mentioned above closed.

Given the comments earlier in this chapter about the positive impact of unions on the adoption of high-commitment management practices (the 'shock effect' of unions), it is not surprising that sophisticated HRM practices are to be found alongside union recognition mainly in larger workplaces and those in the public sector rather than non-union private sector workplaces (Cully et al. 1999, p.111; Machin and Wood 2005; Sisson 1993, p.206). Furthermore, higher union density (the proportion of employees who are trade union members) is also associated with greater joint regulation and more high-commitment management (HCM) practices. There is also evidence that the combination of union recognition and high-commitment management practices has a powerful effect on workplace performance, with 'workplaces with a recognised union and a majority of the HCM practices . . . [performing] better than the average, and better than workplaces without recognition and a minority of these practices' (Cully et al. 1999, p.135). In private sector workplaces where managers withdrew from collective bargaining during the 1990s there was no compensating increase in high-commitment management practices, with lower productivity growth as a consequence (Charlwood 2007). It is not, however, clear that these positive associations will continue, given the evidence presented earlier in this chapter showing that union effects on employers continue to diminish in unionised workplaces. If unions cannot force employers to adopt more HCM practices than non-unionised companies then the differences between working in the union and non-union sectors will gradually disappear and this inevitably reduces the incentive for employees to join unions.

Non-union employee representation

As almost half of workplaces in Britain are effectively union-free, a 'representation gap' (Towers 1997) may have developed where managers operate without any independent employee voice. The representation gap is felt most keenly among the estimated 3 million workers who might join a union but a union does not exist in their workplace (Metcalfe 2004). In Britain, three-quarters of workplaces contain no employee representatives (either union or non-union employee representatives) and almost half of employees do not have an employee representative to speak up for them (Charlwood and Terry 2007, p.324). The absence of representation is important because dissatisfied workers who cannot effectively express their grievances may have little option but to leave the organisation (Hirschman 1971). In the absence of union recognition managers can provide employee voice through direct channels by communicating with workers in team briefings and problem solving, and there is evidence that managers are more responsive to these communications than in listening to unions (Bryson 2004). However, many organisations fail to provide either union or direct channels for employee voice.

Earlier it was mentioned that the state has increasingly intervened in industrial relations, partly to compensate for the decline in joint regulation through trade unions. The European Union Directive for informing and consulting employees, phased into the UK from 2005, provided rights for employees to be informed about the economic situation of their employer's business, employment prospects and substantial changes in work organisation or employment contracts (Hall 2006). This imposes obligations on all organisations, including those without unions, to consult with employee representatives. In Britain, an estimated 7 per cent of workplaces contain a non-union representative and 17 per cent of employees have access to a non-union representative (Charlwood and Terry 2007, p.324). Although workplace union representatives continue to have some effects on employer policies and employees' terms and conditions, the evidence to date reports that non-union forms of employee representation have no effects and are irrelevant (Charlwood and Terry 2007). There is little evidence to date that non-union employee representation, even backed by legislation, meets the basic requirement of representing employee interests to influence employer practices.

Partnership with unions

What of other developments in the unionised sector? In organisations where managers continue to recognise unions, an important innovation has been the signing of partnership agreements with trade unions. The election of 'New Labour' in the UK in 1997 produced a new public policy environment, with the Employment Relations Act 1999 and Fairness at Work programme introducing new rights for trade unions and individual employees (Dickens *et al.* 2005). As already mentioned, this legislative programme involved a statutory route for union recognition, an extension of rights for individual employees, a national minimum wage and closer engagement with the social policies of the European Union. A central aim of this legislative programme has been to 'replace the notion of conflict between employers and employees with the promotion of partnership in the longer term' (HMSO 1998) and reflects the increasing influence of a European approach in the UK.

Managers and unions have contested the meaning of 'partnership' and at times it appears an inherently ambiguous industrial relations aim with no agreed meaning (Undy 1999; Ackers and Payne 1998). As Undy (1999, p.318) has pointed out, 'What one party, or commentator, means by "partnership" is not necessarily shared by others'. As with so many terms in the area of employment relations, key pressure groups such as the Trades Union Congress (TUC), the Confederation of British Industries and the Institute of Directors (IoD) have sought to provide 'widely differing interpretations' of partnership (Undy 1999, p.318), defining the term for their own ends. The Institute of Personnel and Development, for example, explained that partnership 'has more to do with an approach to the relationship between employers and employees, individually and in groups, than it has to do with trade unions' (IPD 1997, p.8). Partnership can therefore be defined in both unitarist and pluralist terms. Rather unsurprisingly, the definition favoured by the TUC is pluralistic, with the stress placed on respecting union influence, whereas the IoD prefers a unitarist definition, whereby employees identify with the employer and trade unions are compliant to the wishes of management.

Despite these different views, the Involvement and Participation Association (IPA), an independent pressure group, developed an influential definition of partnership with leading companies and trade union leaders. This approach was endorsed by leading figures, including representatives from J. Sainsbury plc, the Boddington Group, the Post Office and the leaders of several trade unions (Involvement and Participation Association 1992). This definition requires managers to make several substantive and procedural commitments: declare security of employment as a key corporate objective; share the results of success with employees; and recognise the legitimacy of the employees' right to be informed, consulted and represented. In return, trade unions are required to: renounce rigid job demarcations and commit to flexible working; give sympathetic consideration to the continental model of representation of the whole workforce by means of election of representatives to new works councils; and recognise and then co-promote employee involvement methods.

The signing of partnership agreements is of potential importance in Britain (IRS 1997), and in contrast to critics who thought such agreement would not become widespread (Kelly 2004), employers and unions have signed significantly more partnership agreements than expected, with 248 partnership agreements signed between 1990 and 2007 (Bacon and Samuel 2007). These agreements at the end of 2007 covered almost 10 per cent of all employees and one-third of public sector employees in Britain. Furthermore, four-fifths of all agreements signed survived, suggesting that few employers and unions walked away from these agreements once signed in ongoing workplaces. However, the majority of partnership agreements have been signed in the public rather than the private sector, with private sector employers generally avoiding partnership agreements with trade unions. The growth of agreements in the public sector partly reflects union power in that sector compared to the private sector. In order to modernise public services, the New Labour government, and more importantly the devolved governments of Scotland and Wales, have sought strategic agreements to work closely with unions. These agreements may form the basis for a social democratic model of industrial relations in the public sector in forthcoming years.

Does the popularity of partnership agreements in Britain indicate that managers and unions have found a workable balance between disputed meanings of partnership and a range of other problems associated with partnership agreements? Careful study of the content of partnership agreements shows that few conform to the IPA definition of partnership, mainly because few contain substantive commitments by employers to provide job security for employees or to share the gains of productivity improvements with employees (Samuel and Bacon 2008). Partnership agreements in Britain are biased towards procedural rules over consultation and do not extend joint regulation or involve managers relinquishing control over unilateral determination of substantive terms and conditions. As employers relinquish so little in these agreements, more employers have signed partnership agreements than commonly appreciated.

Employers and unions signing partnership agreements have to deal with at least two critical issues. First, both sides have to commit fully to a single strategy of cooperative industrial relations throughout the organisation and avoid behaving in a short-term, contradictory or opportunistic manner. For example, at the Royal Mail several partnership initiatives have failed because not all managers in the company supported the partnership approach (Bacon and Storey 2000). For some other employers, partnership agreements form part of a longer-term strategy to marginalise trade unions (Claydon 1989; Gall and McKay 1994; Kelly 1996; Smith and Morton 1993).

Whereas one review of partnership agreements in six organisations reported that 'none gave serious consideration to ending recognition' (IDS 1998, p.4), a study of management attempts to restructure industrial relations in 10 organisations (Bacon and Storey 2000) revealed that de-recognition had been more seriously explored. According to Oxenbridge *et al.* (2003), employers working in partnership with unions to implement organisational change are sometimes simultaneously excluding unions from bargaining over issues such as pay.

A second important issue for the future of partnership agreements is whether they deliver greater returns for managers and trade unions. If returns are not forthcoming for either party then enthusiasm for the partnership approach may wane. Kelly (1996) has argued, for example, that unions have more to gain from militancy than cooperation with employers. Partnership is associated by Kelly with eroding the willingness and capacity of union members to resist employers, inhibiting the growth of workplace union organisation and generating apathy among union members; it involves union 'give' and management 'take', results in attempts to drive down terms and conditions of employment, and fails to genuinely represent member grievances. The extent to which Kelly is correct and unions will not benefit from partnership agreements is an interesting question. Kelly (2004) compared similar UK companies with and without partnership agreements and found that partnership firms shed jobs at a faster rate than non-partnership firms in industries marked by employment decline. In contrast, partnership firms in expanding sectors created jobs at a faster rate than non-partnership firms. Partnership appeared to have no impact on wage settlements or union density. In another study of 54 companies, Guest and Peccei (2001, p.207) discovered that the balance of advantage from partnership at work 'is skewed towards management', with improvements only in employment relations, quality and productivity. As few partnership agreements actually contain substantive clauses on job security or sharing gains with employees, gains for employees from partnership are particularly elusive (Samuel and Bacon 2008).

Union organising and new types of union representatives

As many employers have preferred not to recognise unions, or negotiate and consult with unions even where they are recognised, it is not surprising that workers and unions have sought to defend their interests. Unions have increasingly focused on organising workers and recruiting new members as an alternative to partnership (Heery 2002) and reversing falling membership levels and declining collective bargaining coverage. In training a new generation of union organisers to recruit members and organise workplaces (Fiorito and Jarley 2008), it is not surprising to see unions learning lessons from the US in how to organise when employers oppose unions (see Godard 2008). Union avoidance techniques used by employers in the US (Logan 2006) are also being learned by employers in other countries. A significant increase in new recognition deals has occurred in Britain, reflecting the work of union organisers and the backing provided by the statutory union recognition procedure of the Employment Relations Act 1999 (Gall 2004). To date, however, this has slowed rather than reversed the decline of union recognition in Britain, as described in Table 8.4.

Such has been the pace of trade union innovation that unions in Britain have also developed and recruited new types of workplace union representatives focused on single issues. These include union learning representatives (ULRs) and equality representatives, although there are others such as environment representatives. The emergence of new types of workplace union representatives constitutes an important and strategic initiative by unions to service existing members, recruit new members and represent members' interests on specific issues. A key aim in recruiting members into single-issue union posts is to increase membership activity in workplace unions and to work with employers on issues that employers have recently regarded as areas of management prerogative. The impact of these new representatives will have an important influence in the forthcoming years on whether unions are able to encourage employers to increase training provision and improve equal opportunities.

To assess the likely impact of these initiatives it is helpful to consider the case of ULRs as the most developed initiative, with 18,000 ULRs recruited by 2007 working to improve training provision for their members. The government provided important support to ULRs in the Employment Act 2002, which provided them with statutory rights to paid time off for five key tasks: analysing training needs; providing information and advice on training; arranging training; promoting the value of training; and consulting the employer over these activities. Have ULRs been able to increase training provision? Research to date has failed to identify a consistent relationship between ULRs and training, with ULR presence not associated with training among any employee group with the exception of male non-managers in the public sector (Hoque and Bacon 2008). The same research has, however, shown that ULRs may exercise a 'sword of justice' role. Employees who are traditionally less likely to report receiving training (for example, older workers, part-time workers, lower occupational groups, and workers with lower-level academic qualifications) are more likely to report training in workplaces with ULRs present. Whether ULRs are successful in raising training levels will depend on the extent to which employers value these new union representatives, employers are genuinely willing to consult and negotiate on these issues, and employers will provide paid time off from normal work duties for representatives to conduct these activities. A large proportion of ULRs in 2004, for example, did not spend any time on employee training in their role as a union representative and could therefore have little influence on levels of employer-provided training (Bacon and Hoque 2008a). Employer support is essential if these new types of representatives are to be effective, as the amount of time spent on the ULR role is strongly related to the number of hours the employer pays for the ULR to spend time on the role (Bacon and Hoque 2008b). ULRs are more likely to report that they are able to increase employee participation in training where the employer values their role, is willing to negotiate, consult or inform unions on training issues, and pay for ULRs to spend time on their role (Bacon and Hoque 2008b). Although other types of new union representatives are only just developing, it is anticipated that the degree of support from management for their role will affect whether unions are able to influence employer policies and develop workplace union representation through recruiting single-issue union representatives.

Conclusions

The aim of this chapter was to introduce the topic of industrial relations, outline some of the key contemporary developments in industrial relations and consider the implications. It covered management approaches to industrial relations, the reasons employees join unions, the decline of joint regulation and its implications, employer choice in industrial relations, non-union workplaces and employee representation in non-union workplaces, partnership with unions, union organising and new types of union representatives. Employers in liberal market economies and other countries are increasingly less inclined to support joint regulation of industrial relations. As a result, unions have found it increasingly difficult to represent effectively the interests of their existing and new members who continue to join trade unions. Employers avoid union recognition and influence in order to avoid the costs imposed by unions. The state has increasingly legislated on employment issues to protect employees from employer attempts to drive down terms and conditions and evade their responsibility for promoting equitable employment. The state is also the major sponsor of partnership agreements with unions as it attempts to reform public services with unions. Employers also have to deal with more sustained attempts by unions to challenge employers by organising workplaces against the wishes of employers. New types of union representatives focused on specific issues are potentially helpful allies for employers seeking to increase employee participation in training and increase the effectiveness of equal opportunities policies. These new representatives are only likely to be effective, however, if employers are willing to concede management prerogative over these issues.

CASE STUDY 8.1

Union–management partnership at NatBank

Stewart Johnstone

NatBank is a major UK bank with over 60,000 employees in the UK and over 100,000 employees worldwide. The partnership agreement at NatBank was born out of a very poor climate of industrial relations in the late 1990s, culminating in industrial action over pay in 1997. Union representatives and managers admitted that there was a need to end the hostile 'everybody out mentality' that prevailed within the bank whenever an issue arose, and that the 1990s situation of 'arm's-length adversarialism' was simply untenable. Improving employment relations was especially important as competition in the financial service sector was intense, and organisational performance had been disappointing. A formal partnership agreement was signed between NatBank and the recognised trade union in 2000, based upon an adaptation of six principles of partnership espoused by the Trades Union Congress:

The principles of partnership:

1. To secure and promote the long-term success of NatBank.
2. To promote the interests of employees, customers and shareholders.
3. To ensure that NatBank meets customer expectations by having people with the right skills in the right place at the right cost.
4. To facilitate the management of change.
5. To ensure employees are managed fairly and professionally.
6. To promote equality of treatment and opportunity for all, valuing diversity.

Partnership was described by senior managers as a modern and sensible approach to the management of industrial relations centred around a joint commitment to business success. In practice this was said to require greater dialogue and interaction with the trade union, and the ability to consider decisions from both an 'employee' as well as 'business' point of view. A senior manager contrasted this with a non-partnership approach, where the union may simply want what is best for the union/employees, while the business simply wants what is best for the business. For local managers, partnership concerned a more proactive problem-solving approach, and achieving a clear understanding of the rationale behind decisions. It was made clear by the management team, however, that the union representatives and officials need not necessarily agree with decisions. Rather, the focus was on early consultation regarding developments and the opportunity for representatives to provide feedback and input while decisions are still at 'the design stage'. When local representatives had strong feelings on an issue and no agreement could be reached locally, there was the option of escalating it to monthly national consultation for further detailed discussion. However, it was clear that under partnership the business retained the right to make the final decisions.

Similarly, for a senior union official, partnership concerned problem solving, mutual respect, transparency, and greater interaction between the union and the management team. However, he warned that the term 'partnership' for such an approach is perhaps inappropriate and potentially misleading. He suggested that the language of partnership often resulted in a debate regarding whether partnership suggests or requires an 'equal' relationship between unions and employers. He believed that such debates were actually unproductive, and that it is was better to view partnership in a more pragmatic way, as essentially an opportunity for unions to get 'inside the tent'. In turn, this was said to offer unions access to key business decision makers, the provision of better information, and a greater respect for each party's point of view. He suggested that senior management now had a clearer idea of the operation and purpose of trade unions, and equally full-time officials now had a greater appreciation of business issues and decision making. He contrasted partnership with an 'institutional conflict approach', without any real dialogue or regard for the other party's point of view. It was suggested that partnership provided a framework by clarifying the rights and responsibilities of the employer and the union, and setting out the 'rules of the game'.

Overall, several benefits were identified compared to the adversarial approach of the 1990s. A key benefit concerned the ability of the union to influence decision making. There was evidence to suggest that the union was involved across areas including pay and conditions, discipline and grievance, and organisational change. An example of this is the joint development of guidelines outlining various commitments regarding off-shoring practices. At the centre of this agreement were commitments to avoid compulsory redundancies and redeploy staff elsewhere in the business where possible, to provide early consultation, and to provide extensive support for employees who were ultimately displaced. With partnership it was suggested that the union now had a wider remit, especially in relation to organisational change issues, whereas prior to partnership much of the attention centred around pay and conditions. More generally, with partnership management were said to benefit from constructive feedback which assisted their decision making, meaning that pre-emptive changes could be made and leading to the greater legitimacy and acceptance of decisions. For the business, it was suggested that the partnership dialogue also encouraged a longer-term perspective than may otherwise have been the case. On the other hand, the union was said to benefit from the opportunity to have a say, often being consulted at a very early stage in the decision-making process. Though the partnership process was not viewed as one of joint decision making per se, union officials and representatives believed that there was evidence of the consultation process having an impact, and this was also recognised by employees.

Another benefit of partnership was said to be more local decision making and improved employment relations. The emphasis from the union had been on building a solid cadre of local representatives, and there was evidence to suggest that this had been successful. Representatives were active and knowledgeable, and appeared to be well respected by management and employees alike. Representatives described their role under partnership as one of questioning, challenging and persuading, as opposed to simply opposing management proposals. In this regard, a key issue was developing a strong basis on which to question proposals which took into account both business rationale as well as the impact on employees. There also appeared to have been an increase in union legitimacy. Prior to partnership, the union was said to have had few resources or facilities provided by the employer. Much of the work of a union representative was undertaken at home, and it was not unusual for vacancies for representative posts to be left unfilled. Since partnership, credible and active representative roles had been created, all union committee positions were filled, and previously weak trade union organisation was believed to have been revived. Representatives were now able to hold quarterly recruitment events, to distribute promotional materials, and to deliver a presentation at staff inductions for new staff. In addition, representatives were pleased with other arrangements in relation to the provision of sufficient time off for union duties, access to meeting rooms and use of office facilities.

In contrast to the frosty times of the 1990s, relationships between senior management and union officials, as well as between local management and union representatives, appeared to be very good. There was a belief that whereas prior to partnership relationships were best described as 'arm's-length legislative compliance', partnership relationships were characterised by a greater degree of trust and mutual respect. It was proposed that dialogue was now more concerned with business success, and trying to balance the needs of the business on the one hand and the likely impact for employees on the other. Building the necessary relationships was said to have been hard work, but was believed to be worthwhile. Again, this did not mean there had not been some significant disagreements between the union and management, but these were viewed as a natural part of any relationship. It also appeared that union representatives had a good relationship with employees. Though employee understanding of the exact nature of the union representatives' involvement and relationship with management was patchy, most employees perceived the union–management relationship to be generally healthy.

Nevertheless, some challenges remained. It was suggested that sometimes there was a lack of a clear understanding of partnership among actors, and what it means in terms of working relationships and decision making. It was generally agreed to require both early consultation at the design stage and a genuine attempt to consider issues from both a business and employee point of view when making decisions. The emphasis was on an explanation of the rationale for decisions, and an opportunity for the union to comment, question and propose alternatives. However, the ultimate decision resided with management. Occasionally some management and union actors were said to have had difficulties with this style of arrangement, but overall most preferred a more collaborative approach compared with the more adversarial strategies of the 1990s. This related to the challenge of embedding a 'partnership culture' across the entire organisation, especially at middle-management level. Though relationships were said to be strong between senior management and union officials, as well as locally between business managers and representatives, tensions sometimes arose with line managers responsible for actually implementing decisions. It was believed that sometimes agreed procedures were inadvertently overlooked, and that some line managers were still uncomfortable with the requirements of the partnership style of working. Line managers also appeared to occupy a space outside the partnership system, which focused predominantly upon the relationships between senior/business managers and union officials/representatives.

An additional challenge was believed to be winning the buy-in of employees. There was a feeling that some employees had little interest in the union, although most employees did appear to trust the union to work effectively behind the scenes to protect their interests. A particular worry from some union representatives was the danger that they may be perceived to be 'in the bank's pocket', as employees only hear about the final outcomes of a decision, and not the actual process of consultation. Embargoes on information were believed to make it more difficult to demonstrate influence to members. As such, there was a feeling that with partnership it can be difficult to advertise the successes of the union to members, and there was a perception that this may have been easier under traditional bargaining. The representatives stressed that there was a need for a great deal of trust from members that they were actively involved on their behalf and not just management poodles, as demonstrating their effectiveness to members was perceived to be more challenging through the low-key partnership approach.

A final concern was the sustainability of the partnership over time, and in particular the effect of a major organisational crisis such as an economic downturn. Equally, there were concerns if some of the key champions of partnership, both from management and the union, were to leave the organisation. Others also questioned the sustainability of partnership if there was a sudden change in government policy, away from the pro-partnership stance of the last decade. Nevertheless, it seems reasonable to conclude that, despite these challenges, a partnership approach appeared to be fairly well rooted, demonstrating a reasonable degree of success and delivering a variety of benefits to actors.

Questions

1. What were the main drivers for partnership at NatBank?
2. What did 'partnership' mean to managers and trade union officials/representatives?
3. What were the key benefits for management, the trade union and employees?
4. To what extent had partnership increased union effectiveness?
5. Why might line managers have found partnership particularly challenging?
6. What challenges might threaten the sustainability of partnership at NatBank in the future?

Bibliography

Ackers, P. and Payne, J. (1998) 'British trade unions and social partnership: rhetoric, reality and strategy', *International Journal of Human Resource Management*, Vol.9, pp.529–50.

Bacon, N. (1999) 'Union derecognition and the new human relations: a steel industry case study', *Work, Employment and Society*, Vol.13, No.1, pp.1–17.

Bacon, N. (2003) 'Human resource management and industrial relations', in P. Ackers and A. Wilkinson (eds) *Understanding Work and Employment*, Oxford: Oxford University Press, pp.71–88.

Bacon, N. (2008) 'Management strategy and industrial relations', in P. Blyton, N. Bacon, J. Fiorito and E. Heery (eds) *The Sage Handbook of Industrial Relations*, London: Sage, pp.241–57.

Bacon, N. and Hoque, K. (2008a) 'Exploring the link between union learning representatives and employer-provided training in Britain', Paper presented to WIAS, University of Sheffield.

Bacon, N. and Hoque, K. (2008b) 'Union learning representatives and training', Paper for BUIRA Conference, University of West of England, 25–27 June.

Bacon, N. and Samuel, P. (2007) 'Partnership agreement adoption, form and survival in Britain', Paper presented to IIRA Conference, Manchester.

Bacon, N. and Storey, J. (2000) 'New employee relations strategies: towards individualism or partnership', *British Journal of Industrial Relations*, Vol.38, No.3, pp.407–27.

Blanchflower, D.G. and Bryson, A. (2003) 'Changes over time in union relative wage effects in the UK and US revisited', in J.T. Addison and C. Schnabel (eds) *International Handbook of Trade Unions*, Cheltenham: Edward Elgar.

Blanchflower, D.G., Bryson, A. and Forth, J. (2007) 'Workplace industrial relations in Britain, 1980–2004', *Industrial Relations Journal*, Vol.38, No.4, pp.285–302.

Blyton, P. and Turnbull, P. (2004) *The Dynamics of Employee Relations* (3rd edn), Basingstoke: Palgrave Macmillan.

Brown, W. (2008) 'The influence of product markets on industrial relations', in P. Blyton, N. Bacon, J. Fiorito and E. Heery (eds) *The Sage Handbook of Industrial Relations*, London: Sage, pp.113–28.

Brown, W. and Nash, D. (2008) 'What has been happening to collective bargaining under New Labour? Interpreting WERS 2004', *Industrial Relations Journal*, Vol.39, No.2, pp.91–103.

Bryson, A. (2004) 'Managerial responsiveness to union and nonunion worker voice in Britain', *Industrial Relations*, Vol.43, No.1, pp.213–42.

Bryson, A. and Forth, J. (2008) 'The theory and practice of pay setting', in P. Blyton, N. Bacon, J. Fiorito and E. Heery (eds) *The Sage Handbook of Industrial Relations*, London: Sage, pp.92–113.

Bryson, A., Charlwood, A. and Forth, J. (2006) 'Worker voice, managerial response and labour productivity: an empirical investigation', *Industrial Relations Journal*, Vol.37, No.5, pp.438–55.

Budd, J. and Bhave, D. (2008) 'Values, ideologies, and frames of reference in employment relations', in P. Blyton, N. Bacon, J. Fiorito and E. Heery (eds) *The Sage Handbook of Industrial Relations*, London: Sage, pp.92–113.

Charlwood, A. (2007) 'The de-collectivisation of pay setting in Britain 1990–98: incidence, determinants and impact', *Industrial Relations Journal*, Vol.38, No.1, pp.33–50.

Charlwood, A. and Terry, M. (2007) '21st-century models of employee representation: structure, processes and outcomes', *Industrial Relations Journal*, Vol.38, No.4, pp.320–37.

Claydon, T. (1989) 'Union de-recognition in Britain in the 1980s', *British Journal of Industrial Relations*, Vol.27, pp.214–23.

Clegg, H. (1979) *The System of Industrial Relations in Great Britain*, Oxford: Blackwell.

Coupland, C., Blyton, P. and Bacon, N. (2005) 'A longitudinal study of the influence of shop floor work teams on expressions of "us" and "them"', *Human Relations*, Vol.58, No.8, pp.1055–81.

Cressey, P., Eldridge, J. and MacInnes, J. (1985) *Just Managing: Authority and Democracy in Industry*, Milton Keynes: Open University Press.

Cully, M. and Woodland, S. (1996) 'Trade union membership and recognition: an analysis of data from the 1995 Labour Force Survey', *Labour Market Trends*, May, pp.215–25, London: HMSO.

Cully, M., Woodland, S., O'Reilly, A. and Dix, G. (1999) *Britain at Work*, London: Routledge.

D'Art, D. and Turner, T. (1999) 'An attitudinal revolution in Irish industrial relations: the end of "them and us"?', *British Journal of Industrial Relations*, Vol.37, No.1, pp.101–16.

Dickens, L., Hall, M. and Wood, S. (2005) *Review of Research into the Impact of Employment Relations Legislation*, Employment Relations Research Series, No.45, London: DTI.

Dickson, T., McLachlan, M.V., Prior, P. and Swales, K. (1988) 'Big Blue and the union: IBM, individualism and trade union strategy', *Work, Employment and Society*, Vol.2, pp.506–20.

Dunn, S. and Wright, M. (1994) 'Maintaining the "status quo": an analysis of the contents of British collective agreements 1979–1990', *British Journal of Industrial Relations*, Vol.32, pp.23–46.

Edwards, P. (1995) 'The employment relationship', in P. Edwards (ed.) *Industrial Relations*, Oxford: Blackwell, pp.3–26.

Edwards, P., Hall, M., Hyman, R., Marginson, P., Sisson, K., Waddington, J. and Winchester, D. (1998) 'Great Britain: from partial collectivism to neo-liberalism to where?', in A. Ferner and R. Hyman (eds) *Changing Industrial Relations in Europe*, Oxford: Blackwell, pp.1–54.

Fiorito, J. and Jarley, P. (2008) 'Trade union morphology', in P. Blyton, N. Bacon, J. Fiorito and E. Heery (eds) *The Sage Handbook of Industrial Relations*, London: Sage, pp.189–208.

Foulkes, F.K. (1980) *Personnel Policies in Large Non-union Companies*, Englewood Cliffs, NJ: Prentice Hall.

Fox, A. (1966) 'Industrial sociology and industrial relations', *Royal Commission Research Paper No.3*, London: HMSO.

Fox, A. (1974) *Beyond Contract: Work, Power and Trust Relations*, London: Faber and Faber.

Freeman, R.B. and Medoff, J.L. (1984). *What Do Unions Do?*, New York: Basic Books.

Gall, G. (2004) 'Trade union recognition in Britain, 1995–2002: turning a corner?', *Industrial Relations Journal*, Vol.35, No.3, pp.249–70.

Gall, G. and McKay, S. (1994) 'Trade union de-recognition in Britain 1988–94', *British Journal of Industrial Relations*, Vol.32, pp.433–48.

Geary, J. (1995) 'Work practices: the structure of work', in P. Edwards (ed.) *Industrial Relations*, Oxford: Blackwell, pp.368–96.

Godard, J. (2008) 'Union formation', in P. Blyton, N. Bacon, J. Fiorito and E. Heery (eds) *The Sage Handbook of Industrial Relations*, London: Sage, pp.377–405.

Guest, D. and Conway, N. (2004) 'Exploring the paradox of unionised worker dissatisfaction', *Industrial Relations Journal*, Vol.35, No.2, pp.102–21.

Guest, D.E., and Peccei, R. (2001) 'Partnership at work: mutuality and the balance of advantage', *British Journal of Industrial Relations*, Vol.39, No.2, pp.207–36.

Hall, M.J. (2006) 'A cool response to the ICE Regulations? Employer and trade union approaches to the new legal framework for information and consultation', *Industrial Relations Journal*, Vol.37, pp.456–72.

Hamann, K. and Kelly, J. (2008) 'Varieties of capitalism and industrial relations', in P. Blyton, N. Bacon, J. Fiorito and E. Heery (eds) *The Sage Handbook of Industrial Relations*, London: Sage, pp.129–48.

Heery, E. (2002) 'Partnership versus organising: alternative futures for British trade unionism', *Industrial Relations Journal*, Vol.33, No.1, pp.20–35.

Heery, E., Bacon, N., Blyton, P. and Fiorito, J. (2008) 'Introduction: the field of industrial relations', in P. Blyton, N. Bacon, J. Fiorito and E. Heery (eds) *The Sage Handbook of Industrial Relations*, London: Sage, pp.1–32.

Hirschman, A. (1971) *Exit, Voice and Loyalty*, Cambridge, MA: Harvard University Press.
HMSO (1998) '*Fairness at Work*', White Paper, London: HMSO.
Hoque, K. and Bacon, N. (2008) 'Trade unions, union learning representatives and employer-provided training in Britain', *British Journal of Industrial Relations*, December.
Hyman, R. (1997) 'The future of employee representation', *British Journal of Industrial Relations*, Vol.35, No.3, pp.309–36.
IDS (1998) 'Partnership agreements', *IDS Study*, 656, October.
Institute of Directors (1994) Evidence presented to the Employment Committee Enquiry, 'The future of trade unions', HMSO, HC 676-II.
Involvement and Participation Association (1992) *Towards Industrial Partnership: A New Approach to Management Union Relations*, London: IPA.
IPD (1997) *Employment Relations into the 21st Century*, London: Institute of Personnel and Development.
IRS (1997) 'Partnership at work: a survey', *Employment Trends*, 645, December, pp.3–24.
Kelly, J. (1996) 'Union militancy and social partnership', in P. Ackers, C. Smith and P. Smith (eds) *The New Workplace and Trade Unionism*, London: Routledge, pp.41–76.
Kelly, J. (2004) 'Social partnership agreements in Britain: Labour cooperation and compliance', *Industrial Relations*, Vol.43, No.1, pp.267–92.
Kelly, J. and C. Kelly (1991) 'Them and us: social psychology and the "new industrial relations"', *British Journal of Industrial Relations*, Vol.29, No.1, pp.25–48.
Kersley, B., Alpin, C., Forth, J., Bryson, A., Bewley, H., Dix, G. and Oxenbridge, S. (2006) *Inside the Workplace: Findings from the 2004 Workplace Employment Relations Survey*, London: Routledge.
Kochan, T.A., McKersie, R.B. and Cappelli, P. (1984) 'Strategic choice and industrial relations theory', *Industrial Relations*, Vol.23, No.1, pp.16–39.
Kochan, T., Katz, H. and McKersie, B. (1986). *The Transformation of American Industrial Relations*, New York: Basic Books.
Lewin, D. (1987) 'Industrial relations as a strategic variable', in M.M. Kleiner, R.N. Block, M. Roomkin and S.W. Salsburg (eds) *Human Resources and the Performance of the Firm*, Madison, WI: Industrial Relations Research Association, pp.1–41.
Logan, J. (2006) 'The union avoidance industry in the United States', *British Journal of Industrial Relations*, Vol.44, No.4, pp.651–75.
Machin, S. (2000) 'Union decline in Britain', *British Journal of Industrial Relations*, Vol.38, No.4, pp.631–45.
Machin, S. and Wood, S.J. (2005) 'Human resource management as a substitute for trade unions in British workplaces', *Industrial and Labor Relations Review*, Vol.58, No.1, pp.201–18.
McLoughlin, I. and Gourlay, S. (1994) *Enterprise Without Unions: Industrial Relations in the Non-Union Firm*, Milton Keynes: Open University Press.
Metcalfe, D. (2004) *British Unions: Resurgence or Perdition*, London: The Work Foundation.
Millward, N., Stevens, M., Smart, D., and Hawes, W.R. (1992) *Workplace Industrial Relations in Transition*, Aldershot: Dartmouth.
Noon, M. and Hoque, K. (2001) 'Ethnic minorities and equal treatment: the impact of gender, equal opportunities policies and trade unions', *National Institute Economic Review*, Vol.176, No.1, pp.105–16.
Oxenbridge, S., Brown, W., Deakin, S., and Pratten, C. (2003) 'Initial responses to the Statutory Recognition Provisions of the Employment Relations Act 1999', *British Journal of Industrial Relations*, Vol.41, No.2, pp.315–34.
Piore, M.J. and Safford, S. (2006) 'Changing regimes of workplace governance, shifting axes of social mobilisation, and the challenge to industrial relations theory', *Industrial Relations*, Vol.45, No.3, pp.299–325.
Poole, M., Mansfield, R., Gould-Williams, J. and Mendes, P. (2005) 'British Managers' attitudes and behaviour in industrial relations: a twenty-year study', *British Journal of Industrial Relations*, Vol.43, No.1, pp.117–34.
Purcell, J. and Ahlstrand, B. (1994) *Human Resource Management in the Multi-Divisional Company*, Oxford: Oxford University Press.
Purcell, J. and Sisson, K. (1983) 'Strategies and practice in the management of industrial relations', in G. Bain (ed.) *Industrial Relations in Britain*, Oxford: Blackwell.

Ramsey, H. (1975) 'Firms and football teams', *British Journal of Industrial Relations*, Vol.13, No.3, pp.396–400.
Roy, D. (1980) 'Fear stuff, sweet stuff and evil stuff: management's defences against unionization in the south', in T. Nichols (ed.) *Capital and Labour: A Marxist Primer*, Glasgow: Fontana, pp.395–415.
Samuel, P. and Bacon, N. (2008) 'Exploring the content of British partnership agreements signed between 1990 and 2007', Paper for BUIRA Conference, 25–27 June, University of West of England.
Schnabel, C. (2003) 'Determinants of trade union membership', in J.T. Addison and C. Schnabel (eds) *International Handbook of Trade Unions*, Cheltenham, Edward Elgar, pp.13–43.
Schnabel, C. and Wagner, J. (2007) 'Union density and determinants of union membership in 18 EU countries: evidence from micro data, 2002/03', *Industrial Relations Journal*, Vol.38, No.1, pp.5–32.
Scott, A. (1994) *Willing Slaves?* Cambridge: Cambridge University Press.
Sisson, K. (1989) 'Personnel management in transition?', in K. Sisson (ed.) *Personnel Management in Britain*, Oxford: Blackwell.
Sisson, K. (1993) 'In search of HRM', *British Journal of Industrial Relations*, Vol.31, No.2, pp.201–10.
Smith, P. and Morton, G. (1993) 'Union exclusion and decollectivization of industrial relations in contemporary Britain', *British Journal of Industrial Relations*, Vol.31, No.1, pp.97–114.
Strauss, G. (1984) 'Industrial relations: time of change', *Industrial Relations*, Vol.23, No.1: pp.1–15.
Towers, B. (1997) *The Representation Gap*, Oxford: Oxford University Press.
Undy, R. (1999) 'Annual review article: New Labour's "Industrial Relations Settlement": The third way?', *British Journal of Industrial Relations*, Vol.37, No.2, pp.315–36.
Visser, J. (2003) 'Unions and unionism around the world', in J.T. Addison and C. Schnabel (eds) *International Handbook of Trade Unions*, Cheltenham, Edward Elgar, pp.366–414.
Waddington, J. and Whitston, C. (1997) 'Why do people join unions in a period of membership decline?', *British Journal of Industrial Relations*, Vol.35, No.4, pp.515–46.
Walsh, J. (2007) 'Equality and diversity in British workplaces: the 2004 Workplace Employment Relations Survey', *Industrial Relations Journal*, Vol.38, No.4, pp.303–19.
White, M. (2005) 'Cooperative unionism and employee welfare', *Industrial Relations Journal*, Vol.36, No.5, pp.348–66.

EMPLOYEE WELLBEING

CHAPTER 11

Health, safety and wellbeing

Objectives

By the end of this chapter you will be able to:

- explain what is meant by the terms 'safety', 'hazard', 'risk', 'wellbeing' and 'health'
- explain the key points in the main legislation relating to health, safety and wellbeing at work
- explain the reasons for managing employee health, safety and wellbeing
- explain the role of various people and groups in health and safety and wellbeing at work
- describe the Health and Safety Executive's approach to stress management
- explain the main health and safety issues in an international context.

In Chapter 1 we traced the history of people management and considered several approaches to what at that time was referred to as welfare. Some people who adopted the 'hard' human resource management approach tried originally to distance themselves from all these welfare approaches, as they felt that they showed a lack of business awareness. However, reducing accidents and improving occupational ill-health is extremely important for organisations today and many are taking an increasing interest in areas such as managing absenteeism. Health and safety are also coming under Government scrutiny as they want to improve the productivity of the workforce and remove unnecessary bureaucracy. The changing demographics of an ageing workforce combined with what is claimed to be a growing obesity problem in the UK are also likely to mean that the country has a new imperative for employers to become more involved in health if organisations want to be effective and productive. Paton (2010) quotes from a 2010 survey by BUPA which said that 'government, the NHS, private providers and OH (Occupational Health) providers are all going to have their work cut out in dealing with an ageing, sicker working population, while firms with the healthiest (and therefore least absent) and most engaged workforce will be the ones best placed to thrive in an increasingly competitive global environment.'

Not everyone takes such a negative view. ACAS (2010a) emphasise the fact that work is good for people's health but stress the value of a good work–life balance.

This is particularly important if we are to benefit from people working longer as will be necessary with an ageing population and no compulsory retirement age. ACAS (2010a) indicate that the growing awareness of a good work–life balance has made people increasingly conscious of the relationship between our mental and physical health and the job we do, so it is no longer sufficient for employers to just comply with legislation. There is clearly a strong case to be made for organisations to pay more attention to the health, safety and wellbeing of their workforces and to see this as another aspect of their approach to performance management.

Many organisations do realise the importance to their success of a healthy and productive workforce and are already seeking to adopt a more proactive approach. As the economy gradually recovers more employers are focusing on aspects of HR where they can get improvements in employee engagement, which will in turn help them retain talent. Strategies to improve safety and improve health are attractive ways to achieve this and should form a part of the organisation's approach to performance management. As we explained in Chapter 8, performance management in some organisations is being integrated with a wider range of HR processes than was traditionally the case and now involves processes designed to promote wellbeing, engagement and development of potential. Clearly issues relating to health, safety and wellbeing can contribute to this and as these approaches are not necessarily costly they may be particularly attractive to organisations trying to keep their budgets under tight control. Investors in People (IIP), which is perhaps better known for its business tool linking training to the strategic objectives of the organisation (discussed in Chapter 9), have developed a new standard for health and wellbeing. IIP (2010) claims increasing evidence of a direct relationship between developing effective health and wellbeing programmes and increased productivity and that there is an excellent return on investment from these programmes.

> **Did you know?**
>
> The positive effects of work are beneficial not only for employers but employees too and can contribute to their sense of happiness and wellbeing. According to ACAS (2010a), 'work can have a positive impact on our health and wellbeing. Healthy and well-motivated employees can have an equally positive impact on the productivity and effectiveness of a business.'
>
> This seems to be true in some other cultures and there is evidence that work can also contribute to our sense of happiness. In the annual happiness survey carried out in Hong Kong in 2009 those who loved their jobs were happiest, followed by those who loved food and cooking, though when analysed by occupation those who were retired were listed as the happiest of all!
>
> (*Source*: Chiu, 2009)

In this chapter we shall first examine what the terminology means before discussing the law relating to safety and the roles of those involved. Later we shall discuss the changing emphasis on health and wellbeing in more detail.

Definitions

Safety

We define safety as absence from danger and avoidance of injury.

According to this definition, we should expect employers to do everything in their power to keep employees away from danger and free of injury while at work. This does not sound like a great deal to expect from an employer, but there is often a conflict in the employer's mind between increased production, which sometimes may involve some risk taking, and the necessity to keep employees safe and uninjured, which may cost money. Legislation has developed over a number of years to protect workers, and was initially designed to protect those who were weak and particularly vulnerable to exploitation from any employers who, tempted by the lure of increased production, might put their employees at risk of injury. Nowadays, with increasingly flexible patterns of work being available, many employees may work from home or even from their car, for all or part of their working week, so employers will also have to consider the health and safety issues arising from this.

Hazard

A hazard is something that could cause harm to someone. Employers who are being proactive about health and safety therefore have to try to identify potential hazards before they actually do cause any harm. Stranks (2007a) says that a hazard can further be defined in three areas, as follows:

- exposure to harm
- something with the potential to do harm – this can include substances or machines, methods of work and other aspects of work organisation
- the result of departure from the normal situation, which has the potential to cause death, injury, damage or loss.

Risk

The term risk relates to the chances of the hazard actually resulting in harm being done to someone. Once the employer has identified a potential hazard then they have to estimate the chances or risk of someone being harmed by it.

We shall discuss the idea of risk assessment later in this chapter. The emphasis in health and safety today is on the prevention of accidents if possible by eliminating anything that could be a hazard and by predicting the level of risk in various situations. It is not, of course, always possible to eliminate all hazards or minimise all risks in a workplace, but employers are expected to predict potentially dangerous situations and then do something about them to ensure they become less dangerous. The emphasis in modern health and safety is to encourage those who own, manage or work in organisations to take responsibility for health and safety in them. For this to happen, both the workforce and safety representatives also need to be involved, risks need to be assessed and action needs to be taken to reduce these where possible. This is, however, currently a subject of debate as some feel that the UK has become too risk averse, to the extent that this stifles initiative and this will be discussed later in the chapter.

Wellbeing

According to Michaelson et al. (2009) 'personal wellbeing describes people's experiences of their positive and negative emotions, satisfaction, vitality, resilience, self esteem and sense of purpose and meaning. Social well-being is made up of two components, supportive relationships and trust and belonging both of which are critical elements of overall well-being.' The forerunners of HR managers were concerned with employee welfare and much of the legislation about health and safety also uses the term welfare. We have chosen to use the term wellbeing instead of welfare as nowadays welfare has a slightly negative connotation and suggests some degree of dependency. Wellbeing clearly includes dealing with what might be regarded as welfare issues but looks at all aspects of a person's wellbeing and does not focus just on the negative aspects. It also has a more positive feel as the individual also has responsibilities for their own wellbeing so should be working in partnership with others on this.

According to Tehrani *et al.* (2007) people have mental and physical needs for social support, safety and health, and also need to feel that they are not overwhelmed by events and can cope with life. These are all aspects of wellbeing and as a large part of our lives is spent at work it is natural to expect employers to play a part in employees' wellbeing. In the past many employers merely reacted to issues about health and safety and welfare without appreciating the benefits that adopting a more proactive approach could bring them. Many still operate in this way. However, some more progressive employers are adopting a much more proactive approach to health, safety and wellbeing to prevent problems arising in the first place.

Health

> **Did you know?**
> In 2004 a senior pilot was forced to resign and two senior cabin crew were dismissed by Ryanair after the two off-duty crew members travelled on a full plane from Gerona to Dublin. Since there were no seats available for them, they sat in the rear toilets of the plane for both take-off and landing. The captain had allowed them to do this even though it contravened aviation regulations and was obviously potentially hazardous.

Here the concern is for good health. We define good health as being physically and mentally well with body and mind in excellent working order.

This goes further than safety in that the employer is no longer just expected not to do anything to injure their employees, but should seek to promote activities that encourage the good health of the employees. We shall return to a discussion of health promotion activities later in this chapter.

Safety

According to the Health and Safety Executive's (HSE's) *Health and Safety Executive Statistics* (HSE, 2010a) the provisional figures for 2009–10 show there were 151 workers fatally injured at work during this period, which is 31 per cent lower than the average for the previous five years and is also one of the lowest rates for fatal injuries in Europe. At the time of writing the latest figures available for accidents requiring absences of three or more days from work were for 2008–9. These showed an estimated 246,000 non-fatal reportable injuries. Overall there was a loss of 29.3 million working days and of these 24.6 million were due to work-related illness (HSE, 2010b). There is a downward trend both in the number of accidents requiring three or more days off work and in work-related illness but these still amount to a significant loss of work and increased costs to employers (HSE, 2010b). It is claimed that over 40 million potential workdays are lost to business each year and it is estimated that this costs British employers somewhere between £3.3 and £6.5 billion each year (HSE, 2010c).

ACTIVITY 11.1

Sometimes employers are reluctant to spend money on safety improvements as they don't feel this is justified. There are, however, costs associated with accidents. What are the possible costs to an individual employer of accidents at work?

Discussion of Activity 11.1

Obviously, depending on the severity of the injury, there are costs to the injured person in terms of pain and suffering, and possible loss of earnings. There are also costs to the employer, and your list is likely to include at least some of the following:

- cost of lost time and production due to absence caused by injury
- cost of lost time and production due to dealing with the injury
- cost of replacement worker or of training the replacement
- cost of replacing broken machinery or unsafe machinery or equipment
- cost of compensation to injured employee
- higher insurance premiums if the organisation's accident record is not good
- cost involved in carrying out a full investigation into the causes of the accident
- cost of paying fines or even facing imprisonment if the employer was to blame for the accident
- cost of poor morale within the workforce
- cost of people not being willing to work for the organisation because of its poor reputation for safety.

You may have found some other costs involved in accidents as well. Employers should be aware of the hidden costs of accidents; if they carried out a cost–benefit analysis they would probably be amazed at how much accidents were costing them and be more prepared to spend money on accident prevention. In their studies of accidents, the Health and Safety Executive (1995) identified one organisation where the costs of accidents amounted to as much as 37 per cent of profits. This organisation did not have a particularly bad record on health and safety, nor had it suffered any major disasters, fatalities or prosecutions.

We believe that health and safety is an important area of concern for all HRM practitioners, since it is in the organisation's interest to pursue any initiatives that will provide benefits and services which the employees will want and value but that will also fit with the strategic needs of the organisation by enhancing levels of employee performance.

Employers can check for themselves the actual costs both of accidents and work-related incidents in their organisations by using the accident and incident calculators provided by the Health and Safety Executive. They allow employers the choice of two different ways to calculate the annual costs of accidents in their organisation and also of using an interactive tool to calculate costs of other work-related incidents. Now there is really no excuse for employer ignorance of the cost of accidents or work-related incidents in their organisations.

If you would like to see how easy it is for employers to calculate the costs of accidents and work-based incidents by examining these tools for yourself, go to **www.hse.gov.uk/costs/accidentcost_calc/accident_costs_intro.asp** (accessed 6.9.2010).

Legislation

Did you know?

The Corporate Manslaughter and Corporate Homicide Act 2007 came into effect on 6 April 2008 across the UK. The Act set out a new offence for convicting an organisation where a gross failure in the way activities were managed results in a person's death.

The offence does not require organisations to comply with new regulatory standards. But the Act means that those who disregard the safety of others at work, with fatal consequences, are more vulnerable to very serious criminal charges. Courts will look at management systems and practices across the organisation, providing a more effective means for prosecuting the worst corporate failures to manage health and safety properly.

(*Source*: Ministry of Justice, 2008)

Much of the early development of legislation to protect employees at work was closely linked to the historical development of people management. The more enlightened employers were concerned to improve working conditions for their employees and appointed industrial welfare workers to help with this. Less enlightened employers were compelled to pay some attention to the protection of selected groups of employees, and as early as 1840 legislation designed to limit the hours that children worked was passed. In more recent times several new Acts have been passed and regulations issued to protect employees.

The Health and Safety at Work Act 1974 (HASAWA)

In Great Britain the foundation for the system of regulating health and safety at work was introduced by the Health and Safety at Work Act 1974. Although this was a long time ago, HASAWA is still very important today and forms the foundation for much of the later legislation. According to Hackitt (2010), one of the fundamental principles underpinning the Health and Safety at Work Act that still applies today is that 'those who create risk are best placed to manage it'. This means that those who create risks have duties to protect both workers and the public from their actions so that those who are the main risk creators are also the main duty holders in law. According to XpertHR (2010a) the main duty holders are likely to be employers and the self-employed but could also include employees, designers, manufacturers, importers, suppliers and those in charge of premises. In this chapter we shall focus principally on the duty holders who are employers and employees.

Before HASAWA, the legislation that could be used to protect employees at work was patchy and applied to vulnerable groups such as women or children, or to particular industries where there were thought to be high risks. The vast majority of the working population before 1974 were not actually protected by any health or safety legislation. The Health and Safety at Work Act 1974 set up some new bodies such as the Health and Safety Commission (HSC), the Health and Safety Executive (HSE) and reinforced the power of others such as local authorities. In 2008 HSC and HSE merged to form one single body called the Health and Safety Executive (HSE) and this is now the organisation responsible for the promotion of health and safety at work in Great Britain (Hackitt, 2010a). It does continue to work closely with local authorities and the roles of the Health and Safety Executive and the local authorities will be discussed later in the chapter.

HASAWA was the first piece of legislation designed to protect everyone at work, and also to protect others who were not at work, such as customers or even passers-by. It is estimated that it brought an extra 3 million people under the scope of protective safety legislation for the first time.

The main aim of the Act was to provide a comprehensive system of law which would raise standards of safety and health for all persons at work and also protect members of the public who might be affected by their actions.

More than 36 years after the Health and Safety at Work Act 1974 became law it still forms the foundation of health and safety legislation in the UK, so it is important to understand some of the fundamental principles that underpin this important piece of legislation.

ACTIVITY 11.2

Both employers and employees have responsibilities under HASAWA. List what you would expect to be the duties of employers and employees with regard to health and safety.

Duties of employers	Duties of employees

Compare your lists with the following duties summarised from the Health and Safety at Work Act 1974.

Discussion of Activity 11.2

Your list probably included some indication that employers were to take responsibility for having a safe workplace with safe equipment that would not injure anyone, and you also probably thought that employees too should take care not to harm anyone at work. There are no specific rules about lighting or temperature in the way that there are in some other Acts. Instead the Act is trying to involve people and make everyone take some responsibility for their actions. This approach is therefore moving towards a human resource management approach, and health and safety is not just in the domain of the human resource specialist but is shared with others. Sometimes the human resource specialist does have some aspects of health and safety included in their job description, and they may, for example, be expected to chair the safety committee if there is one.

The responsibilities of employers under the Health and Safety at Work Act

Employers have a basic duty of care to their employees to ensure their health, safety and welfare. As well as this rather general duty, they have five other duties. These are:

- to ensure that the workplace itself is safe; that equipment has been maintained correctly and work is safely organised
- that accidents do not occur because of incorrect handling, storage or transportation within the workplace
- that there is training, supervision and information relating to health and safety
- that the workplace itself is maintained adequately and that there are safe ways to get into and out of the buildings
- that provisions for wellbeing are adequate.

All of these duties are expressed in quite general terms and there is nothing in the Act to specify, for example, how much training or information should be given. The words 'so far as is reasonably practicable' are used frequently within HASAWA. The exact meaning of this phrase will be discussed later in this chapter. The employer also has a further specific duty to produce a safety policy statement and we shall also discuss later in the chapter what this involves.

As we said earlier, HASAWA was designed to gain involvement in health and safety from as many sources as possible, so the responsibility was not just one way. Employees also have responsibilities.

The responsibilities of employees under the Health and Safety at Work Act

As you might expect, there are fewer responsibilities for the employees than for the employers. They have three main areas of responsibility under HASAWA in relation to health and safety. These are:

- to take responsibility for their own health and safety, and for any health and safety problems which might be caused to colleagues by their actions or in some cases their failure to act
- not to recklessly interfere with or misuse any machinery, equipment or processes
- to cooperate with employers about health and safety initiatives.

Although they may not seem very onerous responsibilities, they are important since employees who do not follow these guidelines could be disciplined or even face prosecution themselves if an accident occurred for which they were responsible. They should cooperate about health and safety issues, such as wearing protective clothing, if the employer provides it. Since they must take responsibility for their own health and safety and that of others, they must also not do anything to interfere with safety guards, as this could result in injuries to themselves or to other people.

> **Pause for thought 11.1** The phrase 'as far as is reasonably practicable' is used several times in HASAWA. What factors do you think should be considered in determining whether or not something is 'reasonably practicable'?

This phrase means that circumstances, risks and cost need to be considered when an employer is endeavouring to make the workplace safe for employees. It would be very difficult to make anywhere completely safe and eliminate all accidents. Accidents are by definition something that you cannot predict; nevertheless, many situations do occur where it is possible to predict that someone could be injured if improvements are not made, and employers should try to anticipate the likelihood of these types of accident and take steps to prevent them from occurring. 'Reasonably practicable' means that a calculation must be made in which the risk is compared with the sacrifices, cost and level of effort needed to avert that risk. If there is a very slim chance that a comparatively minor accident might occur, but this chance could be eliminated by spending thousands of pounds on new equipment and also by disrupting the workforce, it might not be considered to be reasonably practicable to do so. If, however, the risk was of a serious injury or possibly death, then it would be reasonable to take every step and spend any amount of money to eliminate this risk. The term 'as far as is reasonably practicable' therefore means that the employer should do as much as they can to try to eliminate risks but that they need to review the balance between the risk and the amount of effort required to eliminate that risk.

Control of Substances Hazardous to Health Regulations (COSHH) 1988

This is another far-reaching piece of legislation comprising 19 regulations and 4 approved codes of practice which came into effect on 1 October 1989 and which have subsequently been revised in 1999, 2002 and 2003. Apart from some minor changes to tidy up the 1999 regulations, as these amendments relate to fairly specialised areas they do not alter the main thrust of this legislation and are too detailed to include in an introductory HRM textbook.

COSHH is designed to protect anyone who works with substances that could be hazardous to health. The regulations apply to all workplaces and include all substances with the exception of asbestos, lead, materials that produce ionising radiation and substances underground, which all have their own separate legislation. The legislation basically applies to any other substances that can cause harm by being inhaled, ingested, coming into contact with the skin, or being injected or introduced into the body, so they do cover a very wide range of substances.

COSHH regulations require all employers to carry out an assessment of risks to their employees from substances that are identified in the workplace as being potentially hazardous to either their employees or others who might be affected. Any risks that are identified must then be controlled. This emphasis on assessing risk and then doing something about it is a very different approach to that of HASAWA.

While it would be easy to assume that these regulations would not have much effect on ordinary workplaces, this is not in fact the case, as many of the substances identified as potentially hazardous will be found in any workplace – e.g. fluid for photocopiers or cleaning products – so in reality all workplaces are affected. The main areas that employers should focus on are:

- assessing the risk of substances used and identifying the required precautions
- introducing appropriate measures to control or prevent the risk
- ensuring the correct use of the control measures, and that equipment is regularly maintained
- conducting health surveillance to monitor health of employees where there is a known identifiable risk
- informing and training employees about risks that may arise from their work, and informing them of the necessary precautions to take.

The Framework Directive

The European Union Framework Directive has broad objectives which were implemented in EU member states by 31 December 1992. This established in general terms the European Commission's approach to health and safety. The main objectives of the directive were to introduce measures to encourage improvements in safety and health of workers at work. In order to do this it contains general principles concerning the prevention of occupational risks, the protection of health and safety, the elimination of risk and accident factors, as well as informing, consultation and providing balanced participation in accordance with national laws.

The British response to the EU directive was made in the Management of Health and Safety at Work Regulations 1992, which were accompanied by an approved Code of Practice which came into effect on 1 January 1993. Five further sets of regulations were also implemented in Britain on 1 January 1993 and all these have become known as the 'six-pack'. The 'six-pack' comprised:

- Management of Health and Safety at Work Regulations 1992
- Workplace (Health, Safety and Welfare) Regulations 1992
- Provision and Use of Work Equipment Regulations 1992
- Personal Protective Equipment at Work Regulations 1992
- Health and Safety (Display Screen Equipment) Regulations 1992
- Manual Handling Operations Regulations 1992.

Legislation becomes out of date and does not always meet the requirements of modern organisations, so amendments are often necessary. All of the original 'six-pack' regulations have been amended and updated so the new dates and any significant changes will be included with the regulations as they are discussed. The Provision and Use of Work Equipment was amended in 1998 and the Management of Health and Safety at Work Regulations in 1999. The remaining four regulations were also amended later under the Health and Safety (Miscellaneous Amendments) Regulations 2002.

The Management of Health and Safety at Work Regulations 1999 (MHSWR)

This is the law in the UK that implemented the Framework Directive. The HASAWA covered some parts of the directive but there were also new things that employers needed to do, such as carrying out certain detailed procedures, assessing risks, implementing certain safety measures and communicating with staff on health and safety. According to Stranks (2007a), 'these regulations do not stand alone – all other modern health and safety legislation such as the Workplace (Health, Safety and Welfare) Regulations 1992 and the Provision and Use of Work Equipment Regulations 1998, must be read in conjunction with the general duties under the MHSWR.' This is therefore a very important piece of legislation which has the following key features.

It states that employers shall:

- carry out assessment of health and safety risks to both employees and the public (this may be done in writing or on computer)
- monitor and review protective and preventive measures
- appoint a competent person or persons to be responsible for protective and preventive measures
- establish emergency procedures
- give comprehensible and relevant information and training to employees (the training can be provided by a suitable training provider other than the employer)
- cooperate with any other employers who may share the same work site.

Also, employees shall:

- use equipment in the way in which they have been trained to use it
- report any dangerous situations or any problem areas that they spot in the arrangements that the employer has made for health and safety.

These regulations are intended for use in cases of criminal action against an employer, and may not be used in any civil cases as evidence of negligence.

> **Pause for thought 11.2** To what extent do you feel that the Management of Health and Safety at Work Regulations 1999 differ from the HASAWA 1974?

These regulations are more forceful than HASAWA and specify that employers 'shall' do certain things, whereas HASAWA only expected employers to carry out its provisions 'so far as it is reasonably practicable' to do so.

The new regulations also mean that employers have a legal duty to predict what could go wrong, before it actually happens, and to take preventive action to avoid it happening. They must record the preventive action that they have taken. This is referred to as risk assessment and is the same principle as under COSHH, but it is now applied more widely. This will be discussed more fully later in the chapter.

The new regulations require employers to be proactive and actively manage activities aimed at protecting the health and safety of their employees. This is more in line than previous legislative measures with the human resource approach of being proactive and actively managing human resources.

Workplace (Health, Safety and Welfare) Regulations 1992, amended by the Health and Safety (Miscellaneous Amendments) Regulations 2002

This law is intended to rationalise older pieces of legislation and provide clearer ruling as to exactly what facilities the employer should provide for the employee. As stated earlier it is important that it is read in conjunction with the Management of Health and Safety at Work Regulations (MHSWR) 1999.

Employers shall:

- provide a good working environment with appropriate temperature, ventilation and level of lighting
- carry out maintenance and be responsible for keeping the workplace clean.

The 2002 amendments include further guidance for employers about achieving this, primarily in relation to rest rooms and rest areas. The amendments specify that there should be sufficient seats (with backs) and tables for the number of people likely to use them at any one time.

The 2002 amendment regulations state that employers must ensure they meet the needs of any disabled workers by also providing suitable rest areas for them. Other equipment and facilities, such as workstations, passageways, doors, and washroom facilities, should also be designed to meet the specific needs of disabled workers.

Provision and Use of Work Equipment Regulations 1998, amended by the Health and Safety (Miscellaneous Amendments) Regulations 2002

This law aims to bring together many older laws governing equipment used at work. Employers shall:

- consider when they purchase new equipment the working condition of the equipment and risks that it may pose to employees
- ensure the provision of appropriate levels of lighting and warnings about the safe use of the equipment
- ensure that the equipment is suitable for the use to which it will be put
- provide adequate information and training
- provide adequate protection from any potentially dangerous parts of the equipment or machinery.

Personal Protective Equipment at Work Regulations 1992, amended by the Health and Safety (Miscellaneous Amendments) Regulations 2002

These regulations replace part of more than 20 old pieces of legislation which were concerned with provision of protective equipment for employees. They aim to ensure suitable provision of protective equipment such as head protection, high visibility clothing or safety harnesses. Employers must ensure the equipment is appropriate for the likely type of risks, the specific working conditions in the workplace and the duration for which it is likely to be worn. In addition, they should consider the ergonomic requirements of the job, state of health of the person employed and any particular characteristics of their workstation that might affect the use of the personal protective equipment. Particular attention should also be paid to ensuring that the equipment provided is hygienic and compatible with any additional personal protective equipment that the worker may need to wear simultaneously.

Employers shall:

- ensure that equipment used is suitable for the job to be done
- adequately maintain, clean and replace equipment as necessary
- store it safely when it is not in use
- ensure correct use of the equipment
- inform and train employees in the correct use of the equipment.

Health and Safety (Display Screen Equipment) Regulations 1992, amended by the Health and Safety (Miscellaneous Amendments) Regulations 2002

This law implements the EU's Visual Display Unit Directive and specifies minimum levels of health and safety for people who spend a large part of their time at work working in front of computer screens or who are about to become employed in that capacity. It is primarily aimed at the prevention of damage to their upper limbs, and to prevent eye strain, fatigue and stress.

Employers shall:

- assess the risks and reduce any that are found
- ensure that workstations meet at least the minimum requirements
- ensure that the work is planned to include breaks and changes of activity
- arrange for employees to have their eyes tested regularly at time limits designated by the optician appointed by the employer and provide spectacles if necessary
- provide appropriate training for users or those about to become users of visual display units.

Eyesight tests should be completed as soon as possible after any request, or in the case of someone who is about to start work, before they become a computer user.

Manual Handling Operations Regulations 1992, amended by the Health and Safety (Miscellaneous Amendments) Regulations 2002

This aims to reduce the levels of injury and ill-health associated with manual handling of loads at work.

Employers shall:

- ensure, as far as is practicable, that employees do not need to use risky techniques when handling loads
- assess whether any risks are inherent in the manual handling that has to be done
- take necessary steps to reduce risks by introducing mechanical help, ensuring loads are lighter and assessing the capabilities of the individual
- ensure the provision of information to all employees
- if employees sometimes work on another employer's premises, liaise closely with the other employer.

When trying to determine whether each specific manual handling activity involves any risk, employers should pay particular attention to the following:

- the physical suitability of the employee for safely completing the particular form of manual handling required
- what the person is wearing and its suitability for the job
- the amount of knowledge and training that the person has received
- the results of any risk assessments that have already been completed that relate to the job
- whether the employee has been identified as being one of a group of employees who are particularly at risk
- the results of any health surveillance that has been undertaken.

This legislation is far reaching in its scope although its effects will vary from one organisation to another, depending on the nature of the work undertaken.

Reporting of Injuries, Diseases and Dangerous Occurrences Regulations (RIDDOR) 1995

RIDDOR requires employers to report certain work-related accidents, diseases and dangerous occurrences to the enforcing authorities so that they can identify risks and investigate serious accidents. The following briefly describes some of the circumstances in which reporting should occur:

- The death or major injury of an employee, or of a self-employed person working in the organisation, or of a member of the public must all be reported to the enforcing authorities immediately and this must be followed within 10 days by a completed accident report. Reportable major injuries include fractures, amputation, dislocation, loss of sight.
- If an employee or self-employed person working on your premises suffers an accident or injury which requires that person to be absent from work for at least three days, then a completed accident form must be sent to the enforcing authorities.
- Some work-related diseases, such as occupational dermatitis, skin cancer or occupational asthma have also to be reported on a disease report form to the enforcing authority, as do infections such as hepatitis, tetanus or tuberculosis.
- There may be instances where something occurs which does not actually result in a reportable injury but which could have done. For example, the collapse of a lift or an explosion in a closed vessel are likely to constitute a dangerous occurrence, even if no one is injured. Any dangerous occurrence has to be reported immediately by telephone to the enforcing authorities. An accident report form should also be completed within 10 days of the dangerous occurrence. (Details of where to find more information are given in 'Further study' at the end of the chapter.)

The enforcing authority will be the environmental health department of the local authority if the type of the business is an office, retail or wholesale, warehousing, hotel or catering, sports or leisure, a residential home or place of worship. Accidents or dangerous occurrences which happen in any other type of business will need to be reported to the area office of the Health and Safety Executive. Nowadays accidents and dangerous occurrences can even be reported using the Internet. Have a look at the websites at the end of this chapter for more details of how to do this.

The Working Time Regulations 1998

We discussed the Working Time Regulations 1998 briefly in Chapter 4, but have also included them here, since the hours people work can have a big impact on their health, wellbeing and safety in the workplace though other factors such as liking their job and the amount of support they get from colleagues can mitigate against some of these negative effects (CIPD, 2010a).

It has often been claimed that the UK is the 'long hours capital' of Europe and that working such long hours adversely affects workers' health. In some organisations there is a culture of 'presenteeism', where people are expected to arrive early for work and leave late, forgoing home and social life. While some workers thrive in a long hours culture and live to work, such a culture is likely to hide a great deal of inefficiency and result in increased levels of stress and ill-health for many other workers. These regulations attempt to control the hours worked and control the way the hours are organised. They also establish minimum holiday levels for employees in the UK, although it is frequently claimed that a large number of UK employees actually fail to take all the holiday they are entitled to, either because they are too busy or are too frightened to be away from work for their whole holiday entitlement.

> **Did you know?**
>
> Death from overwork is so common in Japan that they even have a special word for it, *Karoshi*. The first documented case of Karoshi occurred in Japan in 1969 but there have been many cases since. In Japan the spouses of those who have died from Karoshi have won claims for compensation from the companies concerned and each year between 20 and 60 claims for compensation are brought. This is still probably a gross underestimate of the real number of cases of Karoshi in Japan.
>
> (*Source*: Nishiyama and Johnson, 1977)

The recession in 2008 and 2009 caused the percentage of people working more than 45 hours per week in the UK to fall from 20.4 per cent to 19.3 per cent. Philpott (2010) says that this may have been just temporary as there are now some indications that the total number of hours worked each week have been increasing since mid-2009, but the numbers of people working between 18 and 30 hours per week have also increased. He claims it would be more appropriate to talk not of a long hours culture, but of a mixed hours culture as while it is true that one in five workers do work more than 45 hours per week there are also a similar number of people working between 16 and 30 hours per week.

Although the 48-hour working week means workers in the UK still work much longer hours than their counterparts in France, it is nevertheless considerably better than the expectation in countries such as Japan. In Japan it has been documented that many workers regularly work for over 100 hours per week, for many weeks, or even years at a time and that this frequently leads, not surprisingly, to ill-health or even death. Since we work increasingly in a global economy, where people are constantly accessible via mobile phones or email, these long-hour work practices are spreading to the USA and the UK.

From 2009 statutory holiday entitlement is 5.6 weeks. This right applies to all workers and not just employees. (The distinction between workers and employees will be discussed in Chapter 12.) Having rights to holiday is not of much use if workers do not take them and employers should take steps to make sure that workers use their holiday entitlement. They should discourage a culture of presenteeism and regard this as good management practice and as a way of contributing to the prevention of ill health.

Legislation about smoking

Four related pieces of legislation have been introduced in Scotland, Wales, Northern Ireland and England prohibiting smoking in public places, including workplaces, and similar legislation has been introduced throughout the rest of Europe.

The Smoking, Health and Social Care (Scotland) Act 2005 was the first to come into effect and resulted in a ban on smoking in public places, including workplaces from March 2006. A similar ban on smoking in public places came into effect in Wales from 2 April 2007, in Northern Ireland from 30 April 2007 and in England from 1 July 2007. These related pieces of legislation are designed to protect workers who may previously have been affected by passive smoking and also to promote positive health improvements by encouraging smokers to stop.

The Corporate Manslaughter and Corporate Homicide Act 2007

The Corporate Manslaughter and Corporate Homicide Act 2007 made corporate manslaughter a criminal offence from April 2008. This has also increased the interest in health safety and wellbeing as companies found guilty could face an unlimited fine if they are found to have caused death through gross negligence or failures in their safety systems. People working for some organisations such as Crown bodies, previously exempt from prosecution, are now covered by this legislation. While this is to be welcomed, Richard Jones (2007) argues that it does not go far enough and that there are still too many exemptions. He goes on to say that 'HR needs to actively engage workers in helping keep workplaces safe, and should regularly consult them on health and safety issues.' Safety should certainly be of concern to all managers including HR managers and line managers.

Most of the legislation discussed here, with the exception of the anti-smoking legislation, has focused primarily on safety although clearly health and wellbeing are also closely linked to this.

The people and organisations involved in health, safety and wellbeing

We have already discussed at length the roles of employers and employees but there are other health, safety and wellbeing roles currently undertaken by the Health and Safety Executive and local authorities. What do these organisations actually do? How are they organised?

In 1999 John Prescott, who was the Deputy Prime Minister at that time, announced a new impetus for health and safety called Revitalising Health and Safety. He said that the Health and Safety at Work Act 1974 had done its job as evidenced by the fact that the 'number of deaths at work today is a quarter of the 1971 level'. However, he wanted a strategic appraisal of the health and safety framework in order to build on the work of the previous 25 years and to establish a new agenda for the first 25 years of the new century (Prescott, 2000). As a part of the Revitalising Health and Safety impetus, targets were set from 2000 onwards which were to be achieved by 2010. These targets were to reduce the number of days lost due to work-related injuries per 100,000 workers by 30 per cent, to reduce the incidence of work-related ill health by 20 per cent and to reduce the numbers of fatalites at work by 10 per cent. The assessment of whether or not these targets have been achieved will start in autumn 2010 but will only be completed by autumn 2011.

Pause for thought 11.3 To what extent do you think that targets are useful in health, safety and wellbeing? Go to www.hse.gov.uk and check for yourself whether or not these targets have been met. What more can organistions do to become healthy and safe workplaces?

Another concern was to simplify and streamline the number of organisations involved in Health and Safety. The merger of the Health and Safety Commission and the Health and Safety Executive in 2008 was a direct response to that concern but the Conservative–Liberal Democrat Coalition Government subsequently announced further plans to streamline health and asked Lord Young of Graffham, a former cabinet minister, to review health and safety legislation (Woolf and Dowling, 2010).

The Health and Safety Executive (HSE)

The HSE is responsible for promoting better health and safety at work within Great Britain. Its mission is:

> The prevention of death, injury and ill-health to those at work and those affected by work activities (HSE, 2010d).

It consists of policy advisers, inspectors and experts in medicine, science and technology. They are responsible for making provision for enforcing the legislation, for dealing with daily administration and conducting research and for identifying any new risks or hazards that emerge with changes to technology or work practices.

In June 2009 HSE launched a new strategy *The Health and Safety of Great Britain: Be Part of the Solution* and one of its key features is that it sets out to involve all stakeholders in health and safety. Hackitt (2010b) emphasises the fact that while HSE and their local authority partners lead and coordinate health and safety, the success of the strategy relies on everyone playing a part and not just leaving it to these groups. This is particularly important as the UK economic situation improves as traditionally any improvement to the economy has also resulted in an increase in work-related accidents and ill-health.

Alongside local authorities HSE is also an independent regulator for health and safety and their main role is to assist others in preventing work-related accidents and ill-health. Its inspectors can achieve this by conducting workplace inspections and by other more proactive measures such as getting stakeholders involved and providing guidance by giving information and advice.

Did you know?

There are often stories in the news indicating that health and safety organisations have become overzealous and created ridiculous rules. Many of the things that are claimed to be true are myths and the Health and Safety Executive now publishes a list of myths on its website each month. In its list of myths of the month it included the following:

August 2010 – Health and safety bans bunting
July 2010 – Health and safety brings candyfloss to a sticky end
June 2010 – Health and safety risks stop children playing 'pin the tail on the donkey'.
May 2010 – You don't need to secure your load if you are just driving down the road.

(*Source:* HSE, 2010e, *2010 Myths*, HSE)

How would you have reacted to these stories? Would you have thought any of these myths were true?

Local authorities (LA)

Local authorities also have responsibility for enforcement of health and safety in approximately 194,000 workplaces. Under HASAWA, the Secretary of State for Work and Pensions (DWP) can make regulations for local authorities to take on responsibility for certain activities and to ensure that there is no duplication of effort between them and the Health and Safety Executive. The local authority inspectors, normally known as environmental health officers, are responsible for health and safety mainly in the services sector, while the HSE tends to concentrate on the more hazard-prone industries. There is a liaison committee which ensures consistency of approach between the HSE and local authorities. The HSE publishes a wide range of material each year explaining its role and the practical implications of legislation. The Health and Safety Executive can provide guidance, approved codes of practice and regulations.

The Gangmasters Licensing Authority (GLA)

Not all workers are lucky enough to work in well-organised and regulated workplaces even in the UK. The death of 18 Chinese cockle pickers in Morecambe Bay, Lancashire, in 2004 drew attention to the world of unscrupulous operators who employ migrant workers, sometimes illegally, to work in low-skilled jobs. The Gangmasters Licensing Authority was formed to license genuine workforce organisers and providers of migrant workers and has the power to revoke licences where poor practice has occurred. Initially legislation targeted the agricultural sector where gangmasters and migrant workers primarily worked. However, it is claimed by MPs and trade unions that 'legislation to regulate gangmasters in the agricultural sector could be pushing unscrupulous operators into providing workers for care homes instead' (CIPD, 2007). The Labour MP Jim Sheridan who was responsible for legislation creating the GLA has been pushing for a new bill to extend the GLA's scope to other sectors. Sheridan said, 'We believe the GLA's remit could be rolled out universally sector by sector. There are really important health and safety issues here. We don't want workers to be abused or intimidated, but we don't want them in skilled jobs either if they are not qualified' (CIPD, 2007).

The world of work has changed dramatically over the years and there is now a much more diverse workforce working in increasingly flexible ways. These new aims are intended to address this. New health and safety issues arise as people work from home, or while on the move, and the risks to their health and safety also need to be assessed. There are also fewer large employers and more small ones.

The enforcing authorities

We shall now discuss how the current inspection of workplaces and investigation of accidents is shared between HSE inspectors and local authority enforcement officers. Basically the HSE inspectors cover work conducted primarily in factories, building sites, mines, fairgrounds, quarries, railways, chemical plants, offshore and nuclear installations, schools or hospitals. The local authority enforcement officers cover retailing, some warehouses, most offices, hotels, catering, consumer services, sports and leisure activities and places of worship. Both have similar powers of enforcement. These include a right to:

- enter employers' premises
- carry out inspections/investigations
- take equipment or materials on to premises
- take measurements, photographs or recordings
- carry out tests on articles or substances
- examine books and documents
- issue improvement notices
- issue prohibition notices
- issue a Crown notice.

The last three points are very important and we shall consider each in turn. However, sometimes when an enforcing inspector finds a breach of the law which is relatively minor they may feel that improvement notices and prohibition notices are not appropriate.

Informal methods

In the case of a minor breach in legislation the inspector may choose to use informal methods and may simply give the employer or contractor advice about what they should do to comply with the law, and explain the reasons.

Improvement notices

If the inspector feels that an organisation is contravening one of the relevant provisions of legislation then they can issue an improvement notice which will specify that improvements must be made within a specified time limit to bring the equipment or process up to the required standard of safety.

Prohibition notices

If when the inspector visits they feel that there is serious danger or risk of injury to employees, they can issue a prohibition notice which will stop work activity immediately until the risk has been dealt with. In some circumstances a deferred prohibition order may be issued: this would occur, for example, if it would be difficult to stop a process in mid-cycle or if there was no immediate risk of injury.

Crown notices

This is a type of notice which HSE can issue to a Crown organisation such as a government department or the Prison Service. It would be issued under the same sort of circumstances that would merit a prohibition notice or improvement notice for other organisations.

> **Did you know?**
>
> There were 8,054 enforcement notices issued in 2008-9 by the Health and Safety Executive and a further 6,340 by local authorities. The HSE prosecuted 1,245 offences in that year and there were 860 convictions. Some organisations were prosecuted for more than one offence. The organisations found guilty received average penalties of £14,614 per breach and because in many instances the prosecutions related to more than one breach to £20,606 per case.
>
> (See **www.hse.gov.uk/statistics** for latest figures.)

The Health and Safety Commission's Enforcement Policy Statement (2008) states the approach which both the Health and Safety Executive and local authorities should take in relation to law enforcement. The overall aims of the HSC are to protect the health, safety and wellbeing of employees and to safeguard others such as members of the public who may be exposed to risk from the workplace or activity.

Normally in England and Wales most prosecutions would go to a magistrates' court but more serious cases are referred to the Crown Courts. Under the Scottish judicial system the majority of cases go to a sheriff court or before a jury. Organisations and individuals can face prosecution, and prison sentences and unlimited fines can also be given by the Crown Courts.

Any accidents at work that result in death are treated as manslaughter. The police are involved in these cases and have overall responsibility for them. However, there had been general dissatisfaction that the system was not tough enough and that employers were on occasions shirking their responsibilities with regard to health and safety and frequently escaping prosecution even when an employee had died as a result of the company's actions or inactions. The Corporate Manslaughter and Corporate Homicide Act (2007), mentioned earlier, is intended to create a criminal offence of corporate manslaughter for the first time. According to Baker (2007), 'The law is likely to lead to more prosecutions for deaths resulting from an organisation's acts or omissions, and may lead to higher fines. It will certainly lead to greater scrutiny by the courts of the way in which companies organise themselves internally in terms of health and safety.' This should make it easier to examine the conduct of senior managers, and a company can be found guilty of corporate manslaughter if it can be proved that the way they managed and organised their activities led to a death and that this amounted to a gross breach of its duty of care to the employee.

In 2008 the HSE (HSE, 2008) revised its Enforcement Policy Statement to reflect the merger between HSC and HSE and it restated the criteria for whether or not particular incidents or complaints should be investigated. This Policy Statement stresses five main things:

1. *The principle of proportionality.* This means that the severity of the action taken should be in proportion to the level of risk and the seriousness of the breach of law.
2. *Targeting.* The people/organisations who cause the most serious risks or who have failed to control hazards in the workplace adequately should be the ones to be targeted by the inspectors.
3. *Consistency.* For people to have faith in the system and the inspectors they need to feel that they will be treated in a consistently fair way. This does not mean identical treatment for duty holders but involves taking a similar approach when the circumstances seem similar and consequently achieving similar ends.
4. *Transparency.* Every action taken should be clear, with explanations given for any action that is taken so that duty holders know what is expected form them in relation to health, safety and wellbeing.
5. *Accountability.* The enforcing authorities must be held accountable for their actions and so must have policies and standards to be assessed against. They also need to have clear ways for people to make comments or complaints and for dealing with these (HSE, 2008).

Prosecution

If the case is very serious then the inspector may also need to initiate a prosecution. Any decision about whether or not to prosecute will be taken after considering the HSE's Enforcement Policy Statement.

Safety representatives

As we said earlier, there is a duty for employers to consult with and involve safety representatives in the workplace. In October 1978 the Safety Representatives and Safety Committees Regulations came into effect. These regulations form part of the Health and Safety at Work Act, and within a year over 100,000 safety representatives were in post. The regulations provide that any recognised trade union can appoint safety representatives, and they recommend that in general the people who are appointed should have worked for that employer for at least two years so that they have a reasonable range of experience from which to draw. In some trade unions the shop stewards take on the role of safety representatives, while in others the safety representative is a separate post. The people to fill these positions are, however, selected by the trade union, not by the management. Organisations where there are no recognised trade unions can still appoint safety representatives, and they are normally elected by the workforce. As more employers start to appreciate that there are benefits for the business and a clear return on investment to be gained from focussing attention on health, safety and wellbeing, this role could become even more important.

The safety representative's main function is to represent the employee in consultation with the employer on issues relating to health and safety in the workplace, and they can investigate hazards or potential hazards as well as carrying out inspections of the workplace. They are entitled to paid time off to perform their duties and for training to enable them to carry out their duties effectively, and they may also require some facilities such as the use of a telephone, a filing cabinet and a room to conduct interviews. If two or more safety representatives make a written request to management for a safety committee to be established, then the employer is legally obliged to fulfil that request.

The Management of Health and Safety at Work Regulations 1992 (MHSWR) as amended in 1999 add to the Safety Representatives and Safety Committees Regulations 1977 and specify that every employer shall consult safety representatives in good time with regard to:

- the introduction of any measure at the workplace which may substantially affect health or safety of the workforce
- arrangements for appointing or nominating a 'competent person' who is able to assist the employer to carry out risk assessment exercises and help them in carrying out duties in relation to health and safety
- the health and safety information that the employer is supposed to provide to employees
- the planning and organisation of health and safety training
- the health and safety consequences of the introduction of new technology at work.

There are, as you can see, a wide range of duties performed by safety representatives. Safety representatives usually receive excellent training from trades unions for this demanding role and those who take on these roles can also choose to take the training further and use it as part of a professional qualification in health and safety.

Safety officer or safety adviser

None of the legislation actually specifies the need for a safety officer but, as the law has grown in complexity, many organisations have felt that it is necessary to appoint a person to specialise in this area of work. This is a management appointment and must not be confused with the trade union/employee-appointed safety representative. Safety officers are sometimes appointed to advise senior management without being part of any other department and report directly to the board, but in many organisations they form part of the human resource management department. Smaller organisations may not wish to appoint a full-time safety officer and may instead call on the expertise provided by independent consultants to act as safety advisers. It is important that anyone appointed as safety officer or safety adviser has the status and level of competence to provide authoritative advice to management and the workforce on aspects of health and safety.

A competent person

This has a specific meaning in terms of health and safety as the Framework Directive (Article 7), which is discussed later, says that employers must designate 'a competent person' who has practical and theoretical knowledge of particular equipment and who is able to identify any problems that may occur with it. The provision of this directive is reflected in Regulation 6 of the Management of Health and Safety at Work Regulations 1992 and clearly refers to a management nominee, although not necessarily to the safety officer but to someone who because of their knowledge and experience of particular machinery, plant or equipment is able to identify problems or defects in it. That person needs to be competent not just to do the job but to carry out risk assessment for health and safety for employees and the public, and must monitor and review protective and preventive measures. A safety officer may fulfil this role but is not likely to be the only designated competent person, as they are unlikely to have the required level of knowledge or experience for all machinery.

Safety committees

Safety committees have to be established, as we said earlier, if two or more safety representatives request the organisation to do so, but many organisations do not wait for this request, and it is good practice to set up a safety committee in any case. The main objective of a safety committee is to promote cooperation between employers and employees in instigating, developing and carrying out measures to ensure the health and safety at work of employees. In organisations seeking to improve health, safety and wellbeing this provides a useful way of gaining increased employee engagement. Safety committees are likely to provide some or all of the following functions:

- study figures and trends for accidents and notifiable diseases
- examine safety audit reports
- consider reports and factual information provided by inspectors
- consider the reports of safety representatives
- assist in development of safety rules and safe systems of work
- monitor the effectiveness of safety training in the workplace
- monitor the effectiveness of the safety and health communication in the workplace
- encourage publicity for health and safety programmes in the workplace
- provide a link with the appropriate inspectorates.

Membership of the health and safety committee

The membership of the committee should be agreed between management and the employees. The committee should normally include equal numbers of people from management and the workforce and should have representation from different areas of the workforce and different grades of management. People such as the organisation's doctor, nurse or safety officer should also be invited to attend as *ex officio* members. It is a good idea for the person who chairs the committee to have sufficient status within the organisation that they can authorise money to be spent on necessary aspects of health and safety without having to refer all such decisions to higher authority. A senior member of the management team would fulfil this role well, although in many organisations the chair of the safety committee may also alternate between management and the workforce.

Health and safety arrangements

Safety policy statement

You will remember that under HASAWA one of the duties of an employer is to provide a safety policy statement to show each person's responsibilities and the arrangements they have made to carry out the policy. The safety policy applies to all organisations that employ more than five employees. This is supposed to be a document that can be used to show in a practical way how the arrangements for health and safety are to be carried out in the workplace, and it should be designed to have a genuine effect on health and safety working practices. This means that it should be clearly written and should be easily available to any employee, and a copy should preferably be given to each employee. It does not mean that it is a secret document, as some organisations in our experience seem to think, kept locked in a filing cabinet well away from the gaze of employees. In order to encourage awareness of health and safety and produce an effective safety policy document, it is also advisable that a range of people, including workforce representatives, should be involved in its design and that key decision makers have been involved fully in these discussions. In some organisations a person will be chosen to champion the policy and targets for improvements in specific areas of health and safety may also be set. Arrangements should also be made to review the health and safety policy regularly, at least annually, since what is important is whether the policy is having an effect on health and safety in the workplace, rather than how well written it is.

The HSE has examples of policies for health and safety and risk assessment on their website (**www.hse.gov.uk**) and while individual organisations are recommended to design their own policies to suit their organisations the model health and safety policy arranges issues in columns under three headings. These are:

- Statement of general policy
- Responsibility for health and safety
- Actions/arrangements made for health and safety.

Statement of general policy

The safety policy should show management's approach to health and safety and should indicate what management plan to do in relation to different aspects of health and safety such as the prevention of accidents, training for health and safety or the ways for engaging with the workforce about health and safety.

Responsibility for health and safety

The second column should indicate who is actually responsible for each of the specific tasks. The safety policy is basically concerned with people, their duties and their accountability. It could also include a management chart showing the chain of command in respect of health and safety, with a clear statement that the ultimate responsibility for health and safety rests with the board or chief executive or equivalent. The safety policy document should carry at the end the signature of the person with the ultimate responsibility for health and safety at work. There should be a clearly defined role for the safety adviser, if such a position exists, and clear explanation of their relationship to senior management and line management. This part of the document should also indicate the role of those appointed as 'competent persons' to assist the employer in implementing the safety policy.

The action/practical arrangements

This section should establish systems and procedures and the practical arrangements for their implementation. It should also show the system for monitoring safety and for publishing results. The section of the safety policy covering arrangements should be a practical section that is regularly reviewed and updated.

Some of the topics that could be included under the arrangements for managing health and safety are listed below.

- Any specific health and safety risks that arise from the organisation's work activities
- Arrangements for consultation with employees
- Arrangements to ensure that plant and equipment are safe to use
- Arrangements for organising the safe handling and use of substances
- Systems for the provision of information, instruction and supervision
- Ways of ensuring competency for tasks and training
- Methods for dealing with accidents, first aid and work-related ill-health
- Methods to be used for monitoring all aspects of health and safety
- The arrangements that have been made for emergency procedures such as for fire and evacuation
- Details of any specific key areas of risk for jobs in that organisation.

Specific health and safety risks arising from an organisation's work activities

This means that the arrangements for carrying out risk assessments, the results of the risk assessments and the actions taken will all need to be shown, although the findings and resulting actions will need to be shown in a separate document. The HSE's template for a health and safety policy also gives a template for conducting risk assessments and HSE (2010f) suggest both should be prepared at the same time. Risk assessments will be discussed in more detail later in the chapter.

Consultation with employees

We have already discussed the fact that if there is a recognised trade union which has appointed safety representatives then by law they must be consulted about any changes likely to affect the health and safety of their members. If there is not a recognised trade union then the employers must consult their employees directly or through a works council.

Safe plant and equipment

This requirement is taken directly from HASAWA and means that employers must keep vehicles, machinery and equipment in good working order. In the safety policy, the names of people responsible for this should be stated, as should arrangements to deal with problems. Those responsible for checking that new machinery and equipment meets the required standards should also be listed here. Records of maintenance and service history of vehicles should be kept, perhaps separately in a log book.

Safe handling and use of substances

This section relates to those responsible for identifying substances that need a COSHH assessment. Once again the names of people with responsibilities should be listed here. This includes the names of those carrying out the assessments, those responsible for ensuring that any actions needed are taken, those who have to tell employees about the results of the assessments as well as the names of those people who have responsibility for checking the safety of new substances prior to purchase. There should also be an indication as to the frequency of assessments.

Information, instruction and supervision

This should show where health and safety law posters are displayed or where leaflets relating to health and safety are kept. It should also detail where health and safety advice can be obtained and the names of those responsible for supervising the work of trainees or young employees.

Competency for tasks and training

The names of people who provide induction training and job-specific training should be listed here. Some jobs may pose particular risks, for example the risk of back injury to workers involved in the manual handling of heavy or awkwardly shaped goods. Both the jobs and the training needed should also be identified. Training records should be kept for all health and safety training as well as other training and the safety policy should indicate where the records are stored and by whom.

Accidents, first aid and work-related ill-health

In this section any health surveillance required for certain jobs, such as work with flour, asbestos or some chemicals, needs to be identified. This should mean any problems in a worker's health caused by the job will be identified at an early stage so that action can be taken to prevent their health becoming worse. It shows who is responsible for health surveillance and where records are kept.

The locations of first aid boxes need to be shown and first aiders should be listed. Records of all accidents, however trivial, and instances of work-related ill-health should be recorded in the accident book and the location of this book should also be given in the health and safety policy.

Monitoring

It is very important that the policy is used and that good practices are checked regularly. Those who have responsibility for checking that working conditions are safe and that safe practices are being followed should be listed here, as should those who are responsible for carrying out investigations of accidents or investigating work-related causes of sickness absence.

Emergency procedures – fire and evacuation

Obviously it is important that there are adequate safety procedures in place in case there is a need to evacuate the building in an emergency. In this section it is important to state who checks the escape routes and the frequency of these checks. Safety equipment such as fire extinguishers have to be maintained and checked, alarms need to be tested, emergency evacuation drills need to be carried out and records of these must be kept.

Key areas of risk

These will vary depending on the organisation and the type of work undertaken, but might include risks relating to particularly dangerous substances such as asbestos, or to stress or potential violence to staff from members of the public. Each organisation will need to carry out its own risk assessments relating to the areas of risk which are identified.

People need to be aware of their responsibilities as, if something goes wrong and a serious accident occurs, the relevant enforcement officers will want to know who was responsible. These enforcement officers would carry out a full investigation and would also want to examine the safety policy document. If a supervisor did not know that they were responsible for checking that a protective guard was in place, then the employer would have to be able to prove that they had informed the supervisor of their responsibilities and had also trained them adequately in the fulfilment of these responsibilities. Many tasks will of course be delegated to different levels of management and employees do, as we have seen, have some responsibility for their own actions. Senior management cannot, however, abdicate their ultimate responsibility for overall safety within the organisation, and must try to ensure the health and safety of their employees and others affected by their employees' actions. Those who carry the ultimate responsibility for this, such as the board of directors, could face prosecution and possibly a large fine or even a spell in prison for individual directors if their organisation is found to be at fault. Similarly, others with specific responsibilities such as safety officers, human resource managers, line managers or training officers could be charged and convicted of an offence.

First consider the following case study and identify the health, safety and wellbeing issues that you think occur here, then complete Activity 11.3.

CASE STUDY 11.1 Health and safety

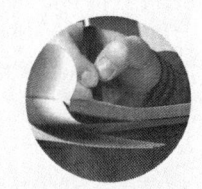

The Sheffley Company employs nearly 330 employees and specialises in the production of steel castings. The organisation has a director, Mr Jones, whose great-grandfather founded the business. There is a new production manager, Mr Tandy; an import and export manager, Ms Jeffries; and an administration manager, Mrs Groves. Mr Tandy has eight line managers reporting to him, who have a total of 280 employees working for them. Mrs Groves has a payroll manager, a canteen manager and a personnel officer reporting to her and Ms Jeffries runs the purchasing, goods inward and goods outward departments, and the warehouse and export sections.

The work involved in the production of steel castings is hazardous and the company has not had a good record with regard to health and safety. It is not only

→

in the production areas that there have been problems – the offices also have suffered rather a large number of accidents which have required employees to have more than three days off work to recover. The office staff are expected to regularly work long hours and work whatever hours are necessary to complete the job. Several are absent with serious long-term illnesses including the payroll manager and of course this puts additional pressure on those who remain. Mrs Groves is beginning to show signs of the strain from doing her own job and that of the absent payroll officer and is suffering from regular headaches and feelings of anxiety.

The new production manager decides that something must be done about the record on health, safety and wellbeing. He decides a punitive approach will work best and in the weekly meeting with the production supervisors he informs them that from next week any employee who does not wear the protective equipment provided will be dismissed. The safety equipment comprises safety boots, safety goggles and overalls.

During the lead-up to the introduction of the safety equipment, notices are put up to explain the disciplinary penalty for non-compliance with the regulation, but information about the use and location of some of the equipment is not provided. Neither the safety representatives nor the safety committee have the opportunity to inspect the new protective equipment or to advise employees on its suitability.

The employees prove to be reluctant to wear the protective goggles which, they complain, pinch their skin and impair their vision. The production manager realises that the enforcement of safety is going to be problematic, and at the next week's meeting informs the supervisors that they do not have to be too rigid in their enforcement of the rules.

Two serious accidents occur just a month later in the production area and a further serious accident occurs in the offices. In the first incident molten metal splashes onto the foot of an employee, causing serious burns. In a separate accident a few days later an employee slips, splashing molten metal close to his eyes. Luckily his sight is saved, but he suffers severe burns and scarring. The accident record in the offices is also unsatisfactory, and one employee is injured when chemicals used in the photocopier spill on her leg, causing a severe itchy rash to develop. She has been having problems at home but has felt she must keep working although her mind has not been on her work all the time. Other employees in the wages office complain of backaches and headaches which they say are caused by poor lighting, uncomfortable chairs and badly adjusted screens on their visual display units.

You should be able to identify some of the many issues raised here about health, safety and the wellbeing of the employees such as the exact nature of the employer and employee responsibilities. The employer in this case, and indeed anyone involved in this area of work, also needs to comply with legislation, so, based on your reading of the chapter so far, you should also be able to identify the key legislation infringed by both the employer and the employees. A full discussion of this case study can be found if you go to our website at **www.pearsoned.co.uk/foothook**.

ACTIVITY 11.3

Design a safety policy statement for Sheffley Company. Remember that this should be a practical document that can be used by people in the organisation. Use the sections and main headings that we have given earlier (see pages 399–401).

Risk assessment

The idea of assessing and controlling risks was introduced to Britain with the Control of Substances Hazardous to Health Regulations 1988, when employers had to assess the risk of harm to people from certain substances being used at work. This was developed further in the 'six-pack' regulations in 1992. The 1992 Code of Practice for the Management of Health and Safety at Work made it a legal duty for employers to assess and record health and safety risks, and to appoint a 'competent person', i.e. a person who has been suitably trained, and who is allowed adequate time and facilities, to perform this role and assist in this and other safety tasks.

Every organisation has to carry out its own risk assessment, and strategies for this should be devised by management after consultation with all interested groups in the workforce.

According to the HSE in the booklet *Five Steps to Risk Assessment* (HSE 2006), the five main steps involved in assessing risks and hazards in the workplace are:

1. Identify the hazards.
2. Decide who might be harmed and how.
3. Evaluate the risks and decide on precautions.
4. Record your findings and implement them.
5. Review your assessment and update if necessary.

Assessments do not have to be carried out by health and safety experts and small organisations may choose to undertake the initial assessment of risk by themselves: alternatively, they may prefer to employ a consultant.

Steps 1 and 2 Identify the hazards and decide who may be harmed by them

Most organisations should be able to carry out the first two steps quite easily and identify sources of risk and then identify those who may be harmed by the risks. Many of the risks will probably be well known to you already such as the risk of slipping in areas where the floor may sometimes be wet, but sometimes even obvious hazards such as this are ignored. Identifying hazards involves looking and talking to people in the area being assessed. It also involves identifying which groups of workers are likely to suffer harm and the type of injury that they are likely to suffer.

Step 3 Evaluate the risks and decide on precautions

Once you have identified the hazards and those likely to be affected by them then you must do something about them. Remember under the Health and Safety at Work Act 1974 you have to do everything that is 'reasonably practicable' to protect people from harm.

Pause for thought 11.4 If the floor is sometimes wet due to cleaning or spillages, what could you do as a precaution?

It is best to try to get rid of the risk if it is possible but if not then ways to minimise the risk should be tried. What could you do to prevent accidents in the case of a wet floor that was slippery in your college/university or workplace?

Your answers should follow the following order if possible. Complete them in the grid below.

Order for trying to control risks	Your response to each of these where there is a wet and slippery floor
1 Try to find a way of doing the job that carries less risk	
2 Ensure people don't come into contact with the hazard	
3 Minimise exposure to the hazard	
4 Issue personal protective clothing	
5 Provide adequate facilities to deal properly with people who have suffered in some way because they come into contact with the problem	

Go to **www.pearsoned.uk/foothook** now to check your answers to this exercise.

Step 4 Record your findings and implement them

Small organisations with five employees or fewer do not have to record their findings but it would be good practice to do so anyway. Workers need to know what is happening as far as minimising risks is concerned and it also helps to involve them more in health and safety. According to the HSE (2006) employers need to show that:

- a proper check was made;
- you asked who might be affected;
- you dealt with all significant hazards, taking into account the number of people who could be involved;
- the precautions are reasonable, and the remaining risk low; and
- you involved your staff or their representatives in the process.

Although it would be excellent if you could tackle all hazards immediately this will probably not be practicable so you need to plan an order of priority. Which are the most dangerous hazards? Which are quick and easy to solve? Are there any temporary solutions that could be used while a longer term solution is being organised? How will you monitor your solutions are working? Who is due to take action on each point and by when?

Step 5 Review your risk assessment and update if necessary

All workplaces are subject to constant change so something that works well at first may, due to changing circumstances or work patterns, no longer be so effective. Therefore the risk assessment needs to be monitored on a regular basis. For some organisations where there is a great deal of change this may involve reviewing risk assessments on a monthly or perhaps even weekly basis, while for other organisations an annual review may be more appropriate unless some unexpected change makes it more urgent to review risks.

> **Pause for thought 11.5** Do you think there is too much emphasis on risk assessment, or not enough?
>
> Michael Gove, the education secretary, believes parents are often frustrated by the lack of adventure in education in schools as activities have been restricted because of health and safety concerns and he says that this will be tackled by Government.
>
> Garath Malone's TV series about the education of boys where he attempts to improve the literacy skills of boys by getting them to do more adventurous and often more dangerous things seems in tune with Gove's views. Blogging teachers responded to the programme by saying it was unreal as they would have to complete mountains of paperwork and face tons of red tape in conducting risk assessments to submit to local authorities before any such activities would be possible. It seems Michael Gove intends to change the health and safety laws to lessen the amount of risk assessment that schools have to do and also wants to change the compensation culture so it becomes more difficult to sue if accidents occur (Millard, 2010).
>
> What do you think? Should there be more opportunities for adventure combined with less risk assessment in schools?
>
> Should it be more difficult for parents of a child injured in an accident at a school to sue?

Wellbeing

One of the earliest roles for HR specialists included that of the welfare officer (Fowler, 1994). The focus of this role was on the wellbeing of employees and it sometimes meant taking a paternalistic viewpoint, i.e. adopting a moral stance and telling people what was best for them. The modern HR function has changed and become more complex, adopting a more strategic and integrated approach to human resource management, a theme taken up in a number of chapters. Individual wellbeing, however, is still a factor which has an obvious impact on employees' ability to function at high levels and add value to their organisation. Employees who cannot concentrate at work or who may even stay away from work because of physical or psychological health problems obviously cannot contribute to their full potential, which has a negative impact on the goal of high-performance working (Incomes Data Services, 2002). In this context, the Engineering Employers' Federation (EEF, 2001) identifies effective stress management as 'a key part of a positive, proactive human resources policy'.

The Health and Safety Executive (HSE) has also been focusing on ways to draw all employers' attention to the benefits to be gained from a more proactive approach. The Revitalising Health and Safety initiatives were started because organisations are operating more and more in new ways with increasingly flexible methods of working. This has been followed by a new strategy called *The Health and Safety of Great Britain: Be Part of the Solution*. The HSE has been consulting and working with employers to demonstrate the business case for improved health and safety measures and for the need to involve everyone in this.

The role of the employer in employee wellbeing

One area of debate on the subject of wellbeing is whether this is a personal and private matter. We have already said that there is a business case for employer involvement in the health and safety of their workforce but should an employer also have a right to enquire into other aspects of the wellbeing of employees that involve their private lives? If so, how far should this go?

> **Pause for thought 11.6** Before you read on, take a few minutes to think about your position on this issue. Make a list of arguments for saying that employers should be concerned about the personal wellbeing of their employees, and a list of reasons why they should not.

Go to our website at **www.pearsoned.co.uk/foothook** for further discussion and to check your arguments with ours.

If an employee's personal problems result in falling standards at work, or even in an event that could be construed as misconduct, this could result in formal disciplinary action. On the whole, managers prefer to handle such issues in an informal manner to preserve good working relationships, and regard formal discipline as an action to be taken if the informal approach fails. This approach is encouraged by the ACAS guidelines on discipline (2009). You will find a fuller discussion of this in Chapter 12. It should suffice to make the point here that the proper use of counselling may obviate the need to embark on formal disciplinary action. According to the Inland Revenue Service (2007) at least one in five employers do provide employee assistance programmes (EAPs) though most are actually funded by the employer and are provided on their behalf by external suppliers. Typically about 10 per cent of the workforce use the EAP in any year but the popularity of EAPs has increased with employers after a legal case in 2002, when it was argued that just having an EAP provided sufficient defence for an employer against stress compensation claims. This was subsequently modified in a 2007 case so that it is not now possible just to rely on this as a defence in stress management cases. Typically the EAP service provided involves help with counselling, often by providing access to telephone helplines and to specialist advisers. Since corporate manslaughter is now a criminal offence employers should certainly be diligent in their responsibilities regarding any health, safety or wellbeing issues that could result in death and should of course take their responsibilities for all health, safety and wellbeing issues equally seriously.

> **Did you know?**
>
> In November 1994, John Walker, a senior social worker with Northumberland County Council, won his case in a high court, claiming that the employer had been negligent in its handling of this employee's stress. Mr Walker had returned to work after suffering a nervous breakdown. After his return to work the employer failed to make adjustments in his workload, and Mr Walker was dismissed on ill-health grounds after he had a second nervous breakdown. The fact that Mr Walker had suffered a first nervous breakdown meant that it could reasonably have been foreseen that the workload was a potential hazard for this employee. Mr Walker received an out of court settlement of £175,000.
>
> (*Source*: Midgley, 1997, p. 36)

Finally, we can justify an employer's interest in the wellbeing of employees with reference to the basic need to develop good working relationships, on the part of individual employees, individual managers, and from a corporate point of view. Abraham Maslow (1954) was one of the first writers to describe motivation in terms of human needs, and these concepts have often been applied to the workplace. One of the needs that Maslow identified is the social need for relationships, and indeed the importance of relationships has been reinforced by the inclusion of this factor in the HSE's list of aspects of stress management. A number of surveys on motivation have identified the importance of good relationships at work, and specifically the relationship between supervisor and subordinate. It is not inappropriate to care about the people we work with. Much has also been written about corporate image, and many employers wish to be recognised as 'good employers', especially since corporate image can affect an organisation's ability to attract and retain good employees and can therefore have a major impact on the success of the organisation.

The reasons for employers to be involved with employees' problems can be summarised as follows:

- to address problems with productivity, standards of work, attendance and turnover
- to meet legal obligations to ensure the health, safety and wellbeing of employees
- to avoid the development of disciplinary problems
- to maintain good employee relations
- to improve performance as a part of the performance management process.

Types of problem and their sources

There can be an infinite range of personal problems faced by workers which could affect their work. Many will arise from sources outside the organisation, such as family breakdown, alcoholism, drug abuse, care duties or bereavement, while others might be the result of bullying, working conditions, excessive workload or some form of discrimination in the workplace. The HR department needs to be clear about each of these issues and have policies and procedures in place to deal with issues such as alcoholism or drug abuse and should certainly also have effective policies to prevent unfair discrimination or bullying within work. It is not within the scope of this textbook to deal with all these specific issues but one area which has caused a lot of concern recently is the area of stress, which we shall focus on next. As you saw in the case of *Walker* v. *Northumberland County Council*, there can be serious repercussions for both the employee and the organisation if an employer fails to deal with stress in an appropriate way.

Stress and stress management

Stress is one major area of concern, and can be regarded as an umbrella term for a range of problems. Stress is manifested when people are dealing with so many pressures that their normal behaviour patterns become affected. Hans Selye (1956 and 1974), a noted writer on stress, used the terms 'eustress' and 'distress' to explain that stress is not always a negative concept. Sometimes people are stimulated by having to deal with a number of issues; this can be exciting and motivating. When it becomes too much and one cannot cope and at the same time continue to behave within the range of one's normal behaviour patterns, this is what Selye refers to as distress. This is what we normally mean when we refer to stress these days (Le Fevre *et al.*, 2003).

What are the causes of stress? There are a wide range of factors that cause stress both in personal relationships and in work relationships (see Figure 11.1); these factors are referred to as stressors. Holmes and Rahe (1967) identified a number of life events as being sources of stress. Ranked at number one as a source of stress was the

Figure 11.1 Some causes of stress

death of one's spouse, and other factors identified included divorce, taking on a high mortgage and taking a holiday.

It is also recognised that circumstances at work such as poor relationships, especially with one's manager or supervisor, and overwork or underemployment can contribute to stress. The case of John Walker mentioned earlier is an example of too high a workload combined with the demanding nature of the work contributing to stress.

The symptoms of stress include the behavioural changes we previously identified that might alert you to the fact that a colleague is under pressure. If not dealt with, the end result can be physical or mental illness leading to mental breakdown.

The Health and Safety Executive (HSE) has played a major role in the development of guidelines for employers on various aspects of stress management. The duty of care addressed in the Health and Safety at Work Act 1974 applies to employees' physical and mental wellbeing, and since these can be affected by stress caused by workplace factors, the duty of care constitutes an obvious legal obligation to pay attention to stress management. The Management of Health and Safety at Work Regulations 1999 also impose a duty on employers to conduct a risk audit on potential hazards in the workplace, which also applies in this area as the effects of stress can be regarded as a hazard.

Organisations can use these standards to measure their achievements in terms of stress management. The stress management standards are not legally enforceable on organisations, but the HSE may use them as evidence that an organisation is not fulfilling its duty with regard to stress management. The HSE has already issued an improvement order against one organisation for failing to manage stress adequately: West Dorset Hospitals NHS Trust in 2003 (reported by Hayden-Smith and Simms, 2003), though Incomes Data Services (2004) report that the Trust has since remedied the situation with suitable interventions.

> **Did you know?**
>
> According to the Health and Safety Executive (2009a):
>
> - The cost to society of work-related stress is about £4 billion per annum.
> - In 2007–8, 13.5 million working days were lost because of stress.
>
> (*Source*: HSE, 2009a)

The standards address six areas of work that should be audited. These are laid out with a brief description of what each entails in Table 11.1. The basic idea is to ascertain what percentages of staff feel that they are able to cope with any work situations in these six areas. According to the International Stress Management Association (2004), 'the target is for all organisations to match the performance of the top 20% of employers that are successfully minimising work-related stress.' Organisations must also be able to show that they have systems in place locally to respond to any individual concerns and should be carrying out risk assessments for stress. As Quinn (2004) points out, the identification of stress factors through such an audit makes the eventuality of stress foreseeable, so employers would be obligated to take some action in such an instance.

Table 11.1 HSE stress management standards

Area of work	The standard	Desirable outcomes that organisations should be working towards
Demands This is about demands caused by the workload, work pattern or the work environment.	Employees should be able to indicate that they can cope with the demands of their job. There should also be systems in place to help deal with any concerns of individuals.	The organisation should ensure hours of work are reasonable and that demands made on the workers are not excessive and that their abilities and skills are matched appropriately to their job. There should be a matching of people's skills to their jobs. There should be systems set up to address concerns that workers may have so that these can be resolved.
Control This is about how much influence an individual has about their job.	Employees should be able to indicate that they get a say in the way they do their work. There should also be systems in place to respond to individual concerns.	Individuals should have control over their pace of work wherever possible. They should get opportunities and be encouraged to use their skills and initiative in their work. They should be encouraged to develop new skills so they can undertake new or more challenging work. The employees should also have a say about when breaks should be taken and be consulted about their work patterns and breaks.
Support This concerns the support mechanisms, or lack of them, from colleagues, line managers, and others such as HR staff. It is also about levels of employee awareness about support.	Employees should be able to indicate that they receive adequate support and information from colleagues and superiors. There should also be evidence of systems in place to adequately address employee concerns.	There should be policies and procedures in place to adequately support staff and there should also be systems in place to enable and encourage managers to support staff. Since support is also sometimes provided by colleagues there should be systems in place to encourage employees to support others. Employees should know about available support and also how to access resources necessary to do their job. They should also get regular and constructive feedback.

Table 11.1 Continued

Area of work	The standard	Desirable outcomes that organisations should be working towards
Relationships This is about encouraging positive behaviour so that conflict is avoided and about creating ways to deal with unacceptable behaviour.	Employees should be able to indicate that they are not subjected to unacceptable behaviour at work such as bullying or harassment and that there are systems in place to deal with these issues.	The organisation should promote positive behaviour to ensure fairness and avoid conflict and employees share information about their work. The organisation should have policies in place to prevent or resolve unacceptable behaviour and employees should be encouraged to report unacceptable behaviour.
Role This concerns the extent to which people understand their role and whether the organisation ensures the individual does not have conflicting roles.	Employees should be able to indicate that they understand their role and responsibilities and there should be systems in place to address individual concerns.	The organisation should provide information about the employees' roles and should try to ensure as far as possible that the different requirements it places on employees are compatible and clear and that the individual understands them. If they have concerns about role conflict or about their role then they should be able to raise them.
Change How much change are employees expected to cope with, and how well prepared are they when they do have to deal with change? Are the arrangements for information sharing and consultation adequate?	Employees should be able to show that the organisation engages with them frequently when undergoing organisational change and that there are systems in place to respond to any concerns they may have.	The organisation should be consulting adequately and providing opportunities for individuals to contribute to and influence the changes. This information needs to be timely and sufficient for employees to understand the reasons for the changes and the likely impact on their jobs. Employees also need to be aware of the timetable for changes and have suitable access to support during the change period.

(*Source:* Adapted from HSE (n.d.), *What are the Management Standards?*)

> **Pause for thought 11.7** Consider any organisation in which you have worked. To what extent do you think that organisation has considered each of the stress management standards?
>
> What is your evidence for this?
>
> How does this compare with the views of others in your class about organisations in which they have worked? Did job roles seem clear and unambiguous? Were you made aware of structures to support you?

As you can see from these standards there are a great many implications for HR departments to ensure that they have not only policies in place but also that they have designed jobs well to ensure there is no role incompatibility or work overload, that individuals understand their roles through induction and subsequent training and that there are support systems in place for those who may be experiencing problems. Management also need training to ensure they respond in an appropriate way to those suffering from stress. This means that they need to recognise that just increasing workloads and hoping that the person can cope is not a satisfactory way to manage but that there is a need for proper analyses of the job and the workload, and to match these to the person's capabilities.

An additional factor to do with employer obligations is that employment tribunals hearing cases of unfair dismissal would expect employers to have conducted a full investigation of the circumstances surrounding an incident of alleged misconduct or incompetence. The investigation should have shown whether this may have arisen as a result of personal problems or stress, particularly in the case of a person who previously had a good work record. Employers would be expected to take any such extenuating circumstances into consideration. You can read more about this in Chapter 13. The point about legal obligations could be summarised in the statement that employers have a duty of care.

Organisational policy and procedures

Policy statements and procedures provide guidelines for all employees. They let managers know how to handle problems, and inform everyone about the help, assistance and support they can expect to receive including the things in the stress management standards. There is a dual role for policies as far as situations requiring counselling are concerned. First, there is a need for policies relating directly to the provision of counselling and, second, an organisation should have policies dealing with workplace behaviour or events that have been identified as causing distress. For instance, in a *Guardian* Careers Section article, Professor Cary Cooper was quoted as saying that bullying probably accounted for a third to a half of all stress-related illness (Venning, 1995).

> **Did you know?**
>
> Some occupational groups and industry groups are more prone to stress than others. According to the HSE, groups that suffer particularly high levels of stress include teachers and nurses, housing and welfare officers, customer service workers and some professional and managerial groups, particularly those in the public sector.
>
> (*Source*: HSE, 2009b)

Policies on bullying and sexual/racial harassment can help to eliminate these unwanted behaviours and promote a less stressful working environment. Many organisations such as banks and retail outlets, where staff handle cash and at the same time have direct contact with the public, have recognised that specialised counselling is necessary to deal with the trauma their employees can suffer after an episode involving violence or a threat of violence. This is true when they have either been directly threatened or witnessed an incident. Employers will obviously have to decide which issues are most important for their organisations, and this may involve surveying employees to discover which issues are of concern to them, and which solutions the employees would most like to take advantage of. The package of wellbeing policies, procedures and benefits an employer offers to employees is often referred to as an 'employee assistance programme'.

Policies should also address the following issues:

- who will be involved in providing counselling, and what are the parameters of their roles
- what type of services will be offered
- issues of confidentiality. (Seenan, 2004)

Health promotion

So far, we have focused primarily on approaches to safety and wellbeing in response to legal requirements and as a way for employers to ensure that they motivate their workers. Recent legislation encourages employers to be proactive about safety and to carry out risk assessments and then take action to reduce or eliminate risks identified. The introduction of the 'fit note' to replace the 'sick note' has changed the focus to one where employees do not have to be 100 per cent fit to return to work but could be fit to do some work. According to Woollen (2010) the previous situation was very restrictive, with GPs only having two choices with the patient either being fit for work or not. The Government's intention appears to be to get employers and employees talking to each other after taking advice from the GP and that the employee could return to do some work before being fully fit. The 'fit note' also aims to make it easier to have a quicker return to work as in the past many employers have not allowed a worker to return until the end of their sick note and since this is often based on an estimate by the GP of the length of time needed for a particular illness, many days which could have been worked productively may have been lost. ACAS (2010b) also feel that since work can be good for health it is better to get people back to work as soon as possible. With a 'fit note' a GP can now indicate that a person 'may be fit for work'. If they choose to say this then they have to indicate one of the following options:

- phased return to work
- amended duties
- altered hours
- workplace adaptations.

Clearly if one of these options is chosen then there should be a discussion with the worker before they return to work (CIPD, 2010b).

Did you know?

According to the CIPD's 2009 annual survey of absence management the average employee absence is for 7.4 days per year but is highest among public sector employees where it is 9.7 days per employee, followed by 9.4 days absence per year in not-for-profit organisations. The average cost of absence is £692.00 per employee. The main causes of absence are due to fairly minor illnesses such as coughs, colds, flu or stomach pains. The next most significant cause of short-term absence is stress.

(*Source*: CIPD, 2009)

Many good employers not only promote measures to promote improvements in safety and wellbeing but also encourage developments to ensure good health among their workforces.

The high cost of absenteeism is a strong financial reason for both individual organisations and the Government to take measures to promote and improve health. According to Griffiths (2009) the current UK recommendation is for moderately intense levels of physical activity for at least 30 minutes every day and the introduction of opportunities for exercise to the workplace could help to alleviate stress, musculoskeletal problems and some common mental health problems. Many people will lapse their membership of gyms after a short period of time because of other pressures in their lives so suggestions to incorporate exercise into work where people may be already spending between 40 and 85 hours a week could be useful. One innovative solution trialled with nurses and office workers was the introduction of a walking work station and though this might not be attractive to everyone, users reported improvements in energy and relief from back pain (Griffiths, 2009).

Many employers already provide some preventative measures such as health screening services and membership of private health insurance schemes for their managers, and some are extending this provision to the workforce as a whole. Increasingly, organisations are actively trying to promote a healthier lifestyle among their employees. Among the measures that have been tried are:

- help for smokers to quit, with support/self-help groups and psychologists giving advice and support

- a healthy diet, with a wider choice of health foods on the menu at work
- supply of free fruit at work
- membership of a health club or purchase of multi-gym exercise equipment for employees to use to get fitter and as a way of tackling obesity
- online assessments of health or lifestyle screening with advice available for lifestyle changes
- stress management programmes
- policies and education programmes on HIV/Aids
- policies and education on substance abuse.

In organisations where these programmes have been made available to all the workforce on a long-term basis, there have been benefits to employees' health, with weight reduction and improvements in blood cholesterol and blood pressure levels, and also improvements in absenteeism rates. It is claimed that the cost of the introduction of this type of programme is more than offset by the savings from lower rates of absenteeism. The CIPD (2006) stated that 'a survey of 97 organisations showed that employees who were participating in "wellness" programmes each incurred between £1,335 and £2,910 less per year in healthcare and absenteeism costs than colleagues who were not participating.'

ACAS (2010a) say that an unhealthy workplace where there are high levels of absence is usually synonymous with poor management and aspects of poor management may include a bullying culture, low productivity and unreasonable work demands being made on the employees. In their opinion, to get employees motivated to go that extra mile there need to be both effective policies and a high level of trust between management and the workforce, with involvement of workers in decisions and open communications. Line managers are also important in ensuring a healthy workplace and they need to be well trained and confident. (Refer back to discussion of the ACAS model workplace in Chapter 1.)

> ### Did you know?
> Some organisations have in the past asked questions at interview or given a medical questionnaire as a method of shortlisting or selecting for employment those they think will be fit and healthy workers. Section 60 of the Equality Act makes it illegal now to ask questions about health or disability either in written or oral form and inclusion of these questions on a reference request is also unlawful.
>
> There are some exceptions; for example it may be necessary for a manager to ask what reasonable adjustments would be needed in the workplace if a candidate is disabled.
>
> (*Source*: XpertHR, 2010b, *Outlook video: Equality Act – Disability*, XpertHR, 4 August)

Absence management

While prevention is always better than cure one of the areas that many HR departments are also becoming increasingly interested in, and which can be used in a complementary way to a wellness programme, is absence management. Westminster City Council 'introduced improved absence management procedures which have reduced its absence rate by more than two days per person per annum and saved it £800,000 annually' (Inland Revenue Service, 2007b). They achieved this by using a mixture of approaches such as the introduction of an employee assistance programme and a new absence management programme which involved return to work interviews and earlier and more positive use of the occupational health department and trigger points. This meant that 'once an employee had more than seven cumulative days' sickness absence in any rolling period, then an enhanced sickness management procedure kicks in. And if sickness absence exceeds 20 days in any one episode, then long-term sickness management procedure applies. Further, when more than eight days of sickness have been recorded over the rolling 365-day period the employee's manager will refer the employee to the council's in-house occupational health service.'

Failure to take steps to reduce risks in the workplace is likely in the future to lead to higher insurance payments for organisations as insurance companies start to link premiums to the way that organisations manage risks of accidents and ill-health. Smokers generally suffer worse health than non-smokers and the charity Action on Smoking and Health (ASH) claims that 34 million working days are lost in Britain each year, just because of smoking. Some employers are becoming more proactive about their employees' health and are introducing measures such as bonuses to encourage smokers to quit. These can, however, prove controversial as non-smokers may then also want to benefit from bonuses.

> **Did you know?**
> A casino worker, Michael Dunn, received £50,000 in an out-of-court settlement after he developed asthma as a result of passive smoking at work.
> (Source: Cacanas, Z., 2004)

International issues in health and safety

Although British health and safety legislation does not apply to workers based outside Britain, employers still have a duty of care towards their employees, no matter where they work. Employees who operate in a global scene need additional knowledge relating to the particular country in which they are working, and this also applies to health and safety. The HR departments in those organisations need to check on health and safety legislation in the countries concerned, and should also carry out a risk assessment of not only the job but also the country, and should evaluate the employee's health. This would help ensure, for example, that they are not sending an asthmatic employee into a very dusty desert environment that would probably make the employee's health worse.

There are also social and ethical responsibilities that large organisations need to take into account when some of their products such as clothing or food is being produced in third world countries for them. Although they produce goods at cheap prices for those in the developed world, this is often at the expense of the workers in that country, by paying people poorly and by allowing them to work in poor health or safety conditions that would not be tolerated in the UK.

Even within Europe we have seen that individual countries can interpret European directives in different ways so the actual health and safety legislation in countries may vary. Attitudes to safety can be different and vary from one culture to another. In cultures where people tend to sue for damages, such as America, people are used to having lots of rules even when they are relaxing, away from work, so on beaches they only swim in the designated areas and obey the lifeguards. In the Greek islands, tourists would seek their own sheltered cove and swim from their own secluded beach so would have to take more responsibility for their own safety. Such differences in cultural expectations do shape attitudes to health and safety, so it is important to take into account the culture of the country and consider this in relation to health and safety. When Disney first opened in Paris some of the instructions on rides such as the requirement 'to exit the ride using your left foot first' jarred a little with Europeans who were used to making such decisions for themselves!

Some employees are sent to work in countries which may be regarded as high risk and where dangers such as kidnapping could occur. Staff need to be briefed as to precautions to take in these countries, as do the local staff, who may actually be more at risk than the expat staff, who probably live in a secure compound and have a driver to transport them safely. Some groups such as humanitarian aid workers are also likely to be at risk, since the nature of their jobs ensure that they are likely to be working in high-risk areas. However, they should still not be exposed to unnecessary risks.

HR departments who have staff working in potentially high-risk countries should carry out risk assessments, relating both to the dangers to health and to potential threats to safety, and should devise suitable emergency plans which can be put in place quickly. They should also devise suitable training programmes, perhaps drawing on local knowledge and expertise, for people undertaking these jobs. The workforce could even be involved in analysing the hazards and designing their own security plans for the compounds in which they live. Training in potential high-risk countries is likely to cover specific issues such as personal safety, office security, compound security, threats to convoys, risk analysis, first aid and emergency evacuation plans.

> **Did you know?**
>
> In response to the killings of three UN workers in West Timor on 6 September 2000, humanitarian workers from around the world marched in protest for better protection. They sent a petition to the UN headquarters demanding 'greater pressure from the UN on national governments to guarantee the safety of humanitarian workers, together with internal measures addressing management accountability, risk assessment and more funding for security provision.'
>
> (*Source*: Hammond, D., 2001)

If this is done the workers are likely to feel and be safer and since health and safety will be perceived as being important, it is likely that they will take more care themselves. Measures such as these can do a great deal to eliminate unnecessary risks, although it is impossible to eliminate all risks completely.

Conclusion

We said at the beginning of this chapter that it is not enough for employers just to be concerned about preventing accidents in order to comply with legislation, although that in itself is a good start. We have shown in this chapter that there has been a change of approach from mere compliance with minimum legal requirements in the legislation prior to HASAWA to the encouragement of increased involvement of all, and nowadays to seeing a business case as well. In difficult economic circumstances many organisations find their profit margins are extremely tight and improving health, safety and wellbeing is one way to give their organisation a cost-effective competitive edge.

This approach to health and safety links with the overall business objectives of maximising efficiency and effectiveness by improving morale and reducing costs, and also allows for some scope for individuality and flexibility in how this is to be achieved. It is the approach to health and safety that we would advocate, and it is a very different approach to the purely legalistic one of just being concerned with not breaking the law. This approach to health and safety involves the following features:

- The need to create a culture in which health, safety and wellbeing are seen to be important to the organisation. The safety policy statement will contribute to this if it is effectively written, known about and acted upon. The legal requirements must be complied with and risk assessments undertaken, as well as information about health and safety gathered and a cost–benefit analysis carried out. If there is to be a culture of health and safety awareness, there also need to be campaigns and publicity, and involvement of top management, individuals and teams. There needs to be regular communication and discussion of health and safety and the contribution that improvements will make to the organisation's overall effectiveness, so that all members of the organisation realise that health and safety are important to the way it operates.
- Commitment from the top to the achievement of progressively higher standards as expressed in the mission statement and safety policy. Top management must not only sign the policy documents but also set a good example in relation to health and safety, and emphasise that it is an area of importance to them and to the future of the organisation by showing their interest and by setting up new systems and monitoring the effectiveness of these systems.
- Commitment throughout the organisation, with all parties clear about their own responsibilities for health and safety, the targets they have to meet and the contribution these make to the organisation's objectives. This should be considered as an aspect of performance management, as individuals and teams would be encouraged to take responsibility for their own actions and to agree and work towards targets when making improvements.
- Managers to demonstrate by their example their commitment to the importance of a safer and healthier work environment. They should also find ways to motivate everyone to make a contribution to health and safety improvements. Prizes and awards to individuals and teams can have an important effect.
- Policies and procedures designed to take account of the importance of a safer and healthier environment. There should also be effective systems to monitor their effectiveness.
- Policies to be backed by adequate resources for equipment and training. Provision of good health and safety costs money but the cost of not providing these can be higher, as any cost–benefit analysis is likely to prove.
- The setting of realistic and attainable targets for everyone in the organisation.
- Encouragement of all to take responsibility for their own actions and involvement of all in health and safety.

Our approach seems to be in line with both ACAS and Investors in People (IIP) in stressing the importance of good management to heath, safety and wellbeing. IIP (2010) say 'Investors in People has learnt that the key determinant of people's wellbeing is how well they are managed and supported. The role that line managers and teams play in providing support to employees, particularly in today's changing climate, is therefore extremely important.' Essentially it is all about good management and ensuring that health, safety and wellbeing are perceived to be an important aspect of performance management and should support the organisation's strategic objectives. In turn this should lead to better performance and provide an excellent return on investment.

REVIEW QUESTIONS

1. Interview people (friends, family or work colleagues from a range of organisations) about their own responsibilities in relation to health and safety and then about their perceptions of other people's roles in their particular organisation. Try to establish how the roles relating to health and safety differ for managers, other employees, human resource managers, safety officers, safety representatives and someone designated to be a 'competent person'. Are these roles the same in different types of organisation? How do they compare with what we said earlier in the chapter about these roles? Is health and safety perceived to be an important part of performance management?

2. Obtain a copy of the safety policy for either your college or your workplace.
   (a) Use this to identify the roles of various people in the organisation in relation to health and safety.
   (b) Use the safety policy to assess whether health and safety are linked to the organisation's strategic objectives.

3. Design a checklist for carrying out a safety inspection in the workplace. Use your checklist to actually carry out an inspection of a designated area either at work or in your college. Write a report about your findings for the safety officer.

4. Write a short report in which you assess the impact of one piece of health and safety legislation on an organisation of your choice.

5. Prepare arguments and then debate the following statements in two teams. Try to persuade the members of the other team to your point of view.

   TEAM A: There is much too much legislation regarding health and safety at work and this is unnecessary as it is in the employers' interests to look after their employees. Legislation merely hinders employers in their ability to run their businesses effectively.

   TEAM B: Legislation is necessary to control employers who would otherwise ignore health and safety issues at the expense of their employees' health, safety and wellbeing.

SELF-CHECK QUESTIONS

Answer the following multiple-choice and short-answer questions. The correct responses are given on pages 496–97 for you to check your understanding of this chapter.

1. Which of the following was the first piece of legislation designed to protect everyone at work, and also to protect others who were not at work, such as customers or passers-by?
   (a) the Factories Act 1961
   (b) the Offices, Shops and Railways Premises Act 1963
   (c) the Fire Precautions Act 1971
   (d) the Health and Safety at Work Act 1974
   (e) the Control of Substances Hazardous to Health Regulations 1988.

2 Which of the following pieces of legislation established the Health and Safety Executive?
   (a) the Factories Act 1961
   (b) the Offices, Shops and Railways Premises Act 1963
   (c) the Fire Precautions Act 1971
   (d) the Health and Safety at Work Act 1974
   (e) the Control of Substances Hazardous to Health Regulations 1988.

3 An improvement notice is issued when:
   (a) something is found to be so dangerous that the factory inspectorate feels it necessary to stop work immediately
   (b) improvements are required by the factory inspectorate but the employer can decide when these should take place
   (c) improvements are required by the factory inspectorate within a specified period to bring the equipment or process up to the required standard
   (d) the required improvement has been made by the employer
   (e) improvements are required by the safety committee to be made within a specified period.

4 The term 'so far as it is reasonably practicable to do so' means:
   (a) that employers must do everything in their power to make the workplace safe
   (b) that employers may weigh up the costs of a safety improvement against the risks when deciding whether to make the improvement
   (c) that employers must assess the risks of substances used and identify the required precautions to be taken
   (d) that employers have a legal duty to predict what may go wrong before it happens
   (e) that employers should be proactive and actively manage health and safety issues.

5 The Management of Health and Safety at Work Regulations contain the following legal requirement:
   (a) that employers must do the best that they can to make the workplace safe
   (b) that employers may weigh up the costs of a safety improvement against the risks when deciding whether to make a safety improvement
   (c) that employers must assess the risks of any substances used by employees and identify the required precautions to be taken
   (d) that employers should carry out an assessment of health and safety risks to both employees and the public
   (e) that employers should carry out an assessment of health and safety risks for their employees only.

6 The term 'six-pack' refers to the following six pieces of legislation:
   (a) the Factories Act 1961, the Offices Shops and Railways Premises Act 1963, the Fire Precautions Act 1971, the Health and Safety at Work Act 1974, the Control of Substances Hazardous to Health Regulations 1988, the Manual Handling Operations Regulations 1992
   (b) the Factories Act 1961, the Offices Shops and Railways Premises Act 1963, the Fire Precautions Act 1971, the Health and Safety at Work Act 1974, the Control of Substances Hazardous to Health Regulations 1988, the Management of Health and Safety at Work Regulations 1992
   (c) the Factories Act 1961, the Health and Safety at Work Act 1974, the Control of Substances Hazardous to Health Regulations 1988, the Management of Health and Safety at Work Regulations 1992, Workplace (Health, Safety and Welfare) Regulations 1992, Provision and Use of Work Equipment Regulations 1992

(d) Management of Health and Safety at Work Regulations 1992, Workplace (Health, Safety and Welfare) Regulations 1992, Provision and Use of Work Equipment Regulations 1992, Personal Protective Equipment at Work Regulations 1992, Health and Safety (Display Screen Equipment) Regulations 1992, Manual Handling Operations Regulations 1992

(e) the Health and Safety at Work Act 1974, the Control of Substances Hazardous to Health Regulations 1988, Management of Health and Safety at Work Regulations 1992, Workplace (Health, Safety and Welfare) Regulations 1992, Provision and Use of Work Equipment Regulations 1992, Personal Protective Equipment at Work Regulations 1992.

Refer back to Case study 11.1 (pages 401–2) and answer the following questions.

7 Describe what the role of the safety committee should have been within the Sheffley Company.

8 Imagine that you are a consultant brought in to advise about health and safety at the Sheffley Company. Write a report to the director in which you outline the improvements that should be made in health and safety at Sheffley, and recommend how these improvements should be introduced.

HR IN THE NEWS

Workforce health on a par with profits and dividends

By Paul Betts

Europe's economies are still stuttering and hopes of recovery have never looked so fragile. This is putting the old continent's companies under even more pressure after a dire couple of years. But companies are their employees, and many of these men and women remain under great pressure, with the shadow of unemployment hanging over many households.

Corporate restructurings are still a daily feature of corporate life, as are factory closures. And the pressure for cost cuts to maintain profitability is unlikely to disappear soon.

This relentless demand for performance can have devastating effects on workforces, as was so tragically the case at France Telecom, which has experienced a rash of suicides during the past 18 months. Suicides have also taken place in other restructuring companies.

In France Renault, Peugeot and EDF have all reported such tragic incidents.

Of course, it is always difficult to say with any certainty that an individual has taken his or her life because of unbearable pressure at work.

Nonetheless, the European Union has already recognised that stress at work could be a problem, and Europe's social partners are discussing an agreement on the issue.

In France, the government has asked companies of more than 1,000 workers to negotiate an anti-stress policy with unions to be adopted by each enterprise. They were given the deadline of the beginning of this month to launch discussions.

This week, a government-appointed commission headed by veteran industrialist Henri Lachmann, chairman of Schneider Electric, delivered a long-awaited report on wellbeing and efficiency at work.

It makes a series of enlightened suggestions, such as the need for business and engineering schools to include social responsibility in the workplace in their curriculums.

It suggests that management training in handling social issues should be compulsory in every company.

But most interesting is the recommendation that social performance should be made a key factor in setting the remuneration of managers.

Danone, whose head of human resources sat on the Lachmann commission, already does this. But few others do.

The report also underlines the fact that the health and wellbeing of the workforce is first and foremost the responsibility of managers, and cannot be outsourced to external advisers as many French companies appear to be doing.

The question now is how to define social performance.

The French report suggests the issue needs to be treated extremely seriously. It suggests the issue is so serious that the board of a company and not just its top management must make it a priority, as much so as delivering profits and dividends to its shareholders.

Financial Times, FT.com, 19/02/2010 (Paul Betts), Reproduced with permission. © The Financial Times Ltd.

Questions

1 To what extent do you think the organisations mentioned here would benefit from using the Health and Safety Executive's stress management standards as a part of their stress policies?

2 In your opinion do you think that measures of social performance should be considered when deciding managers pay? If so, what measures should be used?

3 Do you think that measures of health, safety and wellbeing should be included as a part of the balanced scorecard approach in organisations?

4 To what extent do you think measures of a country's wellbeing should be included when comparing the performance of countries? Should there be something like the balanced scorecard, discussed in Chapter 1, as a gauge of countries' success and prosperity with measures such as a happiness index or metrics about wellbeing being used alongside economic measures?

WHAT NEXT?

Research conducted by Aberdeen University on 13 offshore oil installations applies the balanced scorecard to occupational health. The article also discusses the results of interviews with UK and Norwegian managers on health and safety performance indicators and the reasons for including occupational health and safety as one measure of performance within the balanced scorecard. What do you think about the idea that measures of occupational health should be included in an assessment of an organisation's performance?

> Mearns, K. and J.I. Havold (2003) Occupational health and safety and the balanced scorecard, *The TQM Magazine*, Vol. 15, No. 6, 408–423.

References

Advisory, Conciliation and Arbitration Service (2009) *Discipline and Grievances at Work; The ACAS Guide*, ACAS.

Advisory, Conciliation and Arbitration Service (2010a) Health, work and wellbeing, ACAS, 2.

Advisory, Conciliation and Arbitration Service (2010b) Statement of fitness for work or 'fit note', ACAS (www.acas.co.uk; accessed 13.9.2010).

Baker, J. (2007) Net closes on corporate killing, *People Management*, Vol. 13, No. 5, 8 March, 22.

Cacanas, Z. (2004) *The Guardian*, 24 July.

Chartered Institute of Personnel and Development (2006) *Occupational Health and Organisational Effectiveness*, CIPD (available at www.cipd.co.uk; accessed 10.09.07).

Chartered Institute of Personnel and Development (2007) *Gangmaster Legislation Should be Extended*, CIPD, 31 July (www.cipd.co.uk/news/_articles/gangmasterlegislationshouldbeextended.htm; accessed 10.09.07).

Chartered Institute of Personnel and Development (2009) *Annual Survey Report 2009: Absence Management*, CIPD (www.cipd.co.uk; accessed 10.9.2010).

Chartered Institute of Personnel and Development (2010a) *Factsheet: Working Hours and Time Off Work*, CIPD (www.cipd.co.uk; accessed 11.9.2010).

Chartered Institute of Personnel and Development (2010b) *Factsheet: Absence Measurement and Management*, CIPD (www.cipd.co.uk; accessed 10.9.2010).

Chiu, A, (2009) Food, job best foundations for success in pursuit of happiness, *South China Morning Post*, 8 December.

Engineering Employers' Federation (2001) *Managing Stress at Work*, EEF.

Fowler, A. (1994) Personnel's model army, *Personnel Management*, September, 34–3.

Griffiths, L. (2009) Addressing obesity in the workplace, *Occupational Health*, RBI, Issue 1, 1 February (www.xperthr.co.uk; accessed 6.9.2010).

Hackitt, J. (2010a) *Foreword. The Health and Safety of Britain: Be Part of the Solution*, HSE (www.hse.gov.uk; accessed 8.9.2010).

Hackitt, J. (2010b) *Foreword. The Health and Safety Business Plan 2010–11*, HSE. (www.hse.gov.uk; accessed 8.9.2010).

Hammond, D. (2001) Dangerous liaisons, *People Management*, 30 May, 26–7. (www.peoplemanagement.co.uk/pm/articles/2001/05/674.htm)

Hayden-Smith, J. and R. Simms (2003) Pressure points, *People Management*, 25 September, 17.

Health and Safety Executive (n.d.) *What are the Management Standards?* (available at www.hse.gov.uk/stress/standards/index.htm; accessed 17.09.2010).

Health and Safety Executive (1995) *Be Safe: Save Money. The Costs of Accidents: A Guide for Small Firms*, HSE Books, 4.

Health and Safety Executive (2006) *Five Steps to Risk Assessment*, HSE, INDG 163 rev. 2 (available at www.hse.gov.uk; accessed 8.09.2010).

Health and Safety Executive (2008) *HSE Enforcement Policy Statement – Updated*, HSE (www.hse.gov.uk; accessed 10.9.2010).

Health and Safety Executive (2009a), *How to Tackle Work-related Stress*, HSE (www.hse.gov.uk; accessed 6.8.2010).

Health and Safety Executive (2009b) *Statistics: Stress-related and Psychological Disorders*, HSE (available at www.hse.gov.uk; accessed 17.9.2010).

Health and Safety Executive (2010a), *Health and Safety Executive Statistics: Fatal Injury Statistics*, HSE (www.hse.gov.uk; accessed 6.8.2010).

Health and Safety Executive (2010b) *Self-reported Work-related Illness and Workplace Injuries in 2008–09: Results from the Labour Force Survey*, HSE (www.hse.gov.uk; accessed 7.8.2010).

Health and Safety Executive (2010c) HSE *Revitalising Health and Safety,* HSE (www.hse.gov.uk; accessed 7.8.2010).

Health and Safety Executive (2010d) *The Health and Safety Executive Business Plan 2010/11*, HSE (www.hse.gov.uk; accessed 7.8.2010).

Health and Safety Executive (2010e) *2010 Myths*, HSE (www.hse.gov.uk; accessed 7.9.2010).

Health and Safety Executive (2010f) *Example Health and Safety Policy*, HSE (www.hse.gove.uk; accessed 11.9.2010).

Holmes, T.H. and R.H. Rahe (1967) The social readjustment rating scale, *Journal of Psychosomatic Research*, August, 216.

Incomes Data Services (2002) *IDS Studies Plus: Employee Assistance Programmes*, IDS.

Incomes Data Services (2004) *IDS HR Studies 775: Managing Stress*, IDS.

Inland Revenue Service Employment Review (2007a) *Employee Assistance Programmes: The IRS Report*, IRS 874, 4 June.

Inland Revenue Service Employment Review (2007b) *Westminster City Council's Successful Absence Management Procedure*, IRS 877, 16 July.

International Stress Management Association UK (2004) *Working Together to Reduce Stress at Work*, International Stress Management Association UK.

Investors in People (2010) *Why Should You be Improving Health and Wellbeing?* IIP (www.iip.co.uk; accessed 11.9.2010).

Jones, R. (2007) Manslaughter Act doesn't go far enough, *Personnel Today*, 6 March.

Le Fevre, M., J. Matheny and G.S. Kolt (2003) Eustress, distress, and interpretation in occupational stress, *Journal of Managerial Psychology*, Vol. 18, No. 7, 726–744.

Maslow, A. (1954) *Motivation and Personality*, 2nd edition, Harper & Row.

Michaelson, J., S.Abdallah, N.Steur, S.Thompson and N.Marks (2009) *National Accounts of Well-being*, The New Economics Foundation (www.neweconomics.org/publications/national-accounts-well-being; accessed 16.9.2010).

Midgley, S. (1997) Pressure points, *People Management*, 10 July, 36–39.

Millard, R. (2010) Gareth Malone's lesson in how to teach boys, *The Sunday Times*, 12 September, 16.

Ministry of Justice (2007) Justice for corporate deaths: Royal assent for corporate Manslaughter and Corporate Homicide Act, Ministry of Justice (www.justice.gov.uk/news/newsrelease260707b.htm; accessed 12.09.07).

Nishiyama, K. and J. Johnson (1997) *Karoshi – Death from Overwork: Occupational Health Consequences of the Japanese Production Management*, 6th Draft for *International Journal of Health Services*, 4 February (available at www.workhealth.org/whatsnew/lpkarosh.html; accessed 17.09.2010).

Paton, N. (2010) Future challenges in workplace health, *Occupational Health*, 1 August (www.xperthr.co.uk; accessed 6.9.2010).

Philpott, J. (2010) *Work Audit: Working Hours in the Recession*, CIPD, 1–2.

Quinn, J. (2004) Dodging the draft, *People Management*, 30 June, 17.

Seenan, G. (2004) No frills – and no travelling toilet class, *The Guardian*, 24 July.

Selye, H. (1956) *The Stress of Life*, McGraw-Hill.

Selye, H. (1974) *Stress without Distress*, Lippincott.

Stranks, J. (2007a) *The Health and Safety Handbook: A Practical Guide to Health and Safety Law, Management Policies and Procedures*, Kogan Page.

Tehrani, N., S.Humpage, B.Wilmott and I. Haslam (2007) *Change Agenda: What's Happening with Well-being at Work?* CIPD, 3.

Venning, N. (1995) Taking the bull by the horns, *Guardian Careers Section*, 15 April, 2–3.

Woolf, M. and K. Dowling (2010) Gove's new curriculum, *The Sunday Times*, 12 September, 1.

Woollen, R. (2010) The fit note – friend or foe, *Managing People*, 1 April.

XpertHR (2010a) *Employment Law Reference Manual, Health and Safety*, XpertHR (www.xperthr.co.uk; accessed 10.9.2010).

XpertHR (2010b) *Outlook Video: Equality Act–Disability*, XpertHR (www.xperthr.co.uk; accessed 11.9.2010).

Further study

Books

Advisory, Conciliation and Arbitration Service (2010) *Health, Work and Wellbeing*, ACAS.

This booklet focuses on measures that employers can take to help promote good health in their workforce and also discusses the importance of work for keeping people healthy.

Stranks, J. (2007b) *Health and Safety at Work: An Essential Guide for Managers*, revised 8th edition, Kogan Page.

This is available as an electronic book and as the name implies gives clear practical guidance for managers.

Articles

HSE publications exist on a wide range of topics, too numerous to include here, from general books to detailed explanations of legislation. Some of its leaflets are also available on the web page listed at the end of this chapter.

Internet

Control Risks Group   www.crg.com

The Health and Safety Executive   www.hse.gov.uk

RIDDOR   www.riddor.gov.uk

The site gives information about RIDDOR and has forms which can be downloaded to report accidents and dangerous occurrences, or these can now be reported directly online.

XpertHR   www.xperthr.co.uk

An excellent source of articles from various publications.

WHERE NEXT?
THE FUTURE OF WORK

Managing People

CHAPTER 34

THE FUTURE OF WORK

THE OBJECTIVES OF THIS CHAPTER ARE TO:

1 Outline the likely demand for skills in the UK over the next twenty years

2 Introduce the debate about whether the workforce will need to upskill or downskill in the future

3 Set out the major demographic trends in the UK and their consequences for the supply of skills

4 Discuss the major consequences for HR practices arising from a changing workforce profile

5 Debate the merits of the argument that traditional employment practices will change radically in the future in response to environmental trends

6 Put the case for focusing on labour market and regulatory developments as well as developments in product markets when considering the future of work

In a business world that is increasingly seen as being subject to instability and change, managers are right to be interested in likely future developments so that they can prepare effectively and, hopefully, keep one step ahead of their competitors. Business history is littered with examples of big, powerful corporations that have failed to survive because they did not adapt fast enough in the face of unstoppable developments in technology, changes in customer demand or the innovations of competitors. In a global economy governments are also right to be interested in the same developments so that they can put in place measures which will give their organisations the best chance of competing effectively internationally. The trouble is, as Mark Twain famously wrote, 'prediction is difficult, especially when predictions relate to the future'. People have very different ideas about the ways in which our business environment will evolve in future decades, and they can't all be right.

Differences of opinion about the likely future of working life are particularly diverse. On the one hand there is a highly influential school of thought associated (in the UK) with the work of writers such as Charles Handy and Susan Greenfield which predicts a radically different future for work in western industrialised countries. Not only will the nature of the work people do be different from that done by most workers today, the radical view foresees a future in which the very idea of the 'job' will become increasingly outdated. Forms of self-employment and subcontracting will be the norm, as 'knowledge workers' pursue 'portfolio careers', moving from assignment to assignment and retraining regularly in order to make a living. Others agree that the future of work will develop in important ways, but reject the idea that we are heading quickly and inexorably towards radically different working lives. They expect to witness evolution rather than revolution as current trends continue steadily to adjust expectations about work and the demand for and supply of workers. This is the main message that has come out of many recent studies carried out under the auspices of the ESRC's Future of Work research programme (*see* Nolan 2004 and Taylor 2002). A third view stresses the significance of the changes we have witnessed in the past twenty or thirty years and predicts a future for work which, by contrast, is rather more stable than we have become used to. Instead of further transformation, the tendency will be for earlier changes, such as the move from a mixed to a market economy, the feminisation of the workforce, the rise of the service sector, globalisation of business activity, and the rise of employment law, to bed in as western countries enjoy a period of relative economic stability by the standards of recent history. According to this view, the future of work has to a considerable degree 'already happened'. We now need to adjust more fully to the consequences of developments which are clearly permanent and not temporary.

THE FUTURE DEMAND FOR WORKERS

If current trends are maintained we can expect to see continued increases, year on year, in the number of jobs being created by British organisations. In 2006 there were 37.1 million people of working age in the UK, of whom 30.8 million were in work. Around 1.5 million were unemployed and actively seeking work, while a further 7.9 million people of working age were defined as being 'economically inactive' (ONS 2006a). The total number of jobs has grown steadily in recent years to reach its current peak of 26.7 million. The figure decreased during the recessions of the early 1980s and early 1990s, but the long-term trend has been upwards for over sixty years.

Importantly, this increase in the amount of employment in the UK has occurred at a time when many major industries have seen the introduction of labour-saving technologies and when millions of jobs have effectively been 'exported' to developing countries where labour costs are much cheaper. Major industrial restructuring has occurred, yet the demand for labour over the long term has increased steadily. Provided the economy continues to grow, we can thus expect to see further increased demand for people on the part of employers over the coming decade.

But what sort of skills will employers be looking for? Here too long-term trends paint a clear picture which there is every reason to believe will continue for the foreseeable future. The official method used to classify occupations in the UK was changed in 1999, so it is not possible to make a precise comparison of today's figures with those produced by government statisticians before then. Nonetheless an obvious long-term pattern can be seen in the two sets of statistics presented in Tables 34.1 and 34.2. These show a pronounced switch occurring over a long period of time, and continuing strongly in more recent years, away from skilled, semi-skilled and unskilled manual work towards jobs which require higher-level and more specialised skills. The major growth areas have long been in the professional, technical and managerial occupations.

The change in the occupational profile of the UK workforce has largely been driven by the revolutionary shift that has occurred in the nature of our industries during the past thirty years. In 1978, which was the first year that data was collected on employment by sector, seven million people worked in manufacturing and a further one and a half million in the energy, water, farming and fishing industries. These have all hugely declined since then. Manufacturing now employs only three million (12 per cent of all jobs). Agriculture

Table 34.1 Changes in occupations, 1951–1999

Occupation	% in 1951	% in 1999
Higher professionals	1.9	6.4
Lower professionals	4.7	14.9
Employers and proprietors	5.0	3.4
Managers and administrators	5.5	15.7
Clerks	10.7	14.9
Foremen, supervisors and inspectors	2.6	3.1
Skilled manual	24.9	12.7
Semi-skilled manual	31.5	23.0
Unskilled manual	13.1	5.9

Source: *Labour Force Survey* statistics accessed at www.statistics.gov.uk.

Table 34.2 Changes in occupations, 2001–2006

Occupation	% in 2001	% in 2006
Managers and senior officials	12.9	14.7
Professional occupations	11.7	12.7
Associate professional and technical occupations	13.2	14.2
Administrative and secretarial	14.9	13.5
Skilled trades	9.5	8.4
Personal services	7.5	8.3
Sales and customer services	8.6	8.6
Process, plant and machine operatives	8.7	7.4
Elementary occupations	13.2	12.1

Source: *Labour Force Survey* statistics accessed at www.statistics.gov.uk.

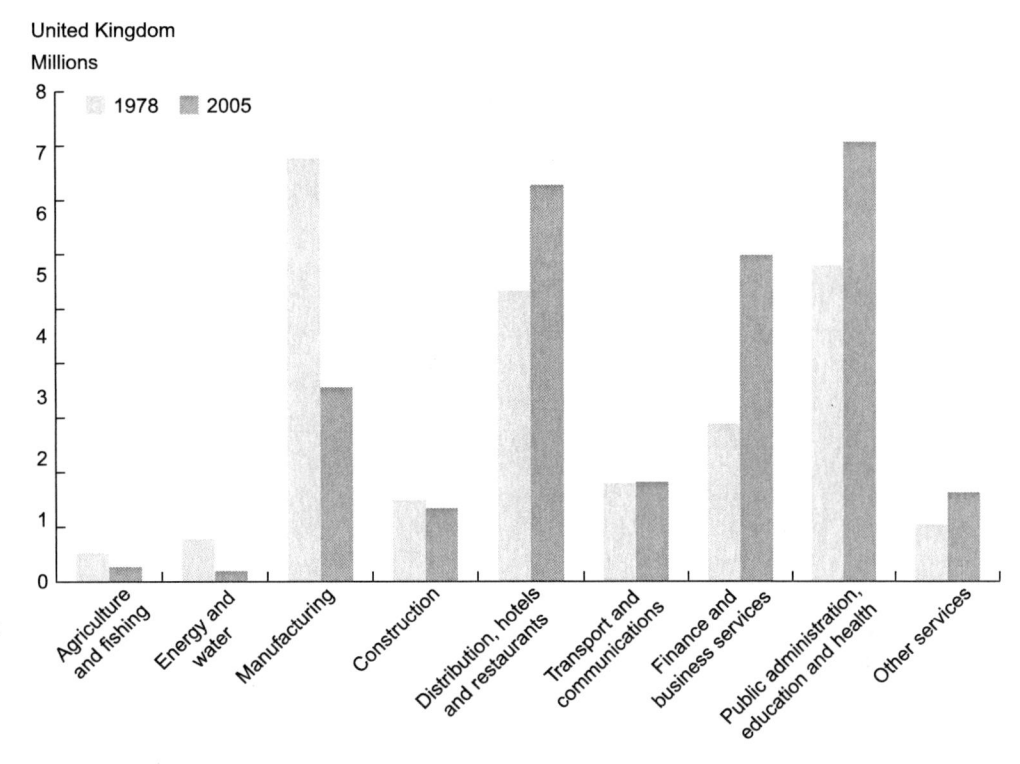

Figure 34.1 Employee jobs: by industry, 1978 (Quarter 2) and 2005 (Quarter 2)

(Source: ONS (2006a: 7))

and fishing account for just 200,000 jobs; energy and water for fewer still (*see* Figure 34.1). The big growth areas have been in retailing, distribution, hotels and restaurants, finance, business services, public administration, education and health. Employment in the financial services sector has grown especially quickly, more than doubling since 1978.

In the most recent years the biggest growth areas in terms of jobs have been in the public sector. Public sector employment fell during the 1990s. Having peaked at 5.9 million in 1991, it reached a 'low point' of 5.1 million in 1998 before climbing back to 5.9 million again. Over 300,000 new jobs have been created in the NHS since 1998 and over 200,000 in education. The expansion of local and central government has led to the creation of 128,000 jobs, a further 45,000 being created in the police service (ONS 2006a, p. 26). Another major employment trend since the 1970s has been a substantial growth in the proportion of people working in small businesses. The small firms sector now employs 55 per cent of the UK workforce.

ACTIVITY 34.1

Why do you think countries such as the UK have seen so great a transformation in their industrial structure since the 1970s? Why are there so many fewer manufacturing jobs and so many more jobs in the service sector? Why are organisations so much more likely to employ small numbers of people than was the case fifty years ago?

One of the most vigorously contested debates among labour market economists concerns the nature of the skills that employers will be looking for in the future, a debate that has very important implications for government education policy, which, as a result, is itself controversial (see Grugulis et al. 2004). In recent years a highly influential group has argued that in the future economies such as the UK's will see a speeding up of the trends identified above. Influenced by figures such as Manuel Castells of Berkeley University in California, it has become common for policymakers to believe that a 'new economy' is rapidly developing which will increasingly be dominated by companies which are 'knowledge-intensive' in nature. According to this 'upskilling thesis', lower-skilled jobs will be rarer and rarer in industrialised countries. Because they can be done far more cheaply in developing economies, they will increasingly be exported overseas.

It follows that the governments such as the UK's should prepare the workforce as best it can for the challenges of a 'high-skill, high-wage economy' in which those who do not have a relevant higher education are going to struggle to make a living. Hence we see the rapid expansion of universities, heavy investment in schools and the provision of all manner of schemes designed to equip unemployed people with new skills.

Critics of Castells tend to look to the writings of a very different American academic guru figure – Harry Braverman. His theories derive from a Marxian perspective as well as from observations of the activities of corporations in the 1960s and 1970s. This contrasting 'deskilling thesis' argues that businesses competing in capitalist economies will always look for ways of cutting their labour costs, and that they do this in part by continually reducing the level of skills required by the people they employ. It follows that, far from leading to a demand for higher-level skills and knowledge, the advent of an economy based on information and communication technologies will *over time* reduce such demand.

Both schools draw on widely documented trends to back up their positions. The upskillers draw attention to the fact that the major growth areas in labour demand are in the higher-skilled occupational categories. Demand for graduates is increasing, demand for lower-skilled people is less strong, and is decreasing in some industries. They also draw attention to the emergence of skills shortages in many industries as employers find it steadily harder to recruit people with the abilities and experience they need.

By contrast, the downskillers draw attention to the growth of call-centre-type operations which use technology to reduce the amount of knowledge and expertise required by customer services staff, and to the increasing use of bureaucratic systems which reduce the number of situations in which people have a discretion to make decisions. They also point to the strong growth in industries such as retailing and hotels which are characterised by employment of people who need only be low skilled and who are relatively low paid. They thus forecast a situation in which the workforce is heavily overqualified and in which graduates are increasingly employed in jobs for which no degree is necessary. They also argue that many of the 'skills' that employers say are in short supply are not in fact 'skills' at all, but are merely 'attributes' or 'characteristics'. The target here is an evolving business language that refers to 'communication skills', 'interpersonal skills', 'teamworking skills', 'problem-solving skills' and 'customer-handling skills'. These, it is argued, have nothing whatever to do with a knowledge-based economy and cannot be gained through formal education.

As with all debates that concern the likely future direction of society, it is difficult to reach firm conclusions about this debate. However, in truth what appears to be happening is that we are seeing the emergence of an 'hourglass' occupational structure in the UK in which half of the jobs are of the 'high-skill/high-pay' variety, and the other half are 'low skill/low pay' (Grugulis *et al.* 2004: 6). The metaphor of the hourglass was originally advanced by Nolan (2001). But it has been popularised and expanded in the highly influential article by Goos and Manning (2003) entitled 'McJobs and Macjobs: the growing polarisation of jobs in the UK'. What seems to be happening is the following:

- Increasing numbers of people are being employed in relatively highly paid, secure, professional and managerial occupations in the finance, private services and public sectors.
- Lower-skilled jobs in manufacturing along with many lower-paid clerical and administrative roles are being 'exported' to countries in Eastern Europe and South East Asia where cheaper labour is readily available.
- But, at the same time, the growing number of higher-paid people are using their disposable income to purchase services which cannot be provided from overseas. Hence there is a simultaneous and rapid growth in demand for hairdressers, beauticians, restaurant workers, and people to work in the media, tourist and entertainment-oriented industries.
- There also remains a great demand for, and shortage of, some groups of skilled workers – plumbers, builders, decorators, etc., whose jobs also, by their nature, cannot be so easily exported.

For the foreseeable future, therefore, we are likely to see growth in demand *both* for people who have gained a higher education or who have specialised higher-level skills *and* for people who have strong interpersonal skills (or attributes) to work in the expanding personal services sector. From a public policy point of view, this means that government is broadly correct to put more investment into higher education, but that it is equally important to make available high-quality, specialised forms of vocational education so that the future needs of all industrial sectors are properly provided for. This latter area is one in which the UK has been conspicuously weaker than other European countries for many years.

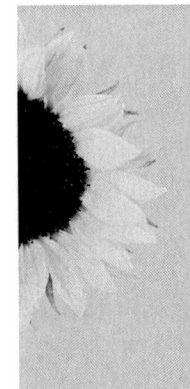

WINDOW ON PRACTICE

In 2006 the Confederation of British Industry (CBI) published a survey of employers which revealed a lack of basic educational skills among new recruits. According to respondents the big problem in the UK is a lack of basic numerical skills among school leavers, but good reading and writing skills are also in short supply. The problem extends to graduate recruits too. The survey suggests that 23 per cent of employers are unhappy with levels of literacy among their graduates and that 13 per cent are concerned about numeracy levels. The response, according to the CBI, is for one in three employers to provide remedial tuition in reading, writing and arithmetic.

Source: M. Green (2006) 'Employers alarmed at skills shortage', *Financial Times*, 21 August.

THE FUTURE SUPPLY OF WORKERS

The UK population currently stands at 59.8 million. This accounts for 13 per cent of the European Union population, eight per cent of the total European population and just under one per cent of the world's total population. Unlike that of most European countries, the UK population is currently growing (Jeffries 2005). This is for two reasons:

1. Birth rates currently exceed death rates. Each year approximately 700,000 babies are born in the UK, while 615,000 people die – a net gain of 85,000 people.
2. Each year it is estimated that around 150,000 more people migrate into the country than emigrate out of it. Total immigration is now in excess of half a million a year.

The population is therefore growing at a rate of nearly a quarter of a million people each year (ONS 2006b). Official estimates state that the total UK population will reach 65 million by 2050, but this figure will be reached a good deal sooner if current levels of immigration continue. This upward trend in the UK population represents a reversal of the position in the in the 1970s and early 1980s – a period of substantial net emigration and relatively low birth rates.

The birth rate increased substantially after the Second World War and continued at relatively high levels until the late 1960s. Over a million babies were born at the peak in 1964. This created the large 'baby boom' generation who are now in their forties and fifties. From 1964 onwards the UK saw a sharp decline in its birth rate, which reached a low point in 1977 when only 657,000 babies were born (i.e. fewer than the number of deaths). This was due in part to the relatively low number of births in the country in the war years (1939–45), in part to the wide availability of the contraceptive pill and abortion, and partly to changes in social attitudes leading to later marriages. The downward trend was reversed somewhat in the 1980s as the baby boomers had children, but fertility rates remain at relatively low levels historically. As a result of these patterns, we have an ageing population. There are many more people in the UK in their forties and fifties than there are in their twenties and thirties (*see* Figure 34.2).

ACTIVITY 34.2

Why do you think that people, on average, choose to have fewer children than they did a generation ago? Can anything be done to reverse the trend? How far should governments see it as their role to encourage more births?

This will mean that there are many more retired people in the future than there are at present, but at the same time the number of adults of working age is projected to increase rather than decrease. Official estimates state that there will be 40.5 million people who are over school leaving age and below retirement age in 2020 as a result of continued net immigration and the equalisation of male and female state pension ages at 65 from 2010. The average age of this group will increase substantially because there will be a higher proportion of older people in the workforce and because younger people are projected

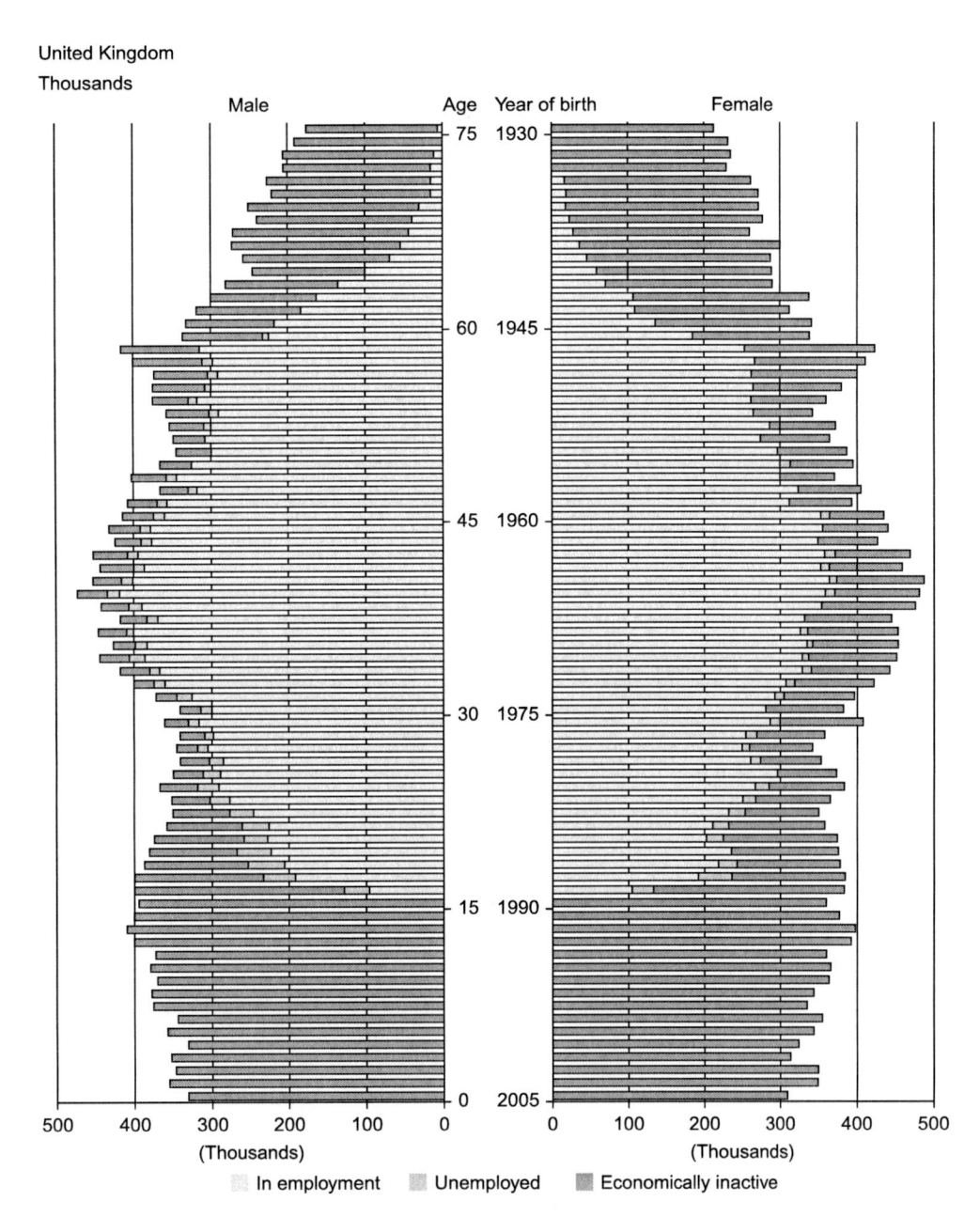

Figure 34.2 Population structure: by age, sex and economic activity, autumn 2005[1]

(Source: ONS (2006a) Labour Force Survey. [1] Not seasonally adjusted)

to choose to stay on in full-time education for longer, on average, than they currently do (Smith *et al.* 2005). We can thus conclude with a degree of confidence both that the supply of labour will increase in the coming two decades and that the profile of the workforce will age significantly.

However, there are important regional differences that it is important to note. The structure, density and growth of the population are by no means likely to be uniform across the whole country. The highest concentrations of older people, for example, are in the resort towns along the south and eastern coasts. Christchurch in Dorset is officially the 'oldest' place in the UK where 33.2 per cent are entitled to draw a state pension. By contrast, pensioners are few and far between in inner London. Tower Hamlets boasts the lowest proportion (only 9.8 per cent), but the numbers are also low in some commuter towns close to London and in cities with large student populations.

The highest concentrations of children are found in Northern Ireland where fertility rates are much higher than elsewhere in the country, while young adults are concentrated in university towns and cities, reflecting the fact that there are now 1.4 million full-time students in the UK. As far as England is concerned, between the 1930s and 2001 the major trend was a movement of people from the north of the country to the south, the southern regions gaining 30,000 people a year on average during this period. Since 2001 there has been an apparent reversal of this long-term trend, the north gaining 35,000 people per year at the expense of the south (Champion 2005). However, as a result of migration and falling fertility rates the populations of Scotland and Wales are both falling. In both countries there are considerably more deaths than births each year and relatively high levels of net emigration.

We can also predict with some certainty that there will be greater diversity among the workforce in terms of ethnicity and national origin as a result of net immigration.

All around the world international migration is increasing. As far as the UK is concerned this means that the long-term trend is towards greater levels of both emigration and immigration (Horsfield 2005). Until the early 1990s the UK had been broadly in balance as far as international migration was concerned for around twenty years. Indeed, for much of the 1970s and during the early 1980s more people left the UK each year than entered it. Since 1993 this trend has changed. Every year there are now substantially more immigrants than emigrants, a gap which widens year on year. People leaving the UK tend to be older on average than the new arrivals. Many leave in order to retire in sunnier climes, while others seek new opportunities in Australasia, the USA, Canada and EU countries. A fair proportion of annual emigration each year involves people who were born overseas returning to their countries of origin, for example following a period studying in a UK university. Historically the main source of immigrants into the UK has been from new Commonwealth countries such as India, Pakistan, Bangladesh and from the Caribbean. However, more recently we have seen a substantial growth in people arriving from other developing countries (such as Somalia) and especially from the countries which joined the European Union in May 2004 (i.e. Poland, Slovakia, Hungary, Cyprus and the Baltic states).

As a result of net immigration the proportion of the UK population which was born overseas increases each year, the vast majority of these people being of working age (Randall and Salt 2005). At the time of the 2001 census just under five million UK residents had been born overseas. This represents 8.3 per cent of the population. This is a great deal higher than was the case at the time of previous censuses. In 1991 the figure was 6.7 per cent, and in 1951 only 4.2 per cent. Here too, however, there is considerable regional variation. Forty-eight per cent of immigrants arriving in the UK settle in London and the south east of England, the largest numbers settling in inner London. The London borough of Brent boasts the highest proportion of foreign-born residents (46.6 per cent). By contrast, the lowest levels (under 3 per cent) are found in the English-Scottish border regions.

If current trends continue the supply of labour across the UK as a whole should be sufficient to meet the growing demand for labour. Chronic skills shortages will be avoided provided government and employers continue to invest in the education and development of people. Importantly, in these respects the UK is a great deal better placed than many of its competitor countries where the population is falling and is ageing at a far faster rate than is the case in Britain. Fertility rates in many southern and eastern European countries have now fallen well below 1.5, meaning that each couple produces on average fewer than 1.5 children. A fertility rate of 2.1 is required to maintain a stable population, yet it is 1.32 in Germany, 1.28 in Italy, 1.27 in Spain and only 1.26 in Poland (United Nations 2005). In the UK immigration allows the maintenance of steady population growth, despite historically low fertility rates (1.66 in 2006). This is in contrast to the position of many countries where immigration rules are more restrictive or where low wages and relatively high unemployment make them less attractive to economic migrants.

The statistics suggest, however, that employers in many regions will continue to face some skills shortages. Provided unemployment remains relatively low, this will tend to push wage rates up beyond the rate of price inflation. The result, as has been the case for the past fifteen years, will be greater pressure on organisations to improve labour productivity by reorganising, merging to achieve economies of scale and outsourcing activities where they can be supplied more efficiently by external providers. It will also be necessary for employers willingly to employ more older people than they have tended to be accustomed to doing. Indeed, in order to meet their demand for labour it is likely that organisations are going to have to target older groups and take steps to make employment attractive to them. There are three distinct groups who have not traditionally found themselves to be in great demand by recruiters:

- people over the age of fifty who are still working,
- people who have taken early retirement/redundancy,
- people who are over the state retirement age.

In the case of the first group, traditional full-time jobs will be sought. The others are more likely to be looking for part-time work or some other form of flexible working. Research strongly suggests that most people have a preference for phased retirement as opposed to full-time work until a retirement day and then leisure (HSBC 2006). Employers who can provide flexibility of this kind will be in a far stronger position to compete for the services of older workers than competitors who do not. Another consequence of an ageing population will be the presence among younger employees of more people with responsibility for caring for elderly relatives. Attracting and retaining them will also require flexible working options.

Aside from flexibility, the other major element that needs to be in place in order to attract and retain older people is a culture which fully respects and values their contribution. A great deal of research has been carried out in recent years looking at attitudes to older workers among managers and younger employees. The conclusion is that people commonly stereotype older workers, just as they tend to stereotype young workers. Older workers tend to be seen as being reliable, stable, mature and experienced, but also as difficult to train, resistant to change, over-cautious, poor with technology, slow and prone to ill health. Organisations which are serious about employing more older people will need to tackle such stereotyping and to ensure that opportunities for development are provided for people of all ages.

However, at the same time, employers need to recognise that people do change as they age and do contribute different qualities than younger colleagues. They thus need to be managed somewhat differently from an HR perspective. It will be necessary, for example, to tailor reward packages to suit the needs of older workers as well as younger ones. Clearly this will include pension arrangements, but may also incorporate other benefits which older employees value more than younger employees such as health insurance.

Organisations often seek a workforce which reflects its core target market. This is particularly true of creative and media industries which need younger employees to ensure that they are in touch with the needs, aspirations and concerns of people in the key 18–30 group. This is a major source of age discrimination in the labour market which is likely, over time, to change. Instead of seeking employees who match their consumers by age, employers will want people of any age who reflect the values and attitudes of more broadly-aged target markets.

The changes to HR practice required as a result of increased numbers of workers from overseas are less profound but equally important. The key here is to make sure that the organisation both gains and retains a reputation for fairness in its labour markets. Once an organisation is perceived to be prone to acting in a discriminatory fashion towards members of ethnic minorities or migrant workers, the reputation is hard to shake off, making it harder to recruit and retain a skilled workforce. In this area perceptions of managers about the fairness of their policies and practices is irrelevant. The perception of the target labour market is all that matters, so we can expect to see organisations in the future 'bending over backwards' to ensure not just that they are committed to equal opportunities and diversity, but that they are seen to be too.

ACTIVITY 34.3

According to the demographers at the United Nations several European countries are going to see substantial falls in their populations over the next forty years due to low fertility rates. It is estimated that the German population will fall from 83 million to 79 million by 2050, and the Italian population from 58 million to 51 million. In Russia the projected fall is from 143 million to 112 million By contrast the British and French populations are projected to increase modestly during this period, while in Turkey the population will increase hugely from 77 million today to 101 million in 2050.

What do you think are the main long-term implications for organisations in these different European countries? What will the effect be on the labour market? What will be the effect on the capacity of public sector organisations to deliver vital public services?

FUTURE CONTRACTUAL ARRANGEMENTS

While there is general agreement among commentators about the nature of the work we will be carrying out in the coming decades and the profile of the workforce that will be employed to carry it out, there is considerable disagreement about the types of contract (both legal and psychological) that will be prevalent. For some years now a diverse group of futurologists have gained considerable influence by predicting substantial changes in this area. The most prominent figure in the UK is Charles Handy, who has published a series of books in which he argues that radical change is in store (*see* Handy 1984, 1989, 1994 and 2001). A broadly similar analysis has been developed by Davidson and Rees Mogg (1997), Rifkin (1995) and Bridges (1995), and more recently by Susan Greenfield (2003a and 2003b). While each of these writers, and others who have advocated the evolution of a similar future for the world of work, justify their conclusion somewhat differently, all predict a switch in the dominant form of work from employment to various forms of self-employment. Moreover, where employment continues, people will be far more likely to work from home (connected to others electronically) and to work for small, highly specialised companies and will neither have nor expect long-term job security.

For Handy the future is one in which portfolio careers will dominate. People will move from employer to employer regularly, often working for two concerns at the same time. There will be periods of self-employment and periods of employment, the conventional working life being likened to that of an actor auditioning for work and moving from production to production on stage, screen and television. There will be periods in between assignments when we will be under-employed, and other periods when we have more than enough work on our plates. Davidson and Rees-Mogg (1997, p. 237) prefer the example of film production companies which assemble a group of talented specialists to work on a project, but when it is over 'the lighting technicians, cameramen, sound engineers and wardrobe specialists will go their separate ways'. Others, including Greenfield (1993, p. 92) go further in arguing that 'the concept of the "job" as we know it may disappear altogether' and that 'firms will perhaps bid for employee time almost on a day-to-day basis'. Insecurity of employment, according to this view, will soon become the norm.

The analysis on which these writers base their predictions is thoughtful and logical and can be persuasive. At root they all argue that greater volatility in the world of employment is inevitable as organisations experience increasing volatility in their product markets. Because employers will no longer operate in markets which are at all stable and predictable, it follows that they will be unable to guarantee any kind of stable employment. For most analysts, increased volatility is seen as being a product of increased competition. Sparrow (2002) uses the term 'hyper-competition' to describe a business environment in which lean, highly productive organisations make use of the latest information and communications technologies to sell their goods and services to anyone, anywhere in a fast-evolving, knowledge-based global economy. In such a world, it is argued, no organisation can be viable if it burdens itself with large numbers of dependent employees expecting to enjoy lengthy, stable careers. Instead organisations will continually be expanding and retracting, forming and dissolving, and hiring different people, with different skill-sets on an 'as needs' basis. Greenfield's conclusion is the same, but for her the change will arise not as a result of increased competition, as she predicts greater cooperation and less competition, but simply because increased technical specialisation will mean that the most efficient and effective enterprises will be those which are small and highly flexible. Rifkin argues that traditional jobs will disappear because technological advances will create a world in which machines do many of the jobs currently performed by people. His future is a world of under-employment in which there are not enough jobs to go round, forcing a large proportion of the workforce either into self-employment or into a working life of short-term employment as and when opportunities arise.

A number of arguments have been advanced in opposition to this radical vision of an employment-free future world of work. Nolan (2004) has led the assault in the UK, drawing on empirical data indicating that in most respects, despite evidence of increased volatility in product markets, traditional, long-term, full-time employment is showing no sign whatever of withering away. Indeed, in some respects the trend is towards greater security, albeit in smaller enterprises. He is contemptuous in his criticisms of those who continue to peddle what he sees as misleading myths:

> Scarcely a week passes without a well-paid visionary heralding the demise of paid work and employment or the growing salience in the new economy of the 'free-worker'. Attention to detail is invariably slight. The great variance in the patterns of work and the consequences of past upheavals in employment are routinely ignored. (Nolan 2004, p. 7)

He goes on to make reference to the real trends that are observable in both the UK and the USA, to many of which we have referred in this and in earlier chapters:

- employment levels (i.e. the number of traditional jobs) are rising and not falling;
- the vast majority of workers continue to be employed in permanent jobs;
- job tenure rates have remained broadly stable for decades;
- around a third of the workforce has been employed (already) for ten years or more by their current employer;
- self-employment has not grown appreciably over the past decade;
- the number of temporary workers has fallen substantially over the past ten years.

While this evidence is very convincing, it is too early to condemn Handy, Rifkin and Greenfield as having been hopelessly wrong in their predictions. It is possible that over the coming few decades they will be proved right. But it is fair to point out that, at least in the case of Handy, the same claims were being made twenty-five years ago about what the world of work would be like today, and in many respects the opposite has turned out to be the case.

One possible reason that the predictions of these futurologists may prove to be inaccurate is their over-reliance on an analysis of what is likely to happen to product markets, ignoring in the process other determinants of employment arrangements such as labour market pressures and the regulatory environment. The evidence suggests that they are right about increasing competition and the need for organisations to become more specialised, flexible and productive, but that they are wrong to ignore other factors in the evolving business environment which serve to push organisations in an opposite direction to that which they would prefer given a free hand. For example, it is very often claimed that in the future, because employers will be unable to guarantee long-term employment, they will instead provide their workers with a capacity for greater 'employability'. People will be recruited and motivated, not with the promise of job security, but with skills development and work experience which will help them to build successful portfolio careers. This is a logical prediction if it is assumed that employers do not have to compete with one another for relatively scarce skills. However, as we have seen throughout this book, in recent years the trend has been towards tighter labour markets in which people increasingly have a choice about where they work and are willing as well as able to switch employers when they become dissatisfied. It is at least arguable that most would-be workers prefer secure employment to employability and portfolio career-building. If so the organisations that will be most successful in attracting and retaining people will be those which maximise job security by offering employment on a permanent basis.

Moreover, in a world in which the quality of staff increasingly provides the key to achieving competitive advantage, it is probable that employers will prefer to nurture high levels of commitment and discretionary effort from their people, rather than hiring and firing them on an as needs basis. In other words, employers may well conclude that a committed, productive workforce is not compatible with highly flexible organisation structures, and that the former is a better route to establishing competitive advantage than the latter.

The potential influence of regulation also needs to be taken into account. In the UK there is general agreement among employers and the political establishment that the best way of securing high levels of employment over the long term is to minimise labour market regulation so as to free businesses of costs which make them less competitive internationally. However, much employment regulation now originates at the European level and would not, for the most part, be on UK statute books were it not for Britain's membership of the European Union. The political establishments of the other larger EU countries have tended to take a different view, believing increased social protection to be necessary as a means of promoting greater security of employment. A perception of insecurity, in their view, tends to reduce people's willingness to spend and to put their savings in riskier types of investment vehicle. The result is less economic growth and a greater propensity to stagnation and recession (European Commission 2000). The outcome, as we have seen in recent years, has been a plethora of new employment legislation aiming to increase security by making it increasingly hard for employers to hire and fire either cheaply or easily. This creates a situation in which any journey on the part of employers towards much more flexible organisational forms is made harder both to embark on and to complete.

Finally it is necessary to point out that some economists are increasingly questioning the commonly held view that the business environment of the future will necessarily be characterised by greater volatility, at least as far as the western industrialised countries are concerned. Indeed already they observe far greater levels of economic stability pertaining in countries such as the UK and the USA that have moved farthest down the road away from manufacturing and towards the establishment of knowledge-based service industries. Kaletsky (2006), for example, argues strongly that manufacturing activities are the major source of volatility and that exporting these overseas, leaving home-based employees to focus on product design and marketing, actually serves to guarantee greater security of employment in a global economy. He gives the title 'platform companies' to organisations like Nokia, Dell and L'Oreal which sell their products internationally, but subcontract the entire manufacturing process to other companies:

> Because the manufacture of physical goods is the most volatile and capital-intensive part of the business process, outsourcing [overseas] does not just transfer jobs and factories – platform companies also outsource to China and other developing countries much of the economic volatility that goes with capital investment, inventory cycles and the unionised factory environment. (p. 21)

Could it be therefore that long-term, stable employment, far from being consigned to the dustbin of history, will actually become more common in the future as organisations increasingly outsource the more volatile elements of their operations and concentrate instead on higher-skilled, value-adding activities? Only time will tell, but an analysis of the major current labour market trends is consistent with this possibility.

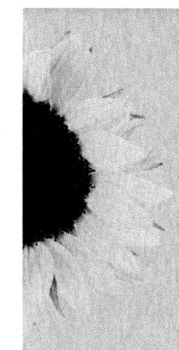

WINDOW ON PRACTICE

In recent years the UK government has made major investments in new technology as a means of improving standards of service delivery in the public services and reducing costs. In 2004 the Gershon Report entitled 'Transformational Government' was published. This identified £21 billion of possible annual savings across government that could be gained by greater efficiency generated by IT. To date the government claims to have saved £9.8 billion.

In order to deliver the government's ambitious agenda in this field, there is a need to recruit IT professionals with the experience and knowledge to develop highly complex systems. This task is proving difficult because there are relatively few people with the required skills and many potential competitors for their services. Critics say that the government will continue to be restricted in its ambitions until it accepts, as it has been reluctant to do, that it needs to pay people at or above the market rate for their services, while also creating clear career paths so that IT people, once recruited, can develop careers by moving across the different government departments. Historically IT people have tended to be hired on a subcontracted basis to work on one-off projects. This no longer works effectively as a means of sourcing scarce skills because private sector competitors are able to offer the prospect of longer-term career growth.

Source: R. Newing (2005) 'Technology: Rethink on careers as IT skills shortages loom', *Financial Times*, 15 June.

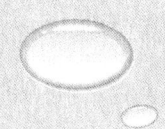

SUMMARY PROPOSITIONS

34.1 The likely future direction of employment practices in the UK has attracted a great deal of attention in recent years and has led to several hotly contested debates.

34.2 The occupations which are growing fastest are higher-level professional, technical and managerial jobs in the public and private sectors, and lower-paid jobs in the private services sector.

34.3 The working population in the UK is likely to grow at a slower rate in the future than it has in the recent past. It is also going to age and become more ethnically diverse.

34.4 Labour markets are likely to tighten further, leading to more skills shortages and a demand for skilled workers from overseas.

34.5 A radical vision for the future of work has been advocated by several influential management thinkers in recent years. They predict many fewer jobs, less job stability and more self-employment.

34.6 The radical vision is increasingly being challenged by researchers who maintain that the organisation of work is unlikely to alter radically in the foreseeable future.

GENERAL DISCUSSION TOPICS

1 What are the major trends in your own organisation's future demand for skills? To what extent do you foresee these being harder to source in the future and why?

2 What purpose does a study of current demographic trends serve from the point of view of the HR function in organisations?

3 Why do you think management writers continue to predict a revolution in the way work is organised in industrialised countries, despite the presence of evidence suggesting a continuation of the approaches that are currently prevalent?

FURTHER READING

Robert Taylor, formerly labour affairs editor of the *Financial Times*, has published five excellent papers over the past few years focusing on different aspects of the future of work. These draw on the large range of academic research that has been contributed to the Economic and Social Research Council's Future of Work programme. You can download these papers without charge at **www.leeds.ac.uk/esrcfutureofwork**.

The government's Office of National Statistics (ONS) also has an excellent website which can be used to gain access to a large range of authoritative articles and statistics concerning demographic trends and the demand and supply of skills in the UK. You will find summaries of the most recent trends in their annual publications *Social Trends* and *Labour Market Review*.

REFERENCES

Bridges, W. (1995) *Jobshift: how to prosper in a workplace without jobs*. London: Nicholas Brealey.

Champion, T. (2005) 'Population movement within the UK', in Office of National Statistics, *Focus on People and Migration*. London: HMSO.

Davidson, J.D. and Rees-Mogg, W. (1997) *The Sovereign Individual: The coming economic revolution. How to survive and prosper in it*. Basingstoke: Macmillan.

European Commission (2000) *The Future of Work*. London. Kogan Page.

Goos, M. and Manning, A. (2003) 'McJobs and Macjobs: the growing polarisation of jobs in the UK', in R. Dickens, P. Gregg and J. Wadsworth (eds), *The Labour Market Under New Labour*. Basingstoke: Palgrave.

Green, M. (2006) 'Employers alarmed at skills shortage', *Financial Times*, 21 August.

Greenfield, S. (2003a) *Tomorrow's People*. London: Penguin/Allen Lane.

Greenfield, S. (2003b) 'Flexible Futures', *People Management*, 23 October, pp. 52–3.

Grugulis, I., Warhurst, C. and Keep, E. (2004) 'What's happening to "Skill"?', in C. Warhurst, I. Grugulis and E. Keep (eds), *The Skills That Matter*. Basingstoke: Palgrave.

Handy, C. (1984) *The Future of Work*. Oxford: Blackwell.

Handy, C. (1989) *The Age of Unreason*. London: Business Books.

Handy, C. (1994) *The Empty Raincoat: Making Sense of the Future*. London: Hutchinson.

Handy, C. (2001) *The Elephant and the Flea: Looking Backwards to the Future*. London: Hutchinson.

Horsfield, G. (2005) 'International migration', in Office of National Statistics, *Focus on People and Migration*. London: HMSO.

HSBC (2006) *The Future of Retirement: What the World Wants*. London: HSBC.

Jeffries, J. (2005) 'The UK population: past, present and future', in Office of National Statistics, *Focus on People and Migration*. London: HMSO.

Kaletsky, A. (2006) 'Why the sun is rising over Britain, not Japan', *The Times*, 10 November, p. 21.

Newing, R. (2005) 'Technology: Rethink on careers as IT skills shortages loom', *Financial Times*, 15 June.

Nolan, P. (2001) 'Shaping things to come', *People Management*, 27 December.

Nolan, P. (2004) *Back to the Future of Work*. At **www.leeds.ac.uk/esrcfutureofwork/downloads/events/colloquium_2004/nolan_paper_0904.pdf**.

ONS (2006a) *Labour Market Review 2006*. London: HMSO.

ONS (2006b) *Social Trends 2006*. London: HMSO.

Randall, M. and Salt, J. (2005) 'The foreign-born population', in Office of National Statistics, *Focus on People and Migration*. London: HMSO.

Rifkin, J. (1995) *The End of Work: The decline of the global labour force and the dawn of the post-market era*. New York: Puttnam.

Smith, C., Tomassini, C., Smallwood, S. and Hawkins, M. (2005) 'The changing age structure of the UK population', in Office of National Statistics, *Focus on People and Migration*. London: HMSO.

Sparrow, P. (2002) 'The Future of work', in D. Holman, T. Wall, C. Clegg, P. Sparrow and A. Howard (eds), *The New Workplace: a guide to the human impact of modern working practices*. Chichester: Wiley.

Taylor, R. (2002) *Britain's World of Work – Myths and Realities*. At **www.leeds.ac.uk/esrcfutureofwork**.

United Nations (2005) *World Population Prospects: The 2004 Revision*. New York: United Nations.

An extensive range of additional materials, including multiple choice questions, answers to questions and links to useful websites can be found on the Human Resource Management Companion Website at www.pearsoned.co.uk/torrington.

INDEX

Index

absence management   439–40
accidents, first aid and work-related ill-health   426
accountability   421
action/practical arrangements   425
acts of absenteeism   115
   see also absence management
Adams' equity theory   354
adjourning, group   193
aggregate labour demand   55–56
alienation   106
alienation of self   105
anthropology   11

behavioural competencies
   advantages of   316
   characteristics of   313–15
   problematic aspects of   316–17
Belbin's team-roles   205
   back-up team-roles   205–06
   value of   206–07
benefits   *see* 'perks' (perquisites) or fringe benefits
benevolent autocracies   389
benign structures   193
'Big Five' dimensions   281–82
biographical information   282–83
blended learning   330
boundedness   8
Boyatzis model   313–14
BPR   *see* business process re-engineering (BPR)
brainstorming   213
   effectiveness   213–14
British health and safety legislation   440
broad-banded pay structures   366–67
bullying   114
business process re-engineering (BPR)   171–75

capitalist labour process   165
coaches   320–22
coaching   320–22
cognitive ability   278, 280–81
coherence/plausibility theories   22
common sense and social science   14
   critical common sense   15–16
   everyday common sense   14–15
communication, patterns of   207–08
   implications for manager   208–09
   member roles   210–11
   task and maintenance functions   209–10
communication skills   197, 454
communication system   187
competence-related pay   369–70
competencies   286, 313
   see also behavioural competencies
   for tasks and training   426
competent person   422–23
competition   42
computer literacy   328
conceptualise phenomena   31

consistency   421
consultation with employees   425
contingencies   245
contractual arrangements, future   460–61
contribution-related pay   369
Control of Substances Hazardous to Health Regulations (COSHH) 1988   410
'core plus' scheme   347
corporate integration, maintaining   239
Corporate Manslaughter and Corporate Homicide Act 2007   416–17
correspondence
   criterion   26
   theories of truth   22
cost of absenteeism   438
   see also absence management
costs of accidents   406
'cottage' industries   339
Cranfield Female FTSE Index 2008   59–60
credit crunch   56
criterion keying   283
criterion-related validity coefficient   278
critical analysis   24
critical common sense   15–16, 23, 27, 34
cultural diversity   198
customer-handling skills   454

deep acting   104
'dehumanising' or 'putting down' customers   116
demand for workers, future   451–56
direct control work design   162–65
discretionary behaviour   282
dual human resourcing strategy   251

economically active   51
economically inactive   50
economic climate   355
economics   11
education and training courses   317–19
e-learning and blended learning   327–30
emergency procedures, fire and evacuation   427
emotional intelligence   217
emotional labour   103–06
emotions and feelings   102
emotion work   103
employee assistance programmes (EAP)   432
employee rewards   338, 345
   choices   353–54
   components of   345–48
   devising pay structures   361–62
   factors influencing organisational approaches   354–55
   economic climate   355
   Equal Pay Act 1970 (EqPA)   356–57
   legal context   355
   National Minimum Wage Regulations 1999   357
   Working Time Regulations 1998   358–59

general design features   362–63
historical and theoretical foundations of   339
   design and debates   341–44
   reward systems   339–41
internal/organisational factors   359–60
job families   367
non-financial reward   348–49
pay determination   360–61
pay progression   367–68
   competence-related pay   369–70
   contribution-related pay   369
   individual performance-related pay (PRP)   368–69
   organisational performance   371
   skills-based pay   370
   team-based pay   370–71
reward management   350–51
   strategy in practice   351–53
single/several structure   363
   broad-banded pay structures   366–67
   graded pay structures   364
   narrow-graded pay structures   364–65
   pay spine   363
time-based mechanisms   342
total reward   349–50
trends   371–72
employee selection   277–78
  HRM, implications for   296–97
  methods   279
   biographical information   282–83
   cognitive ability   280–81
   mixed approaches   286
   performance-based methods   283–86
   personality   271–82
  organization's approach   287–89
  practice, explaining
   as 'best fit'   289–92
   as discourse   294–96
   as interactive decision process   292–94
  psychometric quality   277–78
  trends   286–87
employees union   383–84
employer discrimination   60–61
employment
  see also unemployment
  changing forms of   65–66
  quality of   66, 68–74
  shift from manufacturing to services   62–63
Employment Appeals Tribunal (EAT)   358
'employment insecurity debate'   67
employment relationship   *see* industrial relations
empowering employees   17
enforcing authorities   419
  crown notices   420–21
  improvement notices   420
  informal methods   419
  prohibition notices   420
  prosecution   421

environmental health officers   418
epistemology   21
Equal Pay Act 1970 (EqPA)   356–57
equity or balance theories of work motivation   155
equity theory   155
ethnic heterogeneity   61–62
ethnicity and patterns   55
European Union Framework Directive   410–11
'eustress' and 'distress'   433
everyday common sense   14–15
expectancy theory(ies)   353
  of work motivation   156

'factory-based' system   339
'fear stuff'   388
feelings, emotions and the experience of stress   97–103
  alienation   106
  emotional labour   103–06
  stress, strain and distress   106–08
female heterogeneity   59–60
Five Factor model   *see* 'Big Five' dimensions
Five Steps to Risk Assessment   429
Flexible benefit schemes   347
flexible firm   251
flexible working options   71–74
focal social science disciplines   11
Fordism   164–65, 251
formal groups   185–86
  Virtuoso teams   186
forming, group   192
frame management   32
  process-relational   32
  systems-control   32
framing of reality   31, 32–33
  concepts   31–32
frictional unemployment   52

Gangmasters Licensing Authority (GLA)   418–19
gender-based inequalities   58
general intelligence   278
graded pay structures   364
graduate assessment centres   295–96
groups
  characteristics of   196
   information technology   196
   technology   196
  cohesiveness and performance   189, 195–96
   factors contributing to   189
  development and relationships   102, 192–93
  disadvantages of strong   195
   intergroup conflict   195–96
  formal   185–86
   Virtuoso teams   186
  individual compared with   211–12
   'groupthink'   212–13
   risky-shift phenomenon   212
  informal   186–87

example of   188
major functions of   187
norms   185
values and norms   185
informal social relations   185
group development and maturity   192–93
creative leadership and group development   193
groups and teams   183
see also groups
differences between   183–85
reasons for formation   188–89
'groupthink'   212–13

hazard   404
health   405
health, safety and wellbeing   417
competent person   422–23
enforcing authorities   419
crown notices   420–21
improvement notices   420
informal methods   419
prohibition notices   420
prosecution   421
Gangmasters Licensing Authority (GLA)   418–19
health and safety executive (HSE)   418
local authorities (LA)   418
membership of the health and safety committee   423
safety committees   423
safety officer or safety adviser   422
safety representatives   421–22
health and safety arrangements
accidents, first aid and work-related ill-health   426
action/practical arrangements   425
competency for tasks and training   426
consultation with employees   425
emergency procedures   427
information, instruction and supervision   426
monitoring   426
responsibility for   424–25
risks   425, 427
safe handling and use of substances   426
safe plant and equipment   425–26
safety policy statement   424
statement of general policy   424
The Health and Safety at Work Act 1974 (HASAWA)   407–08
employees, responsibilities of   409–10
employers under   408–09
The Health and Safety Commission's Enforcement Policy Statement (2008)   420
Health and Safety (Display Screen Equipment) Regulations 1992, amended by the Health and Safety (Miscellaneous Amendments) Regulations 2002   413–14
health and safety executive (HSE)   418, 421, 431
stress management standards   435–36

health promotion   437–39
hierarchical structure, nautre   210
hierarchy of needs' theory   *see* Maslow's hierarchy of needs theory
high commitment human resourcing strategies   244, 245–46, 249
high-commitment management (HCM) practices   389
high-performance management approach   277
human resource management (HRM)   227–33
choices and constraints   244–50
dimensions of   232
flexibility and dual human resourcing strategies   250–58
organisational and managerial options   249
practitioners   232
selection, choice and discrimination in   258–66
specialists and other managers   243–44
strategic nature   233
corporate and long-term focus of   239–42
employment relationship   236–39
organisational strategy making   233–36
human resources   228
for future   239
strategy   245
human vulnerabilities   97

implicit contracts   87–88, 89, 93, 112
improvement notices   420
inattentiveness through day-dreaming   114
indulgency pattern   150
industrial relations   381
decline of joint regulation   384–86
implications of   386–88
employees union   383–84
management approaches to   381–83
non-union employee representation   390
non-union workplaces   388–89
partnership with unions   390–92
union organising and new types of union representatives   392–93
informal groups   186–87
see also groups
culture   187
example of   188
functions of   187
interest and fun in work life   187
maintenance of communication system   187
social control, implementation of   187
informal social relations   185
information, instruction and supervision   426
in-house courses   317
initial orientation   88, 90
interactions among members   204–05
co-operation and interactions   205
interest and fun in work life   187
intergroup conflict   195–96
international issues in health and safety   440–41

International Labour Organisation (ILO)   357
interpersonal skills   454
Investors in People (IIP)   403, 442
isolation   340

job
   design   141
   enrichment   154, 165, 166
   evaluation   361
   quality   74
   redesign practices   159
   security   66–67
   simulations   284
Johari window   214
joint regulation of industrial relations   384–86
joking and humour   124

Karoshi   416
keeping information to oneself   114
'key strategic lever'   350

labour   162
   Social/general division of   162
   technical/detailed division of   162
labour demand   42
   aggregate demand   55–56
   changing forms of employment   65–66
   changing patterns   62
   ethnically based labour market inequality   60–61
   ethnic heterogeneity   61–62
   female heterogeneity   59–60
   gender-based inequalities   58
   labour market inequality   56–58
   occupational structure, changes in   63–65
   shift of employment from manufacturing to services   62–63
labour markets   42–44
   discrimination in   57
   ethnicity and patterns   55
   inequality   56–58, 60–61
   job quality   74
   male and female participation   53–55
   participation, patterns of   52–53
   quality of employment   66
      effort and work pressure   68–69
      job security   66–67
      worker discretion and autonomy   67–68
      work–life balance   69–74
   supply of labour   44
labour supply   42, 44
leadership   141
lean production   170
learning
   behaviourist perspective   307
   cognitive approaches   307–08
   constructivist perspective   308
   contracts   326–27

   from experience   308–11
   logs   325
   nature of   307–08
   need identification   311–13
   planned and emergent   311
   social learning theory   308
learning and development, methods
   e-learning and blended learning   327–30
   learning on the job
      learning contracts   326–27
      learning logs   325
      manager coaching and other internal and external coaching   320–22
      mentoring   322–23
      peer relationships   323–24
      self-development   324–25
   off-job methods
      education and training courses   317–19
learning cycle   309
   activists   310
   pragmatists   310
   reflectors   310
   theorists'   310
leaving the organisation at an especially inconvenient time   115
legal context   355
legislation   407
   about smoking   416
   Control of Substances Hazardous to Health Regulations (COSHH) 1988   410
   Corporate Manslaughter and Corporate Homicide Act 2007   416–17
   European Union Framework Directive   410–11
   The Health and Safety at Work Act 1974 (HASAWA)   407–08
      employees, responsibilities of   409–10
      employers under   408–09
   Health and Safety (Display Screen Equipment) Regulations 1992, amended by the Health and Safety (Miscellaneous Amendments) Regulations 2002   413–14
   The Management of Health and Safety at Work Regulations 1999 (MHSWR)   411–12
   Manual Handling Operations Regulations 1992, amended by the Health and Safety (Miscellaneous Amendments) Regulations 2002   414
   Personal Protective Equipment at Work Regulations 1992, amended by the Health and Safety (Miscellaneous Amendments) Regulations 2002   413
   Provision and Use of Work Equipment Regulations 1998, amended by the Health and Safety (Miscellaneous Amendments) Regulations 2002   413
   Reporting of Injuries, Diseases and Dangerous Occurrences Regulations (RIDDOR) 1995   414–15

Working Time Regulations 1998   415–16
Workplace (Health, Safety and Welfare) Regulations 1992, amended by the Health and Safety (Miscellaneous Amendments) Regulations 2002   412
linking motivation, leadership and job design   140–42
local authorities (LA)   418
long-term adaptability   252
long-term unemployment   52
low commitment human resourcing strategy   244, 245–46, 249
low-fidelity simulations   283
　see also situational judgement tests

male and female employees   53–55
management and communication skills   197
Management Learning   14
The Management of Health and Safety at Work Regulations 1999 (MHSWR)   411–12
management of work   6–9
　organisation and   9–12
manager coaching and other internal and external coaching   320–22
managing people   6–7
managing systems   8
manipulation of implicit contracts   145–54
Manual Handling Operations Regulations 1992, amended by the Health and Safety (Miscellaneous Amendments) Regulations 2002   414
market HR sub-strategy   252
Maslow's hierarchy of needs theory   24–27, 29
Maslow's triangle   28
meaninglessness   340
membership   190
　compatibility of members   190
　of the health and safety committee   423
　permanence of group members   190
　size of group   190
mentoring   322–23
minimal compliance with instructions   114
mixed approaches   286–87
mobilising of groups   116
monitoring   426
motivation   96, 141
　in work context   143
motivation theory   25–27

narrow-graded pay structures   364–65
NatBank   394–96
National Minimum Wage Regulations 1999   341, 346, 357
natural learning   324
need-based motivational analyses, inadequacy of   88
need identification, learning   311–13
non-financial reward   348–49

non-union employee representation   390
non-union workplaces   388–89

occupational stress   111
occupational structure, changes in   63–65
occupations, changes in   452
off-job courses   319
opportunistic pilfering or embezzlement   114–15
organisational behaviour   8, 13
organisational groups
　external threat   192
　HR policies and procedures   191–92
　management and leadership   191
　success   192
Organisational human resources and employment relationship   227–30
organisational mischief   111–18
　unintended consequences   112
organisational performance   371
organisational policy and procedures   437
organisational practitioners   10
Organisation Studies   14
organised bullying and harassment   116
organised fiddles   115
organised sabotaging of goods   116
organising and managing work   9–12, 13, 16–20
　social scientific study   10
　theories of   21–24
outdoor-type courses   318
outward bound   *see* outdoor-type courses

partnership   391
part-time working   58
pay determination   360–61
payment by results (PBR)   343
pay progression
　competence-related pay   369–70
　contribution-related pay   369
　individual performance-related pay (PRP)   368–69
　organisational performance   371
　skills-based pay   370
　team-based pay   370–71
pay spine   363
pay structure   362
　broad-banded   366
　devising   361–62
　graded   364
　job families   367
　narrow-graded   364–65
peer relationships   323–24
people management   *see* human resource management (HRM)
'people processing' aspect   265
performance-based methods   283–86
performance-related pay (PRP)   368–69
performing, group   193
'perks' (perquisites) or fringe benefits   346–47
personal identity   182

personality   281–82
    attributes   261
Personal Protective Equipment at Work Regulations 1992, amended by the Health and Safety (Miscellaneous Amendments) Regulations 2002   413
personnel management   229–30
physiological needs   25–26
plausibility criterion   27
political science   11
population
    age structure of   46–48
    ethnicity and   49–50
    national population trends   44–45
    regional population trends   45–46
    workforce   50–52
posh accents   19
positive motivation   144
post-course questionnaire   331
powerlessness   340
practical jokes, organised 'piss-takes' or 'wind-ups'   116
pragmatist theories of truth   22
principle of employment   237
principle of free labour   237
principle of proportionality   421
problem-centred approach   312
problem-solving skills   454
process-relational frame   17
    of organisations   34
    of people   34
process-relational style   111
'process' theories of motivation   139
productive cooperation   141
profile comparison approach   312
prohibition notices   420
prosecution   421
Provision and Use of Work Equipment Regulations 1998, amended by the Health and Safety (Miscellaneous Amendments) Regulations 2002   413
PRP   see performance-related pay (PRP)
psychological factors   12
psychology   11
psychometric model for selection   see employee selection
psychometric standards   278–79
psychometric tests   277–81, 287–90
    in graduate jobs   280–81
punishing of awkward customer   115

quality of employment   66
quality of working life (QWL)   349
questioning   18

rational bureaucratic work organisation   237
rationalistic and bureaucratic personnel management technology   260

Reporting of Injuries, Diseases and Dangerous Occurrences Regulations (RIDDOR) 1995   414–15
residual unemployed   52
responsible autonomy   43
restrictions of output   115
retail prices index (RPI)   355
revitalising health and safety   417
reward management   350–51
    strategy in practice   351–53
reward practice, trends in   360
reward strategy   351
    and business strategy   351
    key choices   353–54
    mistakes   352
risk   404
risk assessment   429
    step 1 – identify the hazards   429
    step 2 – decide who might be harmed and how   429
    step 3 – evaluate the risks and decide on precautions   429
    step 4 – record your findings and implement them   430
    step 5 – review your risk assessment and update   430
risky-shift phenomenon   212
role conflict   200–02
    ambiguity   201
    incompatibility   201
    influences on behaviour   202–03
    and matrix organisation   202
    overload   201
    role stress   202
    sanctions   203
    underload   202
role relationships   198–99
    see also role conflict
    person's role-set   199
    role expectations   200
    role incongruence   199

sabotaging   115, 122
safe plant and equipment   425–26
safety   403–04, 405–06
    committees   423
    needs   26
    officer or safety adviser   422
    policy statement   424
    representatives   421–22
sanctions   203
'sausage machine' approach   264–65
scientific management (Taylorism)   163–64, 168
seasonal unemployment   52
selection method   see employee selection
self-actualisation   25, 98
self-development   307, 324–25
    groups   325

self-estrangement   340
Self-interest and opportunism   200
semi-autonomous work group   154
sensitivity training   214
   Johari window   214
serial thinking   90
service-orientation   286
service-related salary increments   351
setting of group work-output norms   115
sexual harassment   114
sexuality, humour and the struggle for control   122–30
shaping work tasks and gaining cooperation   168–75
short-term adjustment   252
situational interview   284–85
situational judgement tests   283–84
'six-pack'   411, 429
skills-based pay   370
small and medium-sized organisations (SME)   362
smoking   416, 438–39
social and self-categorisation   194
social control, informal control   187
Social/general division of labour   162
social identity theory   194–95
social networks and interpersonal relationships   193
social psychology   11
sociology   11
socio-technical systems   166
soft skills   215–17
spontaneous individual acts of absenteeism   114
stable workforce   42
statement of general policy   424
storming, group   192
strategic exchange   85, 142–43
   perspective   84–86
   relationships   142
stress, causes of   434
stress, strain and distress   106–08
structured interviews   285
subgroup predictive validity   278
successful teams   214–15
   emotional intelligence, role of   217
   skills for   215–17
supply of labour   44
   age structure of population   46–48
   gender composition   48
   population
      ethnicity and   49–50
      national population trends   44–45
      regional population trends   45–46
      workforce   50–52
supply of workers, future   456–60
   see also supply of labour
supporting social science disciplines   11
   see also Focal social science disciplines
surface acting   104

'sweet stuff '   388
'systematic training cycle'   311–12
systems-control framing
   of organisations   34, 264
   of people   34
systems-control orthodoxy   17
systems thinking   8

tacit knowledge   281
targeting   421
Taylor, F.W.   340
Taylorism   163–64, 168
team-based pay   370–71
team leader   140
team work   154, 203, 204
   see also groups
   effective   203–04
teamworking/semi-autonomous workgroups   167
teamworking skills   454
technical/detailed division of labour   162
technology   196
thought showers   see brainstorming
Time-based pay   343
total quality management   248
total reward   349–50
trade union   see union
training and development, evaluation of   330–31
transparency   421
Truck Acts   341
Tuckman's storm   193

unemployed   52
unemployment   61
   frictional   52
   long-term   52
   seasonal   52
union
   employees   383–84
   non-union employee representation   390
   non-union workplaces   388–89
   organising and new types of union representatives   392–93
   partnership with   390–92
union learning representatives (ULR)   392–93

virtual teams   197
   cultural diversity   198
   management and communication skills   197
   organising   197–98
Virtuoso teams   186

Weber, Max   97
wellbeing   404–05, 431
   employer, role of   432–33
   problem and their sources   433
   stress and stress management   433–37
white collar work samples   see situational judgement tests

Wood's theoretical classification of employers' responses to work–life balance 71–72
work design
   direct and indirect control principles of 158–61
   modernity, industrialism and the hesitant embracing of direct control 162–68
   redesign principles 158
work environment
   communications 191
   nature of the task 190–91
   physical setting 191
   technology 191
worker cooperation in production 43
worker discretion and autonomy 67–68
worker motivation 142–43
workforce 50–52
work group 196
   information technology, imact of 196
   semi-autonomous 154
   technology, effect of 196
Working Time Regulations 1998 358–59, 415–16
work intensification 169
work–life balance 68, 69–74
   levels of response to 70

work management *see* management of work
work motivation
   equity or balance theories of 155
   expectancy theories of 156–58
work organisation and management studies 9, 12–14, 18
work orientation 88–91, 143–44
   equity, balance and expectancies in 154–58
   varying and changing 94–97
work orientations 142–43
workplace games 116
Workplace (Health, Safety and Welfare) Regulations 1992, amended by the Health and Safety (Miscellaneous Amendments) Regulations 2002 412
workplace humour 129
work premises
   for group-sanctioned non-work purposes 116
   or equipment for private purposes, using 115, 122
work pressure 68–69
work tasks and gaining cooperation 168–75